MOON

OREGON CAMPING

TOM STIENSTRA

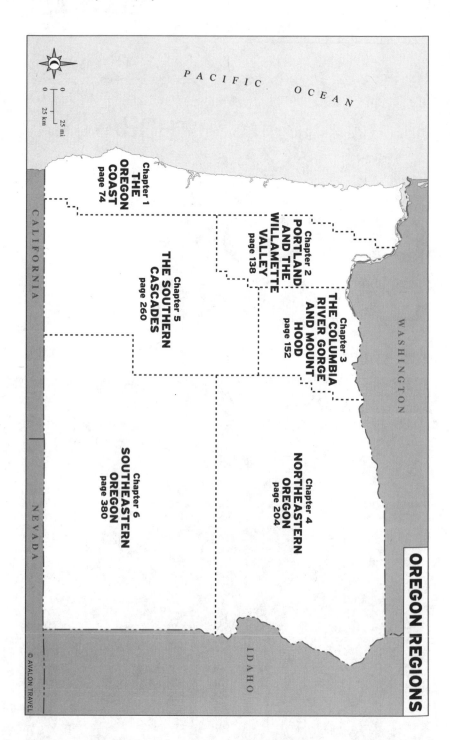

PACIFIC OCEAN

CALIFORNIA

WASHINGTON

NEVADA

IDAHO

Chapter 1
THE OREGON COAST
page 74

Chapter 2
PORTLAND AND THE WILLAMETTE VALLEY
page 138

Chapter 3
THE COLUMBIA RIVER GORGE AND MOUNT HOOD
page 152

Chapter 5
THE SOUTHERN CASCADES
page 260

Chapter 6
SOUTHEASTERN OREGON
page 380

Chapter 4
NORTHEASTERN OREGON
page 204

0 25 mi
0 25 km

OREGON REGIONS

© AVALON TRAVEL

Contents

How to Use This Book
ABOUT THE CAMPGROUND PROFILES

The campgrounds are listed in a consistent, easy-to-read format to help you choose the ideal camping spot. If you already know the name of the specific campground you want to visit, or the name of the surrounding geological area or nearby feature (town, national or state park, forest, mountain, lake, river, etc.), look it up in the index and turn to the corresponding page. Here is a sample profile:

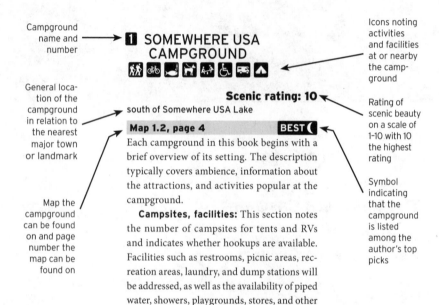

Campground name and number →

General location of the campground in relation to the nearest major town or landmark →

Map the campground can be found on and page number the map can be found on →

Icons noting activities and facilities at or nearby the campground →

Rating of scenic beauty on a scale of 1-10 with 10 the highest rating →

Symbol indicating that the campground is listed among the author's top picks →

1 SOMEWHERE USA CAMPGROUND

Scenic rating: 10

south of Somewhere USA Lake

Map 1.2, page 4 **BEST (**

Each campground in this book begins with a brief overview of its setting. The description typically covers ambience, information about the attractions, and activities popular at the campground.

Campsites, facilities: This section notes the number of campsites for tents and RVs and indicates whether hookups are available. Facilities such as restrooms, picnic areas, recreation areas, laundry, and dump stations will be addressed, as well as the availability of piped water, showers, playgrounds, stores, and other amenities. The campground's pet policy and wheelchair accessibility is also mentioned here.

Reservations, fees: This section notes whether reservations are accepted, and provides rates for tent sites and RV sites. If there are additional fees for parking or pets, or discounted weekly or seasonal rates, they will also be noted here.

Directions: This section provides mile-by-mile driving directions to the campground from the nearest major town or highway.

Contact: This section provides an address, phone number, and website, if available, for the campground.

ABOUT THE ICONS

The icons in this book are designed to provide at-a-glance information on activities, facilities, and services available on-site or within walking distance of each campground.

- 🏔 Hiking trails
- 🚴 Biking trails
- 🏊 Swimming
- 🎣 Fishing
- 🚤 Boating
- 🛶 Canoeing and/or kayaking
- ❄ Winter sports

- ♨ Hot springs
- 🐾 Pets permitted
- 🛝 Playground
- ♿ Wheelchair accessible
- 🚐 RV sites
- ⛺ Tent sites
- 🏅 5 Percent Club

ABOUT THE SCENIC RATING

Each campground profile employs a scenic rating on a scale of 1 to 10, with 1 being the least scenic and 10 being the most scenic. A scenic rating measures only the overall beauty of the campground and environs; it does not take into account noise level, facilities, maintenance, recreation options, or campground management. The setting of a campground with a lower scenic rating may simply not be as picturesque that of as a higher rated campground, however other factors that can influence a trip, such as noise or recreation access, can still affect or enhance your camping trip. Consider both the scenic rating and the profile description before deciding which campground is perfect for you.

MAP SYMBOLS

▦▦▦▦ Expressway	🛡80	Interstate Freeway	✈	Airfield
▦▦▦▦ Primary Road	🛡101	U.S. Highway	✈	Airport
▦▦▦▦ Secondary Road	21	State Highway	○	City/Town
= = = = Unpaved Road	66	County Highway	▲	Mountain
·········· Ferry	⬭ Lake		▲	Park
—··— National Border	⌇ Dry Lake		⟩⟨	Pass
—·—· State Border	⬭ Seasonal Lake		◉	State Capital

ABOUT THE MAPS

This book is divided into chapters based on major regions in the state; an overview map of these regions precedes the table of contents. Each chapter begins with a map of the region, which is further broken down into detail maps. Campgrounds are noted on the detail maps by number.

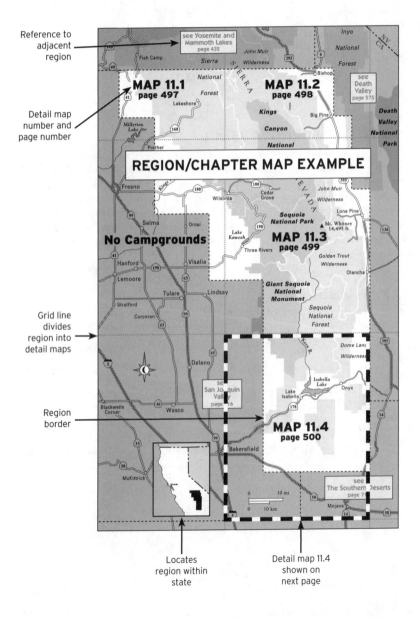

Reference to adjacent region

Detail map number and page number

REGION/CHAPTER MAP EXAMPLE

No Campgrounds

Grid line divides region into detail maps

Region border

Locates region within state

Detail map 11.4 shown on next page

Indicates adja-
cent detail maps
within region

Locates detail
map within
region

Map
number → **Map 11.4**

Sites shown
on detail map → **Sites 105-117**
and the page
range where   **Pages 564-570**
those sites are
listed

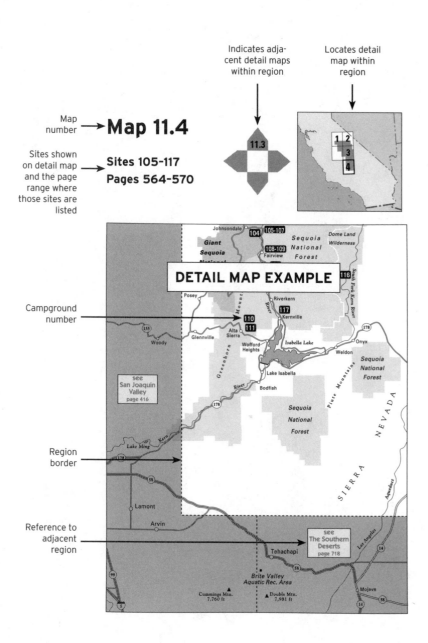

Campground
number

DETAIL MAP EXAMPLE

Region
border

Reference to
adjacent
region

INTRODUCTION

Author's Note

When my family and friends throughout Oregon heard I was writing this book, they all instantly hated me! They figured their favorite spots would be revealed to all. But after reading the book, they don't hate me anymore (except for this one cousin). That is because they have discovered, as I have, that Oregon is filled with beautiful, little-used campgrounds that are perfect jump-off points for adventure—and there are hundreds of outstanding destinations, in addition to their sprinkling of personal favorites.

Looking for *mystery?* There are hundreds of hidden, rarely used campgrounds listed and mapped in this book that most people have never dreamed of. *Excitement?* At many of them, you'll find the sizzle with the steak: the hike to a great lookout or the big fish at the end of your line. *Fun?* The Camping Tips section of this book can help you take the futility out of your trips and put the fun back in. Add it up, put it in your cash register, and you can turn a camping trip into the satisfying adventure it's meant to be, whether it's just an overnight quickie or a month-long expedition.

Going on a camping trip can be like trying to put hiking boots on an octopus. You've tried it too, eh? Instead of a relaxing and fun trip full of adventure, it turns into a scenario called "You Against the World." You might as well try to fight a volcano. But it doesn't have to be that way, and that's what this book is all about. If you give it a chance, the information herein can remove the snarls, confusion, and occasional, volcanic temper explosions that keep people at home, locked away from the action.

It's estimated that 95 percent of American vacationers use only 5 percent of the country's available recreation areas. With this book, you can leave the herd, wander, and be free. You can join the inner circle, the Five Percenters who know the great hidden areas used by so few people. To join the Five Percent Club, take a hard look at the maps for the areas you wish to visit and the corresponding campground listings. As you study the camps, you'll start to feel a sense of excitement building, a feeling that you are about to unlock a door and venture into a world that is rarely viewed. When you feel that excitement, act on it. Parlay that energy into a great trip.

The campground maps and listings can serve in two ways: 1) If you're on the road late in the day and you're stuck for a spot for the night, you can likely find one nearby; or 2) if you are planning a trip, you can tailor a vacation to fit exactly into your plans rather than heading off and hoping—maybe praying—it turns out all right.

For the latter, you may wish to obtain additional maps, particularly if you are venturing into areas governed by the U.S. Forest Service or Bureau of Land Management. Both are federal agencies that offer low-cost maps detailing all hiking trails, lakes, streams, and backcountry camps reached via logging roads. The Resource Guide at the back of this book details how to obtain these and other maps.

Backcountry camps listed in this book are often in primitive and rugged settings but provide the sense of isolation that you may want from a trip. They also provide good jump-off points for backpacking trips, if that's your calling. These camps are often free, and I have listed hundreds of them.

At the other end of the spectrum are the developed parks for RVs. They offer a home away from home, with everything from full hookups to a grocery store and laundry room. Instead of isolation, an RV park provides a place to shower and get outfitted for food and clean clothes. For RV cruisers, it's a place to stay in high style while touring the area. RV

KEEP IT WILD

"Enjoy America's country and leave no trace." That's the motto of the Leave No Trace program, and I strongly support it. Promoting responsible outdoor recreation through education, research, and partnerships is its mission. Look for the Keep It Wild Tips, developed from the policies of Leave No Trace, throughout the Camping Tips portion of this book. This copyrighted information has been reprinted with permission from the Leave No Trace Center for Outdoor Ethics. For more information or materials, please visit www.LNT.org or call 303/442-8222 or 800/332-4100.

parks range in price, depending on location, and an advance deposit may be necessary in summer.

Somewhere between the two extremes are hundreds and hundreds of campgrounds that provide a compromise: beautiful settings and some facilities, with a small overnight fee. Piped water, vault toilets, and picnic tables tend to come with the territory. Fees for these sites are usually in the $10-35 range, with the higher-priced sites located near population centers. Because they offer a bit of both worlds, they are in high demand. Reservations are usually advised, and at state parks, particularly during the summer season, you can expect company. This doesn't mean you need to forgo them in hopes of a less confined environment. For one thing, most state parks have set up quotas so that visitors don't feel as if they've been squeezed in with a shoehorn. For another, the same parks are often uncrowded during the off-season and on weekdays.

Before your trip, you'll want to get organized, and that's when you must start putting boots on that giant octopus. The trick to organization for any task is breaking it down to its key components and then solving each element independent of the others. Remember the octopus. Grab a moving leg, jam on a boot, and make sure it's on tight before reaching for another leg. Do one thing at a time, in order, and all will get done quickly and efficiently.

Now you can become completely organized for your trip in just one week, spending just a little time each evening on a given component. Getting organized is an unnatural act for many. By splitting up the tasks, you take the pressure out of planning and put the fun back in.

As you might figure, this is not a hobby for me, as it is for some part-time writers who publish books. This is my full-time job. Because I spend up to 200 days a year in the field, I understand how seriously people take their fun, what they need to know to make their trips work, as well as their underlying fears that they might get stuck for the night without a spot. I get tons of emails and letters, and I read each one carefully. These have been of great benefit. In the process, I have incorporated dozen of suggestions from readers to make this book they want it to be. Your comments and questions are always welcome and appreciated. As a full-tome outdoors writer, the question I am asked more than any other is: "Where are you going this week?"

All of the answers are in this book.

Best Campgrounds

Can't decide where to stay? Here are my picks for the best Oregon campgrounds in seven different categories.

BEST(Most Scenic

Honey Bear Campground & RV Resort, The Oregon Coast, page 128.
Long Bow Group, Portland and the Willamette Valley, page 148.
Piety Island Boat-In, The Columbia River Gorge and Mount Hood, page 191.
Cove Creek, The Columbia River Gorge and Mount Hood, page 192.
Paul Dennis, The Columbia River Gorge and Mount Hood, page 195.
Anthony Lakes, Northeastern Oregon, page 242.
Scott Lake Walk-In, The Southern Cascades, page 285.
North Waldo, The Southern Cascades, page 300.
Lava Lake, The Southern Cascades, page 322.
Squaw Lake Hike-In, The Southern Cascades, page 373.

BEST(Families

Fort Stevens State Park, The Oregon Coast, page 79.
Honey Bear Campground & RV Resort, The Oregon Coast, page 128.
Cascade Locks Marine Park, The Columbia River Gorge and Mount Hood, page 166.
Hoover and Hoover Group Camp, The Columbia River Gorge and Mount Hood, page 192.
Twin Lakes Resort, The Southern Cascades, page 328.
Indian Mary Park, The Southern Cascades, page 346.
Abbott Creek, The Southern Cascades, page 355.
Lake of the Woods Resort, The Southern Cascades, page 364.
Drews Creek, Southeastern Oregon, page 402.

BEST(Fishing

Waldport/Newport KOA, The Oregon Coast, page 98.
Port of Siuslaw RV Park and Marina, The Oregon Coast, page 104.
Carter Lake, The Oregon Coast, page 106.
Trillium Lake, The Columbia River Gorge and Mount Hood, page 176.
Gone Creek, The Columbia River Gorge and Mount Hood, page 182.
Pelton, The Columbia River Gorge and Mount Hood, page 199.
Belknap Hot Springs Resort, The Southern Cascades, page 274.
Mallard Marsh, The Southern Cascades, page 321.
Trapper Creek, The Southern Cascades, page 337.
Drews Creek, Southeastern Oregon, page 402.

BEST(Hiking

Nehalem Falls, The Oregon Coast, page 82.
Cape Lookout State Park, The Oregon Coast, page 87.
Cape Blanco State Park, The Oregon Coast, page 121.
Eagle Creek, The Columbia River Gorge and Mount Hood, page 166.
Toll Gate, The Columbia River Gorge and Mount Hood, page 174.

Belknap Hot Springs Resort, The Southern Cascades, page 274.
Boulder Flat, The Southern Cascades, page 309.
Natural Bridge, The Southern Cascades, page 354.
Aspen Point, The Southern Cascades, page 364.

BEST❰ Waterfalls

Nehalem Falls, The Oregon Coast, page 82.
Alsea Falls, The Oregon Coast, page 100.
Ainsworth State Park, The Columbia River Gorge and Mount Hood, page 158.
Salmon Creek Falls, The Southern Cascades, page 299.
Susan Creek, The Southern Cascades, page 306.
Steamboat Falls, The Southern Cascades, page 307.
Hemlock Lake, The Southern Cascades, page 314.

BEST❰ Waterfront Campgrounds

Loon Lake Recreation Area, The Oregon Coast, page 113.
Laird Lake, The Oregon Coast, page 123.
Lost Lake, The Columbia River Gorge and Mount Hood, page 170.
Trillium Lake, The Columbia River Gorge and Mount Hood, page 176.
Meditation Point, The Columbia River Gorge and Mount Hood, page 184.
Jubilee Lake, Northeastern Oregon, page 224.
Wallowa Lake State Park, Northeastern Oregon, page 229.
Bull Prairie Lake, Northeastern Oregon, page 238.
Middle Fork, Northeastern Oregon, page 246.
Driftwood, The Southern Cascades, page 287.
Hemlock Lake, The Southern Cascades, page 314.
Gold Lake, The Southern Cascades, page 334.
Bolan Lake, The Southern Cascades, page 353.
Campbell Lake, Southeastern Oregon, page 398.
Dog Lake, Southeastern Oregon, page 401.

BEST❰ Wildlife-Viewing

Cape Lookout State Park, The Oregon Coast, page 87.
Seal Rocks RV Cove, The Oregon Coast, page 96.
Port of Siuslaw RV Park and Marina, The Oregon Coast, page 104.
Harris Beach State Park, The Oregon Coast, page 133.
Pelton, The Columbia River Gorge and Mount Hood, page 199.
Penland Lake, Northeastern Oregon, page 216.
Crooked River Ranch RV Park, The Southern Cascades, page 284.
Bolan Lake, The Southern Cascades, page 353.
Mount Ashland, The Southern Cascades, page 374.
Jackson Creek, Southeastern Oregon, page 394.

Camping Tips

SLEEPING GEAR

On an eve long ago in the mountain pines, my dad, brother, and I had rolled out our sleeping bags and were bedded down for the night. After the pre-trip excitement, a long drive, an evening of trout fishing and a barbecue, we were like three tired doggies who had played too much.

But as I looked up at the stars, I was suddenly wide awake. I was still wired. A half hour later? No change. Wide awake.

And as little kids can do, I had to wake up ol' Dad to tell him about it. "Hey, Dad, I can't sleep."

After the initial grimace, he said: "This is what you do. Watch the sky for a shooting star and tell yourself that you cannot go to sleep until you see at least one shooting star. As you wait and watch, you will start getting tired, and it will be difficult to keep your eyes open. But tell yourself, you must keep watching. Then you'll start to really feel tired. When you finally see a shooting star, you'll go to sleep so fast you won't know what hit you."

Well, I tried it that night and I don't even remember seeing a shooting star, I went to sleep so fast.

It's a good trick, and along with having a good sleeping bag, ground insulation, maybe a tent, or a few tricks for bedding down in a pickup truck or RV, you can get a great night's sleep on every camping trip.

More than 20 years after that camping episode with my dad and brother, we made a trip to the planetarium at the Academy of Sciences in San Francisco to see a show. The lights dimmed, and the ceiling turned into a night sky, filled with stars and a setting moon. A scientist began explaining the phenomena of the heavens.

After a few minutes, I began to feel drowsy. Just then, a shooting star zipped across the planetarium ceiling. I went into such a deep sleep, it was like I was in a coma. I didn't wake up until the show was over, the lights were turned back on, and the people were leaving.

Feeling drowsy, I turned to see if Dad had liked the show. Oh yeah? Not only had he gone to sleep too, but he apparently had no intention of waking up, no matter what. Just like a camping trip.

Sleeping Bags

The first rule of a good nights' sleep is that you must be dry, warm and safe. A good sleeping bag can help plenty. A sleeping bag is a shell filled with heat-retaining insulation. By itself, it is not warm. Your body provides the heat, and the sleeping bag's ability to retain that heat is what makes it warm or cold.

The cheap cotton bags are heavy, bulky, cold, and, when wet, useless. With other options available, their function is limited. Anybody who sleeps outdoors or backpacks should choose otherwise. Use a sleeping bag filled with down or one of the quality poly-fills. Down is light, warm, and aesthetically pleasing to those who don't think camping and technology mix. If you choose a down bag, be sure to keep it double wrapped in plastic garbage bags on your trips to keep it dry. Once it's wet, you'll spend your nights howling at the moon.

The polyfiber-filled bags are not necessarily better than those filled with down, but they can be. Their one key advantage is that even when wet, some poly-fills can retain up to 85 percent of your body heat. This allows you to sleep and get valuable rest even in miserable conditions. In my camping experience, no matter how lucky you may be, there will come a time when you will get caught in an unexpected, violent storm and everything you've got will get wet, including your sleeping bag. That's when a poly-fill bag becomes priceless. You have one and can sleep. Or you don't have one and suffer. It is that simple. Of the synthetic fills, Quallofil made by DuPont is the industry leader.

But just because a sleeping bag uses a

KEEP IT WILD TIP 1: CAMP WITH CARE

1. Choose an existing, legal site. Restrict activities to areas where vegetation is compacted or absent.
2. Camp at least 75 steps (200 feet) from lakes, streams, and trails.
3. Always choose sites that won't be damaged by your stay.
4. Preserve the feeling of solitude by selecting camps that are out of view when possible.
5. Don't dig trenches or build structures or furniture.

high-tech poly-fill doesn't necessarily make it a better bag. There are other factors.

The most important are a bag's temperature rating and weight. The temperature rating of a sleeping bag refers to how cold it can get outside before you start actually feeling cold. Many campers make the mistake of thinking, "I only camp in the summer, so a bag rated at 30 or 40°F should be fine." Later, they find out it isn't so fine, and all it takes is one cold night to convince them of that. When selecting the right temperature rating, visualize the coldest weather you might ever confront, and then get a bag rated for even colder weather.

For instance, if you are a summer camper, you may rarely experience a night in the low 30s or high 20s. A sleeping bag rated at 20°F would be appropriate, keeping you snug, warm, and asleep. For most campers, I advise bags rated at 0 or 10°F.

But guess how the companies come up with their temperature ratings? Usually it's a guy like me field-testing a bag before it is commercially released, and then saying, "Well, it got down to 40°F and I was pretty warm." So they rate it at 30 degrees. Obviously, testers can have different threshold levels for cold, while others base their ratings on how much fill is used.

If you buy a poly-filled sleeping bag, try not to leave it squished in your stuff sack between camping trips. Instead, keep it on a hanger in a closet or use it as a blanket. One thing that can reduce a poly-filled bag's heat-retaining qualities is if the tiny hollow fibers that make up the fill lose their loft. You can avoid this with proper storage.

The weight of a sleeping bag can also be a key factor, especially for backpackers. When you have to carry your gear on your back, every ounce becomes important. Sleeping bags that weigh just 2-3 pounds are available, although they are expensive. But if you hike much, it's worth the price to keep your weight to a minimum. For an overnighter, you can get away with a 4- or 4.5-pound bag without much stress. However, bags weighing five pounds and up should be left back at the car.

I have several sleeping bags; they range from a seven-pounder that feels like a giant sponge to a three-pounder. The heavy-duty model is for pickup-truck camping in cold weather and doubles as a blanket at home. The lightweight bag is for expeditions.

Insulation Pads

Even with the warmest sleeping bag in the world, if you just lay it down on the ground and try to sleep, you will likely get as cold as a winter cucumber. That is because the cold ground will suck the warmth right out of your body. The solution is to have a layer of insulation between you and the ground. For this, you can use a thin Insulite pad, a lightweight Therm-a-Rest inflatable pad, a foam pad or mattress, an airbed, or a cot. Here is a capsule summary of each:

Insulite pads: They are light, inexpensive, roll up quickly for transport, and can double as a seat pad at your camp. The negative side is that in one night, they will compress, making you feel like you are sleeping on granite. But they are light and they help keep you warm in the wilderness.

Therm-a-Rest pads: These are a real

luxury for wilderness travel because they do everything an Insulite pad does, but they also provide a cushion. The negative side is that they are expensive by comparison, and if they get a hole in them, they become worthless without a patch kit. Most wilderness campers carry one "bonus item"—and a full-length Therm-A-Rest is often what they choose.

Foam mattresses, air beds, and cots: These are excellent for car campers. The new line of air beds, especially the thicker ones, are outstanding and inflate quickly with an electric motor inflator that plugs into a power plug or cigarette lighter in your vehicle. Foam mattresses are also excellent; I think they are the most comfortable of all, but their size precludes many from considering them. I've found that cots work great, too. I've always had one and they're great for drive-in tent sites. For camping in the back of a pickup truck with a camper shell, the cots with three-inch legs are best, of course. Here's the trick: Put a blanket over the sleeping surface, then add a Therm-A-Rest pad; you need insulation to keep the cold air beneath you from sucking out the warmth.

A Few Tricks

When surveying a camp area, the most important consideration should be to select a good spot for sleeping. Everything else is secondary. Ideally, you want a flat area that is wind-sheltered and on ground soft enough to drive stakes into. Yeah, and I want to win the lottery, too.

Sometimes, the ground will have a slight slope to it. In that case, always sleep with your head on the uphill side. If you sleep parallel to the slope, every time you roll over, you'll find yourself rolling down the hill. If you sleep with your head on the downhill side, you'll get a headache that feels as if an ax is embedded in your brain.

When you've found a good spot, clear it of all branches, twigs, and rocks, of course. A good tip is to dig a slight indentation in the ground where your hip will fit. Since your body is not flat, but has curves and edges, it will not feel comfortable on flat ground. Some people even get severely bruised on the sides of their hips when sleeping on flat, hard ground. For that reason alone, they learn to hate camping. What a shame, especially when the problem is solved easily with a Therm-a-Rest pad, foam insulation, an air bed, or a cot.

After the ground is prepared, throw a ground cloth over the spot, which will keep much of the morning dew off you. In some areas, particularly where fog is a problem, morning dew can be heavy and get the outside of your sleeping bag quite wet. In that case, you need overhead protection, such as a tent or some kind of roof, like a poncho or tarp with its ends tied to trees.

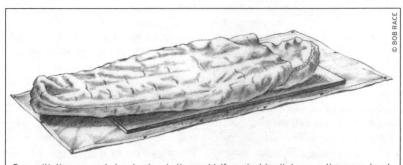

© BOB RACE

Even with the warmest sleeping bag in the world, if you just lay it down on the ground and try to sleep, you will likely get as cold as a winter cucumber. That is because the cold ground will suck the warmth right out of your body. The solution? A sleeping pad.

A Great Nights' Sleep

Some people sleep seven, eight hours at camp, but it comes in 10 installments. They keep waking up. They wake up and half their body is paralyzed. Heh, heh, heh. They can't get comfortable. To solve this, practice camp-style sleeping at home until you get it perfect. At home, you have flexibility and complete control over your sleeping surface. Get it right. Get it just how you like it.

For wilderness travel, my bonus item is an extra inflatable pillow; that's right, I carry two, not one. I inflate them about half full. It puts my head at a perfect comfort zone for deep sleep. Whatever it takes, know how to get a great night's sleep and your entire trip has the chance to feel epic, no matter what you do.

Tents and Weather Protection

All it takes is to get caught in the rain once without a tent and you will never go anywhere without one again. A tent provides protection from rain, wind, and mosquito attacks. In exchange, you can lose a starry night's view, though some tents now even provide moon roofs.

A tent can be as complex as a four-season, tubular-jointed dome with a rain fly or as simple as a tarp roped up to a tree. They can be as cheap as a $10 tube tent, which is nothing more than a hollow piece of plastic, or as expensive as a $500 five-person deluxe expedition, multiroom dome. They vary greatly in size, price, and assembly time. For those who camp infrequently and want to buy a tent without paying much, off-brand models are available at considerable price discounts. My experience in field-testing outdoor gear, though, is that cheap tents often rip at the seams if subjected to regular use. If you plan on getting a good one, plan on doing plenty of shopping and asking lots of questions. With a little bit of homework, you can get the right answers to these questions:

WILL IT KEEP ME DRY?

On many one-person and two-person tents, the rain fly does not extend far enough to keep water off the bottom sidewalls of the tent. In a driving rain, water can also drip from the rain fly and onto those sections of the tent. Eventually, the water can leak through to the inside, particularly through the seams.

You must be able to stake out your rain fly so it completely covers all of the tent. If you are tent shopping and this does not appear possible, then don't buy the tent. To prevent potential leaks, use a seam water-proofer, such as Seam Lock, a glue-like substance that can close potential leak areas on tent seams. For large umbrella tents, keep a patch kit handy. Coleman tents, by the way, are guaranteed to keep campers dry.

Another way to keep water out of your tent is to store all wet garments outside the tent, under a poncho. Moisture from wet clothes stashed in the tent will condense on the interior tent walls. If you bring enough wet clothes into the tent, by the next morning you'll feel as if you're camping in a duck blind.

HOW HARD IS IT TO PUT UP?

If a tent is difficult to erect in full sunlight, you can just about forget it at night, especially the first night out if you arrive late to camp. Some tents can go up in just a few minutes, without requiring help from another camper. This might be the kind of tent you want.

The way to compare put-up times when shopping for tents is to count the number of connecting points from the tent poles to the tent and the number of stakes required. The fewer, the better. Think simple. My two-person-plus-a-dog tent has seven connecting points and, minus the rain fly, requires no stakes. It goes up in a few minutes.

My bigger family tent, which has three rooms with walls (so we can keep our two kids isolated on each side if necessary), takes about a half hour to put up. That's without anybody's help. With their help, add about 15 minutes. Heh, heh.

Another factor is the tent poles themselves. Always make sure the poles are connected by

Tents vary in complexity, size, and price. Be sure to buy the one that's right for you.

an interior bungee cord. It takes only an instant to convert them to a complete pole.

Some outdoor shops have tents on display on their showroom floors. Before buying the tent, have the salesperson take the tent down and put it back up. If it takes him more than five minutes, or he says he doesn't have time, then keep looking.

Is It Roomy Enough?

Don't judge the size of a tent on floor space alone. Some tents that are small on floor space can give the illusion of roominess with a high ceiling. You can be quite comfortable and snug in them.

But remember that a one-person or two-person tent is just that. A two-person tent has room for two people plus gear. That's it. Don't buy a tent expecting it to hold more than it is intended to.

How Much Does It Weigh?

If you're a hiker, this becomes the preeminent question. If it's much more than six or seven pounds, forget it. A 12-pound tent is bad enough, but get it wet and it's like carrying a piano on your back. On the other hand, weight is scarcely a factor if you camp only where you can take your car. My dad, for instance, used to have this giant canvas umbrella tent that folded down to a neat little pack that weighed about 500 pounds.

Family Tents

It is always worth spending the time and money to buy a tent you and your family will be happy with.

Many excellent family tents are available from Cabela's, Coleman, Eureka!, North Face, Remington, and Sierra Designs. Guide-approved expedition tents for groups cost more. Here is a synopsis of some of best tents available:

Cabela's Two- or Three-Room Cabin

800/237-4444
www.cabelas.com
This beautiful tent features two to three rooms, a 10- by 16-foot floor available in different configurations with removable interior walls. Three doors mean everybody doesn't tromp through the center room for access to the side

rooms. It will stand up to wind, rain, and frequent use.

COLEMAN MODIFIED DOME

800/835-3278

www.coleman.com

Coleman Modified Dome tents are available in six different single- and multi-room designs. The pole structure is unique, with all four upright poles and one ridgepole shock-corded together for an integrated system that makes setup extremely fast and easy. Yet, because of the ridgepole's engineering, the tent has passed tests in high winds. Mesh panels in the ceiling are a tremendous plus for ventilation.

COLEMAN WEATHERMASTER

800/835-3278

www.coleman.com

The Weathermaster series features tents with multiple rooms, walls, and ample headroom, and they are guaranteed to keep rain out. The 17- by 9-foot model sleeps six to eight, has a 76-inch ceiling, and has zippered dividers. Since the dividers are removable, you can configure the tent in multiple layouts. The frame is designed with poles adjustable to three different heights to accommodate uneven ground.

KELTY

800/423-2320

www.kelty.com

Kelty offers top-of-the-line tents based on a sleek dome profile. This is a great package, with mesh sides, tops, and doors, along with a full awning fly and coverage for weather protection. Clip sleeves and rubber-tipped poles for easy slide during setup are nice bonuses.

REI

800/423-2320

www.rei.com

REI has 94 backpacking tents and 27 tents available for car camping, including their own designs as well as those from other manufacturers. A great backpacking tent for two is the REI

Half Dome 2 Plus. The Eureka Copper Canyon 6 is one of the better family values.

Bivouac Bags

If you like going light or solo, and choose not to own a tent at all, a bivy bag or tarp can be the way to go. Bivy is short for bivouac bag and pronounced "bivvy" as in dizzy, not "bivy" as in ivy, and can provide the extremely lightweight weather protection you require. A bivy bag is a water-repellent shell in which your sleeping bag fits. It is light and tough, and for some is the perfect alternative to a heavy tent. My own bivy weighs 31 ounces and cost around $250; it's made by OR (Outdoor Research), and I just plain love the thing on expeditions. On the downside, however, some say it can be a bit difficult getting settled just right in it, and others say they feel claustrophobic in such close quarters. Once you get used to a bivy, spend a night in a tent; the tent will feel like a room at the Mirage. For me, not a problem.

The idea of riding out a storm in a bivy can be quite worrisome for some. You can hear the rain hitting you, and sometimes even feel the pounding of the drops through the bivy bag. For some, it can be unsettling to try to sleep under such circumstances. On the other hand, I've always looked forward to it. In cold weather, a bivy also helps keep you warm. I've had just one miserable night in mine. That was when my sleeping bag was a bit wet when I started the night. By the middle of the night, the water was condensing from the sleeping bag on the interior walls of the bivy, and then soaking the bag, like a storm cycle. The night hit only about 45°F but I just about froze to death anyway. Otherwise, I've used it on more than 100 expeditions with great results: warm, dry quarters and deep, restful sleeps by night, and a pack lightened without carrying a tent by day.

Many long-distance hikers are switching to light tarps in the continuing mission to minimize weight. They work great in rain and the spacious feel beneath them is fantastic. You just need a tree to tie to and soft enough ground for stakes, so they don't work above tree line. Tarps are great, except when there are bug problems; then you need some kind of mosquito netting. A bivy or tent solves that, of course.

Pickup Truck Campers

If you own a pickup truck with a camper shell, you can turn it into a self-contained campground with a little work. This can be an ideal way to go: It's fast, portable, and you are guaranteed a dry environment.

But that does not necessarily mean it is a warm environment. In fact, without insulation from the metal truck bed, it can be like trying to sleep on an iceberg. The metal truck bed will get as cold as the air temperature, which is often much colder than the ground temperature. Without insulation, it can be much colder in your camper shell than it would be on the open ground.

When I camp in my rig, I use a large piece of foam for a mattress and insulation. The foam measures four inches thick, 48 inches wide, and 76 inches long. It makes for a bed as comfortable as anything one might ask for. In fact, during the winter, if I don't go camping for a few weeks because of writing obligations, I sometimes will throw the foam on the floor, lay down the old sleeping bag, light a fire, and camp right in my living room. It's in my blood, I tell you. Airbeds and cots are also extremely comfortable and I've used both many times. Whatever you choose, just make sure you have a comfortable sleeping unit. Good sleep makes for great camping trips.

RVs

The problems RVers encounter come from two primary sources: lack of privacy and light intrusion.

The lack of privacy stems from the natural restrictions of where a land yacht can go. Without careful use of the guide section of this book, owners of RVs can find themselves in parking-lot settings, jammed in with plenty of neighbors. Because RVs often have large picture windows, you lose your privacy, causing some late nights; then, come daybreak, light

intrusion forces an early wake up. As a result, you get shorted on your sleep.

The answer is to carry inserts to fit over the inside of your windows. These close off the outside and retain your privacy. And if you don't want to wake up with the sun at daybreak, you don't have to. It will still be dark.

Many campgrounds and RV parks enforce a quiet time. If that is important to you, make sure you don't end up somewhere where a quiet time is optional.

HIKING AND FOOT CARE

We had set up a nice little camp in the woods, and my buddy, Foonsky, was strapping on his hiking boots, sitting against a big Douglas fir.

"New boots," he said with a grin. "But they seem pretty stiff."

We decided to hoof it down the trail for a few hours, exploring the mountain wildlands that are said to hide Bigfoot and other strange creatures. After just a short while on the trail, a sense of peace and calm seemed to settle in. The forest provides the chance to be purified with clean air and the smell of trees, freeing you from all troubles.

But it wasn't long before a look of trouble was on Foonsky's face. And no, it wasn't from seeing Bigfoot.

"Got a hot spot on my toe," he said.

Immediately, we stopped. He pulled off his right boot, then his sock, and inspected the left side of his big toe. Sure enough, a blister had bubbled up, filled with fluid, but hadn't popped. From his medical kit, Foonsky cut a small piece of moleskin to fit over the blister and taped it to hold it in place. In a few minutes we were back on the trail.

A half hour later, there was still no sign of Bigfoot. But Foonsky stopped again and pulled off his other boot. "Another hot spot." On the little toe of his left foot was another small blister, over which he taped a Band-Aid to keep it from further chafing against the inside of his new boot.

In just a few days, ol' Foonsky, a strong, 6-foot-5, 200-plus-pound guy, was walking around like a sore-hoofed horse that had been loaded with a month's worth of supplies and ridden over sharp rocks. Well, it wasn't the distance that had done Foonsky in; it was those blisters. He had them on eight of his 10 toes and was going through Band-Aids, moleskin, and tape like a walking emergency ward. If he'd used any more tape, he would've looked like a mummy from an Egyptian tomb.

If you've ever been in a similar predicament, you know the frustration of wanting to have a good time, wanting to hike and explore the area where you have set up a secluded camp, only to be held up by several blisters. No one is immune—all are created equal before the blister god. You can be forced to bow to it unless you get your act together.

What causes blisters? In almost all cases, it is the simple rubbing of a foot against the rugged interior of a boot. That can be worsened by several factors:

1. A very stiff boot or one in which your foot moves inside as you walk, instead of a boot that flexes as if it were another layer of skin.

2. Thin, ragged, or dirty socks. This is the fastest route to blisters. Thin socks will allow your feet to move inside your boots, ragged socks will allow your skin to chafe directly against the boot's interior, and dirty socks will wrinkle and fold, also rubbing against your feet instead of cushioning them.

3. Soft feet. By themselves, soft feet will not cause blisters, but in combination with a stiff boot or thin socks, they can cause terrible problems. The best way to toughen up your feet is to go barefoot. In fact, some of the biggest, toughest-looking guys you'll ever see, from Hells Angels to pro football players, have feet that are as soft as a baby's butt. Why? Because they never go barefoot and don't hike much.

The Perfect Boot

Every hiker eventually conducts a search for the perfect boot in the mission for ideal foot comfort and freedom from blisters. While there are many entries in this search—in fact, so many that it can be confusing—there is a way to find that perfect boot for you.

To stay blister-free, the most important factors are socks and boot flexibility. If there is

Hiking shoes are perfect for short treks to day-long trips.

KEEP IT WILD TIP 2:
KEEP THE WILDERNESS WILD

1. Let nature's sound prevail. Avoid loud voices and noises.
2. Leave radios and tape players at home. At drive-in camping sites, never open car doors with music playing.
3. Careful guidance is necessary when choosing any games to bring for children. Most toys, especially any kind of gun toys with which children simulate shooting at each other, shouldn't be allowed on a camping trip.
4. Control pets at all times or leave them with a sitter at home.
5. Treat natural heritage with respect. Leave plants, rocks, and historical artifacts where you find them.

---

any foot slippage from a thin sock or a stiff boot, you can rub up a blister in minutes. For instance, I never wear stiff boots and I sometimes wear two fresh sets of SmartWools.

My search for the perfect boot included discussions with the nation's preeminent long-distance hikers, Brian Robinson of Mountain View (7,200 miles in 2001) and Ray Jardine of Oregon (2,700 miles of Pacific Crest Trail in three months). Both believe that the weight of a shoe is the defining factor when selecting hiking footwear. They both go as light as possible, believing that heavy boots will eventually wear you out by forcing you to pick up several pounds on your feet over and over again.

It is absolutely critical to stay away from very stiff boots and thin socks. Always wear the right style boots for what you have in mind and then protect your feet with carefully selected socks. If you are still so unfortunate as to get a blister or two, it means knowing how to treat them fast so they don't turn your walk into a sore-footed endurance test.

Selecting the Right Boots

The first time we did the John Muir Trail, I hiked 400 miles in three months; that is, 150 miles in a two-month general-training program, then 250 miles in three weeks from Mount Whitney to Yosemite Valley. In that span, I got just one blister, suffered on the fourth day of the 250-miler. I treated it immediately and suffered no more. One key is wearing

the right boot, and for me, that means a boot that acts as a thick layer of skin that is flexible and pliable to my foot. I want my feet to fit snugly in them, with no interior movement.

There are four kinds of hiking footwear, most commonly known as: 1. Hiking boots; 2. Hunting boots; 3. Mountaineering boots; 4. Athletic shoes. Select the right one for you or pay the consequences.

One great trick when on a hiking vacation is to bring all four, and then for each hike, wear different footwear. This has many benefits. By changing boots, you change the points of stress for your feet and legs, greatly reducing soreness and the chance of creating a hot spot on a foot. It also allows you to go light on flat trails and heavy on steep trails, where additional boot weight can help with traction in downhill stretches.

HIKING BOOTS

Lightweight hiking boots are basically Gore-Tex walking shoes. They are designed for day walks or short backpacking trips and look like rugged, lightweight athletic shoes, designed with a Gore-Tex top for lightness and a Vibram sole for traction. These are perfect for people who like to walk but rarely carry a heavy backpack. Because they are flexible, they are easy to break in, and with fresh socks, they rarely cause blister problems. Because they are light, general hiking fatigue is greatly reduced. Like many, I've converted over 100 percent to them.

On the negative side, because hiking boots are light, traction can be far from great on steep, gravelly surfaces. In addition, they provide less than ideal ankle support, which can be a problem in rocky areas, such as along a stream where you might want to go trout fishing.

Regardless of the distance you anticipate, they are the footwear of choice. My personal preference is Merrell's, but New Balance, Salomon, Asolo, Zamberlan, Vasque, and others make great hiking boots. Many of the greatest long-distance hikers in America wear trail running shoes.

Hunting Boots

Hunting boots are also called backpacking boots, super boots, or wilderness boots. They feature high ankle support, deep Vibram lug sole, built-in orthotics and arch support, and waterproof exterior.

They have fallen out of favor among campers and backpackers. On the negative side, hunting boots can be quite hot, weigh a ton, and if they get wet, take days to dry. Because they are heavy, they can wear you out. Often, the extra weight can add days to long-distance expeditions, cutting into the number of miles a hiker is capable of on a daily basis.

They are still popular among mountaineers who hunt. Their weight and traction make them good for trekking off-trail or for carrying heavy packs because they provide additional support. They also can stand up to hundreds of miles of wilderness use, constantly being banged against rocks and walked through streams while supporting 200 pounds.

My favorite hunting boot is made by Mendl, out of Germany. I have also used Danner, Cabela's and RedWing.

Mountaineering Boots

Mountaineering boots are identified by midrange tops, laces that extend almost as far as the toe area, and ankle areas that are as stiff as a board. The lack of "give" is what endears them to mountaineers. Their stiffness is preferred when rock-climbing, walking off-trail

on craggy surfaces, or hiking along the edge of streambeds where walking across small rocks can cause you to turn your ankle. Because these boots don't give on rugged, craggy terrain, they reduce ankle injuries and provide better traction.

The drawback to stiff boots is that if you don't have the proper socks and your foot starts slipping around in the boot, blisters will inevitably follow. If you just want to go for a walk or a good tromp with a backpack, then hiking shoes or hunting boots will serve you better.

Vasque makes my favorite mountaineering boots for rock climbing.

At the Store

There are many styles, brands, and price ranges to choose from. If you wander about comparing all their many features, you will get as confused as a kid in a toy store.

Instead, go into the store with your mind clear about what you want, find it, and buy it. If you want the best, expect to spend $85-200 for hiking boots, $100-250 for hunting boots, $250-300 for mountaineering boots. If you go much cheaper, well, then you are getting cheap footwear.

This is one area where you don't want to scrimp, so try not to yelp about the high cost. Instead, walk into the store believing you deserve the best, and that's exactly what you'll pay for.

You don't always get what you pay for, though. Once, I spent $200-plus on some hunting boots that turned out to be miserable blister-makers and I had to throw them out. Even after a year of trying to get my money's worth, I never felt they worked right on the trail. Adios. Move on to what works.

If you plan to use the advice of a shoe salesperson, first look at what kind of boots he or she is wearing. If the salesperson isn't even wearing boots, then their advice may not be worth much. Most people I know who own quality boots, including salespeople, wear them almost daily if their jobs allow, since boots are the best footwear available. However, even these well-meaning folks can offer sketchy advice. Plenty of hikers claim to wear the world's greatest boot! Instead of asking how great the boot is, ask, "How many blisters did you get when you hiked 12 miles a day for a week?"

Enter the store with a precise use and style in mind. Rather than fish for suggestions, tell the salesperson exactly what you want, try two or three brands of the same style, and always try on both boots in a pair simultaneously so you know exactly how they'll feel. If possible, walk up and down stairs with them. Are they too stiff? Are your feet snug yet comfortable, or do they slip? Do they have that "right" kind of feel when you walk?

If you get the appropriate answers to those questions, then you're on your way to blister-free, pleasure-filled days of walking.

Socks

People can spend so much energy selecting the right kind of boots that they virtually overlook wearing the right kind of socks. One goes with the other.

Your socks should be thick enough to cushion your feet as well as fit snugly. Without good socks, you might tie your bootlaces too tight—and that's like putting a tourniquet on your feet. You should have plenty of clean socks on hand, or plan on washing what you have on your trip. As socks are worn, they become compressed, dirty, and damp. If they fold over, you'll rub up a blister in minutes.

My companions believe I go overboard when it comes to socks, that I bring too many and wear too many. But it works, so that's where the complaints stop. So how many do I wear? Well, it varies. On day hikes, I have found a sock called a SmartWool that makes my size 13s feel as if they're walking on pillows. I often wear two of them; that is, two on each foot. Several manufacturers now produce socks that are the equivalent of SmartWools, but are a lot less expensive. SmartWool socks and other similar socks are a synthetic composite. They can partially wick moisture away from the skin.

Some hikers wear multiple socks and it

works for them—a comfortable cotton-poly blend sock on the interior and wool sock on the exterior. This will cushion your foot, provide that just-right snug fit in your boot, and give you some additional warmth and insulation in cold weather. It is critical to keep the interior sock clean. If you wear a sock over and over again, it will compact, lose its cushion, and start wrinkling or folding over while you hike and a blister will be born.

Do not wear thin cotton socks. Your foot can get damp and mix with dirt, which can cause a hot spot to start on your foot. Eventually, you get blisters, lots of them.

Inner Sole

If you are like most folks, the bottoms of your feet are rarely exposed and can be quite soft. You can take additional steps in their care. The best tip is keeping a fresh inner sole footpad in your boot. I prefer Dr. Scholl's gel pad or the equivalent. Some new inner soles can be slippery for a few days, which, if your foot slides around while you're hiking, can cause blisters. Just like new boots and new socks, they need to be broken in before an expedition.

Another cure for soft feet is to get out and walk or jog on a regular basis before your camping trip. On one trip on the Pacific Coast Trail, I ran into the long-distance master Jardine. He swore that going barefoot regularly is the best way to build up foot strength and arch support, while toughening up the bottom of your feet.

If you plan to use a foot pad and wear two heavy socks, you will need to use these items when sizing boots. Do not buy shoes if you're wearing thin cotton socks; wear the socks you're planning to wear when hiking, insert the inner sole, and then see how they feel. That's the only right way to size a hiking boot.

Treating Blisters

The key to treating blisters is fast work at the first sign of a hot spot. If you feel a hot spot, never keep walking, figuring that the problem will go away or that you will work through it. Wrong! Stop immediately and go to work.

Before you remove your socks, check to see if the sock has a wrinkle in it, a likely cause of the problem. If so, either change socks or pull them tight, removing the tiny folds, after taking care of the blister.

To take care of the blister, forget Moleskin. (They changed how they manufacture it and I've found it will slide off the blister while hiking.) Instead, use "Second Skin," which adheres over the top of the blister and does not dislodge. For small blisters, Band-Aids can do the job, but these have to be replaced daily, and sometimes with even more frequency. At night, clean your feet and sleep without socks. That will allow your feet to dry and heal.

Tips in the Field

Three other items that can help your walking are an Ace bandage, a pair of gaiters, and hiking poles.

For sprained ankles and twisted knees, an Ace bandage can be like an insurance policy to get you back on the trail and out of trouble. In many cases, a hiker with a twisted ankle or sprained knee has relied on a good wrap with a four-inch bandage for the added support to get home. Always buy the Ace bandages that come with the clips permanently attached, so you don't have to worry about losing them.

Gaiters are leggings made of Gore-Tex that fit from just below your knees, over your calves, and attach under your boots. They are of particular help when walking in damp areas or in places where rain is common. As your legs brush against ferns or low-lying plants, gaiters deflect the moisture. Without them, pants can get soaked wet in short order.

Many hikers would never hit the trail without hiking poles. Personally, they are not for me; I like to hike in rhythm and keeping my arms swinging effortlessly. I don't like to have to watch where I'm putting my poles all the time. But for those who have trouble with footing, a cranky knee or ankle, or want the upper body workout, poles can be a good fit. If it floats your boat, bring 'em.

Another tip: Should your boots become wet, never try to force-dry them. Some well-meaning folks will try to dry them quickly at the edge of a campfire, or at home, actually put the boots in an oven. While this may dry the boots, it can also loosen the glue that holds them together, ultimately weakening them until one day they fall apart in a heap.

A better bet is to treat the leather so the boots become water-repellent. Silicone-based liquids are the easiest to use and least greasy of the treatments available.

A final tip is to have another pair of lightweight shoes or moccasins that you can wear around camp and, in the process, give your feet the rest they deserve.

CLOTHING AND WEATHER PROTECTION

What started as an innocent pursuit of the perfect campground evolved into one heck of a predicament for Foonsky and me.

We had parked at the end of a logging road and then bushwhacked our way down a canyon to a pristine trout stream. On my first cast—a little flip into the plunge pool of a waterfall—I caught a 16-inch rainbow trout, a real beauty that jumped three times. Magic stuff.

Then, just across the stream, we saw it: The Perfect Camping Spot. On a sandbar on the edge of the forest, there lay a flat spot, high and dry above the river. Nearby was plenty of downed wood collected by past winter storms that we could use for firewood. And, of course, this beautiful trout stream was bubbling along just 40 yards from the site.

But nothing is perfect, right? To reach it, we had to wade across the river, although it didn't appear to be too difficult. The cold water tingled a bit, and the river came up surprisingly high, just above the belt. But it would be worth it to camp at The Perfect Spot.

Once across the river, we put on some dry clothes, set up camp, explored the woods, and fished the stream, catching several nice trout for dinner. But late that afternoon, it started raining. What? Rain in the summertime? Nature makes its own rules. By the next morning, it was still raining, pouring like a Yosemite waterfall from a solid gray sky.

That's when we noticed The Perfect Spot wasn't so perfect. The rain had raised the river level too high for us to wade back across. We were marooned, wet, and hungry.

"Now we're in a heck of a predicament," said Foonsky, the water streaming off him.

Getting cold and wet on a camping trip with no way to warm up is not only unnecessary and uncomfortable, it can be a fast ticket to hypothermia, the number one killer of campers in the woods. By definition, hypothermia is a condition in which body temperature is lowered to the point that it causes illness. It is particularly dangerous because the afflicted are usually unaware it is setting in. The first sign is a sense of apathy, then a state of confusion, which can lead eventually to collapse (or what appears to be sleep), then death.

You must always have a way to get warm and dry in short order, regardless of any conditions you may face. If you have no way of getting dry, then you must take emergency steps to prevent hypothermia. (See the steps detailed in *First Aid and Insect Protection* in this chapter.)

But you should never reach that point. For starters, always have spare sets of clothing tucked away so no matter how cold and wet you might get, you have something dry to put on. On hiking trips, I always carry a second set of clothes, sealed to stay dry, in a plastic garbage bag. I keep a third set waiting back at the truck.

If you are car camping, your vehicle can cause an illusory sense of security. But with an extra set of dry clothes stashed safely away, there is no illusion. The security is real. And remember, no matter how hot the weather is when you start your trip, always be prepared for the worst. Foonsky and I learned the hard way.

So both of us were soaking wet on that sandbar. With no other choice, we tried holing up in the tent for the night. A sleeping bag with Quallofil or another polyester fiberfill can retain warmth even when wet, because the fill is hollow and retains its loft. So as miserable as it was, the night passed without incident.

The rain stopped the next day and the river dropped a bit, but it was still rolling big and angry. Using a stick as a wading staff, Foonsky crossed about 80 percent of the stream before he was dumped, but he made a jump for it and managed to scramble to the riverbank. He waved for me to follow. "No problem," I thought.

It took me 20 minutes to reach nearly the same spot where Foonsky had been dumped. The heavy river current was above my belt and pushing hard. Then, in the flash of an instant, my wading staff slipped on a rock. I teetered in the river current and was knocked over like a bowling pin. I became completely submerged. I went tumbling down the river, heading right toward the waterfall. While underwater, I looked up at the surface, and I can remember how close it seemed yet how out of control I was. Right then, this giant hand appeared, and I grabbed it. It was Foonsky. If it weren't for that hand, I would have sailed right over the waterfall.

My momentum drew Foonsky right into the river, and we scrambled in the current, but I suddenly sensed the river bottom under my knees. On all fours, the two of us clambered ashore. We were safe.

"Thanks, ol' buddy," I said.

"Man, we're wet," he responded. "Let's get to the rig and get some dry clothes on."

The Art of Layering

The most important element for enjoying the outdoor experience in any condition is to stay dry and warm. There is no substitute. You must stay dry and you must stay warm.

Thus comes the theory behind layering, which suggests that as your body temperature fluctuates or the weather shifts, you simply peel off or add available layers as needed—and have a waterproof shell available in case of rain.

The introduction of a new era of outdoor clothing has made it possible for campers to turn choosing clothes into an art form. Like art, it's much more expensive than throwing on a pair of blue jeans, a T-shirt, and some flannel, but, for many, it is worth the price.

KEEP IT WILD TIP 3: TRAVEL LIGHTLY

1. Visit the backcountry in small groups.
2. Below tree line, always stay on designated trails.
3. Don't cut across switchbacks.
4. When traveling cross-country where no trails are available, follow animal trails or spread out with your group so no new routes are created.
5. Read your map and orient yourself with landmarks, a compass, and an altimeter. Avoid marking trails with rock cairns, tree scars, or ribbons.

In putting together your ideal layering system, there are some general considerations. What you need to do is create a system that effectively combines elements of breathability, durability, insulation, rapid drying, water repellence, wicking, and wind resistance, while still being lightweight and offering the necessary freedom of movement, all with just a few garments.

The basic intent of a base layer is to manage moisture. Your base layer will be the first article of clothing you put on and the last to come off. Since your own skin will be churning out the perspiration, the goal of this second skin is to manage the moisture and move it away from you. The best base layers are made of bicomponent knits, that is, blends of polyester and cotton, which provide wicking and insulating properties in one layer.

The way it works is that the side facing your skin is water-hating, while the side away from your skin is water-loving; thus, it pulls or "wicks" moisture through the material. You'll stay dry and happy, even with only one layer on, something not possible with old single-function weaves. The best include Capilene, Driclime, Lifa, Polartec 100, and Thermax. The only time that cotton should become a part of your base layer is if you wish to keep cool, not warm, such as in a hot desert climate where evaporative cooling becomes your friend, not your enemy.

Stretch fleece and microdenier pile also provide a good base layer, though they can be used as a second layer as well. Microdenier pile can be worn alone or layered under or over other pieces; it has excellent wicking capability as well as more windproof potential.

The next layer should be a light cotton shirt or a long-sleeved cotton/wool shirt, or both, depending on the coolness of the day. For pants, many just wear blue jeans when camping, but blue jeans can be hot and tight, and once wet, they tend to stay that way. Putting on wet blue jeans on a cold morning is a torturous way to start the day. A better choice is pants made from nylon with detachable leggings; these are light, have a lot of give, and dry quickly. If the weather is quite warm, nylon shorts that have some room to them can be the best choice. My preference is for The North Face dark-green expedition hiking shorts.

Finally, you should top the entire ensemble off with a thin, windproof, water-resistant layer. You want this layer to breathe, yet not be so porous that rain runs through it. Patagonia's Velocity shell is one of the best; its outer fabric is treated with DWR (Durable Water Repellent finish) and the coating is by Goretex. Patagonia, Marmot, and The North Face and others all offer their own versions. Though condensation will still build up inside, it manages to get rid of enough moisture.

Note: It is critical to know the difference between "water-resistant" and "waterproof." (This is covered under the *Rain Gear* section in this chapter.)

But hey, why does anybody need all this fancy stuff just to go camping? Fair question. You don't have to opt for this aerobic-function fashion statement. It is unnecessary on many camping trips. The fact is that you must be ready for anything when you venture into the outdoors. The new era of outdoor clothing works, and it works better than anything that has come before. Regardless of what you choose, weather should never be a nuisance or cause discomfort. There is no such thing as bad weather, so the saying goes, only bad gear.

Hats

Another word of advice: Always pack along a warm hat for those times when you need to seal in warmth. You lose a large percentage of heat through your head. At night in cold weather, I wear a skullcap. During the day, I almost always wear a wide-brimmed hat, something like those that the legendary outlaws wore 150 years ago. There's actually logic behind it: My hat is made of waterproof canvas, is rigged with a lariat (it can be cinched down when it's windy), and has a wide brim that keeps the tops of my ears from being sunburned. If you're outside a lot, do not wear baseball hats—the tops of your ears will burn to a red crisp. Years ago, that's how an old friend of mine lost his ears to skin cancer.

HEAD LIGHT

I've tried many head lights and the Trail Torch Hat Light is my favorite by a mile (www.halibut. net). It comes with five white and green LED lights in a horizontal row that clips under the bill of your hat. For the best option, order the set with three green lights (for night vision) and two white lights. (At night you'll look like a jet coming in for a landing.)

Vests and Parkas

In cold weather, you should take the layer system one step further with a warm vest and a parka jacket. Vests are especially useful because they provide warmth without the bulkiness of a parka. The warmest vests and parkas are either filled with down or Quallofil, or they are made with a cotton/wool mix. Each has its respective merits and problems. Down fill provides the most warmth for the amount of weight, but becomes useless when wet, closely resembling a wet dishrag. Quallofil keeps much of its heat-retaining quality even when wet, but it is expensive. Vests made of cotton/wool mixes are the most attractive and also are quite warm, but they can be as heavy as a ship's anchor when wet.

Sometimes, the answer is combining a parka with a vest. One of my best camping companions wears a good-looking cotton/wool vest and a parka filled with Quallofil. The vest never gets wet, so weight is not a factor.

Rain Gear

One of the most miserable nights of my life was on a camping trip for which I hadn't brought my rain gear or a tent. Hey, it was early August, the temperature had been in the 90s for weeks, and if anybody had said it was going to rain, I would have told him to consult a brain doctor. But rain it did. And as I got wetter and wetter, I kept saying to myself, "Hey, it's summer, it's not supposed to rain." Then I remembered one of the 10 commandments of camping: Forget your rain gear and you can guarantee it will rain.

To stay dry, you need some form of water-repellent shell. It can be as simple as a $5 poncho made out of plastic or as elaborate as a $300 Gore-Tex jacket-and-pants set. What counts is not how much you spend, but how dry you stay.

The most important thing to realize is that waterproof and water-resistant are completely different things. In addition, there is no such thing as rain gear that is both waterproof and breathable. The more waterproof a jacket is, the less it breathes. Conversely, the more breathable a jacket is, the less waterproof it becomes.

If you wear water-resistant rain gear in a sustained downpour, you'll get soaked. Water-resistant rain gear is appealing because it breathes and will keep you dry in the light stuff, such as mist, fog, even a little splash from a canoe paddle. But in rain? Forget it.

So what is the solution?

I've decided that the best approach is a set of fairly light but 100 percent-waterproof rain gear. I recently bought a hooded jacket and pants from Coleman, and my assessment is that it is the most cost-efficient rain gear I've ever had. All I can say is, hey, it works: I stay dry, it doesn't weigh much, and it didn't cost a fortune.

The absolute best foul weather gear made is by Simms, both jacket and bib. While it is expensive, you will stay dry and warm in any condition but that in which you need a survival suit.

You can also stay dry with any of the waterproof plastics and even heavy-duty rubber-coated outfits made for commercial fishermen. But these are uncomfortable during anything but a heavy rain. Because they are heavy and don't breathe, you'll likely get soaked anyway (that is, from your own sweat), even if it isn't raining hard.

On backpacking trips, I still stash a super-lightweight, water-repellent slicker for day hikes and a poncho, which I throw over my pack at night to keep it dry. But, otherwise, I never go anywhere—*anywhere*—without my rain gear.

Some do just fine with a cheap poncho, and note that ponchos can serve other uses in addition to a raincoat. Ponchos can be used as a ground tarp, as a rain cover for supplies or a backpack, or can be snapped together and roped up to trees in a pinch to provide a quick storm ceiling if you don't have a tent. The problem with ponchos is that in a hard rain, you just don't stay dry. First your legs get wet, then they get soaked. Then your arms follow the same pattern. If you're wearing cotton, you'll find that once part of the garment gets wet, the water spreads until, alas, you are dripping wet, poncho and all. Before long, you start to feel like a walking refrigerator.

One high-cost option is to buy a Gore-Tex rain jacket and pants. Gore-Tex is actually not a fabric, as is commonly believed, but a laminated film that coats a breathable fabric. The result is lightweight, water-repellent, breathable jackets and pants. They are perfect for campers, but they cost a fortune.

Some hiking buddies of mine have complained that the older Gore-Tex rain gear loses its water-repellent quality over time. However, manufacturers insist that this is the result of water seeping through seams, not leaks in the jacket. At each seam, tiny needles have pierced the fabric, and as tiny as the holes are, water will find a way through. An application of Seam Lock, especially at major seams around the shoulders of a jacket, can usually fix the problem.

If you don't want to spend the big bucks for Gore-Tex rain gear but want more rain protection than a poncho affords, a coated nylon jacket is the compromise that many choose. They are inexpensive, have the highest water-repellency of any rain gear, and are warm, providing a good outer shell for your layers of clothing. But they are not without fault. These jackets don't breathe at all, and if you zip them up tight, you can sweat a river.

My brother Rambob gave me a nylon jacket before a mountain-climbing expedition. I wore that cheap special all the way to the top with no complaints; it's warm and 100 percent waterproof. The one problem with nylon comes when temperatures drop below freezing. It gets so stiff that it feels as if you are wearing a straitjacket.

There's one more jacket-construction term to know: DWR, or Durable Water-Repellent finish. All of the top-quality jackets these days are DWR-treated. The DWR causes water to bead on the shell. When the DWR wears off, even a once-waterproof jacket will feel like a wet dishrag.

Also note that ventilation is the key to coolness. The only ventilation on most shells is often the zipper. But waterproof jackets need additional openings. Look for mesh-backed pockets and underarm zippers, as well as cuffs, waists, and hems that can be adjusted to open wide. Storm flaps (the baffle over the zipper) that close with hook-and-loop material or snaps let you leave the zipper open for airflow into the jacket.

Other Gear

What are the three items most commonly

forgotten on a camping trip? A hat, sunglasses, and lip balm.

A hat is crucial, especially when you are visiting high elevations. Without one you are constantly exposed to everything nature can give you. The sun will dehydrate you, sap your energy, sunburn your head, and in worst cases, cause sunstroke. Start with a comfortable hat. Then finish with sunglasses, lip balm, and sunscreen for additional protection. They will help protect you from extreme heat.

To guard against extreme cold, it's a good idea to keep a pair of thin ski gloves stashed away with your emergency clothes, along with a wool ski cap, or a skull cap. The gloves should be thick enough to keep your fingers from stiffening up, but pliable enough to allow full movement so you don't have to take them off to complete simple tasks, like lighting a stove. An alternative to gloves is glovelets, which look like gloves with no fingers. In any case, just because the weather turns cold doesn't mean that your hands have to.

FOOD AND COOKING GEAR

It was a warm, crystal clear day, a perfect day for skydiving. That was exactly the case for my old pal Foonsky, who had never before tried the sport. But a funny thing happened after he jumped out of the plane and pulled on the rip cord: His parachute didn't open.

In total free fall, Foonsky watched the earth below getting closer and closer. Not one to panic, he calmly pulled the ripcord on the emergency parachute. Again, nothing happened. No parachute, no nothing.

The ground was getting ever closer, and as he tried to search for a soft place to land, Foonsky detected a small object shooting up toward him, growing larger as it approached. It looked like a camper.

Figuring this was his last chance, Foonsky shouted as they passed in midair, "Hey, do you know anything about parachutes?"

The other fellow just yelled back as he headed off into space, "Do you know anything about lighting camping stoves?"

Well, Foonsky got lucky and his parachute opened. As for the other guy, well, he's probably in orbit like a NASA weather satellite. If you've ever had a mishap while lighting a camping stove, you know exactly what I'm talking about.

When it comes to camping, all gear is not created equal. Nothing is more important than lighting your stove easily and having it reach full heat without feeling as if you're playing with a short fuse to a miniature bomb. If your stove does not work right, your trip can turn into a disaster, regardless of how well you have planned the other elements. In addition, a bad stove will add an underlying sense of foreboding to your day. You will constantly have the inner suspicion that your darn stove is going to foul up again.

Camping Stoves

If you are buying a camping stove, remember this one critical rule: Do not leave the store with a new stove unless you have been shown exactly how to use it.

Know what you are getting. Many stores that specialize in outdoor recreation equipment now staff experienced campers/employees who will demonstrate the use of every stove they sell. While they're at it, they'll also describe the stoves' respective strengths and weaknesses.

An innovation by Peak 1 is a two-burner butane-powered backpacking stove that allows you to boil water and heat a pot of food simultaneously. While that has long been standard for car campers using Coleman's legendary camp stove, it was previously unheard of for wilderness campers in high-elevation areas. It's a fantastic stove.

The standard Coleman car camping stove, the green one with the two burners, is a legend around the world. Electronic ignition has solved all the old lighting problems.

A stove that has developed a cult-like following is the little Sierra, which burns small twigs and pinecones, then uses a tiny battery-driven fan to develop increased heat and

KEEP IT WILD TIP 4: CAMPFIRES

1. Fire use can scar the backcountry. If a fire ring is not available, use a lightweight stove for cooking.
2. Where fires are permitted, use existing fire rings away from large rocks or overhangs.
3. Don't char rocks by building new rings.
4. Gather sticks from the ground that are no larger than the diameter of your wrist.
5. Don't snap branches of live, dead, or downed trees, which can cause personal injury and also scar the natural setting.
6. Put the fire "dead out" and make sure it's cold before departing. Remove all trash from the fire ring and sprinkle dirt over the site.
7. Remember that some forest fires can be started by a campfire that appears to be out. Hot embers burning deep in the pit can cause tree roots to catch fire and burn underground. If you ever see smoke rising from the ground, seemingly from nowhere, dig down and put the fire out.

cooking ability. It's an excellent alternative for long-distance backpacking trips, as it solves the problem of carrying a fuel bottle, especially on expeditions for which large quantities of fuel would otherwise be needed. Some tinkering with the flame (a very hot one) is required, and they are legal and functional only in the alpine zone where dry wood is available. Also note that in years with high fire danger, the U.S. Forest Service enacts rules prohibiting open flames, and fires are also often prohibited above an elevation of 10,000 feet.

The MSR Whisperlite is an icon among backpackers. I've gone through several of them. It uses white gas in a separate fuel container so you can easily monitor fuel consumption. The one flaw is the connector links from the fuel line. After a few years of heavy use, they can develop leaks; ignite and you've got meltdown.

For heavy, long-term use, ease of cleaning the burner is the most important. If you camp often, especially with a smaller stove, the burner holes will eventually become clogged. Some stoves have a built-in cleaning needle: a quick twist of the knob and you're in business. Others require disassembly and a protracted cleaning session using special tools. If a stove is difficult to clean, you will tend to put off the tiresome chore, and your stove will sputter and pant while you watch that pot of water sitting there, staying cold.

Before making a purchase, have the salesperson show you how to clean the burner head. Except in the case of large, multi-burner family-style camping stoves, which rarely require cleaning, this run-through can do more to determine the long-term value of a stove than any other factor.

Fuels for Camping Stoves

White gas and butane have long been the most popular camp fuels, but a newly developed fuel could dramatically change that.

LPG (liquid petroleum gas) comes in cartridges for easy attachment to a stove or lantern. At room temperature, LPG is delivered in a combustible gaseous form. When you shake the cartridge, the contents sound liquid; that is because the gas liquefies under pressure, which is why it is so easy to use. Large amounts of fuel can be compressed into small canisters.

The following summaries detail the benefits and drawbacks of other available fuels:

Butane: You don't have to worry about explosions when using stoves that burn bottled butane fuel. Butane requires no pouring, pumping, or priming, and butane stoves are the easiest to light. Just turn a knob and light—that's it. On the minus side, because it comes in bottles, you never know precisely how much fuel you have left. And when a bottle is empty, you have a potential piece of litter. (Never litter. Ever.)

The other problem with butane is that it

just plain does not work well in cold weather or when there is little fuel left in the cartridge. Since you cannot predict mountain weather in spring or fall, you might wind up using more fuel than originally projected. That can be frustrating, particularly if your stove starts wheezing when there are still several days left to go. In addition, with most butane cartridges, if there is any chance of the temperature falling below freezing, you often have to sleep with the cartridge to keep it warm. Otherwise, forget about using it come morning.

Butane/Propane: This blend offers higher octane performance than butane alone, solving the cold temperature doldrums somewhat. However, propane burns off before butane, so there's a performance drop as the fuel level in the cartridge lowers.

Coleman Max Performance Fuel: This fuel offers a unique approach to solving the consistent burn challenge facing all pressurized gas cartridges: operating at temperatures at or below 0°F. Using a standard propane/butane blend for high-octane performance, Coleman gets around the drop-off in performance other cartridges experience by using a version of fuel injection. A hose inside the cartridge pulls liquid fuel into the stove, where it vaporizes—a switch from the standard approach of pulling only a gaseous form of the fuel into a stove. By drawing liquid out of the cartridge, Coleman gets around the tendency of propane to burn off first and allows each cartridge to deliver a consistent mix of propane and butane to the stove's burners throughout the cartridge's life.

Denatured alcohol: Though this fuel burns cleanly and quietly and is virtually explosion-proof, it generates much less heat than pressurized or liquid gas fuels.

Kerosene: Never buy a stove that uses kerosene for fuel. Kerosene is smelly and messy, generates low heat, needs priming, and is virtually obsolete as a camp fuel in the United States. As a test, I once tried using a kerosene stove. I could scarcely boil a pot of water. In addition, some kerosene leaked out when the stove was packed, ruining everything it touched. The smell of kerosene never did go away. Kerosene remains popular in Europe only because most

© SABRINA YOUNG

Stoves are available in many sizes and burn a variety of fuels.

campers there haven't yet heard much about white gas. When they do, they will demand it.

Primus Tri-Blend: This blend is made up of 20 percent propane, 70 percent butane, and 10 percent isobutane and is designed to burn with more consistent heat and efficiency than standard propane/butane mixes.

Propane: Now available for single-burner stoves using larger, heavier cartridges to accommodate higher pressures, propane offers the very best performance of any of the pressurized gas canister fuels.

White gas: White gas is the most popular camp fuel in the United States because it is inexpensive and effective—not to mention, sold at most outdoor recreation stores and many supermarkets. It burns hot, has virtually no smell, and evaporates quickly when spilled. If you are caught in wet, miserable weather and can't get a fire going, you can use white gas as an emergency fire starter; however, if you do so, use it sparingly and never on an open flame.

White gas is a popular fuel both for car campers who use the large, two-burner stoves equipped with a fuel tank and a pump and for hikers who carry a lightweight backpacking stove. On the latter, lighting can require priming with a gel called priming paste, which some people dislike. Another problem with white gas is that it can be extremely explosive.

As an example, I once almost burned my beard completely off in a mini-explosion while lighting one of the larger stoves designed for car camping. I was in the middle of cooking dinner when the flame suddenly shut down. Sure enough, the fuel tank was empty, and after refilling it, I pumped the tank 50 or 60 times to regain pressure. When I lit a match, the sucker ignited from three feet away. The resulting explosion was like a stick of dynamite going off, and immediately the smell of burning beard was in the air. In a flash, my once thick, dark beard had been reduced to a mass of little, yellow, burned curlicues.

My error? After filling the tank, I forgot to shut the fuel cock off while pumping up the pressure in the tank. As a result, the stove burners were slowly emitting the gas/air mixture as I pumped the tank, filling the air above the stove. Then, strike a match from even a few feet away and ka-boom!

Building Fires

One summer expedition took me to the Canadian wilderness in British Columbia for a 75-mile canoe trip on the Bowron Lake Circuit, a chain of 13 lakes, six rivers, and seven portages. It is one of the greatest canoe trips in the world, a loop that ends just a few hundred feet from its starting point. But at the first camp at Kibbee Lake, my stove developed a fuel leak at the base of the burner, and the nuclear-like blast that followed just about turned Canada into a giant crater.

As a result, we had to complete the final 70 miles of the trip without a stove, cooking instead on open fires each night. The problem was compounded by the weather. It rained eight of the 10 days. Rain? In Canada, raindrops the size of silver dollars fall so hard they actually bounce on the lake surface. We had to stop paddling a few times to empty the rainwater out of the canoe. At the end of the day, we'd make camp and then face the critical decision: either make a fire or go to bed cold and hungry.

Equipped with an ax, at least we had a chance for success. Although the downed wood was soaked, I was able to make my own fire-starting tinder from the chips of split logs; no matter how hard it rains, the inside of a log is always dry.

In miserable weather, matches don't stay lit long enough to get tinder started. Instead, we used either a candle or the little waxlike fire-starter cubes that remain lit for several minutes. From those, we could get the tinder going. Then we added small, slender strips of wood that had been axed from the interior of the logs. When the flame reached a foot high, we added the logs, their dry interior facing in. By the time the inside of the logs had caught fire, the outside was drying from the heat. It wasn't long before a royal blaze was brightening the rainy night.

That's a worst-case scenario, and I hope you will never face anything like it. Nevertheless, being able to build a good fire and cook on it can be one of the more satisfying elements of a camping trip. At times, just looking into the flames can provide a special satisfaction at the end of a good day.

However, never expect to build a fire for every meal or, in some cases, even to build one at all. Many state and federal campgrounds have been picked clean of downed wood. During the fire season, the danger of forest fires can force rangers to prohibit fires altogether. In either case, you must use your camp stove or go hungry.

But when you can build a fire and the resources for doing so are available, it will enhance the quality of your camping experience. Of the campgrounds listed in this book, those where you are permitted to build fires will usually have fire rings. In primitive areas where you can make your own fire, you should dig a ring eight inches deep, line the edges with rock, and clear all the needles and twigs in a five-foot radius. The next day, when the fire is dead, you can scatter the rocks, fill over the black charcoal with dirt, and then spread pine needles and twigs over it. Nobody will even know you camped there. That's the best way I know to keep a secret spot a real secret.

When you start to build a campfire, the first thing you will notice is that no matter how good your intentions, your fellow campers will not be able to resist moving the wood around. Watch. You'll be getting ready to add a key piece of wood at just the right spot, and your companion will stick his mitts in, confidently believing he has a better idea. He'll shift the fire around and undermine your best-thought-out plans.

So I enforce a rule on camping trips: One person makes the fire while everybody else stands clear or is involved with other camp tasks, such as gathering wood, getting water, putting up tents, or planning dinner. Once the fire is going strong, then it's fair game; anyone adds logs at his or her discretion. But in the early, delicate stages of the campfire, it's best to leave the work to one person.

Before a match is ever struck, you should gather a complete pile of firewood. Then, start small, with the tiniest twigs you can find, and slowly add larger twigs as you go, crisscrossing them like a miniature tepee. Eventually, you will get to the big chunks that produce high heat. The key is to get one piece of wood burning into another, which then burns into another, setting off what I call the chain of flame. Conversely, single pieces of wood set apart from each other will not burn.

On a dry summer evening at a campsite where plenty of wood is available, about the only way you can blow the deal is to get impatient and try to add the big pieces too quickly. Do that and you'll get smoke, not flames, and it won't be long before every one of your fellow campers is poking at your fire. It will drive you crazy, but they just won't be able to help it.

Cooking Gear

I like traveling light, and I've found that all I need for cooking is a pot, small frying pan, metal pot grabber, fork, knife, cup, and matches. If you want to keep the price of food low and also cook customized dinners each night, a small pressure cooker can be just the ticket. (See *Keeping the Price Down* in this chapter.) I store all my gear in one small bag that fits into my pack. If I'm camping out of my four-wheel-drive rig, I can easily keep track of the little bag of cooking gear. Going simple, not complicated, is the key to keeping a camping trip on the right track.

You can get more elaborate by buying complete kits with plates, a coffeepot, large pots, and other cookware, but what really counts is having a single pot that makes you happy. It needs to be just the right size, not too big or small, and stable enough so it won't tip over, even if it is at a slight angle on a fire, filled with water at a full boil. Mine is just six inches wide and 4.5 inches deep. It holds better than a quart of water and has served me well for several hundred camp dinners.

The rest of your cook kit is easy to complete. The frying pan should be small, light-gauge aluminum, and Teflon-coated, with a fold-in handle so it's no hassle to store. A pot grabber is a great addition. This little aluminum gadget clamps to the edge of pots and allows you to lift them and pour water with total control and without burning your fingers. For cleanup, take along a plastic scrubber and a small bottle filled with dish soap, and you're in business.

A sierra cup, a wide aluminum cup with a wire handle, is an ideal item to carry because you can eat out of it as well as use it for drinking. This means no plates to scrub after dinner, so washing up is quick and easy. In addition, if you go for a hike, you can clip its handle to your belt. Some people bring a giant cup called a "Fair Share." In expeditions where food has to be rationed, they manage to get a lot more than their "fair share" because a cup of food looks so small in these giant vessels.

If you opt for a more formal setup, complete with plates, glasses, silverware, and the like, you can end up spending more time preparing and cleaning up after meals than enjoying the country you are exploring. In addition, the more equipment you bring, the more loose ends you will have to deal with, and loose ends can cause plenty of frustration. If you have a choice, go simple.

Remember what Thoreau said: "A man is rich in proportion to what he can do without."

Food and Cooking Tricks

On a trip to the Bob Marshall Wilderness in western Montana, I woke up one morning, yawned, and said, "What've we got for breakfast?"

The silence was ominous. "Well," finally came the response, "we don't have any food left."

"What!?"

"Well, I figured we'd catch trout for meals every other night."

On the return trip, we ended up eating wild berries, buds, and, yes, even roots (not too tasty). When we finally landed the next day at a suburban pizza parlor, we nearly ate the wooden tables.

Running out of food on a camping trip can do more to turn reasonable people into violent grumps than any other event. There's no excuse for it, not when figuring meals can be done precisely and with little effort. You should not go out and buy a bunch of food, throw it in your rig, and head off for yonder. That leaves too much to chance. And if you've ever been really hungry in the woods, you know it's worth a little effort to guard against a day or two of starvation. Here's a three-step solution:

1. Draw up a general meal-by-meal plan and make sure your companions like what's on it.

2. Tell your companions to buy any specialty items (such as a special brand of coffee) on their own and not to expect you to take care of everything.

3. Put all the food on your living room floor and literally plan out every day of your trip, meal by meal, putting the food in plastic bags as you go. That way, you will know exact food quotas and you won't go hungry.

Fish for your dinner? There's one guarantee as far as that goes: If you expect to catch fish for meals, you will most certainly get skunked. If you don't expect to catch fish for meals, you will probably catch so many they'll be coming out of your ears. I've seen it a hundred times.

Keeping the Price Down

"There must be some mistake," I said with a laugh. "Whoever paid $750 for camp food?"

But the amount was as clear as the digital numbers on the cash register: $753.27.

"How is this possible?" I asked the clerk.

"Just add it up," she responded, irritated.

Then I started figuring. The freeze-dried backpack dinners cost $6 apiece. A small pack of beef jerky went for $2, the beef sticks for $0.75, granola bars for $0.50. Multiply it all by four hungry men, including Foonsky.

The dinners alone cost close to $500. Add in the usual goodies—candy, coffee, dried fruit, granola bars, jerky, oatmeal, soup, and

Tang—and I felt as if an earthquake had struck when I saw the tab.

A lot of campers have received similar shocks. In preparation for their trips, campers shop with enthusiasm. Then they pay the bill in horror.

Well, there are solutions, lots of them. You can eat gourmet-style in the outback without having your wallet cleaned out. But it requires do-it-yourself cooking, more planning, and careful shopping. It also means transcending the push-button, I-want-it-now attitude that so many people can't leave behind when they go to the mountains.

Now when Foonsky, Mr. Furnai, Rambob, and I sit down to eat such a meal, we don't call it "eating." We call it "hodgepacking" or "time to pack your hodge." After a particularly long day on the trail, you can do some serious hodgepacking.

If your trip is a shorter one, say for a weekend, consider bringing more fresh food to add some sizzle to the hodge. You can design a hot soup/stew mix that is good enough to eat at home.

Start by bringing a pot of water to a full boil, and then add pasta, ramen noodles, or macaroni. While it simmers, cut in a potato, carrot, onion, and garlic clove, and cook for about 10 minutes. When the vegetables have softened, add in a soup mix or two, maybe some cheese, and you are just about in business. But you can still ruin it and turn your hodge into slodge. Make sure you read the directions on the soup mix to determine cooking time. It can vary widely. In addition, make sure you stir the whole thing up; otherwise, you will get those hidden dry clumps of soup mix that taste like garlic sawdust.

How do I know? Well, it was up near Kearsage Pass in the Sierra Nevada, where, feeling half-starved, I dug into our nightly hodge. I will never forget that first bite—I damn near gagged to death. Foonsky laughed at me, until he took his first bite (a nice big one) and then turned green.

Another way to trim food costs is to make your own beef jerky, the trademark staple of campers for more than 200 years. A tiny packet of beef jerky costs $2, and for that 250-mile expedition, I spent $150 on jerky alone. Never again. Now we make our own and get big strips of jerky that taste better than anything you can buy.

For a crew of four, you can get by with two freeze-dried dinners that you cook right in the container pouch. Liam Furniss discovered that by adding a separate bonus pack of garlic-seasoned mashed potatoes, which cook in 90 seconds; everybody has plenty of food. That goes even for his dad Mo, with his gigantic, crater-of-the-moon "Fair Share" cup.

You can supplement your eats with sweets, nuts, freeze-dried fruits, and drink mixes. In any case, make sure you keep the dinner menu varied. If you and your buddies look into your dinner cups and groan, "Ugh, not this again," you will soon start dreaming of cheeseburgers and french fries instead of hiking, fishing, and finding beautiful campsites.

If you are car camping and have a big ice chest, you can bring virtually anything to eat and drink. If you are on the trail and don't mind paying the price, the newest freeze-dried dinners provide another option.

Some of the biggest advances in the outdoors industry have come in the form of freeze-dried dinners. Some of them are almost good enough to serve in restaurants. Sweet-and-sour pork over rice, tostadas, Burgundy chicken—it sure beats the poopy goop we used to eat, like the old soupy chili-mac dinners that tasted bad and looked so unlike food that consumption was nearly impossible, even for my dog, Rebel. Foonsky usually managed to get it down, but just barely.

To provide an idea of how to plan a menu, consider what my companions and I ate while hiking 250 miles on California's John Muir Trail:

Breakfast: instant soup, oatmeal (never get plain), one beef or jerky stick, coffee or hot chocolate.

Lunch: one beef stick, two jerky sticks, one

HOW TO MAKE BEEF JERKY IN YOUR OWN KITCHEN

Start with a couple of pieces of meat: lean top round, sirloin, or tri-tip. Cut them into 3/16-inch strips across the grain, trimming out the membrane, gristle, and fat. Marinate the strips for 24 hours in a glass dish. The fun begins in picking a marinade. Try two-thirds teriyaki sauce, one-third Worcestershire sauce. You can customize the recipe by adding pepper, ground mustard, bay leaf, red wine vinegar, garlic, and, for the brave, Tabasco sauce.

After a day or so, squeeze out each strip of meat with a rolling pin, lay them in rows on a cooling rack over a cookie sheet, and dry them in the oven at 125°F for 12 hours. Thicker pieces can take as long as 18-24 hours.

That's it. The hardest part is cleaning the cookie sheet when you're done. The easiest part is eating your own homemade jerky while sitting at a lookout on a mountain ridge. The do-it-yourself method for jerky may take a day or so, but it is cheaper and can taste better than any store-bought jerky.

—my thanks to Jeff Patty for this recipe

granola bar, dried fruit, half cup of pistachio nuts, Tang, one small bag of M&Ms.

Dinner: instant soup, one freeze-dried dinner (split between two people), one milk bar, rainbow trout.

What was that last item? Rainbow trout? Right! Unless you plan on it, you can catch them every night.

Trout Dinner

If all this still doesn't sound like your idea of a gourmet but low-cost camping meal, well, you are forgetting the main course: rainbow trout. Remember: If you don't plan on catching them for dinner, you'll probably land more than you can finish in one night's hodgepacking.

Some campers go to great difficulties to cook their trout, bringing along frying pans, butter, grills, tinfoil, and more, but all you need is some seasoned salt and a campfire.

Rinse the gutted trout, and while it's still wet, sprinkle on a good dose of seasoned salt, both inside and out. Clear any burning logs to the side of the campfire, then lay the trout right on the coals, turning it once so both sides are cooked. Sound ridiculous? Sound like you are throwing the fish away? Sound like the fish will burn up? Sound like you will have to eat the campfire ash? Wrong on all counts. The fish cooks perfectly, the ash doesn't stick, and

after cooking trout this way, you may never fry again.

If you can't convince your buddies, who may insist that trout should be fried, then make sure you have butter to fry it in, not oil. Also make sure you cook them all the way through, so the meat strips off the backbone in two nice, clean fillets. The fish should end up looking like one that Sylvester the Cat just drew out of his mouth—only the head, tail, and a perfect skeleton.

FIRST AID AND INSECT PROTECTION

Mountain nights don't get any more perfect, I thought as I lay in my sleeping bag.

The sky looked like a mass of jewels and the air tasted sweet and smelled of pines. A shooting star fireballed across the sky, and I remember thinking, "It just doesn't get any better."

Just then, as I was drifting into sleep, a mysterious buzz appeared from nowhere and deposited itself inside my left ear. Suddenly awake, I whacked my ear with the palm of my hand, hard enough to cause a minor concussion. The buzz disappeared. I pulled out my flashlight and shined it on my palm, and there, lit in the blackness of night, lay the squished intruder: a mosquito, dead amid a stain of blood.

Satisfied, I turned off the light, closed my

KEEP IT WILD TIP 5: SANITATION

If no refuse facility is available:

1. Deposit human waste in "cat holes" dug 6-8 inches deep. Cover and disguise the cat hole when finished.
2. Deposit human waste at least 75 paces (200 feet) from any water source or camp.
3. Use toilet paper sparingly. When finished, carefully burn it in the cat hole, then bury it.
4. If no appropriate burial locations are available, such as in popular wilderness camps above tree line in granite settings, then all human refuse should be double-bagged and packed out.
5. At boat-in campsites, chemical toilets are required. Chemical toilets can also solve the problem of larger groups camping for long stays at one location where no facilities are available.
6. To wash dishes or your body, carry water away from the source and use small amounts of biodegradable soap. Scatter dishwater after all food particles have been removed.
7. Scour your campsites for even the tiniest piece of trash and any other evidence of your stay. Pack out all the trash you can, even if it's not yours. Finding cigarette butts, for instance, provides special irritation for most campers. Pick them up and discard them properly.
8. Never litter. Never. Or you become the enemy of all others.

---

eyes, and thought of the fishing trip planned for the next day. Then I heard them. It was a squadron of mosquitoes making landing patterns around my head. I tried to grab them with an open hand, but they dodged the assault and flew off. Just 30 seconds later, another landed in my left ear. I promptly dispatched the invader with a rip of the palm.

Now I was completely awake, so I got out of my sleeping bag to retrieve some mosquito repellent. But en route, several of the buggers swarmed and nailed me in the back and arms. After I applied the repellent and settled snugly again in my sleeping bag, the mosquitoes would buzz a few inches from my ear. After getting a whiff of the poison, they would fly off. It was like sleeping in a sawmill.

The next day, drowsy from little sleep, I set out to fish. I'd walked but 15 minutes when I brushed against a bush and felt a stinging sensation on the inside of my arm, just above the wrist. I looked down: A tick had his clamps in me. I ripped it out before he could embed his head into my skin.

After catching a few fish, I sat down against a tree to eat lunch and just watch the water go by. My dog, Rebel, sat down next to me and stared at the beef jerky I was munching as if it were a T-bone steak. I finished eating, gave

him a small piece, patted him on the head, and said, "Good dog." Right then, I noticed an itch on my arm where a mosquito had drilled me. I unconsciously scratched it. Two days later, in that exact spot, some nasty red splotches started popping up. Poison oak. By petting my dog and then scratching my arm, I had transferred the oil residue of the poison oak leaves from Rebel's fur to my arm.

When I returned home, Foonsky asked me about the trip.

"Great," I said. "Mosquitoes, ticks, poison oak. Can hardly wait to go back."

"Sorry I missed out," he answered.

Mosquitoes, No-See-Ums, and Horseflies

On a trip to Canada, Foonsky and I were fishing a small lake from the shore when suddenly a black horde of mosquitoes could be seen moving across the lake toward us. It was like when the French army looked across the Rhine and saw the Wehrmacht coming. There was a buzz in the air. We fought them off for a few minutes, then made a fast retreat to the truck and jumped in, content the buggers had been foiled. But in some way still unknown to us, the mosquitoes gained entry to the truck. In 10 minutes, we squished 15 of them as they attempted to plant their oil drills into our skins. Just outside the truck, the black horde waited for us to make a tactical error, such as rolling down a window. It finally took a miraculous hailstorm to squelch the attack.

When it comes to mosquitoes, no-see-ums, gnats, and horseflies, there are times when there is nothing you can do. However, in most situations, you can muster a defense to repel the attack.

When under heavy attack by mosquitoes, the first key is to wear clothing too heavy for them to drill through. Expose a minimum of skin, wear a hat, and tie a bandanna around your neck, preferably one that has been sprayed with repellent. If you try to get by with just a thin cotton T-shirt and nylon shorts, you will be declared a federal mosquito sanctuary.

So, first, your skin must be well covered, with only your hands and face exposed. Second, you should have your companion spray your clothes with repellent. (I prefer Deep Woods Off!) Third, you should dab liquid repellent directly on your skin.

At night, the easiest way to get a good sleep without mosquitoes buzzing in your ear is to sleep in a bug-proof tent. If the nights are warm and you want to see the stars, new tent models are available that have a skylight covered with mosquito netting. If you don't like tents on summer evenings, mosquito netting rigged with an air space at your head can solve the problem. Otherwise, prepare to get bitten, even with the use of mosquito repellent.

A newer option is a battery-powered, clip-on mosquito repellent made by Off! that is also portable. It includes a canister that lasts 12 hours and a small fan, so you can set right next to you. That's right, you don't spray it on.

If your problems are with no-see-ums or biting horseflies, then you need a slightly different approach. No-see-ums are tiny black insects that look like nothing more than a sliver of dirt on your skin. Then you notice something stinging, and when you rub the area, you scratch up a little no-see-um. The results are similar to mosquito bites, making your skin itch, splotch,

and, when you get them bad, swell. In addition to using the techniques described to repel mosquitoes, you should go one step further.

The problem is that no-see-ums are tricky little devils. Somehow, they can actually get under your socks and around your ankles, where they will bite to their hearts' content all night long while you sleep, itch, sleep, and itch some more. The best solution is to apply a liquid repellent to your ankles, then wear clean socks.

Horseflies are another story. They are rarely a problem, but when they get their dander up, they can cause trouble you'll never forget.

Always wear sunglasses when you hike. If you enter an area with flies, the moisture from your eyes will attract them. The sunglasses will keep them from getting in your eyes.

On one trip, Foonsky and I were paddling a canoe along the shoreline of a Lake Quesnel in British Columbia. This giant horsefly, about the size of a fingertip, started dive-bombing the canoe. After 20 minutes, it landed on Foonsky's thigh. He immediately slammed it with an open hand, then let out a blood-curdling "Yeeeee-ow!" that practically sent ripples across the lake. When Foonsky whacked it, the horsefly had somehow turned around and bit him on the hand, leaving a huge red welt.

In the next 10 minutes, that big fly strafed the canoe on more dive-bomb runs. I finally got my canoe paddle, swung it as if it were a baseball bat, and nailed that horsefly as if I'd hit a home run. It landed about 15 feet from the boat, still alive and buzzing in the water. While I was trying to figure what it would take to kill this bugger, a large rainbow trout surfaced and snatched it out of the water, finally avenging the assault.

If you have horsefly or yellow jacket problems, you'd best just leave the area. One, two, or a few can be dealt with. More than that and your fun camping trip will be about as fun as being roped to a tree and stung by an electric shock rod.

On most trips, you will spend time doing everything possible to keep from getting bitten by mosquitoes or no-see-ums. When your attempts fail, you must know what to do next, and fast, especially if you are among those ill-fated campers who get big, red lumps from a bite inflicted from even a microscopic mosquito.

A fluid called After Bite or a dab of ammonia should be applied immediately to the bite. To start the healing process, apply a first-aid gel (not a liquid), such as the one made by Campho-Phenique.

DEET

What is DEET? You're not likely to find the word DEET on any repellent label. That's because DEET stands for N,N diethyl-m-toluamide. If the label contains this scientific name, the repellent contains DEET. Despite fears of DEET-associated health risks and the increased attention given natural alternatives, DEET-based repellents are still acknowledged as by far the best option when serious insect protection is required.

On one trip, I had a small bottle of mosquito repellent in the same pocket as a Swiss army knife. Guess what happened? The mosquito repellent leaked a bit and literally melted the insignia right off the knife. DEET will also melt synthetic clothes. That is why, in bad mosquito country, I'll expose a minimum of skin, just hands and face (with full beard), apply the repellent only to my cheeks and the back of my hands, and perhaps wear a bandanna sprinkled with a few drops as well. That does the trick, with a minimum of exposure to the repellent.

"NATURAL" REPELLENTS

Are natural alternatives a safer choice than DEET? Some are potentially hazardous if ingested, and most are downright painful if they find their way into the eyes or onto mucus membranes. For example, pennyroyal is perhaps the most toxic of the essential oils used to repel insects and can be deadly if taken internally. Other oils used include cedarwood, citronella, and perhaps the most common, eucalyptus and peppermint.

How effective are natural repellents? The average effective repelling time of a citronella product appears to range from 1.5-2 hours, so it must be reapplied to be effective.

What other chemical alternatives are there? Another line of defense against insects is the chemical permethrin, used on clothing, not on skin. Permethrin-based products are designed to repel and kill arthropods or crawling insects, making them a preferred repellent for ticks. The currently available products remain effective—repelling and killing chiggers, mosquitoes, and ticks—for two weeks and through two launderings.

Ticks

Ticks are nasty little vermin that will wait in ambush, jump on unsuspecting prey, and then crawl to a prime location before filling their bodies with their victim's blood.

I call them Dracula bugs, but by any name they can be a terrible camp pest. Ticks rest on grass and low plants and attach themselves to those who brush against the vegetation (dogs are particularly vulnerable). Typically, they can be found no more than 18 inches above ground, and if you stay on the trails, you can usually avoid them.

There are two common species of ticks. The common coastal tick is larger, brownish in color, and prefers to crawl around before putting its clamps on you. The feel of any bug crawling on your skin can be creepy, but consider it a forewarning of assault; you can just pick the tick off and dispatch it. The coastal tick's preferred destination is usually the back of your neck, just where the hairline starts. The other species, the wood tick, is small and black, and when he puts his clamps in, it's immediately painful. When a wood tick gets into a dog for a few days, it can cause a large red welt. In either case, ticks should be removed as soon as possible.

If you have hiked in areas infested with ticks, it is advisable to shower as soon as possible, washing your clothes immediately. If you just leave your clothes in a heap, a tick can crawl out and invade your home. They like warmth, and one way or another, they can end up in your bed. Waking up in the middle of the night with a tick crawling across your chest can be unsettling, to put it mildly.

Once a tick has its clampers in your skin, you must determine how long it has been there. If it has been a short time, the most painless and effective method for removal is to take a pair of sharp tweezers and grasp the little devil, making certain to isolate the mouth area, then pull him out. Reader Johvin Perry sent in the suggestion to coat the tick with Vaseline, which will cut off its oxygen supply, after which it may voluntarily give up the hunt.

If the tick has been in longer, you may wish to have a doctor extract it. Some people will burn a tick with a cigarette or poison it with lighter fluid, but neither is advisable. No matter how you do it, you must take care to remove all of the tick, especially its clawlike mouth.

The wound, however small, should then be cleansed and dressed. First, apply liquid peroxide, which cleans and sterilizes, and then apply a dressing coated with a first-aid gel, such as First-Aid Cream, Campho-Phenique, or Neosporin.

Lyme disease, which can be transmitted by the bite of a deer tick, is rare but common enough to warrant some attention. To prevent tick bites, some people tuck their pant legs into their hiking socks and spray tick repellent, called Permamone, on their pants.

The first symptom of Lyme disease is a bright red, splotchy rash that develops around the bite area. Other possible early symptoms include headache, nausea, fever, and/or a stiff neck. If any of these happen, or if you have any doubts, you should see your doctor immediately. If you do get Lyme disease, don't panic. Doctors say it is easily treated in the early stages with simple antibiotics. If you are nervous about getting Lyme disease, carry a small plastic bag with you when you hike. If a tick manages to get his clampers into you, put the tick in the plastic bag after you pull it out. Then give it to your doctor for analysis to see if the tick is a carrier of the disease.

During the course of my hiking and camping career, I have removed ticks from my skin hundreds of times without any problems. However, if you are worried about ticks, you can buy a tick removal kit from any outdoors store. These kits allow you to remove ticks in such a way that their toxins are guaranteed not to enter your bloodstream.

If you are particularly wary of ticks or perhaps even have nightmares of them, wear long pants that are tucked into your socks, as well as a long-sleeved shirt tucked securely into your pants and held with a belt. Clothing should be light in color, making it easier to see ticks, and tightly woven so ticks have trouble hanging on. On one hike with my mom, Eleanor, I brushed more than 100 ticks off my blue jeans in less than an hour, while she did not pick up a single one on her polyester pants.

Perform tick checks regularly, especially on the back of the neck. The combination of DEET insect repellents applied to the skin and permethrin repellents applied directly to clothing is considered to be the most effective line of defense against ticks.

Poison Oak

After a nice afternoon hike, about a five-miler, I was concerned about possible exposure to poison oak, so I immediately showered and put on clean clothes. Then I settled into a chair with my favorite foamy elixir to watch the end of a baseball game. But the game went on for hours, 18 innings; meanwhile, my dog, tired from the hike, went to sleep on my bare ankles.

A few days later, I had a case of poison oak. My feet looked as though they had been on fire and put out with an ice pick. The lesson? Don't always trust your dog, give him a bath as well, and beware of extra-inning ball games.

You can get poison oak only from direct contact with the oil residue from the plant's leaves. It can be passed in a variety of ways, as direct as skin-to-leaf contact or as indirect as leaf to dog, dog to sofa, sofa to skin. Once you have it, there is little you can do but feel horribly itchy. Applying Caladryl lotion or its equivalent can

© BOWLEGGEDGALLOOT/DREAMSTIME.COM

poison oak

help because it contains antihistamines, which attack and dry the itch.

My pal Furniss offers a tip that may sound crazy but seems to work. You should expose the afflicted area to the hottest water you can stand, then suddenly immerse it in cold water. The hot water opens the skin pores and gets the "itch" out, and the cold water then quickly seals the pores.

In any case, you're a lot better off if you don't get poison oak to begin with. Remember that poison oak can disguise itself. In the spring, it is green; then it gradually turns reddish in the summer. By fall, it becomes a bloody, ugly-looking red. In the winter, it loses its leaves altogether and appears to be nothing more than the barren, brown sticks of a small plant. However, at any time and in any form, its contact with skin can quickly lead to infection.

Some people are more easily afflicted than others, but if you are one of the lucky few who aren't, don't cheer too loudly. While some people can be exposed to the oil residue of poison oak with little or no effect, the body's resistance can gradually be worn down with repeated exposure. At one time, I could

practically play in the stuff and the only symptom would be a few little bumps on the inside of my wrist. Now, more than 15 years later, my resistance has broken down. If I merely brush against poison oak now, in a few days the exposed area can look as if it were used for a track meet.

So regardless of whether you consider yourself vulnerable or not, you should take heed to reduce your exposure. That can be done by staying on trails when you hike and making sure your dog does the same. Remember, the worst stands of poison oak are usually brush-infested areas just off the trail. Also protect yourself by dressing so your skin is completely covered, wearing long-sleeved shirts, long pants, and boots. If you suspect you've been exposed, immediately wash your clothes and then wash yourself with aloe vera, rinsing with a cool shower.

And don't forget to give your dog a bath as well.

Sunburn

The most common injury suffered on camping trips is sunburn, yet some people wear it as a badge of honor, believing that it somehow enhances their virility. Well, it doesn't. Neither do suntans. Too much sun can lead to serious burns or sunstroke.

Both are easy enough to avoid. Use a high-level sunscreen on your skin, apply lip balm, and wear sunglasses and a hat. If any area gets burned, apply first-aid cream, which will soothe and provide moisture to the parched skin.

The best advice is not to get even a suntan. Those who tan are involved in a practice that can eventually ruin their skin and possibly lead to cancer.

Giardia and Cryptosporidium

You have just hiked in to your backwoods spot, you're thirsty and a bit tired, but you smile as you consider the prospects. Everything seems perfect—there's not a stranger in sight, and you have nothing to do but relax with your pals.

You toss down your gear, grab your cup, dip it into the stream, and take a long drink of that ice-cold mountain water. It seems crystal pure and sweeter than anything you've ever tasted. It's not till later that you find out it can be just like drinking a cup of poison.

Whether you camp in the wilderness or not, if you hike, you're going to get thirsty. And if your canteen runs dry, you'll start eyeing any water source. Stop! Do not pass Go. Do not drink.

By drinking what appears to be pure mountain water without first treating it, you can ingest a microscopic protozoan called *Giardia lamblia*. The ensuing abdominal cramps can make you feel like your stomach and intestinal tract are in a knot, ready to explode. With that comes long-term diarrhea that is worse than even a bear could imagine.

Doctors call the disease giardiasis, or giardia for short, but it is difficult to diagnose. One friend of mine who contracted giardia was told he might have stomach cancer before the proper diagnosis was made.

Drinking directly from a stream or lake does not mean you will get giardia, but you are taking a giant chance. There is no reason to assume such a risk, potentially ruining your trip and enduring weeks of misery.

A lot of people are taking that risk. I made a personal survey of campers in the Yosemite National Park wilderness, and found that roughly only one in 10 was equipped with some kind of water-purification system. The result, according to the Public Health Service, is that an average of 4 percent of all backpackers and campers suffer giardiasis. According to the Parasitic Diseases Division of the Center for Infectious Diseases, the rates range from 1 percent to 20 percent across the country.

But if you get giardia, you are not going to care about the statistics. "When I got giardia, I just about wanted to die," said Henry McCarthy, a California camper. "For about 10 days, it was the most terrible thing I have ever experienced. And through the whole thing, I kept thinking? I shouldn't have drunk that water, but it seemed all right at the time."

That is the mistake most campers make. The stream might be running free, gurgling over

Always filter water before drinking.

boulders in the high country, tumbling into deep, oxygenated pools. It looks pure. Then in a few days, the problems suddenly start. Drinking untreated water from mountain streams is a lot like playing Russian roulette. Sooner or later the gun goes off.

STERIPEN

We would never do another wilderness trip without one and I keep mine with me all the time. By using UV light, the SteriPEN destroy viruses, bacteria and protozoa (like Giardia) that can make you sick. Dip your water bottle in a cold stream, purify the water with the UV light in under two minutes, and drink all the cold, clean mountain water you can. It's like having a cooler full of ice-cold water with you all the time. On expeditions of more than four days, make sure you bring extra batteries.

FILTERS

Handheld filters are getting more compact, lighter, easier to use, and often less expensive. Having to boil water or endure chemicals that leave a bad taste in the mouth has been all but eliminated.

With a filter, you just pump and drink. Filtering strains out microscopic contaminants, rendering the water clear and somewhat pure. How pure? That depends on the size of the filter's pores—what manufacturers call pore-size efficiency. A filter with a pore-size efficiency of one micron or smaller will remove protozoa, such as *Giardia lamblia* and cryptosporidium, as well as parasitic eggs and larva, but it takes a pore-size efficiency of less than 0.4 micron to remove bacteria. All but one of the filters recommended here do that.

A good backcountry water filter weighs less than 20 ounces, is easy to grasp, simple to use, and a snap to clean and maintain. At the very least, buy one that will remove protozoa and bacteria. (A number of cheap, pocket-sized filters remove only *Giardia lamblia* and cryptosporidium. That, in my book, is risking your health to save money.) Consider the flow rate, too: A liter per minute is good.

All filters will eventually clog—it's a sign that they've been doing their job. If you force water through a filter that's becoming difficult to pump, you risk injecting a load of microbial nasties into your bottle. Some models can be back-washed, brushed, or, as with ceramic elements, scrubbed to extend their useful lives. And if the filter has a pre-filter to screen out the big stuff, use it: It will give your filter a boost in mileage, which can then top out at about 100 gallons per disposable element. Any of the filters reviewed here will serve well on an outing into the wilds, providing you always play by the manufacturer's rules.

First Need Deluxe: The filter pumps smoothly and puts out more than a liter per minute. The 15-ounce First Need Deluxe from General Ecology does something no other handheld filter will do: It removes protozoa, bacteria, and viruses without using chemicals. Such effectiveness is the result of a fancy three-stage matrix system. The First Need has been around since 1982. Additional cartridges mean you just replace the cartridge, not the entire unit. If you drop the filter and unknowingly crack the cartridge, all the little nasties can get through. A small point worth noting.

Basic Designs Ceramic: It clogs quickly and therefore is not a good choice for long trips. The Basic Designs Ceramic Filter Pump weighs eight ounces and is as stripped-down a filter as you'll find. The pump is simple, easy to use, and quite reliable. The ceramic filter effectively removes protozoa and bacteria, making it ideal and cost effective for backpacking—but it won't protect against viruses. Also, the filter element is too bulbous to work directly from a shallow water source; as with the PentaPure, you'll have to decontaminate a pot, cup, or bottle to transfer your unfiltered water.

Katadyn Hiker Pro: The Katadyn effectively removes protozoa and bacteria. I found it challenging to put any kind of power behind the pump's tiny handle, and the filtered water comes through at a paltry half-liter per minute. It also requires more cleaning than most filters—though the good news is that the element is made of long-lasting ceramic.

MSR MiniWorks: The 14-ounce MiniWorks looks similar to the more expensive WaterWorks, and, like the WaterWorks, is fully field-maintainable, while guarding against protozoa, bacteria, and chemicals. It attaches directly to a standard one-quart Nalgene water bottle. Takes about 90 seconds to filter that quart.

MSR WaterWorks II Ceramic: At 17.4 ounces, the WaterWorks II isn't light. You get a better flow rate (90 seconds per liter), an easy pumping action, and—like the original Mini Filter—a long-lasting ceramic cartridge. This filter is a good match for the person who encounters a lot of dirty water—its three-stage filter weeds out protozoa, bacteria, and chemicals. The MSR can be completely disassembled in the field for troubleshooting and cleaning.

SweetWater WalkAbout: The WalkAbout is perfect for the day hiker or backpacker who obsesses on lightening the load. The filter weighs just 8.5 ounces, is easily cleaned in the field, and removes both protozoa and bacteria: a genuine bargain. There are some trade-offs, however, for its diminutiveness. Water delivery is a tad slow at just under a liter per minute, but filter cartridges are now good for up to 100 gallons.

The big drawback with filters is that if you pump water from a mucky lake, the filter can clog in a few days. Therein lies the weakness. Once plugged up, it is useless, and you have to replace it or take your chances. One trick to extend the filter life is to fill your cook pot with water, let the sediment settle, then pump from there. As an insurance policy, always have a spare filter canister on hand.

Boiling Water

Except for water filtration, this is the only treatment that you can use with complete confidence. According to the federal Parasitic Diseases Division, it takes a few minutes at a rolling boil to be certain you've killed *Giardia lamblia*. At high elevations, boil for 3-5 minutes. A side benefit is that you'll also kill other dangerous bacteria that live undetected in natural waters.

But to be honest, boiling water is a thorn for most people on backcountry trips. For one thing, if you boil water on an open fire, what should taste like crystal-pure mountain water tastes instead like a mouthful of warm ashes. If you don't have a campfire, it wastes stove fuel. And if you are thirsty *now,* forget it. The water takes hours to cool.

The only time boiling always makes sense, however, is when you are preparing dinner. The ash taste will disappear in whatever freeze-dried dinner, soup, or hot drink you make.

Water-Purification Pills

I bring water-purification pills for back-up use only. They are cheap and, in addition, they kill most of the bacteria, regardless of whether you use iodine crystals or potable aqua iodine tablets. The problem is they just don't always kill *Giardia lamblia,* and that is the one critter worth worrying about on your trip. That makes water-treatment pills unreliable and dangerous.

Another key element is the time factor. Depending on the water's temperature, organic content, and pH level, these pills can take a long time to do the job. A minimum wait of 20 minutes is advised. Most people don't like waiting that long, especially when they're hot and thirsty after a hike and thinking, "What the heck, the water looks fine."

And then there is the taste. On one trip, my water filter clogged and we had to use the iodine pills instead. It doesn't take long to get tired of iodine-tinged water. Mountain water should be one of the greatest tasting beverages of the world, but the iodine kills that.

No Treatment

This is your last resort and, using extreme care, can be executed with success. Michael Furniss, the renowned hydrologist, has shown me the difference between safe and dangerous water sources.

When I was in the Boy Scouts, I remember

a scoutmaster actually telling me if you could find water running over a rock for at least five feet, it was a guarantee of its purity. Imagine that. What we've learned is that the safe water sources are almost always small springs in high, craggy mountain areas. The key is making sure no one has been upstream from where you drink. We drink untreated water only when we can see the source, such as a spring.

Furniss mentioned that another potential problem in bypassing water treatment is that even in settings free of *Giardia lamblia,* you can still ingest other bacteria that cause stomach problems.

Hypothermia

No matter how well planned your trip might be, a sudden change in weather can turn it into a puzzle for which there are few answers. Bad weather or an accident can set in motion a dangerous chain of events.

Such a chain of episodes occurred for my brother Rambob and me on a fishing trip one fall day just below the snow line. The weather had suddenly turned very cold, and ice was forming along the shore of the lake. Suddenly, the canoe became terribly imbalanced, and, just that quickly, it flipped. The little life vest seat cushions were useless, and using the canoe as a paddleboard, we tried to kick our way back to shore where my dad was going crazy at the thought of his two sons drowning before his eyes.

It took 17 minutes in that 38-degree water, but we finally made it to shore. When they pulled me out of the water, my legs were dead, not strong enough even to hold up my weight. In fact, I didn't feel so much cold as tired, and I just wanted to lie down and go to sleep.

I closed my eyes, and my brother-in-law, Lloyd Angal, slapped me in the face several times, then got me on my feet and pushed and pulled me about.

In the celebration over our making it to shore, only Lloyd had realized that hypothermia was setting in. Hypothermia is the condition in which the temperature of the body is lowered to the point that it causes poor reasoning, apathy, and collapse. It can look like the afflicted person is just tired and needs to sleep, but that sleep can be the first step toward a coma.

Ultimately, my brother and I shared what little dry clothing remained. Then we began hiking around to get muscle movement, creating internal warmth. We ate whatever munchies were available because the body produces heat by digestion. But most important, we got our heads as dry as possible. More body heat is lost through wet hair than any other single factor.

A few hours later, we were in a pizza parlor replaying the incident, talking about how only a life vest can do the job of a life vest. We decided never again to rely on those little flotation seat cushions that disappear when the boat flips.

We had done everything right to prevent hypothermia: Don't go to sleep, start a physical activity, induce shivering, put dry clothes on, dry your head, and eat something. That's how you fight hypothermia. In a dangerous situation, whether you fall in a lake or a stream or get caught unprepared in a storm, that's how you can stay alive.

After being in that ice-bordered lake for almost 20 minutes and then finally pulling ourselves to the shoreline, we discovered a strange thing. My canoe was flipped right-side up and almost all of its contents were lost: tackle box, flotation cushions, and cooler. But remaining were one paddle and one fishing rod, the trout rod my grandfather had given me for my 12th birthday.

Lloyd gave me a smile. "This means that you are meant to paddle and fish again," he said with a laugh.

Getting Unlost

I could not have been more lost. There I was, a guy who is supposed to know about these things, transfixed by confusion, snow, and hoofprints from a big deer.

I discovered that it is actually quite easy to get lost. If you don't get your bearings, getting found is the difficult part. This occurred on a wilderness trip where I'd hiked in to a remote lake and then set up a base camp for a deer hunt.

"There are some giant bucks up on that rim," confided Mr. Furnai, who lives near the area. "But it takes a mountain man to even get close to them."

That was a challenge I answered. After four-wheeling it to the trailhead, I tromped off with pack and rifle, gut-thumped it up 100 switchbacks over the rim, then followed a creek drainage up to a small but beautiful lake. The area was stark and nearly treeless, with bald granite broken only by large boulders. To keep from getting lost, I marked my route with piles of small rocks to act as directional signs for the return trip.

But at daybreak the next day, I stuck my head out of my tent and found eight inches of snow on the ground. I looked up into a gray sky filled by huge, cascading snowflakes. Visibility was about 50 yards, with fog on the mountain rim. "I better get out of here and get back to my truck," I said to myself. "If my truck gets buried at the trailhead, I'll never get out."

After packing quickly, I started down the mountain. But after 20 minutes, I began to get disoriented. You see, all the little piles of rocks I'd stacked to mark the way were now buried in snow, and I had only a smooth white blanket of snow to guide me. Everything looked the same, and it was snowing even harder now.

Five minutes later, I started chewing on some jerky to keep warm, then suddenly stopped. Where was I? Where was the creek drainage? Isn't this where I was supposed to cross over a creek and start the switchbacks down the mountain?

Right then, I looked down and saw the tracks of a huge deer, the kind Mr. Furnai had talked about. What a predicament: I was lost and snowed in and seeing big hoofprints in the snow. Part of me wanted to abandon all safety and go after that deer, but a little voice in the back of my head won out. "Treat this as an emergency," it said.

The first step in any predicament is to secure your present situation, that is, to make sure it does not get any worse. I unloaded my rifle (too easy to slip, fall, and have a misfire),

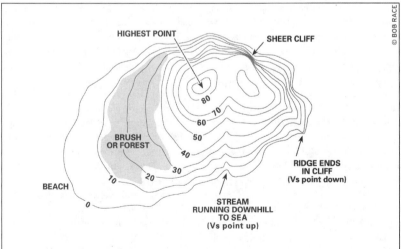

The **topographical map** is easier to read than many believe. Lines close together mean steep gradients; lines farther apart mean gentle gradients; V-shaped sets of lines pointing to higher elevations mean gulleys or stream-beds; V-shaped sets of lines pointing to lower elevations mean ridges.

Rock cairns (small piles of rocks) can act as directional signs to keep you from getting lost.

took stock of my food (three days' worth), camp fuel (plenty), and clothes (rain gear keeping me dry). Then I wondered, "Where the hell am I?"

I took out my map, compass, and altimeter, then opened the map and laid it on the snow. It immediately began collecting snowflakes. I set the compass atop the map and oriented it to north. Because of the fog, there was no way to spot landmarks, such as prominent mountaintops, to verify my position. Then I checked the altimeter, which read 4,900 feet. Well, the elevation at my lake was 5,320 feet. That was critical information.

I scanned the elevation lines on the map and was able to trace the approximate area of my position, somewhere downstream from the lake, yet close to a 4,900-foot elevation. "Right here," I said, pointing to a spot on the map with my finger. "I should pick up the switchback trail down the mountain somewhere off to the left, maybe just 40 or 50 yards away."

Slowly and deliberately, I pushed through the light, powdered snow. In five minutes, I suddenly stopped. To the left, across a 10-foot depression in the snow, appeared a flat spot that veered off to the right. "That's it! That's the crossing."

In minutes, I was working down the switchbacks, on my way, no longer lost. I thought of the hoofprints I had seen, and now that I knew my position, I wanted to head back and spend the day hunting. Then I looked up at the sky, saw it filled with falling snowflakes, and envisioned my truck buried deep in snow. Alas, this time logic won out over dreams.

In a few hours, now trudging through more than a foot of snow, I was at my truck at a spot called Doe Flat, and next to it was a giant, all-terrain U.S. Forest Service vehicle and two rangers.

"Need any help?" I asked them.

They just laughed. "We're here to help you," one answered. "It's a good thing you filed a trip plan with our district office in Gasquet. We wouldn't have known you were out here."

"Winter has arrived," said the other. "If we don't get your truck out now, it will be stuck here until next spring. If we hadn't found you, you might have been here until the end of time."

They connected a chain from the rear axle of their giant rig to the front axle of my truck and started towing me out, back to civilization. On the way to pavement, I figured I had gotten some of the more important lessons of my life. Always file a trip plan and have plenty of food, fuel, and a camp stove you can rely on. Make sure your clothes, weather gear, sleeping bag, and tent will keep you dry and warm. Always carry a compass, altimeter, and map with elevation lines, and know how to use them, practicing in good weather to get the feel of it.

And if you get lost and see the hoofprints of a giant deer, well, there are times when it is best to pass them by.

CATCHING FISH, AVOIDING BEARS, AND HAVING FUN

Feet tired and hot, stomachs growling, we stopped our hike for lunch beside a beautiful little river pool that was catching the flows from a long but gentle waterfall. My brother Rambob passed me a piece of jerky. I took my boots off, then slowly dunked my feet into the cool, foaming water.

I was gazing at a towering peak across a canyon when suddenly, Wham! There was a quick jolt at the heel of my right foot. I pulled my foot out of the water to find that, incredibly, a trout had bitten it.

My brother looked at me as if I had antlers growing out of my head. "Wow!" he exclaimed. "That trout almost caught himself an outdoors writer!"

It's true that in remote areas trout sometimes bite on almost anything, even feet. On one high-country trip, I caught limits of trout using nothing but a bare hook. The only problem is that the fish will often hit the splitshot sinker instead of the hook. Of course, fishing isn't usually that easy. But it gives you an idea of what is possible.

America's wildlands are home to a remarkable abundance of fish and wildlife. Deer browse with little fear of man, bears keep an eye out for your food, and little critters, such as squirrels and chipmunks, are daily companions. Add in the fishing, and you've got yourself a camping trip.

Your camping adventures will evolve into premium outdoor experiences if you can work in a few good fishing trips, avoid bear problems, and occasionally add a little offbeat fun with some camp games.

Trout and Bass

He creeps up on the stream as quietly as an Indian scout, keeping his shadow off the water. With his little spinning rod he'll zip his lure within an inch or two of its desired mark, probing along rocks, the edges of riffles, pocket water, or wherever he can find a change

in river habitat. Rambob is trout fishing, and he's a master at it.

In most cases, he'll catch a trout on his first or second cast. After that, it's time to move up the river, giving no spot much more than five minutes' due. Stick and move, stick and move, stalking the stream like a bobcat zeroing in on an unsuspecting rabbit. He might keep a few trout for dinner, but mostly he releases what he catches. Rambob doesn't necessarily fish for food. It's the feeling that comes with it.

You don't need a million dollars' worth of fancy gear to catch fish. What you need is the right outlook, and that can be learned. That goes regardless of whether you are fishing for trout or bass, the two most popular fisheries in the United States. Your fishing tackle selection should be as simple and clutter-free as possible.

At home, I've got every piece of fishing tackle you might imagine, more than 30 rods and many tackle boxes, racks and cabinets filled with all kinds of stuff. I've got one lure that looks like a chipmunk and another that resembles a miniature can of beer with hooks. If I hear of something new, I want to try it and

brother Rambob's big Almanor trout

usually do. It's a result of my lifelong fascination with the sport.

But if you just want to catch fish, there's an easier way to go. And when I go fishing, I take that path. I don't try to bring everything. It would be impossible. Instead, I bring a relatively small amount of gear. At home, I scan my tackle boxes for equipment and lures, make my selections, and bring just the essentials. Rod, reel, and tackle will fit into a side pocket of my backpack or a small carrying bag.

So what kind of rod should be used on an outdoor trip? For most camper/anglers, I suggest the use of a light, multi-piece spinning rod that will break down to a small size. The lowest-priced, quality six-piece rod on the market is the Daiwa 6.5-foot pack rod, number 6752, which is made of a graphite/glass composite that gives it the quality of a much more expensive model. And it comes in a hard plastic carrying tube for protection. Other major rod manufacturers, such as Fenwick, offer similar premium rods. It's tough to miss with any of them.

The use of graphite/glass composites in fishing rods has made them lighter and more sensitive, yet stronger. The only downside to graphite as a rod material is that it can be brittle. If you rap your rod against something, it can crack or cause a weak spot. That weak spot can eventually snap under even light pressure, like setting a hook or casting. Of course, a bit of care will prevent that from ever occurring.

If you haven't bought a fishing reel in some time, you will be surprised at the quality and price of micro spinning reels on the market. The reels come tiny and strong, with rear-control drag systems. Among others, Abu, Cardinal, Shimano, Sigma all make premium reels. They're worth it. With your purchase, you've just bought a reel that will last for years and years.

The one downside to spinning reels is that after long-term use, the bail spring will weaken. As a result, after casting and beginning to reel, the bail will sometimes not flip over and allow the reel to retrieve the line. Then you have to do it by hand. This can be incredibly frustrating, particularly when stream fishing, where instant line pickup is essential. The solution is to have a new bail spring installed every few years. This is a cheap, quick operation for a tackle expert.

You might own a giant tackle box filled with lures but, on your fishing trip, you are better off to fit just the essentials into a small container. One of the best ways to do that is to use the Plano Micro-Magnum 3414, a tiny two-sided tackle box for trout anglers that fits into a shirt pocket. In mine, I can fit 20 lures in one side of the box and 20 flies, split-shot weights, and snap swivels in the other. For bass lures, which are bigger, you need a slightly larger box, but the same principle applies.

There are more fishing lures on the market than you can imagine, but a few special ones can do the job. I make sure these are in my box on every trip. For trout, I carry a small black Panther Martin spinner with yellow spots, a small gold Kastmaster, a yellow Roostertail, a gold Z-Ray with red spots, a Super Duper, and a Mepps Lightning spinner.

You can take it a step further using insider's wisdom. My old pal Ed "the Dunk" showed me his trick of taking a tiny Dardevle spoon, spray painting it flat black, and dabbing five tiny red dots on it. It's a real killer, particularly in tiny streams where the trout are spooky.

The best trout catcher I've ever used on rivers is a small metal lure called a Met-L Fly. On days when nothing else works, it can be like going to a shooting gallery. The problem is that the lure is nearly impossible to find. Rambob and I consider the few we have remaining so valuable that if the lure is snagged on a rock, a cold swim is deemed mandatory for its retrieval. I've been able snag about five of these and they only get pulled out when fishing turns into Mission Impossible.

For bass, you can also fit all you need into a small plastic tackle box. I have fished with many bass pros, and all of them actually use just a few lures: twist-tail grubs, Senkos, Brush Hog, a white spinner bait, a surface plug called a Zara Spook, and AC plug. At times, like when the bass move into shoreline areas during the spring, shad minnow imitations like those made by Rebel or Rapala can be dynamite. My favorite is the one-inch, blue-silver Rapala. Every spring as the lakes begin to warm and the fish snap out of their winter doldrums, I like to float and paddle around in my small raft. I'll cast that little Rapala along the shoreline and catch and release hundreds of bass, bluegill, and sunfish. The fish are usually sitting close to the shoreline, awaiting my offering.

Fishing Tips

There's an old angler's joke about how you need to think like a fish. But if you're the one getting zilched, you may not think it's so funny.

The irony is that it is your mental approach, what you see and what you miss, that often determines your fishing luck. Some people will spend a lot of money on tackle, lures, and fishing clothes, and that done, just saunter up to a stream or lake, cast out, and wonder why they are not catching fish. The answer is their mental outlook. They are not attuning themselves to their surroundings.

You must live on nature's level, not your own. Try this and you will become aware of things you never believed even existed. Soon you will see things that will allow you to catch fish. You can get a head start by reading about fishing, but to get your degree in fishing, you must attend the University of Nature.

On every fishing trip, regardless of what you fish for, try to follow three hard-and-fast rules:

1. Always approach the fishing spot so you will be undetected.

2. Present your lure, fly, or bait in a manner so it appears completely natural, as if no line was attached.

3. Stick and move, hitting one spot, working it the best you can, then moving to the next.

APPROACH

No one can just walk up to a stream or lake, cast out, and start catching fish as if someone had waved a magic wand. Instead, give the fish credit for being smart. After all, they live there.

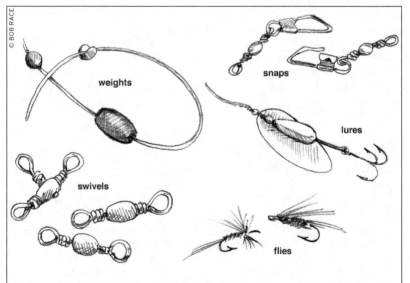

While camping, the only **fishing tackle** you should bring is the essentials: several varying weights, about 20 lures, and about 20 flies, splitshot, and snap swivels. These should all fit into a container just bigger than a deck of cards.

Your approach must be completely undetected by the fish. Fish can sense your presence through sight and sound, though these factors are misinterpreted by most people. By sight, fish rarely actually see you; more often, they see your shadow on the water or the movement of your arm or rod while casting. By sound, they don't necessarily hear you talking, but they do detect the vibrations of your footsteps along the shore, a rock being kicked, or the unnatural plunking sound of a heavy cast hitting the water. Any of these elements can spook them off the bite. In order to fish undetected, you must walk softly, keep your shadow off the water, and keep your casting motion low. All of these key elements become easier at sunrise or sunset, when shadows are on the water. At midday, the sun is at its peak, causing a high level of light penetration in the water. This can make the fish skittish to any foreign presence.

Like a hunter, you must stalk the spots. When my brother Rambob sneaks up on a fishing spot, he is like a burglar sneaking through an unlocked window.

Presentation

Your lure, fly, or bait must appear in the water as if no line were attached, so it looks as natural as possible. My pal Mo Furniss has skin-dived in rivers to watch what the fish see when somebody is fishing.

"You wouldn't believe it," he said. "When the lure hits the water, every trout within 40 feet, like 15, 20 trout, will do a little zigzag. They all see the lure and are aware something is going on. Meanwhile, onshore the guy casting doesn't get a bite and thinks there aren't any fish in the river."

If your offering is aimed at fooling a fish into striking, it must appear as part of the natural habitat, like an insect just hatching or a small fish looking for a spot to hide. That's where you come in.

After you have sneaked up on a fishing spot, you should zip your cast upstream and start your retrieval as soon as it hits the water. If you let the lure sink to the bottom and then start

the retrieval, you have no chance. A minnow, for instance, does not sink to the bottom, then start swimming. On rivers, the retrieval should be more of a drift, as if the "minnow" is in trouble and the current is sweeping it downstream.

When fishing on trout streams, always hike and cast upriver and retrieve as the offering drifts downstream in the current. This is effective because trout will sit almost motionless, pointed upstream, finning against the current. This way, they can see anything coming their direction, and if a potential food morsel arrives, all they need to do is move over a few inches, open their mouths, and they've got an easy lunch. Thus, you must cast upstream.

Conversely, if you cast downstream, your retrieval will bring the lure from behind the fish, where he cannot see it approaching. And I've never seen a trout that had eyes in its tail. In addition, when retrieving a downstream lure, the river current will tend to sweep your lure inshore to the rocks.

Finding Spots

A lot of anglers don't catch fish, and a lot of hikers never see any wildlife. The key is where they are looking.

The rule of the wild is that fish and wildlife will congregate wherever there is a distinct change in the habitat. This is where you should begin your search. To find deer, for instance, forget probing a thick forest, but look for where it breaks into a meadow or a clearcut has splayed a stand of trees. That's where the deer will be.

In a river, it can be where a riffle pours into a small pool, a rapid plunges into a deep hole and flattens, a big boulder in the middle of a long riffle, a shoreline point, a rock pile, a submerged tree. Look for the changes. Conversely, long, straight stretches of shoreline will not hold fish—the habitat is lousy.

On rivers, the most productive areas are often where short riffles tumble into small oxygenated pools. After sneaking up from the downstream side and staying low, you should zip your cast so the lure plops gently into the

© BOB RACE

The rule of the wild is that wildlife will congregate wherever there is a distinct change in habitat. To find where fish are hiding, look where a riffle pours into a small pond, where a rapid plunges into a deep hole and flattens, and around submerged trees, rock piles, and boulders in the middle of a long riffle.

white water just above the pool. Start your retrieval instantly; the lure will drift downstream and plunk into the pool. Bang! That's where the trout will hit. Take a few more casts and then head upstream to the next spot.

With a careful approach and lure presentation and by fishing in the right spots, you have the ticket to many exciting days on the water.

Of Bears and Food

The first time you come nose-to-nose with a bear can make your skin quiver.

Even the sight of mild-mannered black bears, the most common bear in America, can send shock waves through your body. They weigh 250-400 pounds and have large claws and teeth that are made to scare campers. When they bound, the muscles on their shoulders roll like ocean breakers. But in California, you don't have to be scared of them. They aren't interested in you, just your food.

Bears in camping areas are accustomed to sharing the mountains with hikers and campers. They have become specialists in the food-raiding business. As a result, you must be able

to bear-proof your camp or be able to scare the fellow off. Many campgrounds provide bear- and raccoon-proof food lockers. In most wilderness areas, bear-proof food canisters are required. Never leave your food or trash in your car!

Bear-proof food canisters are so effective in wilderness areas at Yosemite, Kings Canyon-Sequoia, and Mount Whitney that I never see bears on trips there anymore—they've given up on backpackers. Instead, they head to the drive-in campgrounds where they can walk right in and often find food sitting out on top of picnic tables.

No problem. Use the bear-proof food lockers. The bear will just move on to the next site on his daily mooching round.

Food Hangs

If you are staying at one of the backpack sites listed in this book, it is unlikely that there will be food lockers available. Your car will not be there, either. The solution is to make a bear-proof food hang, suspending all of your food wrapped in a plastic garbage bag from a rope

© CESLO DINIZ/123RF.COM

Use bear-proof containers to protect your campsite.

GRIZZLY BEAR TERRITORY

If you are hiking in a wilderness area in Canada or Alaska that may have grizzlies, it is necessary to wear bells on your pack. That way the bear will hear you coming and likely get out of your way. Keep talking, singing, or maybe even debating the country's foreign policy, but do not fall into a silent hiking vigil. And if a breeze is blowing in your face, you must make even more noise (a good excuse to rant and rave about the government's domestic affairs). Noise is important because your smell will not be carried in the direction you are hiking. As a result, the bear will not smell you coming.

If a bear can hear you and smell you, it will tend to get out of the way and let you pass without your knowing it was even close by. The exceptions are if you are carrying fish or lots of sweets in your pack or if you are wearing heavy, sweet deodorants or makeup. All of these are bear attractants.

in midair, 10 feet from the trunk of a tree and 20 feet off the ground. (Counterbalancing two bags with a rope thrown over a tree limb is very effective, but finding an appropriate limb can be difficult.)

The food hang is accomplished by tying a rock to a rope, then throwing it over a high but sturdy tree limb. Next, tie your food bag to the rope and hoist it in the air. When you are satisfied with the position of the food bag, tie off the end of the rope to another tree. In an area frequented by bears, a good food bag is a necessity—nothing else will do.

I've been there. On one trip, my pal Foonsky and my brother Rambob left to fish. I was stoking up an evening campfire when I felt the eyes of an intruder on my back. I turned around and saw a big bear heading straight for our camp. In the next half hour, I scared the bear off twice, but then he got a whiff of something sweet in my brother's pack.

The bear rolled into camp like a truck, grabbed the pack, ripped it open, and plucked out the Tang and the Swiss Miss. The 350-pounder then sat astride a nearby log and lapped at the goodies like a thirsty dog drinking water.

Once a bear gets his mitts on your gear, he considers it his. I took two steps toward the pack, and that bear jumped off the log and galloped across the camp right at me. Scientists say a man can't outrun a bear, but they've never

seen how fast I can go up a granite block with a bear on my tail.

Shortly thereafter, Foonsky returned to find me perched on top of the rock and demanded to know how I could let a bear get our Tang. It took all three of us, Foonsky, Rambob, and me, charging at once and shouting like madmen, to clear the bear out of camp and send him off over the ridge. We learned never to let food sit unattended.

The Grizzly

When it comes to grizzlies, well, my friends, you need what we call an attitude adjustment. Or that big ol' bear may just decide to adjust your attitude for you, making your stay at the park a short one.

Grizzlies are nothing like black bears. They are bigger, stronger, have little fear, and take what they want. Some people believe there are many different species of this critter, such as Alaskan brown, silvertip, cinnamon, and Kodiak, but the truth is they are all grizzlies. Any difference in appearance has to do with diet, habitat, and life habits, not speciation. By any name, they all come big.

The first thing you must do is determine if there are grizzlies in the area where you are camping. That can usually be done by asking local rangers. If you are heading into Yellowstone or Glacier National Park, or the Bob Marshall Wilderness of Montana, well, you don't have to ask. They're out there, and they're the biggest and potentially most dangerous critters you could run into.

One general way to figure the size of a bear is from his footprint. Take the width of the footprint in inches, add one to it, and you'll have an estimated length of the bear in feet. For instance, a nine-inch footprint equals a 10-foot bear. Any bear that big is a grizzly. In fact, most grizzly footprints average about 9-10 inches across, and black bears (though they may be brown in color) tend to have footprints only 4.5-6 inches across.

Most encounters with grizzlies occur when hikers fall into a silent march in the wilderness with the wind in their faces, and they walk around a corner and right into a big, unsuspecting grizzly. If you do this and see a big hump just behind its neck, don't think twice. It's a grizzly.

And then what should you do? Get up a tree, that's what. Grizzlies are so big that their claws cannot support their immense weight, and thus they cannot climb trees. And although young grizzlies can climb, they rarely want to get their mitts on you.

If you do get grabbed, every instinct in your body will tell you to fight back. Don't believe it. Play dead. Go limp. Let the bear throw you around a little. After a while, you'll become unexciting play material and the bear will get bored. My grandmother was grabbed by a grizzly in Glacier National Park and, after a few tosses and hugs, was finally left alone to escape.

Some say it's a good idea to tuck your head under his chin, since that way the bear will be unable to bite your head. I'll take a pass on that one. If you are taking action, any action, it's a signal that you are a force to be reckoned with, and he'll likely respond with more aggression. And bears don't lose many wrestling matches.

What grizzlies really like to do, believe it or not, is to pile a lot of sticks and leaves on you. Just let them, and keep perfectly still. Don't fight them; don't run. And when you have a 100 percent chance (not 98 or 99) to dash up a nearby tree, that's when you let fly. Once safely

in a tree, you can hurl down insults and let your aggression out.

In a wilderness camp, there are special precautions you should take. Always hang your food at least 100 yards downwind of camp and get it high; 30 feet is reasonable. In addition, circle your camp with rope and hang the bells from your pack on it. Thus, if a bear walks into your camp, he'll run into the rope, the bells will ring, and everybody will have a chance to get up a tree before ol' griz figures out what's going on. Often, the unexpected ringing of bells is enough to send him off in search of a quieter environment.

You see, more often than not, grizzlies tend to clear the way for campers and hikers. So be smart, don't act like bear bait, and always have a plan if you are confronted by one.

My pal Foonsky had such a plan during a wilderness expedition in Montana's northern Rockies. On our second day of hiking, we started seeing scratch marks on the trees 13-14 feet off the ground.

"Mr. Griz made those," Foonsky said. "With spring here, the grizzlies are coming out of hibernation and using the trees like a cat uses a scratch board to stretch the muscles."

The next day, I noticed Foonsky had a pair of track shoes tied to the back of his pack. I just laughed.

"You're not going to outrun a griz," I said. "In fact, there's hardly any animal out here in the wilderness that man can outrun."

Foonsky just smiled.

"I don't have to outrun a griz," he said. "I just have to outrun you!"

Fun and Games

"Now what are we supposed to do?" the young boy asked his dad.

"Yeah, Dad, think of something," said another son.

Well, Dad thought hard. This was one of the first camping trips he'd taken with his sons and one of the first lessons he received was that kids don't appreciate the philosophic release of mountain quiet. They want action and lots of it. With a glint in his eye, Dad searched around the camp and picked up 15 twigs, breaking them so each was four inches long. He laid them in three separate rows, three twigs in one row, five twigs in another, and seven in the other.

"OK, this game is called 3-5-7," said Dad. "You each take turns picking up sticks. You are allowed to remove all or as few as one twig from a row, but here's the catch: You can pick only from one row per turn. Whoever picks up the last stick left is the loser."

I remember this episode well because those two little boys were my brother Bobby, as in Rambobby, and I. And to this day, we still play 3-5-7 on campouts, with the winner getting to watch the loser clean the dishes. What I have learned in the span of time since that original episode is that it does not matter what your age is: Campers need options for camp fun.

Some evenings, after a long hike or ride, you feel too worn out to take on a serious romp downstream to fish or a climb up to a ridge for a view. That is especially true if you have been in the outback for a week or more. At that point, a lot of campers will spend their time resting and gazing at a map of the area, dreaming of the next day's adventure, or just take a seat against a rock, watching the colors of the sky and mountain panorama change minute by minute. But kids in the push-button video era, and a lot of adults too, want more. After all, "I'm on vacation. I want some fun."

There are several options, such as the 3-5-7 twig game, and they should be just as much a part of your trip planning as arranging your gear.

For kids, plan on games, the more physically challenging the competition, the better. One of the best games is to throw a chunk of wood into a lake and challenge the kids to hit it by throwing rocks. It wreaks havoc on the fishing, but it can keep kids totally absorbed for some time. Target practice with a wrist-rocket slingshot—firing rocks at small targets, like pinecones set on a log—is also all-consuming for kids.

You can also set kids off on little missions near camp, such as looking for the footprints of wildlife, searching out good places to have a "snipe hunt," picking up twigs to get the evening fire started, or having them take the water purifier to a stream to pump some drinking water into a canteen. The latter is an easy, fun, yet important task that will allow kids to feel a sense of equality they often don't get at home.

For adults, the appeal should be more to the intellect. A good example is star and planet identification, and while you are staring into space, you're bound to spot a few asteroids or shooting stars. A star chart can make it easy to find and identify many distinctive stars and constellations, such as Pleiades (the Seven Sisters), Orion, and others from the zodiac, depending on the time of year. With a little research, this can add a unique perspective to your trip. You could point to Polaris, one of the most easily identified of all stars, and note that navigators in the 1400s used it to find their way. Polaris, of course, is the North Star and is at the end of the handle of the Little Dipper. Pinpointing Polaris is quite easy. First find the Big Dipper and then find the outside stars of the ladle of the Big Dipper. They are called the "pointer stars" because they point right at Polaris.

A tree identification book can teach you a few things about your surroundings. It is also a good idea for one member of the party to research the history of the area you have chosen and another to research the geology. With shared knowledge, you end up with a deeper love of wild places.

Another way to add some recreation into your trip is to bring a board game, a number of which have been miniaturized for campers. The most popular are chess, checkers, and cribbage. The latter comes with an equally miniature set of playing cards. And if you bring those little cards, that opens a vast set of other possibilities. With kids along, for instance, just take three queens out of the deck and you can play Old Maid.

But there are more serious card games, and they come with high stakes. Such occurred on one high-country trip where Foonsky, Rambob, and I sat down for a late-afternoon game of poker. In a game of seven-card stud, I caught a straight on the sixth card and felt like a dog licking on a T-bone. Already, I had bet several Skittles and peanut M&Ms on this promising hand.

Then I examined the cards Foonsky had face up. He was showing three sevens, and acting as happy as a grizzly with a pork chop—or a full house. He matched my bet of two peanut M&Ms, then raised me three SweetTarts, one Starburst, and one sour apple Jolly Rancher. Rambob folded, but I matched Foonsky's bet and hoped for the best as the seventh and final card was dealt.

Just after Foonsky glanced at that last card, I saw him sneak a look at my grape stick and beef jerky stash.

"I raise you a grape stick," he said.

Rambob and I both gasped. It was the highest bet ever made, equivalent to a million dollars laid down in Las Vegas. Cannons were going off in my chest. I looked hard at my cards. They looked good, but were they good enough?

Even with a great hand like I had, a grape stick was too much to gamble, my last one with 10 days of trail ahead of us. I shook my head and folded my cards. Foonsky smiled at his victory.

But I still had my grape stick.

Old Tricks Don't Always Work

Most people are born honest, but after a few camping trips, they usually get over it.

I remember some advice I got from Rambob, normally an honest soul, on one camping trip. A giant mosquito had landed on my arm and he alerted me to an expert bit of wisdom.

"Flex your arm muscles," he commanded, watching the mosquito fill with my blood. "He'll get stuck in your arm, then he'll explode."

For some reason, I believed him. We both proceeded to watch the mosquito drill countless holes in my arm.

Alas, the unknowing face sabotage from

their most trusted companions on camping trips. It can arise at any time, usually in the form of advice from a friendly, honest-looking face, as if to say, "What? How can you doubt me?" After that mosquito episode, I was a little more skeptical of my dear old brother. Then the next day, when another mosquito was nailing me in the back of the neck, out came this gem:

"Hold your breath," he commanded. I instinctively obeyed. "That will freeze the mosquito," he said, "then you can squish him."

But in the time I wasted holding my breath, the little bugger was able to fly off without my having the satisfaction of squishing him. When he got home, he probably told his family, "What a dummy I got to drill today!"

Over the years, I have been duped numerous times with dubious advice:

On a grizzly bear attack: "If he grabs you, tuck your head under the grizzly's chin; then he won't be able to bite you in the head." This made sense to me until the first time I saw a nine-foot grizzly 40 yards away. In seconds, I was at the top of a tree, which suddenly seemed to make the most sense.

On coping with animal bites: "If a bear bites you in the arm, don't try to jerk it away. That will just rip up your arm. Instead, force your arm deeper into his mouth. He'll lose his grip and will have to open it to get a firmer hold, and right then you can get away." I was told this in the Boy Scouts. When I was 14, I had a chance to try it out when a friend's dog bit me as I tried to pet it. What happened? When I shoved my arm deeper into his mouth, he bit me three more times.

On cooking breakfast: "The bacon will curl up every time in a camp frying pan. So make sure you have a bacon stretcher to keep it flat." As a 12-year-old Tenderfoot, I spent two hours looking for the bacon stretcher until I figured out the camp leader had forgotten it. It wasn't for several years that I learned that there is no such thing.

On preventing sore muscles: "If you haven't hiked for a long time and you are facing a rough climb, you can keep from getting sore muscles in your legs, back, and shoulders by practicing the 'Dead Man's Walk.' Simply let your entire body go slack, and then take slow, wobbling steps. This will clear your muscles of lactic acid, which causes them to be so sore after a rough hike." Foonsky pulled this one on me. Rambob and I both bought it and tried it while we were hiking up Mount Whitney, which requires a 6,000-foot elevation gain in six miles. In one 45-minute period, about 30 other hikers passed us and looked at us as if we were suffering from some rare form of mental aberration.

Fish won't bite? No problem: "If the fish are not feeding or will not bite, persistent anglers can still catch dinner with little problem. Keep casting across the current, and eventually, as they hover in the stream, the line will feed across their open mouths. Keep reeling and you will hook the fish right in the side of the mouth. This technique is called 'lining.' Never worry if the fish will not bite, because you can always line 'em." Of course, heh, heh, heh, that explains why so many fish get hooked in the side of the mouth.

On keeping bears away: "To keep bears away, urinate around the borders of your camp-ground. If there are a lot of bears in the area, it is advisable to go right on your sleeping bag." Yeah, surrrrrre.

On disposing of trash: "Don't worry about packing out trash. Just bury it. It will regener-ate into the earth and add valuable minerals." Bears, raccoons, skunks, and other critters will dig up your trash as soon as you depart, leav-ing one huge mess for the next camper. Always pack out everything.

Often the advice comes without warning. That was the case after a fishing trip with a fe-male companion, when she outcaught me two to one, the third such trip in a row. I explained this to a shopkeeper, and he nodded, then ex-plained why.

"The male fish are able to detect the female scent on the lure, and thus become aroused into striking."

Of course! That explains everything!

Getting Revenge

I was just a lad when Foonsky pulled the old snipe-hunt trick on me. It took nearly 30 years to get revenge.

You probably know about snipe hunting. The victim is led out at night in the woods by a group, and then is left holding a bag.

"Stay perfectly still and quiet," Foonsky ex-plained. "You don't want to scare the snipe. The rest of us will go back to camp and let the woods settle down. Then when the snipe are least expecting it, we'll form a line and charge through the forest with sticks, beating bushes and trees, and we'll flush the snipe out right to you. Be ready with the bag. When we flush the snipe out, bag it. But until we start our charge, make sure you don't move or make a sound or you will spook the snipe and ruin everything."

I sat out there in the woods with my bag for hours, waiting for the charge. I waited, waited, and waited. Nothing happened. No charge, no snipe. It wasn't until well past midnight that I figured something was wrong. When I finally returned to camp, everybody was sleeping.

Well, I tell ya, don't get mad at your pals for the tricks they pull on you. Get revenge. About 25 years later, on the last day of a camping trip, the time finally came.

"Let's break camp early," Foonsky suggested to Mr. Furnai and me. "Get up before dawn, eat breakfast, pack up, and be on the ridge to watch the sun come up. It will be a fantastic way to end the trip."

"Sounds great to me," I replied. But when Foonsky wasn't looking, I turned his alarm clock ahead three hours. So when the alarm sounded at the appointed 4:30am wake-up time, Mr. Furnai and I knew it was actually only 1:30am.

Foonsky clambered out of his sleeping bag and whistled with a grin. "Time to break camp."

"You go ahead," I answered. "I'll skip break-fast so I can get a little more sleep. At the first sign of dawn, wake me up, and I'll break camp."

"Me, too," said Mr. Furnai.

Foonsky then proceeded to make some cof-fee, cook a breakfast, and eat it, sitting on a log

---

KEEP IT WILD TIP 6: PLAN AHEAD AND PREPARE

1. Learn about the regulations and issues that apply to the area you're visiting.
2. Avoid heavy-use areas.
3. Obtain all maps and permits.
4. Bring extra garbage bags to pack out any refuse you come across.

---

in the black darkness of the forest, waiting for the sun to come up. An hour later, with still no sign of dawn, he checked his clock. It now read 5:30am. "Any minute now we should start seeing some light," he said.

He made another cup of coffee, packed his gear, and sat there in the middle of the night, looking up at the stars, waiting for dawn. "Anytime now," he said. He ended up sitting there all night long.

Revenge is sweet. Before a fishing trip at a lake, I took Foonsky aside and explained that the third member of the party, Jimbobo, was hard of hearing and very sensitive about it. "Don't mention it to him," I advised. "Just talk real loud."

Meanwhile, I had already told Jimbobo the same thing. "Foonsky just can't hear very good."

We had fished less than 20 minutes when Foonsky got a nibble.

"GET A BITE?" shouted Jimbobo.

"YEAH!" yelled back Foonsky, smiling. "BUT I DIDN'T HOOK HIM!"

"MAYBE NEXT TIME!" shouted Jimbobo with a friendly grin.

Well, they spent the entire day yelling at each other from the distance of a few feet. They never did figure it out. Heh, heh, heh.

That is, I thought so, until we made a trip salmon fishing. I got a strike that almost knocked my fishing rod out of the boat. When I grabbed the rod, it felt as if Moby Dick were on the other end. "At least a 25-pounder," I said. "Maybe bigger."

The fish dove, ripped off line, and then bulldogged. "It's acting like a 40-pounder," I

announced, "Huge, just huge. It's going deep. That's how the big ones fight."

Some 15 minutes later, I finally got the "salmon" to the surface. It turned out to be a coffee can that Foonsky had clipped on the line with a snap swivel. By maneuvering the boat, he made the coffee can fight like a big fish.

This all started with a little old snipe hunt years ago. You never know what your pals will try next. Don't get mad. Get revenge.

CAMPING OPTIONS
Boat-In Seclusion

Most campers would never think of trading in their cars, pickup trucks, or RVs for a boat, but people who go by boat on a camping trip enjoy virtually guaranteed seclusion and top-quality outdoor experiences.

Camping with a boat is a do-it-yourself venture in living under primitive circumstances. Yet at the same time, you can bring along any luxury item you wish, from giant coolers, stoves, and lanterns to portable gasoline generators. Weight is almost never an issue.

Many outstanding boat-in campgrounds in beautiful surroundings are available. The best are on the shores of lakes accessible by canoe or skiff, and at offshore islands reached by saltwater cruisers. Several boat-in camps are detailed in this book.

If you want to take the adventure a step further and create your own boat-in camp, perhaps near a special fishing spot, this is a go-for-it deal that provides the best way possible to establish your own secret campsite. But most people who set out freelance style forget three critical items for boat-in camping: a shovel, a

Claim your own boat-in island.

sunshade, and an ax. Here is why these items can make a key difference in your trip:

Shovel: Many lakes and virtually all reservoirs have steep, sloping banks. At reservoirs subject to drawdowns, what was lake bottom in the spring can be a campsite in late summer. If you want a flat area for a tent site, the only answer is to dig one out yourself. A shovel gives you that option.

Sunshade: The flattest spots to camp along lakes often have a tendency to support only sparse tree growth. As a result, a natural shield from sun and rain is rarely available. What? Rain in the summer? Oh yeah, don't get me started. A light tarp, set up with poles and staked ropes, solves the problem.

Ax: Unless you bring your own firewood, which is necessary at some sparsely wooded reservoirs, there is no substitute for a good, sharp ax. With an ax, you can almost always find dry firewood, since the interior of an otherwise wet log will be dry. When the weather turns bad is precisely when you will most want a fire. You may need an ax to get one going.

In the search to create your own personal boat-in campsite, you will find that the flattest areas are usually the tips of peninsulas and points, while the protected back ends of coves are often steeply sloped. At reservoirs, the flattest areas are usually near the mouths of the feeder streams and the points are quite steep. On rivers, there are usually sandbars on the inside of tight bends that make for ideal campsites.

Almost all boat-in campsites developed by government agencies are free of charge, but you are on your own. Only in extremely rare cases is piped water available.

Any way you go, by canoe, skiff, or power cruiser, you end up with a one-in-a-million campsite you can call your own.

Desert Outings

It was a cold, snowy day in Missouri when 10-year-old Rusty Ballinger started dreaming about the vast deserts of the West.

"My dad was reading aloud from a Zane Grey book called *Riders of the Purple Sage*," Ballinger said. "He would get animated when he got to the passages about the desert. It wasn't long before I started to have the same feelings."

That was in 1947. Since then Ballinger has spent a good part of his life exploring the West, camping along the way. "The deserts are the best part. There's something about the uniqueness of each little area you see," Ballinger said. "You're constantly surprised. Just the time of day and the way the sun casts a different color. It's like the lady you care about. One time she smiles, the next time she's pensive. The desert is like that. If you love nature, you can love the desert. After a while, you can't help but love it."

A desert adventure is not just an antidote for a case of cabin fever in the winter. Whether you go by RV, pickup truck, car, or on foot, it provides its own special qualities.

If you go camping in the desert, your approach has to be as unique as the setting. For starters, don't plan on any campfires, but bring a camp stove instead. And unlike in the mountains, do not camp near a water hole. That's because an animal, such as a badger, coyote, or desert bighorn, might be desperate for water, and if you set up camp in the animal's way, you may be forcing a confrontation.

In some areas, there is a danger of flash floods. An intense rain can fall in one area, collect in a pool, then suddenly burst through a narrow canyon. If you are in its path, you could be injured or drowned. The lesson? Never camp in a gully.

"Some people might wonder 'What good is this place?'" Ballinger said. "The answer is that it is good for looking at. It is one of the world's unique places."

CAMP ETHICS AND POLITICS

The perfect place to set up a base camp turned out to be not so perfect. In fact, according to Doug Williams of California, it did not even exist.

Williams and his son, James, had driven deep into Angeles National Forest, prepared to set up camp and then explore the surrounding area on foot. But when they reached their destination, no campground existed.

"I wanted a primitive camp in a national forest where I could teach my son some basics," said the senior Williams. "But when we got there, there wasn't much left of the camp, and it had been closed. It was obvious that the area had been vandalized."

It turned out not to be an isolated incident. A lack of outdoor ethics practiced by a few people using the unsupervised campgrounds available on national forestland has caused the U.S. Forest Service to close a few of them and make extensive repairs to others.

"There have been sites closed, especially in Angeles and San Bernardino National Forests in Southern California," said David Flohr, regional campground coordinator for the U.S. Forest Service. "It's an urban type of thing, affecting forests near urban areas, and not just Los Angeles. They get a lot of urban users and they bring with them a lot of the same ethics they have in the city. They get drinking and they're not afraid to do things. They vandalize and run. Of course, it is a public facility, so they think nobody is getting hurt."

But somebody is getting hurt, starting with the next person who wants to use the campground. And if the ranger district budget doesn't have enough money to pay for repairs, the campground is then closed for the next arrivals. Just ask Doug and James Williams.

In an era of considerable fiscal restraint for the U.S. Forest Service, vandalized campgrounds could face closure instead of repair. Williams had just a taste of it, but Flohr, as camping coordinator, gets a steady diet.

"It starts with behavior," Flohr said. "General rowdiness, drinking, partying, and then vandalism. It goes all the way from the felt-tip pen things (graffiti) to total destruction, blowing up toilet buildings with dynamite. I have seen toilets destroyed totally with shotguns. They burn up tables, burn barriers. They'll burn up signs for firewood, even the shingles right off the roofs of the bathrooms. They'll shoot anything, garbage cans, signs. It

KEEP IT WILD TIP 7: RESPECT OTHER USERS

1. Horseback riders have priority over hikers. Step to the downhill side of the trail and talk softly when encountering horseback riders.
2. Hikers and horseback riders have priority over mountain bikers. When mountain bikers encounter other users even on wide trails, they should pass at an extremely slow speed. On very narrow trails, they should dismount and get off to the side so hikers or horseback riders can pass without having their trip disrupted.
3. Mountain bikes aren't permitted on most single-track trails and are expressly prohibited in designated wilderness areas and all sections of the Pacific Crest Trail. Mountain bikers breaking these rules should be confronted and told to dismount and walk their bikes until they reach a legal area.
4. It's illegal for horseback riders to break off branches that may be in the path of wilderness trails.
5. Horseback riders on overnight trips are prohibited from camping in many areas and are usually required to keep stock animals in specific areas where they can do no damage to the landscape.

can get a little hairy. A favorite is to remove the stool out of a toilet building. We've had people fall in the open hole."

The National Park Service had similar problems some years back, especially with rampant littering. Park Director Bill Mott responded by creating an interpretive program that attempts to teach visitors the wise use of natural areas, and to have all park workers set examples by picking up litter and reminding others to do the same.

The U.S. Forest Service has responded with a similar program, making brochures available that detail the wise use of national forests. The four most popular brochures are titled: "Rules for Visitors to the National Forest," "Recreation in the National Forests," "Is the Water Safe?" and "Backcountry Safety Tips." These include details on campfires, drinking water from lakes or streams, hypothermia, safety, and outdoor ethics.

Flohr said even experienced campers sometimes cross over the ethics line unintentionally. The most common example, he said, is when campers toss garbage into the outhouse toilet, rather than packing it out in a plastic garbage bag.

"They throw it in the vault toilet bowls, which just fills them up," Flohr said. "That creates an extremely high cost to pump it. You know why? Because some poor guy has to pick that stuff out piece by piece. It can't be pumped."

At most backcountry sites, the U.S. Forest Service has implemented a program called "Pack it in, pack it out," even posting signs that remind all visitors to do so. But a lot of people don't do it, and others may even uproot the signs and burn them for firewood.

On a trip to a secluded lake near Carson Pass in the Sierra Nevada, I arrived at a small, little-known camp where the picnic table had been spray painted and garbage had been strewn about. A pristine place, the true temple of God, had been defiled.

Getting Along with Fellow Campers

The most important thing about a camping, fishing, or hunting trip is not where you go, how many fish you catch, or how many shots you fire. It often has little to do with how beautiful the view is, how easily the campfire lights, or how sunny the days are.

Oh yeah? Then what is the most important factor? The answer: The people you are with. It is that simple.

Who would you rather camp with? Your

enemy at work or your dream mate in a good mood? Heh, heh. You get the idea. A camping trip is a fairly close-knit experience, and you can make lifetime friends or lifelong enemies in the process. That is why your choice of companions is so important. Your own behavior is equally consequential.

Yet most people spend more time putting together their camping gear than considering why they enjoy or hate the company of their chosen companions. Here are 10 rules of behavior for good camping mates:

1. **No whining:** Nothing is more irritating than being around a whiner. It goes right to the heart of adventure, since often the only difference between a hardship and an escapade is simply whether or not an individual has the spirit for it. The people who do can turn a rugged day in the outdoors into a cherished memory. Those who don't can ruin it with their incessant sniveling.

2. **Activities must be agreed upon:** Always have a meeting of the minds with your companions over the general game plan. Then everybody will possess an equal stake in the outcome of the trip. This is absolutely critical. Otherwise they will feel like merely an addendum to your trip, not an equal participant, and a whiner will be born (see number one).

3. **Nobody's in charge:** It is impossible to be genuine friends if one person is always telling another what to do, especially if the orders involve simple camp tasks. You need to share the space on the same emotional plane, and the only way to do that is to have a semblance of equality, regardless of differences in experience. Just try ordering your mate around at home for a few days. You'll quickly see the results, and they aren't pretty.

4. **Equal chances at the fun stuff:** It's fun to build the fire, fun to get the first cast at the best fishing spot, and fun to hoist the bagged food for a bear-proof food hang. It is not fun to clean the dishes, collect firewood, or cook every night. So obviously, there must be an equal distribution of the fun stuff and the not-fun stuff,

and everybody on the trip must get a shot at the good and the bad.

5. **No heroes:** No awards are bestowed for achievement in the outdoors, yet some guys treat mountain peaks, big fish, and big game as if they are prizes in a trophy competition. Actually, nobody cares how wonderful you are, which is always a surprise to trophy chasers. What people care about is the heart of the adventure, the gut-level stuff.

6. **Agree on a wake-up time:** It is a good idea to agree on a general wake-up time before closing your eyes for the night, and that goes regardless of whether you want to sleep in late or get up at dawn. Then you can proceed on course regardless of what time you crawl out of your sleeping bag in the morning, without the risk of whining (see number one).

7. **Think of the other guy:** Be self-aware instead of self-absorbed. A good test is to count the number of times you say, "What do you think?" A lot of potential problems can be solved quickly by actually listening to the answer.

8. **Solo responsibilities:** There are a number of essential camp duties on all trips, and while they should be shared equally, most should be completed solo. That means that when it is time for you to cook, you don't have to worry about me changing the recipe on you. It means that when it is my turn to make the fire, you keep your mitts out of it.

9. **Don't let money get in the way:** Of course everybody should share equally in trip expenses, such as the cost of food, and it should be split up before you head out yonder. Don't let somebody pay extra, because that person will likely try to control the trip. Conversely, don't let somebody weasel out of paying a fair share.

10. **Accordance on the food plan:** Always have complete agreement on what you plan to eat each day. Don't figure that just because you like Steamboat's Sludge, everybody else will, too, especially youngsters. Always, always, always check for food allergies, such as nuts, onions, or cheese, and make sure each person brings his or her own personal coffee brand.

Some people drink only decaffeinated; others might gag on anything but Burma monkey beans.

Obviously, it is difficult to find companions who will agree on all of these elements. This is why many campers say that the best camping buddies they'll ever have are their mates, who know all about them and like them anyway.

OUTDOORS WITH KIDS

How do you get a youngster excited about the outdoors? How do you compete with the television and remote control? How do you prove to a kid that success comes from persistence, spirit, and logic, which the outdoors teaches, and not from pushing buttons?

The answer is in the Ten Camping Commandments for Kids. These are lessons that will get youngsters excited about the outdoors and that will make sure adults help the process along, not kill it. I've put this list together with the help of my own kids, Jeremy and Kris, and their mother, Stephani. Some of the commandments are obvious, some are not, but all are important:

1. Take children to places where there is a guarantee of action. A good example is camping in a park where large numbers of wildlife can be viewed, such as squirrels, chipmunks, deer, and even bears. Other good choices include fishing at a small pond loaded with bluegill or hunting in a spot where a kid can shoot a .22 at pinecones all day. Boys and girls want action, not solitude.

2. Enthusiasm is contagious. If you aren't excited about an adventure, you can't expect a child to be. Show a genuine zest for life in the outdoors, and point out everything as if it is the first time you have ever seen it.

3. Always, always, always be seated when talking to someone small. This allows the adult and child to be on the same level. That is why fishing in a small boat is perfect for adults and kids. Nothing is worse for youngsters than having a big person look down at them and give them orders. What fun is that?

4. Always *show* how to do something, whether it is gathering sticks for a campfire, cleaning a trout, or tying a knot. Never tell—always show. A button usually clicks to "off"

when a kid is lectured. But kids can learn behavior patterns and outdoor skills by watching adults, even when the adults are not aware they are being watched.

5. Let kids be kids. Let the adventure happen, rather than trying to force it within some preconceived plan. If they get sidetracked watching pollywogs, chasing butterflies, or sneaking up on chipmunks, let them be. A youngster can have more fun turning over rocks and looking at different kinds of bugs than sitting in one spot, waiting for a fish to bite.

6. Expect short attention spans. Instead of getting frustrated about it, use it to your advantage. How? By bringing along a bag of candy and snacks. Where there is a lull in the camp activity, out comes the bag. Don't let them know what goodies await, so each one becomes a surprise.

7. Make absolutely certain the child's sleeping bag is clean, dry, and warm. Nothing is worse than discomfort when trying to sleep, but a refreshing sleep makes for a positive attitude the next day. In addition, kids can become quite scared of animals at night. A parent should not wait for any signs of this, but always play the part of the outdoor guardian, the one who will take care of everything.

8. Kids quickly relate to outdoor ethics. They will enjoy eating everything they kill, building a safe campfire, and picking up all their litter, and they will develop a sense of pride that goes with it. A good idea is to bring extra plastic garbage bags to pick up any trash you come across. Kids long remember when they do something right that somebody else has done wrong.

9. If you want youngsters hooked on the outdoors for life, take a close-up photograph of them holding up fish they have caught, blowing on the campfire, or completing other camp tasks. Young children can forget how much fun they had, but they never forget if they have a picture of it.

10. The least important word you can ever say to a kid is "I." Keep track of how often you are saying "Thank you" and "What do you think?" If you don't say them very often, you'll lose out. Finally, the most important words of all are: "I am proud of you."

PREDICTING WEATHER

Foonsky climbed out of his sleeping bag, glanced at the nearby meadow, and scowled hard.

"It doesn't look good," he said. "Doesn't look good at all."

I looked at my adventure companion of 20 years, noting his discontent. Then I looked at the meadow and immediately understood why: *"When the grass is dry at morning light, look for rain before the night."*

"How bad you figure?" I asked him.

"We'll know soon enough, I reckon," Foonsky answered. *"Short notice, soon to pass. Long notice, long it will last."*

When you are out in the wild, spending your days fishing and your nights camping, you learn to rely on yourself to predict the weather. It can make or break you. If a storm hits the unprepared, it can quash the trip and possibly endanger the participants. But if you are ready, a potential hardship can be an adventure.

You can't rely on TV weather forecasters, people who don't even know that when all the cows on a hill are facing north, it will rain that night for sure. God forbid if the cows are all sitting. But what do you expect from TV?

Foonsky made a campfire, started boiling some water for coffee and soup, and we started to plan the day. In the process, I noticed the smoke of the campfire: It was sluggish, drifting and hovering.

"You notice the smoke?" I asked, chewing on a piece of homemade jerky.

"Not good," Foonsky said. "Not good." He knew that sluggish, hovering smoke indicates rain.

"You'd think we'd have been smart enough to know last night that this was coming," Foonsky said. "Did you take a look at the moon or the clouds?"

"I didn't look at either," I answered. "Too busy eating the trout we caught." You see, if the moon is clear and white, the weather will be good the next day. But if there is a ring around the moon, the number of stars you can count inside the ring equals the number of days until the next rain. As for clouds, the high, thin ones—called cirrus—indicate a change in the weather.

We were quiet for a while, planning our strategy, but as we did so, some terrible things happened: A chipmunk scampered past with his tail high, a small flock of geese flew by very low, and a little sparrow perched on a tree limb quite close to the trunk.

"We're in for trouble," I told Foonsky.

"I know, I know," he answered. "I saw 'em, too. And come to think of it, no crickets were chirping last night either."

"Damn, that's right!"

These are all signs of an approaching storm. Foonsky pointed at the smoke of the campfire and shook his head as if he had just been condemned. Sure enough, now the smoke was blowing toward the north, a sign of a south wind. *"When the wind is from the south, the rain is in its mouth."*

"We'd best stay hunkered down until it passes," Foonsky said.

I nodded. "Let's gather as much firewood now as we can, get our gear covered up, then plan our meals."

"Then we'll get a poker game going."

As we accomplished these camp tasks, the sky clouded up, then darkened. Within an hour, we had gathered enough firewood to make a large pile, enough wood to keep a fire going no matter how hard it rained. The day's meals had been separated out of the food bag so it wouldn't have to be retrieved during the storm. We buttoned two ponchos together, staked two of the corners with ropes to the ground, and tied the other two with ropes to different tree limbs to create a slanted roof/shelter.

As the first raindrop fell with that magic sound on our poncho roof, Foonsky was just starting to shuffle the cards.

"Cut for deal," he said.

Just as I did so, it started to rain a bit harder. I pulled out another piece of beef jerky and

started chewing on it. It was just another day in paradise.

Weather lore can be valuable. Here is the list I have compiled over the years:

When the grass is dry at morning light,
Look for rain before the night.
Short notice, soon to pass.
Long notice, long it will last.

When the wind is from the east,
'Tis fit for neither man nor beast.
When the wind is from the south,
The rain is in its mouth.
When the wind is from the west,
Then it is the very best.

Red sky at night, sailors' delight.
Red sky in the morning, sailors take warning.

When all the cows are pointed north,
Within a day rain will come forth.

Onion skins very thin, mild winter coming in.
Onion skins very tough, winter's going to be very rough.

When your boots make the squeak of snow,
Then very cold temperatures will surely show.

If a goose flies high, fair weather ahead.
If a goose flies low, foul weather will come instead.

Small signs provided by nature and wildlife can also be translated to provide a variety of weather information:

A thick coat on a woolly caterpillar means a big, early snow is coming.

Chipmunks will run with their tails up before a rain.

Bees always stay near their hives before a rainstorm.

When the birds are perched on large limbs near tree trunks, an intense but short storm will arrive.

CAMPING GEAR CHECKLIST

COOKING GEAR

- Camp stove and fuel
- Dish soap and scrubber
- Fire-starter cubes
- Heavy-duty paper plates
- Ice chest and drinks
- Itemized food, separated by groups
- Knife, fork, cup
- Large, heavy-duty garbage bags
- Matches stored in resealable (such as Ziploc) bags
- One lighter for each camper
- Paper towels
- Plastic spatula and stir spoon
- Pot grabber or pot holder
- Salt, pepper, spices
- Two pots and no-stick pan
- Water jug or lightweight plastic "cube"

Optional Cooking Gear

- Aluminum foil
- Ax or hatchet
- Barbecue tongs
- Can opener
- Candles
- Dustpan
- Grill or hibachi
- Plastic clothespins
- Tablecloth
- Whisk broom
- Wood or charcoal for barbecue

CLOTHING

- Cotton/canvas pants
- Gore-Tex parka or jacket
- Gore-Tex rain pants
- Lightweight, breathable shirt
- Lightweight fleece jacket
- Medium-weight fleece vest
- Polypropylene underwear
- Rain jacket and pants, or poncho
- Sunglasses
- Waterproofed, oilskin wide-brimmed hat

Optional Clothing

- Gloves
- Shorts
- Ski cap

HIKING GEAR

- Backpack or daypack
- Hiking boots
- Fresh bootlaces
- Innersole or foot cushion (for expeditions)
- Moleskin and medical tape
- SmartWool (or equivalent) socks
- Water-purification system

Optional Hiking Gear

- Backup lightweight shoes or moccasins
- Gaiters
- Water-repellent boot treatment

SLEEPING GEAR

- Ground tarp
- Sleeping bag
- Tent or bivy bag
- Therm-a-Rest pad

Optional Sleeping Gear

- Air bed
- Cot
- Catalytic heater

- Foam pad for truck bed
- Mosquito netting
- Mr. Heater and propane tank (for use in pickup truck camper shell)
- Pillow (even in wilderness)
- RV windshield light screen
- Seam Lock for tent stitching

FIRST AID

- Ace bandage
- After-Bite for mosquito bites (before you scratch them)
- Aspirin
- Biodegradable soap
- Caladryl for poison oak
- Campho-Phenique gel for bites (after you scratch them)
- Mosquito repellent
- Lip balm
- Medical tape to affix pads
- Neosporin for cuts
- Roller gauze
- Sterile gauze pads
- Sunscreen
- Tweezers

Optional First Aid

- Athletic tape for sprained ankle
- Cell phone or coins for phone calls
- Extra set of matches
- Mirror for signaling
- Thermometer

RECREATION GEAR

- All required permits and licenses
- Fishing reel with fresh line
- Fishing rod

- Knife
- Leatherman tool or needle-nose pliers
- Small tackle box with flies, floats, hooks, lures, snap swivels, and splitshot

Optional Recreation Gear

- Backpacking cribbage board
- Deck of cards
- Folding chairs
- Guidebooks
- Hammock
- Mountain bike
- Reading material

OTHER NECESSITIES

- Duct tape
- Extra plastic garbage bags
- Flashlight and batteries
- Lantern and fuel
- Maps
- Nylon rope for food hang
- Spade for cat hole
- Toilet paper
- Toothbrush and toothpaste
- Towelettes
- Wristwatch

OTHER OPTIONAL ITEMS

- Altimeter
- Assorted bungee cords
- Binoculars
- Camera with fresh battery and digital card or film
- Compass
- Feminine hygiene products
- GPS unit
- Handkerchief
- Notebook and pen

On the coast, if groups of seabirds are flying a mile inland, look for major winds.

If crickets are chirping very loudly during the evening, the next day will be clear and warm.

If the smoke of a campfire at night rises in a thin spiral, good weather is assured for the next day.

If the smoke of a campfire at night is sluggish, drifting and hovering, it will rain the next day.

If there is a ring around the moon, count the number of stars inside the ring, and that is how many days until the next rain.

If the moon is clear and white, the weather will be good the next day.

High, thin clouds, or cirrus, indicate a change in the weather.

Oval-shaped lenticular clouds indicate high winds.

Two levels of clouds moving in different directions indicate changing weather soon.

Huge, dark, billowing clouds, called cumulonimbus, suddenly forming on warm afternoons in the mountains mean that a short but intense thunderstorm with lightning can be expected.

When squirrels are busy gathering food for extended periods, it means good weather is ahead in the short term, but a hard winter is ahead in the long term.

And God forbid if all the cows are sitting down....

THE OREGON COAST

Want to treat yourself to a trip you'll treasure forever? Set up camp on one of the most dramatic coasts in North America. The Oregon Coast is home to tidewater rock gardens, cliff-top views that seem to stretch to forever, vast sand dunes, protected bays, beautiful streams with salmon and steelhead, and three major national forests. The most spectacular region may be the Oregon Dunes National Recreation Area, which spans roughly from Coos Bay north past Florence to near the mouth of the Siuslaw River. Whenever I visit, I'm instantly transported to another universe. I have a photo of the dunes in my office. While I'm writing, I often look at the image of a lone raptor soaring past a pyramid of sand—it's my window to this other world.

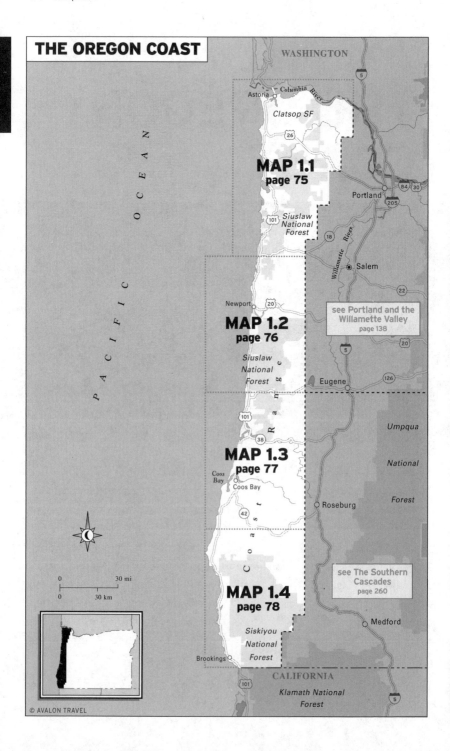

THE OREGON COAST

WASHINGTON

Astoria

Columbia River

Clatsop SF

MAP 1.1
page 75

Portland

Siuslaw
National
Forest

Willamette River

Salem

see Portland and the
Willamette Valley
page 138

Newport

MAP 1.2
page 76

Siuslaw
National
Forest

Eugene

P A C I F I C   O C E A N

C o a s t   R a n g e

Umpqua

National

Forest

MAP 1.3
page 77

Coos
Bay

Coos Bay

Roseburg

see The Southern
Cascades
page 260

MAP 1.4
page 78

Medford

Siskiyou

National

Forest

Brookings

CALIFORNIA

Klamath National
Forest

0   30 mi
0   30 km

© AVALON TRAVEL

Map 1.1

**Sites 1-31
Pages 79-92**

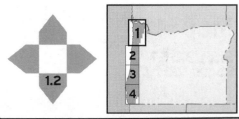

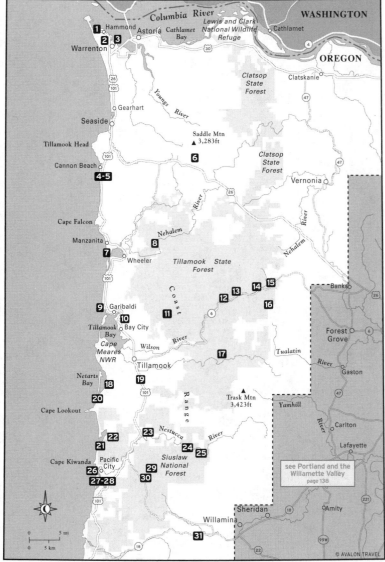

Map 1.2
Sites 32-57
Pages 92-103

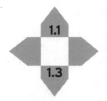

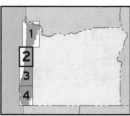

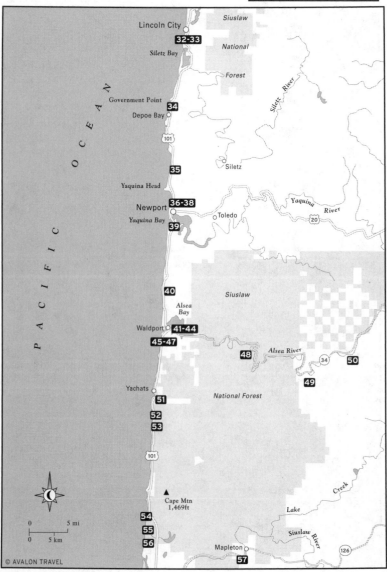

Lincoln City
32-33

Siuslaw

National

Forest

Siletz Bay

Siletz River

Government Point
34
Depoe Bay

101

Siletz River

35

Siletz

Yaquina Head

36-38
Newport
Yaquina Bay
39
Toledo

Yaquina River

20

40

Alsea Bay

Siuslaw

Waldport
41-44
45-47

48

Alsea River

34

50

49

Yachats
51

National Forest

52

53

101

▲ Cape Mtn
1,469ft

Creek

Lake

54

0   5 mi

0   5 km

55

56

Siuslaw River

Mapleton
57

126

© AVALON TRAVEL

Map 1.3

Sites 58-97
Pages 103-120

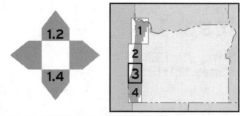

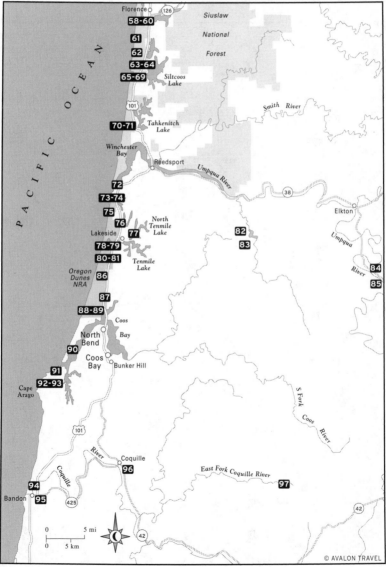

Map 1.4

Sites 98-132
Pages 121-135

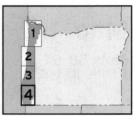

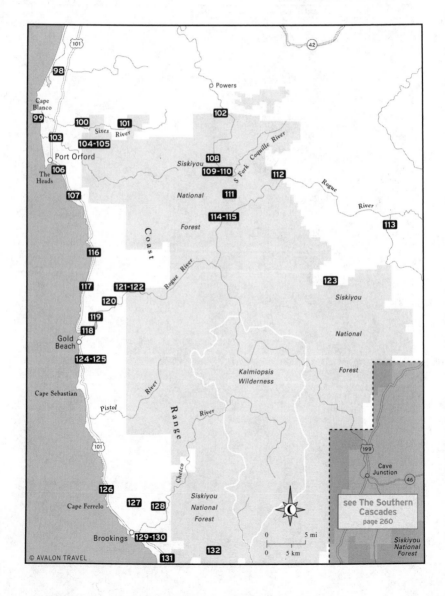

1 FORT STEVENS STATE PARK

🚶 🚴 🏊 🛶 ⛴ 🐴 🧗 ♿ 🚐 ⛺

Scenic rating: 8

at the mouth of the Columbia River

Map 1.1, page 75   **BEST (**

This classic spot is set at the northern tip of Oregon, right where the Columbia River enters the Pacific Ocean. At 3,700 acres, the park offers nine miles of biking trails, six miles of hiking trails, swimming, boating, fishing, and wildlife-viewing in a landscape of forests, wetlands, and dunes. The trailhead for the Oregon Coast Trail is here as well. History buffs will find a museum, tours of the fort and artillery batteries, and the remains of the *Peter Iredale* shipwreck.

Campsites, facilities: There are 476 sites with full or partial hookups for tents or RVs up to 60 feet long, 19 sites for tents or small RVs (no hookups), a camping area for hikers and bicyclists, and 15 yurts. Picnic tables and fire grills are provided. Drinking water, restrooms with flush toilets and showers, dump station, a transfer and recycling station, two picnic shelters, firewood, and a playground are available. Boat docks and launching facilities are nearby. Some facilities are wheelchair accessible. Leashed pets are permitted.

Reservations, fees: Reservations are accepted at 800/452-5687 or www.oregonstateparks.org ($8 reservation fee). RV sites are $30-32 per night, tent sites are $22 per night, $6 per night per person for hikers/bikers, yurts are $46 per night, $7 per night per additional vehicle. Some credit cards are accepted. Open year-round.

Directions: From Portland, turn west on U.S. 26 and drive 73 miles to the junction with U.S. 101. Turn right (north) on U.S. 101 and drive about 15 miles (about 0.25 mile past the Camp Rilea Army Base). Turn west on Perkins Road/Highway 104 at the sign for Fort Stevens State Park and drive about one mile to Ocean View Cemetery Road. Turn left and drive about 2.5 miles (Ocean View Cemetery Road becomes Ridge Road) to the park entrance.

Contact: Fort Stevens State Park, 503/861-1671 or 800/551-6949, www.oregonstateparks.org.

2 ASTORIA/WARRENTON SEASIDE KOA

🚶 🚴 🏊 🛶 ⛴ 🏊 🐴 🧗 ♿ 🚐 ⛺

Scenic rating: 3

near Fort Stevens State Park

Map 1.1, page 75

This campground is nestled in a wooded area adjacent to Fort Stevens State Park, and tours of that historical military site can be arranged. This camp provides an excellent alternative if the state park campground is full. A host of activities are available in the immediate area, including beachcombing, bicycling, deep-sea fishing, hiking, and kayaking. Horse stables are within 10 miles.

Campsites, facilities: There are 311 sites with full or partial hookups for tents or RVs of any length, 54 cabins, and eight deluxe lodges. Some sites are pull-through. Picnic tables and fire pits are provided. Cable TV, 30- and 50-amp service, Wi-Fi, restrooms with flush toilets and showers, coin laundry, meeting room, firewood, limited groceries, ice, snack bar, RV supplies, propane gas, and a picnic area are available. Recreational facilities include a playground, game room, bicycle rentals, miniature golf, horseshoe pits, spa, and a heated indoor swimming pool. Some facilities are wheelchair accessible. Leashed pets are permitted with some restrictions.

Reservations, fees: Reservations are accepted at 800/562-8506. RV sites start at $51 per night, $5.50 per person per night for more than two people, $1 per pet per night, $5 per night per additional vehicle unless towed. Some credit cards are accepted. Open year-round.

Directions: From Portland, turn west on U.S. 26 and drive 73 miles to the junction with U.S. 101. Turn right (north) on U.S. 101 and drive about 15 miles (about 0.25 mile past the Camp Rilea Army Base). Turn west on Perkins Road/Highway 104 at the sign for Fort Stevens State

Park and drive about one mile to Ocean View Cemetery Road. Turn left and drive about 2.5 miles (Ocean View Cemetery Road becomes Ridge Road) to the campground directly across from the state park.

Contact: Astoria/Warrenton Seaside KOA, 503/861-2606, www.koa.com.

🚩 KAMPERS WEST RV PARK

🚶 🚴 🏊 🎣 🐕 🚐 ⛺

Scenic rating: 7

near Fort Stevens State Park

Map 1.1, page 75

Just four miles from Fort Stevens State Park, this privately run camp offers full RV services. Nearby recreation possibilities include an 18-hole golf course, hiking trails, and marked bike trails.

Campsites, facilities: There are 160 sites with full or partial (30-amp) hookups for RVs of any length, a small area for tents only, and three park-model cabins. Drinking water and picnic tables are provided, and some sites have fire pits. Restrooms with flush toilets and showers, propane gas, dump station, coin laundry, firewood, cable TV, fish-cleaning and crab-cooking stations, and ice are available. A store and a café are within two miles. Leashed pets are permitted.

Reservations, fees: Reservations are accepted. RV sites are $40 per night, tent sites are $30 per night, and cabins are $52 per night, $5 per each additional person or vehicle per night. Some credit cards are accepted. Open year-round.

Directions: From Portland, turn west on U.S. 30 and drive 105 miles north and west to Astoria and the junction of U.S. 101. Turn south and drive 6.5 miles to the Warrenton/Hammond Junction. Turn right (west) on Warrenton and drive 1.5 miles to the campground on the right.

Contact: Kampers West RV Park, 503/861-1814, www.kamperswest.com.

🚩 SEA RANCH RV PARK

🚶 🚴 🏊 🎣 🐎 🚐 ⛺

Scenic rating: 9

in Cannon Beach

Map 1.1, page 75

This park is set in a wooded area with nearby access to the beach. Activities at the camp include stream fishing, horseback riding, and swimming on the seashore. A golf course is six miles away, and the historic Lewis and Clark Trail is nearby. Elk hunters camp here in season. The beach and the town of Cannon Beach are within walking distance of the park.

Campsites, facilities: There are 80 sites with full or partial hookups for tents or RVs up to 40 feet long and seven cabins. Picnic tables and fire rings are provided. Restrooms with flush toilets and showers, horse rentals, firewood, and a dump station are available. Supplies are available within two miles. Leashed pets are permitted.

Reservations, fees: Reservations are accepted. RV sites are $50-55 per night, tent sites are $40 per night, cabins are $95-105 per night, $3-15 per person per night for more than two people, $4 per night per additional vehicle, and $3-25 per pet per night. Monthly rates are available. Some credit cards are accepted. Open year-round.

Directions: From Portland on I-5, turn west on U.S. 26 and drive 73 miles to the junction with U.S. 101. Turn south on U.S. 101 and drive three miles to the Cannon Beach exit. Take that exit and drive on Fir Street for 0.3 mile to the park on the left.

Contact: Sea Ranch RV Park, 503/436-2815, www.searanchrv.com.

5 RV RESORT AT CANNON BEACH

Scenic rating: 9

near Ecola State Park

Map 1.1, page 75

This private resort is located about seven blocks from one of the nicest beaches in the region and about two miles from Ecola State Park. From the town of Cannon Beach, you can walk for miles in either direction. Nearby recreational facilities include marked bike trails, a riding stable, and tennis courts. The city shuttle service stops here.

Campsites, facilities: There are 99 sites with full hookups for RVs of any length; some sites are pull-through. Picnic tables and fire pits are provided. Restrooms with flush toilets and showers, cable TV, propane gas, firewood, recreation hall, playground, horseshoe pits, basketball court, convenience store, spa, coin laundry, ice, gasoline, playground, and a heated swimming pool (year-round) are available. Some facilities are wheelchair accessible. Leashed pets are permitted.

Reservations, fees: Reservations are accepted at 800/847-2231. Sites are $37-52 per night, $3 per person per night for more than two people. Weekly and monthly rates available. Some credit cards are accepted. Open year-round.

Directions: From Portland on I-5, turn west on U.S. 26 and drive 73 miles to the junction with U.S. 101. Turn south on U.S. 101 and drive four miles to the second Cannon Beach exit at Milepost 29.5. Exit on the left (east) and drive 200 feet to the resort.

Contact: RV Resort at Cannon Beach, 503/436-2231, www.cbrvresort.com.

6 SADDLE MOUNTAIN STATE NATURAL AREA

Scenic rating: 7

on Saddle Mountain

Map 1.1, page 75

This inland camp offers a good alternative to the many beachfront parks. A 2.5-mile trail climbs to the top of Saddle Mountain, a great lookout on clear days. The park is a real find for the naturalist interested in rare and unusual varieties of plants, many of which have established themselves along the slopes of this isolated mountain.

Campsites, facilities: There are 10 primitive walk-in tent sites and a grassy overflow area for tents. Picnic tables and fire grills are provided. Drinking water (seasonal), garbage bins, flush and vault toilets (seasonal), and a picnic area are available. Leashed pets are permitted.

Reservations, fees: Reservations are not accepted. Sites are $11 per night, $7 per night per additional vehicle. Open March-October.

Directions: From Portland, turn west on U.S. 26 and drive about 63 miles to just before Necanicum Junction and Saddle Mountain Road. Turn right (north) on Saddle Mountain Road and drive seven miles to the park. The road dead-ends at the park.

Contact: Ecola State Park, 503/436-2844 or 800/551-6949 (this number reaches Ecola State Park, which manages Saddle Mountain), www.oregonstateparks.org.

7 NEHALEM BAY STATE PARK

Scenic rating: 7

on Nehalem Bay

Map 1.1, page 75

This state park on a sandy point separating the Pacific Ocean from Nehalem Bay features six miles of beach frontage. There is no ocean view from the campsites, but the sites are about 150 yards from the ocean. In 2008, beachcombers discovered a pair of historic cannons at low tide, likely dating back to an 1846 shipwreck. Crabbing and fishing on the bay are popular. The Oregon Coast Trail passes through the park. A horse camp with corrals and a 7.5-mile equestrian trail are available. There is also a two-mile bike trail. The neighboring towns of Manzanita and Nehalem offer fine dining and shopping. An airport is adjacent to the park, and there are airstrip fly-in campsites.

Campsites, facilities: There are 265 sites with partial hookups for tents or RVs up to 60 feet long, a camping area for hikers and bicyclists, and six primitive fly-in sites next to the airport. There are also 18 yurts and 17 equestrian sites with stock corrals. Drinking water, picnic tables, and fire grills are provided. Restrooms with flush toilets and showers, dump station, playgrounds, firewood, and a meeting hall are available. Boat-launching facilities are nearby on Nehalem Bay, and an airstrip is adjacent to the park. Some facilities are wheelchair accessible. Leashed pets are permitted.

Reservations, fees: Reservations are accepted at 800/452-5687 or www.oregonstateparks.org ($8 reservation fee). Sites are $29 per night, $7 per night per additional vehicle, and $6 per person per night for hikers/bikers. Yurts are $45-55 per night; horse sites are $21 per night. Fly-in sites are $11 per night, not including tie-down. Some credit cards are accepted. Open year-round.

Directions: From Portland, drive west on U.S. 26 for 73 miles to the junction with U.S. 101. Turn south on U.S. 101 and drive 19 miles to Manzanita. Continue south on U.S. 101 for 0.75 mile to Necarney City Road. Turn right and drive 0.2 mile to a stop sign. Turn right and drive 0.75 mile to the park entrance.

Contact: Nehalem Bay State Park, 503/368-5154 or 800/551-6949, www.oregonstateparks.org.

8 NEHALEM FALLS

Scenic rating: 10

in Tillamook State Forest

Map 1.1, page 75　　　　　　**BEST (**

This beautiful campground, amid old-growth hemlock and spruce, is located within a two-minute walk of lovely Nehalem Falls. Note that swimming in the pool below the falls is hazardous and not advised. A half-mile loop trail follows the Nehalem River, where fishing and swimming are options.

Campsites, facilities: There are 14 sites for tents or RVs up to 40 feet long, six walk-in tent sites, and one group site for up to 20 people. Picnic tables and fire grills are provided. Drinking water, vault toilets, garbage bins, and a recycling center are available. A camp host is on-site. Some facilities are wheelchair accessible. Leashed pets are permitted.

Reservations, fees: Reservations are accepted for the group site only online at www.oregon.gov. Sites are $15 per night, $5 per night per additional vehicle, walk-in sites are $10 per night, and the group site is $50 per night. Open May-mid-September.

Directions: From Tillamook on U.S. 101 northbound, drive 22 miles to Highway 53. Turn right (east) and drive 1.3 miles to Miami Foley Road. Turn right (south) and drive one mile to Foss Road (narrow and rough). Turn left and drive seven miles to the campground on the left.

Contact: Tillamook State Forest, Tillamook District, 503/842-2545, www.oregon.gov.

9 BARVIEW JETTY CAMPGROUND

Scenic rating: 7

near Garibaldi

Map 1.1, page 75

This Tillamook County park covers 160 acres and is located near the beach, in a wooded area adjacent to Tillamook Bay. The sites are set on grassy hills. Nearby recreation options include an 18-hole golf course, surf and scuba fishing, and a full-service marina.

Campsites, facilities: There are 242 tent sites, 73 sites with full hookups for tents or RVs of any length, and 20 hiker/biker sites. Some sites are pull-through. Groups can be accommodated. Picnic tables and fire pits are provided. Drinking water, restrooms with flush toilets and showers, a dump station, a fish-cleaning station, Wi-Fi, and a day-use area are available. A camp host is on site. Propane gas, store, café, and ice are within one mile. Some facilities are wheelchair accessible. Leashed pets are permitted.

Reservations, fees: Reservations are accepted ($10 reservation fee) at 503/322-3522 or www. co.tillamook.or.us. Sites are $29-39 per night, $5 per night per each additional vehicle, $7 per night per additional tent, $8 per person per night for hiker/biker sites, $5 per pet. Some credit cards are accepted. Open year-round.

Directions: From Tillamook, drive north on U.S. 101 for 12 miles to the park on the left (two miles north of the town of Garibaldi).

Contact: Barview Jetty Campground, Tillamook County, 503/322-3522, www. co.tillamook.or.us/gov/parks.

🔟 PORT OF GARIBALDI RV PARK

Scenic rating: 7

on Tillamook Bay

Map 1.1, page 75

This park along the shore of Tillamook Bay is a prime retreat for beachcombing, clamming, crabbing, deep-sea fishing, scuba diving, and surf fishing. The nearby town of Tillamook is home to a cheese factory and a historical museum. Cape Meares State Park, where you can hike through the national wildlife preserve and see how the seabirds nest along the cliffs,

makes a good side trip. There is also a golf course nearby.

Campsites, facilities: There are 48 sites with full (50-amp) hookups for RVs of any length. Picnic tables are provided. Drinking water, restrooms with flush toilets and showers, Wi-Fi, cable TV, convenience store, and a coin laundry are available. Propane gas, café, and ice are within one mile. Boat docks, launching facilities, and rentals are nearby. Some facilities are wheelchair accessible. Leashed pets are permitted.

Reservations, fees: Reservations are accepted. RV sites are $32 per night. There is a fee ($2 per day) for more than one pet. Weekly and monthly rates are available. Some credit cards are accepted. Open year-round.

Directions: From Tillamook and U.S. 101, drive north for 10 miles to 7th Street. Turn left on 7th Street and drive to the park on the left (just over the tracks).

Contact: Port of Garibaldi RV Park, 606 S. Biak Ave., 503/322-3292, http://portofgaribaldi.org.

🔢 KILCHIS RIVER PARK

Scenic rating: 8

on the Kilchis River

Map 1.1, page 75

Riverfront campsites are the highlight at this Tillamook County campground. The campground is forested and gets moderate use. Hiking trails are available. Other recreational options include boating, fishing, and swimming.

Campsites, facilities: There are 63 sites for tents or RVs of any length (no hookups) and 27 hiker/biker sites. Picnic tables and fire pits are provided. Drinking water, flush toilets, coin showers, playground, garbage bins, boat launch, day-use area, dump station, basketball court, and a volleyball court are available. A camp host is on-site. Some facilities are wheelchair accessible. Leashed pets are permitted.

Reservations, fees: Reservations are accepted ($10 reservation fee) at 503/842-6694 or www.co.tillamook.or.us. Sites are $14-24 per night, $5 per night per additional vehicle, $7 per night per additional tent, $8 per person per night for hiker/biker sites, and $5 per pet. Open May-October.

Directions: From Tillamook and U.S. 101, take the Alderbrook Loop/Kilches Park exit. Turn onto Alderbrook Loop and drive northeast for approximately one mile to Kilchis River Road. Turn right and drive approximately four miles to the park at the end of the road.

Contact: Kilchis River Park, Tillamook County, 503/842-6694, www.co.tillamook.or.us/gov/parks.

12 JONES CREEK

Scenic rating: 7
on the Wilson River in Tillamook State Forest

Map 1.1, page 75

Set in a forest of alder, fir, hemlock, and spruce, campsites here are spacious and private. The adjacent Wilson River provides opportunities for steelhead and salmon fishing (artificial lures only). A scenic 3.8-mile trail runs along the riverfront. The camp fills up on weekends July-Labor Day.

Campsites, facilities: There are 28 sites for tents or RVs of any length, 14 walk-in tent sites, and one group site for up to 20 people. Picnic tables and fire grills are provided. Drinking water, vault toilets, garbage bins, firewood, and a horseshoe pit are available. A camp host is on-site. Some facilities are wheelchair accessible. Leashed pets are permitted.

Reservations, fees: Reservations are accepted for the group site only online at www.oregon.gov. Sites are $15 per night, $5 per night per additional vehicle, walk-in sites are $10 per night, and the group site is $50 per night. Open May-mid-September.

Directions: From Portland, turn west on U.S. 26 and drive 24 miles to Highway 6. Turn west on Highway 6 and drive 28 miles to Milepost 22.7 and North Fork Road. Turn right and drive 0.25 mile to the campground on the left.

Contact: Tillamook State Forest, Tillamook District, 503/842-2545, www.oregon.gov.

13 ELK CREEK WALK-IN

Scenic rating: 7
on Elk Creek in Tillamook State Forest

Map 1.1, page 75

This small campground is set among alder, fir, and maple on Elk Creek and borders the Wilson River. The Elk Mountain trailhead is here and a good swimming hole is nearby.

Campsites, facilities: There are 14 walk-in tent sites. Picnic tables and fire grills are provided. Drinking water and vault toilets are available. Garbage must be packed out. Some facilities are wheelchair accessible. Leashed pets are permitted.

Reservations, fees: Reservations are not accepted. Sites are $10 per night, $5 per night per additional vehicle. Open mid-May-October.

Directions: From Portland, turn west on U.S. 26 and drive 24 miles to Highway 6. Turn west on Highway 6 and drive 23 miles to Milepost 28 and the campground entrance road on the right. Turn right on Elk Creek Road and drive 0.5 mile to the campground on the left.

Contact: Tillamook State Forest, Forest Grove District, 503/357-2191, www.oregon.gov.

14 JORDAN CREEK OHV

Scenic rating: 6
near Jordan Creek in Tillamook State Forest

Map 1.1, page 75

This off-highway vehicle (OHV) camp is set at the bottom of a scenic, steep canyon next to Jordan Creek. Wooded campsites are clustered around a central parking area, and the park caters to OHV campers. There are almost

40 miles of OHV trails, varying from moderate to difficult. Note that in order to ride an ATV on roads, you need an ATV sticker, a driver's license, and a spark arrestor. There's no fishing in Jordan Creek.

Campsites, facilities: There are six sites for tents or RVs of any length. Overflow RV camping is allowed in the main parking lot. Picnic tables and fire grills are provided. Garbage bins and vault toilets are available. There is no drinking water. Leashed pets are permitted.

Reservations, fees: Reservations are not accepted. Sites are $15 per night, $5 per night per additional vehicle. (Motorcycles, ATVs, and 4x4s taken in on trailers do not count as extra vehicles.) Open mid-May-mid-September.

Directions: From Tillamook on U.S. 101, turn east on Highway 6 and drive 17.9 miles to Jordan Creek Road. Turn right and drive 2.2 miles to the campground on the right.

Contact: Tillamook State Forest, Tillamook District, 503/842-2545, www.oregon.gov.

15 GALES CREEK

Scenic rating: 7
on Gales Creek in Tillamook State Forest

Map 1.1, page 75

Gales Creek runs through this heavily forested camp. The Gales Creek Trailhead is accessible from camp, providing access to hiking and mountain biking opportunities. A day-use picnic area is also available.

Campsites, facilities: There are 17 sites for tents or RVs up to 35 feet long and four walk-in tent sites. Picnic tables and fire grills are provided. Garbage bins, vault toilets, and drinking water are available. A camp host is on-site. Some facilities are wheelchair accessible. Leashed pets are permitted.

Reservations, fees: Reservations are not accepted. RV sites are $15 per night, walk-in tent sites are $10 per night, and an additional vehicle is $5 per night. Open mid-May-October.

Directions: From Portland, turn west on U.S.

26 and drive 24 miles to Highway 6. Turn west on Highway 6 and drive 17 miles to the campground entrance road (Rogers Road) on the right at Milepost 35. Turn right on Rogers Road and drive one mile to the campground.

Contact: Tillamook State Forest, Forest Grove District, 503/357-2191, www.oregon.gov.

16 BROWNS CAMP OHV

Scenic rating: 6
in Tillamook State Forest

Map 1.1, page 75

This camp is located next to the Devil's Lake Fork of the Wilson River and has sites with and without tree cover. Surrounded by miles of OHV trails, it caters to off-highway vehicle campers. Don't expect peace and quiet. No fishing is allowed here.

Campsites, facilities: There are 30 sites for tents or RVs up to 45 feet long. Picnic tables and fire grills are provided. Drinking water, garbage bins, and vault toilets are available. Some facilities are wheelchair accessible. Leashed pets are permitted.

Reservations, fees: Reservations are not accepted. Sites are $15 per night, $5 per night per additional vehicle. Open April-October.

Directions: From Portland, turn west on U.S. 26 and drive 24 miles to Highway 6. Turn west on Highway 6 and drive 19 miles to Beaver Dam Road. Turn left (south) and drive 2.5 miles to Scoggins Road. Turn left (southeast) and drive 0.5 mile to the campground.

Contact: Tillamook State Forest, Forest Grove District, 503/357-2191, www.oregon.gov.

17 TRASK RIVER PARK

Scenic rating: 7
on the Trask River

Map 1.1, page 75

This is a popular campground and park that

gets moderate use primarily from the locals in Tillamook County. Some campsites are shaded. Fishing for trout and steelhead is available in season; check current fishing regulations.

Campsites, facilities: There are 112 sites for tents or RVs of any length (no hookups), two group camps for up to 48 people, and a hiker/biker area. Picnic tables and fire pits are provided. Drinking water, vault toilets, garbage service, and a day-use area are available. A camp host is on-site. Some facilities are wheelchair accessible. Leashed pets are permitted.

Reservations, fees: Reservations are accepted ($10 reservation fee) at 503/842-4559 or www. co.tillamook.or.us. Sites are $19-29 per night, group sites are $90 per night, $5 per night per additional vehicle, $7 per night per additional tent, $8 per person per night for hiker/biker sites, and $5 pet fee. Some credit cards are accepted. Open year-round.

Directions: From Tillamook and U.S. 101, turn east on 3rd Street. Drive 2.5 miles to Trask River Road. Turn right and drive 1.5 miles, turning left to stay on Trask River Road. Continue 10 miles to the park.

Contact: Trask River Park, Tillamook County, 503/842-4559, www.co.tillamook.or.us/gov/parks.

18 NETARTS BAY GARDEN RV PARK RESORT

Scenic rating: 8

on Netarts Bay in Tillamook

Map 1.1, page 75

This camp is one of three on the east shore of Netarts Bay. A golf course is eight miles away. Sunsets and wildlife-viewing are notable here. Some sites are filled with rentals for the summer season.

Campsites, facilities: There are 83 sites with full hookups for RVs of any length; some are pull-through sites. Picnic tables are provided, and fire rings are available at some sites. Drinking water, restrooms with flush toilets and showers, propane gas, Wi-Fi, convenience store, in-park office, a meeting room, coin laundry, playground, horseshoe pits, fish-cleaning station, crab-cooking facilities, crab bait, and ice are available. Boat docks, launching facilities, and rentals are available on-site. A store and a café are within one mile. Leashed pets are permitted, with a two-pet maximum.

Reservations, fees: Reservations are recommended. Sites are $32-43 per night, $6 per night per extra person, $6 per night per additional vehicle. Winter, weekly, and monthly rates are available. Some credit cards are accepted. Open year-round.

Directions: From Tillamook and Netarts Highway/Highway 131, drive west on Netarts Highway for six miles to the campground entrance.

Contact: Netarts Bay Garden RV Resort, 2260 Bilyeu Ave., 503/842-7774, www.netartsbay.com.

19 PLEASANT VALLEY RV PARK

Scenic rating: 8

on the Tillamook River

Map 1.1, page 75

Pleasant Valley RV Park sits along the Tillamook River. The park is very clean and provides easy access to many recreation options in the immediate area.

Campsites, facilities: There are 76 pull-through sites with full or partial hookups for RVs of any length, plus two cabins. Picnic tables and fire rings are provided. Drinking water, restrooms with flush toilets and showers, propane gas, dump station, firewood, a meeting room, cable TV, Wi-Fi, convenience store, coin laundry, ice, and a playground are available. Boat-launching facilities are nearby. Leashed pets are permitted.

Reservations, fees: Reservations are accepted. Sites are $29-34 per night, $2 per person per night for more than two people; cabins are $25-29 per night. Some credit cards are accepted. Open year-round.

Directions: From Tillamook and U.S. 101, drive south on U.S. 101 for seven miles to the campground entrance on the right (west).

Contact: Pleasant Valley RV Park, 503/842-4779, www.pleasantvalleyrvpark.com.

20 CAPE LOOKOUT STATE PARK

Scenic rating: 8

near Netarts Bay

Map 1.1, page 75   **BEST (**

This park is set on a sand spit between Netarts Bay and the Pacific. There are more than eight miles of wooded trails, including the Cape Lookout Trail, which follows the headland for more than two miles. Another walk will take you out through a variety of estuarine habitats along the five-mile sand spit that extends between the ocean and Netarts Bay. With many species to view, this area is a paradise for birdwatchers. You might also catch the local hang gliders and paragliders that frequent the park. Fishing is another option here.

Campsites, facilities: There are 170 sites for tents or RVs (no hookups), 38 sites with full hookups for RVs up to 60 feet long, a tent camping area for hikers and bicyclists, two group tent sites for up to 25 people each, three cabins, and 13 yurts. Picnic tables and fire grills are provided. Restrooms with flush toilets and showers, dump station, garbage bins, meeting hall and picnic shelter, summer interpretive programs, and firewood are available. Some facilities are wheelchair accessible. Leashed pets are permitted.

Reservations, fees: Reservations are accepted at 800/452-5687 or www.oregonstateparks.org ($8 reservation fee). RV sites are $29-31 per night, tent sites are $21 per night, hikers/bikers sites are $6 per person per night, group sites are

$78 per night, cabins are $88 per night s, and yurts are $45 per night, $7 per night per additional vehicle. Some credit cards are accepted. Open year-round.

Directions: From Tillamook and U.S. 101, turn east on 3rd Street (becomes Netarts Highway). Drive approximately five miles to Whiskey Creek Road. Turn left and drive approximately seven miles to the park on the right.

Contact: Cape Lookout State Park, 503/842-4981, www.oregonstateparks.org.

21 WHALEN ISLAND PARK

Scenic rating: 6

in the Sandlake Estuary

Map 1.1, page 75

This park is located in the Sandlake Estuary and is close to the beach and Nestucca Bay. The campground is fairly open and has a few trees.

Campsites, facilities: There are 34 sites for tents or RVs of any length (no hookups) and 11 hiker/biker sites. Picnic tables and fire pits are provided. Drinking water, flush and chemical toilets, dump station, a day-use area, and a boat launch are available. A camp host is on-site during the summer. Some facilities are wheelchair accessible. Leashed pets are permitted.

Reservations, fees: Reservations are accepted ($11 reservation fee). Sites are $16-27 per night, $6 per night per additional vehicle, $8 per night per additional tent, $9 per person per night for hiker/biker sites, and a $6 pet fee. Open year-round.

Directions: From Tillamook and U.S. 101, drive south for 11 miles to Sand Lake Road. Turn right (west) and drive approximately 55 miles to a stop sign. Turn left to stay on Sand Lake Road. Continue 4.75 miles south to the park entrance road on the right.

Contact: Whalen Island Park, Tillamook County, 503/965-6085, www.co.tillamook.or.us/gov/parks.

22 SANDBEACH, EAST DUNES, AND WEST WINDS OHV

Scenic rating: 5

in Siuslaw National Forest

Map 1.1, page 75

Sandbeach campground is set along the shore of Sand Lake, which is actually more like an estuary than a lake since the ocean is just around the bend. This area is known for its beaches with large sand dunes, which are popular with off-road-vehicle enthusiasts. It's noisy and can be windy. East Dunes and West Winds, which used to be the overflow parking area, are nearby. This is the only coastal U.S. Forest Service camping area for many miles, and it's quite popular. If you're planning a trip for midsummer, be sure to reserve far in advance. Holiday permits are required ($10 at the district office) for three-day holiday weekends.

Campsites, facilities: There are 82 sites for tents or RVs up to 30 feet long. Picnic tables and fire pits are provided. Drinking water, garbage bins, and flush toilets are available. A camp host is on-site at each campground. Leashed pets are permitted.

Reservations, fees: Reservations are accepted for Sandbeach and East Dunes during the summer season at 877/444-6777 ($10 reservation fee) or www.recreation.gov ($9 reservation fee). Sites at Sandbeach and East Dunes are $25 per night. Sites at West Winds (first-come, first-served) are $25 per night. Additional vehicles cost $8 per night at all campgrounds. Open year-round.

Directions: From Tillamook on U.S. 101, drive south for 11 miles to County Road 8. Turn right (west) on County Road 8 and drive approximately 12 miles to the campground.

Contact: Siuslaw National Forest, Hebo Ranger District, 503/392-5100, www.fs.usda.gov/siuslaw.

23 CAMPER COVE RV PARK & CAMPGROUND

Scenic rating: 6

near Cloverdale

Map 1.1, page 75

This small, wooded campground along Beaver Creek is set just far enough off the highway to provide quiet. The park can be used as a base camp for anglers, with seasonal steelhead and salmon fishing in the nearby Nestucca River. It gets crowded here, especially in the summer, so be sure to make a reservation if possible. Ocean beaches are four miles away.

Campsites, facilities: There are 25 sites for RVs up to 45 feet; 11 sites have full hookups, while 14 sites have partial hookups (30 amp). There are also 25 walk-in tent sites and one cabin. Picnic tables and fire pits are provided. Drinking water, restrooms with flush toilets and coin showers, dump station, firewood, recreation hall, coin laundry, and ice are available. Some facilities are wheelchair accessible. Leashed pets are permitted.

Reservations, fees: Reservations are accepted. RV sites are $34 per night, tent sites are $23 per night, $6 per person per night for more than two people, $6 per night per additional vehicle. The cabin is $45 per night. Weekly and monthly rates are available. Open year-round.

Directions: From Tillamook and U.S. 101, drive south on U.S. 101 for 12 miles to the park entrance on the right (west), three miles north of Beaver.

Contact: Camper Cove RV Park & Campground, 19620 Hwy. 101 S., 503/664-4364, www.campercovervpark.cm.

24 ROCKY BEND GROUP

Scenic rating: 5

on the Nestucca River in Siuslaw National Forest

Map 1.1, page 75

At time of publication, Rocky Bend was under renovation with plans to turn the campground into a group site. Contact the ranger station for further updates.

This campground along the Nestucca River is a little-known, secluded spot that provides guaranteed peace and quiet. There isn't much in the way of recreational activities, but clamming, fishing, hiking, and swimming are available along the coast, a relatively short drive away.

Campsites, facilities: There are six tent sites. Picnic tables and fire pits are provided. Vault toilets are available. There is no drinking water and garbage must be packed out. Leashed pets are permitted.

Reservations, fees: Reservations are not accepted. There is no fee for camping, however the campground may enter the reservation system on a fee basis in the future. Open year-round.

Directions: On U.S. 101 southwest of Portland, drive to the tiny town of Beaver and Blaine Road. Turn east on Blaine Road (keep right; Blaine Road turns into Nestucca River Access Road) and drive 15.5 miles to the campground on the right.

Contact: Siuslaw National Forest, Hebo Ranger District, 503/392-5100, www.fs.usda.gov/siuslaw.

25 DOVRE, FAN CREEK, ALDER GLEN, AND ELK BEND

Scenic rating: 5

on the Nestucca River

Map 1.1, page 75

This is a series of four BLM campgrounds set along the Nestucca River. The camps, separated by alder trees and shrubs, are near the river, and some have river views. Tourists don't know about these spots. The Nestucca is a gentle river, with the water not deep enough for swimming.

Campsites, facilities: Dovre has 10 sites, Fan Creek has 11 sites, and Alder Glen has 11 sites; all sites are for tents or small RVs. Elk Bend has five walk-in sites. Picnic tables and fire grills are provided. Drinking water and vault toilets are available. Garbage must be packed out. Some facilities, including a fishing pier at Alder Glen, are wheelchair accessible. Leashed pets are permitted.

Reservations, fees: Reservations are not accepted. Sites at Dovre, Fan Creek, and Alder Glen are $10 per night, $5 per night per additional vehicle with a limit of two vehicles per site. There is no fee to camp at Elk Bend. Dovre, Fan Creek, and Alder Glen are open late May-early September; Elk Bend is open year-round.

Directions: On U.S. 101 southwest of Portland, drive to the tiny town of Beaver and Blaine Road. Turn east on Blaine Road (keep right; Blaine Road turns into Nestucca River Access Road) and drive 17.5 miles to Alder Glen. Continue east for seven more miles to reach Fan Creek and nine more miles to reach Dovre.

Contact: Bureau of Land Management, Salem District, 503/815-1134 or 503/375-5646, www.blm.gov.

26 WOODS COUNTY PARK

Scenic rating: 6

on the Kilchis River

Map 1.1, page 75

This small Tillamook County park is not well known outside the local area and gets fairly light use. The campground is grassy with few trees. Salmon fishing is a possibility; check current regulations.

Campsites, facilities: There are seven tent sites and five sites for RVs up to 45 feet long. Picnic tables and fire pits are provided. Drinking water, flush toilets, garbage containers, and a day-use area are available. A camp host is on-site. Leashed pets are permitted.

Reservations, fees: Reservations are accepted ($10 reservation fee) at 503/965-5001 or www.co.tillamook.or.us. Sites are $19-39 per night, $5 per night per additional vehicle, $7 per night per additional tent, and a $5 pet fee. Open May-October, weather permitting.

Directions: From Tillamook and U.S. 101, drive approximately 25 miles south to Resort Drive. Turn right (west) and drive three miles (road changes to Brooten Drive) to the park on the right.

Contact: Woods County Park, Tillamook County, 503/965-5001, www.co.tillamook.or.us/gov/parks.

27 CAPE KIWANDA RV RESORT

Scenic rating: 8

near Cape Kiwanda State Park

Map 1.1, page 75

This park is set a short distance from Cape Kiwanda State Park, which is open for day use only. Highlights at the park include a boat launch and hiking trails that lead out to the cape. Four miles south at Nestucca Spit, there is another day-use park, providing additional recreational options. The point extends about three miles and is a good spot for bird-watching. The campsites do not have ocean views, but the ocean is across the road and within walking distance. Surfing is an option.

Campsites, facilities: There are 116 sites with full or partial hookups for RVs up to 65 feet long, 10 tent sites, and 14 camping cabins, 8 cottages, and 3 camping cottages. Some sites are pull-through. Picnic tables and fire rings are provided. Drinking water, restrooms with flush toilets and showers, dump station, Wi-Fi, a heated swimming pool (year-round), hot tub, an exercise room, firewood, a recreation hall, coin laundry, propane, a seafood market, deli, gift shop, ATM, sandboard rentals, and a playground are available. Gasoline, a store, and a café are within one mile. Boat docks, launching facilities, and kayak rentals are nearby. Some facilities are wheelchair accessible. Leashed pets are permitted.

Reservations, fees: Reservations are recommended. RV sites are $32.95-54.95 per night, tent sites are $22.95-36.95 per night, $4 per person per night for more than two people, and $4 per night per additional vehicle. Weekly and monthly rates are available. Fall and winter discounts are available. Some credit cards are accepted. Open year-round.

Directions: From Tillamook and U.S. 101, drive south on U.S. 101 for 25 miles to the Pacific City exit and Brooten Road. Turn right on Brooten Road and drive three miles toward Pacific City and Three Capes Drive. Turn left, cross the bridge, and bear right on Three Capes Drive. Continue one mile north to the park on the right.

Contact: Cape Kiwanda RV Resort, 503/965-6230, www.capekiwandarvresort.com.

28 WEBB PARK

Scenic rating: 7

near Cape Kiwanda

Map 1.1, page 75

This public campground provides an excellent

alternative to the more crowded commercial RV parks off U.S. 101. Although not as developed, it offers a quiet, private setting and access to the ocean. Fishing and swimming are among your options here. The camp is adjacent to Cape Kiwanda and provides convenient access to the beach.

Campsites, facilities: There are 30 sites for tents or RVs (no hookups), eight sites with partial hookups for RVs up to 40 feet long, and seven hiker/biker sites. Picnic tables and fire pits are provided. Drinking water, a dump station, fish-cleaning station, and restrooms with flush toilets and showers are available. Beach launching is nearby. Some facilities are wheelchair accessible. Leashed pets are permitted.

Reservations, fees: Reservations are accepted ($10 reservation fee) at 503/965-5001 or www.co.tillamook.or.us. Sites are $24-39 per night, $5 per night per additional vehicle, $7 per night per additional tent, $8 per person per night for hiker/biker sites, and a $5 pet fee. Some credit cards are accepted. Open year-round.

Directions: From Tillamook and U.S. 101, drive south on U.S. 101 for 25 miles to the Pacific City exit and Highway 30. From Pacific City, turn right (north) and drive to the four-way stop at McPhillips Drive. Turn left on McPhillips Drive and drive 0.5 mile to Cape Kiwanda and the park on the right.

Contact: Webb Park, Tillamook County Parks, 503/965-5001, www.co.tillamook.or.us/gov/parks.

29 HEBO LAKE

Scenic rating: 7

on Hebo Lake in Siuslaw National Forest

Map 1.1, page 75

This U.S. Forest Service campground along the shore of Hebo Lake is a secluded spot with sites nestled under trees. The trailhead for the eight-mile-long Pioneer-Indian Trail is located in the campground. The trail around the lake is wheelchair accessible.

Campsites, facilities: There are six sites for trailers or RVs up to 18 feet long and six tent sites. Picnic tables and fire pits are provided. Drinking water, garbage bins, and vault toilets are available. Boats with electric motors are allowed on the lake, but gas motors are not. Some facilities are wheelchair accessible. Leashed pets are permitted.

Reservations, fees: Reservations are accepted at 877/444-6777 ($10 reservation fee) or www.recreation.gov ($9 reservation fee). Sites are $18 per night, $5 per night per additional vehicle. Open from mid-April to mid-November, weather permitting.

Directions: On U.S. 101 southwest of Portland, drive to the town of Hebo and Highway 22. Turn east on Highway 22 and drive 0.25 mile to Forest Road 14. Turn left (east) and drive five miles to the campground on the right.

Contact: Siuslaw National Forest, Hebo Ranger District, 503/392-5100, www.fs.usda.gov/siuslaw.

30 CASTLE ROCK GROUP

Scenic rating: 4

on Three Rivers in Siuslaw National Forest

Map 1.1, page 75

This tiny spot along Three Rivers provides group tent campers with an inland alternative to the large beachfront RV parks popular on the Oregon coast. Fishing can be good here. The gated camp is located along the edge of Highway 22 in an open meadow.

Campsites, facilities: There is one group site for up to 50 people. Picnic tables, fire pits, garbage bins, and a vault toilet are provided. There is no drinking water. Leashed pets are permitted.

Reservations, fees: Reservations are accepted at 877/444-6777 ($10 reservation fee) or www.recreation.gov ($9 reservation fee). The site is $75 per night. A gate code is required for access. Open year-round, weather permitting.

Directions: On U.S. 101 southwest of Portland,

drive to the town of Hebo and Highway 22. Turn east on Highway 22 and drive five miles to the campground on the right.

Contact: Siuslaw National Forest, Hebo Ranger District, 503/392-5100, www.fs.usda. gov/siuslaw.

31 WANDERING SPIRIT RV PARK

Scenic rating: 6

on Rock Creek

Map 1.1, page 75

The major draw here is the nearby casino, but there is the added benefit of shaded sites next to Rock Creek, which provides fishing and swimming options. The Yamhill River is 0.5 mile away. Fishing is good for steelhead and salmon in season. Golf courses and wineries are available within 10 miles. There is a combination of monthly rentals and overnighters at this park.

Campsites, facilities: There are 129 sites with full hookups (30 and 50 amps) for RVs up to 45 feet long, 11 tent sites, and eight park-model cabins. Some sites are pull-through. Group camping available. Drinking water, cable TV, Wi-Fi, restrooms with showers, dump station, coin laundry, RV storage, RV supplies, and a convenience store are available. Propane, a clubhouse, basketball hoop, an exercise room, and a game room are also available on-site. A 24-hour free bus shuttles campers to and from the Spirit Mountain Casino, restaurants, and shops less than two miles away. Some facilities are wheelchair accessible. Leashed pets are permitted.

Reservations, fees: Reservations are accepted at 800/390-6980. RV sites are $50 per night, tent sites are $18 per night, $4 per person per night for more than two people. Weekly and monthly rates are available. Some credit cards are accepted. Open year-round.

Directions: From Salem, drive west on Highway 22 about 25 miles to Highway 18.

Turn west on Highway 18 and drive seven miles to the park on the left.

Contact: Wandering Spirit RV Park, 503/879-5700, www.wanderingspiritrvpark.com.

32 DEVIL'S LAKE STATE PARK

Scenic rating: 7

on Devil's Lake

Map 1.2, page 76

Oregon's only coastal camp in the midst of a city, Devil's Lake is the center of summertime activity. A take-your-pick deal: You can boat, canoe, fish, kayak, or water-ski. A walking path extends from the campground to the boat launch 0.25 mile away. For something different, head west and explore the seven miles of beaches. Lincoln City also has a number of arts and crafts galleries and a weekend farmers market during the summer. East Devil's Lake is two miles east and offers a boat ramp and picnic facilities.

Campsites, facilities: There are 54 sites for tents or small RVs (no hookups), 33 sites for tents or RVs up to 55 feet long (full hookups), 10 yurts, and a separate area for hikers and bikers. Picnic tables and fire grills are provided. Drinking water, cable TV, garbage bins, restrooms with flush toilets and showers, an amphitheater, and firewood are available. Boat docks and launching facilities are nearby. Some facilities are wheelchair accessible. Leashed pets are permitted.

Reservations, fees: Reservations are accepted at 800/452-5687 or www.oregonstateparks.org ($8 reservation fee). Sites are $21-31 per night, $7 per night per additional vehicle, $6 per person per night for hikers/bikers, and yurts are $45 per night. Boat mooring is $10 per night. Some credit cards are accepted. Open year-round.

Directions: From Lincoln City and U.S. 101, take the 6th Street exit. Drive east on 6th Street for one block to the park on the right.

Contact: Devil's Lake State Park, 541/994-2002 or 800/551-6949, www.oregonstateparks.org.

33 KOA LINCOLN CITY

Scenic rating: 7

on Devil's Lake

Map 1.2, page 76

This area offers opportunities for beachcombing, fishing, and tidepool-viewing along a seven-mile stretch of beach. Nearby recreation options include a casino, factory outlets, a golf course, skateboard park, and tennis courts.

Campsites, facilities: There are 15 tent sites and 81 sites with full or partial hookups for RVs up to 60 feet long, including some pull-through sites, and 30- and 50-amp service is available. There are also 14 cabins. Picnic tables and some fire pits are provided. Drinking water, cable TV, Wi-Fi, restrooms with flush toilets and showers, dump station, convenience store, snack bar, gift shop, propane gas, ice, RV supplies, video and DVD rentals, coin laundry, firewood, and a playground are available. Some facilities are wheelchair accessible. Leashed pets are permitted, with certain restrictions.

Reservations, fees: Reservations are accepted at 800/562-3316. RV sites are $23-40 per night, tent sites are $21-30 per night, $4-5 per person per night for more than two people, $5 per night per additional vehicle. Some credit cards are accepted. Open year-round.

Directions: From Portland, drive south on Highway 99 West to Highway 18. Turn west on Highway 18 and drive 47 miles to U.S. 101. Turn south on U.S. 101 and drive 1.5 miles to East Devil's Lake Road. Turn east on East Devil's Lake Road and drive one mile to the park on the left.

Contact: KOA Lincoln City, 541/994-2961, www.koa.com.

34 SEA AND SAND RV PARK

Scenic rating: 9

near Siletz Bay

Map 1.2, page 76

Beachcombing for fossils and agates is popular at this oceanfront park near Gleneden Beach on Siletz Bay. Some sites have ocean views and pleasant terraces. The Siletz River and numerous small creeks are in the area. The park is located 3.5 miles north of Depoe Bay.

Campsites, facilities: There are 114 sites with full hookups for RVs up to 40 feet long. Picnic tables are provided and some sites have fire rings. Drinking water, restrooms with flush toilets and showers, cable TV, dump station, firewood, and a coin laundry are available. A store, café, and ice are within one mile. Leashed pets are permitted with breed restrictions.

Reservations, fees: Reservations are accepted. Sites are $39-79 per night, $5 per person per night for more than two people, and $10 per night per additional vehicle unless towed. Rates higher on weekends and holidays. Weekly discounts available. Open year-round.

Directions: From Lincoln City and U.S. 101, drive south for nine miles on U.S. 101 to the park entrance (on the beach side of the highway).

Contact: Sea and Sand RV Park, 541/764-2313 or 877/821-2231, www.seaandsandrvpark.com.

35 BEVERLY BEACH STATE PARK

Scenic rating: 7

near Newport

Map 1.2, page 76

This beautiful campground is set in a wooded, grassy area on the east side of U.S. 101. Treed campsites sit along Spencer Creek. A tunnel leads under the roadway to a beach that stretches from Yaguna Head to the Otter Rock headlands. A one-mile hiking trail is available.

Just a mile to the north lies a small day-use state park called Devil's Punchbowl, named for an unusual bowl-shaped rock formation with caverns under it where the waves rumble about. For some great ocean views, head north one more mile to the Otter Crest Wayside. The Oregon Coast Aquarium is within a few minutes' drive.

Campsites, facilities: There are 128 sites for tents or small RVs, 128 sites with full or partial hookups for tents or RVs up to 65 feet long, a special camping area for hikers and bicyclists, and three group sites for tents or RVs (no hookups) that can accommodate up to 25 people each. There is also a village of 21 yurts. Picnic tables and fire grills are provided. Drinking water, restrooms with flush toilets and showers, cable TV, a playground, a day-use area, garbage bins, and a dump station are available. Some facilities are wheelchair accessible. Leashed pets are permitted.

Reservations, fees: Reservations are accepted at 800/452-5687 or www.oregonstateparks.org ($8 reservation fee). Sites are $21-31 per night, $7 per night per additional vehicle, $6 per person per night for hikers/bikers, $45 per night for yurts, and $75-78 for group sites. Some credit cards are accepted. Open year-round.

Directions: From Newport and U.S. 101, drive north on U.S. 101 for seven miles to the park entrance on the east side.

Contact: Beverly Beach State Park, 541/265-9278 or 800/551-6949, www.oregonstateparks.org.

36 AGATE BEACH RV PARK

Scenic rating: 6

near Newport

Map 1.2, page 76

This park is located about 0.5 mile from Agate Beach Wayside, a small state park with beach access. Agate hunting can be good. Sometimes, a layer of sand covers the agates, and you have to dig a bit. But other times, wave action clears the sand, unveiling the agates at low tides. Beverly Beach State Park is 4.5 miles north. About half of the sites are filled with monthly rentals. There are no ocean views from the campsites.

Campsites, facilities: There are 32 sites with full or partial hookups for RVs up to 40 feet long. Picnic tables are provided. Drinking water, cable TV, a restroom with flush toilets and showers, a dump station, and a coin laundry room are available. A store and ice are within one mile. Leashed pets are permitted, with some restrictions.

Reservations, fees: Reservations are accepted. Sites are $25 per night, $20 per night per additional vehicle. Some credit cards are accepted. Open year-round.

Directions: From Newport and U.S. 101, drive to the north end of town. The park is on the east side of the road.

Contact: Agate Beach RV Park, 6138 N. Coast Highway, Newport, 541/265-7670.

37 HARBOR VILLAGE RV PARK

Scenic rating: 6

on Yaquina Bay

Map 1.2, page 76

This wooded and landscaped park is set near the shore of Yaquina Bay. Nearby recreation options include clamming, crabbing, deep-sea fishing, an 18-hole golf course, hiking trails, and a full-service marina.

Campsites, facilities: There are 40 sites with full hookups for RVs up to 35 feet long. Note that there are also 100 sites for full-time renters and a mobile-home park for ages 55 and up. Picnic tables are provided. Drinking water, cable TV, Wi-Fi, restrooms with flush toilets and showers, and a coin laundry are available. Propane gas, a store, and a café are within one mile. Boat docks, launching facilities, and rentals are nearby. Leashed pets are permitted.

Reservations, fees: Reservations are

accepted. Sites are $40 per night, $5 per person per night for more than two people. Weekly and monthly rates are available. Some credit cards are accepted. Open year-round.

Directions: In Newport, drive south on John Moore Road for 0.5 mile to the bay and Bay Boulevard. Bear left and drive a short distance to the park entrance on the left.

Contact: Harbor Village RV Park, 541/265-5088, www.harborvillagervpark.com.

38 PORT OF NEWPORT MARINA AND RV PARK

🚶 🚴 🏄 🎣 🐕 ♿ 🚐

Scenic rating: 7

on Yaquina Bay

Map 1.2, page 76

This public park is set along the shore of Yaquina Bay near Newport, a resort town that offers a variety of attractions. Among them are ocean fishing, a museum and aquarium at the nearby Hatfield Marine Science Center, the Undersea Garden, the Waxworks, Ripley's Believe It or Not, and the Lincoln County Historical Society Museum. Nearby recreation options include an 18-hole golf course, hiking trails, and a full-service marina.

Campsites, facilities: There are 143 sites with full hookups for RVs up to 45 feet long. Restrooms with flush toilets and showers, cable TV, Wi-Fi, modem access, dump station, convenience store, coin laundry, fish-cleaning station, and ice are available. A marina with boat docks and launching facilities is available onsite. Some facilities are wheelchair accessible. Leashed pets are permitted.

Reservations, fees: Reservations are accepted at 541/867-3321. Sites with hookups are $33-50 per night, sites without hookups are $22 per night, $3 per person per night for more than two people, $3 for each pet. Discounted rates Nov. 1-May 1. Weekly rates are available. Some credit cards are accepted. Open year-round.

Directions: From Newport and U.S. 101, drive south for 0.5 mile (over the bridge) to Marine Science Drive. Turn right (east) and drive 0.5 mile to the park entrance on the left.

Contact: Port of Newport Marina and RV Park, 541/867-3321, www.portofnewport.com.

39 SOUTH BEACH STATE PARK

🚶 🚴 🏄 🛶 🚣 🏊 🐕 ♿ 🚐 ⛺

Scenic rating: 7

near Newport

Map 1.2, page 76

This park along the beach offers opportunities for beachcombing, boating, crabbing, fishing, hiking, and windsurfing. The Oregon Coast Trail passes right through the park. A nature trail circles the campground, and there are hiking and bicycling trails to the beach. A primitive hike-in campground is also available. A naturalist provides campground talks during the summer season. Kayak trips are an option during the summer. The park is within walking distance of Oregon Aquarium. Newport attractions include the Hatfield Marine Science Center, the Undersea Garden, the Waxworks, Ripley's Believe It or Not, and the Lincoln County Historical Society Museum.

Campsites, facilities: There are 227 sites with partial hookups for tents or RVs up to 45 feet long, 60 primitive tent sites, a dispersed camping area (without designated sites) for hikers and bicyclists, and an overflow area for RVs. There are also three group sites for up to 25 people each and 27 yurts. Picnic tables and fire grills are provided. Drinking water, restrooms with flush toilets and showers, garbage bins, recycling, a dump station, Wi-Fi, horseshoe pits, playground, a day-use area, meeting hall, and firewood are available. A camp host is onsite. Some facilities are wheelchair accessible. Leashed pets are permitted.

Reservations, fees: Reservations are accepted at 800/452-5687 or www.oregonstateparks.org ($8 reservation fee). Sites are $21-29 per night, $7 per night per additional vehicle, $6 per person per night for hikers/bicyclists (3-night limit), $75-78 per night for group sites, and $45-55 per night for yurts. Some credit cards are accepted. Open year-round.

Directions: From Newport and U.S. 101, drive south for three miles to the park entrance on the right.

Contact: South Beach State Park, 541/867-4715 or 800/551-6949, www.oregonstateparks.org.

40 SEAL ROCKS RV COVE

Scenic rating: 8

near Seal Rock State Park

Map 1.2, page 76   BEST (

This RV park is situated on the rugged coastline near Seal Rock State Park (open for day use only), where you may find seals, sea lions, and a variety of birds. The ocean views are stunning, and some sites have views.

Campsites, facilities: There are 28 sites with full hookups (30 and 50 amps) for RVs of any length and 16 tent sites with 20-amp electricity. Some sites are pull-through. Picnic tables and fire rings are provided. Drinking water, firewood, restrooms with flush toilets and showers, Wi-Fi, and cable TV are available. Pets are permitted.

Reservations, fees: Reservations are accepted. RV sites are $31-55 per night, tent sites are $20-23 per night, $1-4 per person per night for more than two people, and there's a $5 one-time fee for an additional vehicle unless towed. Winter and weekly rates are available. Open year-round.

Directions: From Newport and U.S. 101, drive south for 10 miles to the town of Seal Rock. Continue south on U.S. 101 for 0.25 mile to the park entrance on the left.

Contact: Seal Rocks RV Cove, 541/563-3955, www.sealrocksrv.com.

41 DRIFT CREEK LANDING

Scenic rating: 6

on the Alsea River

Map 1.2, page 76

Drift Creek Landing is set along the shore of the Alsea River in a heavily treed and mountainous area. The Oregon Coast Aquarium is 15 miles away, and an 18-hole golf course is nearby. There are 10 mobile homes with long-term renters on this property, and more than one-third of the RV sites are taken by monthly renters.

Campsites, facilities: There are 50 sites with full hookups for RVs of any length, six sites for tents, and three cabins. Drinking water and picnic tables are provided. Restroom with flush toilets and showers, cable TV, propane gas, recreation hall, convenience store, snack bar, coin laundry, boat docks, boat rentals, moorage, and launching facilities are available. Leashed pets are permitted.

Reservations, fees: Reservations are accepted. RV sites are $28-32 per night, and tent sites are $15-17 per night; it's $2 per person per night for more than two people and $5 per night per additional vehicle. Weekly, monthly, and group discounts. Some credit cards are accepted. Open year-round.

Directions: From Newport and U.S. 101, drive south for 14 miles to Waldport and Highway 34. Turn east on Highway 34 and drive 3.8 miles to the campground.

Contact: Drift Creek Landing, 541/563-3610, www.driftcreeklandingrv.com.

42 ALSEA RIVER RV PARK & MARINA

Scenic rating: 6

on the Alsea River

Map 1.2, page 76

This campground is one of several along the shore of the Alsea River. Kayaking and canoeing are popular, as is watching the elk herd across the river. Some of the sites here are filled with monthly rentals.

Campsites, facilities: There are 23 sites with full or partial hookups for RVs to 45 feet, five sites for tents, and one cabin. Picnic tables are provided and fire pits are available on request. Drinking water, restrooms with flush toilets and showers, coin laundry, recreation room, bait and tackle, boat docks, boat rentals, and launching facilities are available. Some facilities are wheelchair accessible. Leashed pets are permitted.

Reservations, fees: Reservations are accepted at 877/770-6137. RV sites are $30-32 per night, tent sites are $20 per night, $5 per person per night for more than two people, and $5 per night per additional vehicle. Some credit cards are accepted. Open year-round.

Directions: From Newport and U.S. 101, drive south for 14 miles to Waldport and Highway 34. Turn east on Highway 34 and drive four miles to the entrance on the left.

Contact: Alsea River RV Park & Marina, 541/563-3401, www.alseariverrvpark.com.

43 ROVER'S RV PARK

Scenic rating: 7

on the Alsea River

Map 1.2, page 76

This park is set along the shore of the Alsea River, about 3.5 miles from the ocean. The park is filled primarily with monthly rentals, although several RV sites are reserved for short-term campers. Campsites are rented on a space-available basis.

Campsites, facilities: There are 34 sites with full or partial hookups for RVs up to 40 feet long. Picnic tables are provided. Drinking water, cable TV, Wi-Fi, restrooms with flush toilets and showers, a picnic area, ice, off-leash dog run, and a coin laundry are available. A store is within 1.5 miles. Boat docks are nearby. Propane gas and boat launching facilities are

available 3.5 miles away. Leashed pets are permitted.

Reservations, fees: Reservations are accepted. RV sites are $30-40 per night, $5 per person per night for more than two people, $5 per night per additional vehicle. Weekly and monthly rates available. Open year-round.

Directions: From Newport and U.S. 101, drive south for 14 miles to Waldport and Highway 34. Turn east on Highway 34 and drive 3.3 miles to the park entrance on the left.

Contact: Rover's RV Park, 541/563-3485, www.roversrvpark.com.

44 TAYLOR'S LANDING RV PARK

Scenic rating: 9

on the Alsea River

Map 1.2, page 76

This wooded campground is set along the scenic Alsea River. Fall, when the salmon fishing is best, is the prime time here, and the park often fills up. Recreation options include hiking trails, marked bike trails, the Oregon Coast Aquarium, the Sea Lion Caves, and a marina.

Campsites, facilities: There are 81 sites for tents or RVs of any length (full hookups). Picnic tables are provided. Drinking water, cable TV, Wi-Fi, and restrooms with flush toilets and showers, propane gas, a café, coin laundry, community fire ring, and boat docks and rentals are available. Boat launching facilities are nearby. Leashed pets are permitted.

Reservations, fees: Reservations are accepted. Sites are $27 per night, $1 per person per night for more than two people. Weekly and monthly rates are available. Open year-round.

Directions: From Newport and U.S. 101, drive south for 14 miles to Waldport and Highway 34. Turn east on Highway 34 and drive seven miles to the entrance on the right.

Contact: Taylor's Landing RV Park, 541/528-3388, www.taylorslandingrvparkmarina.com.

45 WALDPORT/ NEWPORT KOA

Scenic rating: 8

on Alsea Bay

Map 1.2, page 76   BEST (

This pretty park, set amid some of the oldest pine trees in Oregon, is located within walking distance of the beach, the bay, and downtown Waldport—and to top it off, some of the campsites have beautiful ocean views. Alsea Bay's sandy and rocky shoreline makes this area a favorite with anglers. The crabbing and clamming can also be quite good. Kite flying is popular. South Beach State Park, about five miles north on U.S. 101, offers more fishing and a boat ramp along Beaver Creek. It's open for day use only. Other nearby recreation options include hiking trails, marked bike trails, the Oregon Coast Aquarium, the Sea Lion Caves, and a marina.

Campsites, facilities: There are 10 tent sites and 66 sites for RVs up to 60 feet long (full hookups), and 20 cabins. Picnic tables and fire pits are provided. Drinking water, cable TV, restrooms with flush toilets and showers, Wi-Fi, recreation room, propane gas, dump station, store, café, coin laundry, playground, bicycle rentals, and ice are available. Boat docks, launching facilities, and boat rentals are nearby. A café is within one mile. Some facilities are wheelchair accessible. Leashed pets are permitted, with certain restrictions.

Reservations, fees: Reservations are accepted at 800/562-3443. RV sites are $42.50-48.50 per night, tent sites are $25.50-31.50 per night, $7 per person per night for more than two people. Some credit cards are accepted. Open year-round.

Directions: From Newport and U.S. 101, drive south for approximately 14 miles to Milepost 155 at the north end of the Alsea Bay Bridge. The park is on the west side of the bridge.

Contact: Waldport/Newport KOA, 541/563-2250, www.koa.com.

46 BEACHSIDE STATE RECREATION SITE

Scenic rating: 7

near Alsea Bay

Map 1.2, page 76

This state park offers about nine miles of beach and is not far from Alsea Bay and the Alsea River. Sites are close to the beach. Nearby attractions include clamming, crabbing, and fishing, as well as hiking and driving tours, tidepools, an aquarium, three lighthouses, science centers, and visitors centers. South Beach State Park, about five miles north on U.S. 101, offers more fishing and a boat ramp along Beaver Creek (day use only).

Campsites, facilities: There are 24 sites for tents, 32 sites with partial hookups for RVs up to 40 feet long, two yurts, and a special camping area for hikers and bicyclists. Picnic tables and fire grills are provided. Drinking water, garbage bins, restrooms with flush toilets and showers, recycling, and firewood are available. A horseshoe pit is available nearby. Some facilities are wheelchair accessible. Leashed pets are permitted.

Reservations, fees: Reservations are accepted at 800/452-5687 or www.oregonstateparks.org ($8 reservation fee). Sites are $21-29 per night, $7 per night per additional vehicle, $6 per person per night for hikers/bicyclists, and yurts are $45-55 per night. Some credit cards are accepted. Open mid-March-October, weather permitting.

Directions: From Newport and U.S. 101, drive south for 16 miles to Waldport. Continue south on U.S. 101 for four miles to the park entrance on the west side of the road.

Contact: Beachside State Recreation Site, 541/563-3220, www.oregonstateparks.org.

47 TILLICUM BEACH

Scenic rating: 8

in Siuslaw National Forest

Map 1.2, page 76

Oceanview campsites are a big draw at this campground just south of Beachside State Park. Since it's just off the highway and along the water, this camp fills up very quickly in the summer, so expect crowds. Nearby forest roads provide access to streams in the mountains east of the beach area.

Campsites, facilities: There are 61 sites for tents or RVs up to 60 feet long; some sites have partial hookups. Picnic tables and fire grills are provided. Flush toilets, garbage bins, firewood, and drinking water are available. Leashed pets are permitted.

Reservations, fees: Reservations are required May-September at 877/444-6777 or www.recreation.gov ($9-10 reservation fee). Sites are $26-33 per night, $6 per night per additional vehicle. Open year-round, with reduced capacity in winter.

Directions: From Newport and U.S. 101, drive south for 14 miles to Waldport. Continue south on U.S. 101 for 4.5 miles to the campground entrance on the right.

Contact: Siuslaw National Forest, Central Coast Ranger District, 541/563-8400, www.fs.usda.gov/siuslaw.

48 CANAL CREEK

Scenic rating: 5

on Canal Creek in Siuslaw National Forest

Map 1.2, page 76

There's one key thing you must know: Vehicles must be able to cross a small creek to access this site. That accomplished, this pleasant little campground is just off the beaten path in a large, wooded, open area along Canal Creek. It feels remote because of the creek that runs through the campground and the historic homesites nearby, with old fruit trees on the grounds. Yet it has easy access and is close to the coast and all the amenities. The climate here is relatively mild, but, on the other hand, there is the rain in winter—lots of it.

Campsites, facilities: There are two group sites for tents or RVs up to 22 feet. A small group site holds up to 50 people; a larger site holds up to 100 people. Picnic tables and fire grills are provided. Vault toilets are available. There is no drinking water and garbage must be packed out. The group site has a picnic shelter and a play area. Leashed pets are permitted.

Reservations, fees: Reservations are required May-September at 877/444-6777 or www.recreation.gov ($9-10 reservation fee). Sites are $140-200 per night. Open mid-May-mid-September.

Directions: From Albany, drive west on U.S. 20 for 15 miles to Philomath and Highway 34. Turn south on Highway 34 and drive 52 miles to Forest Road 3462. Turn left (south) and drive four miles to the camp.

Contact: Siuslaw National Forest, Central Coast Ranger District, 541/563-3211 or 541/547-8400, www.fs.usda.gov/siuslaw.

49 BLACKBERRY

Scenic rating: 7

on the Alsea River in Siuslaw National Forest

Map 1.2, page 76

Blackberry makes a good base camp for a fishing trip on the Alsea River. The U.S. Forest Service provides boat launches and picnic areas at several spots along this stretch of river. Often, there is a camp host who can give you inside information on nearby recreational opportunities. Large fir trees and lawns separate the sites.

Campsites, facilities: There are 32 sites for tents or RVs of any length. Picnic tables and fire grills are provided. Drinking water, garbage bins, and flush toilets are available. There is no firewood. A boat ramp is on-site. Leashed pets are permitted.

Reservations, fees: Reservations are accepted May-September at 877/444-6777 or www.recreation.gov ($9-10 reservation fee). Sites are $24 per night, $7 per night per additional vehicle. Open year-round.

Directions: From Albany, drive west on U.S. 20 for 15 miles to Philomath and Highway 34. Turn south on Highway 34 and drive 41 miles to the campground entrance on the left.

Contact: Siuslaw National Forest, Central Coast Ranger District, 541/563-8400, www.fs.usda.gov/siuslaw.

50 ALSEA FALLS
🚶‍♂️🏊‍♂️🎣🐎⛰️♿🚐⛺

Scenic rating: 8
adjacent to the south fork of the Alsea River

Map 1.2, page 76   **BEST (**

Enjoy the beautiful surroundings of Alsea Falls by exploring the trails that wander through this park and lead to a picnic area by the falls. Trails to McBee Park and Green Peak Falls are accessible from the campground along the south fork of the river. The campsites are situated in a 40-year-old forest of Douglas fir and vine maple. On a warm day, Alsea Falls offers cool relief along the river. The area was named after its original inhabitants, the Alsea people.

Campsites, facilities: There are 16 sites for tents or RVs up to 32 feet long. Group camping is also available. Picnic tables and fire pits are provided. Drinking water, vault toilets, and garbage bins are available. A camp host is onsite. Some facilities are wheelchair accessible. Leashed pets are permitted.

Reservations, fees: Reservations are not accepted. Sites are $12 per night, the group site is $20 per night, $5 per night per additional vehicle. Open mid-May-early September.

Directions: From Albany, drive west on U.S. 20 for nine miles to Corvallis. Turn left (south) onto Highway 99 and drive 15 miles to County Road 45120. Turn right (west) and drive five

miles to Alpine Junction. Continue along the South Fork Alsea Access Road for nine miles to the campground on the right.

Contact: Bureau of Land Management, Salem District Office, 503/375-5646, www.blm.gov.

51 CAPE PERPETUA
🚶‍♂️🏊‍♂️🎣♿🚐⛺

Scenic rating: 8
on Cape Perpetua in Siuslaw National Forest

Map 1.2, page 76

This U.S. Forest Service campground is set along Cape Creek in the Cape Perpetua Scenic Area. The visitor information center provides hiking and driving maps to guide you through this spectacular region; maps highlight the tidepools and picnic spots. The coastal cliffs are perfect for whale-watching December-March. Neptune State Park is just south and offers additional rugged coastline vistas.

Campsites, facilities: There are 38 sites for tents or RVs up to 45 feet long, plus one group site that can accommodate up to 50 people and 102 vehicles. Picnic tables and fire grills are provided. Flush toilets, drinking water, dump station, firewood, and garbage bins are available. A camp host is on-site. Some facilities are wheelchair accessible. Leashed pets are permitted.

Reservations, fees: Reservations are accepted at 877/444-6777 or www.recreation.gov ($9-10 reservation fee). Sites are $26 per night, $7 per night per additional vehicle; group sites are $127.50 per night. Open May-September.

Directions: From Newport and U.S. 101, drive south for 23 miles to Yachats. Continue three miles south on U.S. 101 to the entrance on the left.

Contact: Siuslaw National Forest, Central Coast Ranger District, 541/563-8400, www.fs.usda.gov/siuslaw; Cape Perpetua Visitors Center, 541/547-3289.

52 SEA PERCH RV PARK

Scenic rating: 8

near Cape Perpetua

Map 1.2, page 76

Sea Perch sits right in the middle of one of the most scenic areas on the Oregon coast. This private park just south of Cape Perpetua has sites 75 feet from the beach and lawn areas, plus its own shell museum and gift shop. Surf fishing and windsurfing are options here, or head to Cape Perpetua for whale-watching and tidepooling. Big rigs are welcome here.

Campsites, facilities: There are 24 sites with full or partial (20, 30, and 50 amp) hookups for RVs of any length, and five ocean villas. Some sites are pull-through. Picnic tables are provided. Drinking water, restrooms with flush toilets and coin showers, dump station, firewood, coin laundry, ice, convenience store, Wi-Fi, picnic area, horseshoe pit, clubroom with recreation hall, exercise room, kitchen, TV, and a beach are available. Leashed pets are permitted.

Reservations, fees: Reservations are accepted. Sites are $70-90 per night, $5 per person per night for more than four, $10 per night for an additional vehicle; villa rates are $125-250 per night. Weekly and monthly rates are available. Some credit cards are accepted. Open year-round.

Directions: From Newport and U.S. 101, drive south for 23 miles to Yachats. Continue south on U.S. 101 for 6.5 miles to the campground at Milepost 171 on the right.

Contact: Sea Perch RV Park, 541/547-3505, www.seaperchrvpark.com.

53 ROCK CREEK

Scenic rating: 7

on Rock Creek in Siuslaw National Forest

Map 1.2, page 76

This little campground is set along Rock Creek just 0.25 mile from the ocean. It's a premium spot for coastal-highway travelers, although it can get packed very quickly. An excellent side trip is to Cape Perpetua, a designated scenic area a few miles up the coast. The cape offers beautiful ocean views and a visitors center that will supply you with information on nature trails, picnic spots, tidepools, and where to find the best viewpoints in the area.

Campsites, facilities: There are 15 sites for tents or RVs up to 22 feet long (limit 8 people per site). Fire grills and picnic tables are provided. Flush toilets, garbage bins, and drinking water are available. Leashed pets are permitted.

Reservations, fees: Reservations are accepted at 877/444-6777 or www.recreation.gov ($9-10 reservation fee). Sites are $26 per night, $7 per night per additional vehicle. Open mid-May-September.

Directions: From Newport and U.S. 101, drive south for 23 miles to Yachats. Continue south on U.S. 101 for 10 miles to the campground entrance on the left.

Contact: Siuslaw National Forest, Waldport Central Coast Ranger District, 541/563-3211 8400 or 541/547-3679 (concessionaire), www.fs.usda.gov/siuslaw.

54 CARL G. WASHBURNE STATE PARK

Scenic rating: 7

near Florence

Map 1.2, page 76

Even though busy Highway 101 lies right next to Washburne State Park, a bank of native plants shields campers from most road noise, so you hear the roar of the ocean instead of traffic. Sites are spacious, with some abutting China Creek, and elk are frequent visitors. Short hikes lead from the campground to a two-mile-long beach, extensive tidepools along the base of the cliffs, and a three-mile trail to Heceta Head Lighthouse. Just three miles south of the park are the Sea Lion Caves, where an elevator takes visitors down into a cavern for an insider's view of the life of a sea lion.

Campsites, facilities: There are 56 sites for tents or RVs up to 45 feet long (full and partial hookups), seven primitive walk-in sites, two yurts, and a hiker/biker camping area. Picnic tables, fire pits, drinking water, garbage bins, and a dump station are provided. Firewood and restrooms with flush toilets and showers are available. Leashed pets are permitted.

Reservations, fees: Reservations are not accepted, except for yurts. Sites are $21-31 per night, $5 per person per night for hikers/bicyclists, and yurts are $44-54 per night; $7 per night per additional vehicle. Some credit cards are accepted. Open year-round.

Directions: From Florence and U.S. 101, drive north for 12.5 miles to the park entrance road (it is well signed, 10 miles south of the town of Yachats). Turn east and drive a short distance to the park.

Contact: Carl G. Washburne State Park, 541/547-3416 or 800/551-6949, www.oregonstateparks.org.

55 ALDER DUNE

Scenic rating: 7
near Alder Lake in Siuslaw National Forest

Map 1.2, page 76

This wooded campground is situated near four lakes—Alder Lake, Dune Lake, Mercer Lake (the largest), and Sutton Lake. A boat launch is available at Sutton Lake. An excellent recreation option is to explore the expansive sand dunes in the area by foot (there is no off-road-vehicle access here). Side trips include the Sea Lion Caves, Darlington State Park, Jessie M. Honeyman Memorial State Park, and the Indian Forest, just four miles north.

Campsites, facilities: There are 38 sites for tents or self-contained RVs (no hookups) up to 62 feet long (limit 8 people per site). Picnic tables and fire grills are provided. Flush toilets,

garbage bins, and drinking water are available. Leashed pets are permitted.

Reservations, fees: Reservations are accepted May-September at 877/444-6777 or www.recreation.gov ($9-10 reservation fee). Sites are $24 per night, $7 per each additional vehicle. Open year-round, weather permitting.

Directions: From Florence and U.S. 101, drive north for eight miles to the campground on the left.

Contact: Siuslaw National Forest, Central Coast Ranger District, 541/271-6000, www.fs.usda.gov/siuslaw.

56 SUTTON

Scenic rating: 7
near Sutton Lake in Siuslaw National Forest

Map 1.2, page 76

This campground is located adjacent to Sutton Creek, not far from Sutton Lake. Vegetation provides some privacy between sites. Holman Vista on Sutton Beach Road offers a beautiful view of the dunes and ocean. Wading and fishing are both popular. A hiking trail system leads from the camp out to the dunes. There is no off-road-vehicle access here. An alternative camp is Alder Dune to the north.

Campsites, facilities: There are 66 sites for tents or RVs up to 30 feet; 20 sites have partial hookups. There are also three group sites; one group site accommodates up to 30 people and two group sites accommodate up to 100 people. Picnic tables and fire grills are provided. Flush toilets, garbage bins, and drinking water are available. A boat ramp is nearby. Leashed pets are permitted.

Reservations, fees: Reservations are accepted at 877/444-6777 or www.recreation.gov ($9-10 reservation fee). Sites are $24-29 per night and $95-200 per night for group sites. Open year-round.

Directions: From Eugene, drive west on Highway 126 for 61 miles to Florence and U.S. 101. Turn north on U.S. 101 and drive six miles to Sutton Beach Road (Forest Road 794). Turn left (northwest) and drive 1.5 miles to the campground entrance.

Contact: Siuslaw National Forest, Central Coast Ranger District, 541/271-6000, www.fs.usda.gov/siuslaw.

57 MAPLE LANE RV PARK AND MARINA
🚶 🎣 � 🐕 �︎ ⛺

Scenic rating: 5

on the Siuslaw River

Map 1.2, page 76

This park along the shore of the Siuslaw River in Mapleton is close to hiking trails. The general area is surrounded by Siuslaw National Forest land. A U.S. Forest Service map details nearby backcountry side-trip options. Fall is the most popular time of the year here, as it's prime time for salmon fishing on the Siuslaw. Most sites are taken by monthly renters.

Campsites, facilities: There are 45 sites with full (30 and 50 amp) hookups for RVs up to 40 feet long, 10 tent sites, and two park models. Some sites are pull-through. Drinking water, restrooms with flush toilets and showers, a coin laundry, cable TV, Wi-Fi, and propane gas are available. A bait and tackle shop is open during the fishing season. Boat docks, moorage, and launching facilities are on-site. A store, café, and ice are nearby. Small leashed pets (under 15 pounds) are permitted.

Reservations, fees: Reservations are accepted. RV sites are $30-35 per night, tent sites are $20-25 per night, $5 per night for more than two people, and $10 per night per additional vehicle. Weekly and monthly rates are available. Open year-round.

Directions: From Eugene, drive west on Highway 126 for 47 miles to Mapleton. Continue on Highway 126 for 0.25 mile past the business district to the park entrance on the left.

Contact: Maple Lane RV Park and Marina,

541/268-4822, www.maplelanervparkandmarina.com.

58 HARBOR VISTA COUNTY PARK
🚶 🎣 � 🐕 🚴 ♿ 🚗 ⛺

Scenic rating: 6

near Florence

Map 1.3, page 77

This county park out among the dunes near the entrance to the harbor offers a great lookout point from its observation deck. The park is perched above the North Jetty of the Siuslaw River and encompasses 15 acres. Beach access is one mile away. A number of side trips are available, including to the Sea Lion Caves, Darlington State Park, Jessie M. Honeyman Memorial State Park, and the Indian Forest, just four miles north. Florence also has displays of Native American dwellings and crafts.

Campsites, facilities: There are 38 sites with partial hookups for tents or RVs up to 60 feet long. Picnic tables, fire rings, and garbage bins are provided. Restrooms with flush toilets and coin showers, dump station, drinking water, and a playground are available. A camp host is on-site. Some facilities are wheelchair accessible. Leashed pets are permitted.

Reservations, fees: Reservations are accepted at 541/682-2000 or www.ecomm.lanecounty.org/parks ($10 reservation fee). Sites are $25-27.50 per night, $7 per night for additional vehicle. Some credit cards are accepted. Open year-round.

Directions: From Florence and U.S. 101, drive north for four miles to 35th Street. Turn left and drive one mile to where it dead-ends into Rhododendron Drive. Turn right and drive 1.4 miles to North Jetty Road. Turn left and drive half a block to Harbor Vista Road. Turn left and continue to the campground at 87658 Harbor Vista Road.

Note: Follow these exact directions. Previous visitors to this park taking a different route will discover that part of Harbor Vista Road is now gated.

Contact: Harbor Vista County Park, 541/902-2114, www.co.lane.or.us.

59 WAYSIDE RV PARK

Scenic rating: 5

near Florence

Map 1.3, page 77

Adjacent to this landscaped RV park is a 28-unit mobile home park for ages 55 and up. Some sites at the RV park are taken by monthly rentals. Nearby recreation options include two golf courses and a riding stable, two miles away.

Campsites, facilities: There are 25 sites with full hookups for RVs of any length. Picnic tables are provided. Restrooms with flush toilets and showers, recreation room, storage sheds, Wi-Fi, and a coin laundry are available. Propane gas, a store, ice, a café, and a restaurant are within two miles. Boat-launching facilities are nearby. Some facilities are wheelchair accessible. Small leashed pets are permitted.

Reservations, fees: Reservations are accepted. Sites are $39 per night, $2 per person per night for more than two people. Weekly and monthly rates are available. Open year-round.

Directions: From Florence and U.S. 101, drive north for 1.8 miles to the park on the right.

Contact: Wayside RV Park, 3760 Highway 101, Florence, 541/997-6451.

60 PORT OF SIUSLAW RV PARK AND MARINA

Scenic rating: 8

on the Siuslaw River

Map 1.3, page 77   **BEST (**

This public resort can be found along the Siuslaw River in a grassy, urban setting. Anglers with boats will find that the U.S. 101 bridge support pilings make good spots for crabbing, as well as fishing for perch and flounder. A new set of docks with drinking water, electricity, gasoline, security, and a fish-cleaning station are available. The Sea Lion Caves and estuary are a bonus for wildlife lovers, and nearby lakes make swimming and waterskiing a possibility. Golf is within driving distance, and horses can be rented about nine miles away.

Campsites, facilities: There are 13 tent sites and 92 sites with full or partial hookups for tents or RVs of any length, plus a hiker/biker camp area. Picnic tables are provided. Drinking water, restrooms with flush toilets and showers, cable TV, dump station, coin laundry, Wi-Fi, gazebo, fish-cleaning station, and boat docks are available. A camp host is on-site. A café, grocery store, and ice are within one mile. Some facilities are wheelchair accessible. Leashed pets are permitted.

Reservations, fees: Reservations are accepted at 541/997-3040 or www.portofsiuslaw.com ($10 reservation fee). Sites are $28-39 per night, hiker/biker sites are $9 per night, $5 per each additional person, $2 per night per additional vehicle. Weekly and monthly rates available. Some credit cards are accepted. Open year-round.

Directions: From Florence and U.S. 101, drive south to Nopal Street. Turn left (east) and drive two blocks to 1st Street. Turn left and drive 0.25 mile to the park at the end of the road.

Contact: Port of Siuslaw RV Park and Marina, 541/997-3040, www.portofsiuslaw.com.

61 JESSIE M. HONEYMAN MEMORIAL STATE PARK

Scenic rating: 7

near Cleowax Lake

Map 1.3, page 77

This popular state park is within walking distance of the shore of Cleowox Lake and adjacent to the dunes of the Oregon Dunes National Recreation Area. Dunes stretch for two miles between the park and the ocean. The dunes here are quite impressive, with some reaching to 500 feet. In the winter, the area is open to OHV use. For thrill-seekers, sandboard rentals (for sand-boarding on the dunes) are available in nearby Florence. The two lakes in the park offer facilities for boating, fishing, and swimming. A one-mile hiking trail with access to the dunes is available in the park, and off-road-vehicle trails are nearby in the sand dunes.

Campsites, facilities: There are 187 sites for tents or RVs (no hookups) up to 60 feet long, 168 sites with full or partial hookups for RVs, a camping area for hikers and bicyclists, six group tent areas for up to 25 people and 10 vehicles each, and 10 yurts. Picnic tables, garbage bins, and fire grills are provided. Drinking water, restrooms with flush toilets and showers, a dump station, seasonal interpretive programs, a playground, an amphitheater, and firewood are available. A meeting hall and picnic shelters can be reserved. Boat docks and launching facilities are nearby. Some facilities are wheelchair accessible. Leashed pets are permitted.

Reservations, fees: Reservations are accepted at 800/452-5687 or www.oregonstateparks.org ($8 reservation fee). Sites are $29-31 per night, $7 per night per additional vehicle, $5 per person per night for hikers/bicyclists, $44-54 per night for yurts, and $77 per night for group sites. Some credit cards are accepted. Open year-round.

Directions: From Florence and U.S. 101, drive south for three miles to the park entrance on the west side of the road.

Contact: Jessie M. Honeyman Memorial State Park, 541/997-3641 or 800/551-6949, www.oregonstateparks.org.

62 LAKESHORE RV PARK
🏊 🛶 🚤 🦌 🚐

Scenic rating: 5

on Woahink Lake

Map 1.3, page 77

Here's a prime area for vacationers. This park is set along the shore of Woahink Lake, a popular spot to fish for bass, bluegill, catfish, crappie, perch, and trout. It's adjacent to Jessie M. Honeyman Memorial State Park and the Oregon Dunes National Recreation Area. Off-road-vehicle access to the dunes is four miles northeast and three miles south of the park. Hiking trails through the dunes can be found at Honeyman Memorial State Park. Some sites are filled with monthly rentals.

Campsites, facilities: There are 20 sites with full 30-amp hookups for RVs of any length; some are pull-through sites. Picnic tables are provided. Drinking water, restrooms with flush toilets and showers, cable TV, recreation hall, Wi-Fi, storage sheds, boat docks, and a coin laundry are available. A café is within three miles. Leashed pets are permitted.

Reservations, fees: Reservations are accepted at 541/997-2741. Sites are $34 per night, $2 per person per night for more than two people. Weekly and monthly rates are available. Open year-round.

Directions: From Florence and U.S. 101, drive south for four miles to Milepost 195. The park is on the left (east side of road).

Contact: Lakeshore RV Park, 541/997-2741, www.lakeshorerv.com.

63 MERCER LAKE RESORT
🏊 🛶 🚤 🦌 🚐

Scenic rating: 7

on Mercer Lake

Map 1.3, page 77

This resort is in a forested setting situated above the shore of Mercer Lake, one of a number of lakes that have formed among the ancient dunes in this area. The 375-acre lake has 11 miles of shoreline and numerous coves. Fishing for rainbow trout and largemouth bass in the stocked lake is the most popular activity. A sandy swimming beach is also available, and the ocean is four miles away.

Campsites, facilities: There are 10 sites with full or partial hookups for RVs up to 40 feet long and 10 cabins. Some sites are pull-through.

Picnic tables are provided. No open fires are allowed. Drinking water, restrooms with flush toilets and showers, dump station, coin laundry, cable TV, convenience store, bait, snacks, and ice are available. Boat docks, launching facilities, and fishing boat rentals are on-site. Leashed pets are permitted.

Reservations, fees: Reservations are accepted at 800/355-3633. Sites are $35-40 per night, $5 per night per each additional person, $5 per night per additional vehicle, $5 per night per pet. Some credit cards are accepted. Open year-round.

Directions: From Florence and U.S. 101, drive north for five miles to Mercer Lake Road. Turn east and drive just under one mile to Bay Berry Lane. Turn left and drive to the resort.

Contact: Mercer Lake Resort, 541/997-3633, www.mlroregon.com.

64 CARTER LAKE

Scenic rating: 9

on Carter Lake in Oregon Dunes National Recreation Area

Map 1.3, page 77   **BEST (**

At time of publication, the campground was closed due to high-water damage in 2017. Call for updates.

This campground sits on the north shore of Carter Lake, and you can fish almost right from your campsite. Boating and fishing are permitted on this long, narrow lake, which is set among dunes overgrown with vegetation. The nearby Taylor Dunes Trail is a half-mile, wheelchair-accessible trail to the dunes past Taylor Lake. Hiking is allowed in the dunes, but there is no off-road-vehicle access here. If you want off-road access, head north one mile to Siltcoos Road, turn west, and drive 1.3 miles to Driftwood II.

Campsites, facilities: There are 22 sites for tents or RVs up to 30 feet long. Some sites are pull-through. Picnic tables, garbage service, and fire pits are provided. Drinking water, flush toilets, and firewood are available. A camp host is on-site. Leashed pets are permitted.

Reservations, fees: Reservations are accepted at 877/444-6777 ($10 reservation fee) or www.recreation.gov ($9 reservation fee). Sites are $22 per night, $5 per night per additional vehicle. Open May-September.

Directions: From Florence and U.S. 101, drive south for 8.5 miles to Forest Road 1084. Turn right on Forest Road 1084 and drive west 200 yards to the camp.

Contact: Oregon Dunes National Recreation Area, Visitors Center, 541/271-3611, www.fs.usda.gov/siuslaw.

65 DRIFTWOOD II

Scenic rating: 6

near Siltcoos Lake in Oregon Dunes National Recreation Area

Map 1.3, page 77

Primarily a campground for off-road vehicles, Driftwood II is set near the ocean, but without an ocean view, in the Oregon Dunes National Recreation Area. It has off-road-vehicle access. Several small lakes, the Siltcoos River, and Siltcoos Lake are nearby. Note that ATV use is prohibited between 10pm and 6am.

Campsites, facilities: There are 62 sites for tents or RVs up to 59 feet long, including nine pull-through sites. Picnic tables, garbage service, and fire grills are provided at back-in sites but not at the pull-through sites. Drinking water and restrooms with flush toilets and showers are available. Boat docks, launching facilities, and rentals can be found about four miles away on Siltcoos Lake. Some facilities are wheelchair accessible. Leashed pets are permitted.

Reservations, fees: Reservations are accepted at 877/444-6777 ($10 reservation fee) or www.recreation.gov ($9 reservation fee); search for "Driftwood." Sites are $25 per night. Open year-round.

Directions: From Florence and U.S. 101, drive

south for seven miles to Siltcoos Beach Road. Turn right and drive 1.5 miles west to the campground.

Contact: Oregon Dunes National Recreation Area, Visitors Center 541/271-6000 or 541/271-3611, www.fs.usda.gov/siuslaw.

66 LAGOON

Scenic rating: 9

near Siltcoos Lake in Oregon Dunes National Recreation Area

Map 1.3, page 77

One of several campgrounds in the area, this camp is located along the lagoon, about one mile from Siltcoos Lake and set 0.5 mile inland with access to the Siltcoos River. The Lagoon Trail offers prime wildlife-viewing for marine birds and other aquatic species.

Campsites, facilities: There are 41 sites for tents or RVs of any length. Picnic tables, garbage service, and fire grills are provided. Drinking water and flush and vault toilets are available. A camp host is on-site. Boat docks, launching facilities, and rentals are nearby on Siltcoos Lake. A dump station is within five miles. Some facilities are wheelchair accessible. Leashed pets are permitted.

Reservations, fees: Reservations are accepted at 877/444-6777 ($10 reservation fee) or www.recreation.gov ($9 reservation fee). Sites are $22 per night. Open year-round.

Directions: From Florence and U.S. 101, drive south for seven miles to Siltcoos Beach Road. Turn right on Siltcoos Beach Road and drive west for 1.2 miles to the campground.

Contact: Oregon Dunes National Recreation Area, Visitors Center 541/271-6000 or 541/271-3611, www.fs.usda.gov/siuslaw.

67 DARLINGS RESORT AND MARINA

Scenic rating: 7

on Siltcoos Lake

Map 1.3, page 77

This park, in a rural area along the north shore of Siltcoos Lake, is adjacent to the extensive Oregon Dunes National Recreation Area. Sites are right on the lake; fish from your picnic table. An access point to the dunes for hikers and off-road vehicles is just across the highway. The lake has a full-service marina. About half the sites are taken by monthly rentals.

Campsites, facilities: There are 13 sites with partial hookups for RVs up to 38 feet long. Picnic tables and fire pits are provided. Drinking water, restrooms with flush toilets and showers, firewood, convenience store, deli, cable TV, boat docks, boat rentals, launching facilities, and a coin laundry are available. Some facilities are wheelchair accessible. Leashed pets are permitted.

Reservations, fees: Reservations are accepted. Sites are $38-42 per night, $5 per night per additional person, $5 per night per additional vehicle. Off-season and monthly rates are available. Some credit cards are accepted. Open May to November 1.

Directions: From Florence and U.S. 101, drive south for five miles to North Beach Road. Turn left (east) and drive 0.25 mile to Darlings Loop Road. Turn right and drive 0.25 mile to the resort.

Contact: Darlings Resort and Marina, 541/997-2841, www.darlingsresortrv.com.

68 TYEE

Scenic rating: 6

on the Siltcoos River in Oregon Dunes National Recreation Area

Map 1.3, page 77

This wooded campground along the shore of

the Siltcoos River provides an alternative to Driftwood II and Lagoon. Fishing is permitted at the nearby lake, where there is a canoe portage trail and a boat ramp. Off-road-vehicle access to the dunes is available from Driftwood II, and there are hiking trails in the area.

Campsites, facilities: There are 16 sites for tents or RVs up to 30 feet long. Picnic tables, garbage service, and fire grills are provided. Drinking water and vault toilets are available. A camp host is on-site. A store, boat docks, launching facilities, and rentals are nearby. Leashed pets are permitted.

Reservations, fees: Reservations are accepted at 877/444-6777 ($10 reservation fee) or www.recreation.gov ($9 reservation fee). Sites are $22 per night, $5 per night per each additional vehicle. Open May-September.

Directions: From Florence and U.S. 101, drive south for six miles to the Westlake turnoff. Take that exit and continue a short distance to the campground.

Contact: Oregon Dunes National Recreation Area, Visitors Center 541/271-6000 or 541/271-3611, www.fs.usda.gov/siuslaw.

69 WAXMYRTLE

Scenic rating: 7
near Siltcoos Lake in Oregon Dunes National Recreation Area

Map 1.3, page 77

One of three camps in the immediate vicinity, Waxmyrtle is adjacent to Lagoon and less than a mile from Driftwood II. The camp is near the Siltcoos River and a couple of miles from Siltcoos Lake, a good-sized lake with boating facilities where you can fish. A pleasant hiking trail here meanders through the dunes and along the estuary.

Campsites, facilities: There are 57 sites for tents or RVs of any length; some sites are pull-through. Picnic tables, garbage service, and fire grills are provided. Drinking water and flush toilets are available. A camp host is on-site. Boat docks, launching facilities, and rentals are nearby on Siltcoos Lake. Leashed pets are permitted.

Reservations, fees: Reservations are accepted at 877/444-6777 ($10 reservation fee) or www.recreation.gov ($9 reservation fee). Sites are $22 per night. Open year-round.

Directions: From Florence and U.S. 101, drive south for seven miles to Siltcoos Beach Road. Turn right and drive 1.3 miles west to the campground.

Contact: Oregon Dunes National Recreation Area, Visitors Center 541/271-6000 or 541/271-3611, www.fs.usda.gov/siuslaw.

70 TAHKENITCH LANDING

Scenic rating: 6
near Tahkenitch Lake in Oregon Dunes National Recreation Area

Map 1.3, page 77

This camp overlooking Tahkenitch Lake (Lake of Many Fingers) has easy access to excellent fishing.

Campsites, facilities: There are 28 sites for tents or RVs up to 40 feet long. Picnic tables, fire grills, and garbage service are provided. There is no drinking water. Vault toilets, boat-launching facilities, and a floating dock are available. A camp host is on-site. Some facilities are wheelchair accessible. Leashed pets are permitted.

Reservations, fees: Reservations are accepted at 877/444-6777 ($10 reservation fee) or www.recreation.gov ($9 reservation fee). Sites are $22 per night, $5 per night per additional vehicle. Open year-round.

Directions: From Florence and U.S. 101, drive south for 14 miles to the campground on the east side of the road.

Contact: Oregon Dunes National Recreation Area, Visitors Center 541/271-6000 or 541/271-3611, www.fs.usda.gov/siuslaw.

71 TAHKENITCH

Scenic rating: 7

near Tahkenitch Lake in Oregon Dunes National Recreation Area

Map 1.3, page 77

This very pretty campground with dense vegetation is set in a wooded area across the highway from Tahkenitch Lake, which has numerous coves and backwater areas for fishing. A hiking trail close to the camp goes through the dunes out to the beach, as well as to Threemile Lake. If this camp is full, Tahkenitch Landing provides space nearby.

Campsites, facilities: There are 26 sites for tents or RVs up to 30 feet long. Some sites are pull-through. Picnic tables, garbage service, and fire grills are provided. Drinking water, firewood, and flush toilets are available. A camp host is on-site. Boat docks and launching facilities are on the lake across the highway. Some facilities are wheelchair accessible. Leashed pets are permitted.

Reservations, fees: Reservations are accepted at 877/444-6777 ($10 reservation fee) or www.recreation.gov ($9 reservation fee). Sites are $22-44 per night, $5 per night per additional vehicle. Open mid-May-September.

Directions: From Florence and U.S. 101, drive south for 14 miles. The campground entrance is on the right.

Contact: Oregon Dunes National Recreation Area, Visitors Center 541/271-6000 or 541/271-3611, www.fs.usda.gov/siuslaw.

72 HALF MOON BAY RV PARK

Scenic rating: 5

adjacent to Oregon Dunes National Recreation Area at Winchester Bay

Map 1.3, page 77

This Douglas County park offers sport fishing and crabbing, lighthouse tours, and beach-combing. If you're looking for tranquility, however, keep in mind that this campground bills itself as *the* campground for the "off-road enthusiast."

Campsites, facilities: There are 45 sites for RVs of any length (no hook-ups) and five group sites for 3-5 RVs each. Picnic tables and fire rings are provided. Drinking water and vault toilets are available. Leashed pets are permitted.

Reservations, fees: Reservations are accepted ($10 reservation fee) at 541/957-7001 or www.co.douglas.or.us/parks. Sites are $25 per night, $5 per night per additional vehicle; the group sites are $60-75 per night. Discounts for Douglas County residents. Some credit cards are accepted. Open year-round.

Directions: From Reedsport and U.S. 101, drive south for three miles to Salmon Harbor Drive near Winchester Bay. Turn right (west) and drive one mile to the campground.

Contact: Half Moon Bay RV Park, 1645 Salmon Harbor Drive, Winchester Bay, 541/957-7001, www.co.douglas.or.us/parks.

73 DISCOVERY POINT RESORT & RV PARK

Scenic rating: 7

on Winchester Bay

Map 1.3, page 77

This resort sits on the shore of Winchester Bay, adjacent to sandy dunes, in a fishing village near the mouth of the Umpqua River. The park was designed around motor sports, and ATVs are available for rent. It is somewhat noisy, but that's what most people come for.

Campsites, facilities: There are five tent sites, 70 sites with full hookups for RVs of any length, 13 cabins, and six condos. Some sites are pull-through. Picnic tables and fire pits are provided at most sites. Restrooms with flush toilets and showers, drinking water, cable TV, convenience store, coin laundry, and ice are available. A dump station and propane gas are within one mile. Boat docks and launching facilities are nearby. Leashed pets are permitted.

Reservations, fees: Reservations are accepted. RV sites are $35-38 per night, tent sites are $20 per night, cabins are $55-175 per night, condos are $325 per night, $7 per night per each additional vehicle. Some credit cards are accepted. Open year-round.

Directions: From Reedsport and U.S. 101, drive south for two miles to Winchester Bay and Salmon Harbor Drive. Turn right at Salmon Harbor Drive and proceed west for one mile to the resort on the left.

Contact: Discovery Point Resort & RV Park, 541/271-3443, www.discoverypointresort.com; ATV rentals, 541/271-9357.

74 WINDY COVE COUNTY PARK

🏃 🏊 ⛵ 🚣 🦌 ♿ 🚐 ⛺

Scenic rating: 7

adjacent to Salmon Harbor at Winchester Bay

Map 1.3, page 77

This Douglas County park actually comprises two campgrounds, Windy Cove A and B. Set near ocean beaches and sand dunes, both offer a variety of additional recreational opportunities, including an 18-hole golf course, hiking trails, and a lighthouse.

Campsites, facilities: There are 94 sites for RVs up to 60 feet long and two cabins, Most sites have full or partial hookups. Picnic tables and fire pits are provided. Drinking water, restrooms with flush toilets and showers, a playground, Wi-Fi, and cable TV are available. Propane gas, dump station, a store, café, and ice are within two miles. Boat docks, launching facilities, boat charters, and rentals are nearby. Some facilities are wheelchair accessible. Leashed pets are permitted.

Reservations, fees: Reservations are accepted at 541/957-7001 ($10 reservation fee). Sites are $17-25 per night, $3 per night per additional vehicle, cabins are $70 per night. Discounts for Douglas County residents. Some credit cards

are accepted. Windy A campsites are closed in winter, but Windy B and the Windy A cabin are open year-round.

Directions: From Reedsport and U.S. 101, drive south for three miles to the Windy Cove exit near Winchester Bay. Take that exit and drive west to the park on the left.

Contact: Windy Cove County Park, Windy B, 541/271-5634; Windy A, 541/271-4138, www.co.douglas.or.us/parks.

75 UMPQUA LIGHTHOUSE STATE PARK

🏃 🏊 ⛵ 🚐 🐴 🚐 ⛺

Scenic rating: 7

on the Umpqua River

Map 1.3, page 77

This park is located near Lake Marie and less than a mile from Salmon Harbor on Winchester Bay. A one-mile trail circles Lake Marie, and swimming and non-motorized boating are allowed. Near the mouth of the Umpqua River, this unusual area features dunes as high as 500 feet. Hiking trails lead out of the park and into the Oregon Dunes National Recreation Area. The park offers more than two miles of beach access on the ocean and 0.5 mile along the Umpqua River. The adjacent lighthouse is still in operation, and tours are available during the summer season.

Campsites, facilities: There are 23 sites for tents or RVs up to 45 feet long (no hookups), 8 sites with partial hookups, 12 sites with full hookups for RVs up to 45 feet long, a hiker/bicyclist camp, two cabins, two rustic yurts, and six deluxe yurts. Picnic tables and fire pits are provided. Drinking water, garbage bins, restrooms with flush toilets and showers, and firewood are available. Boat docks and launching facilities are on the Umpqua River. Leashed pets are permitted; one yurt is pet-friendly.

Reservations, fees: Reservations are accepted at 800/452-5687 or www.oregonstateparks.org ($8 reservation fee). Sites are $19-29 per night, $7 per night for an additional vehicle, $5 per person per night for hikers/bikers, $41-51 per night for cabins, $41 per night for rustic yurts, and $80-90 for deluxe yurts. Some credit cards are accepted. Open year-round.

Directions: From Reedsport and U.S. 101, drive south for six miles to Umpqua Lighthouse Road. Turn right (west) and drive one mile to the park.

Contact: Umpqua Lighthouse State Park, 541/271-4118 or 800/551-6949, www.oregonstateparks.org.

76 WILLIAM M. TUGMAN STATE PARK

Scenic rating: 7
on Eel Lake

Map 1.3, page 77

This campground is set along the shore of Eel Lake, which offers almost five miles of shoreline for boating, fishing, sailing, and swimming. It's perfect for bass fishing. A boat ramp is available, but there is a 10-mph speed limit for boats. Oregon Dunes National Recreation Area is across the highway. Hiking is available just a few miles north at Umpqua Lighthouse State Park. A developed, 2.5-mile trail along the south end of the lake allows hikers to get away from the developed areas of the park and explore the lake's many outlets.

Campsites, facilities: There are 93 sites with partial hookups for tents or RVs up to 50 feet long, a camping area for hikers and bicyclists, and 16 yurts. Drinking water, fire rings, and picnic tables are provided. Restrooms with flush toilets and showers, dump station, firewood, and a picnic shelter are available. Boat docks and launching facilities are nearby. Some facilities are wheelchair accessible. Leashed pets are permitted; eight yurts are pet-friendly.

Reservations, fees: Reservations are accepted at 800/452-5687 or www.oregonstateparks.org ($8 reservation fee). Sites are $24 per night, $7 per night per additional vehicle, $5 per person

per night for hikers/bicyclists, and $44-54 per night for yurts. Some credit cards are accepted. Open year-round.

Directions: From Reedsport and U.S. 101, drive south for eight miles to the park entrance on the left (east side of the road).

Contact: William H. Tugman State Park, 541/759-3604, www.oregonstateparks.org.

77 TENMILE LAKE COUNTY PARK

Scenic rating: 5
on Tenmile Lake in Lakeside

Map 1.3, page 77

Set on the shore of Tenmile Lake, this campground draws anglers eager to fish for rainbow and cutthroat trout, largemouth bass, and catfish. Waterskiing, wakeboarding, and sailing are other recreation options.

Campsites, facilities: There are 45 sites for RVs with partial hookups. Picnic tables and fire pits are provided. Drinking water, restrooms with showers and flush toilets, a dump station, fish-cleaning station, fishing dock, boat launch facilities, swimming and wading beach, horseshoe pits, and a reservable picnic shelter are available. Some facilities are wheelchair accessible. Leashed pets are permitted.

Reservations, fees: Reservations are accepted at 541/396-7755 ($12 reservation fee). Sites are $20-25 per night, $5 per night per additional vehicle. Some credit cards are accepted. Open year-round.

Directions: In Coos Bay, take Highway 101 north for 14 miles to Airport Way. Turn right on Airport Way and drive 0.5 mile to N. 8th Street. Turn right on N. 8th Street and drive a short distance to Park Avenue. Turn left on Park Avenue. The park entrance will be on the left.

Contact: Tenmile Lake County Park, 170 S. 12th St., Lakeside, 541/396-7759, www.co.coos.or.us.

78 NORTH LAKE RESORT AND MARINA

🏊 🚣 � 🏕 🐕 ♿ 🚐 ⛺

Scenic rating: 8

on Tenmile Lake

Map 1.3, page 77

This 40-acre resort along the shore of Tenmile Lake is wooded and secluded, has a private beach, and makes the perfect layover spot for U.S. 101 travelers. The lake has a full-service marina, and bass fishing can be good here. About 25 percent of the sites are taken by summer season rentals.

Campsites, facilities: There are 24 tent sites and 75 sites with full or partial hookups for RVs of any length. Picnic tables are provided and most sites have fire pits. Restrooms with flush toilets and coin showers, dump station, firewood, convenience store, ice, Wi-Fi, cable TV, drinking water, coin laundry, horseshoe pits, and a volleyball court are available. Boat docks, launching facilities, a fish-cleaning station, and a marina are also available. A café and boat rentals are nearby. Some facilities are wheelchair accessible. Leashed pets are permitted.

Reservations, fees: Reservations are accepted. Tent sites are $25 per night; RV sites are $32 per night. Some credit cards are accepted. Open April-October.

Directions: From Reedsport and U.S. 101, drive south on U.S. 101 for 11 miles to the Lakeside exit. Take that exit east into town for 0.75 mile (across the railroad tracks) to North Lake Road. Turn left (north) and drive 0.5 mile to the resort on the left.

Contact: North Lake Resort and Marina, 541/759-3515, www.northlakeresort.com.

79 OSPREY POINT RV RESORT

🚶 🏊 🚣 🚤 🏕 🐕 🚐 ⛺

Scenic rating: 7

on Tenmile Lake

Map 1.3, page 77

Tenmile is one of Oregon's premier bass fishing lakes and yet is located only three miles from the ocean. The resort is situated in a large, open area adjacent to Tenmile Lake and 0.5 mile from North Lake. A navigable canal connects the lakes. The Oregon Dunes National Recreation Area provides nearby hiking trails, and Elliot State Forest offers wooded trails. With weekend barbecues and occasional live entertainment, Osprey Point is more a destination resort than an overnight stop.

Campsites, facilities: There are 132 sites for tents or RVs of any size (full hookups), a grassy area for tents, and five park-model cabins. Picnic tables and fire pits are provided. Drinking water, restrooms with flush toilets and showers, cable TV, Wi-Fi, dump station, coin laundry, restaurant, cocktail lounge, convenience store, full-service marina with boat rentals, boat docks, launch, fishing pier, fish-cleaning station, horseshoe pits, volleyball, tetherball, recreation hall, video arcade, and a pizza parlor are available. Leashed pets are permitted.

Reservations, fees: Reservations are accepted. RV sites are $36-47 per night, tent sites are $25 per night, $4 per person per night for more than two people, $3.50 per night per extra vehicle. Monthly and off-season rates are available. Some credit cards are accepted. Open year-round.

Directions: From Reedport, drive north on U.S. 101 for 11 miles to the Lakeside exit. Take that exit east into town for 0.75 mile (across the railroad tracks) to North Lake Road. Turn left (north) on North Lake Road and drive 0.5 mile to the resort on the right.

Contact: Osprey Point RV Resort, 541/759-2801, www.ospreypoint.net.

80 EEL CREEK

Scenic rating: 8

near Eel Lake in Oregon Dunes National Recreation Area

Map 1.3, page 77

This campground along Eel Creek is located near both Eel and Tenmile Lakes. Although Tenmile Lake allows waterskiing, Eel Lake does not. Nearby trails offer access to the Umpqua Dunes Scenic Area, where you'll find spectacular scenery in an area closed to off-road vehicles. Off-road access is available at Spinreel.

Campsites, facilities: There are 38 sites, including one double site, for tents or RVs up to 50 feet long. Some sites are pull-through. Picnic tables, garbage service, and fire grills are provided. Drinking water, flush toilets, and firewood are available. A camp host is on-site. Boat docks, launching facilities, and rentals are nearby. Leashed pets are permitted.

Reservations, fees: Reservations are accepted at 877/444-6777 ($10 reservation fee) or www.recreation.gov ($9 reservation fee). Sites are $22 per night, the double site is $44 per night, $5 per night per additional vehicle. Open mid-May-September.

Directions: From Reedsport and U.S. 101, drive south for 10.5 miles to the park entrance.

Contact: Oregon Dunes National Recreation Area, Visitors Center 541/271-6000 or 541/271-3611, www.fs.usda.gov/siuslaw.

81 SPINREEL

Scenic rating: 6

on Tenmile Creek in Oregon Dunes National Recreation Area

Map 1.3, page 77

Spinreel campground is set several miles inland at the outlet of Tenmile Lake in the Oregon Dunes National Recreation Area. A boat launch (for drift boats and canoes) is near the camp. Primarily for off-road-vehicle enthusiasts, Spinreel's other recreational opportunities include hiking trails and off-road-vehicle access to the dunes. Off-road-vehicle rentals are available adjacent to the camp.

Campsites, facilities: There are 37 sites for tents or RVs up to 61 feet long. Picnic tables and fire grills are provided. Drinking water, garbage service, and flush toilets are available. Firewood, store, ATV rentals, and a coin laundry are nearby. Boat docks, launching facilities, and rentals are on Tenmile Lake. Some facilities are wheelchair accessible. Leashed pets are permitted.

Reservations, fees: Reservations are accepted at 877/444-6777 ($10 reservation fee) or www.recreation.gov ($9 reservation fee). Sites are $25 per night. Open year-round.

Directions: From Coos Bay, drive north on U.S. 101 for 10 miles to the campground entrance road (well signed). Turn northwest and drive one mile to the campground.

Contact: Oregon Dunes National Recreation Area, Visitors Center 541/271-6000 or 541/271-3611, www.fs.usda.gov/siuslaw.

82 LOON LAKE RECREATION AREA

Scenic rating: 8

on Loon Lake

Map 1.3, page 77 **BEST(**

Loon Lake was created 1,400 years ago when a nearby mountain crumbled and slid downhill, damming a creek with house-sized boulders. Today, the lake is half a mile wide and nearly two miles long, covers 260 acres, and is more than 100 feet deep in places. Its ideal location provides a warm, wind-sheltered summer climate for various water activities. A nature trail leads to a waterfall about half a mile away. Evening interpretive programs are held during summer weekends.

Campsites, facilities: There are 52 sites for tents or RVs up to 35 feet; some are double sites that can accommodate up to 12 people. Picnic tables and fire pits are provided. Drinking water, restrooms with flush toilets and showers, garbage bins, basketball court, firewood, playground, horseshoe pits, fish-cleaning station, a sand beach, and a boat ramp are available. Some facilities are wheelchair accessible, including the fishing pier. Leashed pets are permitted in the campground, but not on the beach or in the day-use area.

Reservations, fees: Reservations are accepted at 877/444-6777 ($10 reservation fee) or www.recreation.gov ($9 reservation fee). Sites are $18 per night, $36 per night for group sites. Open late May-September, weather permitting.

Directions: From Eugene, drive south on I-5 to Exit 162 and Highway 38. Turn west on Highway 38 and drive 43 miles to Milepost 13.5 and the County Road 3 exit. Turn left (south) and drive 7.5 miles to the campground on the right.

Contact: Bureau of Land Management, Coos Bay District Office, 541/756-0100 (winter), 541/599-2254 (summer), www.blm.gov.

83 LOON LAKE LODGE AND RV RESORT

🏃 🚲 🏊 🛶 🚤 🚐 ⛺

Scenic rating: 8

on Loon Lake

Map 1.3, page 77

This resort boasts one mile of lake frontage and nestles among the tall trees on pretty Loon Lake. It's not a long drive from either U.S. 101 or I-5, making it an ideal layover spot for travelers eager to get off the highway. The lake offers good bass fishing, boating, swimming, and waterskiing.

Campsites, facilities: There are 24 tent sites, 40 sites with full or partial hookups for tents or RVs up to 40 feet long, four group sites for up to 20-30 people each, 10 cabins, a lakefront house, four yurts, and a six-unit motel. Some RV sites are pull-through. Picnic tables and fire rings are provided. Pit toilets, flush toilets, showers, and drinking water are available. A

general store with deli, Wi-Fi, cable TV, firewood, ice, gasoline and propane, beach access, boat ramp, dock, marina, and boat rentals are also available. Leashed pets are permitted, with certain restrictions.

Reservations, fees: Reservations are accepted. Tent sites are $17-35 per night, RV sites are $30-55 per night, $7 per person per night for more than five, $7 per night per additional vehicle. Weekly and monthly rates are available. Some credit cards are accepted. Open April 1-November 1.

Directions: From Eugene, drive south on I-5 to Exit 162 and Highway 38. Turn west on Highway 38 and drive 20 miles through the town of Elkton. Continue on Highway 38 for another 22 miles until you cross a large bridge and reach Loon Lake Road. Turn left at Loon Lake Road and drive nine miles to the resort.

Contact: Loon Lake Lodge and RV Resort, 541/599-2244, www.loonlakerv.com.

84 EAGLEVIEW GROUP CAMPGROUND

🏊 🛶 🏕 ♿ 🚐 ⛺

Scenic rating: 5

on the Umpqua River

Map 1.3, page 77

In a canyon surrounded by deep forest, this lovely spot along the Umpqua River is perfectly suited for weddings, family reunions, and group outings or retreats.

Campsites, facilities: There are 10 sites that can accommodate up to 100 people in tents or RVs. Picnic tables and fire grills are provided. Drinking water, garbage service, vault toilets, a dump station, river access, horseshoe pits, a group area with a large fire pit, and a large covered pavilion are available. A grassy area invites games of croquet, bocce ball, or Frisbee. A camp host is on-site. Some facilities are wheelchair accessible. Leashed pets are permitted.

Reservations, fees: Reservations are required at 877/444-6777 or www.recreation.gov

($10 reservation fee). The site is $145 per night. Open May 11-September 24.

Directions: From Roseburg, drive north on I-5 to Exit 136 and Highway 138. Take that exit and drive west on Highway 138 for 12 miles. Cross Bullock Bridge and immediately turn right onto Bullock Road/County Road 57. Drive one mile to Eagleview Campground on the right. GPS Coordinates: 43.497363, -123.4927

Contact: Bureau of Land Management, Roseburg District, 541/440-4930, www.blm.gov.

85 TYEE

Scenic rating: 7

on the Umpqua River

Map 1.3, page 77

Here's a classic spot along the Umpqua River with great salmon, smallmouth bass, and steelhead fishing in season. Boat launches are available a few miles upstream and downstream of the campground. Eagleview Group camp, a BLM campground, is one mile away.

Campsites, facilities: There are 15 sites for tents or RVs up to 70 feet long. Picnic tables and fire grills are provided. Drinking water, garbage service, vault toilets, river access, a day-use area with horseshoe pits, and a pavilion are available. A camp host is on-site. A store is within one mile. Some facilities are wheelchair accessible. Leashed pets are permitted.

Reservations, fees: Reservations are not accepted. Sites are $10 per night, $4 per night for each additional vehicle. Open late March-mid-November.

Directions: From Roseburg, drive north on I-5 to Exit 136 and Highway 138. Take that exit and drive west on Highway 138 for 12 miles. Cross Bullock Bridge and continue to County Road 57. Turn right and drive 0.5 mile to the campground entrance.

Contact: Bureau of Land Management, Roseburg District, 541/440-4930, www.blm.gov.

86 RILEY RANCH COUNTY PARK

Scenic rating: 5

on Butterfield Lake near Oregon Dunes National Recreation Area

Map 1.3, page 77

This 135-acre campground, located right next door to Oregon Dunes National Recreation Area, provides access to an Off-Highway Vehicle area. ATVs and equestrian groups are both welcome here and plans are afoot for an ATV learning center. Butterfield Lake offers anglers in non-motorized boats the chance for trout, bass, and crappie.

Campsites, facilities: There are 90 sites with partial hookups for RVs and two camping cabins. Picnic tables and fire pits are provided. Drinking water, restrooms with showers and flush toilets, fishing dock, boat launch facilities, swimming and wading beach, and horseshoe pits are available. A camp host is on-site and a dump station is four miles away. Some facilities are wheelchair accessible. Leashed pets are permitted.

Reservations, fees: Reservations are accepted at 541/396-7755 ($12 reservation fee). Sites are $32 per night, $5 per night per additional vehicle. Some credit cards are accepted. Open year-round.

Directions: Riley Ranch County Park is four miles south of Tenmile County Park at Milepost 227 on Highway 101.

Contact: Riley Ranch County Park, 93507 Riley Ranch Lane, North Bend, 541/396-7759, www.co.coos.or.us.

87 OREGON DUNES KOA

Scenic rating: 5

north of North Bend, next to the Oregon Dunes National Recreation Area

Map 1.3, page 77

This ATV-friendly park was winner of KOA

Founder's and President's Award for 2013. It has direct access to Oregon Dunes National Recreation Area, which offers miles of ATV trails. The fairly open campground features a landscape of grass, young trees, and a small lake. The ocean is a 15-minute drive away. Mill Casino is about six miles south on U.S. 101. Freshwater and ocean fishing are nearby. A golf course is about five miles away.

Campsites, facilities: There are 62 sites for tents or RVs of any size (full hookups), six tent sites, nine camping cabins, and three deluxe cabins. Most sites are pull-through, and 30- and 50-amp service is available. Picnic tables and fire pits are provided for RV sites. Drinking water, restrooms with flush toilets and showers, Wi-Fi, cable TV, coin laundry, convenience store, game room, playground, seasonal organized activities, firewood, propane gas, horseshoe pits, and a picnic shelter are available. ATV rentals are nearby. Some facilities are wheelchair accessible. Leashed pets are permitted, except in cabins.

Reservations, fees: Reservations are accepted at 800/562-4236. Tent sites are $33-44 per night, RV sites are $56-61 per night, $4 per person per night for more than two people, $4.50 per night per additional vehicle. Some credit cards are accepted. Open year-round.

Directions: From Coos Bay, drive north on U.S. 101 past North Bend for nine miles to Milepost 229. The campground entrance road is on the left.

Contact: Oregon Dunes KOA, 541/756-4851, www.oregonduneskoa.com.

88 WILD MARE HORSE CAMP

Scenic rating: 7

in Oregon Dunes National Recreation Area

Map 1.3, page 77

This horse camp has paved parking, with single and double corrals. No off-road vehicles are allowed within the campground. Horses can be ridden straight out into the dunes and to the ocean; they cannot be ridden on developed trails, such as Bluebill Lake Trail. The heavily treed shoreline gives rise to treed sites with some bushes.

Campsites, facilities: There are 11 horse campsites for tents or RVs up to 61 feet long. There is a maximum of two vehicles per site. Picnic tables and fire pits are provided. Drinking water, vault toilets, 12 corrals, and garbage bins are available. Leashed pets are permitted.

Reservations, fees: Reservations are accepted at 877/444-6777 ($10 reservation fee) or www.recreation.gov ($9 reservation fee). Sites are $22 per night. Some credit cards are accepted. Open year-round.

Directions: From Coos Bay, drive north on U.S. 101 for 1.5 miles to Horsfall Dunes and Beach Access Road. Turn left and drive west for one mile to the campground access road. Turn right and drive 0.75 mile to the campground on the left.

Contact: Oregon Dunes National Recreation Area, Visitors Center 541/271-6000 or 541/271-3611, www.fs.usda.gov/siuslaw.

89 BLUEBILL

Scenic rating: 6

on Bluebill Lake in Oregon Dunes National Recreation Area

Map 1.3, page 77

This campground gets very little camping pressure, although there are some good hiking trails available. It's located next to little Bluebill Lake, which sometimes dries up during the summer. A one-mile trail goes around the lakebed. The camp is a short distance from Horsfall Lake, which is surrounded by private property. If you continue west on the forest road, you'll come to a picnicking and parking area near the beach. This spot provides off-road-vehicle access to the dunes at the Horsfall day-use area and Horsfall Beach.

Campsites, facilities: There are 19 sites for

tents or RVs of any length. Picnic tables, garbage service, and fire grills are provided. Vault toilets and drinking water are available. A camp host is on-site. Leashed pets are permitted.

Reservations, fees: Reservations are accepted at 877/444-6777 ($10 reservation fee) or www.recreation.gov ($9 reservation fee). Sites are $20 per night. Open April-September.

Directions: From Coos Bay, drive north on U.S. 101 for 1.5 miles north to Horsfall Dunes and Beach Access Road. Turn west and drive one mile to Horsfall Road. Turn northwest and drive two miles to the campground entrance.

Contact: Oregon Dunes National Recreation Area, Visitors Center 541/271-6000 or 541/271-3611, www.fs.usda.gov/siuslaw.

90 HORSFALL

Scenic rating: 4

in Oregon Dunes National Recreation Area

Map 1.3, page 77

Horsfall campground is actually a nice, large paved area for parking RVs; it's the staging area for off-road-vehicle access into the southern section of Oregon Dunes National Recreation Area. If Horsfall is full, try nearby Horsfall Beach, an overflow area with 34 tent and RV sites.

Campsites, facilities: There are 102 sites for RVs up to 52 feet long. Picnic tables and fire rings are provided. Drinking water, garbage service, restrooms with flush toilets and coin showers are available. Some facilities are wheelchair accessible. Leashed pets are permitted.

Reservations, fees: Reservations are accepted at 877/444-6777 ($10 reservation fee) or www.recreation.gov ($9 reservation fee). Sites are $25 per night. Open year-round.

Directions: From Coos Bay, drive north on U.S. 101 for 1.5 miles to Horsfall Road. Turn west on Horsfall Road and drive about one mile to the campground access road. Turn on the campground access road (well signed) and drive 0.5 mile to the campground.

Contact: Oregon Dunes National Recreation Area, Visitors Center 541/271-6000 or 541/271-3611, www.fs.usda.gov/siuslaw.

91 SUNSET BAY STATE PARK

Scenic rating: 8

near Sunset Bay

Map 1.3, page 77

Scenic Sunset Bay sits on the beautiful Oregon Coast, amid coastal forest and headlands. The sandy beach is secluded, protected by cliffs and conifers, and tidepooling is a popular activity. A series of hiking trails leads to Shore Acres and Cape Arago Parks. Clamming and fishing is available in nearby Charleston. Golfing and swimming are some of the recreation options here.

Campsites, facilities: There are 65 sites for tents or self-contained RVs, 65 sites with full or partial hookups for tents or RVs up to 47 feet long, a separate area for hikers and bicyclists, eight yurts, and two group camps for up to 25 and 250 people, respectively. Drinking water, picnic tables, garbage bins, and fire grills are provided. Restrooms with flush toilets and showers, a fish-cleaning station, boat ramp, and firewood are available. A camp host is on-site. A gazebo and meeting hall can be reserved at nearby Shore Acres. A restaurant is within three miles. Some facilities are wheelchair accessible. Leashed pets are permitted, except in yurts; one yurt is pet friendly.

Reservations, fees: Reservations are accepted at 800/452-5687 or www.oregonstateparks.org ($8 reservation fee). Sites are $19-29 per night, $7 per night per additional vehicle, $5 per person per night for hikers/bicyclists, $41-51 per night for yurts, and $71 per night for group camps. Some credit cards are accepted. Open year-round.

Directions: In Coos Bay, take the Charleston/State Parks exit to Empire Coos Bay Highway. Drive west to Newmark Avenue. Bear left and continue to Cape Arago Highway. Turn left and drive about five miles south to Charleston and cross the South Slough Bridge. Continue on Cape Arago Highway about three miles to the park entrance on the left.

Contact: Sunset Bay State Park, 541/888-3778 x221 or 800/551-6949, www.oregonstateparks. org.

92 BASTENDORFF BEACH PARK

Scenic rating: 8

near Cape Arago State Park

Map 1.3, page 77

This campground is surrounded by large trees and provides access to the ocean and a small lake. Nearby activities include boating, clamming, crabbing, dune buggy riding, fishing, golfing, swimming, and whale-watching. Swimmers should be aware of undertows and sneaker waves. Horses may be rented near Bandon. A nice side trip is to Shore Acres State Park and Botanical Gardens, about 2.5 miles away.

Campsites, facilities: There are 25 tent sites, 74 sites with partial hookups for tents or RVs (of any length), and two cabins. An 18-site group camp is also available. Picnic tables and fire pits are provided. Drinking water, restrooms with flush toilets and coin showers, and two dump stations are available. A fish-cleaning station, horseshoe pits, playground, basketball courts, a softball/volleyball lawn, and a picnic area are also available. Some facilities are wheelchair accessible. Leashed pets are permitted.

Reservations, fees: Reservations are accepted for groups, cabins, and the picnic area at 541/396-7755 ($12 reservation fee) or online; individual campsites can be reserved only online. RV sites are $20-26 per night, tent sites are $18-20 per night, $5 per night per additional vehicle, and cabins are $45 per night. Call for group camping rates. Winter rates are lower. Some credit cards are accepted. Open year-round.

Directions: In Coos Bay, take the Charleston/ State Parks exit to Empire Coos Bay Highway. Drive west to Newmark Avenue. Bear left and continue to Cape Arago Highway. Turn left and drive about five miles south to Charleston and cross the South Slough Bridge. Continue on Cape Arago Highway for 1.25 miles to the park entrance.

Contact: Bastendorff Beach Park, 541/396-7759, www.co.coos.co.or.us.

93 CHARLESTON MARINA RV PARK

Scenic rating: 7

on Coos Bay

Map 1.3, page 77

This large, developed public park and marina is located near Charleston on the Pacific Ocean. Recreational activities in and near the campground include boating, clamming, crabbing, fishing (halibut, salmon, and tuna), hiking, huckleberry and blackberry picking, and swimming.

Campsites, facilities: There are 100 sites for RVs up to 50 feet long (full hookups) and three yurts. Picnic tables are provided. No open fires are allowed. Drinking water, satellite TV, Wi-Fi, restrooms with showers, dump station, coin laundry, playground, fish-cleaning station, crab-cooking facilities, and propane gas are available. A marina with a boarding dock and launch ramp are on-site. Some facilities are wheelchair accessible. Leashed pets are permitted.

Reservations, fees: Reservations are accepted at 541/888-9512 or rvpark@charlestonmarina. com. RV sites are $33-37 per night, yurts are $55 per night, $3 per night per additional vehicle. Weekly and monthly rates are available. Some credit cards are accepted. Open year-round.

Directions: In Coos Bay, take the Charleston/ State Parks exit to Empire Coos Bay Highway. Drive west to Newmark Avenue. Bear left and continue to Cape Arago Highway. Turn left and drive about five miles south to Charleston and cross the South Slough Bridge. Continue to Boat Basin Drive. Turn right and drive 0.2 mile to Kingfisher Drive. Turn right and drive 200 feet to the campground on the left.

Contact: Charleston Marina RV Park, 541/888-9512, www.charlestonmarina.com.

94 BULLARDS BEACH STATE PARK

Scenic rating: 7

on the Coquille River

Map 1.3, page 77

The Coquille River, which has good fishing in season for both boaters and crabbers, is the centerpiece of this park with four miles of shore access. If fishing is not your thing, the park also has several hiking trails. The Coquille River Lighthouse is at the end of the road that wanders through the park; during the summer, there are tours to the tower. Equestrians can explore the seven-mile horse trail.

Campsites, facilities: There are 185 sites with full or partial hookups for tents or RVs up to 64 feet long, a primitive horse camp with eight sites and three corrals, and 13 yurts. Drinking water, garbage bins, picnic tables, and fire grills are provided. Restrooms with flush toilets and showers, dump station, playground, firewood, a yurt meeting hall, and picnic shelters are available. Boat docks and launching facilities are in the park on the Coquille River. Some facilities are wheelchair accessible. Leashed pets are permitted; one yurt is pet friendly.

Reservations, fees: Reservations are accepted at 800/452-5687 or www.oregonstate-parks.org ($8 reservation fee). Sites are $26-29 per night, $7 per vehicle per night, and yurts are $41-51 per night. Horse camping is $19 per night. Some credit cards are accepted. Open year-round.

Directions: In Coos Bay, drive south on U.S.

101 for about 22 miles to the park on the right (west side of road), two miles north of Bandon.

Contact: Bullards Beach State Park, 541/347-3501 (May-Sept.) or 800/551-6949 (Oct.-Apr.), www.oregonstateparks.org.

95 BANDON RV PARK

Scenic rating: 6

near Bullards Beach State Park

Map 1.3, page 77

This in-town RV park is a good base for many adventures. Some sites are filled with renters, primarily anglers, for the summer season. Rock hounds will enjoy combing for agates and other semiprecious stones hidden along the beaches, while kids can explore the West Coast Game Park Walk-Through Safari petting zoo seven miles south of town. Bandon State Park, four miles south of town, has a nice wading spot in the creek at the north end of the park. Nearby recreation opportunities include two 18-hole golf courses, a riding stable, and tennis courts. Bullards Beach is about 2.5 miles north. Nice folks run this place.

Campsites, facilities: There are 45 sites with full hookups for RVs of any length; some are pull-through sites. Picnic tables are provided at most sites. No open fires are allowed. Restrooms with flush toilets and showers, cable TV, Wi-Fi, and a coin laundry are available. Propane gas and a store are within two blocks. Boat docks and launching facilities are nearby. Some facilities are wheelchair accessible. Leashed pets are permitted.

Reservations, fees: Reservations are accepted. Sites are $32 per night, $2 per person per night for more than two people. Monthly rates are available. Some credit cards are accepted. Open year-round.

Directions: From Coos Bay, drive south on U.S. 101 for 26 miles to Bandon and the Highway 42S junction. Continue south on U.S. 101 for one block to the park (located on the right at 935 2nd Street Southeast).

Contact: Bandon RV Park, 541/347-4122, www.bandonrvpark.com.

96 LAVERNE AND WEST LAVERNE GROUP CAMP

Scenic rating: 9

in Fairview on the north fork of the Coquille River

Map 1.3, page 77

This beautiful, 350-acre park sits on a river with a small waterfall and many trees, including a myrtle grove and old-growth Douglas fir. Mountain bikers can take an old wagon road, and golfers can enjoy any of several courses. There are a few hiking trails and a very popular swimming hole. You can fish for salmon, steelhead, and trout, and the wildlife includes bears, cougars, deer, elk, and raccoons. You can take a side trip to the museums at Myrtle Point and Coos Bay, which display local indigenous items, or an old stagecoach house in Dora.

Campsites, facilities: There are 30 tent sites and 46 RV sites with partial hookups for RVs of any length at Laverne. One cabin is also available. There is a large group site at West Laverne B that includes 22 RV sites with partial hookups and an overflow area for dry camping. Picnic tables and fire pits are provided. Drinking water, restrooms with flush toilets and coin showers, garbage bins, dump station, ice, playground, a picnic area that can be reserved, swimming hole (unsupervised), horseshoe pits, and volleyball and softball areas are available. A restaurant is within 1.5 miles. Propane gas, a store, and gasoline are within five miles. Some facilities are wheelchair accessible. Leashed pets are permitted.

Reservations, fees: Reservations are accepted for the group site and cabin ($12 reservation fee) at 541/396-7755 or online; individual campsites can be reserved only online. RV sites are $20 per night, tent sites are $15 per night, $5 per night per each additional vehicle. The cabin is $45 per night. Call for group rates. Some credit cards are accepted. Open year-round.

Directions: From Coos Bay, drive south on U.S. 101 for six miles to the junction with Highway 42. Turn east and drive 11 miles to Coquille and West Central. Turn left and drive 0.5 mile to Fairview McKinley Road. Turn right and drive eight miles to the Fairview Store. Continue east another five miles (past the store) to the park on the right.

Contact: Laverne County Park, Coos County, 541-396-7759, www.co.coos.or.us.

97 PARK CREEK

Scenic rating: 7

near Coquille

Map 1.3, page 77

Want to be by yourself? You came to the right place. This pretty little campground offers peaceful, shady campsites under an old-growth canopy of Douglas fir, myrtle, red cedar, and western hemlock. Relax and enjoy nearby Park Creek and Middle Creek.

Campsites, facilities: There are 15 sites for tents or small RVs. Picnic tables and fire grills are provided. Vault toilets are available. There is no drinking water. Leashed pets are permitted.

Reservations, fees: Reservations are not accepted. There is no fee for camping. Open mid-May-September 30 with a stay limit of 14 days.

Directions: From Coos Bay, drive south on U.S. 101 for six miles to the junction with Highway 42. Turn east and drive 11 miles to Coquille and Coquille Fairview Road. Turn left (east) on Coquille Fairview Road and drive 7.5 miles to Fairview and Coos Bay Wagon Road. Turn right and drive four miles to Middle Creek Access Road. Turn left (east) and drive nine miles to the campground on the right.

Contact: Bureau of Land Management, Coos Bay District, 541/756-0100, www.blm.gov.

98 KOA BANDON/ PORT ORFORD

🚶 🏊 🐴 �̲ 🚐 ⛺

Scenic rating: 7

near the Elk River

Map 1.4, page 78

Winner of the "Best of the Best" award from *Trailer Life,* this spot is considered just a lay-over camp, but it offers large, secluded sites nestled among big trees and coastal ferns. A pool and spa are available. During the summer season, a daily pancake breakfast and ice cream social are held. The Elk and Sixes Rivers, where the fishing can be good, are minutes away, and Cape Blanco State Park is just a few miles down the road.

Campsites, facilities: There are 46 tent sites and 26 pull-through sites, some with full hookups (20-, 30-, and 50-amp), for RVs of any length. Six cabins are also available. Picnic tables and fire rings are provided. Restrooms with flush toilets and showers, cable TV, Wi-Fi, snack bar, propane gas, dump station, firewood, recreation hall, convenience store, coin laundry, seasonal heated swimming pool, spa, off-leash dog park, horseshoe pits, basketball court, ice, and a playground are available. Leashed pets are permitted.

Reservations, fees: Reservations are accepted at 800/562-3298. Sites are $39-48 per night, $3-7 per person per night for more than two people, and $5 per night per additional vehicle. Some credit cards are accepted. Open March-November.

Directions: From Bandon, drive south on U.S. 101 for 16 miles to the campground at Milepost 286 near Langlois, on the west side of the highway.

Contact: KOA Bandon/Port Orford, 541/348-2358, www.koa.com.

99 CAPE BLANCO STATE PARK

🚶 🚲 🛶 🏊 🚐 🐴 ♿ 🚌 ⛺

Scenic rating: 8

between the Sixes and Elk Rivers

Map 1.4, page 78   **BEST (**

This large park is named for the white *(blanco)* chalk appearance of the sea cliffs here, which rise 200 feet above the ocean. Sea lions inhabit the offshore rocks, and trails and a road lead to the black sand beach below the cliffs. The park offers good fishing access to the Sixes River, which runs for more than two miles through meadows and forests. There are seven miles of trails for horseback riding available and more than eight miles of hiking trails, some with ocean views. Tours of the lighthouse and historic Hughes House are available (Wed.-Mon.).

Campsites, facilities: There are 52 sites with partial hookups for tents or RVs up to 65 feet long. Other options include an equestrian camp with eight sites, a hiker/bicyclist camping area, four cabins, and four primitive group sites for tents or RVs for up to 25 people. Garbage bins, picnic tables, drinking water, and fire grills are provided. Firewood and restrooms with flush toilets and showers are available. Some facilities are wheelchair accessible. Leashed pets are permitted; one cabin is pet friendly.

Reservations, fees: Reservations are not accepted for single sites, but are accepted for cabins, the group site, and the horse camp at 800/452-5687 or www.oregonstateparks.org ($8 reservation fee). Single sites are $22 per night, $7 per night per additional vehicle. The horse camp is $17 per night; the hiker/biker sites are $5 per person per night. The group site is $71 per night for the first 25 people, then $3 per each additional person per night. The cabins are $41-51 per night. Some credit cards are accepted. Open year-round.

Directions: From Coos Bay, turn south on U.S. 101 and drive approximately 46 miles (south of Sixes, five miles north of Port Orford) to Cape Blanco Road. Turn right (northwest) and drive five miles to the campground on the left.

Contact: Humbug Mountain State Park, 541/332-6774 or 800/551-6949, www.oregonstateparks.org. (This park is under the same management as Humbug Mountain State Park.)

100 EDSON CREEK CAMPGROUND

Scenic rating: 6

on the Sixes River

Map 1.4, page 78

This is a popular campground along the banks of the Sixes River. Edson is similar to Sixes River Campground, except it has less tree cover and Sixes River has the benefit of a boat ramp.

Campsites, facilities: There are 27 sites for tents or RVs up to 30 feet long, and five group sites for 15-50 people each. Picnic tables and fire grills are provided. Drinking water, vault toilets, garbage service, a boat launch, and a camp host are available. Some facilities are wheelchair accessible. Leashed pets are permitted.

Reservations, fees: Reservations are not accepted for single sites but are required for group sites at 877/444-6777 or www.recreation.gov ($10 reservation fee). Sites are $8-16 per night and $4 per night for each additional vehicle, with a 14-day stay limit. The group sites are $30 per night. Open mid-May-September 30, weather permitting.

Directions: From Coos Bay, drive south on U.S. 101 for 40 miles to Sixes and Sixes River Road/County Road 184. Turn left (east) on Sixes River Road and drive four miles to the campground entrance on the left. It's located before the Edson Creek Bridge.

Contact: Bureau of Land Management, Coos Bay District, 541/756-0100, www.blm.gov.

101 SIXES RIVER

Scenic rating: 6

on the Sixes River

Map 1.4, page 78

Set along the banks of the Sixes River at an elevation of 4,303 feet, this camp is a favorite of anglers, miners, and nature lovers. There are opportunities to pan or sluice for gold year-round or through a special limited permit. Dredging is permitted from July 15 through September. The camp roads are paved.

Campsites, facilities: There are 19 sites for tents or small RVs. Picnic tables and fire grills are provided. Vault toilets are available. Some facilities are wheelchair accessible. A camp host is on-site. Leashed pets are permitted.

Reservations, fees: Reservations are not accepted. Sites are $8 per night, $4 per night for an additional vehicle, with a 14-day stay limit. Open late-May-September.

Directions: From Coos Bay, drive south on U.S. 101 for 40 miles to Sixes and Sixes River Road/County Road 184. Turn left (east) on Sixes River Road and drive 11 miles to the campground on the right. The last 0.5 mile is an unpaved road.

Contact: Bureau of Land Management, Coos Bay District, 541/756-0100, www.blm.gov.

102 POWERS COUNTY PARK

Scenic rating: 9

near the south fork of the Coquille River

Map 1.4, page 78

This private and secluded public park in a wooded, mountainous area is a great stop for travelers going between I-5 and the coast. A 30-acre lake at the park provides a spot for visitors to boat and fish for trout. The lake is stocked with bass, catfish, crappie, and trout. Only electric boat motors are allowed. Swimming is not recommended because of the algae in the lake. A bike trail is available. On display at the park are an old steam donkey and a hand-carved totem pole. The biggest cedar tree in Oregon is reputed to be about 12 miles away.

Campsites, facilities: There are 30 sites for tents or RVs up to 54 feet long and 40 sites with partial hookups (20- and 30-amp). Primitive camping for large groups and three cabins are also available. Picnic tables, fire pits, drinking water, restrooms with flush toilets and showers, a dump station, fish-cleaning station, and picnic shelters are provided. Recreational facilities include a boat ramp, horseshoe pits, playground, basketball and volleyball courts, tennis courts, and a softball field. Supplies are available within one mile. Some facilities are wheelchair accessible. Leashed pets are permitted.

Reservations, fees: Reservations ($12 reservation fee) are accepted online for the RV sites; cabins can be reserved online or at 541/396-7755. RV sites are $20 per night, tent sites are $15 per night, and cabins are $45 per night. Call for group rates. Some credit cards are accepted. Open year-round.

Directions: From Coos Bay, drive south on U.S. 101 for six miles to the junction with Highway 42. Turn east and drive 20 miles to Myrtle Point. Continue on Highway 42 to the Powers Highway (Highway 242) exit. Turn right (southwest) and drive 19 miles to the park on the right.

Contact: Powers County Park, Coos County, 541/439-2791, www.co.coos.or.us/ccpark.

103 ELK RIVER CAMPGROUND

Scenic rating: 7

near the Elk River

Map 1.4, page 78

This quiet and restful camp makes an excellent base for fall and winter fishing on the Elk River, which is known for its premier salmon fishing. A one-mile private access road goes to the river, so guests get their personal fishing holes. About half of the sites are taken by monthly rentals.

Campsites, facilities: There are 50 sites with full hookups for RVs up to 40 feet long; some sites are pull-through. There is also a large open area for tent camping. Picnic tables are provided. No open fires are allowed. Drinking water, restrooms with showers, dump station, Wi-Fi, cable TV, and a coin laundry are available. Recreational facilities include a sports field and a boat ramp. Some facilities are wheelchair accessible. Leashed pets are permitted.

Reservations, fees: Reservations are recommended. RV sites are $25 per night, tent sites are $10 per person. Weekly and monthly rates are available. Open year-round.

Directions: From Port Orford, drive north on U.S. 101 for 1.5 miles to Elk River Road (Milepost 297). Turn right (east) on Elk River Road and drive 1.8 miles to the campground on the left.

Contact: Elk River Campground, 541/332-2255.

104 LAIRD LAKE

Scenic rating: 8

on Laird Lake in Rogue River-Siskiyou National Forest

Map 1.4, page 78   **BEST (**

This secluded campground is set at 1,600 feet elevation, along the shore of pretty Laird Lake (six feet at its deepest point). Some old-growth cedar logs are in the lake. Most campers have no idea such a place exists in the area. This very private and scenic spot can be just what you're looking for if you're tired of fighting the crowds at the more developed camps along U.S. 101.

Campsites, facilities: There are four sites for tents or RVs up to 25 feet long. Picnic tables, fire rings, and a vault toilet are provided. There is no drinking water and garbage must be packed out. Leashed pets are permitted.

Reservations, fees: Reservations are not accepted. There is no fee for camping. Open year-round.

Directions: From Port Orford, drive north on

U.S. 101 for three miles to County Road 208. Turn right and drive 7.5 miles southeast (the road becomes Forest Road 5325). Continue for 15.5 miles (the road bears to the right when you reach the gravel) to the campground. The road is paved for 11 miles and is gravel for the last 4.5 miles to the campground.

Contact: Rogue River-Siskiyou National Forest, Powers Ranger District, 541/439-6200, www.fs.usda.gov/rogue-siskiyou.

105 BUTLER BAR

Scenic rating: 6
on the Elk River in Rogue River-Siskiyou National Forest

Map 1.4, page 78

This campground, at an elevation of 800 feet, is set back from the shore of the Elk River and surrounded by old-growth and hardwood forest, with some reforested areas nearby. Across the river is the Grassy Knob Wilderness, which has no trails and is generally too rugged to hike. Check fishing regulations before fishing.

Campsites, facilities: There are seven sites for tents. Picnic tables and fire grills are provided. Vault toilets are available. There is no drinking water, but river water may be filtered. Garbage must be packed out. Leashed pets are permitted.

Reservations, fees: Reservations are not accepted. There is no fee for camping. Open year-round, weather permitting.

Directions: From Port Orford, drive north on U.S. 101 for three miles to County Road 208. Turn right and drive 7.5 miles southeast (the road becomes Forest Road 5325). Continue for 7.5 miles to the campground. The road is paved.

Contact: Rogue River-Siskiyou National Forest, Powers Ranger District, 541/439-6200, www.fs.usda.gov/rogue-siskiyou.

106 PORT ORFORD RV VILLAGE

Scenic rating: 5
near the Elk and Sixes Rivers

Map 1.4, page 78

Each evening, an informal group campfire and happy hour enliven this campground. Other nice touches include a small gazebo where you can get free coffee each morning and a patio where you can sit. Fishing is good during the fall and winter on the nearby Elk and Sixes Rivers, and the campground has a smokehouse, freezer, and fish-cleaning station. Some sites here are taken by summer season rentals or permanent residents.

Campsites, facilities: There are 47 sites with full or partial hookups for RVs of any length and one rental trailer. Some sites are pull-through. Picnic tables are provided. Flush toilets and showers, propane gas, dump station, horseshoe pits, basketball, recreation hall, Wi-Fi, cable TV, book and video library, fish-cleaning station, crab cooker, and a coin laundry are available. Boat docks and launching facilities are nearby. Lake, river, and ocean are all within 1.5 miles. Leashed pets are permitted.

Reservations, fees: Reservations are accepted. Sites are $29 per night, $2 per person per night for more than two people, and $5 per night for additional vehicle. Open year-round.

Directions: In Port Orford on U.S. 101, drive to Madrona Avenue. Turn east and drive one block to Port Orford Loop. Turn left (north) and drive 0.5 mile to the camp on the left side.

Contact: Port Orford RV Village, 541/332-1041, www.portorfordrv.com.

107 HUMBUG MOUNTAIN STATE PARK

🏃 🚴 🏊 🐕 ♿ 🚐 ⛺

Scenic rating: 7

near Port Orford

Map 1.4, page 78

Humbug Mountain, at 1,756 feet elevation, looms over its namesake state park. Fortunately, this natural guardian affords the campground some of the warmest weather on the coast by blocking cold winds from the ocean. Windsurfing and scuba diving are popular, as is hiking the three-mile trail to Humbug Peak. Both ocean and freshwater fishing are accessible nearby.

Campsites, facilities: There are 56 sites for tents or RVs (no hookups), 39 sites with partial hookups for RVs up to 55 feet long, and hiker/bicyclist sites. Some sites are pull-through. Fire grills, picnic tables, garbage bins, and drinking water are provided. Firewood and restrooms with flush toilets and showers are available. A camp host is on-site. Some facilities are wheelchair accessible. Leashed pets are permitted.

Reservations, fees: Reservations are accepted at 541/332-6774. Sites are $17-22 per night, $7 per night per additional vehicle, and $5 per person per night for hikers/bicyclists. Some credit cards are accepted. Open year-round.

Directions: From Port Orford, drive south on U.S. 101 for six miles to the park entrance on the left.

Contact: Humbug Mountain State Park, 541/332-6774 or 800/551-6949, www.oregonstateparks.org.

108 MYRTLE GROVE

🏃 🐕 ⛺

Scenic rating: 6

on the south fork of the Coquille River in Rogue River-Siskiyou National Forest

Map 1.4, page 78

This U.S. Forest Service campground is located along the south fork of the Coquille River, a little downstream from Daphne Grove, at an elevation of 500 feet. No fishing is allowed. Campsites are set under a canopy of big leaf maple and Douglas fir in a narrow, steep canyon. The Big Tree Observation Site, home to a huge Port Orford cedar, is a few miles away. The trail that runs adjacent to Elk Creek provides a prime hike. (The road to Big Tree may be closed because of slides, so be sure to check with the ranger district in advance.)

Campsites, facilities: There are five tent sites. Picnic tables and fire grills are provided. Vault toilets and garbage bins are available. There is no drinking water. Leashed pets are permitted.

Reservations, fees: Reservations are not accepted. There is no fee for camping. Open year-round.

Directions: From Coos Bay, drive south on U.S. 101 for six miles to the junction with Highway 42. Turn east and drive 20 miles to Myrtle Point. Continue on Highway 42 to Powers Highway (Highway 242). Turn right (southwest) and drive 18 miles (the road becomes County Road 90) to Powers. Continue for 4.3 miles (the road becomes Forest Road 33). Turn south and drive to the camp. The road is paved all the way to the camp.

Contact: Rogue River-Siskiyou National Forest, Powers Ranger District, 541/439-6200 or 541/439-6217, www.fs.usda.gov/rogue-siskiyou.

109 DAPHNE GROVE

🏕 ♿ 🚐 ⛺

Scenic rating: 7

on the south fork of the Coquille River in Rogue River-Siskiyou National Forest

Map 1.4, page 78

This prime spot is far enough out of the way to attract little attention. At 1,000 feet elevation, it sits along the south fork of the Coquille River and is surrounded by old-growth cedar, Douglas fir, and maple. No fishing is allowed. The road is paved all the way to, and in, the campground, a plus for RVs and "city cars."

Campsites, facilities: There are 14 sites for tents or RVs up to 35 feet long. Picnic tables, garbage bins, and fire grills are provided. Drinking water and vault toilets are available. Some facilities are wheelchair accessible. Leashed pets are permitted.

Reservations, fees: Reservations are not accepted. Sites are $6 per night, $3 per night per additional vehicle. Open year-round.

Directions: From Coos Bay, drive south on U.S. 101 for six miles to the junction with Highway 42. Turn east and drive 20 miles to Myrtle Point. Continue on Highway 42 to Powers Highway (Highway 242). Turn right (southwest) and drive 18 miles (the road becomes County Road 90) to Powers. Continue for 4.3 miles (the road becomes Forest Road 33). Continue for 10.5 miles to the campground entrance.

Contact: Rogue River-Siskiyou National Forest, Powers Ranger District, 541/439-6200, www.fs.usda.gov/rogue-siskiyou.

110 ISLAND

Scenic rating: 7

near Coquille River Falls

Map 1.4, page 78

Island Camp is an excellent base camp for hikers with many trailheads nearby. It is located along the south fork of the Coquille River at 1,000-foot elevation in Rogue River-Siskiyou National Forest. Nearby hiking opportunities include the Azalea Lake Trail, Panther Ridge Trail, Coquille River Falls Trail, and Sucker Creek Trail. Note: Do not confuse this Island Campground with the Island Campground in Umpqua National Forest.

Campsites, facilities: There are five sites for tents or RVs to 16 feet. Picnic tables and fire rings are provided. Vault toilets and garbage bins are available, but there is no drinking water. Leashed pets are permitted.

Reservations, fees: Reservations are not

accepted. Sites are $6 per night. Open year-round, with limited winter services.

Directions: From Coos Bay, drive south on U.S. 101 for six miles to the junction with Highway 42. Turn east and drive 20 miles to Myrtle Point. Continue on Highway 42 to Powers Highway (Highway 242). Turn right (southwest) and drive 18 miles (the road becomes County Road 90) to Powers. Drive south 17 miles on Forest Service Road 3300 to the campground.

Contact: Rogue River-Siskiyou National Forest, Powers Ranger District, 541/439-6200, www.fs.usda.gov/rogue-siskiyou.

111 SRU LAKE

Scenic rating: 8

on Sru Lake in Rogue River-Siskiyou National Forest

Map 1.4, page 78

Sru (pronounced "Shrew") campground is set along the shore of one-acre Sru Lake at 2,200 feet elevation in rich, old-growth forest. Sru is more of a pond than a lake, but it is stocked with trout in the spring. Get there early—the fish are generally gone by midsummer. The trailheads for the Panther Ridge Trail and Coquille River Falls Trail are a 10-minute drive from the campground. It's strongly advised that you obtain a U.S. Forest Service map detailing the backcountry roads and trails.

Campsites, facilities: There are six sites for tents or RVs up to 21 feet long. Picnic tables and fire rings are provided. Vault toilets are available. There is no drinking water, and garbage must be packed out. Leashed pets are permitted.

Reservations, fees: Reservations are not accepted. There is no fee for camping. Open year-round, weather permitting.

Directions: From Coos Bay, drive south on U.S. 101 for six miles to the junction with Highway 42. Turn east and drive 20 miles to Myrtle Point. Continue on Highway 42 to

Powers Highway (Highway 242). Turn right (southwest) and drive 18 miles (the road becomes County Road 90) to Powers. Continue for 4.3 miles (the road becomes Forest Road 33). Continue on Forest Road 33 for 15 miles to the South Fork Coquille River Bridge. Continue on Forest Road 33 for 0.5 mile to Forest Road 3347 (paved road). Turn right and drive one mile to the camp.

Contact: Rogue River-Siskiyou National Forest, Powers Ranger District, 541/439-6200, www.fs.usda.gov/rogue-siskiyou.

112 TUCKER FLAT

Scenic rating: 7

on the Rogue River

Map 1.4, page 78

Above the clear waters of Mule Creek, this campground borders the Wild Rogue Wilderness. Tucker Flat offers a trailhead into the Wild Rogue Wilderness and lots of evidence of historic mining. Mosquitoes can be a problem, and bears occasionally wander through. The historic Rogue River Ranch is just 0.25 mile away, and the museum and other buildings are open during the summer. The Rogue River Ranch is on the National Register of Historic Places. There are also scenic bridges along Mule Creek. Tucker Flat campground can also be reached by hiking the Rogue River Trail or by floating the Rogue River and hiking up past the Rogue River Ranch. Campers and hikers are advised to stop by the Medford BLM office for maps.

Campsites, facilities: There are six primitive tent sites. Picnic tables and fire grills are provided. Vault toilets and bear-proof trash cans are available. There is no drinking water. Some facilities are wheelchair accessible. Leashed pets are permitted.

Reservations, fees: Reservations are not accepted. There is no fee for camping. Open May-October, weather permitting.

Directions: From Grants Pass, drive one mile

north on I-5 to Exit 61. Take that exit and drive west on Merlin-Galice Access Road for 20 miles to the Grave Creek Bridge (the second bridge over the Rogue River). Cross the bridge and drive a short distance to BLM Road 34-8-1. Turn left and drive 16 miles to BLM Road 32-8-31. Turn left and drive seven miles to BLM Road 32-9-14.2. Turn left and drive 15 miles to the campground (around the bend from the Rogue River Ranch). RV travel is discouraged as the roads are curvy, one-lane, and a combination of paved and gravel.

Contact: Bureau of Land Management, Medford District, 541/618-2200, www.blm.gov.

113 ALMEDA PARK

Scenic rating: 6

on the Rogue River

Map 1.4, page 78

This rustic park, located along the Rogue River and featuring a grassy area, is popular for rafting and swimming. One of the main put-in points for floating the lower section of the river can be found right here. Fishing is also available. The Rogue River Trail is four miles west.

Campsites, facilities: There are 34 sites for tents or RVs of any length (no hookups) and two group sites for tents or RVs for up to 30 people. Some sites are pull-through. Picnic tables and fire pits are provided. Drinking water, vault toilets, garbage bins, a dump station, and a boat ramp are available. A seasonal camp host is on-site. Some facilities are wheelchair accessible. Leashed pets are permitted.

Reservations, fees: Reservations are accepted ($8 reservation fee) at reserveamerica. com. Sites are $20 per night, $5 per night per additional vehicle. The group sites are $40 per night for up to 12 people, and $3 per person per night for more than 12 people. Cash is the only payment method accepted. Open year-round.

Directions: From Grants Pass, drive north on I-5 for 3.5 miles to Exit 61 (Merlin-Galice Road). Take that exit and drive on

Merlin-Galice Road for 19 miles to the park on the right. The park is approximately 16 miles west of Merlin.

Contact: Josephine County Parks, 541/474-5285, www.co.josephine.or.us.

114 ROCK CREEK

Scenic rating: 6

near the south fork of the Coquille River in Rogue River-Siskiyou National Forest

Map 1.4, page 78

This little-known camp (elevation 1,400 feet) in a tree-shaded canyon is surrounded by old-growth forest and some reforested areas. It is set near Rock Creek, just upstream from its confluence with the south fork of the Coquille River. No fishing is allowed. For a good side trip, take the one-mile climb to Azalea Lake, a small, shallow lake where there are some hike-in campsites. In July, the azaleas are spectacular.

Campsites, facilities: There are seven sites for tents or RVs up to 16 feet long. Picnic tables and fire grills are provided. Vault toilets, garbage bins, and firewood are available. There is no drinking water, but river water may be filtered. Leashed pets are permitted.

Reservations, fees: Reservations are not accepted. Sites are $6 per night, $3 per night per additional vehicle. Open year-round, with limited winter facilities.

Directions: From Coos Bay, drive south on U.S. 101 for six miles to the junction with Highway 42. Turn east and drive 20 miles to Myrtle Point. Continue on Highway 42 to Powers Highway (Highway 242). Turn right (southwest) and drive 18 miles (the road becomes County Road 90) to Powers. Continue for 4.3 miles (the road becomes Forest Road 33). Continue on Forest Road 33 for 15 miles to the South Fork Coquille River Bridge. Continue on Forest Road 33 for 0.5 mile to Forest Road 3347 (paved road). Turn right and drive 0.5 mile to the camp.

Contact: Rogue River-Siskiyou National Forest, Powers Ranger District, 541/439-6200, www.fs.usda.gov/rogue-siskiyou.

115 FOSTER BAR

Scenic rating: 5

on the Rogue River in Rogue River-Siskiyou National Forest

Map 1.4, page 78

This camping area is set near the banks of the Rogue River. There's a take-out point for rafters. Hiking opportunities are good nearby, and you can also fish from the river bar. Agness RV Park provides a nearby camping alternative.

Campsites, facilities: There are eight sites for tents. Drinking water, flush toilets, garbage bins, and boat-launching facilities are available. A camp host is on-site. Leashed pets are permitted.

Reservations, fees: Reservations are not accepted. Sites are $5 per night, $3 per night per additional vehicle. Open year-round.

Directions: From Gold Beach on U.S. 101, turn east on County Road 595 and drive 35 miles (it becomes Forest Road 33) to the junction for Illahe and Foster Bar. Turn right on County Road 375 and drive five miles to the campground.

Contact: Rogue River-Siskiyou National Forest, Gold Beach Ranger District, 541/247-3600, www.fs.usda.gov/rogue-siskiyou.

116 HONEY BEAR CAMPGROUND & RV RESORT

Scenic rating: 10

near Gold Beach

Map 1.4, page 78   **BEST (**

This campground offers wooded sites with ocean views. The owners have built a huge, authentic chalet, which contains a German deli, recreation area, and a big dance floor. On summer nights, they hold dances with live music. A restaurant is available on-site with authentic German food. A fishing pond is stocked with trout.

Campsites, facilities: There are 20 sites for tents or RVs (no hookups) and 65 sites with full hookups for RVs of any length. Thirty are pull-through sites with full hookups and 15 have patios. Picnic tables and fire rings are provided. Restrooms with flush toilets and showers, drinking water, cable TV, Wi-Fi, dump station, firewood, recreation hall, restaurant and kitchen, convenience store, coin laundry, ice, and a playground are available. Some facilities are wheelchair accessible. Leashed pets are permitted.

Reservations, fees: Reservations are accepted at 800/822-4444. RV sites are $30-60 per night, tent sites are $25 per night, $4 per person per night for more than two people, and $3 per night per additional vehicle. Children under age 12 and pets are free. Monthly and winter rates available. Open year-round, weather permitting.

Directions: From Gold Beach, drive north on U.S. 101 for eight miles to Ophir Road near Milepost 321. Turn right and drive two miles to the campground on the right side of the road.

Contact: Honey Bear Campground & RV Resort, 541/247-2765, www.honeybearrv.com.

117 NESIKA BEACH RV PARK

Scenic rating: 7

near Gold Beach

Map 1.4, page 78

This RV park next to Nesika Beach is a good layover spot for U.S. 101 cruisers. An 18-hole golf course is close by. There are many long-term rentals here.

Campsites, facilities: There are six tent sites and 32 sites with full or partial hookups for RVs of any length; some sites are pull-through. Picnic tables are provided, and some tent sites

have fire rings. Drinking water, restrooms with flush toilets and showers, a dump station, convenience store, coin laundry, cable TV, propane, and ice are available. Leashed pets are permitted.

Reservations, fees: Reservations are accepted. RV sites are $30-35 per night, tent sites are $18 per night, $4 per person per night for more than two people. Weekly and monthly rates are available. Open year-round.

Directions: From Gold Beach, drive north on U.S. 101 for six miles to Nesika Road. Turn left and drive 0.75 mile west to the park on the right.

Contact: Nesika Beach RV Park, 541/247-6077, www.nbrvp.com.

118 INDIAN CREEK RESORT

Scenic rating: 7

on the Rogue River

Map 1.4, page 78

This campground is set along the Rogue River on the outskirts of the town of Gold Beach. A few sites have river views. Nearby recreation options include boat trips on the Rogue.

Campsites, facilities: There are 26 tent sites and 90 sites with full hookups for RVs of any length; some sites are pull-through. Picnic tables are provided, and each seven-site carousel has barbecues and sinks. Drinking water, restrooms with flush toilets and showers, cable TV, Wi-Fi, firewood, recreation hall, convenience store, sauna, café, coin laundry, ice, horseshoes and croquet, and a playground are available. Propane gas is within two miles. Boat docks, launching facilities, and rentals are nearby. Some facilities are wheelchair accessible. Leashed pets are permitted.

Reservations, fees: Reservations are accepted at 541/247-7704. RV sites are $25-40 per night, tent sites are $20-25 per night, $2 per person per night for more than two people. Weekly, monthly, and winter rates are available. Some credit cards are accepted. Open year-round, with limited winter facilities.

Directions: On U.S. 101, drive to the northern end of Gold Beach to Jerry's Flat Road (just south of the Patterson Bridge). Turn left (east) on Jerry's Flat Road and drive 0.5 mile to the resort.

Contact: Indian Creek Resort, 541/247-7704, www.indiancreekrv.com.

119 LUCKY LODGE RV PARK

Scenic rating: 6

on the Rogue River

Map 1.4, page 78

Lucky Lodge is a good layover spot for U.S. 101 travelers who want to get off the highway circuit. Set on the shore of the Rogue River, it offers opportunities for boating, fishing, and swimming. Most sites have a view of the river. Nearby recreation options include hiking trails. About two-thirds of the sites are occupied by monthly renters.

Campsites, facilities: There are 31 sites with full hookups for RVs of any length, three tent sites, and one cabin. Picnic tables are provided. Drinking water, restrooms with flush toilets and showers, propane gas, a recreation hall, and coin laundry are available. Boat docks and rentals are within eight miles. Some facilities are wheelchair accessible. Leashed pets are permitted.

Reservations, fees: Reservations are accepted online. RV sites are $25-35 per night, tent sites are $22 per night, $5 per person per night for more than two people, $1 per each additional vehicle. Open year-round.

Directions: From Gold Beach, drive north on U.S. 101 for four miles (on the north side of the Rogue River) to Rogue River Road. Turn right (east) and drive 3.5 miles to North Bank River Road. Turn right and drive 4.5 miles to the park on the right.

Contact: Lucky Lodge RV Park, 541/247-7618, www.luckylodgervpark.net.

120 KIMBALL CREEK BEND RV RESORT

Scenic rating: 6

on the Rogue River

Map 1.4, page 78

Kimball Creek campground on the scenic Rogue River is just far enough from the coast to provide quiet and its own distinct character. The resort offers guided fishing trips and sells tickets for jet boat tours. Nearby recreation options include an 18-hole golf course, hiking trails, and boating facilities. Note that about one-third of the sites are monthly rentals.

Campsites, facilities: There are 62 sites with full hookups for RVs of any length, 13 tent sites, one park-model cabin, and three motel rooms. Some sites are pull-through. Group camping is available. Picnic tables are provided and there are fire rings at some sites. Drinking water, restrooms with flush toilets and showers, Wi-Fi, cable TV, dump station, recreation hall with library, convenience store with fishing licenses, coin laundry, and ice are available. Boat docks are on-site, and launching facilities are nearby. Leashed pets are permitted.

Reservations, fees: Reservations are accepted at 888/814-0633. RV sites are $28.50-40.50 per night, tent sites are $25 per night, $3 per person per night for more than two people. Some credit cards are accepted. Open year-round.

Directions: From Gold Beach, drive north on U.S. 101 for one mile (on the north side of the Rogue River) to Rogue River Road. Turn right (east) and drive about eight miles to the resort on the right.

Contact: Kimball Creek Bend RV Resort, 541/247-7580, www.kimballcreek.com.

121 QUOSATANA

Scenic rating: 6

on the Rogue River in Rogue River-Siskiyou National Forest

Map 1.4, page 78

This campground is set along the banks of the Rogue River, upstream from the much smaller Lobster Creek Campground. The campground features a large, grassy area and a barrier-free trail around the campground. Ocean access is just a short drive away, and the quaint town of Gold Beach offers a decent side trip. Nearby Otter Point State Park (day-use only) has further recreation options. The Shrader Old-Growth Trail, Lower Rogue River Trail, and Myrtle Tree Trail provide nearby hiking opportunities. Quosatana makes a good base camp for a hiking or fishing trip.

Campsites, facilities: There are 43 sites for tents or RVs up to 32 feet long. Drinking water, fire grills, garbage bins, and picnic tables are provided. Flush toilets, dump station, fish-cleaning station, and a boat ramp are available. A camp host is on-site. Some facilities are wheelchair accessible. Leashed pets are permitted.

Reservations, fees: Reservations are not accepted. Sites are $15 per night, $3 per night per additional vehicle. Open year-round.

Directions: From Gold Beach on U.S. 101, turn east on County Road 595 and drive 14.5 miles (it becomes Forest Road 33) to the campground on the left.

Contact: Rogue River-Siskiyou National Forest, Gold Beach Ranger District, 541/247-3600, www.fs.usda.gov/rogue-siskiyou.

122 LOBSTER CREEK

Scenic rating: 6

on the Rogue River in Rogue River-Siskiyou National Forest

Map 1.4, page 78

This small campground on a river bar along the Rogue River is about a 15-minute drive from Gold Beach, and it makes a good base for a fishing or hiking trip. The area is heavily forested with myrtle and Douglas fir, and the Shrader Old-Growth Trail and Myrtle Tree Trail are nearby.

Campsites, facilities: There are seven sites for tents or RVs up to 26 feet long. Fire rings and picnic tables are provided. Drinking water, flush toilets, and garbage bins are available, as is a boat launch. A camp host is on-site. Leashed pets are permitted.

Reservations, fees: Reservations are not accepted. Sites are $10 per night, $3 per night per additional vehicle. Camping is also permitted on a gravel bar area for $5 per night. Open year-round, weather permitting.

Directions: From Gold Beach on U.S. 101, turn east on County Road 595 and drive 10 miles (it becomes Forest Road 33) to the campground on the left.

Contact: Rogue River-Siskiyou National Forest, Gold Beach Ranger District, 541/247-3600, www.fs.usda.gov/rogue-siskiyou.

123 SAM BROWN

Scenic rating: 4

near Grants Pass in Rogue River-Siskiyou National Forest

Map 1.4, page 78

This campground is located in an isolated area near Grants Pass along Briggs Creek in a valley of pine and Douglas fir. It is set at an elevation of 2,500 feet. Many sites lie in the shade of trees, and a creek runs along one side of the campground. Briggs Creek Trail, Dutchy Creek

Trail, and Taylor Creek Trail are nearby and are popular for hiking and horseback riding. An amphitheater is available for small group presentations. Although the campground was spared, the Biscuit Fire of 2002 did burn nearby areas.

Campsites, facilities: There are 27 sites for tents or RVs of any length at Sam Brown and seven equestrian tent sites with small corrals down the road at Sam Brown Horse Camp. Picnic tables and fire rings or grills are provided. Drinking water and vault toilets are available at the horse camp. A picnic shelter, solar shower, and an amphitheater are available. Some facilities are wheelchair accessible. Leashed pets are permitted.

Reservations, fees: Reservations are not accepted. Sites are $5 per night, $2 per night per additional vehicle. Open late May-mid-October, weather permitting.

Directions: From Grants Pass, drive north on I-5 for 3.5 miles to Exit 61 (Merlin-Galice Road). Take that exit and drive northwest for 12.5 miles to Forest Road 25. Turn left on Forest Road 25 and head southwest for 14 miles to the campground.

Contact: Rogue River-Siskiyou National Forest, Wild Rivers Ranger District, 541/471-6500, www.fs.usda.gov/rogue-siskiyou.

124 IRELAND'S OCEAN VIEW RV PARK

Scenic rating: 8

in Gold Beach

Map 1.4, page 78

This spot is situated on the beach in the quaint little town of Gold Beach, only one mile from the famous Rogue River. The park is very clean and features blacktop roads and grass beside each site. Recreation options include beachcombing, boating, and fishing. Great ocean views are possible from the observatory/lighthouse.

Campsites, facilities: There are 31 sites with full hookups (20-, 30-, and 50-amp) for RVs up to 40 feet long; some sites are pull-through. Picnic tables are provided. No open fires are allowed. Cable TV, restrooms with flush toilets and showers, coin laundry, and Wi-Fi are available. Some facilities are wheelchair accessible. Leashed pets are permitted.

Reservations, fees: Reservations are recommended. Sites are $32-40 per night. Weekly and monthly rates are available. Open year-round.

Directions: On U.S. 101, drive to the southern end of Gold Beach (U.S. 101 becomes Ellensburg Avenue). The park is located at 20272 Ellensburg Avenue, across from the U.S. Forest Service office.

Contact: Ireland's Ocean View RV Park, 541/247-0148, www.irelandsrvpark.com.

125 OCEANSIDE RV PARK

Scenic rating: 5

in Gold Beach

Map 1.4, page 78

Set 100 yards from the ocean, this park is close to beachcombing terrain, marked bike trails, and boating facilities. The park is also adjacent to the mouth of the Rogue River, in the Port of Gold Beach.

Campsites, facilities: There are 30 sites with full hookups, 50 sites with partial hookups, and 10 sites with no hookups for RVs up to 40 feet long; some sites are pull-through. There are also two yurts. Picnic tables and community fire rings are provided. Drinking water, restrooms with flush toilets and showers, coin laundry, Wi-Fi, cable TV, a convenience store, picnic area, and ice are available. Propane gas, a store, and a café are within two miles. Boat docks and launching facilities are nearby. Leashed pets are permitted.

Reservations, fees: Reservations are recommended. Sites are $31-35 per night, $1 per person per night for more than two people; yurts are $40 per night. Weekly, monthly, and winter rates are available. Some credit cards are accepted. Open year-round.

Directions: On U.S. 101, drive to central Gold Beach and the intersection with Moore Street. Turn west and drive two blocks to Airport Way. Turn right and drive three blocks to South Jetty Road. Turn left and look for the park on the left.

Contact: Oceanside RV Park, 541/247-2301, www.oceansidervl.com.

126 WHALESHEAD BEACH RESORT

Scenic rating: 7

near Brookings

Map 1.4, page 78

This resort, about 0.25 mile from the beach, is set in a forested area with a small stream nearby. Activities at and around the camp include ocean and river fishing, jet boat trips, whale-watching excursions, and a golf course (13 miles away). Each campsite has a deck, and many cabins have an ocean view. One unique feature, a tunnel connects the campground to a trail to the beach.

Campsites, facilities: There are 35 sites with full hookups for RVs up to 60 feet long and 50 cabins. Picnic tables are provided at some sites. Cable TV, restrooms with showers, coin laundry, limited groceries, ice, and propane gas are available. Wi-Fi is available at the office. A dump station is six miles away. Leashed pets are permitted.

Reservations, fees: Reservations are recommended. Sites are $40 per night, $10 per person per night for more than two people. Some credit cards are accepted. Open year-round.

Directions: From Brookings, drive seven miles north on U.S. 101 until you pass Harris Beach. Look for the resort on the right.

Contact: Whaleshead Beach Resort, 541/469-7446, www.whalesheadresort.com.

127 ALFRED A. LOEB STATE PARK

Scenic rating: 8

near the Chetco River

Map 1.4, page 78

This park is set in a canyon formed by the Chetco River. The campsites are set in a beautiful old myrtle grove. The 0.75-mile River View Trail follows the Chetco River to a redwood grove. Swimming, fishing, and rafting are popular activities. Nature programs and interpretive tours are available by request.

Campsites, facilities: There are 48 sites with partial hookups for tents or RVs up to 50 feet long and three log cabins. Picnic tables, drinking water, garbage bins, and fire grills are provided. Restrooms with flush toilets and showers and firewood are available. A camp host is on-site. Some facilities are wheelchair accessible. Leashed pets are permitted, but not in cabins.

Reservations, fees: Reservations are accepted for cabins only at 800/452-5687 or www.oregonstateparks.org ($8 reservation fee). Sites are $22 per night, $7 per night per additional vehicle; cabins are $40-50 per night. Some credit cards are accepted. Open year-round.

Directions: On U.S. 101, drive south to Brookings and County Road 784 (North Bank Chetco River Road). Turn northeast and drive eight miles northeast on North Bank Road to the park entrance on the right.

Contact: Alfred A. Loeb State Park, 541/469-2021 or 800/551-6949, www.oregonstateparks.org.

128 HARRIS BEACH STATE PARK

Scenic rating: 8

near Brookings

Map 1.4, page 78   **BEST (**

This park is prime with wildlife-watching opportunities. Not only is it home to Bird Island, a breeding site for the tufted puffin and other rare birds, but gray whales, harbor seals, and sea lions can be spotted here as well. Tidepooling is also popular. Sites are shaded and well-spaced with plenty of beach and nature trails leading from the campground. In the fall and winter, the nearby Chetco River attracts good runs of salmon and steelhead, respectively.

Campsites, facilities: There are 59 sites for tents or RVs up to 50 feet (no hookups), 80 sites with full or partial hookups for RVs up to 60 feet long, a hiker/biker camp, and six yurts. Picnic tables, garbage bins, and fire grills are provided. Drinking water, cable TV, Wi-Fi, restrooms with flush toilets and showers, a dump station, coin laundry, and firewood are available. A camp host is on-site. Some facilities are wheelchair accessible. Leashed pets are permitted in campsites.

Reservations, fees: Reservations are accepted at 800/452-5687 or www.oregonstateparks.org ($8 reservation fee). Sites are $28-30 per night, $5 per night per additional vehicle, $5 per night per person for hikers/bikers, $20 per night for group tent sites, and $43-53 per night for yurts. Some credit cards are accepted. Open year-round.

Directions: From Brookings, drive north on U.S. 101 for two miles to the park entrance on the left (west side of road).

Contact: Harris Beach State Park, 541/469-2021, www.oregonstateparks.org.

129 BEACHFRONT RV PARK

Scenic rating: 8

near Brookings

Map 1.4, page 78

Beachfront RV Park, located just this side of the Oregon/California border on the Pacific Ocean, makes a great layover spot. Oceanfront sites are available, and recreational activities include boating, fishing, and swimming. Beach access is available from the park. Plan your trip early, as sites usually book up for the entire summer season. Nearby Harris Beach State Park, with its beach access and hiking trails, makes a good side trip.

Campsites, facilities: There are 13 tent sites and 138 sites with full or partial hookups for RVs of any length; some sites are pull-through. Picnic tables and some fire pits are provided. Restrooms with showers, dump station, cable TV, Wi-Fi, public phone, coin laundry, restaurant, ice, and a marina with a boat ramp, boat dock, and snacks are available. Supplies are available nearby. Some facilities are wheelchair accessible. Leashed pets are permitted.

Reservations, fees: Reservations are accepted at 800/441-0856. Tent sites are $27 per night, RV sites are $32-51 per night, $2 per person per night for more than four people. Weekly rates are available. Some credit cards are accepted. Open year-round.

Directions: From Brookings, drive south on U.S. 101 for 2.5 miles to Benham Lane. Turn west on Benham Lane and drive 1.5 miles (it becomes Lower Harbor Road) to Boat Basin Road. Turn left and drive two blocks to the park on the right.

Contact: Beachfront RV Park, 541/469-5867 or 800/441-0856, www.beachfrontrvpark.com.

130 ATRIVERS EDGE RV RESORT

Scenic rating: 7

on the Chetco River

Map 1.4, page 78

This resort lies along the banks of the Chetco River, just upstream from Brookings Harbor. A favorite spot for anglers, it features salmon and steelhead trips on the Chetco in the fall and winter. Deep-sea trips for salmon or rockfish are available nearby in the summer. This resort looks like the Rhine Valley in Germany, a pretty canyon between the trees and the river. A golf course is nearby.

Campsites, facilities: There are 114 sites with full hookups for RVs of any length; some are pull-through. Group camping, eight cabins, a yurt, a hut, and a teepee are also available. Picnic tables are provided, and fire rings are at some sites. Restrooms with flush toilets and showers, Wi-Fi, cable TV, propane gas, dump station, recreation hall with kitchen, exercise equipment, coin laundry, and a recycling station are available. Some facilities are wheelchair accessible. Leashed pets are permitted in the campgrounds only.

Reservations, fees: Reservations are recommended at 541/469-3356. RV sites are $39-47 per night, $3 per person per night for more than two people. Cabins are $46-58 per night, yurts are $86 per night, the Hideaway Hut is $44 per night, and the teepee is $35 per night. Call for group rates. Some credit cards are accepted. Open year-round.

Directions: On U.S. 101, drive to the southern end of Brookings (harbor side) and to South Bank Chetco River Road (a cloverleaf exit). Turn east on South Bank Chetco River Road and drive 1.5 miles to the resort entrance on the left (a slanted left turn, through the pillars, well signed).

Contact: AtRivers Edge RV Resort, 541/469-3356, www.atriversedge.com.

131 SEA BIRD RV PARK

Scenic rating: 5

near Brookings

Map 1.4, page 78

Sea Bird is one of several parks in the area. Nearby recreation options include marked bike trails, a full-service marina, and tennis courts. A nice, neat park, it features paved roads and gravel/granite sites. There is also a beach for surfing near the park. In summer, most of the sites are reserved for the season. An 18-hole golf course is within 2.5 miles.

Campsites, facilities: There are 60 sites with full or partial hookups for RVs of any length; some are pull-through sites. Picnic tables are provided. No open fires are allowed. Restrooms

with flush toilets and showers, dump station, cable TV, high-speed modem access, recreation hall, and a coin laundry are available. Boat docks, launching facilities, and rentals are nearby. Some facilities are wheelchair accessible. Leashed pets are permitted.

Reservations, fees: Reservations are recommended. Sites are $32 per night, $4 per person per night for more than two people, $20 per night for additional vehicle or boat not fitting in the space. Weekly and monthly rates are available. Open year-round.

Directions: In Brookings, drive south on U.S. 101 to the Chetco River Bridge. Continue 0.25 mile south on U.S. 101 to the park entrance on the left.

Contact: Sea Bird RV Park, 541/469-3512, www.seabirdrv.com.

132 LUDLUM

Scenic rating: 5

near Brookings in Rogue River-Siskiyou National Forest

Map 1.4, page 78

This small campground is a local favorite, with fine fishing and a great swimming hole in Wheeler Creek. The well-spaced sites offer a nice sense of seclusion. There is an old-fashioned hand pump, and if you put in the work you'll be rewarded with some of the best water you've ever tasted. The Oregon Redwoods hiking trail is located about one mile off U.S. 101 and eight miles south of the campground on Winchuck River Road. The trail has beautiful old-growth redwoods and is worth the trip.

Campsites, facilities: There are seven sites for tents or RVs up to 30 feet. Picnic tables and fire rings are provided. Hand-pumped drinking water and vault toilets are available. Also available for rent is Ludlum House (March-November), a renovated 1930s two-story house; there are no beds or electricity, but there is a food prep area, a sink, and a woodstove. Bring your own firewood.

Reservations, fees: Reservations are accepted for Ludlum House at 877/444-6777 ($10 reservation fee) or www.recreation.gov ($9 reservation fee). Sites are $10 per night, $3 for each additional vehicle. Ludlum House is $60 per night for up to 10 people, $5 for each additional person. Open mid-May-early December, weather permitting.

Directions: From Brookings, take U.S. 101 south to Winchuck River Road. Drive 11 miles then take the right fork to Forest Service Road 1108 (a gravel road) and continue 1.5 miles to campground.

Contact: Rogue River-Siskiyou National Forest, Gold Beach Ranger District, 541/247-3600, www.fs.usda.gov/rogue-siskiyou.

PORTLAND AND THE WILLAMETTE VALLEY

© DAVIDGN / DREAMSTIME.COM

Portland is an excellent recreation hub, with the Columbia River corridor and Mount Hood to the east, and Eugene and the McKenzie and Willamette Rivers to the south. In between lies Silver Falls State Park, Oregon's largest state park, with a seven-mile hike past 10 awesome waterfalls, some falling more than 100 feet from their brinks. The Willamette Valley stretches from Portland to Cottage Grove and provides a great jumping-off point to adventure. Lakes are plentiful, including Cottage Grove Reservoir, Dorena Lake, Fall Creek Reservoir, and Green Peter Reservoir on the Santiam River. Slow two-lane highways border the streams and provide routes to the coast that can be used to create a loop trip, with many hidden campgrounds to choose from while en route.

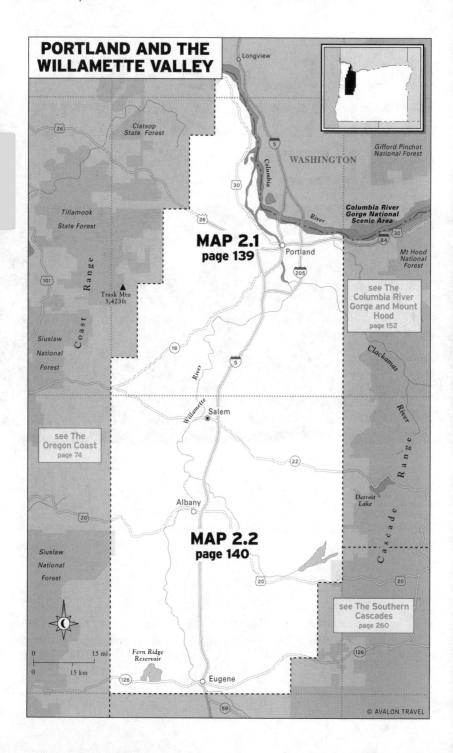

PORTLAND AND THE WILLAMETTE VALLEY

Longview

WASHINGTON

Clatsop State Forest

Gifford Pinchot National Forest

Tillamook State Forest

Columbia River

Columbia River Gorge National Scenic Area

Mt Hood National Forest

MAP 2.1
page 139

Portland

Coast Range

Trask Mtn 3,423ft

Siuslaw National Forest

see The Columbia River Gorge and Mount Hood
page 152

Clackamas River

Willamette River

Salem

see The Oregon Coast
page 74

Cascade Range

Albany

Detroit Lake

MAP 2.2
page 140

Siuslaw National Forest

see The Southern Cascades
page 260

Fern Ridge Reservoir

0   15 mi
0   15 km

Eugene

© AVALON TRAVEL

Map **2.1**

Sites 1-6
Pages 141-143

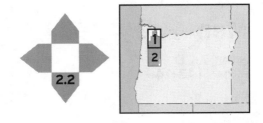

2.2

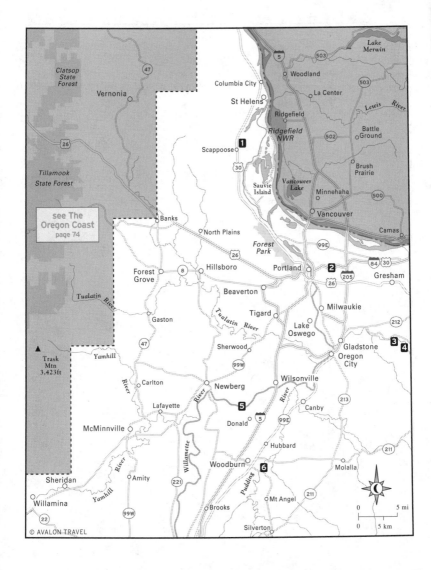

Map 2.2

Sites 7-20
Pages 143-149

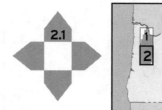

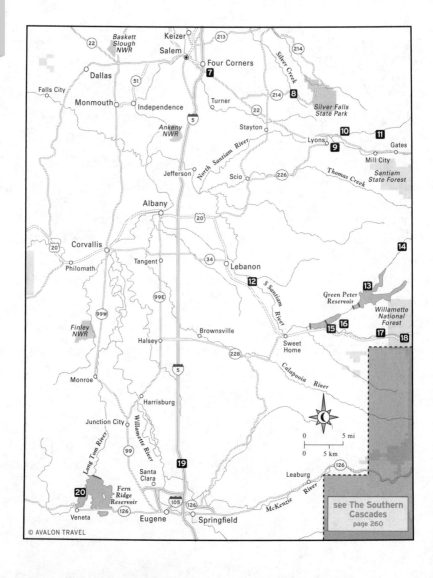

© AVALON TRAVEL

1 SCAPPOOSE RV PARK

Scenic rating: 6

in Scappoose

Map 2.1, page 139

This county-operated RV park neighbors the rural Scappoose airport, making it a convenient spot for private pilots. The sites are partially shaded with maple, oak, and spruce trees. Set on the edge of a dike, it is less than a mile from the Columbia River and about a 30-minute drive from Portland.

Campsites, facilities: There are four tent sites in dispersed areas and seven sites for RVs up to 41 feet long, six with full (30 amp) hookups. Picnic tables and fire grills are provided. Drinking water, a restroom with flush toilets and showers, a dump station, a playground, and horseshoe pits are available. Some facilities are wheelchair accessible. Leashed pets are permitted.

Reservations, fees: Reservations are accepted online or by phone at 503/366-3984. RV sites are $18-22 per night, tent sites are $7 per night, $7 per night for an additional vehicle. Open year-round.

Directions: From Portland, turn west on U.S. 30 and drive to Scappoose. Continue one mile north on U.S. 30 to West Lane Road. Turn right (east) and drive 0.75 mile to Honeyman Road. Turn left and drive one block to the park on the right.

Contact: Columbia County, Parks and Recreation, 503/397-2353, www.co.columbia. or.us; Scappoose RV Park, 503/543-3225.

2 PORTLAND FAIRVIEW RV PARK

Scenic rating: 7

east of Portland

Map 2.1, page 139

This is a massive yet pretty RV park located eight miles east of downtown Portland. The setting is peaceful, with the entire park landscaped, edged by tall conifers. A small brook runs nearby. Many I-5 ramblers have a chance to unwind for a spell here.

Campsites, facilities: There are 407 sites with full hookups (50 amps) for RVs of any length; most sites are pull-through. Picnic tables are provided. Drinking water and restrooms with flush toilets and showers, a barbecue and picnic area, horseshoe pits, seasonal swimming pool, basketball, recreation and fitness centers, Wi-Fi, satellite TV, coin laundry, and parking for boats and tow vehicles are available. Some facilities are wheelchair accessible. Leashed pets are permitted, with some breed restrictions.

Reservations, fees: Reservations are accepted online. Sites are $63.50 per night. Monthly and group rates available. Open year-round.

Directions: From I-84/Highway 30 in Portland, take Exit 14 and turn north on NE 207th Avenue. Drive on NE 207th Avenue to NE Sandy Boulevard. Turn right on NE Sandy Boulevard and drive a short distance to the park.

Contact: Portland Fairview RV Park, 877/777-1047, www.rvonthego.com; Encore RV Resorts, Thousand Trails, 877/570-2267.

3 BARTON PARK

Scenic rating: 6

near the Clackamas River

Map 2.1, page 139

Getting here may seem a bit of a maze, but the trip is well worth it. This camp is set on the Clackamas River and is surrounded by woods and tall trees. The river can provide good salmon and steelhead fishing.

Campsites, facilities: There are 98 sites for tents or RVs up to 40 feet; sites have partial hookups, and some sites are pull-through. Picnic tables and fire rings are provided. Restrooms with flush toilets and showers, a dump station, picnic area, and firewood are available. Recreational facilities include horseshoe pits, a playground, volleyball court, softball field, and boat ramp. Supplies are available within one mile. A camp host is on-site. Some facilities are wheelchair accessible. Leashed pets are permitted. Gates are locked 10pm-6am daily.

Reservations, fees: Reservations are recommended ($8 reservation fee). Sites are $26 per night, $5 per night per additional vehicle. Some credit cards are accepted. Open May-September; Barton East is open through October 31.

Directions: From Portland, drive south on I-5 to I-205. Turn east and drive about 20 miles to Exit 12, the Clackamas/Estacada exit (Highway 212). Turn east on Highway 212/224 and drive 3.2 miles to the Carver exit/Rock Creek junction. Turn right on Highway 224 and drive about 6.5 miles to the town of Barton and Baker's Ferry Road. Turn right and drive 0.2 mile to Barton Park Road. Turn left and drive to the park on the left.

Contact: Clackamas County Parks Department, 503/742-4414, www.clackamas.us; Park Ranger, 503/637-3015.

4 METZLER PARK

Scenic rating: 8

on Clear Creek

Map 2.1, page 139

This county campground on a small stream not far from the Clackamas River is a hot spot for fishing, picnicking, and swimming. Be sure to make your reservation early at this very popular park.

Campsites, facilities: There are 112 sites; 103 sites have water and electrical hookups, while 9 primitive sites are for tents or RVs up to 40 feet long. There is one group site for tents only and one bunkhouse. Picnic tables and fire pits are provided. Restrooms with flush toilets and showers, a dump station, playground, picnic areas, firewood, and a recreation field with baseball, basketball, and volleyball are

available. Propane and ice are within five miles. Some facilities are wheelchair accessible. Leashed pets are permitted. Gates are locked 10pm-6am daily.

Reservations, fees: Reservations are recommended ($8 reservation fee). Sites with hookups are $26 per night, tent sites are $21 per night, the group site is $60 per night, and the bunk house is $30 per night; $5 per night per additional vehicle. Some credit cards are accepted. Open May-September.

Directions: From Portland, drive south on I-5 to I-205. Turn east and drive about 20 miles to Exit 12, the Clackamas/Estacada exit (Highway 212). Turn east on Highway 212/224 and drive 3.2 miles to the Carver exit/Rock Creek junction. Turn right on Highway 224 and drive approximately 15 miles to Estacada and Highway 211. Turn right, crossing a bridge, and drive four miles to Tucker Road. Turn right and drive 0.5 mile to Metzler Park Road. Turn left and drive 1.6 miles to the park entrance.

Contact: Clackamas County Parks Department, 503/742-4414, www.clackamas.us; Park Ranger, 503/630-4743.

5 CHAMPOEG STATE HERITAGE AREA

Scenic rating: 7

on the Willamette River

Map 2.1, page 139

Champoeg State Heritage Area lies on the south bank of the Willamette River and features an interpretive center, a botanical garden with native plants, and hiking and bike trails. A junior ranger program is available during the summer. The log cabin museum, the historic Newell House, and the visitors center are also worth a tour. Some of the best sturgeon fishing in North America is on the Willamette River below Oregon City Falls (also called Willamette Falls). I caught my biggest fish here in 2009, a nine-foot sturgeon that weighed 400 pounds.

The best fishing guide to the area is Charlie Foster.

Campsites, facilities: There are 67 sites with partial hookups (water and electricity) for tents or RVs of any length and 8 sites with full hookups. There are also three group tent areas that accommodate a maximum of 25 people each, six walk-in sites, six cabins, six yurts, a hiker/biker camp, and a 10-site tent and RV group area with electric hookups only. Picnic tables and fire grills are provided. Restrooms with flush toilets and showers, drinking water, garbage bins, a dump station, meeting hall, picnic area, off-leash dog park, disc golf, ice, and firewood are available. Boat docking facilities are nearby. Some facilities are wheelchair accessible. Leashed pets are permitted.

Reservations, fees: Reservations are accepted at 800/452-5687 or www.oregonstateparks.org ($8 reservation fee). RV sites are $26-29 per night, tent sites are $19 per night, $5 per person per night for hiker/biker sites, the group tent camps are $71 per night, the group RV/tent camp is $102 per night, $10 per RV after the first 10 units; yurts and cabins are $41-51 per night, $5 per night per additional vehicle. Some credit cards are accepted. Open year-round.

Directions: From Portland, drive south on I-5 to Exit 278, the Donald/Aurora exit. Take that exit and turn right (west) on Ehlen Road and drive three miles to Case Road. Turn right (north) and drive 4.5 miles (the road becomes Champoeg Road) to the park on the right.

Contact: Champoeg State Heritage Area, 503/678-1251 or 800/551-6949, www.oregonstateparks.org; Charlie Foster's NW Sturgeon Adventures, 503/820-1189, www.nwsturgeonadventures.com.

6 FEYRER PARK

Scenic rating: 5

on the Molalla River

Map 2.1, page 139

On the scenic Molalla River, this county park offers swimming and excellent salmon fishing. A superb option for weary I-5 cruisers, the park is only 30 minutes off the highway and provides a peaceful, serene environment.

Campsites, facilities: There are 20 sites with partial hookups for tents or RVs up to 40 feet long. Picnic tables and fire rings are provided. Drinking water, restrooms with showers, a dump station, and picnic areas are available. There are also a playground, horseshoe pits, volleyball, and softball. A boat ramp is nearby. Supplies are available within three miles. Some facilities are wheelchair accessible. Leashed pets are permitted.

Reservations, fees: Reservations are recommended ($8 reservation fee). Sites are $26 per night, $5 per night per additional vehicle. Some credit cards are accepted. Open May-September.

Directions: From Portland, drive south on I-5 to Woodburn. Take Exit 271 and drive east on Highway 214; continue (the road changes to Highway 211 at the crossing with Highway 99E) to Molalla and Mathias Road. Turn right and drive 0.25 mile to Feyrer Park Road. Turn right and drive three miles to the park on the left.

Contact: Clackamas County Parks Department, 503/742-4414, www.clackamas.us; park ranger, 503/829-6621.

7 SALEM CAMPGROUND & RVS

Scenic rating: 5

in Salem

Map 2.2, page 140

This park with shaded sites is located next to I-5 in Salem; expect to hear traffic noise. A picnic area and a lake for swimming are within walking distance, and a nine-hole golf course and hiking trails are nearby. This is a good overnight campground, but not a destination place.

Campsites, facilities: There are 195 sites with full hookups (20, 30, and 50 amps) for RVs of any length; 90 sites are pull-through. There are also 25 tent sites. Picnic tables are provided, and barbecues are available upon request. Group facilities are available. Restrooms with flush toilets and showers, propane, a dump station, a game room, convenience store, coin laundry, ice, a playground, cable TV, Wi-Fi, and drinking water are available. A café is within one mile. Some facilities are wheelchair accessible. Leashed pets are permitted; no pit bulls or rottweilers are allowed.

Reservations, fees: Reservations are accepted at 800/826-9605. Sites are $30-36 per night, $5 per person per night for more than two people. Weekly, monthly, and group rates are available. Some credit cards are accepted. Open year-round.

Directions: From Salem on I-5, take Exit 253 to Highway 22. Turn east and drive 0.25 mile to Lancaster Drive. Turn right on Lancaster Drive and continue 0.1 mile to Hagers Grove Road. Turn right on Hagers Grove Road and drive a short distance to the campground at the end of the road.

Contact: Salem Campground & RVs, 503/581-6736 or 800/826-9605, www.salemrv.com.

8 SILVER FALLS STATE PARK

Scenic rating: 8

near Salem

Map 2.2, page 140

Oregon's largest state park, Silver Falls covers more than 8,700 acres. Numerous trails crisscross the area, one of which is a seven-mile jaunt that meanders past 10 majestic waterfalls (some more than 100 feet high) in the rainforest of Silver Creek Canyon. Four of these falls have an amphitheater-like surrounding where you can walk behind the falls and feel the misty spray. A horse camp and a 14-mile equestrian trail are available in the park. Fitness-conscious campers can check out the three-mile jogging trail or the four-mile bike trail. There are also a rustic nature lodge and group lodging facilities. Pets are not allowed on the Canyon Trail.

Campsites, facilities: There are 45 sites for tents or self-contained RVs (no hookups), 52 sites with partial hookups for tents or RVs up to 60 feet long, two group tent sites for up to 50-75 people each, two group RV areas, five horse sites, a group horse camp, and 14 cabins. Picnic tables and fire grills are provided. Drinking water, garbage bins, restrooms with flush toilets and showers, a dump station, an amphitheater, firewood, ice, and a playground are available. Some facilities are wheelchair accessible. Leashed pets are permitted in the campground.

Reservations, fees: Reservations are accepted at 800/452-5687 or www. reserveamerica.com ($8 reservation fee). RV sites are $26 per night, tent sites are $19 per night, $5 per night for an additional vehicle. The group tent site is $71 per night; the group RV sites are $102 per night for the first 10 units and then $10 per additional unit. Horse campsites are $19-58 per night. Cabins are $41-51 per night. Some credit cards are accepted. RV sites are open year-round, tent sites April-October.

Directions: From Salem on I-5, take Exit 253 to Highway 22. Turn east and drive five miles to Highway 214. Turn left (east) and drive 15 miles to the park.

Contact: Silver Falls State Park, 503/873-8681, 503/873-4395, or 800/551-6949, 503/873-3890 (trail rides), www.oregonstateparks.org.

9 JOHN NEAL MEMORIAL PARK

Scenic rating: 6

on the North Santiam River

Map 2.2, page 140

This camp is set on the banks of the North Santiam River, offering good boating and trout fishing possibilities. The park covers about 27 acres, and there are hiking trails. Other recreation options include exploring lakes and trails in the adjacent national forest land or visiting Silver Falls State Park.

Campsites, facilities: There are 23 sites for tents or self-contained RVs up to 30 feet long, and a group site for up to 100 people (12 RVs). Picnic tables and fire pits are provided. Restrooms with flush toilets and showers, garbage bins, and drinking water are available. Recreational facilities include a boat ramp, playground, horseshoe pits, picnic areas, and a recreation field. Ice and a grocery store are within one mile. Some facilities are wheelchair accessible. Leashed pets are permitted.

Reservations, fees: Reservations are recommended ($12 reservation fee). Sites are $24 per night, $7 per night per additional vehicle, and $200 per night for group sites ($50 reservation fee). Senior discounts available. Some credit cards are accepted for reservations. Open mid-April-mid-September, weather permitting.

Directions: From Salem, drive east on Highway 22 for about 20 miles to Highway 226. Turn right and drive south for two miles to Lyons and John Neal Park Road. Turn left (east) and drive a short distance to the campground on the left.

Contact: Linn County Parks Department, 541/967-3917, www.linnparks.com.

10 FISHERMEN'S BEND
🚶 🚲 🎣 ⛴ 🐴 👪 ♿ 🚐 ⛰

Scenic rating: 7
on the North Santiam River

Map 2.2, page 140

Fishermen's Bend is a popular spot for anglers of all ages, and the sites are spacious. The campground was renovated in 2005. A barrier-free fishing and river viewing area and a network of trails provide access to more than a mile of river. There's a one-mile, self-guided nature trail, and the nature center has a variety of displays. The amphitheater has films and activities on weekends. The front gate closes at 10pm.

Campsites, facilities: There are 54 sites with full or partial hookups for tents and RVs up to 38 feet long; some sites are pull-through. There

are also three group sites (for up to 60 people each) and two cabins. Picnic tables and fire pits are provided. Drinking water, restrooms with flush toilets and showers, a dump station, and garbage containers are available. A boat ramp, fishing pier, day-use area with playgrounds, baseball fields, volleyball and basketball courts, horseshoe pits, firewood, and a picnic shelter are also available. Some facilities are wheelchair accessible. Leashed pets are permitted.

Reservations, fees: Reservations are accepted for some campsites, the cabins, and the group sites at 888/444-6777 or www.recreation.gov ($10 reservation fee). Sites are $16-28 per night, $5 per night per each additional vehicle. Group sites are $85-105 per night. Cabins are $40 per night. Open May-October.

Directions: From Salem on I-5, take Exit 253 to Highway 22. Turn east and drive 30 miles to the campground on the right.

Contact: Bureau of Land Management, Salem District Office, 503/897-2406, www.blm.gov.

11 ELKHORN VALLEY
🚶 🏊 🎣 🐴 🚐 ⛰

Scenic rating: 7
on the Little North Santiam River

Map 2.2, page 140

This pretty campground along the Little North Santiam River, not far from the north fork of the Santiam River, has easy access and on-site hosts and is only a short drive away from a major metropolitan area. Swimming is good here during the summer, and the campground is popular with families. The front gate is locked 10pm-7am daily. This site offers an alternative to Shady Cove, which is about 10 miles to the east.

Campsites, facilities: There are 23 sites for tents or RVs up to 24 feet long. Picnic tables and fire grills are provided. Vault toilets, garbage service, and drinking water are available. Some facilities are wheelchair accessible. Leashed pets are permitted.

Reservations, fees: Reservations are not

accepted. Sites are $14 per night, $5 per night per additional vehicle. There is a 14-day stay limit. Open late May-early September.

Directions: From Salem on I-5, take Exit 253 to Highway 22. Turn east and drive 25 miles to Elkhorn Road (Little North Fork Road). Turn left (northeast) and drive nine miles to the campground on the left.

Contact: Bureau of Land Management, Salem District Office, 503/897-2406, www.blm.gov.

12 WATERLOO COUNTY PARK

Scenic rating: 8

on the South Santiam River

Map 2.2, page 140

This campground features more than a mile of South Santiam River frontage. Field sports, fishing, picnicking, and swimming are options here. Small boats with trolling motors are the only boats allowed here. A golf course is within five miles.

Campsites, facilities: There are 120 sites for tents or RVs of any length; most have partial hookups. Fire pits and picnic tables are provided. Drinking water, restrooms with flush toilets and showers, a dump station, boat ramps, two playgrounds, day-use area, off-leash dog park, and picnic shelters are available. Some facilities are wheelchair accessible. Leashed pets are permitted.

Reservations, fees: Reservations are accepted at 541/967-3917 or www.linnparks.com ($12 reservation fee). Sites are $24-29 per night, $7 per night for an additional vehicle. Senior discounts available. Some credit cards are accepted for reservations. Open year-round.

Directions: From Albany, drive east on U.S. 20 for about 20 miles through Lebanon to the Waterloo exit. Turn left (north) at the Waterloo exit and drive approximately two miles to the camp on the right. The camp is on the south side of the South Santiam River, five miles east of Lebanon.

Contact: Linn County Parks Department, 541/967-3917, www.linnparks.com.

13 WHITCOMB CREEK COUNTY PARK

Scenic rating: 8

on Green Peter Reservoir

Map 2.2, page 140

This camp, located on the north shore of Green Peter Reservoir, is in a wooded area with lots of ferns, which gives it a rainforest feel. Anglers appreciate that Oregon Department of Fish and Wildlife stocks trout here. Other recreation options include hiking, picnicking, sailing, swimming, and waterskiing. Two boat ramps are on the reservoir about a mile from camp.

Campsites, facilities: There are 39 sites for tents or RVs up to 30 feet long (no hookups) and one group tent and RV area for up to 100 people. Picnic tables and fire pits are provided. Drinking water is available to haul; vault toilets, garbage bins, and a boat ramp are also available. Supplies are within 15 miles. Some facilities are wheelchair accessible. Leashed pets are permitted.

Reservations, fees: Reservations are accepted at 541/967-3917 or www.linnparks.com ($12 reservation fee). Sites are $22 per night, $7 per night per additional vehicle; the group site is $250 per night, plus a $50 reservation fee. Senior discounts available. Some credit cards are accepted. Open mid-April-mid-September.

Directions: From Albany, drive east on U.S. 20 for about 35 miles (through Lebanon and Sweet Home) to the Quartzville Road exit (near Foster Reservoir). Turn left (north) on Quartzville Road and drive 15 miles to the park.

Contact: Linn County Parks Department, 541/967-3917, www.linnparks.com.

14 YELLOWBOTTOM

Scenic rating: 7

on Quartzville Creek

Map 2.2, page 140

Out-of-town visitors always miss this campground across the road from Quartzville Creek. It's nestled under a canopy of old-growth forest. The Rhododendron Trail, which is just under a mile, provides a challenging hike through forest and patches of rhododendrons. Some folks pan for gold here, and swimming is popular in the creek. Though primitive, the camp is ideal for a quiet getaway weekend.

Campsites, facilities: There are 22 sites for tents or RVs up to 28 feet long, including some pull-through sites. Picnic tables, garbage bins, and fire grills are provided. Drinking water, vault toilets, and firewood are available. A camp host is on-site seasonally. Some facilities are wheelchair accessible. Leashed pets are permitted.

Reservations, fees: Reservations are not accepted. Sites are $12 per night, with a 14-day stay limit, $5 per night for an additional vehicle. Open mid-June–early September.

Directions: From Albany, drive east on U.S. 20 for about 35 miles (through Sweet Home) to Quartzville Road. Turn left (northeast) on Quartzville Road and drive 24 miles to the campground on the left.

Contact: Bureau of Land Management, Salem District, 503/897-2406 or 503/375-5646, www.blm.gov.

15 RIVER BEND COUNTY PARK

Scenic rating: 8

on the South Santiam River

Map 2.2, page 140

When River Bend opened in 2005, it was an instant hit. The park has plenty of hiking trails, the river current is calm in summer, and there are swimming beaches. The campground is in a woodsy setting of firs and ferns. Additional water activities include fishing and inner tubing, a favorite. A golf course is within 15 miles.

Campsites, facilities: There are 10 sites for tents and self-contained RVs (no hookups), 74 sites with partial hookups for tents and RVs of any length, a group camp for up to 50 people, and five cabins. Picnic tables and fire rings are provided. Drinking water, restrooms with flush toilets and showers, a dump station, picnic area, athletic field, interpretive display, fishing area, and swimming and tubing area are available. An enclosed group shelter is also available. Some facilities are wheelchair accessible. Leashed pets are permitted.

Reservations, fees: Reservations are accepted at 541/967-3917 or www.linnparks.com ($12 reservation fee). Sites are $25-31 per night, $7 per night per additional vehicle, $65 per cabin per night. Senior discounts available. Some credit cards are accepted for reservations. Open year-round, with limited winter services.

Directions: From Albany, drive east on U.S. 20 to Sweet Home. Continue east on U.S. 20 for five miles to the park on the left.

Contact: Linn County Parks Department, 541/967-3917, www.linnparks.com.

16 SUNNYSIDE COUNTY PARK

Scenic rating: 8

on Foster Reservoir

Map 2.2, page 140

Sunnyside is Linn County's most popular park. Recreation options at this 98-acre park include boating, fishing, swimming, and waterskiing. A golf course is within 15 miles.

Campsites, facilities: There are 165 sites for tents or RVs of any length; most sites have partial hookups. There are also three group sites for up to 80 people each. Picnic tables and fire rings are provided; there is also a community fire ring. Drinking water, restrooms with flush toilets and showers, a dump station, playground, dog park, stocked fishing ponds, fish-cleaning station, picnic shelter (available by reservation), volleyball courts, firewood, a boat ramp, and moorage are available. Supplies are available within three miles. Some facilities are wheelchair accessible. Leashed pets are permitted.

Reservations, fees: Reservations are accepted at 541/967-3917 or www.linnparks.com ($12 reservation fee, $50 reservation fee for group site). Individual sites are $30-72 per night, $7 per night for an additional vehicle; group sites are $208 per night (reserve by phone). Senior discounts available. Open mid-March-early November.

Directions: From Albany, drive east on U.S. 20 for about 35 miles (through Lebanon and Sweet Home) to the Quartzville Road exit (near Foster Reservoir). Turn left (north) on Quartzville Road and drive one mile to the campground on the right. The camp is on the south side of Foster Reservoir.

Contact: Linn County Parks Department, 541/967-3917, www.linnparks.com.

17 CASCADIA STATE PARK

Scenic rating: 7

on the Santiam River

Map 2.2, page 140

Cascadia State Park is set along the banks of the Santiam River. The highlight of this 258-acre park is Soda Creek Falls, with a fun 0.75-mile hike to reach it. Another riverside trail leads through groves of Douglas fir and provides good fishing access. This is a choice spot for a less crowded getaway, and also for reunions and meetings for families, Boy Scouts, and other groups.

Campsites, facilities: There are 25 primitive sites for tents or self-contained RVs up to 35 feet long, and two group tent areas for up to 100 people each. Picnic tables, garbage bins, and fire grills are provided. Drinking water, flush and vault toilets, and firewood are available. A camp host is on-site. Some facilities are wheelchair accessible. Leashed pets are permitted.

Reservations, fees: Reservations are accepted for group tent areas only at 800/452-5687 or www.reserveamerica.com ($8 reservation fee). Tent sites are $17 per night, $5 per night for an additional vehicle. Hiker/biker sites are $5 per night. Group tent sites are $71 per night for up to 25 people and $3 per night for each additional person. Some credit cards are accepted. Open May-September, weather permitting.

Directions: From Albany, drive east on U.S. 20 for 40 miles to the park on the left (14 miles east of the town of Sweet Home).

Contact: Cascadia State Park, 541/367-6021 or 800/551-6949, www.oregonstateparks.org.

18 LONG BOW GROUP

Scenic rating: 10

on the South Santiam River

Map 2.2, page 140   **BEST (**

Long Bow campground is located at 1,200 feet in elevation on the South Santiam River. It's a pretty spot with fishing, hiking, and swimming options and a natural amphitheater on-site.

Note: No tents or trailers are allowed at the campground. Instead, your group will camp at one of six shelters that can hold a combined total of 48 people. The reservation fee covers all six shelters.

Campsites, facilities: There are six sites with shelters for up to 48 people. Picnic tables and fire grills are provided. Drinking water, vault toilets, and a sheltered cooking and dining area are available. Leashed pets are permitted.

Reservations, fees: Reservations are accepted at 877/444-6777 or www.recreation.gov ($9-10 reservation fee). Sites are $125 per night. Open May-September, weather permitting.

Directions: From Albany, drive east on U.S. 20 for 43 miles (17 miles past Sweet Home) to Forest Road 2032. Turn right and drive 0.5 mile to the camp on the left.

Contact: Willamette National Forest, Sweet Home Ranger District, 541/367-5168, www. fs.usda.gov/willamette.

19 ARMITAGE PARK

Scenic rating: 7

north of Eugene

Map 2.2, page 140

This 57-acre county park sits on the banks of the McKenzie River outside Eugene. Hiking opportunities include the 0.5-mile Crilly Nature Trail through deciduous forest common around this river. Over the years, my brother Rambob, cousins Andy and Neil, and I have caught a lot of trout on the McKenzie in this area. Hopefully you will too.

Campsites, facilities: There are 32 sites for tents or RVs and two group sites for up to 16-20 people each. Some sites are pull-through. Picnic tables and fire rings are provided. Drinking water and restrooms with flush toilets are available. A boat ramp, volleyball courts, horseshoe pits, Wi-Fi, and a two-acre dog park are available. Some facilities are wheelchair accessible. Leashed pets are permitted.

Reservations, fees: Reservations are accepted ($10 reservation fee) at 541/682-2000 or http://reservations.lanecounty.org. RV sites are $40-43 per night, tent sites are $30 per night, group sites are $85 per night, $7 for each additional vehicle. Open year-round.

Directions: From Portland, take I-5 to the Eugene area. Take Exit 195A-B and drive 0.7 mile toward Florence/Junction City. Merge onto Belt Line Highway and drive one mile to the Coburg exit. Take that exit and drive 0.2 mile to N. Coburg Road. Turn right on N. Coburg Road and drive 1.8 miles to the campground at 90064 Coburg Road.

Contact: Lane County Parks, 541/682-2000, www.lanecounty.org.

20 RICHARDSON PARK

Scenic rating: 7

on Fern Ridge Reservoir

Map 2.2, page 140

This pretty Lane County park is a favorite for sailing and sailboarding, as the wind is consistent. Boating and waterskiing are also popular. There is a walking trail that doubles as a bike trail. A kiosk display in the park features the historic Applegate Trail. Additional activities include fishing, swimming (unsupervised), and wildlife-viewing. The Corps of Engineers has wildlife areas nearby.

Campsites, facilities: There are 88 sites with partial hookups for tents or RVs of any length; some sites are pull-through. Picnic tables and fire pits are provided. Drinking water, restrooms with flush toilets and coin showers, a dump station, picnic areas, sand volleyball area, swimming area, three picnic shelters, playground, amphitheater, and garbage bins are available. A seasonally attended marina offers minimal supplies including ice, a boat launch, and transient boat docks. There is a small town within five miles. Some facilities are wheelchair accessible. Leashed pets are permitted.

Reservations, fees: Reservations are recommended at 541/682-2000 or www.lanecounty.org/parks ($10 reservation fee). RV sites are $25-27.50 per night, tent sites are $20 per night, $7 per night per additional vehicle. Maximum stay is 14 days within a 30-day period. Some credit cards are accepted. Open April-mid-October.

Directions: In Eugene on I-5, drive to Exit 195B and Belt Line Road. Turn west on Belt Line Road and drive 6.5 miles to the Junction City Airport exit and Highway 99. Take that exit, turn left on Highway 99, and drive north for 0.5 mile to Clear Lake Road (the first stoplight). Turn left and drive 8.25 miles to the campground on the left.

Contact: Richardson Park, 541/935-2005 or 541/682-2000, www.lanecounty.org; marina, 541/935-2005.

THE COLUMBIA RIVER GORGE AND MOUNT HOOD

The Columbia River area is a living history lesson, a geological wonder, and a recreation paradise. This waterway carves a deep gorge through the Cascade Range that divides Oregon. The transformation of the Gorge area from forest to grasslands to high desert is quick and striking. Driving west to east from the Portland area, you will pass along the wooded foothills of the Cascade Range to the south. When you pass Hood River, the world suddenly changes: The trees disappear and in their place are rolling grasslands that seem to extend forever. It is often hot and dry here, with strong winds blowing straight down the river. However, the entire time you are within the realm of Mount Hood, an 11,239-foot, diamond-shaped mountain whose flanks support stellar destinations with campsites and small, forested lakes. Mount Hood and its surrounding national forest provide numerous opportunities for camping, fishing, and hiking.

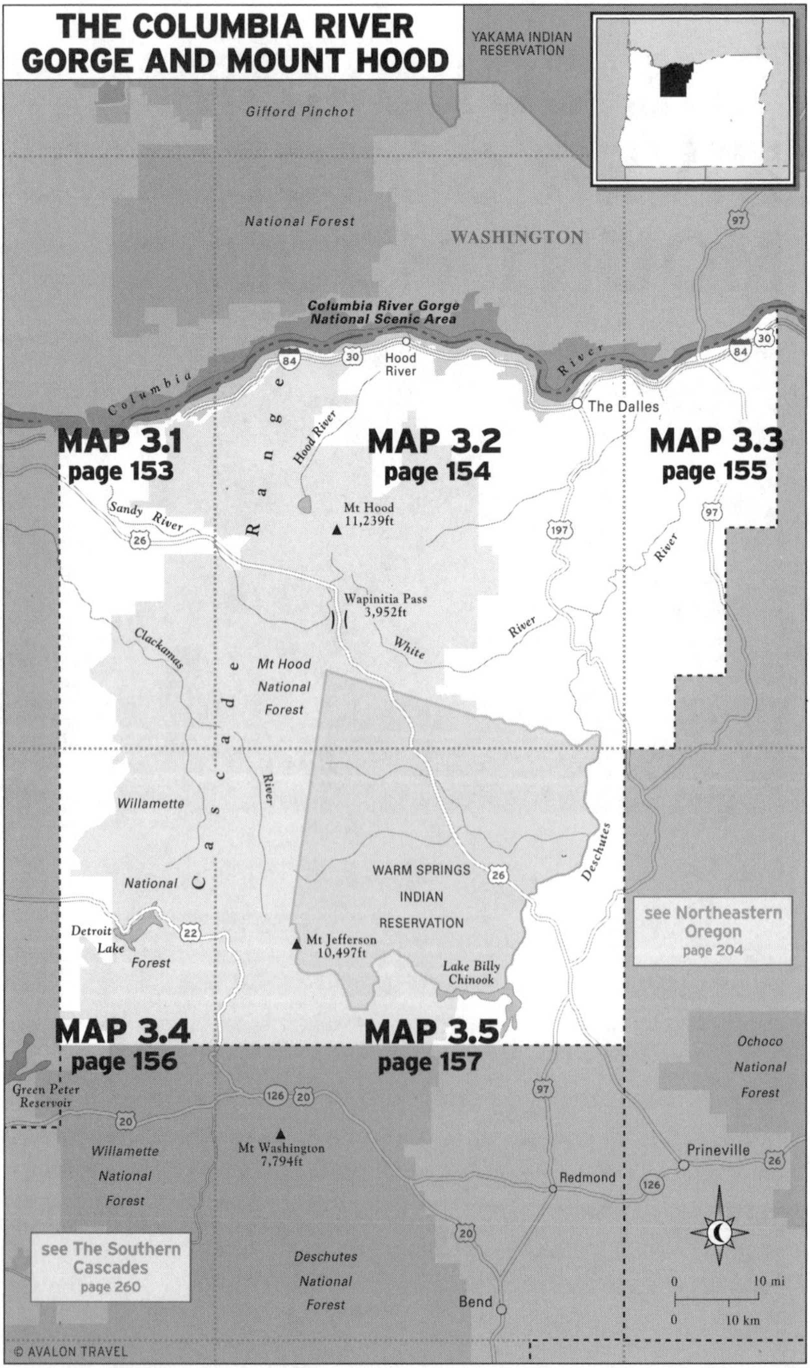
THE COLUMBIA RIVER GORGE AND MOUNT HOOD
YAKAMA INDIAN RESERVATION
Gifford Pinchot
National Forest
WASHINGTON
Columbia River Gorge National Scenic Area
Columbia
River
Hood River
The Dalles
84
30
97
MAP 3.1
page 153
MAP 3.2
page 154
MAP 3.3
page 155
Hood River
Sandy River
26
Cascade Range
Mt Hood
11,239ft
197
Wapinitia Pass
3,952ft
White River
Clackamas River
Mt Hood National Forest
Willamette National Forest
WARM SPRINGS INDIAN RESERVATION
Deschutes
26
see Northeastern Oregon
page 204
Detroit Lake
22
Mt Jefferson
10,497ft
Lake Billy Chinook
MAP 3.4
page 156
MAP 3.5
page 157
Ochoco National Forest
Green Peter Reservoir
126
20
97
Mt Washington
7,794ft
Willamette National Forest
Prineville
Redmond
126
26
20
see The Southern Cascades
page 260
Deschutes National Forest
Bend
0
10 mi
0
10 km
© AVALON TRAVEL

Map 3.1

Sites 1-18
Pages 158-165

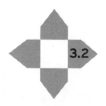

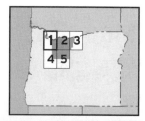

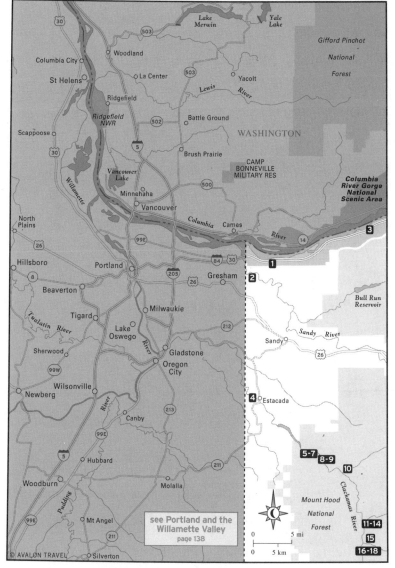

see Portland and the
Willamette Valley
page 138

© AVALON TRAVEL

Map 3.2

Sites 19-68
Pages 166-187

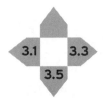

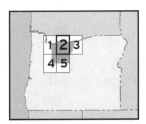

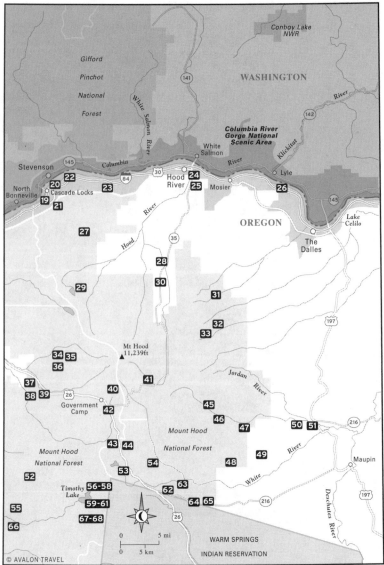

Map **3.3**

Sites 69-71
Pages 188-189

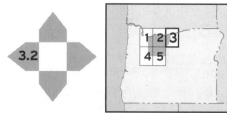

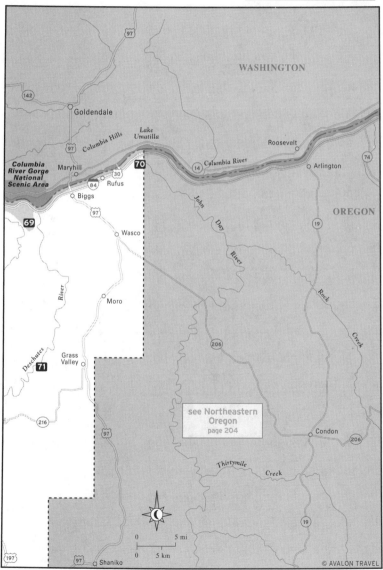

Map 3.4

Sites 72-79
Pages 189-192

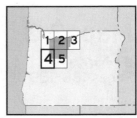

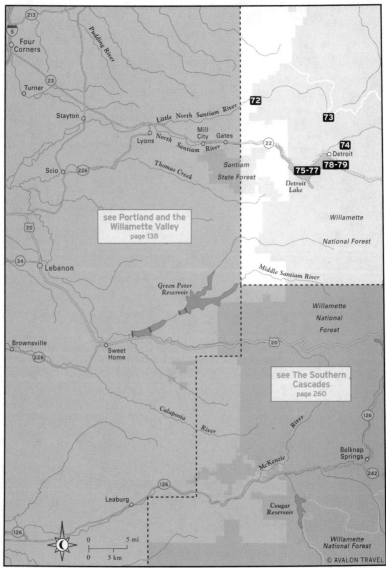

see Portland and the
Willamette Valley
page 138

see The Southern
Cascades
page 260

© AVALON TRAVEL

Map **3.5**

Sites 80-99
Pages 193-201

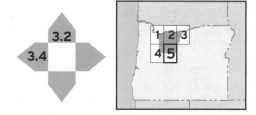

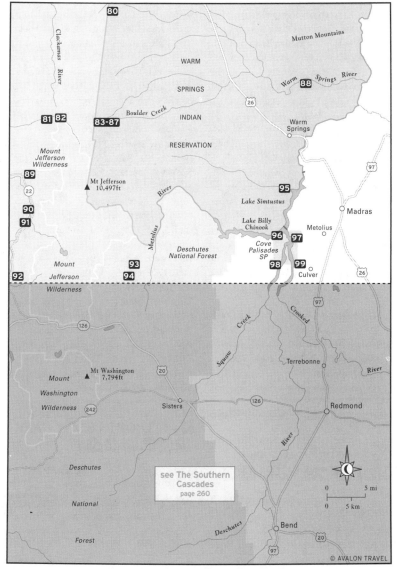

1 CROWN POINT RV PARK

Scenic rating: 6

near the Columbia River

Map 3.1, page 153

This little park is located near the Columbia River along scenic U.S. 30. Nearby Crown Point State Park is open during the day and offers views of the Columbia River Gorge and the historic Vista House, a memorial built in 1918 to honor Oregon's pioneers. Multnomah Falls offers another possible side trip.

Campsites, facilities: There are 21 sites with full hookups for RVs of any length. One site is pull-through. Picnic tables are provided. Drinking water, restrooms with flush toilets and coin showers, Wi-Fi, and a coin laundry are available. A store and ice are within walking distance. Leashed pets are permitted.

Reservations, fees: Reservations are accepted. Sites are $40 per night. Open year-round.

Directions: From Portland on I-84 eastbound, drive 16 miles to Exit 22 and Corbett. Take that exit and turn right on Corbett Hill Road. Drive 1.5 miles to a Y intersection with East Historic Columbia River Highway. Bear left and drive 0.25 mile to the park on the right.

Note: The recommended route has a 10 percent grade for 1.5 miles. An alternate route: From Portland on I-84 eastbound, drive to Exit 18/Lewis and Clark State Park. Take that exit and drive to East Historic Columbia River Highway and continue seven miles to the park on the right.

Contact: Crown Point RV Park, 503/695-5207.

2 OXBOW REGIONAL PARK

Scenic rating: 7

on the Sandy River

Map 3.1, page 153

This 1,200-acre park along the Sandy River, a short distance from the Columbia River Gorge, is a designated national scenic waterway. Fishing, non-motorized boating, and swimming are permitted here. The water is usually calm, and canoes, kayaks, and rafts are allowed. About 200 acres of the park are old-growth Douglas fir forest. There are several miles of hiking trails.

Campsites, facilities: There are 57 sites for tents or RVs up to 35 feet long and 10 pull-through sites for RVs. There are no hookups. Two group sites accommodate 25 and 150 people. Picnic tables, fire pits, and barbecues are provided. Drinking water, flush and vault toilets, showers, firewood, an amphitheater, horseshoe pits, and a playground are available. Boat-launching facilities are on-site. Gates lock at official sunset and open at 6:30am. Services are approximately 10 miles away. Some facilities are wheelchair accessible.

Reservations, fees: Reservations are accepted at 800/452 5687. Sites are $22 per night, $5 per night per additional vehicle. The group sites are $2.50 per person per night. There is a park entrance fee of $5 per vehicle for the first day only. Open year-round.

Directions: From Portland on I-84, drive to Exit 17/Troutdale. Take that exit and drive on the frontage road for 0.5 mile to 257th Street. Turn right (south) on 257th Street and drive three miles to Division Street. Turn left and drive seven miles to the park entrance on the left.

Contact: Metro Regional Parks and Greenspaces, Oxbow Regional Park, 503/663-4708, www.oregonmetro.gov.

3 AINSWORTH STATE PARK

Scenic rating: 8

along the Columbia River Gorge

Map 3.1, page 153   **BEST (**

Note: This park was affected by the 2017 wildfires. Contact the park to confirm access and services.

Set along the scenic Columbia River Gorge,

Ainsworth State Park is waterfall central, with famous Multnomah Falls a highlight. A 1.3-mile trail leads from the campground to Horsetail Falls and the Nesmith Point Trail shares a great view of St. Peter's Dome. Anglers should check out the Bonneville Fish Hatchery about five miles away.

Campsites, facilities: There are 43 sites with full hookups for RVs up to 60 feet long, seven walk-in tent sites, and a designated bike-in camping area. Picnic tables and fire grills are provided. Drinking water, restrooms with flush toilets and showers, garbage bins, a dump station, playground, camp host, amphitheater with occasional interpretive programs, and firewood are available. Some facilities are wheelchair accessible. Leashed pets are permitted.

Reservations, fees: Reservations are accepted at 800/452-5687 or www.reserveamerica.com ($8 reservation fee). Sites with full hookups are $24 per night, walk-in tent sites are $17 per night, $7 per night per each additional vehicle. Some credit cards accepted. Open mid-March-late October, weather permitting.

Directions: From Portland on I-84 eastbound, drive 35 miles to Exit 35. Turn southwest on the Columbia River Scenic Highway and continue a short distance to the park; the park is 17 miles east of Troutdale. An alternate route is to take the historic Columbia River Highway, a designated scenic highway, all the way from Portland (37 miles).

Contact: Ainsworth State Park, 503/695-2301 or 800/551-6949, www.oregonstateparks.org.

◢ MILO MCIVER STATE PARK
🏃 🎣 ⛴ 🚣 🐕 ♿ 🚐 ⛺

Scenic rating: 7

on the Clackamas River

Map 3.1, page 153

Though only 45 minutes from Portland, this park is far enough off the beaten track to provide a feeling of separation from the metropolitan area. It sits along the banks of the Clackamas River and has a boat ramp. There is fishing for salmon and steelhead in season; check current regulations. They also offer seasonal kayak tours. Trails for hiking are available, and a 4.5-mile equestrian trail is also accessible; bicycles are not allowed on trails. A fish hatchery is a nearby point of interest. Every September, actors participate in a Civil War reenactment here.

Campsites, facilities: There are 44 sites with partial hookups for RVs up to 50 feet long, nine primitive tent sites, one hiker/bicyclist site, and three group tent areas for up to 50 people each. Picnic tables and fire grills are provided. Drinking water, garbage bins, restrooms with flush toilets and showers, a dump station, picnic shelters, and firewood are available. Boat-launching facilities (canoes, inflatables, and kayaks), a model airplane field, and a 27-hole disc golf course are nearby. Group facilities are available. Some facilities are wheelchair accessible. Leashed pets are permitted, and there is a designated area for off-leash dog runs.

Reservations, fees: Reservations are accepted at 800/452-5687 or www.reserveamerica.com ($8 reservation fee). Tent sites are $18 per night, RV sites are $24 per night, $7 per night per each additional vehicle. Hiker/biker sites are $5 per person per night and group sites are $75 per night for up to 25 people, $3 per each additional person. Some credit cards are accepted. Open mid-March-October.

Directions: From Portland, drive east on U.S. 26 to Gresham. Continue 11 miles to Sandy and Highway 211. Turn right (south) and drive six miles to a junction. Turn south (still Highway 211) and drive one mile to Hayden Road. Turn right and drive one mile to Springwater Road. Turn right and drive one mile to the park on the right.

Contact: Milo McIver State Park, 503/630-6147, 503/630-7150, or 800/551-6949, www.oregonstateparks.org.

5 PROMONTORY

Scenic rating: 7

on North Fork Reservoir

Map 3.1, page 153

This Portland General Electric camp on North Fork Reservoir is part of a large recreation area and park. The reservoir, actually a dammed-up overflow of the Clackamas River, encompasses 350 acres. The water is calm and ideal for boating, and the trout fishing is excellent. A trail connects the campground to the marina. A one-acre lake is available for children's fishing.

Campsites, facilities: There are 69 sites for tents or self-contained RVs up to 35 feet long (no hookups) and 11 yomes (canvas cabins). There is also a group area for up to 35 people for tents or small self-contained RVs. Picnic tables and fire rings are provided. Restrooms with flush toilets and showers, garbage bins, a playground, horseshoes, a children's fishing pond, and covered picnic shelters are available. Some facilities are wheelchair accessible. Leashed pets are permitted.

Reservations, fees: Reservations are accepted at 503/630-7229 or www.portland-general.com/parks ($6 reservation fee). Sites are $18 per night, $30 per night for a yome. Some credit cards are accepted. Open mid-May-mid-September.

Directions: From Portland, drive east on U.S. 26 to Gresham. Continue 11 miles to Sandy and Highway 211. Turn right (south) and drive six miles to a junction. Turn south (still Highway 211) and drive six miles to Estacada. Continue south on Highway 224 and drive seven miles to the campground on the right. The route is well signed.

Contact: Portland General Electric, 503/464-8515, www.portlandgeneral.com/parks; store and marina, 503/630-5152; campground, 503/630-7229.

6 LAZY BEND

Scenic rating: 8

on the Clackamas River in Mount Hood National Forest

Map 3.1, page 153

This campground is situated at 800 feet elevation along the banks of the Clackamas River near the large North Fork Reservoir. It's far enough off the highway to provide a secluded, primitive feeling, though it fills quickly on weekends and holidays. There's only catch-and-release fishing in the Clackamas.

Campsites, facilities: There are five sites for tents or RVs up to 23 feet long and 13 sites for tents only. Picnic tables, garbage service, and fireplaces are provided. Drinking water and flush toilets are available. Leashed pets are permitted.

Reservations, fees: Reservations are accepted at 877/444-6777 ($10 reservation fee) or www.recreation.gov ($9 reservation fee). Sites are $21-23 per night, $8 per night per additional vehicle. Open early May-late September, weather permitting.

Directions: From Portland, drive south on U.S. 205 to the junction with Highway 24. Take the Highway 224/Estacada exit and turn left (south) onto Highway 224. Drive approximately 13 miles to Estacada. Continue south on Highway 224 for 10.5 miles to the campground on the right.

Contact: Mount Hood National Forest, Clackamas River Ranger District, 503/630-6861, www.fs.usda.gov/mthood.

7 ARMSTRONG

Scenic rating: 5

on the Clackamas River in Mount Hood National Forest

Map 3.1, page 153

Armstrong campground is set at an elevation of 900 feet along the banks of the Clackamas

River and offers good fishing access. Fishing is catch-and-release only.

Campsites, facilities: There are four sites for tents or RVs up to 40 feet long and seven sites for tents only. Picnic tables and fire rings are provided. Vault toilets and drinking water are available. Garbage service is available in the summer only. Some facilities are wheelchair accessible. Leashed pets are permitted.

Reservations, fees: Reservations are accepted at 877/444-6777 ($10 reservation fee) or www.recreation.gov ($9 reservation fee). Sites are $19-20 per night, $8 per night per additional vehicle. Open year-round, with limited winter services.

Directions: From Portland, drive south on U.S. 205 to the junction with Highway 24. Take the Highway 224/Estacada exit and turn left (south) onto Highway 224. Drive approximately 13 miles to Estacada. Continue south on Highway 224 for 15 miles to the campground on the right.

Contact: Mount Hood National Forest, Clackamas River Ranger District, 503/630-6861, www.fs.usda.gov/mthood.

8 CARTER BRIDGE

Scenic rating: 5

on the Clackamas River in Mount Hood National Forest

Map 3.1, page 153

This small, flat campground is popular with anglers. The Clackamas River flows along one end, and the other end borders the highway, with peripheral traffic noise.

Campsites, facilities: There are 15 sites for tents or RVs up to 28 feet long. Picnic tables and fire pits are provided. Vault toilets and garbage bins are available. There is no drinking water. Some facilities are wheelchair accessible. Leashed pets are permitted.

Reservations, fees: Reservations are not accepted. Sites are $16 per night, $8 per night

per additional vehicle. Open late May-early September, weather permitting.

Directions: From Portland, drive south on U.S. 205 to the junction with Highway 24. Take the Highway 224/Estacada exit and turn left (south) onto Highway 224. Drive approximately 13 miles to Estacada. Continue south on Highway 224 for 15.2 miles to the campground on the left.

Contact: Mount Hood National Forest, Clackamas River Ranger District, 503/630-6861, www.fs.usda.gov/mthood.

9 LOCKABY

Scenic rating: 6

on the Clackamas River in Mount Hood National Forest

Map 3.1, page 153

This campground sits at an elevation of 900 feet along the banks of the Clackamas River, next to Armstrong. Fishing in the Clackamas River is catch-and-release only.

Campsites, facilities: There are 30 sites for tents or RVs up to 15 feet long. Picnic tables, fireplaces, drinking water, garbage service, vault toilets, and firewood are available. A camp host is on-site. Leashed pets are permitted.

Reservations, fees: Reservations are accepted at 877/444-6777 ($10 reservation fee) or www.recreation.gov ($9 reservation fee). Sites are $22-23 per night, $8 per night per additional vehicle. Open late May-early September.

Directions: From Portland, drive south on U.S. 205 to the junction with Highway 24. Take the Highway 224/Estacada exit and turn left (south) onto Highway 224. Drive approximately 13 miles to Estacada. Continue south on Highway 224 for 15.3 miles to the campground on the left.

Contact: Mount Hood National Forest, Clackamas River Ranger District, Estacada Ranger Station, 503/630-6861, www.fs.usda.gov/mthood.

10 ROARING RIVER

Scenic rating: 8

on the Roaring River in Mount Hood National Forest

Map 3.1, page 153

Set among old-growth cedars at the confluence of the Roaring and Clackamas Rivers at an elevation of 1,000 feet, this campground has access to the Dry Ridge Trail. The trail starts in camp, and it's a butt-kicker of an uphill climb. Several other trails into the adjacent roadless area are accessible from camp.

Campsites, facilities: There are 14 sites for tents or RVs up to 16 feet long. Picnic tables and fireplaces are provided. Garbage service, drinking water, and vault toilets are available. Leashed pets are permitted.

Reservations, fees: Reservations are accepted at 877/444-6777 ($10 reservation fee) or www.recreation.gov ($9 reservation fee). Sites are $19-20 per night, $8 per night per additional vehicle. Open mid-May-mid-September, weather permitting.

Directions: From Portland, drive south on U.S. 205 to the junction with Highway 24. Take the Highway 224/Estacada exit and turn left (south) onto Highway 224. Drive approximately 13 miles to Estacada. Continue south on Highway 224 for 18 miles to the campground on the left.

Contact: Mount Hood National Forest, Clackamas River Ranger District, 503/630-6861, www.fs.usda.gov/mthood.

11 SUNSTRIP

Scenic rating: 3

on the Clackamas River in Mount Hood National Forest

Map 3.1, page 153

This campground on the banks of the Clackamas River offers fishing and rafting access. One of several camps along the Highway 224 corridor, Sunstrip is a favorite with rafting and kayaking enthusiasts and can fill up quickly on weekends. The elevation is 1,000 feet. Note: This campground, squeezed between the river and the highway and traversed by power lines, may be a turnoff for those wanting another kind of experience.

Campsites, facilities: There are nine sites for tents or RVs up to 60 feet long. Picnic tables and fireplaces are provided. Garbage service, firewood, and vault toilets are available. There is no drinking water. A camp host is on-site. Leashed pets are permitted.

Reservations, fees: Reservations are accepted at 877/444-6777 ($10 reservation fee) or www.recreation.gov ($9 reservation fee). Sites are $19-20 per night, $8 per night per additional vehicle. Open year-round, with limited winter services.

Directions: From Portland, drive south on U.S. 205 to the junction with Highway 24. Take the Highway 224/Estacada exit and turn left (south) onto Highway 224. Drive approximately 13 miles to Estacada. Continue south on Highway 224 for 19 miles to the campground.

Contact: Mount Hood National Forest, Clackamas River Ranger District, 503/630-6861, www.fs.usda.gov/mthood.

12 RAINBOW

Scenic rating: 6

on the Oak Grove Fork of the Clackamas River in Mount Hood National Forest

Map 3.1, page 153

Rainbow campground sits at an elevation of 1,400 feet along the banks of the Oak Grove Fork of the Clackamas River, not far from where it empties into the Clackamas River. The camp is less than a quarter mile from Ripplebrook Campground.

Campsites, facilities: There are 17 sites for tents only. Picnic tables and fire grills are provided. Drinking water and vault toilets are available. Garbage service is available during the summer. Leashed pets are permitted.

Reservations, fees: Reservations are accepted at 877/444-6777 ($10 reservation fee) or www. recreation.gov ($9 reservation fee). Sites are $19-20 per night, $8 per night per additional vehicle. Open year-round, with limited winter services.

Directions: From Portland, drive south on U.S. 205 to the junction with Highway 24. Take the Highway 224/Estacada exit and turn left (south) onto Highway 224. Drive approximately 13 miles to Estacada. Continue south on Highway 224 and drive 27 miles in national forest (the road becomes Forest Road 46). Continue south and drive about 100 yards to the campground on the right.

Contact: Mount Hood National Forest, Clackamas River Ranger District, 503/630-6861, www.fs.usda.gov/mthood.

13 INDIAN HENRY
🏕️ 🎣 🐕 ♿ 🚐 ⛺

Scenic rating: 8

on the Clackamas River in Mount Hood National Forest

Map 3.1, page 153

One of the most popular campgrounds in the Clackamas River Ranger District, Indian Henry hugs the banks of the Clackamas River at an elevation of 1,250 feet and has a wheelchair-accessible trail. Group campsites and an amphitheater are available. The nearby Clackamas River Trail has fishing access.

Sadly, this popular site has a great deal of dead and dying hazard trees. Only a small portion may be open for overnight camping and until the Forest Service determines the best course of action. Call for updates.

Campsites, facilities: There are 36 sites for tents or RVs up to 40 feet long, 46 sites for tents only, eight group tent sites for up to 30 people, and three yurts. Picnic tables, garbage service, and fire grills are provided. Flush toilets, firewood, and drinking water are available. A

camp host is on-site. Some facilities are wheelchair accessible. Leashed pets are permitted.

Reservations, fees: Reservations are accepted at 877/444-6777 ($10 reservation fee) or www. recreation.gov ($9 reservation fee). Sites are $22-23 per night, $8 per night per additional vehicle; group sites are $56 per night; yurts are $42 per night. Open late May-early September, weather permitting.

Directions: From Portland, drive south on U.S. 205 to the junction with Highway 24. Take the Highway 224/Estacada exit and turn left (south) onto Highway 224. Drive approximately 13 miles to Estacada. Continue south on Highway 224 for 23 miles to Forest Road 4620. Turn right and drive 0.5 mile southeast to the campground on the left.

Contact: Mount Hood National Forest, Clackamas River Ranger District, 503/630-6861, www.fs.usda.gov/mthood.

14 RIPPLEBROOK
🏕️ 🎣 🐕 🚐

Scenic rating: 7

on the Oak Grove Fork of the Clackamas River in Mount Hood National Forest

Map 3.1, page 153

Shaded sites with river views are a highlight at this campground along the banks of the Oak Grove Fork of the Clackamas River, where anglers are limited to artificial lures and catch-and-release only. Note: The road to this camp experiences slides and washouts; check current status before making a trip.

Campsites, facilities: There are five sites for RVs up to 19 feet long and nine sites for tents only. Picnic tables, garbage service, and fire grills are provided. Vault toilets are available, but there is no drinking water. Leashed pets are permitted.

Reservations, fees: Reservations are accepted at 877/444-6777 ($10 reservation fee) or www. recreation.gov ($9 reservation fee). Sites are $19-20 per night, $8 per night per additional vehicle. Open late April-late September, weather permitting.

Directions: From Portland, drive south on U.S. 205 to the junction with Highway 24. Take the Highway 224/Estacada exit and turn left (south) onto Highway 224. Drive approximately 13 miles to Estacada. Continue south on Highway 224 for 26.5 miles to the campground entrance on the left.

Contact: Mount Hood National Forest, Clackamas River Ranger District, 503/630-6861, www.fs.usda.gov/mthood.

15 RIVERSIDE

Scenic rating: 8

on the Clackamas River in Mount Hood National Forest

Map 3.1, page 153

The banks of the Clackamas River are home to this campground (elevation 1,400 feet). A worthwhile trail leaves the camp and follows the river for four miles north. Fishing is another option here, and several old forest roads in the vicinity make excellent mountain-biking trails.

Campsites, facilities: There are 13 sites for tents only and three sites for tents or RVs up to 24 feet long. Picnic tables, garbage service, and fire grills are provided. Vault toilets and drinking water are available. Some facilities are wheelchair accessible. Leashed pets are permitted; no horses are allowed in the campground.

Reservations, fees: Reservations are accepted at 877/444-6777 ($10 reservation fee) or www.recreation.gov ($9 reservation fee). Sites are $19-20 per night, $8 per night per additional vehicle. Open mid-May-late September, weather permitting.

Directions: From Portland, drive south on U.S. 205 to the junction with Highway 24. Take the Highway 224/Estacada exit and turn left (south) onto Highway 224. Drive approximately 13 miles to Estacada. Continue south

on Highway 224 for 27 miles and into national forest (Highway 224 becomes Forest Road 46). Continue 2.5 miles south on Forest Road 46 to the campground on the right.

Contact: Mount Hood National Forest, Clackamas River Ranger District, 503/630-6861, www.fs.usda.gov/mthood.

16 RIVERFORD

Scenic rating: 4

on the Clackamas and Collawash Rivers in Mount Hood National Forest

Map 3.1, page 153

This campground, just a two-minute walk from the confluence of the Clackamas and Collawash Rivers, offers access to good fishing. Otherwise, it's small, and the sites provide little privacy. It is set at an elevation of 1,500 feet. Although there is no drinking water at this camp, drinking water is available 0.75 mile away at Riverside Campground.

Campsites, facilities: There are eight sites for tents and two sites for RVs up to 16 feet long. Picnic tables and fire grills are provided. A vault toilet is available. Garbage service is provided in the summer. There is no drinking water. Leashed pets are permitted.

Reservations, fees: Reservations are not accepted. Sites are $19-20 per night, $8 per night per additional vehicle. Open year-round, with limited winter services.

Directions: From Portland, drive south on U.S. 205 to the junction with Highway 24. Take the Highway 224/Estacada exit and turn left (south) onto Highway 224. Drive approximately 13 miles to Estacada. Continue south on Highway 224 for 27 miles in national forest (the road becomes Forest Road 46). Continue south on Forest Road 46 for 3.5 miles to the campground on the right.

Contact: Mount Hood National Forest, Clackamas River Ranger District, 503/630-6861, www.fs.usda.gov/mthood.

17 RAAB GROUP

Scenic rating: 7

on the Collawash River in Mount Hood National Forest

Map 3.1, page 153

Raab Group camp (1,500 feet elevation) is located along the banks of the Collawash River, about a mile from its confluence with the Clackamas River. Raab gets moderate use, but it's usually quiet and has a nice, secluded atmosphere with lots of privacy among the sites.

Campsites, facilities: There are three group sites for tents or RVs up to 26 feet long and three tent-only group sites. Sites can accommodate 30-60 people. Picnic tables, garbage service, and fire grills are provided. Vault toilets are available. There is no drinking water in the campground; water is available one mile away at Two Rivers Picnic Area. Leashed pets are permitted.

Reservations, fees: Reservations are accepted at 877/444-6777 ($10 reservation fee) or www.recreation.gov ($9 reservation fee). Sites are $55-76 per night. Open late May-early September, weather permitting.

Directions: From Portland, drive south on U.S. 205 to the junction with Highway 24. Take the Highway 224/Estacada exit and turn left (south) onto Highway 224. Drive approximately 13 miles to Estacada. Continue south on Highway 224 for 27 miles in national forest (the road becomes Forest Road 46). Continue south on Forest Road 46 for 2.5 miles to Forest Road 63. Turn right and drive 1.5 miles to the campground on the right.

Contact: Mount Hood National Forest, Clackamas River Ranger District, 503/630-6861, www.fs.usda.gov/mthood.

18 KINGFISHER

Scenic rating: 7

on the Hot Springs Fork of the Collawash River in Mount Hood National Forest

Map 3.1, page 153

This pretty campground, surrounded by old-growth forest, sits on the banks of the Hot Springs Fork of the Collawash River and provides fishing access. Catch-and-release is allowed on the main fork of the Collawash, but the streams are closed to fishing. It's about three miles from Bagby Hot Springs, a U.S. Forest Service day-use area. The hot springs are an easy 1.5-mile hike from the day-use area. The camp sits at 1,250 feet elevation.

Campsites, facilities: There are 16 sites for tents only, seven sites for tents or RVs up to 66 feet long, and a few double sites. Picnic tables and fireplaces are provided. Garbage service is provided during the summer. Vault toilets and drinking water are available. Leashed pets are permitted.

Reservations, fees: Reservations are accepted at 877/444-6777 ($10 reservation fee) or www.recreation.gov ($9 reservation fee). Sites are $21-42 per night, $8 per night per additional vehicle. Open year-round, weather permitting, with limited winter facilities.

Directions: From Portland, drive south on U.S. 205 to the junction with Highway 24. Take the Highway 224/Estacada exit and turn left (south) onto Highway 224. Drive approximately 13 miles to Estacada. Continue south on Highway 224 for 27 miles in national forest (the road becomes Forest Road 46). Continue south on Forest Road 46 for 3.5 miles to Forest Road 63. Turn right and drive three miles to Forest Road 70. Turn right again and drive one mile to the campground on the left.

Contact: Mount Hood National Forest, Clackamas River Ranger District, 503/630-6861, www.fs.usda.gov/mthood.

19 EAGLE CREEK

Scenic rating: 8

near the Columbia Wilderness in Mount Hood National Forest

Map 3.2, page 154   **BEST(**

Eagle Creek is the oldest Forest Service Camp in America. Set at 400 feet elevation among old-growth Douglas fir and hemlock, it makes a good base camp for a hiking trip. The Eagle Creek Trail leaves the campground and travels 13 miles to Wahtum Lake, where it intersects with the Pacific Crest Trail. A primitive campground sits at the 7.5-mile point. The upper seven miles of the trail pass through the Hatfield Wilderness.

Campsites, facilities: There are 16 sites for tents or RVs up to 20 feet long and one group site for up to 90 people. Picnic tables and fire grills are provided. Drinking water, garbage bins, and vault toilets are available. A camp host is on-site. Boat docks and launching facilities are nearby on the Columbia River. Some facilities are wheelchair accessible. Leashed pets are permitted.

Reservations, fees: Reservations are not accepted for single sites and are required for the Eagle Creek Overlook group site at 877/444-6777 ($10 reservation fee) or www.recreation. gov ($9 reservation fee). Sites are $15 per night, $5 per night per additional vehicle; the group site is $75-125. Open May 1-September 30.

Directions: From Portland, drive east on I-84 for 41 miles to Bonneville. Continue east for two miles to the campground.

Contact: Columbia River Gorge National Scenic Area, 541/308-1700, www.fs.usda.gov/crgnsa.

20 CASCADE LOCKS MARINE PARK

Scenic rating: 8

in Cascade Locks

Map 3.2, page 154   **BEST(**

This public riverfront park covers 23 acres and offers a museum and boat rides. The salmon fishing is excellent here. Stern-wheeler dinner cruises are available. Hiking trails and tennis courts are nearby; the Pacific Crest Trail is within one mile.

Campsites, facilities: There are 15 sites for tents or RVs of any length; 11 sites have partial hookups (max. 8 people per site). Picnic tables are provided. Drinking water (May-Oct.), restrooms with flush toilets and showers, a dump station, boat docks, launching facilities, Wi-Fi, book exchange, a picnic area, and a playground are available. A camp host is on-site. Propane gas, gasoline, a store, café, coin laundry, and ice are within one mile. Some facilities are wheelchair accessible. Leashed pets are permitted.

Reservations, fees: Reservations are accepted at 509/637-6911 ($5 reservation fee). Sites are $15-35 per night, hiker/biker sites are $5 per night, $5 per night per each additional vehicle. Winter rates available November-April. Some credit cards are accepted. Open year-round, with limited winter facilities.

Directions: From Portland, drive east on I-84 for 44 miles to Cascade Locks. Take Exit 44/Cascade Locks to Wanapa Street. Turn left and drive 0.5 mile to the sign for the park on the left (well signed). Please note: There is a 12-foot clearance into Marine Park.

Contact: Port of Cascade Locks, Cascade Locks Marine Park, 541/374-8619, www.portofcascadelocks.org.

21 KOA CASCADE LOCKS

Scenic rating: 5

near the Columbia River

Map 3.2, page 154

This KOA is a good layover spot for RVers touring the Columbia River corridor. The campground offers level, shaded RV sites and grassy tent sites. A pancake breakfast is available on weekends during the summer season. Nearby recreation options include bike trails, hiking trails, and tennis courts. The 200-acre Cascade Locks Marine Park is close by and offers everything from museums to boat trips.

Campsites, facilities: There are 33 sites for tents, 78 sites with full or partial hookups for RVs of any length, and 13 cabins and cottages. Most RV sites are pull-through. Picnic tables and fire pits are provided. Restrooms with flush toilets and showers, drinking water, propane gas, a dump station, firewood, a spa, cable TV, Wi-Fi, a recreation hall, convenience store, coin laundry, ice, a playground, bicycle rentals, and a heated seasonal swimming pool are available. A café is within one mile. Some facilities are wheelchair accessible. Leashed pets are permitted.

Reservations, fees: Reservations are accepted at 800/562-8698. Sites are $27-42 per night, $5 per person per night for more than two people. Cabins are $45-69 per night; cottages are $55-129 per night. Some credit cards are accepted. Open February-October 15.

Directions: From Portland, drive east on I-84 for 44 miles to Cascade Locks and Exit 44. Take that exit to Forest Lane. Turn east on Forest Lane and drive one mile to the campground on the left.

Contact: KOA Cascade Locks, 541/374-8668, www.koa.com.

22 HERMAN CREEK HORSE CAMP

Scenic rating: 9

near the Pacific Crest Trail in Mount Hood National Forest

Map 3.2, page 154

This rustic campground sits at 300 feet elevation and is about half a mile from Herman Creek, not far from the Pacific Crest Trail. This area, separated from Washington by the Columbia River, is particularly beautiful. The campsites are spacious, and the many recreation options include biking, boating, fishing, and hiking. Stock hay must be certified weed-free.

Note: This campground has been day-use only due to hazard trees. Call for updates.

Campsites, facilities: There are seven sites for tents or RVs of any length; some sites have stalls. Picnic tables and fire grills are provided. Drinking water, garbage bins, restrooms with flush toilets, and stock-handling facilities are available. A camp host is on-site. Leashed pets are permitted.

Reservations, fees: Reservations are not accepted. Sites are $10 per night, $5 per night per additional vehicle. Open May 1-September 30.

Directions: From Portland, drive east on I-84 for 44 miles to Cascade Locks and Exit 44. Take that exit and drive straight ahead (east) onto Wanapa Street and drive back under the highway. Continue 1.5 miles (the road becomes Herman Creek Road) to the campground on the right.

Contact: Columbia River Gorge National Scenic Area, 541/308-1700, www.fs.usda.gov/crgnsa.

23 WYETH

Scenic rating: 5

on Gordon Creek in Mount Hood National Forest

Map 3.2, page 154

Wyeth makes a good layover spot for Columbia River corridor cruisers. The camp (100 feet elevation) borders Gordon Creek, near the Columbia River. Recreation options include biking, boating, fishing, and hiking.

Campsites, facilities: There are 14 sites for tents or RVs up to 30 feet long and three group sites for 30 people. Fire grills and picnic tables are provided. A flush toilet is available; call for drinking water availability. A camp host is on-site. Some facilities are wheelchair accessible. Leashed pets are permitted.

Reservations, fees: Reservations are accepted and recommended at 877/444-6777 ($10 reservation fee) or www.recreation.gov ($9 reservation fee). Sites are $20 per night, $5 per night per additional vehicle, group sites are $30 per night. Open May 1-September 30.

Directions: From Portland, drive east on I-84 for 44 miles to Cascade Locks. Continue east on I-84 for seven miles to Wyeth and Exit 51. Turn right and drive 0.25 mile to the campground entrance.

Contact: Columbia River Gorge National Scenic Area, 541/308-1700, www.fs.usda.gov/crgnsa.

24 VIENTO STATE PARK

Scenic rating: 8

along the Columbia River Gorge

Map 3.2, page 154

This park along the Columbia River Gorge offers scenic hiking trails and some of the best windsurfing in the Gorge. Just 12 miles to the east, old U.S. 30 skirts the Columbia River, offering a picturesque drive. Viento has a day-use picnic area right next to a babbling creek. Look for weekend interpretive programs during the summer. There are several other day-use state parks along I-84 just west of Viento, including Seneca Fouts, Vinzenz Lausmann, and Wygant. All offer quality hiking trails and scenic views.

Campsites, facilities: There are 56 sites with partial hookups for RVs up to 30 feet long (with some up to 40 feet long) and 18 tent sites. Picnic tables and fire grills are provided. Drinking water, garbage bins, restrooms with flush toilets and showers, firewood, and a playground are available. Some facilities are wheelchair accessible. Leashed pets are permitted.

Reservations, fees: Reservations are accepted at 800/452-5687 or www.oregonstateparks.reserveamerica.com ($8 reservation fee). RV sites are $22 per night, tent sites are $17 per night, $7 per night per additional vehicle. Some credit cards are accepted. Open mid-April-October, weather permitting.

Directions: From Portland, drive east on I-84 for 56 miles to Exit 56 (eight miles west of Hood River). Take Exit 56 and drive to the park entrance. The park is set on both sides of I-84.

Contact: Viento State Park, 541-374-8811 or 800/551-6949, www.oregonstateparks.org.

25 TUCKER COUNTY PARK

Scenic rating: 6

on the Hood River

Map 3.2, page 154

This county park along the banks of the Hood River is just far enough out of the way to be missed by most of the tourist traffic. Many people who choose this county park come for the windsurfing. Other recreation opportunities include rafting and kayaking. Fishing is not allowed at the park.

Campsites, facilities: There are 70 sites for tents or RVs and 20 sites with water-only hookups for tents or RVs up to 34 feet long. Picnic tables and fire rings are provided. Drinking water, restrooms with flush toilets and showers, reservable picnic shelter, and a playground are available. A store, café, gasoline, and ice are within three miles. Some facilities are wheelchair accessible. Leashed pets are permitted.

Reservations, fees: Reservations are not accepted. RV and tent sites are $20-30 per night, hiker/biker sites are $5 per night, $10 per night per additional tent, and $5 per night per additional vehicle. Open April-October.

Directions: From Portland, turn east on I-84 and drive about 65 miles to the town of Hood River and Exit 62. Take the exit and drive east on Cascade Street, continuing to 13th Street (first light). Turn right (south) and drive through and out of town; 13th Street becomes Tucker Road and then Dee Highway (Highway 281). Follow the signs to Parkdale. The park is four miles out of town on the right.

Contact: Hood River County Parks, 541/387-6889 or 541/386-4477, www.co.hood-river.or.us.

26 MEMALOOSE STATE PARK
🐕 🚶 🚐 ⛰️

Scenic rating: 7

in the Columbia River Gorge

Map 3.2, page 154

This park borrows its name from nearby Memaloose Island, which Native Americans used as a sacred burial ground. Situated along the hottest part of the scenic Columbia River Gorge, the campground makes a prime layover spot for campers cruising the Oregon/Washington border. Nature programs and interpretive events are held here. This popular camp receives a good deal of traffic, so plan on arriving early to claim a spot, even if you have a reservation.

Campsites, facilities: There are 66 tent sites and 43 sites with full hookups for RVs up to 60 feet long. Picnic tables and fire grills are provided. Drinking water, garbage bins, restrooms with flush toilets and showers, a dump station, playground, and firewood are available. Leashed pets are permitted.

Reservations, fees: Reservations are accepted at 800/452-5687 or www.reserveamerica.com ($8 reservation fee). RV sites with full hookups are $29 per night, tent sites are $19 per night, $7 per night per additional vehicle. Some credit cards are accepted. Open mid-March-October.

Directions: Memaloose State Park is accessible only to westbound traffic on I-84. From The Dalles, drive west on I-84 for 11 miles to the signed turnoff. (The park is about 75 miles east of Portland.)

If eastbound on I-84, take Exit 76. Drive under the freeway to the I-84 west on-ramp. Once on I-84 west, drive 2.5 miles to the sign for Rest Area/Memaloose State Park. Drive into the rest area and take an immediate right into the campground.

Contact: Memaloose State Park, 541/478-3008 or 800/551-6949, www.oregonstateparks.org.

27 WAHTUM LAKE CAMPGROUND
🚶 🚣 🚐 🐕 ⛰️

Scenic rating: 9

east of the Mark O. Hatfield Wilderness on Wahtum Lake in Mount Hood National Forest

Map 3.2, page 154

Located at 3,900 feet elevation, this small but popular campsite is situated among old-growth Douglas fir trees above a beautiful and pristine alpine lake. Follow a short stair-step trail down to the edge of Wahtum Lake and fish some of the stocked and native rainbow trout. Or continue on another mile or so following the Pacific Crest Trail/Eagle Creek 440 Trail around the perimeter of the lake. Non-motorized boating is allowed.

Note: The campground was temporarily closed due to road damage. Call the ranger station for updates.

Campsites, facilities: There are five sites for tents only. Picnic tables and fire pits are provided. Vault toilets and garbage bins are available. There is no drinking water. Leashed pets are permitted.

Reservations, fees: Reservations are not

accepted. Sites are $15 per night, $8 extra vehicle fee. Open late May-early September, weather permitting.

Directions: From Hood River, take Highway 35 South for about 14 miles and turn right on Woodworth Road. Continue three miles to the intersection with Highway 281. Turn right onto Highway 281 and travel approximately six miles to Dee; turn left on Lost Lake Road. Continue seven miles, then turn right onto Forest Service Road 13. Drive six miles, then turn right onto Forest Service Road 1310 and drive two miles to the campground on the right.

GPS Coordinates: 45.57731, -121.79247

Contact: Mount Hood National Forest, Hood River Ranger District, 541/352-6002, www.fs.usda.gov/mthood.

28 KINNICKKINNICK

Scenic rating: 5

on Laurence Lake in Mount Hood National Forest

Map 3.2, page 154

Kinnickkinnick campground sits on a peninsula that juts into Laurence Lake; only non-motorized boats are allowed on the lake. Campsite privacy varies because of the fairly sparse tree cover, and more than half of the sites are a short walk from your vehicle.

Campsites, facilities: There are 20 walk-in tent sites. Picnic tables and fire rings with fire grills are provided. There is no drinking water. Vault toilets, garbage bins, and a boat ramp are available. Some facilities are wheelchair accessible. Leashed pets are permitted.

Reservations, fees: Reservations are not accepted. Sites are $16 per night, $8 per night per additional vehicle. Open May-September, weather permitting.

Directions: From Portland, drive 62 miles west on I-84 to the city of Hood River. Take Exit 64 and drive about 14 miles south on Highway 35 to the town of Mount Hood and Cooper Spur Road. Turn right and drive three miles

to Parkdale and Clear Creek Road. Turn left (south) and drive three miles to the Laurence Lake turnoff. Turn right on Forest Road 2840 (Laurence Lake Road) and drive four miles to the campground on the right.

Contact: Mount Hood National Forest, Hood River Ranger District, 541/352-6002, www.fs.usda.gov/mthood.

29 LOST LAKE

Scenic rating: 9

on Lost Lake in Mount Hood National Forest

Map 3.2, page 154   **BEST (**

Only non-motorized boats are allowed on this clear, 240-acre lake set against the Cascade Range. The campground is nestled in an old-growth forest of cedar, Douglas fir, and hemlock trees at 3,200 feet elevation. Many sites have a lake view, and the campground affords a great view of Mount Hood.

Campsites, facilities: There are 125 sites for tents or RVs up to 32 feet long and several group sites. A horse camp with a corral is also available. Picnic tables and fire rings with grills are provided. Drinking water, vault toilets, garbage containers, a dump station, and a covered picnic shelter are available. Cabins, a grocery store, showers, beach picnic areas, a boat launch, and boat rentals are nearby. Some facilities are wheelchair accessible, including a barrier-free boat launch and fishing pier, as well as 3.5 miles of barrier-free trails. Leashed pets are permitted.

Reservations, fees: Reservations are accepted at 877/444-6777 ($10 reservation fee) or www.recreation.gov ($9 reservation fee). Single sites are $27-32 per night for up to three tents, $8 per night per additional vehicle; group sites are $44-55 per night and can accommodate up to 50 people. Some credit cards are accepted. Open mid-May-mid-October, weather permitting.

Directions: From Portland, drive 62 miles east on I-84 to the city of Hood River. Take

Exit 62/Westcliff to Cascade Street. Drive east on Cascade Street to 13th Street. Turn right on 13th Street and drive through Hood River Heights. The road turns into Dee Highway. Continue seven miles to Lost Lake Road/Forest Road 13. Turn right and drive seven miles to the campground.

Contact: Mount Hood National Forest, Hood River Ranger District, 541/352-6002; Lost Lake Resort, 541/386-6366, www.fs.usda.gov/mthood.

30 TOLL BRIDGE PARK

Scenic rating: 5

on the Hood River

Map 3.2, page 154

The wild Hood River runs through this campground in a woodsy setting. Fishing for trout is an obvious recreational option; stargazing is another, as there is no light pollution here.

Campsites, facilities: There are 21 sites for tents only, 20 sites with full hookups for RVs of any length, 40 sites with partial hookups, and two group sites for up to 50 people. Picnic tables and fire rings are provided. Drinking water, restrooms with flush toilets and showers, a dump station, and a playground are available. Groceries and fishing tackle are available eight miles away in Odell. Some facilities are wheelchair accessible. Leashed pets are permitted.

Reservations, fees: Reservations are strongly advised and are accepted via email at reservations@co.hood-river.or.us ($10 reservation fee). RV sites are $25-40 per night, tent sites are $20 per night, $10 per night per additional tent, and $5 per night per additional vehicle; group sites are $60-80 per night. Open April 1-November 1.

Directions: From Portland, take I-84 east for about 65 miles to Exit 64. Take that exit and drive south to Highway 35. Take Highway 35 south and drive 14.5 miles to Toll Bridge Road. Turn right (west) onto Toll Bridge Road and

drive 0.25 mile to the park entrance on the right.

GPS Coordinates: 45.518603567584144, -121.56850576400757

Contact: Hood River County Parks, 541/387-6889 or 541/352-5522, www.co.hood-river.or.us.

31 KNEBAL SPRINGS

Scenic rating: 6

near Knebal Springs in Mount Hood National Forest

Map 3.2, page 154

This spot (4,000 feet elevation) is in a semi-primitive area near Knebal Springs, an ephemeral water source. The Knebal Springs Trail begins at the campground. There is a nice, level family trail available for biking or horseback riding. Another trail from the camp provides access to a network of trails in the area. A U.S. Forest Service map is advised.

Campsites, facilities: There are eight sites for tents or RVs up to 22 feet long. Picnic tables and fire grills are provided. There is no drinking water. Vault toilets and horse-loading and -tending facilities are available. Garbage must be packed out. Leashed pets are permitted.

Reservations, fees: Reservations are not accepted. Sites are $12 per night, $5 per each additional vehicle. Open mid-May-October, weather permitting. Winter camping is permitted; there are no services and no fee.

Directions: From Portland, turn east on I-84 and drive about 90 miles to Exit 87. Take Exit 87 and turn south on U.S. 197; drive 13 miles to Dufur and Dufur Valley Road. Turn right on Dufur Valley Road and drive west for 12 miles to Forest Road 44. Continue west on Forest Road 44 for four miles to Forest Road 4430. Turn right and drive four miles to Forest Road 1720. Turn left (southwest) and drive one mile to the campground.

Contact: Mount Hood National Forest, Barlow

Ranger District, 541/467-2291, www.fs.usda.gov/mthood.

32 EIGHTMILE CROSSING

Scenic rating: 7

on Eightmile Creek in Mount Hood National Forest

Map 3.2, page 154

This campground sits at an elevation of 4,200 feet along Eightmile Creek. Although pretty and shaded, with sites scattered along the banks of the creek, it gets relatively little camping pressure. From the day-use area, you have access to a nice hiking trail that runs along Eightmile Creek. In addition, a 0.75-mile wheelchair-accessible trail links Eightmile Campground to Lower Crossing Campground. The fishing can be good here, so bring your gear.

Campsites, facilities: There are 21 sites for tents or RVs up to 30 feet long. Picnic tables and fire grills are provided. Vault toilets are available. No drinking water is available, and garbage must be packed out. Some facilities are wheelchair accessible. Leashed pets are permitted.

Reservations, fees: Reservations are not accepted. Sites are $15 per night, $8 per each additional vehicle. Open June-mid-October, weather permitting.

Directions: From Portland, turn east on I-84 and drive about 90 miles to Exit 87. Take Exit 87 and turn south on U.S. 197; drive 13 miles to Dufur and Dufur Valley Road. Turn right on Dufur Valley Road and drive west for 12 miles to Forest Road 44. Continue west on Forest Road 44 for four miles to Forest Road 4430. Turn right and drive 0.5 mile to the campground.

Contact: Mount Hood National Forest, Barlow Ranger District, 541/467-2291, www.fs.usda.gov/mthood.

33 PEBBLE FORD

Scenic rating: 6

in Mount Hood National Forest

Map 3.2, page 154

This is just a little camping spot by the side of a gravel forest road. Primitive and quiet, it's an alternative to the better-known Eightmile Crossing. There are some quality hiking trails in the area if you're willing to drive two or three miles. The elevation is 4,200 feet.

Campsites, facilities: There are three sites for tents or RVs up to 16 feet long. Picnic tables and fire grills are provided. Vault toilets are available. There is no drinking water. Leashed pets are permitted.

Reservations, fees: Reservations are not accepted. Sites are $12-14 per night, $8 per each additional vehicle. Open June-early October, weather permitting.

Directions: From Portland, turn east on I-84 and drive about 90 miles to Exit 87. Take Exit 87 and turn south on U.S. 197; drive 13 miles to Dufur and Dufur Valley Road. Turn right on Dufur Valley Road and drive west for 12 miles to Forest Road 44. Continue west on Forest Road 44 for five miles to Forest Road 130. Turn left (south) and drive a short distance to the campground on the left.

Contact: Mount Hood National Forest, Barlow Ranger District, 541/467-2291, www.fs.usda.gov/mthood.

34 MCNEIL

Scenic rating: 5

on the Clear Fork of the Sandy River in Mount Hood National Forest

Map 3.2, page 154

McNeil campground (2,040 feet elevation) is located in Old Maid Flat, a special geological area along the Clear Fork of the Sandy River. There's a good view of Mount Hood from the campground entrance. Several trails nearby provide access to the wilderness backcountry.

Campsites, facilities: There are 34 sites for tents or RVs up to 22 feet long. Picnic tables and vault toilets are provided. There is no drinking water. Leashed pets are permitted.

Reservations, fees: Reservations are not accepted. Sites are $16-18 per night, $8 per night per additional vehicle; $2 per night charge during holidays. Open May-October, weather permitting.

Directions: From Portland, drive 40 miles east on U.S. 26 to Zigzag. Turn left on County Road 18/East Lolo Pass Road and drive 4.5 miles to Forest Road 1825. Turn right on Forest Road 1825, drive less than one mile, bear right onto a bridge to stay on Forest Road 1825, and drive 0.25 mile to the campground on the left.

Contact: Mount Hood National Forest, Zigzag Ranger District, 503/622-3191, www.fs.usda.gov/mthood.

35 RILEY HORSE CAMP

Scenic rating: 6

near the Clear Fork of the Sandy River in Mount Hood National Forest

Map 3.2, page 154

Riley Horse Camp is close to McNeil and offers the same opportunities, except Riley provides stock facilities and is reserved for horse camping only on holidays. Secluded in an area of Douglas fir and lodgepole pine at 2,100 feet elevation, Riley is a popular base camp for horsepacking trips.

Campsites, facilities: There are 14 sites for tents or RVs up to 45 feet long. Picnic tables and fire grills are provided. Vault toilets, garbage bins, and firewood are available. There is no drinking water. Corrals and hitching posts for horses are available. Leashed pets are permitted.

Reservations, fees: Reservations are accepted for 10 equestrian sites at 877/444-6777 ($10 reservation fee) or www.recreation.gov ($9

reservation fee). Sites are $19-21 per night, $8 per night per additional vehicle. Open May-September, weather permitting.

Directions: From Portland, drive 40 miles east on U.S. 26 to Zigzag. Turn left (northeast) on County Road 18/East Lolo Pass Road and drive 4.5 miles to Forest Road 1825. Turn right and drive 0.5 mile to Forest Road 380. Turn right and drive 100 yards to the camp.

Contact: Mount Hood National Forest, Zigzag Ranger District, 503/622-3191, www.fs.usda.gov/mthood.

36 LOST CREEK

Scenic rating: 8

on Lost Creek in Mount Hood National Forest

Map 3.2, page 154

This campground near McNeil and Riley has some of the same opportunities. Set in a cool, lush area on a creek at 2,600 feet elevation, it's barrier-free and offers an interpretive nature trail about one mile long, as well as a wheelchair-accessible fishing pier.

Campsites, facilities: There are eight sites for tents or RVs up to 40 feet long, including some pull-through sites, five walk-in sites, and two yomes that can accommodate up to six people. Picnic tables and fire grills are provided. Drinking water, garbage service, and vault toilets are available. Some facilities are wheelchair accessible. Leashed pets are permitted.

Reservations, fees: Reservations are accepted at 877/444-6777 ($10 reservation fee) or www.recreation.gov ($9 reservation fee). Sites are $21-22 per night, yomes are $42 per night, $8 per night per additional vehicle. Open May-late September.

Directions: From Portland, drive 40 miles east on U.S. 26 to Zigzag. Turn left (northeast) on County Road 18/East Lolo Pass Road and drive 4.5 miles to Forest Road 1825. Turn right and drive for less than a mile and bear right at the fork, which keeps you on Forest Road 1825. Continue across the Sandy River Bridge and drive approximately two miles and bear right at the Y junction. The campground is less than a mile past the junction.

Contact: Mount Hood National Forest, Zigzag Ranger District, 503/622-3191, www.fs.usda.gov/mthood.

37 TOLL GATE

Scenic rating: 8

on the Zigzag River in Mount Hood National Forest

Map 3.2, page 154 **BEST (**

This shady campground along the banks of the Zigzag River near Rhododendron is extremely popular, and finding a site on a summer weekend can be next to impossible. Luckily, you can make a reservation. There are numerous hiking trails in the area. The nearest one leads east for several miles along the river. The campground features a historic Civilian Conservation Corps shelter from the 1930s, which can be used by campers for day use.

Campsites, facilities: There are four sites for tents or RVs up to 40 feet long and six sites for tents only. Picnic tables and fire grills are provided. Drinking water, garbage service, firewood, a group picnic area (available by reservation), and vault toilets are available. A camp host is on-site. Leashed pets are permitted.

Reservations, fees: Reservations are accepted at 877/444-6777 ($10 reservation fee) or www.recreation.gov ($9 reservation fee). Sites are $22-43 per night, $8 per night per additional vehicle. Open late May-early September, weather permitting.

Directions: From Portland, drive east on U.S. 26 for 40 miles to Zigzag. Continue 2.5 miles southeast on U.S. 26 to the campground entrance.

Contact: Mount Hood National Forest, Zigzag Ranger District, 503/622-3191, www.fs.usda.gov/mthood.

38 GREEN CANYON

Scenic rating: 8

on the Salmon River in Mount Hood National Forest

Map 3.2, page 154

Few out-of-towners know about this winner. But the locals do, and they keep the place hopping in the summer. The camp sits at 1,600 feet elevation along the banks of the Salmon River. A long trail cuts through the area and parallels the river, passing through a magnificent old-growth forest.

Campsites, facilities: There are 15 sites for tents or RVs up to 22 feet long. Picnic tables and fire grills are provided. Garbage bins and vault toilets are available. There is no drinking water. A store, café, and ice are within five miles. Leashed pets are permitted.

Reservations, fees: Reservations are not accepted. Sites are $21 per night, $8 per night per additional vehicle, $2 additional fee on certain holidays. Open May-October, weather permitting.

Directions: From Portland, drive east on U.S. 26 for 39 miles to Forest Road 2618 (Salmon River Road) near Zigzag. Turn right and drive 4.5 miles to the campground on the right.

Contact: Mount Hood National Forest, Zigzag Ranger District, 503/622-3191, www.fs.usda.gov/mthood.

39 CAMP CREEK

Scenic rating: 8

near the Zigzag River in Mount Hood National Forest

Map 3.2, page 154

This campground (2,200 feet elevation) sits along Camp Creek, not far from the Zigzag River. It looks similar to Toll Gate, but larger and farther from the road. A hiking trail runs through camp and along the river; another one leads south to Still Creek. This campground, along with Toll Gate to the west, is very popular—you'll probably need a reservation.

Campsites, facilities: There are 22 single sites and three double sites for tents or RVs up to 45 feet long. Picnic tables and fire grills are provided. Drinking water, vault toilets, and garbage bins are available. A camp host is on-site. Some facilities are wheelchair accessible. Leashed pets are permitted.

Reservations, fees: Reservations are accepted Memorial Day-Labor Day at 877/444-6777 ($10 reservation fee) or www.recreation.gov ($9 reservation fee). Single sites are $19-22 per night, $43 for a double site, and $8 per night per additional vehicle, $2 additional fee on holidays. Open May-September, weather permitting.

Directions: From Portland, drive east on U.S. 26 for 40 miles to Zigzag. Continue southeast on U.S. 26 for about four miles to the camp on the right.

Contact: Mount Hood National Forest, Zigzag Ranger District, 503/622-3191, www.fs.usda.gov/mthood.

40 ALPINE

Scenic rating: 8

near the Pacific Crest Trail in Mount Hood National Forest

Map 3.2, page 154

The small Alpine campground is set on the south slope of Mount Hood at 5,400 feet elevation, one mile from the Timberline Ski Area lodge. If you can bear some traffic noise, you'll be rewarded with big trees, a mountain feel, and year-round skiing and snowboarding less than one mile away. The Pacific Crest Trail is accessible from the Timberline Lodge. It can get quite crowded here on weekends. In the shoulder seasons, come prepared for cold nights.

Campsites, facilities: There are 16 sites for tents or RVs up to 16 feet long. Picnic tables and fire grills are provided. Drinking water, a portable toilet, and garbage service are available.

Some facilities are wheelchair accessible. Leashed pets are permitted.

Reservations, fees: Reservations are not accepted. Sites are $22 per night, $8 per night per additional vehicle, $2 additional fee on holidays. Open mid-July-September, weather permitting.

Directions: From Portland, drive east on U.S. 26 for 55 miles to the small town of Government Camp. Continue east for one mile to Timberline Road (Forest Road 173). Turn left and drive 4.5 miles to the campground on the left.

Contact: Mount Hood National Forest, Zigzag Ranger District, 503/622-3191, www.fs.usda.gov/mthood.

41 NOTTINGHAM

Scenic rating: 7

near the East Fork of the Hood River

Map 3.2, page 154

Nottingham campground, situated at 3,300 feet in elevation on the East Fork of the Hood River, has a variety of shady and sunny spots. The primary tree cover is Douglas fir and ponderosa pine. The Tamanawas Falls Trail (near Sherwood Camp) is three miles away, and the Gumjuwac Trail is 1.5 miles north. Fishing is only fair because of the swift water and lack of pools.

Campsites, facilities: There are 23 sites for tents or RVs up to 32 feet long. Picnic tables and fire rings are provided. A portable toilet and garbage bins are available. There is no drinking water. Some facilities are wheelchair accessible. Leashed pets are permitted.

Reservations, fees: Reservations are not accepted. Sites are $12 per night, $7 per night per additional vehicle. Open May-October, weather permitting.

Directions: From Mount Hood, drive south on Highway 35 for 13 miles to the camp on the right.

Contact: Mount Hood National Forest, Hood

River Ranger District, 541/352-6002, www. fs.usda.gov/mthood.

42 STILL CREEK

Scenic rating: 6
on Still Creek in Mount Hood National Forest

Map 3.2, page 154

This primitive camp, shaded primarily by fir and hemlock, sits along Still Creek where the creek pours off Mount Hood's south slope. Adjacent to Summit Meadows and the site of a pioneer gravesite from the Oregon Trail days, it's a great place for mountain views, sunsets, and wildlife. Anglers should bring along their rods: The fishing in Still Creek can be excellent. The camp sits at 3,600 feet elevation.

Campsites, facilities: There are 10 sites for tents or RVs up to 40 feet long and 17 sites for tents only. Picnic tables and fire grills are provided. Vault toilets, drinking water, and garbage service are available. Leashed pets are permitted.

Reservations, fees: Reservations are accepted at 877/444-6777 ($10 reservation fee) or www. recreation.gov ($9 reservation fee). Sites are $22-23 per night, $8 per night per additional vehicle. Open mid-June-mid-September, weather permitting.

Directions: From Portland, drive 55 miles east on U.S. 26 to Government Camp. Continue east on U.S. 26 for one mile to Forest Road 2650. Turn right and drive south for 500 yards to the campground.

Contact: Mount Hood National Forest, Zigzag Ranger District, 503/622-3191, www.fs.usda. gov/mthood.

43 TRILLIUM LAKE

Scenic rating: 9
on Trillium Lake in Mount Hood National Forest

Map 3.2, page 154   BEST (

This campground (3,600 feet elevation) hugs the shores of Trillium Lake, which is about half a mile long and a quarter mile wide. Fishing is good in the evening here, and the nearby boat ramp makes this an ideal camp for anglers. The lake is great for canoes, rafts, and small rowboats. Trillium Lake is an extremely popular vacation destination, so expect plenty of company. Reservations are highly recommended.

Campsites, facilities: There are 41 sites for tents or RVs of any length, 21 sites for tents only, one group site for up to 30 people, and one yurt. Picnic tables and fire grills are provided. Vault toilets and drinking water are available. Boat docks and launching facilities are available on the lake, but no motors are allowed. Some facilities are wheelchair accessible. Leashed pets are permitted.

Reservations, fees: Reservations are accepted at 877/444-6777 ($10 reservation fee) or www. recreation.gov ($9 reservation fee). Sites are $22-24 per night, the yurt is $42 per night, the group site is $90 per night, $8 per night per additional vehicle. Open late May-late September, weather permitting.

Directions: From Portland, drive east on U.S. 26 for 55 miles to the small town of Government Camp. Continue east on U.S. 26 for 1.5 miles to Forest Road 2656. Turn right and drive 1.3 miles to the campground on the right.

Contact: Mount Hood National Forest, Zigzag Ranger District, 503/622-3191, www.fs.usda. gov/mthood.

44 FROG LAKE

Scenic rating: 6

near the Pacific Crest Trail in Mount Hood National Forest

Map 3.2, page 154

This classic spot in the Cascade Range is situated on the shore of little Frog Lake (more of a pond than a lake), at an elevation of 3,800 feet and a short distance from the Pacific Crest Trail. Several other trails lead to nearby lakes. Clear Lake, to the south, provides a possible day trip and offers more recreation options.

Campsites, facilities: There are 23 sites for tents or RVs up to 35 feet long and nine sites for tents only. Picnic tables and fire rings are provided. Drinking water, vault toilets, garbage bins, and firewood are available. A camp host is on-site. Boat-launching facilities are nearby; no motorized boats are allowed. Some facilities are wheelchair accessible. Leashed pets are permitted.

Reservations, fees: Reservations are accepted at 877/444-6777 ($10 reservation fee) or www.recreation.gov ($9 reservation fee). Sites are $22-24 per night, $8 per night per additional vehicle. Open mid-May-mid-September, weather permitting.

Directions: From Portland, drive east on U.S. 26 for 57 miles to the junction with Highway 35 (two miles past Government Camp). Take that exit, bear right onto Highway 35, and drive seven miles to Forest Road 2610. Turn left and drive 0.5 mile to the campground.

Contact: Mount Hood National Forest, Hood River Ranger District, 541/352-6002, www.fs.usda.gov/mthood; park phone, 503/622-3191.

45 BADGER LAKE

Scenic rating: 8

on Badger Lake in Mount Hood National Forest

Map 3.2, page 154

This campground (4,400 feet elevation) sits along the shore of Badger Lake. Non-motorized boating is permitted if you can manage to get a boat in here over the rough roads. No trailers are allowed on the campground road. The camp is adjacent to the Badger Creek Wilderness, and numerous trails provide access to the backcountry. Badger Creek Trail heads out of camp, northeast along Badger Creek for several miles.

Campsites, facilities: There are four sites for tents only, accessible only by high-clearance vehicles. Picnic tables and fire grills are provided. Vault toilets are available. There is no drinking water, and garbage must be packed out. Leashed pets are permitted.

Reservations, fees: Reservations are not accepted. There is no fee for camping. Wilderness regulations apply. Open June-September, weather permitting.

Directions: From Portland, drive east on I-84 for 65 miles to Hood River, Exit 64 and Highway 35. Turn right (south) on Highway 35 and drive 37 miles to Forest Road 48. Turn left and drive 16 miles to Forest Road 4860. Turn left (north) and drive eight miles to Forest Road 140. Bear right and drive four miles to the lake. The last two miles on this primitive road require a high-clearance vehicle.

Contact: Mount Hood National Forest, Barlow Ranger District, 541/467-2291, www.fs.usda.gov/mthood.

46 BONNEY MEADOW

Scenic rating: 9

in Mount Hood National Forest

Map 3.2, page 154

This primitive campground is on the east side of the Cascade Range at an elevation of 4,800 feet. As a result, there is little water in the area, and also very few people, so you're liable to have the place all to yourself. Bonney Meadow Trail leaves from the campground and travels 1.5 miles up to a group of small lakes. This trail provides great mountain views.

Campsites, facilities: There are six sites for tents or RVs up to 16 feet long. Picnic tables and fire grills are provided. Vault toilets are available. There is no drinking water and garbage must be packed out. Leashed pets are permitted.

Reservations, fees: Reservations are not accepted. There is no fee for camping. Open June-early October, weather permitting.

Directions: From Portland, turn east on I-84 and drive 65 miles to the town of Hood River, Exit 64 and Highway 35. Turn right (south) on Highway 35 and drive 37 miles to Forest Road 48. Turn left and drive 14 miles to Forest Road 4890. Turn left and drive four miles north to Forest Road 4891. Turn right and drive a short distance to the campground.

Contact: Mount Hood National Forest, Barlow Ranger District, 541/467-2291, www.fs.usda.gov/mthood.

47 BONNEY CROSSING
🏃 🏊 🚻 🚐 ⛺

Scenic rating: 7

on Badger Creek in Mount Hood National Forest

Map 3.2, page 154

Bonney Crossing campground at 2,200 feet elevation along Badger Creek is the trailhead for the Badger Creek Trail, which provides access to the Badger Creek Wilderness. The camp gets fairly light use and is usually very quiet. Fishing is available in the creek and is usually pretty good. Horse campers are welcome here.

Campsites, facilities: There are eight sites for tents or RVs up to 16 feet long. Picnic tables and fire grills are provided. Vault toilets are available. There is no drinking water, and garbage must be packed out. Stock facilities include horse corrals. Leashed pets are permitted.

Reservations, fees: Reservations are not accepted. Sites are $12-14 per night, $5 per each additional vehicle. Open mid-April-mid-October, weather permitting.

Directions: From The Dalles, drive south on

U.S. 197 for 32 miles to Tygh Valley. Take the Tygh Valley exit to Tygh Valley Road. Turn west and drive 0.25 mile to Wamic Market Road (County Road 226). Turn right (west) and drive eight miles to Wamic. Continue through Wamic and drive seven miles to Forest Road 4810. Bear right and drive three miles to Forest Road 4811. Turn right and drive two miles to a junction with Forest Road 2710. Turn right and drive three miles to the campground on the right.

Contact: Mount Hood National Forest, Barlow Ranger District, 541/467-2291, www.fs.usda.gov/mthood.

48 FOREST CREEK
🏃 🏊 🚻 🚐 ⛺

Scenic rating: 6

on Forest Creek in Mount Hood National Forest

Map 3.2, page 154

This is a very old camp that borders Forest Creek on the original Barlow Trail, once used by early settlers. Shaded by an old-growth Douglas fir and ponderosa pine forest, you'll camp amid solitude. The elevation here is 3,000 feet. See a U.S. Forest Service map for specific roads and trails.

Campsites, facilities: There are eight sites for tents or RVs up to 16 feet long. Picnic tables and fire grills are provided. No drinking water is available. Vault toilets are available. Garbage must be packed out. Leashed pets are permitted.

Reservations, fees: Reservations are not accepted. Sites are $12-14 per night, $8 per each additional vehicle. Open June-early October, weather permitting.

Directions: From Portland, turn east on I-84 and drive 91 miles to The Dalles/Exit 87/Highway 197. Turn south and drive 31 miles to Tygh Valley and Wamic Market Road. Turn right and drive west for six miles to Forest Road 48. Continue west and drive 12.5 miles southwest to Forest Road 4885. Turn left and drive one mile to Forest Road 3530. Turn left and drive a short distance to the campground.

Contact: Mount Hood National Forest, Barlow Ranger District, 541/467-2291, www.fs.usda. gov/mthood.

49 ROCK CREEK RESERVOIR

Scenic rating: 7

on Rock Creek Reservoir in Mount Hood National Forest

Map 3.2, page 154

Fishing is excellent, and the environment is perfect for canoes or rafts at this campground along the shore of Rock Creek Reservoir. Enjoy views of Mount Hood from the day-use area (Northwest Forest Pass required). No hiking trails are in the immediate vicinity, but there are many old forest roads that are ideal for walking or mountain biking. The camp sits at 2,200 feet elevation.

Campsites, facilities: There are 28 sites for tents or RVs up to 35 feet long and five sites for tents only. Picnic tables, garbage service, and fire grills are provided. Vault toilets, drinking water, and firewood are available. Water disposal sites are located throughout the campground. There are boat docks nearby, but no motorboats are allowed on the reservoir. Some facilities are wheelchair accessible. Leashed pets are permitted.

Reservations, fees: Reservations are accepted at 877/444-6777 ($10 reservation fee) or www. recreation.gov ($9 reservation fee). Sites are $22-24 per night, $8 per night per additional vehicle. Open late May-early October.

Directions: From Portland, turn east on I-84 and drive 91 miles to The Dalles/Exit 87/ Highway 197. Turn south and drive 31 miles to Tygh Valley and Wamic Market Road. Turn right and drive west for six miles to Forest Road 48. Turn west and drive one mile to Forest Road 4820. Turn west and drive a short distance to the campground.

Contact: Mount Hood National Forest, Barlow Ranger District, 541/467-2291, www.fs.usda. gov/mthood.

50 PINE HOLLOW LAKESIDE RESORT

Scenic rating: 8

on Pine Hollow Reservoir

Map 3.2, page 154

This resort on the shore of Pine Hollow Reservoir is the best game in town for RV campers, with some shaded lakefront sites and scenic views. Year-round boating, fishing, swimming, and waterskiing are some recreation options here.

Campsites, facilities: There are 15 tent sites, 63 sites with partial hookups for RVs of any length, nine cabins, a camp trailer, and a two-bedroom house. Picnic tables and fire pits are provided. Drinking water, restrooms with flush toilets and coin showers, propane gas, a dump station, firewood, a convenience store, café, arcade, volleyball, horseshoe pits, playground, coin laundry, and ice are available. Boat docks, launching facilities, and boat and personal watercraft rentals are on-site. Some facilities are wheelchair accessible. Leashed pets are permitted.

Reservations, fees: Reservations are accepted. Tent sites are $28 per night, RV sites are $35 per night, $10 per each additional tent, $5 per person per night for more than two people, $5 per night per additional vehicle, and $5 per pet per night. Cabins start at $65 per night (no pets). Some credit cards are accepted. Open mid-March-October.

Directions: From Portland, turn east on I-84 and drive 91 miles to The Dalles/Exit 87/Highway 197. Turn south on Highway 197 and drive 31 miles to Tygh Valley and Wamic Market Road. Turn right (west) and drive four miles to Ross Road. Turn right (north) and drive 3.5 miles to the resort on the right.

Contact: Pine Hollow Lakeside Resort, 541/544-2271, www.pinehollowlakeside.com.

51 HUNT PARK

🚶🚴🎣🏕♿🚐⛺

Scenic rating: 6

near Badger Creek

Map 3.2, page 154

This Wasco County campground is set near the confluence of Badger and Tygh Creeks. Hiking trails, marked bike trails, and tennis courts are nearby, and fishing and rafting are available on the Deschutes River.

Campsites, facilities: There are 150 tent sites, 141 sites with full or partial hookups for RVs of any length (many are pull-through), and a group site for tents only that can accommodate up to 1,000 people. Picnic tables are provided, and some sites have fire rings. Drinking water, restrooms with flush toilets and coin showers, a dump station, garbage bins, a basketball court, Wi-Fi, and reservable picnic shelters are available. Horse facilities, including stalls and an arena, are also available. A camp host is on-site. A store, café, and ice are within two miles. Some facilities are wheelchair accessible. Leashed pets are permitted.

Reservations, fees: Reservations are accepted at 541/483-2288. RV sites are $20 per night, tent sites are $15 per night, $3 per night per additional vehicle. The group site is $7.50 per person per night for up to 100 people, $5 per person per night for larger groups. Open May-October.

Directions: From Portland, turn east on I-84 and drive 91 miles to The Dalles/Exit 87/Highway 197. Turn south on Highway 197 and drive 31 miles to Tygh Valley and Main Street. Turn right on Main Street and drive two blocks to Fairgrounds Road. Turn right and drive one mile to the fairgrounds on the right.

Contact: Wasco County, 541/483-2288, co.wasco.or.us.

52 HIDEAWAY LAKE

🚶🛶🎣🚐🏕🚐⛺

Scenic rating: 9

near the Rock Lakes Basin in Mount Hood National Forest

Map 3.2, page 154

This jewel of a spot features a small, deep lake where non-motorized boats are allowed, but they must be carried about 100 yards to the lake. The campsites are separate and scattered around the shore. At the north end of the lake, an 8.5-mile loop trail passes a number of lakes in the Rock Lakes Basin, all of which support populations of rainbow and brook trout. If you don't want to make the whole trip in a day, you can camp overnight at Serene Lake. See a U.S. Forest Service map for information.

Campsites, facilities: There are nine sites for tents or small RVs up to 16 feet long. Picnic tables and fire grills are provided. Vault toilets are available. There is no drinking water. Leashed pets are permitted.

Reservations, fees: Reservations are not accepted. Sites are $19-21 per night, $8 per night per additional vehicle. Open mid-June-late September, weather permitting.

Directions: From Portland, drive south on U.S. 205 to the junction with Highway 224/Estacada. Take the exit and turn left onto Highway 224, heading south. Drive approximately 13 miles to Estacada. Continue south on Highway 224 and drive 27 miles to Forest Road 57. Turn left (east) and drive 7.5 miles to Forest Road 58. Turn left (north) and drive three miles to Forest Road 5830. Turn left (northwest) and drive 5.5 miles to the campground on the left.

Contact: Mount Hood National Forest, Clackamas River Ranger District, 503/630-6861, www.fs.usda.gov/mthood.

53 CLEAR LAKE

Scenic rating: 4

near the Pacific Crest Trail in Mount Hood National Forest

Map 3.2, page 154

This campground is located along the shore of Clear Lake, a spot favored by anglers, swimmers, and windsurfers, but as a reservoir, it is subject to water-level fluctuations. The boating speed limit is 10 mph. This wooded camp features shady sites and is set at 3,600 feet elevation. The camp sometimes gets noisy from the revels of the party set. If you want quiet, this spot is probably not for you. A nearby trail heads north from the lake and provides access to the Pacific Crest Trail and Frog Lake, both good recreation options.

Campsites, facilities: There are 16 sites for tents or RVs up to 30 feet long, 12 sites for tents only, one lookout cabin for four people (winter only), and an overflow camping area. Picnic tables and fire grills are provided. Drinking water, garbage bins, firewood, and vault toilets are available. Some facilities are wheelchair accessible. Boat-launching facilities are nearby. Leashed pets are permitted.

Reservations, fees: Reservations are accepted at 877/444-6777 ($10 reservation fee) or www.recreation.gov ($9 reservation fee). Sites are $22-24 per night, overflow camping is $15 per night, $8 per night per additional vehicle; the lookout cabin is $50 per night. Open mid-May–late September, weather permitting.

Directions: From Portland, drive east on U.S. 26 for 57 miles to the junction with Highway 35 (two miles past Government Camp). Bear right (southeast) on U.S. 26 and drive nine miles to Forest Road 2630. Turn right (south) and drive one mile to the campground on the right.

Contact: Mount Hood National Forest, Hood River Ranger District, 541/352-6002, www.fs.usda.gov/mthood.

54 BARLOW CREEK

Scenic rating: 7

on Barlow Creek in Mount Hood National Forest

Map 3.2, page 154

One of several primitive U.S. Forest Service camps in the immediate vicinity, this campground is set along Barlow Creek at an elevation of 3,100 feet. It is on Old Barlow Road, which was the wagon trail for early settlers in this area. If this campground is full, Barlow Crossing Campground is one mile southeast on Forest Road 3530.

Campsites, facilities: There are three sites for tents. Picnic tables and fire grills are provided. Vault toilets are available. There is no drinking water, and garbage must be packed out. Leashed pets are permitted.

Reservations, fees: Reservations are not accepted. Sites are $12 per night. Open May-September, weather permitting.

Directions: From Portland, drive east on U.S. 26 for 57 miles to the junction with Highway 35 (two miles past Government Camp). Stay on U.S. 26 and continue 12 miles to Forest Road 43. Turn left and drive five miles to Forest Road 3530. Turn left (north) and drive 1.5 miles to the campground on the left.

Contact: Mount Hood National Forest, Hood River Ranger District, 541/352-6002, www.fs.usda.gov/mthood.

55 LAKE HARRIET

Scenic rating: 5

on Lake Harriet in Mount Hood National Forest

Map 3.2, page 154

Formed by a dam on the Oak Grove Fork of the Clackamas River, this little lake is a popular spot during the summer. Rowboats and boats with small motors are permitted, but only non-motorized boats are encouraged. The lake is stocked regularly and can provide good fishing for a variety of trout, including brook, brown, cutthroat, and rainbow. Anglers often stand shoulder to shoulder in summer. Road and infrastructure improvements may be under installation.

Campsites, facilities: There are 11 sites for tents or RVs up to 40 feet long. Picnic tables and fire grills are provided. Drinking water and vault toilets are available. Garbage service is provided in the summer. A fishing pier and boat-launching facilities are on the lake. Some facilities are wheelchair accessible. Leashed pets are permitted.

Reservations, fees: Reservations are accepted at 877/444-6777 ($10 reservation fee) or www.recreation.gov ($9 reservation fee). Sites are $16 per night, $8 per night per additional vehicle. Open year-round, weather permitting, with limited winter services.

Directions: From Portland, drive south on U.S. 205 to the junction with Highway 224/Estacada. Take the exit and turn left onto Highway 224, heading south. Drive approximately 13 miles to Estacada. Continue south on Highway 224 and drive 27 miles to Forest Road 57. Turn east and drive 7.5 miles to Forest Road 4630. Turn left and drive two miles to the campground on the left.

Contact: Mount Hood National Forest, Clackamas River Ranger District, 503/630-6861, www.fs.usda.gov/mthood.

56 GONE CREEK

Scenic rating: 8
on Timothy Lake in Mount Hood National Forest

Map 3.2, page 154 **BEST(**

This campground, set along the south shore of Timothy Lake at 3,200 feet elevation, is one of five camps at the lake. Timothy Lake provides good fishing for brook trout, cutthroat trout, kokanee salmon, and rainbow trout. Boats with motors are allowed, but a 10-mph speed limit keeps it quiet. Several trails in the

area—including the Pacific Crest Trail—provide access to a number of small mountain lakes.

Campsites, facilities: There are 50 sites for tents or RVs up to 45 feet long. Picnic tables and fire grills are provided. Drinking water, garbage service, vault toilets, and firewood are available. A boat ramp is nearby. Leashed pets are permitted.

Reservations, fees: Reservations are accepted at 877/444-6777 ($10 reservation fee) or www.recreation.gov ($9 reservation fee). Sites are $20 per night, $8 per night per additional vehicle. Open mid-May-early September, weather permitting.

Directions: From Portland, drive on U.S. 26 for 55 miles (just past the town of Government Camp) to the junction with Highway 35. Bear southeast, staying on U.S. 26, and drive 15 miles to Forest Road 42 (Skyline Road). Turn right and drive eight miles to Forest Road 57. Turn right and drive one mile west to the campground on the right.

Contact: Mount Hood National Forest, Zigzag Ranger District, 503/622-3191, www.fs.usda.gov/mthood.

57 OAK FORK

Scenic rating: 8
on Timothy Lake in Mount Hood National Forest

Map 3.2, page 154

Heavy timber and bear grass surround this forested camp along the south shore of Timothy Lake, where fishing is good for brook trout, cutthroat trout, kokanee salmon, and rainbow trout. Boats with motors are allowed, but a 10-mph speed limit is enforced. Oak Fork is located just east of Hoodview and Gone Creek campgrounds, at an elevation of 3,200 feet. Several area trails—including the Pacific Crest—provide access to various small mountain lakes.

The campground underwent a face-lift in

2017, including the addition of more cabins. Call to confirm access.

Campsites, facilities: There are 47 sites for tents or RVs up to 45 feet long. Picnic tables and fire grills are provided. Drinking water, firewood, and vault toilets are available. A boat ramp and launching facilities are nearby; the speed limit on the lake is 10 mph. Leashed pets are permitted.

Reservations, fees: Reservations are accepted at 877/444-6777 ($10 reservation fee) or www. recreation.gov ($9 reservation fee). Sites are $16-20 per night, $8 per night per additional vehicle; cabins are $45 per night. Open May-early October, weather permitting.

Directions: From Portland, turn east on U.S. 26 and drive 57 miles (just past the town of Government Camp) to the junction with Highway 35. Bear southeast, staying on U.S. 26, and drive 15 miles to Forest Road 42 (Skyline Road). Turn right and drive eight miles to Forest Road 57. Turn right and drive three miles to the camp on the right.

Contact: Mount Hood National Forest, Zigzag Ranger District, 503/622-3191, www.fs.usda. gov/mthood.

58 PINE POINT

Scenic rating: 8

on Timothy Lake in Mount Hood National Forest

Map 3.2, page 154

One of five camps on Timothy Lake, Pine Point spot sits at an elevation of 3,400 feet on the southwest shore. This camp has lake access and more open vegetation than the other Timothy Lake campgrounds. There's good fishing for brook trout, cutthroat trout, kokanee salmon, and rainbow trout, and a 10-mph speed limit keeps it pleasant for everyone. The trail that leads around the lake and to the Pacific Crest Trail passes along this campground.

Campsites, facilities: There are 24 sites for tents or RVs up to 45 feet long, including 13

single sites, six double sites for up to 12 people, and five group sites for up to 18 people each. Picnic tables, garbage service, and fire grills are provided. Drinking water and vault toilets are available. A boat ramp, launching facilities, and fishing pier are nearby; the speed limit on the lake is 10 mph. Leashed pets are permitted.

Reservations, fees: Reservations are accepted at 877/444-6777 ($10 reservation fee) or www. recreation.gov ($9 reservation fee). Single sites are $20 per night, $40 per night for a double site, $8 per night per additional vehicle, and group sites are $60-120 per night. Open late May-mid-September, weather permitting.

Directions: From Portland, turn east on U.S. 26 and drive 57 miles (just past the town of Government Camp) to the junction with Highway 35. Bear southeast, staying on U.S. 26, and drive 15 miles to Forest Road 42 (Skyline Road). Turn right and drive eight miles to Forest Road 57. Turn right and drive four miles to the park on the right.

Contact: Mount Hood National Forest, Zigzag Ranger District, 503/622-3191, www.fs.usda. gov/mthood.

59 HOODVIEW

Scenic rating: 9

on Timothy Lake in Mount Hood National Forest

Map 3.2, page 154

Here's another camp along the south shore of Timothy Lake; this one is set at 3,200 feet elevation. Timothy Lake provides good fishing for brook trout, cutthroat trout, kokanee salmon, and rainbow trout. Motorized boats are allowed, and the speed limit is 10 mph. A trail out of camp branches south for a few miles and, if followed to the east, eventually leads to the Pacific Crest Trail.

Campsites, facilities: There are 43 sites for tents or RVs up to 45 feet long. Picnic tables and fire grills are provided. Vault toilets, drinking water, garbage service, and firewood are available. A boat ramp is nearby. Leashed pets are permitted.

Reservations, fees: Reservations are accepted at 877/444-6777 ($10 reservation fee) or www. recreation.gov ($9 reservation fee). Sites are $20 per night, $8 per night per additional vehicle. Open mid-May-mid-September, weather permitting.

Directions: From Portland, turn east on U.S. 26 and drive 57 miles (just past the town of Government Camp) to the junction with Highway 35. Bear southeast, staying on U.S. 26, and drive 15 miles to Forest Road 42 (Skyline Road). Turn right and drive eight miles to Forest Road 57. Turn right and drive three miles to the campground on the right.

Contact: Mount Hood National Forest, Zigzag Ranger District, 503/622-3191, www.fs.usda. gov/mthood.

60 MEDITATION POINT
🚶 🚵 🏊 ⛵ 🐾 ⛺

Scenic rating: 9
on Timothy Lake in Mount Hood National Forest

Map 3.2, page 154 **BEST (**

Accessible only by foot or boat, this remote and rustic camp sits at 3,200 feet elevation and offers the most secluded location along Timothy Lake. It's one of two campgrounds on the north shore of the lake, which means you'll get a quieter, less crowded environment, though you'll have to bring your own water. The lake has a 10-mph speed limit for boaters. Timothy Lake Trail makes a 14-mile loop around the lake.

Campsites, facilities: There are five boat-in or walk-in tent sites. Picnic tables and fire grills are provided. Vault toilets are available. There is no drinking water, and garbage must be packed out. Boat docks and launching facilities are nearby. Leashed pets are permitted.

Reservations, fees: Reservations are not accepted. Access from PGE Day Use Area requires a $5 fee or a Northwest Forest Pass.

Walk-in sites are $5 per night. Open late May-mid-September, weather permitting.

Directions: From Portland, drive east on U.S. 26 and drive 57 miles to the junction with Highway 35 (2 miles past Government Camp). Bear right (southeast), staying on U.S. 26, and continue for 15 miles to Forest Road 42/Skyline Road. Turn right and drive eight miles south to Forest Road 57. Turn right and drive five miles, passing Pine Point Campground and crossing the Timothy Lake Dam. Park in the day-use area and hike one mile or take a boat to the north shore of the lake.

Contact: Mount Hood National Forest, Zigzag Ranger District, 503/622-3191, www.fs.usda. gov/mthood.

61 LITTLE CRATER LAKE
🚶 🏊 🐾 🚐 ⛺

Scenic rating: 7
on Clear Creek in Mount Hood National Forest

Map 3.2, page 154

Little Crater campground (3,200 feet elevation) nestles against Crater Creek and scenic Little Crater Lake. This camp is popular with hunters in the fall. Both the drinking water and the lake water are spring fed, and the beautiful turquoise water is numbingly cold. The Pacific Crest Trail is located near camp, providing hiking trail access. Fishing is poor at Little Crater Lake. Little Timothy Lake lies about 10 miles away; note the 10-mph speed limit for boats. Bring your mosquito repellent—you'll need it.

Campsites, facilities: There are eight sites for tents or RVs up to 35 feet long and seven sites for tents only. Picnic tables, garbage bins, and fire grills are provided. Vault toilets, firewood, and drinking water are available. Leashed pets are permitted.

Reservations, fees: Reservations are accepted at 877/444-6777 ($10 reservation fee) or www. recreation.gov ($9 reservation fee). Sites are $21-23 per night, $8 per night per additional vehicle. Open May-mid-September, weather permitting.

Directions: From Portland, drive east on U.S. 26 for 57 miles to the junction with Highway 35 (2 miles past Government Camp). Bear right (southeast), staying on U.S. 26, and drive 15 miles to Forest Road 42 (Skyline Road). Turn right and drive about six miles to Forest Road 58. Turn right and drive about 2.5 miles to the campground on the left.

Contact: Mount Hood National Forest, Zigzag Ranger District, 503/622-3191, www.fs.usda.gov/mthood.

62 CLEAR CREEK CROSSING

Scenic rating: 7

on Clear Creek in Mount Hood National Forest

Map 3.2, page 154

This secluded, little-known spot hugs the banks of Clear Creek at an elevation of 3,600 feet. Clear Creek Trail, a very pretty walk, begins at the campground. Fishing and hiking are two recreation options here.

Campsites, facilities: There are seven sites for tents or RVs up to 16 feet long. Picnic tables and fire grills are provided. Vault toilets are available. There is no drinking water, and garbage must be packed out. Leashed pets are permitted.

Reservations, fees: Reservations are not accepted. Sites are $12 per night, $8 per night per each additional vehicle. Open May-September, weather permitting.

Directions: From Portland, drive east on U.S. 26 for 55 miles to Government Camp. Continue three miles to a junction and bear right, staying on U.S. 26, and drive south for 12 miles to Highway 216. Turn left (east) on Highway 216 and drive two miles to Forest Road 2130. Turn left (north) on Forest Road 2130 and drive three miles to the campground.

Contact: Mount Hood National Forest, Barlow Ranger District, 541/467-2291, www.fs.usda.gov/mthood.

63 KEEPS MILL

Scenic rating: 9

on Clear Creek in Mount Hood National Forest

Map 3.2, page 154

This small, pretty campground is situated at the confluence of Clear Creek and the White River. No RVs are permitted. The elevation is 2,600 feet. Many hiking trails, some with awesome views of the White River Canyon, crisscross the area, but be warned: These are butt-kicking canyon climbs. The road in is rough, but the drive is worth it.

Campsites, facilities: There are five sites for tents only. The road to the campground is not good for trailers. Picnic tables and fire grills are provided. Vault toilets are available. There is no drinking water, and garbage must be packed out. Leashed pets are permitted.

Reservations, fees: Reservations are not accepted. There is no fee for camping. Open May-September, weather permitting.

Directions: From Portland, drive east on U.S. 26 for 55 miles to Government Camp. Continue three miles to a junction, turn right on U.S. 26, and drive south for 12 miles to Highway 216. Turn left (east) on Highway 216 and drive three miles to Forest Road 2120. Turn left (north) on Forest Road 2120 and drive three miles to the campground.

Contact: Mount Hood National Forest, Barlow Ranger District, 541/467-2291, www.fs.usda.gov/mthood.

64 BEAR SPRINGS

Scenic rating: 6

on Indian Creek in Mount Hood National Forest

Map 3.2, page 154

This campground is set along the banks of Indian Creek on the border of the Warm Springs Indian Reservation and features both secluded and open sites set in old-growth forest. The elevation is 3,000 feet.

Campsites, facilities: There are 19 single sites and two double sites for tents or RVs up to 32 feet long; sites can be combined into group sites. Picnic tables and fire grills are provided. Drinking water, garbage bins, vault toilets, and firewood are available. Leashed pets are permitted.

Reservations, fees: Reservations are accepted for the group sites at 877/444-6777 ($10 reservation fee) or www.recreation.gov ($9 reservation fee). Group sites are $51-76 per night, sites are $13 per night and $8 per night for each additional vehicle. Open June-September, weather permitting.

Directions: From Portland, drive east on U.S. 26 for 55 miles to Government Camp. Continue three miles to a junction and bear right, staying on U.S. 26, and drive south for 12 miles to Highway 216. Turn left (east) on Highway 216 and drive four miles to Reservation Road. Turn right (east) on Reservation Road and look for the campground on the right.

Contact: Mount Hood National Forest, Barlow Ranger District, 541/467-2291, www.fs.usda.gov/mthood.

65 MCCUBBINS GULCH

Scenic rating: 5

in Mount Hood National Forest

Map 3.2, page 154

This small, primitive camp sits alongside a small creek at 3,000 feet in elevation and offers decent fishing and off-highway vehicle (OHV) recreation. A 40-mile network of OHV trails runs through the surrounding forest, with access right from camp. So, though out of the way, this camp gets heavy use; claim a spot early in the day. To the south is the Warm Springs Indian Reservation; do not trespass, as large fines are assessed to those prosecuted. Bear Springs provides a nearby camping alternative.

Campsites, facilities: There are 15 sites for tents and RVs up to 25 feet long and four sites in an overflow area. Picnic tables and fire grills

are provided. Vault toilets are available. There is no drinking water, and garbage must be packed out. Leashed pets are permitted.

Reservations, fees: Reservations are not accepted. Sites are $12 per night, $8 for each additional vehicle; overflow sites are $11 per night. Open May-September, weather permitting.

Directions: From Portland, drive east on U.S. 26 for 55 miles to Government Camp. Continue three miles to a junction and bear right, staying on U.S. 26, and drive south for 12 miles to Highway 216. Turn left (east) on Highway 216 and drive six miles to Forest Road 2110. Take a sharp left and drive 1.5 miles to the campground entrance on the right.

Contact: Mount Hood National Forest, Barlow Ranger District, 541/467-2291, www.fs.usda.gov/mthood.

66 SHELLROCK CREEK

Scenic rating: 6

on Shellrock Creek in Mount Hood National Forest

Map 3.2, page 154

This quiet little campground (2,200 feet elevation) occupies a nice spot on Shellrock Creek and has been used primarily as an overflow area for Lake Harriet campground. You can hear the sound of the creek throughout the campground. Small trout can be caught here, but remember that on the Clackamas River it's catch-and-release only. Obtain a U.S. Forest Service map for details on the backcountry roads and trails.

Campsites, facilities: There are eight sites for tents or RVs up to 16 feet long. Picnic tables and fire grills are provided. Vault toilets are available. There is no drinking water and garbage must be packed out. Leashed pets are permitted.

Reservations, fees: Reservations are not accepted. Sites are $19 per night, $8 per night per additional vehicle. Open year-round, with limited winter services.

Directions: From Portland, drive south on U.S. 205 to the junction with Highway 24. Take the Highway 224/Estacada exit and turn left (south) onto Highway 224. Drive approximately 13 miles to Estacada. Continue south on Highway 224 for 27 miles in national forest (the road becomes Forest Road 46) to Forest Road 57. Turn left (east) and drive 7.5 miles to Forest Road 58. Turn left and drive north one mile to the campground on the left.

Contact: Mount Hood National Forest, Clackamas River Ranger District, Estacada Ranger Station, 503/630-6861, www.fs.usda.gov/mthood.

67 JOE GRAHAM HORSE CAMP

Scenic rating: 8

near Clackamas Lake in Mount Hood National Forest

Map 3.2, page 154

Named for a forest ranger, this campground sits at 3,250 feet elevation among majestic Douglas fir and hemlock, just north of tiny Clackamas Lake. The adjacent wet meadow is home to a wide variety of wildlife. It's one of two campgrounds in the area that allow horses. Timothy Lake (the setting for the Gone Creek, Hoodview, Meditation Point, Oak Fork, and Pine Point camps) provides a nearby alternative to the northwest. The Pacific Crest Trail is just east of camp.

Campsites, facilities: There are 14 sites for tents, horse trailers, or RVs up to 45 feet long; 11 have corrals, and two have hitching rails. Picnic tables, hitching posts, garbage service, and fire grills are provided. Drinking water and vault toilets are available. Leashed pets are permitted.

Reservations, fees: Reservations are accepted at 877/444-6777 ($10 reservation fee) or www.recreation.gov ($9 reservation fee). Sites are $21-23 per night, $8 per night per additional

vehicle, $2 additional charge during holidays. Open mid-May–mid-October, weather permitting.

Directions: From Portland, turn east on U.S. 26 and drive 57 miles (just past the town of Government Camp) to the junction with Highway 35. Bear right, continuing southeast on U.S. 26, and drive 15 miles to Forest Road 42 (Skyline Road). Turn right and drive eight miles to the campground on the left.

Contact: Mount Hood National Forest, Zigzag Ranger District, 503/622-3191, www.fs.usda.gov/mthood.

68 CLACKAMAS LAKE

Scenic rating: 7

near the Clackamas River in Mount Hood National Forest

Map 3.2, page 154

This camp, set at 3,400 feet elevation, is a good place to go to escape the hordes of people at the lakeside sites in neighboring camps. The Pacific Crest Trail passes nearby, and Timothy Lake requires little more than a one-mile hike from camp. The Clackamas Lake Historic Ranger Station, a visitors center built in the early 1900s, is worth a visit and is still using the old hand crank-style phones once used in lookout towers and guard stations. This is a popular spot for campers with horses. The Forest Service continues to update the facilities.

Campsites, facilities: There are 49 sites for tents or RVs up to 45 feet long. There are also 11 equestrian sites with hitch rails and corrals. Drinking water, garbage service, fire grills, and picnic tables are provided. Vault toilets are available. Boat docks and launching facilities are nearby at Timothy Lake, but only nonmotorized boats are allowed. Leashed pets are permitted.

Reservations, fees: Reservations are accepted at 877/444-6777 ($10 reservation fee) or www.recreation.gov ($9 reservation fee). Sites are $21 per night, $8 per night per additional vehicle. Open May-mid-September, weather permitting.

Directions: From Portland, turn east on U.S. 26 and drive 57 miles (just past the town of Government Camp) to the junction with Highway 35. Bear southeast, staying on U.S. 26, and drive 15 miles to Forest Road 42 (Skyline Road). Turn right and drive eight miles to Forest Road 57. Continue 500 feet (on Forest Road 42) past the Clackamas Lake Historic Ranger Station to Forest Road 4270. Turn left and drive 0.5 mile to the campground on the left.

Contact: Mount Hood National Forest, Zigzag Ranger District, 503/622-3191, www.fs.usda.gov/mthood.

69 DESCHUTES RIVER STATE RECREATION AREA

🏃 🚴 🛶 🏊 🚣 🐕 ♿ 🚐 ⛺

Scenic rating: 7

on the Deschutes River

Map 3.3, page 155

This tree-shaded park along the Deschutes River in the Deschutes Canyon offers bicycling and hiking trails and good steelhead fishing in season. The river-level Atiyeh Deschutes River Trail is a favorite jaunt for hikers. Reservation-only equestrian trail riding is available March-June. A small day-use state park called Heritage Landing, which has a boat ramp and restroom facilities, is located across the river. The U.S. Army Corps of Engineers offers a free train ride and tour of the dam at The Dalles during the summer. Good rafting is a bonus here. For 25 miles upstream, the river is mostly inaccessible by car. Many anglers launch boats here and then go upstream to steelhead fishing grounds. Note that boat fishing is not allowed here; you must wade into the river or fish from shore.

Campsites, facilities: There are 34 sites with partial hookups for tents or RVs up to 50 feet, 25 primitive sites for tents or self-contained RVs up to 30 feet, and four group areas for RVs and tents, which can hold up to 25 people and

five RVs each. Picnic tables and fire grills are provided, but campfires are prohibited July 1-September 30. Drinking water (seasonal), garbage bins, and flush toilets are available. Some facilities are wheelchair accessible. Leashed pets are permitted.

Reservations, fees: Reservations are accepted at 800/452-5687 or www.reserveamerica.com ($8 reservation fee). Sites with partial hookups are $22 per night, primitive sites are $10 per night, $7 per night per additional vehicle. Group sites are $71 per night. Some credit cards are accepted. Open year-round, with limited services November-March.

Directions: From Portland, turn east on I-84 and drive about 90 miles to The Dalles. Continue east on I-84 for 12 miles to Exit 97/Deschutes State Recreation Area, turn right, and drive 50 feet to Biggs-Rufus Highway. Turn left and drive about three miles, cross the Deschutes River, and turn right to the campground entrance.

Contact: Deschutes River State Recreation Area, 541/739-2322 or 800/452-5687, www.oregonstateparks.org.

70 LEPAGE PARK

🏊 🛶 🚣 🐕 ♿ 🚐 ⛺

Scenic rating: 6

on the John Day River

Map 3.3, page 155

Half of the campsites are adjacent to the John Day River and the other half are on the opposite side of the road at this partially shaded campground. The John Day River feeds into the Columbia just 0.12 mile north of the campground. Rattlesnakes are occasionally seen in the area but are not abundant. Anglers come for the smallmouth bass and catfish during the summer. The day-use area has a swimming beach, lawn, boat launch, and boat docks. There are several other campgrounds nearby.

Campsites, facilities: There is a grassy area with 20 walk-in sites for tents and 22 sites with partial hookups for tents or RVs up to 56 feet long; some sites are pull-through. Picnic tables and fire pits are provided. Drinking water, restrooms with flush toilets and showers, and pit toilets are available. A boat ramp, docks, dump station, fish-cleaning station, and garbage containers are also available. Food, gasoline, and coin laundry are available five miles away in the town of Rufus. Some facilities are wheelchair accessible. Leashed pets are permitted.

Reservations, fees: Reservations are accepted at 877/444-6777 ($10 reservation fee) or www.recreation.gov ($10 reservation fee). RV sites are $22-25 per night and tent sites are $15-17 per night. Some credit cards are accepted. Open April 1-October 31.

Directions: From Portland on I-84, drive east 120 miles (30 miles past The Dalles) to Exit 114, the John Day River Recreation Area. The campground is just off I-84.

Contact: Army Corps of Engineers, Portland District, 503/808-5150; LePage Park, 541/739-2713.

71 BEAVERTAIL

Scenic rating: 6

on the Deschutes River

Map 3.3, page 155

This isolated campground is set at an elevation of 2,900 feet along the banks of the Deschutes River, one of the classic steelhead streams in the Pacific Northwest. The camp provides fishing and rafting options. The open landscape affords canyon views. This is my favorite put-in spot for a drift boat for fishing float trips on the Deschutes. I've made the trip from Beavertail to the mouth of the Deschutes, ideal in four days, camping at Bureau of Land Management (BLM) boat-in sites along the river and fly-fishing for steelhead. A boating pass is required to float the river. There are 12 other BLM campgrounds along upper and lower Deschutes River Road. The hardest part is getting used to the freight trains that rumble through the canyon at night.

Campsites, facilities: There are 15 sites for tents or RVs up to 30 feet long and two group sites for up to 16 people. Picnic tables, garbage bins, and fire grills are provided. No campfires are allowed June 1-October 15. Drinking water and vault toilets are available. Boat-launching facilities are at the campground. Some facilities are wheelchair accessible. Leashed pets are permitted.

Reservations, fees: Reservations are not accepted. Sites are $8-12 per night, $2 per night per additional vehicle, with a 14-day stay limit. Group sites are $25-35 per night. Open year-round.

Directions: From Portland, drive east on U.S. 84 to The Dalles and Highway 197. Turn south and drive to Maupin. Continue through Maupin, cross the bridge, and within a mile look for Deschutes River Road on your left. Turn left on Deschutes River Road and drive 21 miles northeast to the campground.

Contact: Bureau of Land Management, Prineville District, 541/416-6700, www.blm.gov/or/districts/prineville.

72 SHADY COVE

Scenic rating: 7

on the Little North Santiam River in Willamette National Forest

Map 3.4, page 156

Shady Cove campground is on the Little North Santiam River in the recently designated Opal Creek Scenic Recreation Area. The Little North Santiam Trail runs adjacent to the campground.

Campsites, facilities: There are 13 sites for tents or RVs up to 16 feet long. Picnic tables, garbage service (summer only), fire grills, and vault toilets are available. There is no drinking water. Leashed pets are permitted.

Reservations, fees: Reservations are not accepted. Single sites are $8 per night, multiple sites are $16 per night, $5 per night per additional vehicle. Open year-round, weather permitting.

Directions: From Salem on I-5, take Exit 253 to Highway 22. Turn east and drive 23 miles to Mehama and North Fork Road (Marion County Road). Turn left and drive 17 miles northeast to the fork. Bear right on Forest Road 2207 and continue for two miles to the campground on the right.

Contact: Willamette National Forest, Detroit Ranger District, 503/854-3366, www.fs.usda. gov/willamette.

73 ELK LAKE

Scenic rating: 9
near Bull of the Woods Wilderness

Map 3.4, page 156

This remote and primitive campground (3,700 feet elevation) borders the shore of Elk Lake, where boating, fishing, and swimming can be quite good in the summer. Wildflower blooms can be beautiful in the nearby meadows. Several trails in the area provide access to the Bull of the Woods Wilderness (operated by Mount Hood National Forest) and the newly designated Opal Creek Wilderness. The campground also offers beautiful views of Battle Ax Mountain.

Campsites, facilities: There are 17 sites for tents only. Pit toilets are available. There is no drinking water, and garbage must be packed out. Primitive boat-launching facilities are available. Leashed pets are permitted.

Reservations, fees: Reservations are not accepted. Single sites are $10 per night, double sites are $20 per night, $5 per each additional vehicle. Open June-October, weather permitting.

Directions: From Salem on I-5, take Exit 253, turn east on Highway 22, and drive 52 miles to Detroit. Turn left on Forest Road 46/ Breitenbush Road and drive 4.5 miles to Forest Road 4696/Elk Lake Road. Turn left and drive

less than one mile to Forest Road 4697. Turn left and drive 9.5 miles to the campground on the left. The road is extremely rough for the last five miles; high-clearance vehicles are recommended.

Contact: Willamette National Forest, Detroit Ranger District, 503/854-3366, www.fs.usda. gov/willamette.

74 HUMBUG

Scenic rating: 9
on the Breitenbush River in Willamette National Forest

Map 3.4, page 156

Fishing and hiking are popular at this campground along the banks of the Breitenbush River, about four miles from where it empties into Detroit Lake. The lake offers many other recreation opportunities. The Humbug Flat Trailhead is behind Sites 9 and 10, and a scenic stroll through an old-growth forest follows the Breitenbush River. The rhododendrons put on a spectacular show May-July.

Campsites, facilities: There are 21 sites for tents or RVs up to 30 feet long. Picnic tables and fire grills are provided. Garbage service (summer only), drinking water, firewood, and vault toilets are available. Leashed pets are permitted.

Reservations, fees: Reservations are not accepted. Sites are $15-20 per night, $7 per night per additional vehicle. Open year-round, weather permitting, with limited winter facilities.

Directions: From Salem on I-5, take Exit 253, turn east on Highway 22, and drive 52 miles to Detroit. Turn left on Forest Road 46/ Breitenbush Road and drive five miles northeast to the campground on the right.

Contact: Willamette National Forest, Detroit Ranger District, 503/854-3366, www.fs.usda. gov/willamette.

75 DETROIT LAKE STATE RECREATION AREA

Scenic rating: 7

on Detroit Lake in Willamette National Forest

Map 3.4, page 156

This campground is set at 1,600 feet elevation along the shore of Detroit Lake, which is 400 feet deep, 9 miles long, and has more than 32 miles of shoreline. The park offers a fishing dock and a moorage area, and a boat ramp and bathhouse are available nearby at the Mongold Day Use Area. The heavily stocked lake is crowded on the opening day of trout season in late April.

Campsites, facilities: There are 178 sites with full or partial hookups for RVs up to 60 feet long, 98 tent sites, and 82 boat slips. Fire grills and picnic tables are provided. Drinking water, restrooms with flush toilets and showers, garbage bins, and firewood are available. Recreation facilities include two playgrounds, swimming areas, horseshoe pits, basketball and volleyball courts, an amphitheater, a gift shop, ice, firewood, and a visitors center. A camp host is on-site. Two boat docks and launching facilities are on-site. Some facilities are wheelchair accessible. Leashed pets are permitted.

Reservations, fees: Reservations are accepted at 800/452-5687 or www.reserveamerica.com ($8 reservation fee). RV sites are $26-29 per night, tent sites are $19 per night, $7 per night per additional vehicle. Boating moorage is $10 per night. Some credit cards are accepted. Open year-round.

Directions: From Salem, drive east on Highway 22 for 50 miles to the park entrance on the right (located 2 miles west of Detroit).

Contact: Detroit Lake State Recreation Area, 800/551-6949, 503/854-3406 or 503/854-3346, www.oregonstateparks.org.

76 PIETY ISLAND BOAT-IN

Scenic rating: 10

on Detroit Lake in Willamette National Forest

Map 3.4, page 156   **BEST (**

This island gets crowded and has a reputation for sometimes attracting rowdy groups. Other campgrounds along the shore have drinking water. Piety Island Trail climbs 1.5 miles to the top of the island. You'll find great vistas on this island, which sits at 1,600 feet in elevation.

Campsites, facilities: This is an island campground with 22 tent sites accessible only by boat. Picnic tables and fire grills are provided. Vault toilets are available. There is no drinking water. Boat docks, launching facilities, and rentals are nearby. Leashed pets are permitted.

Reservations, fees: Reservations are not accepted. Single sites are $10 per night; double sites are $20 per night. Open year-round, weather permitting.

Directions: From Salem, drive east on Highway 22 for 45 miles to Detroit Lake. Continue east on Highway 22 along the north side of the lake to the boat ramp (three miles west of the town of Detroit). Launch your boat and head southeast to the island in the middle of the lake. The campground is on the east side of the island.

Contact: Willamette National Forest, Detroit Ranger District, 503/854-3366, www.fs.usda.gov/willamette.

77 SOUTHSHORE

Scenic rating: 9

on Detroit Lake in Willamette National Forest

Map 3.4, page 156

This popular camp hugs the south shore of Detroit Lake, where fishing, swimming, and waterskiing are some of the recreation options. The Stahlman Point Trailhead is about half a mile from camp. There's a day-use area for picnicking and swimming. The views of the lake and surrounding mountains are outstanding.

Campsites, facilities: There are eight walk-in tent sites and 24 sites for tents or RVs up to 30 feet long. Fire grills, garbage service, and picnic tables are provided. Vault toilets, drinking water, and firewood are available. Boat-launching facilities are nearby at a day-use area. Some facilities are wheelchair accessible. Leashed pets are permitted.

Reservations, fees: Reservations are accepted at 877/444-6777 ($10 reservation fee) or www. recreation.gov ($9 reservation fee). Sites are $20 for a single site, $38 for double site, and $7 per night per additional vehicle. Open May-late September, with a gate preventing access during the off-season.

Directions: From Salem, drive east on Highway 22 for 52 miles to Detroit. Continue southeast on Highway 22 for 2.5 miles to Forest Road 10 (Blowout Road). Turn right and drive four miles to the campground on the right.

Contact: Willamette National Forest, Detroit Ranger District, 503/854-3366, www.fs.usda. gov/willamette.

78 COVE CREEK

Scenic rating: 10
on Detroit Lake in Willamette National Forest

Map 3.4, page 156   **BEST (**

Cove Creek is a popular campground, and it gets high use in the summer. Situated in a forest, the campground is located on the south side of the lake, about one mile from both Hoover and Southshore campgrounds. Water sports are popular, and both waterskiing and personal watercraft are allowed.

Campsites, facilities: There are 63 sites for tents or RVs of any length and one group site for up to 70 people. Picnic tables and fire rings are provided. Drinking water, restrooms with flush toilets and coin showers, garbage bins, firewood, and a boat ramp are available. Some

facilities are wheelchair accessible. Leashed pets are permitted.

Reservations, fees: Reservations are accepted only for the group site at 877/444-6777 ($10 reservation fee) or www.recreation.gov ($9 reservation fee). Single sites are $22 per night, double sites are $40 per night, $7 per night per additional vehicle. Group sites are $197 per night and require a two-night minimum stay on weekends. Open May-September, with a gate preventing access in the off-season.

Directions: From Salem, drive east on Highway 22 for 52 miles to Detroit. Continue southeast on Highway 22 for 2.5 miles to Forest Road 10 (Blowout Road). Turn right and drive three miles to the campground on the right.

Contact: Willamette National Forest, Detroit Ranger District, 503/854-3366, www. fs.usda.gov/willamette; park information, 503/854-3251.

79 HOOVER AND HOOVER GROUP

Scenic rating: 9
on Detroit Lake in Willamette National Forest

Map 3.4, page 156

Hoover campground is located along the eastern arm of Detroit Lake at an elevation of 1,600 feet near the mouth of the Santiam River. It offers fishing, boating, swimming, and hiking. You're likely to see osprey fishing during the day, a truly special sight. The camp features a wheelchair-accessible fishing area and an interpretive trail. The group campground has nice, open sites and direct access to the lake.

Campsites, facilities: There are 37 sites for tents or RVs up to 30 feet long and one group site for tents or RVs up to 30 feet long that accommodates up to 70 people and 20 vehicles. Picnic tables, garbage service, and fire grills are provided. Flush toilets and drinking water are available. Boat docks and launching facilities are nearby. Some facilities are wheelchair accessible. Leashed pets are permitted.

Reservations, fees: Reservations are accepted at 877/444-6777 ($10 reservation fee) or www.recreation.gov ($9 reservation fee). Single sites are $22 per night, double sites are $40 per night, $7 per night per additional vehicle. The group site is $197 per night. Open mid-May-mid-September; a gate prevents access in the off-season.

Directions: From Salem, drive east on Highway 22 for 52 miles to Detroit. Continue southeast on Highway 22 for 2.5 miles to Forest Road 10 (Blowout Road). Turn right and drive one mile to the campground on the right.

Contact: Willamette National Forest, Detroit Ranger District, 503/854-3366, www.fs.usda.gov/willamette.

80 SUMMIT LAKE

Scenic rating: 6

on Summit Lake in Mount Hood National Forest

Map 3.5, page 157

This idyllic camp is set in a remote area along the western slopes of the Cascade Range at an elevation of 4,200 feet. On the shore of little Summit Lake, the camp is primitive but a jewel. It's a perfect alternative to the more crowded camps at Timothy Lake, and you have access to all the same recreation options by driving just a short distance north. Non-motorized boats are allowed.

Campsites, facilities: There are eight tent sites. Fire grills, garbage service, and picnic tables are provided. Vault toilets are available. There is no drinking water. Leashed pets are permitted.

Reservations, fees: Reservations are not accepted. Sites are $17-19 per night, $8 per each additional vehicle, $2 charge on holidays. Open mid-July-September, weather permitting.

Directions: From Portland, turn east on U.S. 26 and drive 57 miles (just past the town of Government Camp) to the junction with Highway 35. Bear southeast, staying on U.S. 26, and drive 15 miles to Forest Road 42 (Skyline

Road). Turn right and drive 12 miles south to Forest Road 141 (a dirt road). Turn right and drive west two miles to the campground on the left.

Contact: Mount Hood National Forest, Zigzag Ranger District, 503/622-3191, www.fs.usda.gov/mthood.

81 CLEATER BEND GROUP CAMP

Scenic rating: 8

near the Breitenbush River in Willamette National Forest

Map 3.5, page 157

Creek views and pretty, shaded sites are the highlights of Cleater Bend, situated on the banks of the Breitenbush River at 2,200 feet elevation. This camp is 0.25 mile from Breitenbush and is a good option if that campground is full. Nearby recreation options include fishing access along the Breitenbush River, the South Breitenbush Gorge National Recreation Trail (three miles away), and Breitenbush Hot Springs (just over a mile away).

Campsites, facilities: The site can accommodate a group camp for up to 45 people in tents or RVs up to 28 feet long. Picnic tables and fire grills are provided. Garbage service, drinking water, vault toilets, and firewood are available. Some facilities are wheelchair accessible. Leashed pets are permitted.

Reservations, fees: Reservations are accepted at 877/444-6777 ($10 reservation fee) or www.recreation.gov ($9 reservation fee). The site is $132 per night. Open May-September; a gate prevents access during the off-season.

Directions: From Salem on I-5, take Exit 253, turn east on Highway 22, and drive 50 miles to Detroit. Turn left on Forest Road 46/Breitenbush Road and drive nine miles to the campground on the right.

Contact: Willamette National Forest, Detroit Ranger District, 503/854-3366, www.fs.usda.gov/willamette.

82 BREITENBUSH

Scenic rating: 8

on the Breitenbush River in Willamette National Forest

Map 3.5, page 157

There is fishing access at this campground along the Breitenbush River. Nearby recreation options include the South Breitenbush Gorge National Recreation Trail, three miles away, and Breitenbush Hot Springs, just over a mile away. If this campground is crowded, try nearby Cleater Bend.

Campsites, facilities: There are 30 sites for tents or RVs up to 24 feet long (longer trailers may be difficult to park and turn). Picnic tables and fire grills are provided. Drinking water, vault toilets, garbage service, and firewood are available. Some facilities are wheelchair accessible. Leashed pets are permitted.

Reservations, fees: Reservations are accepted at 877/444-6777 ($10 reservation fee) or www.recreation.gov ($9 reservation fee). Sites are $16 per night for a single site, $30 per night for a double site, and $7 per night per additional vehicle. Open May-September; a gate prevents access during the off-season.

Directions: From Salem on I-5, take Exit 253, turn east on Highway 22, and drive 50 miles to Detroit. Turn left (north) on Forest Road 46/Breitenbush Road and drive 10 miles to the campground on the right.

Contact: Willamette National Forest, Detroit Ranger District, 503/854-3366, www.fs.usda.gov/willamette.

83 LOWER LAKE

Scenic rating: 7

near Olallie Lake in Mount Hood National Forest

Map 3.5, page 157

This sunny, open campground is set at an elevation of 4,600 feet, about 0.75 mile from Lower Lake, a small but deep lake that's perfect for fishing and swimming. It's also less than a mile from Olallie Lake and near a network of trails that provide access to other nearby lakes. It's advisable to obtain a U.S. Forest Service map that details the backcountry roads and trails.

Campsites, facilities: There are eight sites for tents or RVs up to 16 feet long. Picnic tables and fire grills are provided. Vault toilets and garbage service are available. There is no drinking water. Leashed pets are permitted.

Reservations, fees: Reservations are not accepted. Sites are $16-20 per night, $5 per each additional vehicle. Open July-October.

Directions: From Portland, drive south on U.S. 205 to the junction with Highway 24. Take the Highway 224/Estacada exit and turn left (south) onto Highway 224. Drive approximately 13 miles to Estacada. Continue south on Highway 224 and drive 27 miles in national forest (the road becomes Forest Road 46). Continue south on Forest Road 46 for 20 miles to Forest Road 4690. Turn left on Forest Road 4690 and drive southeast for 8.2 miles to Forest Road 4220. Turn right (south) and drive about 4.5 miles of rough road to the campground on the right.

Contact: Mount Hood National Forest, Clackamas River Ranger District, 503/630-6861, www.fs.usda.gov/mthood.

84 CAMP TEN

Scenic rating: 9

on Olallie Lake in Mount Hood National Forest

Map 3.5, page 157

Here's a camp along the shore of Olallie Lake, a popular area. Camp Ten sits at an elevation of 5,000 feet, on the lake's western shore in the midst of the Olallie Lake Scenic Area, which is home to a number of pristine mountain lakes and a network of hiking trails. (See a U.S. Forest Service map for trail locations.) Boats without motors—including canoes, kayaks, and rafts—are permitted on the lake.

Campsites, facilities: There are 10 sites for tents or RVs up to 16 feet long. Picnic tables, garbage service, and fire grills are provided. Vault toilets are available. There is no drinking water. Leashed pets are permitted.

Reservations, fees: Reservations are not accepted. Sites are $15-20 per night, $5 per night for each additional vehicle. Open July-October, weather permitting.

Directions: From Portland, drive south on U.S. 205 to the junction with Highway 24. Take the Highway 224/Estacada exit and turn left (south) onto Highway 224. Drive approximately 13 miles to Estacada. Continue south on Highway 224 and drive 27 miles in national forest (the road becomes Forest Road 46). Continue south on Forest Road 46 for 20 miles to Forest Road 4690. Turn left on Forest Road 4690 and drive southeast for 8.2 miles to Forest Road 4220. Turn right (south) and drive about six miles of rough road to the campground.

Contact: Mount Hood National Forest, Clackamas River Ranger District, 503/630-6861, www.fs.usda.gov/mthood.

85 PAUL DENNIS
🚶 ⛵ � 🏠 🚐 ⛺

Scenic rating: 10
on Olallie Lake in Mount Hood National Forest

Map 3.5, page 157   **BEST (**

This campground, set at an elevation of 5,000 feet, borders the north shore of Olallie Lake. From here, you can see the reflection of Mount Jefferson (10,497 feet). Boats with motors are not permitted on the lake. A trail from camp leads to Long Lake (just east of the border of the Warm Springs Indian Reservation), Monon Lake, and Nep-Te-Pa Lake. It's advisable to obtain a U.S. Forest Service map.

Campsites, facilities: There are 17 sites for tents or RVs up to 16 feet long (trailers not recommended) and three hike-in tent sites. Picnic tables, garbage service, and fire grills are provided. Pit toilets are available. There is

no drinking water. A store and ice are nearby. Leashed pets are permitted.

Reservations, fees: Reservations are not accepted. Sites are $15-20 per night, $5 per each additional vehicle. Open July-October, weather permitting.

Directions: From Portland, drive south on U.S. 205 to the junction with Highway 24. Take the Highway 224/Estacada exit and turn left (south) onto Highway 224. Drive approximately 13 miles to Estacada. Continue south on Highway 224 and drive 27 miles in national forest (the road becomes Forest Road 46). Continue south on Forest Road 46 for 20 miles to Forest Road 4690. Turn left and drive southeast for 8.2 miles to Forest Road 4220. Turn right (south) and drive 6.2 miles to Forest Road 4220-170. Turn left and drive 0.12 mile to the campground.

Contact: Mount Hood National Forest, Clackamas River Ranger District, 503/630-6861, www.fs.usda.gov/mthood.

86 PENINSULA
🚶 ⛵ � 🏠 🚐 ⛺

Scenic rating: 10
on Olallie Lake in Mount Hood National Forest

Map 3.5, page 157

Peninsula, the largest of several campgrounds along Olallie Lake, is set at an elevation of 5,000 feet on the south shore. An amphitheater is located near the campground, and rangers present campfire programs during the summer. Non-motorized boats are permitted on the lake, and nearby trails lead to a number of smaller lakes in the area, such as Long Lake, Monon Lake, and Nep-Te-Pa Lake.

Campsites, facilities: There are 35 sites for tents or RVs up to 24 feet long, one double site, and six walk-in tent sites that can also be used as a group site. Picnic tables, garbage service, and fire grills are provided. Vault toilets are available. There is no drinking water. Leashed pets are permitted.

Reservations, fees: Reservations are not

accepted. Sites are $15-40 per night, $6 per night per additional vehicle, and $6 per night for walk-in sites. Open July-October, weather permitting.

Directions: From Portland, drive south on U.S. 205 to the junction with Highway 24. Take the Highway 224/Estacada exit and turn left (south) onto Highway 224. Drive approximately 13 miles to Estacada. Continue south on Highway 224 and drive 27 miles in national forest (the road becomes Forest Road 46). Continue south on Forest Road 46 for 20 miles to Forest Road 4690. Turn left and drive southeast for 8.2 miles to Forest Road 4220. Turn right (south) and drive 6.5 miles of rough road to the campground on the left.

Contact: Mount Hood National Forest, Clackamas River Ranger District, 503/630-6861, www.fs.usda.gov/mthood.

87 OLALLIE MEADOWS

Scenic rating: 8
near Olallie Lake in Mount Hood National Forest

Map 3.5, page 157

Olallie Meadows is set at 4,500 feet elevation along a large and peaceful alpine meadow about three miles from Olallie Lake. Non-motorized boats are allowed on Olallie Lake. The Pacific Crest Trail passes very close to the campground.

Campsites, facilities: There are seven sites for tents or RVs up to 16 feet long. Picnic tables, garbage service, and fire grills are provided. Vault toilets are available. There is no drinking water. Leashed pets are permitted.

Reservations, fees: Reservations are not accepted. Sites are $15-20 per night, $5 per night for each additional vehicle. Open July-October, weather permitting.

Directions: From Portland, drive south on U.S. 205 to the junction with Highway 24. Take the Highway 224/Estacada exit and turn left (south) onto Highway 224. Drive

approximately 13 miles to Estacada. Continue south on Highway 224 and drive 27 miles in national forest (the road becomes Forest Road 46). Continue south on Forest Road 46 for 20 miles to Forest Road 4690. Turn left and drive southeast for 8.2 miles to Forest Road 4220. Turn right (south) and drive 1.5 miles to the campground on the left.

Contact: Mount Hood National Forest, Clackamas River Ranger District, 503/630-6861, www.fs.usda.gov/mthood.

88 KAH-NEE-TA RESORT

Scenic rating: 7
on the Warm Springs Indian Reservation

Map 3.5, page 157

This resort features a stellar-rated, full-concept spa, with the bonus of a nearby casino. It is also the only public camp on the east side of the Warm Springs Indian Reservation; there are no other camps within 30 miles. The Warm Springs River runs nearby. Recreation options in the area include an 18-hole golf course, miniature golf, biking and hiking trails, a riding stable, and tennis courts.

Campsites, facilities: There are 51 sites with full hookups for RVs of any length. Some sites are pull-through. A motel, 20 teepees, and a cottage are also available. Some picnic tables are provided. Cable TV, restrooms with flush toilets and coin showers, propane gas, a dump station, seasonal concession stand, coin laundry, ice, a playground, a spa, mineral baths, and an Olympic-sized, spring-fed swimming pool with a 170- and a 140-foot water slide are available. Some facilities are wheelchair accessible. Leashed pets are permitted, but some areas are restricted.

Reservations, fees: Reservations are accepted at 800/554-4786. RV sites are $28-72 per night, teepees are $99-125 per night. Rates are for two people; $10-15 per each additional person. The resort fee is $16. There is a two-night minimum on weekends, and a three-night minimum on holiday weekends. Some credit cards are accepted. Open year-round.

Directions: From Portland, turn east on U.S. 26 and drive about 105 miles to Warm Springs and Agency Hot Springs Road on the left. Turn left and drive 11 miles northeast to Kah-Nee-Ta and the resort on the right.

Contact: Kah-Nee-Ta Resort, 800/554-4786, www.kahneeta.com.

89 WHISPERING FALLS

Scenic rating: 10

on the North Santiam River near Detroit Lake in Willamette National Forest

Map 3.5, page 157

This popular campground sits on the banks of the North Santiam River, where you can fish. If the campsites at Detroit Lake are crowded, this camp provides a more secluded option, and it's only about a 10-minute drive from the lake. Ospreys sometimes nest near the campground.

Campsites, facilities: There are 16 sites for tents or RVs up to 30 feet long. Picnic tables, garbage service, and fire grills are provided. Drinking water and flush toilets are available. Bring your own firewood. Leashed pets are permitted.

Reservations, fees: Reservations are accepted at 877/444-6777 ($10 reservation fee) or www.recreation.gov ($9 reservation fee). Single sites are $16 per night, double sites are $30 per night, $7 per night per additional vehicle. Open late April-mid-September; a gate prevents access in the off-season.

Directions: From Salem, drive east on Highway 22 for 50 miles to Detroit. Continue east on Highway 22 for eight miles to the campground on the right.

Contact: Willamette National Forest, Detroit Ranger District, 503/854-3366, www.fs.usda.gov/willamette.

90 RIVERSIDE

Scenic rating: 7

on the North Santiam River in Willamette National Forest

Map 3.5, page 157

This campground is set at an elevation of 2,400 feet along the banks of the North Santiam River, where the fishing can be good. A point of interest, the Marion Forks Fish Hatchery and interpretive site lies just 2.5 miles south. Other day-trip options include the Mount Jefferson Wilderness, directly to the east in Willamette National Forest, and Minto Mountain Trail, three miles east.

Campsites, facilities: There are 35 sites for tents or RVs up to 24 feet long and two sites for tents only. Picnic tables and fire grills are provided. Drinking water, vault toilets, and graywater disposal sites are available. Leashed pets are permitted.

Reservations, fees: Reservations are accepted for RV sites at 877/444-6777 ($10 reservation fee) or www.recreation.gov ($9 reservation fee). Sites are $16 per night, $7 per night per additional vehicle. Open late May-September; a gate prevents access during the off-season.

Directions: From Salem, drive east on Highway 22 for 50 miles to Detroit. Continue southeast on Highway 22 for 14 miles to the campground on the right.

Contact: Willamette National Forest, Detroit Ranger District, 503/854-3366, www.fs.usda.gov/willamette.

91 MARION FORKS

Scenic rating: 8

on the Santiam River in Willamette National Forest

Map 3.5, page 157

Situated along Marion Creek at 2,500 feet in elevation, this campground is adjacent to the Marion Forks Fish Hatchery. A U.S. Forest

Service guard station and a restaurant are across Highway 22. The area boasts some quality hiking trails; the nearest is Independence Rock Trail, 0.25 mile north of the campground.

Campsites, facilities: There are 15 sites for tents or RVs up to 24 feet long. Picnic tables, fire grills, and garbage containers are provided. Vault toilets are available. There is no drinking water. Leashed pets are permitted.

Reservations, fees: Reservations are not accepted. Single sites are $10 per night, double sites are $20 per night, $5 per night per additional vehicle. Open year-round, weather permitting, with no winter services.

Directions: From Salem, drive east on Highway 22 for 50 miles to Detroit. Continue southeast on Highway 22 for 16 miles to the campground on the left.

Contact: Willamette National Forest, Detroit Ranger District, 503/854-3366, www.fs.usda. gov/willamette.

92 BIG MEADOWS HORSE CAMP

Scenic rating: 10

near Mount Jefferson Wilderness in Willamette National Forest

Map 3.5, page 157

Built by the U.S. Forest Service with the support of a horse club, this camp is used heavily by equestrians riding into the Big Meadows area and the adjacent Mount Jefferson Wilderness. There's no local forage, so bring your own weed-free certified hay. If you're not a horse lover, you may want to stick with Riverside or Marion Forks.

Campsites, facilities: There are nine sites for tents or RVs up to 36 feet long. Picnic tables, garbage service, fire grills, hitching rack, loading rack, and enclosed four-horse corrals are provided at each site. Drinking water, vault toilets, firewood, and stock water troughs are available. Some facilities are wheelchair accessible. Leashed pets are permitted.

Reservations, fees: Reservations are not accepted. Sites are $14 per night, $7 per night per additional vehicle. Open June-October, weather permitting.

Directions: From Salem, drive east on Highway 22 for 50 miles to Detroit. Continue southeast on Highway 22 for 27 miles to Big Meadows Road (Forest Road 2267). Turn left and drive one mile to Forest Road 2257. Turn left and drive 0.5 mile to the campground on the left.

Contact: Willamette National Forest, Detroit Ranger District, 503/854-3366, www.fs.usda. gov/willamette.

93 SHEEP SPRINGS HORSE CAMP

Scenic rating: 7

near the Mount Jefferson Wilderness in Deschutes National Forest

Map 3.5, page 157

This well-shaded equestrian camp with privacy screening between sites is near the trailhead for the Metolius-Windigo Horse Trail, which heads northeast into the Mount Jefferson Wilderness and south to Black Butte. Contact the U.S. Forest Service for details and maps of the backcountry. The camp is set at an elevation of 3,200 feet.

Campsites, facilities: There are 11 sites for tents or RVs up to 45 feet long. Fire grills are provided. Drinking water, vault toilets, garbage bins, and corrals and box stalls for horses are available.

Reservations, fees: Reservations are accepted until the end of September at 877/444-6777 ($10 reservation fee) or www.recreation.gov ($9 reservation fee). Sites are $14-16 per night, $8 per night per additional vehicle. Open early May-mid-September, weather permitting.

Directions: From Albany, drive east on U.S. 20 for 87 miles to the sign for Jack Lake (located one mile east of Suttle Lake) and Suttle-Sherman Road. Turn left on Forest Road 12

and drive eight miles to Forest Road 1260. Turn left and drive 1.5 miles to Forest Road 1260-200. Turn right and drive 1.5 miles to the campground on the right.

Contact: Deschutes National Forest, Sisters Ranger District, 541/549-7700, www.fs.usda. gov/centraloregon.

94 JACK CREEK

Scenic rating: 5

near Mount Jefferson Wilderness in Deschutes National Forest

Map 3.5, page 157

A more primitive alternative to the other camps in the area, this campground sits along the banks of Jack Creek in an open setting among ponderosa pine. Sites are large and well shaded and the elevation is 3,100 feet. To protect the bull trout habitat, no fishing is permitted here.

Campsites, facilities: There are 20 sites for tents or RVs up to 50 feet long. Some of the larger sites can accommodate up to seven cars and 20 people. Picnic tables and fire grills are provided. Vault toilets and garbage bins are available. There is no drinking water. Leashed pets are permitted.

Reservations, fees: Reservations are accepted mid-April-September at 877/444-6777 ($10 reservation fee) or www.recreation.gov ($9 reservation fee). Sites are $12 per night, $6 per night per additional vehicle. Open mid-April-mid-October.

Directions: From Albany, drive east on U.S. 20 for 87 miles to the sign for Jack Lake (located one mile east of Suttle Lake) and Suttle-Sherman Road. Turn left on Forest Road 12 and drive five miles to Forest Road 1230. Turn left and drive 0.75 mile to Forest Road 1232. Turn left and drive 0.25 mile to the campground on the left.

Contact: Deschutes National Forest, Sisters Ranger District, 541/549-7700, www.fs.usda. gov/centraloregon.

95 PELTON

Scenic rating: 8

on Lake Simtustus in Deschutes National Forest

Map 3.5, page 157   **BEST (**

This campground claims 0.5 mile of shoreline along the north side of Lake Simtustus. Campsites here are shaded with juniper in an area of rolling hills and sagebrush. One section of the lake is accessible for water skis and personal watercraft. Simtustus is a trophy fishing lake for kokanee and brown, bull, and rainbow trout. Just north of the park is the Pelton Wildlife Overlook, where you can view a variety of waterfowl, such as great blue herons, ducks, geese, and shorebirds, as well as eagles and other raptors. Cove Palisades State Park, about 15 miles south, provides additional recreational opportunities.

Campsites, facilities: There are 68 sites, some with partial hookups, for tents or RVs up to 56 feet long, two group sites for up to 12 people, and 13 yomes (canvas cabins). Picnic tables and fire grills are provided. Drinking water, restrooms with flush toilets and showers, garbage service, a restaurant, general store, ice, and fishing supplies are available. Also, a full-service marina with boat rentals, marine fuel, a boat launch, boat dock, fishing pier, moorage, swimming beach, volleyball courts, horseshoe pits, and a playground are available. Some facilities are wheelchair accessible. Leashed pets are permitted, and a dog run area is available.

Reservations, fees: Reservations are accepted at 541/325-5292 or www.portlandgeneral.com/parks. Sites are $18-25 per night; the group sites are $36-50 per night; yomes are $30-60 per night. Some credit cards are accepted. Open late-April-late-September.

Directions: From Portland, drive south on U.S. 26 for 108 miles to the town of Warm Springs. Continue south two miles to Pelton Dam Road. Turn right and drive three miles to the campground on the right.

Contact: PGE Campground office, 503/464-8515 or 541/475-0516 (store and marina), www.portlandgeneral.com/parks.

96 PERRY SOUTH

Scenic rating: 6

on Lake Billy Chinook in Deschutes National Forest

Map 3.5, page 157

Perry South campground is located near the shore of the Metolius arm of Lake Billy Chinook. The lake borders the Warm Springs Indian Reservation and can get very crowded and noisy, as it attracts powerboat/water-ski enthusiasts. Recreation options include waterskiing and fishing for bass and panfish, and one of Oregon's nicest golf courses is nearby.

Campsites, facilities: There are 63 sites for tents or RVs up to 95 feet long. Picnic tables, garbage service, and fire grills are provided. Drinking water, vault toilets, firewood, a fish-cleaning station, boat docks, and launching facilities are available. A camp host is on-site. Some facilities are wheelchair accessible. Leashed pets are permitted.

Reservations, fees: Reservations are accepted for some sites at 877/444-6777 ($10 reservation fee) or www.recreation.gov ($9 reservation fee). Sites are $18-20 per night, $8-10 per night per additional vehicle, $2 additional charge during holidays. Open May-September, weather permitting.

Directions: From Bend, drive north on U.S. 97 to Redmond, then continue north for 15 miles to the Culver Highway. Take the Culver Highway north to Culver, and continue two miles to Gem Lane. Turn left and drive two miles to Frazier Drive. Turn left and drive a short distance to Peck Road. Turn right and drive through Cove Palisades State Park to Jordan Road at the shore of Lake Billy Chinook. Turn left on Jordan Road and drive about 10 miles (over the bridge) to County Road 64. Continue (bearing left) and drive

about eight miles to the campground entrance on the left (on the upper end of the Metolius Fork of Lake Billy Chinook).

Contact: Deschutes National Forest, Sisters Ranger District, 541/549-7700, www.fs.usda.gov/centraloregon.

97 MONTY

Scenic rating: 5

on the Metolius River in Deschutes National Forest

Map 3.5, page 157

Remote Monty campground is set at 2,000 feet elevation and gets light use. Trout fishing can be good along the banks of the Metolius River, near where it empties into Lake Billy Chinook. The river runs fast through this area, so swimming and boating are not advised; however, it is an ideal put-in for kayaks. Warm Springs Indian Reservation is across the river.

Campsites, facilities: There are 32 sites for tents or RVs up to 20 feet long. Picnic tables, garbage service, and fire grills are provided. Firewood and pit toilets are available. There is no drinking water. Boat docks and launching facilities are nearby at Perry South. Leashed pets are permitted.

Reservations, fees: Reservations are accepted for some sites at 877/444-6777 ($10 reservation fee) or www.recreation.gov ($9 reservation fee). Sites are $14 per night, $7 per night per additional vehicle. Open June-mid-September, weather permitting.

Directions: From Bend, drive north on U.S. 97 to Redmond and continue north for 15 miles to the Culver Highway. Take the Culver Highway north to Culver and continue two miles to Gem Lane. Turn left and drive two miles to Frazier Drive. Turn left and drive a short distance to Peck Road. Turn right and drive through Cove Palisades State Park to Jordan Road at the shore of Lake Billy Chinook. Turn left on Jordan Road and drive about 10 miles (over the bridge) to County

Road 64. Turn left and drive about 13 miles to the campground entrance (on the Metolius River above the headwaters of Lake Billy Chinook). The last five miles are very rough. **Contact:** Deschutes National Forest, Sisters Ranger District, 541/549-7700, www.fs.usda. gov/centraloregon.

98 COVE PALISADES STATE PARK

Scenic rating: 7

on Lake Billy Chinook

Map 3.5, page 157

This park is a mile away from the shore of Lake Billy Chinook, where some lakeshore cabins are available. Here in Oregon's high-desert region, summers are warm and sunny with fairly mild but cold winters. Lofty cliffs surround the lake, and about 10 miles of hiking trails crisscross the area. Two popular special events are held here annually: Lake Billy Chinook Day in September and the Eagle Watch in February.

Campsites, facilities: There are two campgrounds: Crooked River Campground offers 88 sites with partial hookups for tents or RVs and three deluxe cabins; Deschutes Campground has 91 tent sites, 85 sites with full hookups for RVs up to 60 feet long, and three group tent areas for up to 25 people each. Picnic tables and fire grills are provided. Drinking water, garbage bins, restrooms with flush toilets and showers, a dump station, firewood, a convenience store, amphitheater, horseshoe pit, playground, and ice are available. Boat docks, launching facilities, a marina, boat rentals, fish-cleaning station, and a restaurant are nearby. Some facilities are wheelchair accessible. Leashed pets are permitted, and there is a designated pet exercise area.

Reservations, fees: Reservations are accepted at 800/452-5687 or www.reserveamerica.com ($8 reservation fee). RV sites with full hookups are $28-30 per night, tent sites are $20 per night, cabins are $85-95 per night, the group areas are $75 per night, $7 per night per additional vehicle. Some credit cards are accepted. Crooked River Campground is open mid-February to mid-December; Deschutes Campground is open May-mid-September.

Directions: From Bend, drive north on U.S. 97 for 13 miles to Redmond and continue north for 15 miles to the Culver Highway. Take the Culver Highway north to Culver and continue two miles to Gem Lane. Turn left and drive two miles to Frazier Drive. Turn left and drive a short distance to Peck Road. Turn right and drive to the park entrance.

Contact: Cove Palisades State Park, 541/546-3412 or 800/551-6949, www.oregonstateparks. org.

99 KOA REDMOND

Scenic rating: 6

near Lake Billy Chinook

Map 3.5, page 157

This KOA has a relaxing atmosphere, with some mountain views. It is set about seven miles from Lake Billy Chinook, a steep-sided reservoir formed where the Crooked River, Deschutes River, Metolius River, and Squaw Creek all merge. Like much of the country east of the Cascades, this is a high-desert area.

Campsites, facilities: There are 22 tent sites and 58 sites with full or partial hookups for RVs of any length; most sites are pull-through. There are also six cabins. Drinking water, fire pits, and picnic tables are provided. Restrooms with flush toilets and showers, propane gas, a dump station, firewood, a convenience store, coin laundry, ice, and a playground are available. Recreational activities include a dog run, Pebble Puppies, seasonal heated pool, bicycle rentals, volleyball, horseshoe pits, and tetherball. Boat docks and launching facilities are nearby. Some facilities are wheelchair accessible. Leashed pets are permitted.

Reservations, fees: Reservations are accepted at 800/562-1992. Sites are $25-44 per night, $2-5 per person per night for more than two people. Some credit cards are accepted. Open year-round.

Directions: From Madras, drive south on U.S. 97 for nine miles to Jericho Lane. Turn left (east) and drive 0.5 mile to the campground on the right.

Contact: KOA Redmond, 541/546-3046, www.koa.com.

NORTHEASTERN OREGON

Even longtime residents often overlook Northeastern Oregon. With its high desert abutting the craggy Blue Mountains, it just doesn't look like the archetypal Oregon. In this corner of the state, you'll find Wallowa-Whitman National Forest and little-known sections of Malheur, Ochoco, and Umatilla National Forests. The Hells Canyon National Recreation Area, Idaho, and the Snake River border this region to the east. Among the highlights are the John Day River and its headwaters, the Strawberry Mountain Wilderness in Malheur National Forest, and various sections of the linked John Day Fossil Beds National Monument. One of the prettiest spots is Wallowa Lake State Park, where 9,000-foot snowcapped mountains surround a pristine lake on three sides. My favorite destinations are the Wallowa Mountains and the Eagle Cap Wilderness, a wildlife paradise with bears, bighorn sheep, deer, elk, and mountain lions.

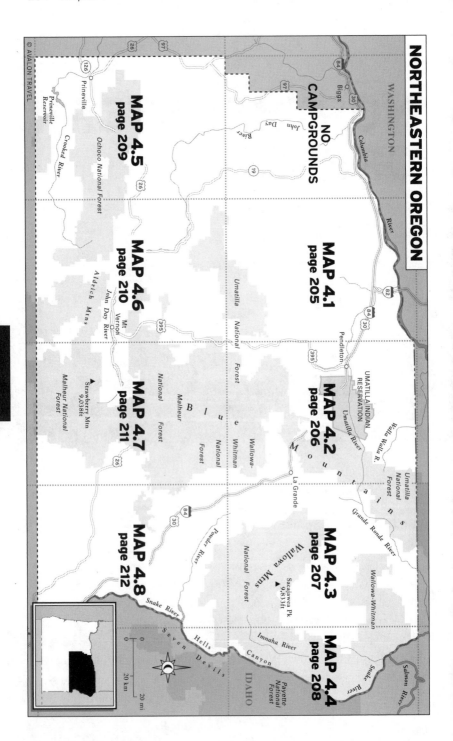

NORTHEASTERN OREGON

MAP 4.5
page 209

MAP 4.6
page 210

MAP 4.7
page 211

MAP 4.8
page 212

NO CAMPGROUNDS

MAP 4.1
page 205

MAP 4.2
page 206

MAP 4.3
page 207

MAP 4.4
page 208

WASHINGTON

IDAHO

© AVALON TRAVEL

Map 4.1

**Sites 1-9
Pages 213-216**

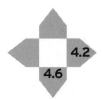

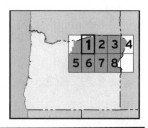

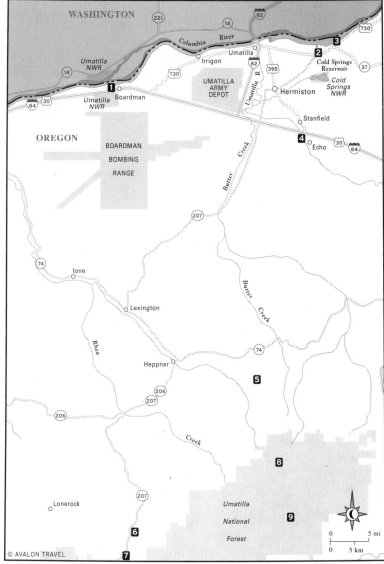

Map 4.2

Sites 10-26
Pages 217-223

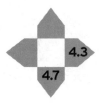

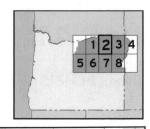

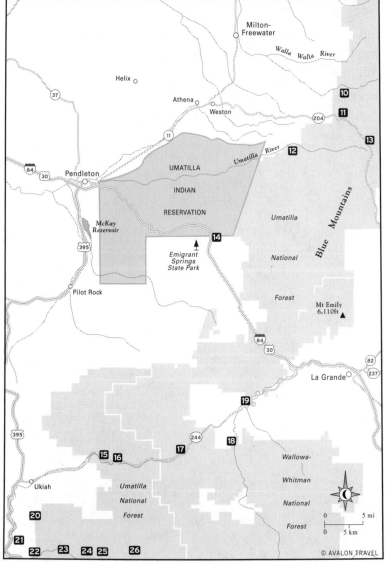

Map 4.3

Sites 27-42
Pages 224-230

4.4

4.8

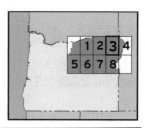

| 1 | 2 | 3 | 4 |
| 5 | 6 | 7 | 8 |

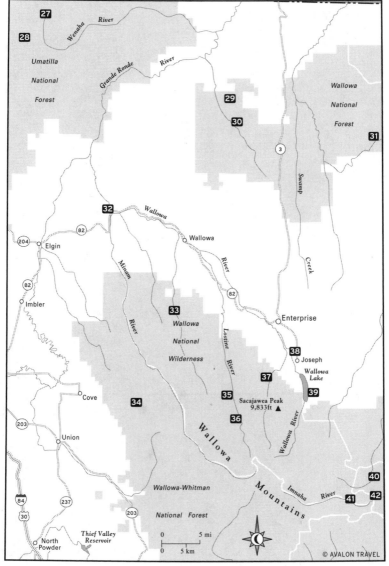

27

28

Wenaha River

Umatilla

National

Forest

Grande Ronde River

29

30

3

Swamp

Wallowa

National

Forest

31

Wallowa

32

204

82

Elgin

Wallowa

River

Wallowa

82

Imbler

Minam River

33

Wallowa

National

Wilderness

Lostine River

82

Enterprise

38

Joseph

Wallowa
Lake

37

39

Cove

34

35

Sacajawea Peak
9,833ft ▲

36

203

Union

Wallowa

Wallowa-Whitman

84

30

237

203

National   Forest

Mountains

Imnaha River

40

41

42

North
Powder

Thief Valley
Reservoir

0   5 mi

0   5 km

© AVALON TRAVEL

Map 4.4

Sites 43-46
Pages 230-231

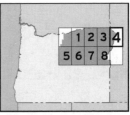

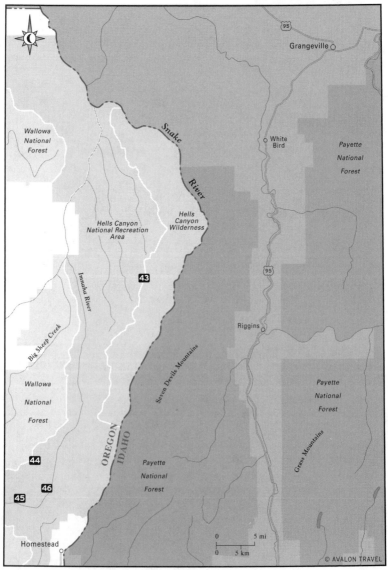

Map 4.5

Sites 47-60
Pages 232-237

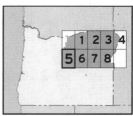

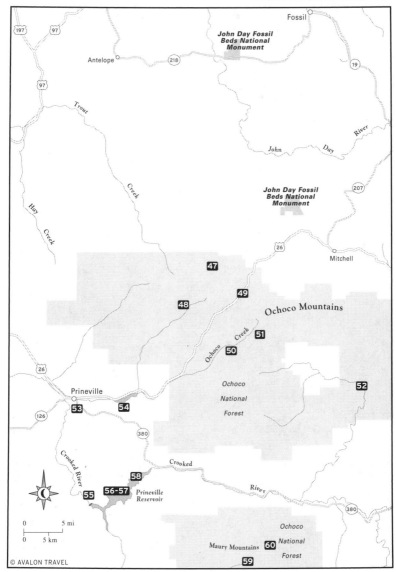

Map 4.6

Sites 61-67
Pages 238-240

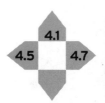

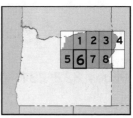

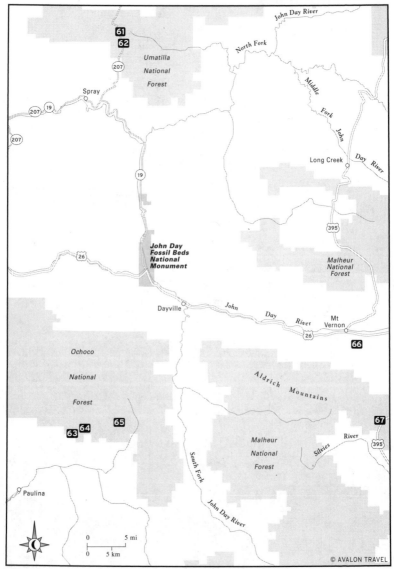

Map 4.7

Sites 68-100
Pages 241-254

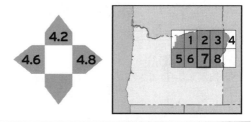

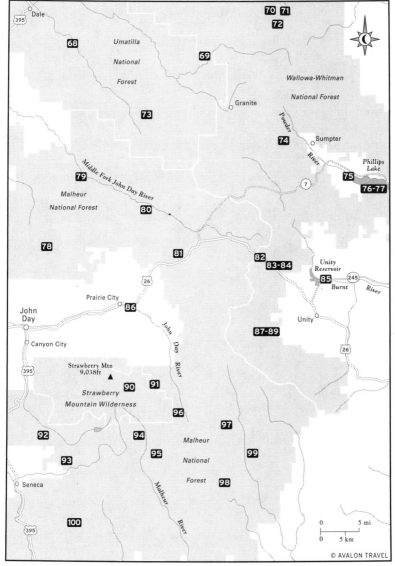

Dale
395
68
Umatilla
National
Forest
69
Granite
70 71
72
Wallowa-Whitman
National Forest
Powder River
73
74
Sumpter
79
Middle Fork John Day River
Phillips Lake
75
76-77
Malheur
National Forest
80
7
78
81
82
83-84
Unity Reservoir
85
245
Burnt River
26
86
Prairie City
Unity
John Day
John Day River
26
Canyon City
395
Strawberry Mtn
9,038ft
Strawberry
Mountain Wilderness
90
91
96
97
92
94
95
99
93
Malheur
National
Forest
98
Seneca
100
395
Malheur River

0 ___ 5 mi
0 ___ 5 km

© AVALON TRAVEL

Map 4.8

Sites 101-108
Pages 254-257

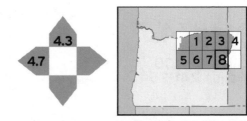

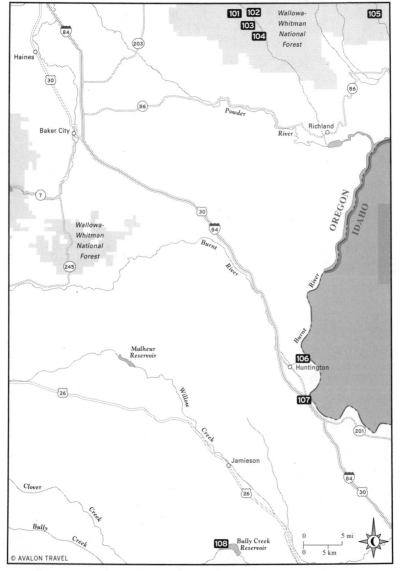

© AVALON TRAVEL

1 BOARDMAN MARINA AND RV PARK

🚴 ⛵ 🚣 🛶 🐕 ♿ 🚐 ⛺

Scenic rating: 7

on the Columbia River

Map 4.1, page 205

This public campground is set on the Columbia River among linden, maple, and sycamore trees. Some sites are located along the riverbank. In addition to fishing for bass, crappie, and walleye, nearby recreation options include a marina and golf course (five miles away).

Campsites, facilities: There are 63 sites with full hookups for tents or RVs of any length and four sites for tents only; some sites are pull-through. Picnic tables and fire pits are provided. Drinking water, restrooms with flush toilets and showers, a dump station, garbage bins, coin laundry, a day-use area with picnic shelters, a pay phone, Wi-Fi, seasonal firewood and ice for sale, children's playground, and a boat dock, pump-out station, fish-cleaning station, and launch are available. Recreational facilities include a basketball court, softball fields, horseshoe pits, sand volleyball, and a hiking/biking path along the river. A boat marina and grocery store are available within one mile. Some facilities are wheelchair accessible. Leashed pets are permitted.

Reservations, fees: Reservations are accepted at 888/481-7217. Sites are $26-32 per night, $5 per night per extra vehicle. Some credit cards are accepted. Open year-round, with limited winter facilities.

Directions: From Portland on I-84 eastbound, drive 164 miles to Boardman and Exit 164. Take that exit and turn left (north) on Main Street. Drive 0.25 mile over the railroad bridge, bear left, and continue 0.2 mile to the Y intersection and the park on the right.

Contact: Boardman Marina and RV Park, Boardman Park and Recreation District, 541/481-7217 or 888/481-7217, www.boardmanmarinapark.com.

2 HAT ROCK CAMPGROUND

🥾 🚴 ⛵ 🚣 🛶 🐕 ♿ 🚐 ⛺

Scenic rating: 7

near the Columbia River

Map 4.1, page 205

Hat Rock State Park is a day-use area with a boat launch along the banks of the Columbia River. The campground itself is very pretty, with lots of trees, and offers close access to the river and fishing.

Campsites, facilities: There are eight tent sites and 60 sites with full or partial hookups for RVs of any length; some sites are pull-through. Picnic tables and fire pits are provided. Drinking water, restrooms with flush toilets and showers, a dump station, convenience store, café, coin laundry, volleyball and basketball courts, ballfield, horseshoe pits, seasonal swimming pool, Wi-Fi, firewood, and ice are available. Boat docks and launching facilities are nearby. Some facilities are wheelchair accessible. Leashed pets are permitted.

Reservations, fees: Reservations are accepted. Sites are $28-32 per night, $3 per person per night for more than two people. Weekly and monthly rates are available. Some credit cards are accepted. Open year-round.

Directions: From Portland, drive east on U.S. 84 for roughly 170 miles past Boardman to the junction of U.S. 84 and U.S. 730. Turn northeast on U.S. 730 and drive 18 miles to the junction with I-82. Continue east on U.S. 730 for seven miles to the state park access road. Turn left (north) and drive 0.5 mile to the park on the left.

Contact: Hat Rock Campground, 541/567-4188, www.hatrockcampground.com; Hat Rock Store 541/567-0917.

3 SAND STATION RECREATION AREA

🚶 🏊 💺 🐕 🚐 ⛺

Scenic rating: 5

on Lake Wallula

Map 4.1, page 205

This eight-acre park offers hiking, picnicking, swimming, and fishing for smallmouth bass and steelhead, salmon, and sturgeon in season. It has a shaded day-use area and campsites on the beach.

Campsites, facilities: There are five sites (no hookups) for tents or RVs and space for an additional 5-10 tents near the beach. Picnic tables, sun shelters, and fire grills are provided. Vault toilets and a swimming beach are available. There is no drinking water and garbage must be packed out. A grocery store is located within three miles, a boat ramp is about two miles away, and a golf course is nine miles away. Leashed pets are permitted.

Reservations, fees: Reservations are not accepted. There is no fee for camping. Open year-round, weather permitting.

Directions: In Umatilla, drive north on I Street to U.S. 730/Columbia River Highway. Turn right onto U.S. 730/Columbia River Highway and drive 11 miles to the park entrance on the left.

Contact: U.S. Army Corps of Engineers, Walla Walla District, 541/922-2268, www.nww.usace.army.mil.

4 FORT HENRIETTA RV PARK

🚶 🚴 🏊 💺 🐕 🚐 ⛺

Scenic rating: 7

on the Umatilla River

Map 4.1, page 205

This park, located in the historic community of Echo, sits along the Umatilla River. It provides a quiet, pleasant layover spot for travelers cruising I-84. The river has some good trout fishing, and a nine-hole public golf course is a short drive away.

Campsites, facilities: There are seven sites with full hookups (including cable TV) for RVs of any length, two pull-through sites with partial hookups, and an area for dispersed tent camping. Picnic tables are provided. Drinking water, restrooms with flush toilets and showers, and a dump station are available. The camp is within walking distance of two restaurants. Leashed pets are permitted.

Reservations, fees: Reservations available at 541/571-3597. Sites are $20-26 per night, $2 per person per night for more than two people. Open year-round.

Directions: From Pendleton, drive west on I-84 to Exit 188 and the Echo Highway. Take the exit, turn left (southeast), and drive one mile; cross the railroad tracks and continue 0.5 mile to Dupont Street. Turn right (south) and drive 0.3 mile to Main Street. Turn left (west) and drive one block to the park on the left.

Contact: Echo City Hall, 541/571-3597, www.echo-oregon.com.

5 CUTSFORTH PARK

🚶 🚴 💺 🐕 🛶 ♿ 🚐 ⛺

Scenic rating: 8

on Willow Creek

Map 4.1, page 205

Cutsforth is a secluded and private county park set beside a small, wheelchair-accessible pond in a quiet, wooded area. In winter, the park serves as a staging area for snowmobilers, and in spring mushroom hunting is an attraction.

Campsites, facilities: There are 54 sites, most with full or partial hookups, for tents or RVs up to 42 feet long, and two cabins. Horse pens and a large building with kitchen facilities are available for rent. Picnic tables and fire rings are provided at most sites. Restrooms with flush toilets, vault toilets, coin showers, a dump station, horseshoe pits, firewood, ice, gazebo, a community building, and a playground are available. Supplies are available in Heppner (22 miles away). Some facilities are wheelchair accessible. Leashed pets are permitted.

Reservations, fees: Reservations are accepted ($12 reservation fee) at 541/989-8214 or www.morrowcountyparks.org. Sites with hookups are $20-26 per night, dry sites are $17 per night, $2 per night per additional vehicle, and $3 per night per horse. Cabins are $45 per night. Weekly and monthly rates are available. Open mid-May-mid-November, weather permitting.

Directions: From Pendleton on I-84, drive west for 27 miles to Exit 182 and Highway 207 (Heppner Highway). Turn south and drive 32 miles to Lexington and Highway 74. Turn left (southeast) on Highway 74 (becomes Highway 207) and drive 10 miles to Heppner. Continue south on Highway 207 for 0.5 mile to Willow Creek Road. Turn left on Willow Creek Road and drive 23 miles to the park.

Contact: Morrow County Public Works, 541/989-8214, www.morrowcountyparks.org.

6 ANSON WRIGHT MEMORIAL PARK

Scenic rating: 7

on Rock Creek

Map 4.1, page 205

Set among wooded hills along a small stream, this county park offers visitors hiking opportunities and prime trout fishing in a stocked, wheelchair-accessible pond. Attractions in the area include Emigrant Springs State Park, Hardman Ghost Town (10 miles away), and the Pendleton Mills. There's also a nearby opal mine, accessible with permission only.

Campsites, facilities: There are 52 sites with full hookups for tents or RVs up to 42 feet long; most sites are pull-through. There is also one cabin. Picnic tables and fire rings are provided. Restrooms with coin showers, a picnic area, dump station, firewood, and a playground are provided. Some facilities are wheelchair accessible. Leashed pets are permitted.

Reservations, fees: Reservations are accepted ($12 reservation fee). Sites are $26 per night, dry sites are $17 per night, and $2 per night per additional vehicle. Cabins are $45 per night. Weekly and monthly rates are available. Open mid-May-end of October, weather permitting.

Directions: From Pendleton, drive west on I-84 for 27 miles to Exit 182 and Highway 207 (Heppner Highway). Turn south and drive 32 miles to Lexington and Highway 74. Turn left (south) on Highway 74 (becomes Highway 20) and drive 10 miles to Heppner. Continue south on Highway 207 for 11 miles to Ruggs and a fork. Bear left at the fork (still Highway 207) and drive 12 miles to the park on the right.

Contact: Morrow County Public Works, 541/989-8214, www.morrowcountyparks.org.

7 MORROW COUNTY OHV PARK

Scenic rating: 5

in Morrow County Park

Map 4.1, page 205

This 6,200-acre park is very popular. It is designed primarily for OHV use and has more than 150 miles of trails specifically for off-highway vehicles. There is a day-use area and the campground itself is wooded.

Campsites, facilities: There are 83 sites, most with full hookups, for tents or RVs of any length, five tent-only sites, four group sites for up to 10 people each in an open gravel lot (no trees), and six cabins. Picnic tables and fire rings are provided at some sites. Drinking water, showers, flush toilets, dump station, firewood, coin ATV wash rack, helmet rental, propane, a seasonal restaurant, playground, and a day-use area are available. Some facilities are wheelchair accessible. Leashed pets are permitted.

Reservations, fees: Reservations are accepted at 541/989-8214 or www.morrowcountyparks.org ($12 reservation fee). Sites with hookups are $26 per night, dry sites are $17 per night, and $2 per night per additional vehicle. Cabins are $45-80 per night. Weekly and monthly rates are available. Open mid-May-mid-November, weather permitting; call ahead December-February.

Directions: From Pendleton, drive west on I-84 for 27 miles to Exit 182 and Highway 207 (Heppner Highway). Turn south and drive 32 miles to Lexington and Highway 74. Turn left (south) on Highway 74 (becomes Highway 20) and drive 10 miles to Heppner. Continue south on Highway 207 for 11 miles to Ruggs and a fork. Bear left at the fork (still Highway 207) and drive 22 miles to the park on the right.

Contact: Morrow County Public Works, 541/989-8214, www.morrowcountyparks.org.

8 PENLAND LAKE

Scenic rating: 10

near Penland Lake in the Umatilla National Forest

Map 4.1, page 205   **BEST (**

This campground (4,950 feet elevation) has partial tree cover, so there are many open spaces. The lake is small, and electric-motor boats are allowed. The fishing can be good at times, with rainbow trout and bluegill the primary fish species. Hiking and bicycling are popular on the nearby trails. The wildlife-viewing can be outstanding; species include bear, deer, and elk, as well as grouse and other birds.

Campsites, facilities: There are seven sites for tents and one site for RVs up to 50 feet long. Picnic tables and fire rings are provided. Vault toilets are available. There is no drinking water. Garbage must be packed out. A boat ramp is nearby. Leashed pets are permitted.

Reservations, fees: Reservations are not accepted. Sites are $8 per night. Open May-October, weather permitting. A 14-day stay limit is enforced.

Directions: From Heppner, drive south on Highway 207 to Willow Creek Road (Forest Road 54/County Road 678). Turn left (east) and drive 23 miles to Forest Road 21. Turn right

(gravel road) and drive three miles to Forest Road 2103. Turn left and drive two miles to the lake and campground.

Contact: Umatilla National Forest, Heppner Ranger District, 541/676-9187, www.fs.usda.gov/umatilla.

9 DIVIDE WELL

Scenic rating: 5

in Umatilla National Forest

Map 4.1, page 205

Divide Well is a primitive campground, but it is busy in the summer, and even occasionally used for reunions. Set at 4,700 feet elevation, it can serve as a good base camp for a hunting trip. Mule deer and Rocky Mountain elk can be spotted in the surrounding ponderosa pine and fir forest. Potamus Point Scenic Overlook, offering a spectacular view of the John Day River drainage, is 11 miles south of the camp on Forest Road 5316 and provides a good opportunity to see bighorn sheep.

Campsites, facilities: There are eight sites for tents or RVs up to 20 feet long and three group sites. A vault toilet is provided. There is no drinking water, and garbage must be packed out. Leashed pets are permitted.

Reservations, fees: Reservations are not accepted. There is no fee for camping. Open late May-November, weather permitting. A 14-day stay limit is enforced.

Directions: From Pendleton, drive south on U.S. 395 for 48 miles to Ukiah and Highway 244. Turn right (the road becomes Forest Road 53) and drive west on Forest Road 53 for about 14 miles to Forest Road 5327. Turn left (south) and drive seven miles to the campground on the right. A U.S. Forest Service map is recommended.

Contact: Umatilla National Forest, North Fork John Day Ranger District, 541-427-3231, www.fs.usda.gov/umatilla.

10 WOODWARD

Scenic rating: 7

near Langdon Lake in Umatilla National Forest

Map 4.2, page 206

Nestled among the trees at an elevation of 4,950 feet, this popular campground has a view of Langdon Lake (though campers do not have access to the private lake). A flat trail encircles the campground, and there is some privacy screening between the sites.

Campsites, facilities: There are 15 sites for tents or RVs up to 28 feet long. Picnic tables, garbage bins, and fire grills are provided. Drinking water and vault toilets are available. Leashed pets are permitted.

Reservations, fees: Reservations are not accepted. Sites are $12 per night, $5 per each additional vehicle. Open late June-September, weather permitting. A 14-day stay limit is enforced.

Directions: From Pendleton on I-84, turn north on Highway 11 and drive approximately 27 miles to Weston and Highway 204. Turn right (southeast) on Highway 204 and drive 17 miles to the campground on the right (near Langdon Lake).

Contact: Umatilla National Forest, Walla Walla Ranger District, 509/522-6290, www.fs.usda.gov/umatilla.

11 TARGET MEADOWS

Scenic rating: 6

near the south fork of the Walla Walla River in Umatilla National Forest

Map 4.2, page 206

This quiet campground with shady sites and a sunny meadow is situated at 4,800 feet elevation. The camp is adjacent to the Burnt Cabin Trailhead, which leads to the south fork of the Walla Walla River Trail and an old military site.

Campsites, facilities: There are 16 sites for tents or RVs up to 28 feet long and two sites for tents only. Picnic tables and fire grills are provided. Garbage bins, drinking water, and vault toilets are available. Leashed pets are permitted.

Reservations, fees: Reservations are not accepted. Sites are $12 per night for up to two vehicles, $5 per each additional vehicle. Open late June-mid-November, weather permitting. A 14-day stay limit is enforced.

Directions: From Pendleton, drive north on Highway 11 for 16 miles to Highway 204 near Weston. Turn right (southeast) on Highway 204 and drive 17.5 miles to Forest Road 64. Turn left and drive 0.5 mile to Forest Road 6401. Turn left (north) and drive two miles to Road 6401-050. Turn right (north) and drive 0.5 mile to the camp.

Contact: Umatilla National Forest, Walla Walla Ranger District, 509/522-6290, www.fs.usda.gov/umatilla.

12 UMATILLA FORKS

Scenic rating: 3

along the Umatilla River in Umatilla National Forest

Map 4.2, page 206

Umatilla Forks campground lies in a canyon between the South and North Forks of the Umatilla River at an elevation of 2,400 feet. Expect warm temperatures in mid- to late summer; tree cover provides some relief. Fishing on the Umatilla River is catch-and-release only, and hiking is possible in the North Fork Umatilla Wilderness.

Campsites, facilities: There are eight sites for tents or RVs up to 28 feet long and seven sites for tents only. Picnic tables and fire grills are provided. Drinking water and vault toilets are available. Garbage must be packed out. Leashed pets are permitted.

Reservations, fees: Reservations are not accepted. Sites are $10 per night for up to two vehicles, $5 per each additional vehicle. Open

May-October, weather permitting. A 14-day stay limit is enforced.

Directions: From Pendleton, drive north on Highway 11 for about 25 miles to Athena and Pambrun Road. Turn right on Pambrun Road and drive five miles to Spring Hollow Road. Turn left on Spring Hollow Road (it becomes Thorn Hollow Road) and drive about 6.5 miles to Bingham Road (River Road). Turn left on Bingham Road (River Road), cross the railroad tracks, and follow signs for about five miles to Gibbon. Cross the railroad tracks at Gibbon and continue on Bingham Road (it becomes Forest Road 32) about 11 miles to the campground on the right.

Contact: Umatilla National Forest, Walla Walla Ranger District, 509/522-6290, www.fs.usda.gov/umatilla.

13 WOODLAND

Scenic rating: 4
in Umatilla National Forest

Map 4.2, page 206

Primitive Woodland campground is set at 5,200 feet elevation with easy highway access—and related road noise. The camp has both shaded and sunny sites and can be a perfect spot for I-84 cruisers looking for a short detour. During fall, the area is popular with hunters; hikers and mountain bikers will enjoy the area the rest of the year.

Campsites, facilities: There are six sites for tents or RVs up to 28 feet long. Picnic tables, fire grills, and vault toilets are provided. There is no drinking water. Garbage must be packed out. Leashed pets are permitted.

Reservations, fees: Reservations are not accepted. Sites are $8 per night for up to two vehicles, $5 per each additional vehicle. Open mid-June-mid-November, weather permitting. A 14-day stay limit is enforced.

Directions: From Pendleton, drive north on Highway 11 for 16 miles to Highway 204 near Weston. Turn right (southeast) on Highway 204

and drive 23 miles. The campground is just off the highway on the left.

Contact: Umatilla National Forest, Walla Walla Ranger District, 509/522-6290, www.fs.usda.gov/umatilla.

14 EMIGRANT SPRINGS STATE HERITAGE AREA

Scenic rating: 7
near the Umatilla Indian Reservation

Map 4.2, page 206

Emigrant Springs sits in old-growth forest at the summit of the Blue Mountains. The campground is popular with horse campers and offers wildlife-watching opportunities. The nearby Oregon Trail and Pendleton Woolen Mills provide interesting side trips.

Campsites, facilities: There are 32 sites for tents, 18 sites with full hookups for RVs of any length, a designated horse camp (closed in winter), a group tent site, and seven cabins. Picnic tables, fire grills, and horse corrals are provided. Drinking water, garbage bins, restrooms with flush toilets and showers, firewood, some horse facilities, a reservable community building with kitchen, basketball court, amphitheater, and baseball field are available. Some facilities are wheelchair accessible. Leashed pets are permitted.

Reservations, fees: Reservations are accepted at 800/452-5687 or www.reserveamerica.com ($8 reservation fee). RV sites are $22-24 per night, tent sites are $17 per night, cabins are $41-51 per night, equestrian sites are $17 per night, and the group site is $71 per night for up to 25 people ($3 per person for more than 25). Additional vehicles are $7 per night. Some credit cards are accepted. Open May 1-mid-October, with only the cabins and five campsites open year-round. (Water is off mid-Oct.-mid-Apr.).

Directions: From Pendleton, drive southeast on I-84 for 26 miles to Exit 234. Take that exit to Old Oregon Trail Road (frontage road) and drive 0.5 mile to the park on the right.

Contact: Emigrant Springs State Heritage Area, 541/983-2277 or 800/551-6949, www.oregonstateparks.org.

15 LANE CREEK

Scenic rating: 4
on Camas Creek in Umatilla National Forest

Map 4.2, page 206

This primitive campground (3,850 feet elevation) borders Camas Creek and Lane Creek, just inside the forest boundary, and provides easy access to all the amenities of town. It's a popular stop for overnighters passing through the area. Some of the sites close to the highway get traffic noise. Highlights in the area include hot springs (privately owned) and good hunting and fishing. A U.S. Forest Service map details the back roads.

Campsites, facilities: There are six sites for tents or RVs up to 28 feet long and one group site for up to 25 people. Picnic tables and fire grills are provided. Vault toilets are available. There is no drinking water, and garbage must be packed out. Leashed pets are permitted.

Reservations, fees: Reservations are not accepted. Sites are $8 per night for up to two vehicles, $5 per each additional vehicle, and $25 per night for the group site. Open April-November, weather permitting. A 14-day stay limit is enforced.

Directions: From Pendleton, drive south on U.S. 395 for 50 miles to Ukiah and Highway 244. Turn east on Highway 244 and drive nine miles to the campground on the left.

Contact: Umatilla National Forest, North Fork John Day Ranger District, 541/427-3231, www.fs.usda.gov/umatilla.

16 BEAR WALLOW CREEK

Scenic rating: 5
on Bear Wallow Creek in Umatilla National Forest

Map 4.2, page 206

Situated near the confluence of Bear Wallow and Camus Creeks at an elevation of 3,900 feet, Bear Wallow is one of three off Highway 244 (the others are Lane Creek and Frazier). Quiet and primitive, the camp is used primarily in the summer. A 0.5-mile, wheelchair-accessible, interpretive trail meanders next to Bear Wallow Creek, highlighting the steelhead habitat.

Campsites, facilities: There are three sites for tents or RVs up to 28 feet long and four sites for smaller RVs or tents. Picnic tables and fire grills are provided. Vault toilets are available. No drinking water is available and garbage must be packed out. Some facilities are wheelchair accessible. Leashed pets are permitted.

Reservations, fees: Reservations are not accepted. Sites are $8 per night for up to two vehicles, $5 per each additional vehicle. Open April-November, weather permitting. A 14-day stay limit is enforced.

Directions: From Pendleton, drive south on U.S. 395 for 50 miles to Ukiah and Highway 244. Turn east on Highway 244 and drive 10 miles to the camp on the left.

Contact: Umatilla National Forest, North Fork John Day Ranger District, 541/427-3231, www.fs.usda.gov/umatilla.

17 FRAZIER

Scenic rating: 5
on Frazier Creek in Umatilla National Forest

Map 4.2, page 206

With nearly 130 miles of OHV and motorcycle trails at the Winom-Frazier Off-Highway-Vehicle Complex, this camp is popular in the summer with the OHV crowd. The campground is set at 4,300 feet elevation along the banks of Frazier Creek. It is a popular hunting area in the fall, and some fishing is available in the area. It's advisable to obtain a map of Umatilla National Forest. On weekends, it's not a good spot for the traditional camper looking for quiet and solitude. Lehman Hot Springs, one mile away, provides a side-trip option.

Campsites, facilities: There are 15 sites for tents or RVs up to 28 feet long and five group sites. Picnic tables and fire grills are provided. An OHV loading ramp and vault toilets are available. There is no drinking water, and garbage must be packed out. Some facilities are wheelchair accessible. Leashed pets are permitted. A 14-day stay limit is enforced.

Reservations, fees: Reservations are not accepted. Sites are $10 per night for up to two vehicles; group sites are $25 per night. Open April-November, weather permitting.

Directions: From Pendleton, drive south on U.S. 395 for 50 miles to Ukiah and Highway 244. Turn left (east) on Highway 244 and drive 18 miles to Forest Road 5226. Turn right (south) and drive 0.5 mile to the campground.

Contact: Umatilla National Forest, North Fork John Day Ranger District, 541/427-3231, www. fs.usda.gov/umatilla.

18 SPOOL CART

🚶 ♨ 🛶 🐴 ♿ 🚐 ⛺

Scenic rating: 6

on the Grande Ronde River in
Wallowa-Whitman National Forest

Map 4.2, page 206

Spool Cart gets its name from the large cable spools that were delivered here by train and then transported to logging sites on a cart. The wooded campground sits at 3,500 feet elevation on the banks of the Grande Ronde River; sites offer privacy. The camp is popular with hunters in the fall, and the gurgling Grande Ronde offers fishing for bull trout. Hilgard Junction State Park to the north provides numerous recreation options, and the Oregon Interpretive Trail Park at Blue Crossing is nearby.

Campsites, facilities: There are 12 sites for tents or RVs up to 22 feet long. Picnic tables and fire grills are provided. Vault toilets are available. There is no drinking water, and garbage must be packed out. Some facilities are wheelchair accessible. Leashed pets are permitted.

Reservations, fees: Reservations are not accepted. Sites are $5 per night per vehicle. Open late May-late November.

Directions: From Pendleton, drive southeast on U.S. 84 for 42 miles to Highway 244. Turn southwest on Highway 244 and drive 13 miles to Forest Road 51. Turn left (south) and drive five miles to the campground on the right.

Contact: Wallowa-Whitman National Forest, LaGrande Ranger District, 541/963-7186, www. fs.usda.gov/wallowa-whitman.

19 BIRD TRACK SPRINGS

🚶 ㊰ 🛶 🐴 ♿ 🚐 ⛺

Scenic rating: 7

near the Grande Ronde River in
Wallowa-Whitman National Forest

Map 4.2, page 206

Bird Track Springs is located at 3,100 feet elevation and is about a five-minute walk from the Grande Ronde River. The spacious campsites are right off the highway in surrounding woods of primarily ponderosa pine and white fir. The Bird Track Springs Interpretive Trail, across the campground, offers a hiking and bird-watching opportunity.

Campsites, facilities: There are 22 sites for tents or RVs up to 22 feet long. Picnic tables and fire rings are provided. Vault toilets are available. There is no drinking water, and garbage must be packed out. A camp host is on-site in the summer. Some facilities are wheelchair accessible. Leashed pets are permitted.

Reservations, fees: Reservations are not accepted. Sites are $5 per night per vehicle. Open mid-May-November, weather permitting.

Directions: From Pendleton, drive southeast on U.S. 84 for 42 miles to Highway 244. Turn right (southwest) and drive seven miles to the campground on the left.

Contact: Wallowa-Whitman National Forest, LaGrande Ranger District, 541/963-7186, www.fs.usda.gov/wallowa-whitman.

20 DRIFT FENCE
🏃 🐴 🚐 ⛺

Scenic rating: 5
near Ross Springs in Umatilla National Forest

Map 4.2, page 206

Get this: Drift Fence is not marked on the Umatilla National Forest Map. The camp, set at 4,250 feet elevation, is adjacent to Blue Mountain National Forest Scenic Byway. With some elk and deer in the area, hunting is a highlight here. The Bridge Creek Interpretive Trail, three miles northwest of the campground off Forest Road 52, leads to a beautiful view of open meadow with various wildflowers and wildlife. Elk may be seen roaming in the Bridge Creek area.

Campsites, facilities: There are six sites for tents or RVs up to 30 feet long and one group site. Picnic tables are provided. A pit toilet is available. There is no drinking water, and garbage must be packed out. Leashed pets are permitted.

Reservations, fees: Reservations are not accepted. There is no fee for camping. Open May-November, weather permitting. A 14-day stay limit is enforced.

Directions: From Pendleton, drive south on U.S. 395 for 50 miles to Highway 244. Turn east on Highway 244 and drive one mile to Ukiah and Forest Road 52. Turn right (south) on Forest Road 52 and drive eight miles to the campground on the right.

Contact: Umatilla National Forest, North Fork John Day Ranger District, 541/427-3231, www.fs.usda.gov/umatilla.

21 UKIAH-DALE FOREST STATE SCENIC CORRIDOR
🏊 🐴 🚐 ⛺

Scenic rating: 7
near the North Fork of the John Day River

Map 4.2, page 206

Fishing is a prime activity at this Camas Creek campground, nestled near the banks of the north fork of the John Day River at an elevation of 3,140 feet. It's a good layover for visitors cruising U.S. 395 looking for a shady spot for the night. Emigrant Springs State Park near Pendleton is a possible side trip.

Campsites, facilities: There are 27 sites for tents or self-contained RVs of any length. Picnic tables and fire pits are provided. Drinking water, firewood, and restrooms with flush toilets are available. Leashed pets are permitted.

Reservations, fees: Reservations are not accepted. Sites are $10 per night, $7 per night per additional vehicle. Open May-mid-October.

Directions: From Pendleton, drive south on U.S. 39 for 50 miles to Highway 244 (near Ukiah). Continue south on U.S. 395 for three miles to the park.

Contact: Emigrant Springs State Heritage Park, 541/983-2277 or 800/551-6949, www.oregonstateparks.org.

22 TOLLBRIDGE
🏊 🐴 ♿ 🚐 ⛺

Scenic rating: 4
on the north fork of the John Day River in Umatilla National Forest

Map 4.2, page 206

This small, secluded campground (elevation 3,800 feet) lies at the confluence of Desolation Creek and the north fork of the John Day River and is adjacent to the Bridge Creek Wildlife Area. It can be beautiful or ugly, depending upon which direction you look. It's dusty in the summer, and there's sparse tree cover. Hunting and fishing are two options here, or explore the geological interpretive sign in the camp.

Campsites, facilities: There are five sites for tents or RVs up to 26 feet long. Picnic tables and fire grills are provided. A vault toilet is available. There is no drinking water, and garbage must be packed out. Some facilities are wheelchair accessible. Leashed pets are permitted.

Reservations, fees: Reservations are not accepted. Sites are $8 per night for up to two vehicles, $5 per each additional vehicle. Open April-November, weather permitting. A 14-day stay limit is enforced.

Directions: From Pendleton, drive south on U.S. 395 for 50 miles to the intersection with Highway 244. Continue south on U.S. 395 for 18 miles to Forest Road 55 (1 mile north of Dale). Turn left and drive 0.5 mile southeast to Forest Road 10 and the campground access road. Drive a short distance to the campground.

Contact: Umatilla National Forest, North Fork John Day Ranger District, 541/427-3231, www.fs.usda.gov/umatilla.

23 GOLD DREDGE CAMP

Scenic rating: 7

on the north fork of the John Day River in Umatilla National Forest

Map 4.2, page 206

Gold Dredge lies along the banks of the north fork of the John Day River, a federally designated Wild and Scenic River. This camp is an excellent launch point for recreation: swimming, fishing, rafting (spring only), float-tubing, and hunting (fall) are among the many activities. Dredge tailings from old mining activity are visible from the camp. At the end of Forest Road 5506, you can access a trailhead that heads into the adjacent North Fork John Day Wilderness. Special fishing regulations are in effect for the North Fork John Day River; check Oregon fishing regulations before heading out.

Parking is provided at Big Creek Bridge for the North Fork John Day Wilderness Trailhead

and the OHV trail that leads to the Winom-Frazier OHV Complex. Those driving to the end of Forest Road 5506 will need a high-clearance vehicle.

Campsites, facilities: There are seven sites for tents or RVs up to 28 feet long and one group site for up to 50 people. Picnic tables are provided. Vault toilets are available. There is no drinking water, and garbage must be packed out. Some facilities are wheelchair accessible. Leashed pets are permitted.

Reservations, fees: Reservations are not accepted. Sites are $8 per night for up to two vehicles. The group site is $25 per night. Open May-November, weather permitting. A 14-day stay limit is enforced.

Directions: From Pendleton, drive south on U.S. 395 for 62 miles to Forest Road 55 (1 mile north of Dale). Turn left and drive six miles to the crossroads. Continue straight onto Forest Road 5506 and drive 2.5 miles to the campground on the right. Note: The last two miles of road are very rough.

Contact: Umatilla National Forest, North Fork John Day Ranger District, 541/427-3231, www.fs.usda.gov/umatilla.

24 DRIFTWOOD

Scenic rating: 6

on the north fork of the John Day River in Umatilla National Forest

Map 4.2, page 206

This tiny campground with ponderosa pine and Douglas fir cover sits on the banks of the north fork of the John Day River at an elevation of 2,500 feet. Recreational opportunities at this remote spot include fishing, float tubing, hunting, rafting, and swimming.

Campsites, facilities: There are six sites for tents or RVs up to 28 feet long. Fire grills and picnic tables are provided. A vault toilet is available. No drinking water is available. Garbage must be packed out. Leashed pets are permitted. A 14-day stay limit is enforced.

Reservations, fees: Reservations are not accepted. Sites are $8 per night for up to two vehicles, $5 per each additional vehicle. Open April-November, weather permitting.

Directions: From Pendleton, drive south on U.S. 395 for 62 miles to Forest Road 55 (1 mile north of Dale; it's easier to find if you know the marker, Texas Bar Road). Turn left and drive six miles to the crossroads. Continue straight ahead onto Forest Road 5506 and drive one mile to the campground on the right. Note: The last two miles of road are very rough.

Contact: Umatilla National Forest, North Fork John Day Ranger District, 541/427-3231, www.fs.usda.gov/umatilla.

25 ORIENTAL CAMPGROUND

Scenic rating: 4

on the north fork of the John Day River in Umatilla National Forest

Map 4.2, page 206

Oriental Creek nestles in a stand of mixed conifer at 3,500 feet elevation along the banks of the north fork of the John Day River. Evidence of old mining activity is visible here. The campground is popular with horse campers, motorcyclists, and off-roaders alike. Hunting and fishing are two possible activities, and nearby trails provide access to the North Fork John Day Wilderness. (No mountain bikes or motorcycles are permitted in the wilderness area.) Be advised that the road into this campground is rough and narrow in places.

Campsites, facilities: There are seven primitive tent sites that are available for group camping. Pit toilets and picnic tables are available. There is no drinking water, and garbage must be packed out. Leashed pets are permitted.

Reservations, fees: Reservations are not accepted. Sites are $8 per night for up to two vehicles, group camping is $25 per night. Open April-November, weather permitting. A 14-day stay limit is enforced.

Directions: From Pendleton, drive south on U.S. 395 for 62 miles to Forest Road 55 (1 mile north of Dale; it's easier to find if you know the marker, Texas Bar Road). Turn left and drive six miles to the crossroads. Continue straight ahead onto Forest Road 5506 and drive six miles to the campground on the right. This road is rough and not recommended for trailers.

Contact: Umatilla National Forest, North Fork John Day Ranger District, 541/427-3231, www.fs.usda.gov/umatilla.

26 WINOM CAMPGROUND

Scenic rating: 2

on Winom Creek in Umatilla National Forest

Map 4.2, page 206

Winom Creek campground is set at 5,000 feet elevation and provides access to the Winom-Frazier Off-Highway-Vehicle Complex, with 130 miles of OHV trails of varying difficulty. The complex was developed in the late 1980s for OHV enthusiasts and has worn in well. The camp is also near the North Fork John Day Wilderness, perfect for hikers. (Check the campground bulletin boards for detailed maps of the terrain.)

Campsites, facilities: There are seven sites for tents or RVs up to 28 feet long and three group sites for up to 40 people. Picnic tables and fire rings are provided. Vault toilets and an OHV loading ramp are available. There is no drinking water, and garbage must be packed out. Two of the group sites have picnic shelters. Leashed pets are permitted.

Reservations, fees: Reservations are not accepted. Sites are $10 per night for up to two vehicles, the group sites are $25 per night. Open May-early November, weather permitting. A 14-day stay limit is enforced.

Directions: From Pendleton, drive south on U.S. 395 for 50 miles to Highway 244. Turn east on Highway 244 and drive one mile to Ukiah and Forest Road 52. Turn right (south) on Forest Road 52 and drive 20 miles to Forest

Road 440. Turn right and drive one mile to the campground on the right. The last mile of the access road is narrow and steep.

Contact: Umatilla National Forest, North Fork John Day Ranger District, 541/427-3231, www.fs.usda.gov/umatilla.

27 MOTTET

Scenic rating: 6

near the south fork of the Walla Walla River in Umatilla National Forest

Map 4.3, page 207

Mottet sits perched at 5,200 feet elevation along a ridge top, surrounded by a heavily timbered forest. Far from the beaten path, it's quite primitive and relatively unknown, so you're almost guaranteed privacy. A trailhead across the road leads down to the south fork of the Walla Walla River. The drinking water comes straight from an icy cold spring.

Campsites, facilities: There are six sites for tents or RVs up to 22 feet. Picnic tables and fire grills are provided. Spring water and vault toilets are available. Garbage must be packed out. Leashed pets are permitted.

Reservations, fees: Reservations are not accepted. Sites are $8 per night for up to two vehicles, $5 per each additional vehicle. Open early July-November, weather permitting. A 14-day stay limit is enforced.

Directions: From Pendleton, drive north on Highway 11 for 16 miles to Highway 204 near Weston. Turn right (southeast) on Highway 204 and drive 17.5 miles to Forest Road 64. Turn left and drive about 15 miles to Forest Road 6403. Turn left and drive about two miles to the campground on the left. The road is rough for the last two miles.

Contact: Umatilla National Forest, Walla Walla Ranger District, 509/522-6290, www.fs.usda.gov/umatilla.

28 JUBILEE LAKE

Scenic rating: 8

on Jubilee Lake in Umatilla National Forest

Map 4.3, page 207   **BEST (**

Jubilee Lake is the largest and most popular campground in Umatilla National Forest, and it fills up on weekends and holidays. Located along the shore of 90-acre Jubilee Lake (elevation 4,800 feet), this spot offers good fishing, hiking, and swimming. Electric boat motors are permitted on the lake, but gas-powered motors are prohibited. A 2.8-mile trail loops around the lake and provides different levels of accessibility for those in wheelchairs; fishing access is available along the trail.

Campsites, facilities: There are 48 sites for tents and RVs up to 28 feet long and five tent-only sites. Picnic tables and fire grills are provided. Drinking water, firewood, picnic areas, and restrooms with flush toilets are available. Boat docks and launching facilities are nearby. Garbage bins are available during the summer. Some facilities are wheelchair accessible. Leashed pets are permitted.

Reservations, fees: Reservations are not accepted. Sites are $17-24 per night for up to two vehicles, $5 per night for each additional vehicle. Open late June-mid-October, weather permitting. A 14-day stay limit is enforced.

Directions: From Pendleton, drive north on Highway 11 for 16 miles to Highway 204 near Weston. Turn right (southeast) on Highway 204 and drive 17.5 miles to Forest Road 64. Turn left and drive 12 miles northeast to Forest Road 6400-250. Turn right (south) and drive 0.5 mile to the camp.

Contact: Umatilla National Forest, Walla Walla Ranger District, 509/522-6290, www.fs.usda.gov/umatilla.

29 DOUGHERTY SPRINGS

Scenic rating: 5

near Dougherty Springs in Wallowa-Whitman National Forest

Map 4.3, page 207

This wooded, primitive campground (elevation 5,100 feet) adjacent to Dougherty Springs is one in a series of remote camps set near natural springs. The camp is in a grassy open area with sparse Douglas and white fir. Birds, deer, elk, and small mammals can be seen in the area. Hells Canyon National Recreation Area to the east provides many recreation options.

Campsites, facilities: There are eight sites for tents only and four sites for tents or RVs up to 22 feet long. Picnic tables and fire rings are provided. Vault toilets are available. There is no drinking water, and garbage must be packed out. Leashed pets are permitted.

Reservations, fees: Reservations are not accepted. There is no fee for camping. Open June-October, weather permitting.

Directions: From LaGrande, drive northeast on Highway 82 for 64 miles to Enterprise and Highway 3. Turn north on Highway 3 and drive 15 miles to Forest Road 46. Turn right (northeast) and drive 30 miles to the campground on the left.

Contact: Hells Canyon National Recreation Area, Wallowa Mountains Visitors Center, 541/426-5546, www.fs.usda.gov/wallowa-whitman.

30 COYOTE

Scenic rating: 4

near Coyote Springs in Wallowa-Whitman National Forest

Map 4.3, page 207

Coyote campground is set at 4,800 feet elevation and adjacent to Coyote Springs. This is the largest of the three primitive camps in the vicinity, offering open sites and privacy.

Campsites, facilities: There are eight sites for tents or RVs up to 22 feet long and 21 sites for tents only. Picnic tables and fire rings are provided. Vault toilets are available. There is no drinking water, and garbage must be packed out. Leashed pets are permitted.

Reservations, fees: Reservations are not accepted. There is no fee for camping. Open May-November, weather permitting.

Directions: From LaGrande, drive northeast on Highway 82 for 64 miles to Enterprise and Highway 3. Turn north on Highway 3 and drive 15 miles to Forest Road 46. Turn right (northeast) and drive 25 miles to the campground on the left.

Contact: Wallowa-Whitman National Forest, Wallowa Valley Ranger District, Wallowa Mountains Visitors Center, 541/426-5546, www.fs.usda.gov/wallowa-whitman.

31 VIGNE

Scenic rating: 5

on Chesnimnus Creek in Wallowa-Whitman National Forest

Map 4.3, page 207

Vigne campground sits at 3,500 feet elevation on the banks of Chesnimus Creek. The campground has pretty riverside sites shaded by Douglas and white fir. Recreation opportunities include fishing and exploring a few of the many hiking trails in the area.

Campsites, facilities: There are six sites for tents or RVs up to 22 feet long. Picnic tables and fire rings are provided. Drinking water and vault toilets are available. Garbage must be packed out. Leashed pets are permitted.

Reservations, fees: Reservations are not accepted. Sites are $6 per night. Open May-November, weather permitting.

Directions: From LaGrande, drive northeast on Highway 82 for 64 miles to Enterprise and Highway 3. Turn north on Highway 3 and drive 15 miles to Forest Road 46. Turn right (northeast) and drive 10 miles to Forest Road

4625. Turn right (east) and drive 10 miles to the campground. The last 10 miles are potholed and rough.

Contact: Wallowa-Whitman National Forest, Wallowa Valley Ranger District, Wallowa Mountains Visitors Center, 541/426-5546, www.fs.usda.gov/wallowa-whitman.

32 MINAM STATE PARK

Scenic rating: 7

near the Grande Ronde River

Map 4.3, page 207

This small and pretty park is well worth the detour off I-84 necessary to get there. Once you do, you'll be greeted by large pines towering above the sharp valley, cut through by the Wallowa River. Rafting and fishing for steelhead are popular activities, and the area is teeming with wildlife, including bears, cougars, deer, elk, and the occasional Rocky Mountain bighorn sheep downriver.

Campsites, facilities: There are 22 primitive sites for tents or self-contained RVs up to 71 feet. Picnic tables and fire grills are provided. Drinking water is available May-mid-October. Garbage bins and vault toilets are available. Raft rentals are available nearby. Leashed pets are permitted.

Reservations, fees: Reservations are not accepted. Sites are $10 per night, $7 per night for an additional vehicle. Open April-October.

Directions: From LaGrande, drive northeast on Highway 82 for 18 miles to Elgin, then continue 14 miles to the park entrance road. Turn left (north) and drive two miles to the park.

Contact: Minam State Park, 541/432-8855 or 800/551-6949, www.oregonstateparks.org.

33 BOUNDARY

Scenic rating: 6

near the Eagle Cap Wilderness in Wallowa-Whitman National Forest

Map 4.3, page 207

This pretty and primitive campground is set 100 yards from the banks of Bear Creek at 3,600 feet elevation and is heavily wooded with Douglas, red, tamarack, and white fir. Recreation options here include hiking, fishing, and horseback riding. Nearby trails provide access to the Eagle Cap Wilderness. This is another in a series of little-known, primitive sites in the area.

Campsites, facilities: There are eight primitive tent sites. Picnic tables and fire rings are provided. Vault toilets are available. There is no drinking water, and garbage must be packed out. Leashed pets are permitted.

Reservations, fees: Reservations are not accepted. There is no fee for camping. Open mid-June-November, weather permitting.

Directions: From LaGrande, drive north on Highway 82 for 46 miles to Wallowa and Forest Road 8250. Turn south and drive eight miles to Forest Road 8250-040. Bear right (south) and drive 0.75 mile to the camp.

Contact: Wallowa-Whitman National Forest, Eagle Cap Ranger District, Wallowa Mountains Visitors Center, 541/426-5546, www.fs.usda.gov/wallowa-whitman.

34 MOSS SPRINGS

Scenic rating: 7

near the Eagle Cap Wilderness in Wallowa-Whitman National Forest

Map 4.3, page 207

At 6,000 feet elevation, Moss Springs campground is heavily forested with spruce and fir and has good views of the Grande Ronde Valley in some locations. The camp is popular with horse packers, and there is a loading ramp on-site. A trailhead provides access to the Eagle Cap Wilderness, a good jumping-off point for a multi-day backpacking trip. (Obtain a map of Wallowa-Whitman National Forest for detailed trail information.) The Breshears OHV Trail and the Mount Fanny Mountain bike trails are just north of the camp.

Campsites, facilities: There are eight sites for tents and RVs up to 16 feet long. Picnic tables and fire grills are provided. No drinking water is provided, but water is available for stock. Horse facilities and vault toilets are available. Garbage must be packed out. Some facilities are wheelchair accessible. Leashed pets are permitted.

Reservations, fees: Reservations are not accepted. Sites are $5 per night per vehicle. Open June-mid-October, weather permitting.

Directions: From LaGrande, drive east on Highway 237 for 15 miles to Cove and County Road 65 (signed for Moss Springs). Turn right (southeast) and drive 1.5 miles to Forest Road 6220. Turn left (east) and drive eight miles to the camp entrance. Note: The last five miles are on a steep gravel road.

Contact: Wallowa-Whitman National Forest, LaGrande Ranger District, 541/963-7186, www. fs.usda.gov/wallowa-whitman.

35 SHADY

Scenic rating: 6
on the Lostine River in Wallowa-Whitman National Forest

Map 4.3, page 207

Shady campground sits along the banks of the Lostine River at an elevation of 5,400 feet. The camp has wooded as well as meadow areas. It is close to trails that provide access to the Eagle Cap Wilderness, a beautiful and pristine area that's perfect for an extended backpacking trip. You can sometimes spot mountain sheep in the area.

Campsites, facilities: There are 13 sites for tents or RVs up to 16 feet long. Picnic tables

and fire grills are provided. Vault toilets are available. There is no drinking water, and garbage must be packed out. Leashed pets are permitted.

Reservations, fees: Reservations are not accepted. Sites are $6 per night. Open mid-June-November, weather permitting.

Directions: From LaGrande, turn north on Highway 82 and drive 52 miles to Lostine and Forest Road 8210. Turn right (south) and drive 15 miles to the campground.

Contact: Wallowa-Whitman National Forest, Eagle Cap Ranger District, 541/426-5546, www. fs.usda.gov/wallowa-whitman.

36 TWO PAN

Scenic rating: 6
on the Lostine River in Wallowa-Whitman National Forest

Map 4.3, page 207

Two Pan lies at the end of a forest road on the banks of the Lostine River. At 5,600 feet elevation, this camp is a prime jumping-off spot for a multi-day wilderness adventure. Adjacent trails provide access to numerous lakes and streams in the Eagle Cap Wilderness. If full, another campground option is Williamson, seven miles north on Forest Road 8210.

Campsites, facilities: There are nine sites for tents or RVs up to 16 feet. Picnic tables and fire grills are provided. Vault toilets are available at the trailhead. There is no drinking water, and garbage must be packed out. Leashed pets are permitted.

Reservations, fees: Reservations are not accepted. Sites are $5 per night. One free Wilderness Visitor Permit per group is required. Registration and self-issued permits are located at each trailhead. There is no fee for camping. Open mid-June-November, weather permitting.

Directions: From LaGrande, turn north on Highway 82 and drive 52 miles to Lostine and

Forest Road 8210. Turn right (south) and drive 17 miles to the campground.

Contact: Wallowa-Whitman National Forest, Eagle Cap Ranger District, Wallowa Mountains Visitors Center, 541/426-5546, www.fs.usda. gov/wallowa-whitman.

37 HURRICANE CREEK

Scenic rating: 5

near the Eagle Cap Wilderness in Wallowa-Whitman National Forest

Map 4.3, page 207

Set along Hurricane Creek at an elevation of 5,000 feet, this campground is on the edge of the Eagle Cap Wilderness and provides a good place to begin a backcountry backpacking trip. Sites are wooded, and some sit close to the creek—perfect for fishing. There is no access for medium to large RVs, which gives the camp more of a wilderness environment. Obtaining maps of the area from the ranger district is essential.

Campsites, facilities: There are 12 sites for tents only. Picnic tables and fire grills are provided. Vault toilets are available. There is no drinking water, and garbage must be packed out. Leashed pets are permitted.

Reservations, fees: Reservations are not accepted. Sites are $6 per night. Open mid-June-November, weather permitting.

Directions: From LaGrande, turn north on Highway 82 and drive 62 miles to Enterprise and Hurricane Creek Road. Turn right (south) on Hurricane Creek Road and drive five miles to Hurricane Grange Hall and Forest Road 8205; bear right (off the paved road) and drive two miles to the campground on the left.

Contact: Wallowa-Whitman National Forest, Eagle Cap Ranger District, 541/426-5546, www. fs.usda.gov/wallowa-whitman.

38 MOUNTAIN VIEW MOTEL AND RV PARK

Scenic rating: 3

near Wallowa Lake

Map 4.3, page 207

Mountain View is centrally located for exploring the greater Wallowa Lake area. Fishing and jet boating are available only a mile away at Wallowa Lake, and nearby recreational facilities include bike paths, a golf course, hiking trails, and a riding stable. The park has a creek with a swimming hole and offers views of the Seven Devils Mountains and of the Eagle Cap Wilderness.

Campsites, facilities: There are 30 sites with partial hookups (one pull-through) for RVs up to 39 feet, a grassy area for tents, three cabins, and six motel rooms. Picnic tables and portable fire pits are provided. Restrooms with flush toilets and showers (seasonal), a dump station, Wi-Fi, firewood, and coin laundry are available. Propane gas, a store, and café are within two miles. Some facilities are wheelchair accessible. Leashed pets are permitted with breed restrictions.

Reservations, fees: Reservations are accepted. RV sites are $30-45 per night, tent sites are $20-35 per night, $5 per person per night for more than four people. Some credit cards are accepted. Open year-round.

Directions: From LaGrande, turn north on Highway 82 and drive 62 miles to Enterprise and the junction with Highway 3. Continue north on Highway 82 for four miles to the campground on the right (1.5 miles north of Joseph).

Contact: Mountain View Motel and RV Park, 541/432-2982, www.mtviewmotel-rvpark.com.

39 WALLOWA LAKE STATE PARK

Scenic rating: 8

on Wallowa Lake

Map 4.3, page 207 **BEST (**

Surrounded by snowy peaks, Wallowa Lake is a large lake with plenty of fishing and boating, including waterskiing and parasailing. Recreational activities include canoeing, horseback riding, and hiking. Bumper boats, miniature golf, and an artist community provide other diversions. Other highlights include a pretty one-mile nature trail and trailheads that provide access into the Eagle Cap Wilderness and Hells Canyon gorge. A marina is nearby for boaters and anglers. Picnicking, swimming, and wildlife-viewing are a few of the other activities available to visitors.

Campsites, facilities: There are 121 sites with full hookups for RVs of any length, 88 tent sites, three group tent areas for up to 25 people each, and two yurts. Picnic tables and fire rings are provided. Garbage bins, drinking water, restrooms with flush toilets and showers, a dump station, and firewood are available. A store, café, and ice are within one mile. Boat docks, launching facilities, and rentals are nearby. Some facilities are wheelchair accessible. Leashed pets are permitted.

Reservations, fees: Reservations are accepted at 800/452-5687 or www.reserveamerica.com ($8 reservation fee). RV sites are $30 per night, tent sites are $20 per night, hiker/biker sites are $5 per person per night, group areas are $74 per night, yurts are $43-53 per night, $7 per night per additional vehicle. Some credit cards are accepted. Open year-round, with limited availability in winter (no water).

Directions: From LaGrande, turn north on Highway 82 and drive 62 miles to Enterprise and the junction with Highway 3. Continue south on Highway 82 to Joseph. Continue for six miles to the south shore of the lake and the campground.

Contact: Wallowa Lake State Park, 541/432-4185, www.oregonstateparks.org.

40 LICK CREEK

Scenic rating: 7

on Lick Creek in Wallowa-Whitman National Forest

Map 4.3, page 207

Located along the banks of Lick Creek in Hells Canyon National Recreation Area, this secluded and pretty campground sits in parklike surroundings at an elevation of 5,400 feet. Interspersed throughout the campground, tall Douglas fir, lodgepole pine, tamarack, and white fir provide a wildlife habitat for the area's birds and small animals.

Campsites, facilities: There are seven sites for tents only and five sites for tents or RVs up to 30 feet long. Picnic tables and fire rings are provided. Vault toilets are available. There is no drinking water, and garbage must be packed out. Some facilities are wheelchair accessible. Leashed pets are permitted.

Reservations, fees: Reservations are not accepted. Sites are $6 per night. Open mid-June-late November, weather permitting.

Directions: From LaGrande, turn north on Highway 82 and drive 64 miles to Enterprise. Continue south on Highway 82 to Joseph and Highway 350. Turn left (east) and drive 7.5 miles to Forest Road 39. Turn right (south) and drive 15 miles to the campground.

Contact: Hells Canyon National Recreation Area, Wallowa Mountains Visitors Center, 541/426-5546, www.fs.usda.gov/wallowa-whitman.

41 COVERDALE

Scenic rating: 7

near the Imnaha River

Map 4.3, page 207

Located at 4,300 feet in elevation along the Imnaha River, this campground is in a lushly forested drainage area. Wildflower viewing can be spectacular and fishing can be good. Hiking trails are nearby.

Campsites, facilities: There are seven sites for tents only and two sites for tents or RVs up to 24 feet long. Picnic tables and fire rings are provided. Vault toilets are available. There is no drinking water. Garbage must be packed out. Leashed pets are permitted.

Reservations, fees: Reservations are not accepted. Sites are $6 per night. Open June-October, weather permitting.

Directions: From Joseph, drive east on Highway 350 for eight miles to Wallowa Mountain Loop Road (Forest Road 39). Turn right and drive approximately 38 miles to Forest Road 3960. Turn right and drive four miles to the campground on the left.

Contact: Hells Canyon National Recreation Area, Wallowa Mountains Visitors Center, 541/426-5546, www.fs.usda.gov/wallowa-whitman.

42 OLLOKOT

Scenic rating: 5

on the Imnaha River in Wallowa-Whitman National Forest

Map 4.3, page 207

This campground sits on the banks of the Imnaha River in Hells Canyon National Recreation Area at an elevation of 4,000 feet. It's named for Chief Joseph's brother, a member of the Nez Perce tribe. For those seeking a little more solitude, this could be the spot.

Campsites, facilities: There are 12 sites for tents or RVs up to 30 feet long. Picnic tables and fire rings are provided. Drinking water, vault toilets, and an interpretive display are available. Garbage must be packed out. Some facilities are wheelchair accessible. Leashed pets are permitted.

Reservations, fees: Reservations are not accepted. Sites are $8 per night. Open June-late November, weather permitting.

Directions: From I-84 at LaGrande, turn north on Highway 82 and drive 64 miles to Enterprise. Continue six miles south to Joseph and Highway 350. Turn left (east) on Highway 350 and drive eight miles to Forest Road 39. Turn right (south) on Forest Road 39 and drive 30 miles to the campground on the left.

Contact: Hells Canyon National Recreation Area, Wallowa Mountains Visitors Center, 541/426-5546, www.fs.usda.gov/wallowa-whitman.

43 SADDLE CREEK

Scenic rating: 8

near the Hells Canyon Wilderness in Wallowa-Whitman National Forest

Map 4.4, page 208

Saddle Creek campground is set at 6,800 feet, nestled in on a ridge between two canyons with excellent views of the Seven Devils Mountains. Trees are scarce here because of past wildfires. Nearby trails provide access to Saddle Creek and Hells Canyon National Recreation Area.

Campsites, facilities: There are seven sites for tents. Picnic tables and fire rings are provided. Vault toilets are available. There is no drinking water, and garbage must be packed out. Leashed pets are permitted. Some facilities are wheelchair accessible. Note: RVs and trailers are not recommended on the access road.

Reservations, fees: Reservations are not accepted. There is no fee for camping. Open July-mid-November, weather permitting.

Directions: From LaGrande, turn north on Highway 82 and drive 64 miles to Enterprise. Continue south on Highway 82 and drive six miles to Joseph and Highway 350. Turn left (east) on Highway 350 and drive 30 miles to the small town of Imnaha and Forest Road 4240. Drive straight up the hill on Forest Road 4240 and continue 19 miles (on a gravel road) to the campground.

Contact: Hells Canyon National Recreation Area, Wallowa Mountains Visitors Center, 541/426-5546 or 541/426-5522, www.fs.usda. gov/wallowa-whitman.

44 BLACKHORSE

Scenic rating: 7

on the Imnaha River in Wallowa-Whitman National Forest

Map 4.4, page 208

This campground along the banks of the Imnaha River in Hells Canyon National Recreation Area is located in a secluded section of Wallowa-Whitman National Forest at an elevation of 4,000 feet.

Campsites, facilities: There are 15 single sites and one double site for tents or RVs up to 30 feet long. Picnic tables and fire rings are provided. Vault toilets are available. There is no drinking water, and garbage must be packed out. Some facilities are wheelchair accessible. Leashed pets are permitted.

Reservations, fees: Reservations are not accepted. Sites are $8 per night. Open June-late November, weather permitting.

Directions: From I-84 at LaGrande, turn north on Highway 82 and drive 64 miles to Enterprise. Continue six miles south to Joseph and Highway 350. Turn left (east) and drive eight miles on Highway 350 to Forest Road 39. Turn right (south) on Forest Road 39 and drive 29 miles to the campground.

Contact: Hells Canyon National Recreation Area, Wallowa Mountains Visitors Center, 541/426-5546, www.fs.usda.gov/ wallowa-whitman.

45 HIDDEN

Scenic rating: 6

on the Imnaha River in Wallowa-Whitman National Forest

Map 4.4, page 208

River views and spacious sites can be found at this campground in a pretty spot along the banks of the Imnaha River in the Hells Canyon National Recreation Area. It's essential to obtain a map of Wallowa-Whitman National Forest that details back roads and hiking trails. If full, Coverdale Campground is an option, just four miles northeast on Forest Road 3960.

Campsites, facilities: There are 10 sites for tents or small, self-contained RVs. Picnic tables and fire rings are provided. Vault toilets are available. There is no drinking water, and garbage must be packed out. Some facilities are wheelchair accessible. Leashed pets are permitted.

Reservations, fees: Reservations are not accepted. Sites are $6 per night. Open June-late November, weather permitting.

Directions: From LaGrande, drive east on Highway 82 for 64 miles to Enterprise. Continue six miles south to Joseph and Highway 350. Turn left (east) and drive eight miles to Wallowa Mountain Loop Road (Forest Road 39). Turn right (south) and drive 30 miles to Forest Road 3960. Turn right (southwest) and drive seven miles to the campground.

Contact: Hells Canyon National Recreation Area, Wallowa Mountains Visitors Center, 541/426-5546, www.fs.usda.gov/ wallowa-whitman.

46 INDIAN CROSSING

Scenic rating: 6

on the Imnaha River in Wallowa-Whitman National Forest

Map 4.4, page 208

Indian Crossing is situated at an elevation of

4,500 feet and is more developed than nearby Hidden Campground. A trailhead for the Eagle Cap Wilderness is near; obtain a U.S. Forest Service map for trail options.

Campsites, facilities: There are 14 sites for tents or RVs up to 30 feet long. Picnic tables and fire rings are provided. Drinking water, vault toilets, and horse facilities are available. Garbage must be packed out. Some facilities are wheelchair accessible. Leashed pets are permitted.

Reservations, fees: Reservations are not accepted. Sites are $6 per night. Open June-late November, weather permitting.

Directions: From LaGrande, turn north on Highway 82 and drive 62 miles to Enterprise. Continue on Highway 82 for six miles to Joseph and Highway 350. Turn left (east) on Highway 350 and drive eight miles to Forest Road 39. Turn right (south) and drive about 30 miles to Forest Road 3960. Turn right and drive 10 miles to the campground at the end of the road.

Contact: Hells Canyon National Recreation Area, Wallowa Mountains Visitors Center, 541/426-5546, www.fs.usda.gov/wallowa-whitman.

47 WHISTLER

Scenic rating: 7

in Ochoco National Forest

Map 4.5, page 209

Whistler is a trailhead camp for the Wildcat Trail, which heads into the Mill Creek Wilderness. The area is extremely popular with rock hounds, who search for agates, jasper, and thunder eggs. (Digging and collecting are forbidden in wilderness areas, however.) Though primitive, this pretty camp in a conifer forest guarantees quiet and privacy.

Campsites, facilities: There are two large open areas for dispersed tent camping. A picnic table and a vault toilet are provided. There is no drinking water and garbage must be

packed out. Horses are welcome. Leashed pets are permitted.

Reservations, fees: Reservations are not accepted. There is no fee for camping. Open late May-late October, weather permitting.

Directions: From Prineville, drive east on U.S. 26 for about 30 miles to Forest Road 27 (just east of Bandit Spring State Rest Area, near Ochoco Pass). Turn left on Forest Road 27 and drive nine miles to the campground entrance on the left. Note: Trailers are not recommended on this road.

Contact: Ochoco National Forest, Lookout Mountain Ranger District, 541/416-6500, www.fs.usda.gov/centraloregon.

48 WILDCAT

Scenic rating: 4

on the east fork of Mill Creek in Ochoco National Forest

Map 4.5, page 209

Surrounded by conifer forest, Wildcat campground sits at an elevation of 3,700 feet in a cool canyon. Situated along the east fork of Mill Creek, the quiet camp is near the Twin Pillars Trailhead, which provides access into the Mill Creek Wilderness. No climbing is allowed in the wilderness. Ochoco Lake and Ochoco Lake State Park to the south provide side-trip possibilities.

Campsites, facilities: There are 17 sites for tents or RVs up to 30 feet long. Picnic tables and fire grills are provided. Drinking water and vault toilets are available. Garbage must be packed out. Leashed pets are permitted.

Reservations, fees: Reservations are not accepted. Sites are $15 per night for one vehicle, $7 per night for each additional vehicle. Open mid-May-late October, weather permitting.

Directions: From Prineville, drive east on U.S. 26 for nine miles to Mill Creek Road (Forest Road 33). Turn left on Mill Creek Road and drive about 10 miles to the campground.

Contact: Ochoco National Forest, Lookout

Mountain Ranger District, 541/416-6500, www.fs.usda.gov/centraloregon.

49 OCHOCO DIVIDE
🏃 🚵 🏕 ♿ 🚐 ⛺

Scenic rating: 5
in Ochoco National Forest

Map 4.5, page 209

This quiet campground is set at an elevation of 4,700 feet in a ponderosa pine forest. Hiking is available along a forest road near the camp and at nearby Marks Creek and Bandit Springs. This is a quick jump off U.S. 26; campers tend to set up in the afternoon and leave early in the morning, so you may get the place to yourself.

Campsites, facilities: There are 28 sites for tents or RVs up to 30 feet long, with a separate area of walk-in and bike-in sites, and a group site for groups of touring cyclists (up to 35 people). Picnic tables and fire pits are provided. Vault toilets are available. There is no drinking water, and garbage must be packed out. Some facilities are wheelchair accessible. Leashed pets are permitted.

Reservations, fees: Reservations are accepted for the group site only at 877/444-6777 ($10 reservation fee) or www.recreation.gov ($9 reservation fee). Sites are $13 per night, plus $6 per night for each additional vehicle; hike-in/bike-in sites are $13 per person per night; and the group site is $35 per night. Open late May-mid-October, weather permitting.

Directions: From Prineville, drive east on U.S. 26 for 30 miles to the campground at the summit of Ochoco Pass.

Contact: Ochoco National Forest, Lookout Mountain Ranger District, 541/416-6500, www.fs.usda.gov/centraloregon.

50 OCHOCO CAMPGROUND
🏃 🚵 🏊 🏕 🐕 ♿ 🚐 ⛺

Scenic rating: 4
in Ochoco National Forest

Map 4.5, page 209

Ochoco Campground sits at an elevation of 4,000 feet along Ochoco Creek amid pine and aspen trees. There's fair fishing for rainbow trout, and hiking is nearby in the Lookout Mountain Recreation Area—that's 15,000 acres without roads. But hey, the truth is: Don't expect privacy and solitude at this campground. The log shelter and picnic area are often reserved for weddings, family reunions, and other group events.

Campsites, facilities: There are five sites for tents or RVs up to 24 feet long and one group site. Picnic tables and fire rings are provided. Drinking water, garbage bins, vault toilets, and a picnic shelter (by reservation) are available. Some facilities are wheelchair accessible. Leashed pets are permitted.

Reservations, fees: Reservations are accepted for the group site only at 877/444-6777 ($10 reservation fee) or www.recreation.gov ($9 reservation fee). Sites are $15 per night, $7 per night per each additional vehicle. The group site is $60-100 per night. Open mid-May-October, weather permitting.

Directions: From Prineville, drive east on U.S. 26 for 16.5 miles to County Road 23. Turn right on County Road 23 and drive nine miles (County Road 23 becomes Forest Road 42) to the campground, across from the Ochoco Ranger Station.

Contact: Ochoco National Forest, Lookout Mountain Ranger District, 541/416-6500, www.fs.usda.gov/centraloregon.

51 WALTON LAKE

Scenic rating: 7

on Walton Lake in Ochoco National Forest

Map 4.5, page 209

This campground, surrounded by meadows and ponderosa pine, borders the shore of small Walton Lake. Fishing and swimming are popular; the lake is stocked with rainbow trout, and the fishing can range from middle-of-the-road right up to downright excellent. Only non-motorized boats or boats with electric motors are allowed on the lake. Hikers can explore a nearby trail that leads south to Round Mountain.

Campsites, facilities: There are 21 sites for tents or RVs up to 28 feet long, six sites for tents only, and two group sites. Picnic tables, garbage bins, and fire grills are provided. Drinking water and vault toilets are available. Boat-launching facilities are nearby (only electric motors are allowed). Some facilities are wheelchair accessible. Leashed pets are permitted.

Reservations, fees: Reservations accepted only for the group sites at 877/444-6777 or www.recreation.gov ($9-10 reservation fee). Sites are $15 per night, $7 per each additional vehicle, and group sites are $60-100 per night. Open mid-May-mid-September, weather permitting.

Directions: From Prineville, drive east on U.S. 26 for 16.5 miles to County Road 23. Turn right (northeast) and drive nine miles (County Road 23 becomes Forest Road 42) to the Ochoco Ranger Station and Forest Road 22. Turn left and drive north on Forest Road 22 for seven miles to the campground.

Contact: Ochoco National Forest, Lookout Mountain Ranger District, 541/416-6500, www.fs.usda.gov/centraloregon.

52 DEEP CREEK

Scenic rating: 5

on the north fork of the Crooked River in Ochoco National Forest

Map 4.5, page 209

This small camp on the edge of the high desert (4,200 feet elevation) gets little use, but it's in a nice spot. Located right at the confluence of Deep Creek and the north fork of the Crooked River, the pretty, shady sites allow for river access and fishing.

Campsites, facilities: There are six sites for tents or RVs up to 22 feet long. Picnic tables and fire grills are provided. Drinking water and vault toilets are available. Garbage must be packed out. Leashed pets are permitted.

Reservations, fees: Reservations are not accepted. Sites are $8 per night for one vehicle, $3 per each additional vehicle. Open mid-May-mid-October, weather permitting.

Directions: From Prineville, drive east on U.S. 26 for 16.5 miles to County Route 23. Turn right (northeast) and drive 8.5 miles (it becomes Forest Road 42). Continue east on Forest Road 42 (paved road) for 23.5 miles to the campground on the right.

Contact: Ochoco National Forest, Lookout Mountain Ranger District, 541/416-6500, www.fs.usda.gov/centraloregon.

53 CROOK COUNTY RV PARK

Scenic rating: 6

near the Crooked River

Map 4.5, page 209

This five-acre public campground sits in a landscaped, grassy area near the Crooked River, where fly-fishing is popular. The camp is located right next to the Crook County Fairgrounds, which offers seasonal expositions, horse races, and rodeos.

Campsites, facilities: There are 81 sites for tents or RVs up to 70 feet long (full hookups);

most sites are pull-through. In addition, there are nine tent sites and two log cabins available. Picnic tables are provided. Fire pits are provided at the tent sites. Restrooms with flush toilets and showers, a dump station, cable TV, and Wi-Fi are available. A convenience store, restaurant, ice, gasoline, and propane are available within one mile. Some facilities are wheelchair accessible. Leashed pets are permitted, with restrictions on some breeds.

Reservations, fees: Reservations are accepted at 800/609-2599. RV sites are $38 per night, tent sites are $16 per night, cabins are $40-50 per night, $5 per additional person, $5 per night per additional vehicle. Weekly and monthly rates are available. Some discounts available. Some credit cards are accepted. Open year-round.

Directions: From Redmond, drive east on Highway 126 for 18 miles to Prineville (Highway 126 becomes 3rd Street) and Main Street. Turn right on Main Street and drive about 0.5 mile south to the campground on the left, before the fairgrounds.

Contact: Crook County RV Park, 541/447-2599, www.ccprd.org.

54 OCHOCO LAKE

Scenic rating: 6

on Ochoco Lake

Map 4.5, page 209

This is one of the nicer camps along U.S. 26 in eastern Oregon. The campground is located on the shore of Ochoco Lake, where boating and fishing are popular pastimes. Some quality hiking trails can be found in the area.

Campsites, facilities: There are 22 primitive sites for tents or self-contained RVs up to 50 feet long and a special hiker/biker area. Picnic tables and fire grills are provided. Drinking water, firewood, restrooms with showers and flush toilets, ice, garbage bins, a fish-cleaning station, and boat-launching facilities are available. A camp host is on-site. Some facilities

are wheelchair accessible. Leashed pets are permitted.

Reservations, fees: Reservations are not accepted. Sites are $16 per night, $5 per person per night for hike-in/bike-in sites, and $7 per night per additional vehicle. Some credit cards are accepted. Open April-October, weather permitting.

Directions: From Prineville, drive east on U.S. 26 for seven miles to the park entrance on the right.

Contact: Crook County Parks and Recreation, 541/447-1209, http://ccprd.org.

55 CHIMNEY ROCK

Scenic rating: 6

on the Crooked River

Map 4.5, page 209

Chimney Rock Campground is one of eight Bureau of Land Management (BLM) camps along a six-mile stretch of Highway 27. This well-spaced campground is a favorite for picnicking and wildlife-viewing. The Chimney Rock Trailhead, just across the highway, is the jumping-off point for the 1.7-mile, moderately difficult hike to Chimney Rock. There are numerous scenic overlooks along the trail, and wildlife sightings are common. Crooked River is open to fishing year-round. The elevation here is 3,000 feet.

Campsites, facilities: There are 14 sites for tents or RVs of any length and a group site for up to 16 people. Picnic tables and fire rings are provided. Vault toilets, drinking water, and garbage bins are available. Some facilities are wheelchair accessible, including a fishing dock. Leashed pets are permitted.

Reservations, fees: Reservations are not accepted. Sites are $8 per night, the group site is $16 per night, $2 per night for an additional vehicle. Open year-round; there is no fee for camping November-March.

Directions: In Prineville, drive south on Highway 27 for 16.4 miles to the campground.

Contact: Bureau of Land Management, Prineville District, 541/416-6700, www.blm. gov.

56 PRINEVILLE RESERVOIR STATE PARK
🏃🏊🛶🛥🏕🐕♿🚐⛰

Scenic rating: 7
on Prineville Reservoir

Map 4.5, page 209

This state park is set along the shore of Prineville Reservoir, which formed with the damming of the Crooked River. This is one of two campgrounds on the reservoir (the other is Prineville Reservoir Resort). Boating, fishing, swimming, and waterskiing are popular activities here; the nearby boat docks and ramp are a bonus. The reservoir supports rainbow and cutthroat trout, small and largemouth bass, catfish, and crappie; you can even ice fish in the winter.

Campsites, facilities: There are 22 sites with partial hookups and 22 sites with full hookups for RVs up to 40 feet long, 23 tent sites, and five deluxe cabins. Picnic tables and fire pits are provided. Drinking water, garbage bins, restrooms with flush toilets and showers, ice, and firewood are available. Boat docks, launching facilities, and moorings that can be reserved are nearby. Some facilities are wheelchair accessible. Leashed pets are permitted.

Reservations, fees: Reservations are accepted at 800/452-5687 or www.reserveamerica.com ($8 reservation fee). RV sites are $29-31, tent sites are $21 per night, cabins are $87-97 per night, boat moorage is $10, $7 per night per additional vehicle. Some credit cards are accepted. Open year-round.

Directions: From Prineville, drive east on U.S. 26 for one mile to Combs Flat Road. Turn right (south) and drive one mile to Juniper Canyon Road. Turn right (south) and drive 18 miles to the campground.

Contact: Prineville Reservoir State Park, 541/447-4363 or 800/551-6949, www.oregon-stateparks.org.

57 PRINEVILLE RESERVOIR RESORT
🏃🚴🏊🛶🛥🏕🐕♿🚐⛰

Scenic rating: 6
on Prineville Reservoir

Map 4.5, page 209

This resort sits on the shore of Prineville Reservoir in the high desert, a good spot for water sports and fishing. The mostly shaded sites are a combination of dirt and gravel. The camp features easy access to the reservoir and some colorful rock formations to check out.

Campsites, facilities: There are 70 sites with partial hookups (including four pull-through sites and 36 waterfront sites) for tents or RVs of any length, seven motel rooms, and one primitive cabin. Picnic tables and fire rings are provided. Drinking water, restrooms with flush toilets and coin showers, propane gas, a dump station, firewood, a convenience store, a café, and ice are available. A full-service marina with boat ramp, boat fuel, boat rentals, fish-cleaning station, and fishing licenses are on-site. Some facilities are wheelchair accessible. Leashed pets are permitted.

Reservations, fees: Reservations are accepted at 541/447-7468 ($9 reservation fee). Sites are $29-31 per night, the cabin is $40-50 per night. Some credit cards are accepted. Open May-mid-October, weather permitting.

Directions: From Prineville, drive east on U.S. 26 for one mile to Combs Flat Road. Turn right (south) and drive one mile to Juniper Canyon Road. Turn right (south) and drive 18 miles to the resort at the end of the road.

Contact: Prineville Reservoir Resort, 541/447-7468, www.prinevillereservoirresort.com.

58 JASPER POINT STATE PARK

🚶 🏊 🎣 🚣 🐴 🚐 ⛺

Scenic rating: 7

on Prineville Reservoir

Map 4.5, page 209

Jasper Point is a quiet alternative to Prineville Reservoir State Park. The park is not as popular as Prineville; although it does fill up on summer weekends, it's used mainly by locals. Although the park is named Jasper Point, the setting is in a cove and the views are not as good as those at Prineville Reservoir State Park. A 1.75-mile trail connects the two campgrounds, and another 0.7-mile trail runs along the shoreline.

Campsites, facilities: There are 27 sites with partial hookups for tents or RVs of any length. There is also one cabin. Picnic tables and fire pits are provided. Drinking water, vault toilets, garbage containers, a day-use area, and a boat launch are available. Leashed pets are permitted.

Reservations, fees: Reservations are accepted for the cabin only at 800/452-5687 or www.reserveamerica.com ($8 reservation fee). Sites are $29 per night, the cabin is $97 per night, $7 per night per additional vehicle. Open May-September.

Directions: From Prineville, drive east on U.S. 26 for one mile to Combs Flat Road. Turn right (south) and drive one mile to Juniper Canyon Road. Turn right (south) and drive 21 miles to the campground.

Contact: Jasper Point State Park, 541/447-4363 or 800/551-6949, www.oregonstateparks.org.

59 ANTELOPE FLAT RESERVOIR

🎣 🚐 🏊 🐴 🚐 ⛺

Scenic rating: 6

on Antelope Flat Reservoir in Ochoco National Forest

Map 4.5, page 209

This pretty spot is situated along the west shore of Antelope Flat Reservoir amid ponderosa pine and juniper. The campground is on the edge of the high desert at an elevation of 4,600 feet. It features wide sites and easy access to the lake. Trout fishing can sometimes be good in the spring, and boating with motors is permitted. This is also a good lake for canoes.

Campsites, facilities: There are 24 sites for tents or RVs up to 30 feet long. Picnic tables and fire grills are provided. Drinking water and vault toilets are available. Garbage must be packed out. Boat-launching facilities are nearby. Leashed pets are permitted.

Reservations, fees: Reservations are not accepted. Sites are $8 per night, $3 per night for each additional vehicle. Open early May-late October, weather permitting.

Directions: From Prineville, drive southeast on Combs Flat Road (Paulina Highway) for 30 miles to Forest Road 17 (Antelope Reservoir Junction). Turn right on Forest Road 17 and drive about 10 miles to Forest Road 1700-600. Drive 0.25 mile on Forest Road 1700-600 to the campground.

Contact: Ochoco National Forest, Lookout Mountain Ranger District, 541/416-6500, www.fs.usda.gov/centraloregon.

60 WILEY FLAT

🚶 🐴 🚐 ⛺

Scenic rating: 3

on Wiley Creek in Ochoco National Forest

Map 4.5, page 209

Wiley Flat campground is set along Wiley Creek in a nice, hidden spot with minimal crowds. It is popular with horseback riders and seasonal hunters. Tower Point Lookout is one mile north of the camp. A map of Ochoco National Forest details nearby access roads.

Campsites, facilities: There are five sites for tents or RVs up to 30 feet long. Picnic tables and fire grills are provided. Vault toilets are available. There is no drinking water, and garbage must be packed out. Leashed pets are permitted.

Reservations, fees: Reservations are not accepted. There is no fee for camping. Open mid-June-late October, weather permitting.

Directions: From Prineville, drive southeast on the Paulina Highway (Combs Flat Road) for 34 miles to Forest Road 16. Turn right (southeast) and drive 10 miles to Forest Road 1600-400. Turn right (west) and drive one mile to the camp.

Contact: Ochoco National Forest, Lookout Mountain Ranger District, 541/416-6500, www.fs.usda.gov/centraloregon.

61 BULL PRAIRIE LAKE

Scenic rating: 8
on Bull Prairie Lake in Umatilla National Forest

Map 4.6, page 210	BEST (

Set on the shore of Bull Prairie Lake, a 28-acre lake at 4,000 feet elevation, this spot attracts little attention from out-of-towners, yet it offers plenty of recreation opportunities, making it an ideal vacation destination. Boating (no motors permitted), fishing for blue gill and trout, hunting, and swimming are some of the attractions here. A hiking trail circles the lake.

Campsites, facilities: There are 28 sites for tents or RVs up to 31 feet long and one group site for up to 25 people. Picnic tables and fire grills are provided. Vault toilets are available. Drinking water and garbage bins are available late May-mid-October. Boat docks and a boat ramp are on-site. Some facilities are wheelchair accessible, including the boat ramp. Leashed pets are permitted.

Reservations, fees: Reservations are not accepted. Single sites are $14, double sites are $19, the group site is $28, $5 per night for an additional vehicle. Open year-round, weather permitting; there is no fee for camping after the water is turned off in mid-October.

Directions: From Heppner, drive south on Highway 207 for roughly 35 miles to the national forest boundary and continue four miles to Forest Road 2039 (paved). Turn left and drive three miles northeast to the campground on the right.

Contact: Umatilla National Forest, Heppner Ranger District, 541/676-9187, www.fs.usda.gov/umatilla.

62 FAIRVIEW

Scenic rating: 5
near Bull Prairie Lake in Umatilla National Forest

Map 4.6, page 210

This small, rugged campground is located in a remote area at 4,300 feet elevation near Mahogany Butte and adjacent to Fairview Springs. Known by very few people, it's very easy to miss and not even marked on Umatilla National Forest maps. Hunters use it primarily as a base camp. Bull Prairie Lake is only four miles away.

Campsites, facilities: There are five sites for tents or RVs up to 16 feet long. Picnic tables and fire grills are provided. Vault toilets are available. Drinking water is available May-October. Garbage must be packed out. Boat docks and launching facilities are nearby at Bull Prairie Lake. Leashed pets are permitted.

Reservations, fees: Reservations are not accepted. There is no fee for camping. Open May-October, weather permitting.

Directions: From Heppner, drive south on Highway 207 for roughly 35 miles to the national forest boundary. Continue four miles to Forest Road 2039 (the turnoff for Bull Prairie Lake). Continue on Highway 207 for one mile to Forest Road 400 (if you pass through an immediate series of hairpin turns, you have gone too far). Turn west and drive 500 yards to the campground.

Contact: Umatilla National Forest, Heppner Ranger District, 541/676-9187, www.fs.usda.gov/umatilla.

63 WOLF CREEK

Scenic rating: 5

on Wolf Creek in Ochoco National Forest

Map 4.6, page 210

Wolf Creek and Wolf Creek Industrial Camp, located just across the road, are set along the banks of Wolf Creek, a nice trout stream that runs through Ochoco National Forest. The elevation is 4,000 feet.

Campsites, facilities: There are 16 sites for tents or RVs up to 20 feet long. Picnic tables and fire grills are provided. Vault toilets are available. There is no drinking water, and garbage must be packed out. Leashed pets are permitted.

Reservations, fees: Reservations are not accepted. Sites are $6 per night, with a 14-day stay limit, and $3 per night for an additional vehicle. Open May-November, weather permitting.

Directions: From Prineville, drive southeast on Combs Flat Road (Paulina Highway) for 55 miles to Paulina. Continue east for 3.5 miles to County Road 112. Turn left (north) and drive 6.5 miles to Forest Road 42. Turn left (north) and drive 1.5 miles to the campground on the right.

Contact: Ochoco National Forest, Paulina Ranger District, 541/477-6900, www.fs.usda.gov/centraloregon.

64 SUGAR CREEK

Scenic rating: 6

on Sugar Creek in Ochoco National Forest

Map 4.6, page 210

This small, quiet, and remote campground sits along the banks of Sugar Creek at an elevation of 4,000 feet in a forest of ponderosa pine. A 0.5-mile trail loops along the creek. The camp also offers a covered group shelter in the day-use area and a wheelchair-accessible trail. Bald eagles occasionally nest in the area.

Campsites, facilities: There are 17 sites for tents or RVs up to 22 feet long. Picnic tables and fire grills are provided. Drinking water, a picnic shelter, and vault toilets are available. Garbage must be packed out. Some facilities are wheelchair accessible. Leashed pets are permitted.

Reservations, fees: Reservations are not accepted. Sites are $8 per night for one vehicle and $3 per night for an additional vehicle. Open May-November with a 14-day stay limit.

Directions: From Prineville, drive southeast on Combs Flat Road (Paulina Highway) for 55 miles to Paulina. Continue east and drive 3.5 miles to a fork with County Road 112. Bear left at the fork onto County Road 112 and drive 7.5 miles to Forest Road 58. Bear right on Forest Road 58 and continue for 1.3 miles to the campground on the right.

Contact: Ochoco National Forest, Paulina Ranger District, 541/477-6900, www.fs.usda.gov/centraloregon.

65 FRAZIER

Scenic rating: 4

on Frazier Creek in Ochoco National Forest

Map 4.6, page 210

Frazier is a small, remote, and little-used campground located at an elevation of 4,600 feet. The landscape is open, grassy, and sprinkled with a few large pine trees. Some dirt roads adjacent to the camp are good for mountain biking in summer, and the camp's meadow setting is occasionally the site of family reunions during summer holidays.

Campsites, facilities: There are nine sites for tents or RVs up to 22 feet long. Picnic tables and fire grills are provided. Vault toilets are available. There is no drinking water, and garbage must be packed out. Leashed pets are permitted.

Reservations, fees: Reservations are not accepted. There is no fee for camping. The stay limit is 14 days. Open May-November, weather permitting.

Directions: From Prineville, drive southeast on Combs Flat Road (Paulina Highway) for 55 miles to Paulina. Continue east and drive 3.5 miles to a fork with County Road 112. Bear left at the fork onto County Road 112 and drive 2.5 miles to County Road 135/Puett Road. Turn right (east) and drive 10 miles to Forest Road 58. Turn right and drive six miles to Forest Road 58-500. Turn left and drive two miles (bearing to the left) to the campground.

Contact: Ochoco National Forest, Paulina Ranger District, 541/477-6900, www.fs.usda. gov/centraloregon.

66 CLYDE HOLLIDAY STATE RECREATION SITE

Scenic rating: 7
near the John Day River

Map 4.6, page 210

Clyde Holliday campground borders the John Day River, a spawning site for steelhead. Sites are private and shaded with cottonwood trees. Wildlife is prevalent in the area; watch for mule deer and elk near the campsites.

Campsites, facilities: There are 31 sites with partial hookups for tents or RVs up to 60 feet long, a hiker/biker tent area, and two tepees. Picnic tables and fire grills are provided. Drinking water, restrooms with showers and flush toilets, firewood, ice, a dump station, and horseshoe pits are available. Some facilities

are wheelchair accessible. Leashed pets are permitted.

Reservations, fees: Reservations are not accepted for campsites but are required for the tepees at 800/452-5687 or www.reserveamerica. com ($8 reservation fee). Sites are $24 per night, $5 per person per night for hike-in/bike-in sites, $44 per night for tepees, $7 per night for an additional vehicle. Open March-November, weather permitting.

Directions: From John Day, drive west on U.S. 26 for six miles to the park on the left.

Contact: Clyde Holliday State Recreation Site, 541/932-4453 or 800/551-6949, www.oregonstateparks.org.

67 STARR

Scenic rating: 4
on Starr Ridge in Malheur National Forest

Map 4.6, page 210

A good layover spot for travelers on U.S. 395, Starr happens to be adjacent to Starr Ridge, a snow play area popular in winter for skiing and sledding. The camp itself doesn't offer much in the way of recreation, but to the northeast is the Strawberry Mountain Wilderness, which has a number of lakes, streams, and trails. The camp sits at an elevation of 5,100 feet.

Campsites, facilities: There are eight sites for tents or RVs up to 22 feet long and one group site for 5-20 people. Picnic tables and fire rings are provided. Vault toilets are available. There is no drinking water, and garbage must be packed out. Some facilities are wheelchair accessible. Leashed pets are permitted.

Reservations, fees: Reservations are not accepted. Sites are $6 per night, $3 per night for an additional vehicle. Open late May-November, weather permitting.

Directions: From John Day, drive south on U.S. 395 for 15 miles to the campground on the right.

Contact: Malheur National Forest, Blue

Mountain Ranger District, 541/575-3000, www.fs.usda.gov/malheur.

68 WELCH CREEK

Scenic rating: 4

on Desolation Creek in Umatilla National Forest

Map 4.7, page 211

Welch Creek is a primitive camp set on the banks of Desolation Creek. Road noise and dust may be a problem for some, and there's little privacy among sites. The camp features trail access to the Desolation Area, both for non-motorized and motorized traffic. Hunting and fishing are popular here.

Campsites, facilities: There are five sites for tents or RVs up to 30 feet long and one group site. Picnic tables and fire rings are provided. A vault toilet is available. There is no drinking water. Garbage must be packed out. Leashed pets are permitted.

Reservations, fees: Reservations are not accepted. Sites are $8 per night for two vehicles, $5 per night for each additional vehicle, and the group site is $25 per night. Open late May-early November, weather permitting. A 14-day stay limit is enforced.

Directions: From Pendleton, drive south on U.S. 395 for 62 miles to Forest Road 55 (one mile north of Dale; it's easier to find if you know the marker, Texas Bar Road). Turn left and drive one mile to Forest Road 10. Turn right and drive 13 miles to the campground on the right.

Contact: Umatilla National Forest, North Fork John Day Ranger District, 541/427-3231, www.fs.usda.gov/umatilla.

69 NORTH FORK JOHN DAY

Scenic rating: 6

on the north fork of the John Day River in Umatilla National Forest

Map 4.7, page 211

Set along the banks of the north fork of the John Day River at an elevation of 5,200 feet, this campground sits in a stand of lodgepole pine at the intersection of Elkhorn and Blue Mountain National Forest Scenic Byways. The campground has a great view of salmon spawning in the river in spring and fall and also makes an ideal launch point for a wilderness backpacking trip. Trails from camp lead into the North Fork John Day Wilderness. A horse-handling area is also available for wilderness users. No mountain bikes or motorcycles are permitted in the wilderness.

Campsites, facilities: There are 15 sites for tents or RVs up to 28 feet long, five sites for tents only, and one group site. Picnic tables and fire rings are provided. Vault toilets are available. There is no drinking water. Garbage must be packed out. Some facilities are wheelchair accessible. Leashed pets are permitted.

Reservations, fees: Reservations are not accepted. Sites are $8 per night for two vehicles, $5 per night for an additional vehicle, and $25 for the group site. Open June-November, weather permitting. A 14-day stay limit is enforced.

For trailhead use, a Northwest Forest Pass is required ($5 daily fee or $30 annual fee per parked vehicle).

Directions: From Pendleton, drive south on U.S. 395 for 50 miles to Highway 244. Turn east on Highway 244 and drive one mile to Ukiah and Forest Road 52. Turn right (south) on Forest Road 52 and drive 36 miles to the campground on the right.

Contact: Umatilla National Forest, North Fork John Day Ranger District, 541/427-3231, www.fs.usda.gov/umatilla.

70 ANTHONY LAKES

Scenic rating: 10

on Anthony Lake in Wallowa-Whitman National
Forest

Map 4.7, page 211   **BEST (**

This campground (7,100 feet elevation) is adjacent to Anthony Lake, where non-motorized
boating is permitted. Sites are wooded, providing good screening between them. Alas,
mosquitoes are often in particular abundance.
Several smaller lakes within two miles by car
or trail are ideal for trout fishing from a canoe,
float tube, or raft. Sometimes mountain goats
can be seen from the Elkhorn Crest Trail,
which begins near here. Weekends and holidays the campground tends to fill up.

Campsites, facilities: There are 10 sites for
tents, 32 sites for RVs up to 22 feet long, and one
group site for up to 75 people. (There are also
10 walk-in sites for tents only; follow the lakeshore trail toward the south end of the lake.)
Drinking water, fire grills, garbage bins (summer only), and picnic tables are provided. Vault
toilets are available. Garbage must be packed
out the rest of the year. Boat-launching facilities are nearby. Some facilities are wheelchair
accessible. Leashed pets are permitted.

Reservations, fees: Reservations are accepted
for the group site only at 877/444-6777 ($10 res-
ervation fee) or www.recreation.gov ($9 reser-
vation fee). Sites are $10-14 per night, $5-8 per
night per additional vehicle, and $50 per night
for the group site. Open June-late September,
weather permitting.

Directions: From Baker City on I-84, turn
north on U.S. 30. Drive north for 10 miles
to Haines and County Road 1146 (signed
for Anthony Lakes Ski Resort). Turn left on
County Road 1146 and drive 20 miles (the road
becomes Forest Road 73) to the campground
on the left.

Contact: Wallowa-Whitman National Forest,
Whitman Ranger District, 541/523-6391, www.
fs.usda.gov/wallowa-whitman.

71 GRANDE RONDE LAKE

Scenic rating: 8

on Grande Ronde Lake in Wallowa-Whitman
National Forest

Map 4.7, page 211

Grande Ronde campground sits amid Douglas
and white fir at an elevation of 6,800 feet along
the shore of Grande Ronde Lake. Trout fishing
can be good at this small lake, and mountain
goats are sometimes seen in the area. Several
trails lie to the south, near Anthony Lake.

Campsites, facilities: There are eight sites for
tents or RVs up to 16 feet long. Picnic tables
and fire grills are provided. Drinking water
and vault toilets are available. Garbage must
be packed out. Boat launching facilities are
nearby. Some facilities are wheelchair accessible. Leashed pets are permitted.

Reservations, fees: Reservations are not accepted. Single sites are $10 per night, double
sites are 18 per night, $5 per night per each ad-
ditional vehicle. Open late June-September,
weather permitting.

Directions: Drive on I-84 to Baker City and
U.S. 30. From Baker City, drive north on U.S. 30
for 10 miles to Haines and County Road 1146
(signed for Anthony Lakes Ski Resort). Turn
left on County Road 1146 and drive 20 miles
(the road becomes Forest Road 73) to the campground on the right.

Contact: Wallowa-Whitman National Forest,
Whitman Ranger District, 541/523-6391, www.
fs.usda.gov/wallowa-whitman.

72 MUD LAKE

Scenic rating: 7

on Mud Lake in Wallowa-Whitman National
Forest

Map 4.7, page 211

Set at an elevation of 7,100 feet, tiny yet pleasant Mud Lake campground is filled with lots
of vegetation and sees relatively little use.

The campground is situated in fir forest on the shore of small Mud Lake, where the trout fishing can be fairly good. Mud Lake is shallow and more marshy than muddy. Bring your mosquito repellent.

Campsites, facilities: There are eight sites for tents or RVs up to 16 feet long and one group site for up to 60 people. Picnic tables and fire grills are provided. Drinking water and vault toilets are available. Garbage must be packed out. Boat launching facilities are nearby at Anthony Lake. Leashed pets are permitted.

Reservations, fees: Reservations are accepted for the group site only at 877/444-6777 ($10 reservation fee) or www.recreation.gov ($9 reservation fee). Sites are $8 per night, $4 per night per additional vehicle, and the group site is $50 per night. Open June-late September, weather permitting.

Directions: Drive on I-84 to Baker City and U.S. 30. From Baker City, drive north on U.S. 30 for 10 miles to Haines and County Road 1146 (signed for Anthony Lakes Ski Resort). Turn left on County Road 1146 and drive 21 miles (the road becomes Forest Road 73) to the campground on the right.

Contact: Wallowa-Whitman National Forest, Whitman Ranger District, 541/523-6391, www.fs.usda.gov/wallowa-whitman.

73 OLIVE LAKE

Scenic rating: 9

on Olive Lake in Umatilla National Forest

Map 4.7, page 211

This campground (6,100 feet elevation) is nestled along the shore of Olive Lake, between two sections of the North Fork John Day Wilderness. Dammed to hold an increased volume of water, the glacial lake is a beautiful tint of blue. Motorized boats are allowed, but waterskiing is prohibited. Fishing is fair for kokanee salmon and brook, cutthroat, and rainbow trout. A 2.5-mile trail circles the lake. Nearby trails provide access to the wilderness;

motorbikes and mountain bikes are not permitted in the wilderness. Sections of the old wooden pipeline for the historic Fremont Powerhouse can still be seen. The old mining town of Granite is 12 miles east of camp.

Campsites, facilities: There are 23 sites for tents or RVs up to 40 feet long, five sites for tents only, and two group sites that can accommodate up to 25 people and five RVs. Picnic tables and fire grills are provided. Vault toilets are available. There is no drinking water, and garbage must be packed out. Two boat docks, launching facilities, and picnic areas are available. A camp host is on-site. Some facilities are wheelchair accessible. Leashed pets are permitted.

Reservations, fees: Reservations are not accepted. Sites are $12 per night for up to two vehicles, $5 per night per additional vehicle, and $25 per night for the group camp. Open Memorial Day-November, weather permitting. A 14-day stay limit is enforced.

Directions: From Pendleton, drive south on U.S. 395 for 62 miles to Forest Road 55 (1 mile north of Dale). Turn right and drive 0.5 mile to Forest Road 10. Turn right on Forest Road 10 and drive 26 miles to Forest Road 480. Turn right and drive 0.5 mile to the campground.

Contact: Umatilla National Forest, North Fork John Day Ranger District, 541/427-3231, www.fs.usda.gov/umatilla.

74 MCCULLY FORKS

Scenic rating: 5

on McCully Creek in Wallowa-Whitman National Forest

Map 4.7, page 211

Here's an easy-access campground that's tiny and primitive. Set at 4,600 feet elevation along the banks of McCully Creek, McCully Forks gets moderately heavy use and is often full on weekends. Wedged between highway and mountains, sites are wooded with alder and cottonwood; highway noise can be audible.

Campsites, facilities: There are seven sites for tents or small trailers. Picnic tables and fire grills are provided. Vault toilets are available. There is no drinking water, and garbage must be packed out. Some facilities are wheelchair accessible. Leashed pets are permitted.

Reservations, fees: Reservations are not accepted. Sites are $6 per night. Open late May-late October, weather permitting.

Directions: From Baker City, drive southwest on Highway 7 for 29 miles (bear west at Salisbury) to Sumpter. Continue three miles past Sumpter (the road becomes Forest Road 24) to the campground on the right.

Contact: Wallowa-Whitman National Forest, Whitman Ranger District, 541/523-6391, www.fs.usda.gov/wallowa-whitman.

75 UNION CREEK
🚶 🚴 ♒ ⛵ 🚤 🏕 ♿ 🧺 ⛺

Scenic rating: 8
on Phillips Lake in Wallowa-Whitman National Forest

Map 4.7, page 211

Union Creek campground along the north shore of Phillips Lake is easy to reach, yet missed by most I-84 travelers. It's the largest of three camps on the lake and the only one with drinking water. An old narrow-gauge railroad has been restored and runs up the valley from McEwen Depot (six miles from the campground) to Sumpter (10 miles away). Visit Sumpter to see an old dredge.

Campsites, facilities: There are 74 sites for tents or RVs up to 32 feet long, two double sites, two group sites for 20-50 people, and an overflow camping area; some sites have full hookups. Drinking water, garbage bins (summer only), and picnic tables are provided. Flush toilets, a dump station, firewood, and ice are available. There is a seasonal concession stand for packaged goods and fishing tackle. Boat docks and launching facilities are adjacent to the campground. Some facilities are wheelchair accessible. Leashed pets are permitted.

Reservations, fees: Reservations are accepted at 877/444-6777 ($10 reservation fee) or www.recreation.gov ($9 reservation fee). Sites are $12-22 per night, double sites are $34 per night (full hookups), the group sites are $60 per night, the overflow area is $12 per night, $6-8 per night per additional vehicle. Open May-September, weather permitting.

Directions: From Baker City, drive southwest on Highway 7 for 20 miles to the campground on the left.

Contact: Wallowa-Whitman National Forest, Whitman Ranger District, 541/523-6391, www.fs.usda.gov/wallowa-whitman.

76 SOUTHWEST SHORE
🚶 ♒ ⛵ 🚤 🦌 🧺 ⛺

Scenic rating: 7
on Phillips Lake in Wallowa-Whitman National Forest

Map 4.7, page 211

Southwest Shore is one of two primitive campgrounds on Phillips Lake, a four-mile-long reservoir created by the Mason Dam on the Powder River. Set at 4,120 feet elevation, the camp borders the south shore of the lake; the boat ramp here is usable only when water is high in the reservoir. An old narrow-gauge railroad runs out of McEwen Depot (six miles from the campground) to Sumpter (10 miles away) for an interesting side trip.

Campsites, facilities: There are 16 sites for tents or RVs up to 24 feet long. Fire grills and vault toilets are available. There is no drinking water, and garbage must be packed out. A boat ramp is adjacent to the campground. Leashed pets are permitted.

Reservations, fees: Reservations are not accepted. Sites are $10 per night, $4 per night per additional vehicle. Open May-October, weather permitting.

Directions: From Baker City, drive southwest on Highway 7 for 24 miles (just past Phillips Lake) to Hudspeth Lane (County Road 667). Turn left (south) on Hudspeth Lane and drive two miles to Forest Road 2220. Turn left (southeast) and drive 2.5 miles to the campground on the left.

Contact: Wallowa-Whitman National Forest, Whitman Ranger District, 541/523-6391, www.fs.usda.gov/wallowa-whitman.

77 MILLERS LANE

Scenic rating: 7
on Phillips Lake in Wallowa-Whitman National Forest

Map 4.7, page 211

Millers Lane is one of two primitive camps on Phillips Lake (the other is Southwest Shore). Phillips Lake is a long, narrow reservoir (and the largest in the region), and this small campground is situated along the south shore at an elevation of 4,120 feet. The camp is also near an old narrow-gauge railroad that runs out of McEwen Depot.

Campsites, facilities: There are eight sites for tents or RVs up to 20 feet long. Picnic tables and fire grills are provided. Vault toilets are available. There is no drinking water, and garbage must be packed out. A boat ramp is at Southwest Shore. Leashed pets are permitted.

Reservations, fees: Reservations are not accepted. Sites are $10 per night, $4 per night per additional vehicle. Open May-October, weather permitting.

Directions: From Baker City, drive southwest on Highway 7 for 24 miles (just past Phillips Lake) to Hudspeth Lane (County Road 667). Turn left (south) on Hudspeth Lane and drive two miles to Forest Road 2220. Turn left (southeast) and drive 3.5 miles to the campground on the left.

Contact: Wallowa-Whitman National Forest, Whitman Ranger District, 541/523-6391, www.fs.usda.gov/wallowa-whitman.

78 MAGONE LAKE

Scenic rating: 8
on Magone Lake in Malheur National Forest

Map 4.7, page 211

This campground is set along the shore of little Magone Lake at an elevation of 5,500 feet. A 1.8-mile trail rings the lake, and the section extending from the beach area to the campground (about 0.25 mile) is wheelchair accessible. A 0.5-mile trail leads to Magone Slide, an unusual geological formation. Canoeing, fishing, sailing, and swimming are some of the popular activities at this lake. Easy-access bike trails can be found within 0.25 mile of the campground. Just so you know, Magone is pronounced "Ma-Goon." Got it?

Campsites, facilities: There are 19 sites for tents or RVs up to 40 feet long (some pull-through), three sites for tents only, and a separate group camp (with picnic shelter) for up to 75 people. Picnic tables and fire grills are provided. Drinking water, flush toilets, a boat ramp, and a beach area are available. A camp host is on-site. Boat docks are nearby. Some facilities, including a fishing pier, are wheelchair accessible. Leashed pets are permitted.

Reservations, fees: Reservations are required for the group site and group picnic shelter at 877/444-6777 ($10 reservation fee) or www.recreation.gov ($9 reservation fee). Sites are $13 per night, $25-60 per night for the group site, $6.50 per night per additional vehicle. Open late May-November, weather permitting.

Directions: From John Day, drive east on U.S. 26 for eight miles to County Road 18. Turn north and drive 10 miles to Forest Road 3620. Turn left (west) on Forest Road 3620 and drive 1.5 miles to Forest Road 3618. Turn right (northwest) and drive 1.5 miles to the campground. Note: The road is paved all the way.

Contact: Malheur National Forest, Blue Mountain Ranger District, 541/575-3000, www.fs.usda.gov/malheur.

79 LOWER CAMP CREEK

Scenic rating: 5

in Malheur National Forest

Map 4.7, page 211

Lower Camp Creek is set at 5,026 feet elevation on the edge of a remote national forest. The camp is small and primitive, with a creek nearby, and is often overlooked, so you may have the place to yourself. In fall, a few hunters will often hunker down here and use it as their base camp.

Campsites, facilities: There are six sites for tents or RVs up to 40 feet long. Picnic tables, fire rings, and vault toilets are provided. There is no drinking water. Garbage must be packed out. Some facilities are wheelchair accessible. Leashed pets are permitted.

Reservations, fees: Reservations are not accepted. Sites are $6 per night for single sites, $3 per night per additional vehicle. Open late May-November, weather permitting.

Directions: From John Day, drive east on U.S. 26 for eight miles to County Road 18. Turn north and drive eight miles to Four Corners. Turn right on Forest Road 36 and drive 12 miles to the campground on the left.

Contact: Malheur National Forest, Blue Mountain Ranger District, 541/573-4300, www.fs.usda.gov/malheur.

80 MIDDLE FORK

Scenic rating: 6

on the Middle Fork of the John Day River in Malheur National Forest

Map 4.7, page 211 **BEST**

Scattered along the banks of the Middle Fork of the John Day River at 4,100 feet elevation, these rustic campsites are easy to reach off a paved road. Besides wildlife-viewing and berry picking, the main activity at this camp is fishing, so bring along your fly rod and pinch down your barbs for catch-and-release. The John Day is a state scenic waterway.

Campsites, facilities: There are nine single sites and one double site for tents or RVs up to 22 feet long. Picnic tables and fire rings are provided. Vault toilets are available. There is no drinking water, and garbage must be packed out. Some facilities are wheelchair accessible. Leashed pets are permitted.

Reservations, fees: Reservations are not accepted. Sites are $8 per night, $4 per night per additional vehicle. Open late May-November, weather permitting.

Directions: From John Day, drive northeast on U.S. 26 for 28 miles to Highway 7. Turn left (north) and drive one mile to County Road 20. Turn left and drive five miles to the campground on the left.

Contact: Malheur National Forest, Blue Mountain Ranger District, 541/575-3000, www.fs.usda.gov/malheur.

81 DIXIE

Scenic rating: 5

near Dixie Summit in Malheur National Forest

Map 4.7, page 211

Perched at Dixie Summit (elevation 5,000 feet), this camp, just off U.S. 26, is close enough to provide easy access to nearby Bridge Creek, where you can toss in a fishing line. Dixie draws overnighters but otherwise gets light use. The Sumpter Valley Railroad interpretive site is one mile west on U.S. 26.

Campsites, facilities: There are 11 sites for tents or RVs up to 22 feet long and one group site for 20-50 people. Picnic tables, vault toilets, and fire rings are provided. No drinking water is available and garbage must be packed out. A store, café, gas, and ice are available within nine miles. Some facilities are wheelchair accessible. Leashed pets are permitted.

Reservations, fees: Reservations are not accepted. Sites are $8 per night, $4 per night for an additional vehicle. Open late May-November, weather permitting.

Directions: From John Day, drive northeast on U.S. 26 for 24 miles to Forest Road 365. Turn left and drive 0.25 mile to the campground on the left.

Contact: Malheur National Forest, Blue Mountain Ranger District, 541/575-3000, www.fs.usda.gov/malheur.

82 WETMORE

Scenic rating: 7

on the Middle Fork of the Burnt River in Wallowa-Whitman National Forest

Map 4.7, page 211

This campground, set at an elevation of 4,320 feet near the Middle Fork of the Burnt River, makes a nice base camp for a fishing or hiking trip. The stream can provide good trout fishing. (Trails are detailed on maps of Wallowa-Whitman National Forest.) An excellent 0.5-mile, wheelchair-accessible trail passes through old-growth forest—watch for bald eagles.

Campsites, facilities: There are 10 single sites and one double site for tents or RVs up to 16 feet long. Picnic tables and fire grills are provided. Vault toilets and drinking water (seasonal) are available. Garbage must be packed out. Some facilities are wheelchair accessible. Leashed pets are permitted.

Reservations, fees: Reservations are not accepted. Sites are $5 per night, $5 per each additional vehicle. Open mid-May-mid-October, weather permitting.

Directions: From John Day, drive east on U.S. 26 for 29 miles to Austin Junction. Continue east on U.S. 26 for 10 miles to the campground on the left.

Contact: Wallowa-Whitman National Forest, Whitman Ranger District, 541/523-6391, www.fs.usda.gov/wallowa-whitman.

83 OREGON

Scenic rating: 6

near Austin Junction in Wallowa-Whitman National Forest

Map 4.7, page 211

Oregon campground sits at 4,880 feet elevation just off U.S. 26 surrounded by hillside as well as Douglas fir, tamarack, and white fir. It is the staging area for all-terrain vehicle (ATV) enthusiasts, and the popular Blue Mountain OHV Trailhead is here; several trails crisscross the area. Bald eagles nest in the area.

Campsites, facilities: There are eight sites for tents or RVs up to 28 feet long. Picnic tables and fire grills are provided. Vault toilets are available. There is no drinking water, and garbage must be packed out. Leashed pets are permitted.

Reservations, fees: Reservations are not accepted. Sites are $5 per night, $5 per each additional vehicle. Open mid-May-mid-October, weather permitting.

Directions: From John Day, drive east on U.S. 26 for 29 miles to Austin Junction. Continue east for 20 miles to the campground.

Contact: Wallowa-Whitman National Forest, Whitman Ranger District, 541/523-6391, www.fs.usda.gov/wallowa-whitman.

84 YELLOW PINE

Scenic rating: 7

near Middle Fork Burnt River in Wallowa-Whitman National Forest

Map 4.7, page 211

Yellow Pine is similar to Oregon Campground, but larger; highlights include easy access and good recreation potential. The camp offers a number of hiking trails, including a 0.5-mile-long, wheelchair-accessible trail that connects to the Wetmore Campground. Keep an eye out for bald eagles in this area.

Campsites, facilities: There are 21 sites for

tents or RVs up to 28 feet long, including one double site; some single sites can combine into a group site for 20-50 people. Picnic tables and fire grills are provided. Vault toilets and drinking water (seasonal) are available. Garbage must be packed out. Some facilities are wheelchair accessible. Leashed pets are permitted.

Reservations, fees: Reservations are not accepted. Sites are $6 per night. Call for group rates. Open late mid-May-mid-October, weather permitting.

Directions: From John Day, drive east on U.S. 26 for 29 miles to Austin Junction. Continue east for 21 miles to the campground.

Contact: Wallowa-Whitman National Forest, Whitman Ranger District, 541/523-6391, www.fs.usda.gov/wallowa-whitman.

85 UNITY LAKE STATE RECREATION SITE

🚶 🚴 🏊 💧 🚐 🏕 ♿ 🚗 ⛺

Scenic rating: 7

on Unity Reservoir

Map 4.7, page 211

The grassy setting of Unity Lake contrasts nicely with the bordering sagebrush and cheatgrass of the high desert. This camp, set along the east shore of Unity Reservoir, is a popular spot in good weather. Campers can choose from boating, fishing, hiking, picnicking, swimming, or enjoying the scenic views.

Campsites, facilities: There are 35 sites with partial hookups for tents or RVs up to 40 feet long, a hiker/biker tent area, and two rustic cabins. Picnic tables, garbage bins, and fire rings are provided. Drinking water, restrooms with flush toilets and showers, a dump station, horseshoe pits, ice, and firewood are available. Boat docks and launching facilities are nearby. Some facilities are wheelchair accessible. Leashed pets are permitted.

Reservations, fees: Reservations are not accepted for campsites but are required for cabins at 800/452-5687 or www.reserveamerica.com ($8 reservation fee). Sites are $24 per night,

cabins are $44-54 per night, $5 per person per night for hike-in/bike-in sites, $7 per night for an additional vehicle. Open year-round, weather permitting.

Directions: From John Day, drive east on U.S. 26 for 50 miles to Highway 245. Turn left (north) on Highway 245 and drive three miles to the park on the left.

Contact: Unity Lake State Recreation Site, 541/446-3470 or 800/452-5687, www.oregonstateparks.org.

86 DEPOT PARK

🚶 🚴 🏊 🐕 🏕 ♿ 🚗 ⛺

Scenic rating: 6

on the John Day River

Map 4.7, page 211

Depot Park is a more developed alternative to the many U.S. Forest Service campgrounds in the area. This urban park sits on grassy flatlands and provides access to the John Day River, a good trout fishing spot. The camp features a historic rail depot on the premises, as well as a related museum. A nearby attraction, the Strawberry Mountain Wilderness, has prime hiking trails.

Campsites, facilities: There are 20 sites for tents or RVs up to 35 feet long (full hookups); some sites are pull-through. There is also a grassy area offering dispersed camping for hikers/bikers and tents. Picnic tables and barbecues are provided. Restrooms with flush toilets and showers, a dump station, playground, and covered picnic area are available. A camp host is on-site seasonally. Some facilities are wheelchair accessible. Leashed pets are permitted.

Reservations, fees: Reservations are not accepted. Sites are $16-20 per night, $10 per night for the hike-in/bike-in sites, $4 per night per additional vehicle. Monthly rates are available. Open May-November, weather permitting.

Directions: From John Day, drive east on U.S. 26 for 13 miles to Prairie City and the junction of U.S. 26 and Main Street. Turn right (south) on Main Street and drive 0.5 mile to the park (well signed).

Contact: Prairie City Hall, 541/820-3605, www.prairiecityoregon.com.

87 ELK CREEK CAMPGROUND

Scenic rating: 5

in Wallowa-Whitman National Forest

Map 4.7, page 211

Elk Creek campground is small, primitive, and remote. It has no designated campsites, but rather an area for dispersed-style tent camping. Its primary use is for OHV riders, with nearby OHV trail access.

Campsites, facilities: There is a dispersed camping area that accommodates roughly 10 tents or small RVs. Picnic tables and fire rings are provided. Vault toilets are available. There is no drinking water. Garbage must be packed out. Leashed pets are permitted.

Reservations, fees: Reservations are not accepted. Sites are $5 per night. Open mid-May-mid-October, weather permitting.

Directions: From John Day, drive east on U.S. 26 for 49 miles to Unity and County Road 600. Turn right on County Road 600 and drive west for six miles (the road becomes Forest Road 6005/South Fork Road). Continue past the forest boundary for three miles to the campground on the right.

Contact: Wallowa-Whitman National Forest, Whitman Ranger District, 541/523-6391, www. fs.usda.gov/wallowa-whitman.

88 STEVENS CAMPGROUND

Scenic rating: 5

on the south fork of the Burnt River in Wallowa-Whitman National Forest

Map 4.7, page 211

This campground sits at an elevation of 4,480

feet along the banks of the south fork of the Burnt River and provides an alternative to the other small camps along the river. The trout fishing is often good here.

Campsites, facilities: There are six single sites and one double site for tents or RVs up to 30 feet. Picnic tables and fire grills are provided. There is no drinking water, and garbage must be packed out. Vault toilets are available. Leashed pets are permitted.

Reservations, fees: Reservations are not accepted. Sites are $5 per night, $5 per night per additional vehicle. Open mid-May-mid-October, weather permitting.

Directions: From John Day, drive east on U.S. 26 for 49 miles to Unity and County Road 600. Turn right on County Road 600 and drive west for six miles (the road becomes Forest Road 6005/South Fork Road). Continue past the forest boundary for two miles to the campground on the right.

Contact: Wallowa-Whitman National Forest, Whitman Ranger District, 541/523-6391, www. fs.usda.gov/wallowa-whitman.

89 SOUTH FORK

Scenic rating: 5

on the south fork of the Burnt River in Wallowa-Whitman National Forest

Map 4.7, page 211

A gem of a spot, South Fork offers drinking water, privacy, and scenery. The campground (4,400 feet elevation) is set on the banks of the south fork of the Burnt River, a nice trout creek with good evening bites for anglers who know how to sneak-fish. An OHV staging area with trail access is across the road from the campground.

Campsites, facilities: There are 12 sites for tents or RVs up to 28 feet long and two sites for tents only; most sites are pull-through. Picnic tables and fire grills are provided. There are vault toilets, and drinking water is available seasonally. Garbage must be packed out. Some facilities are wheelchair accessible. Leashed pets are permitted.

Reservations, fees: Reservations are not accepted. Sites are $5 per night, $5 per night per additional vehicle. Open mid-May-mid-October, weather permitting.

Directions: From John Day, drive east on U.S. 26 for 49 miles to Unity and County Road 600. Turn right on County Road 600 and drive west for six miles (the road becomes Forest Road 6005/South Fork Road). Continue past the forest boundary for one mile to the campground on the left.

Contact: Wallowa-Whitman National Forest, Whitman Ranger District, 541/523-6391, www. fs.usda.gov/wallowa-whitman.

90 STRAWBERRY

Scenic rating: 7

on Strawberry Creek in Malheur National Forest

Map 4.7, page 211

At 5,700 feet elevation, this campground hugs the banks of Strawberry Creek. Nearby trails provide access to the Strawberry Mountain Wilderness, Strawberry Lake, and Strawberry Falls. This pretty area features a variety of hiking and hunting options, as well as fishing in Strawberry Creek.

Campsites, facilities: There are 10 sites for tents. Picnic tables and fire rings are provided. Drinking water and vault toilets are available. Garbage must be packed out. Some facilities are wheelchair accessible. Leashed pets are permitted.

Reservations, fees: Reservations are not accepted. Sites are $8 per night, $4 per night for an additional vehicle. Open late May-November, weather permitting.

Directions: From John Day, drive east on U.S. 26 for 13 miles to Prairie City and County Road 62. Turn right (southeast) and drive 0.5 mile to County Road 60. Turn right and drive south on County Road 60 for 8.5 miles (County Road 60

becomes Forest Road 6001). Continue 2.5 miles to the campground on the left.

Contact: Malheur National Forest, Prairie City Ranger District, 541/820-3800, www.fs.usda. gov/malheur.

91 SLIDE CREEK

Scenic rating: 5

in Malheur National Forest

Map 4.7, page 211

Slide Creek has tiny, overlooked sites known by a handful of backcountry equestrians. It is set at 4,900 feet in Malheur National Forest with a nearby creek to provide water for horses.

Campsites, facilities: There are three sites for tents or RVs up to 40 feet long. Picnic tables and fire rings are provided. Vault toilets, corrals, and hitching posts are available. There is no drinking water, and garbage must be packed out. Some facilities are wheelchair accessible. Leashed pets are permitted.

Reservations, fees: Reservations are not accepted. There is no fee for camping. Open late May-November, weather permitting.

Directions: From John Day, drive east on U.S. 26 for 13 miles to Prairie City and County Road 62. Turn right (southeast) and drive 0.5 mile to County Road 60. Turn right and drive south on County Road 60 for 8.5 miles (County Road 60 becomes Forest Road 6001). Continue on Forest Road 6001 to the campground on the right.

Contact: Malheur National Forest, Prairie City Ranger District, 541/820-3800, www.fs.usda. gov/malheur.

92 WICKIUP

Scenic rating: 5

on Wickiup Creek in Malheur National Forest

Map 4.7, page 211

This campground sits at an elevation of 4,300 feet along the forks of Wickiup Creek and

Canyon Creek at a historic site; many of its original Civilian Conservation Corps structures are still in place. There is limited fishing in the creek. To the north are numerous trails that lead into the Strawberry Mountain Wilderness. Horses are not allowed within the campground except for loading and unloading.

Campsites, facilities: There are six sites for tents or RVs up to 22 feet long, including one group site for 5-20 people. Picnic tables and fire rings are provided. A vault toilet is available. There is no drinking water, and garbage must be packed out. Some facilities are wheelchair accessible. Leashed pets are permitted.

Reservations, fees: Reservations are not accepted. Sites are $5 per night, $3 per night per additional vehicle. Open late May-November, weather permitting.

Directions: From John Day, drive south on U.S. 395 for 10 miles to Forest Road 15. Turn left (southeast) and drive eight miles to the campground on the right.

Contact: Malheur National Forest, Blue Mountain Ranger District, 541/575-3000, www.fs.usda.gov/malheur.

93 PARISH CABIN

Scenic rating: 6
on Little Bear Creek in Malheur National Forest

Map 4.7, page 211

Parish Cabin campground sits along the banks of Little Bear Creek at an elevation of 4,900 feet. This is a pretty spot that's not heavily used, and the road is paved all the way to the campground. The creek offers limited fishing. The place is popular with groups of families and hunters in season.

Campsites, facilities: There are 19 sites for tents or RVs up to 22 feet long and one group site for up to 50 people. Picnic tables and fire rings are provided. Vault toilets are available. Drinking water may be available. Garbage must be packed out. Some facilities are wheelchair accessible. Leashed pets are permitted.

Reservations, fees: Reservations are not accepted. Sites are $8 per night, $4 per night per additional vehicle. Open late May-November, weather permitting.

Directions: From John Day, drive south on U.S. 395 for 10 miles to Forest Road 15. Turn left and drive 16 miles southeast to Forest Road 16. Turn right onto Forest Road 16 and drive a short distance to the campground on the right.

Contact: Malheur National Forest, Blue Mountain Ranger District, 541/575-3000, www.fs.usda.gov/malheur.

94 MURRAY CAMPGROUND

Scenic rating: 7
in Malheur National Forest

Map 4.7, page 211

Murray Elk Creek is set at an elevation of 5,200 feet with nearby Forest Service roads that provide access to the Strawberry Mountain Wilderness. The camp is used primarily as a layover for those heading into the wilderness to fish or hunt. Note that fishing is restricted to the use of artificial lures with a single, barbless hook.

Campsites, facilities: There are five sites for tents or RVs up to 40 feet long. Picnic tables and fire rings are provided. Vault toilets are available. There is no drinking water, and garbage must be packed out. Some facilities are wheelchair accessible. Leashed pets are permitted.

Reservations, fees: Reservations are not accepted. Sites are $8 per night, $4 per night for an additional vehicle. Open late May-November, weather permitting.

Directions: From John Day, drive east on U.S. 26 for 13 miles to Prairie City and County Road 62. Turn right and drive 24 miles to Forest Road 16. Turn right and follow signs to the campground on the right.

Contact: Malheur National Forest, Prairie City Ranger District, 541/820-3800, www.fs.usda.gov/malheur.

95 BIG CREEK

Scenic rating: 6

near the Strawberry Mountain Wilderness in
Malheur National Forest

Map 4.7, page 211

At 5,100 feet elevation, this campground hugs
the banks of Big Creek. Nearby forest roads
provide access to the Strawberry Mountain
Wilderness. Other recreation options include
fishing and mountain biking. Note that fishing
is restricted to the use of artificial lures with a
single, barbless hook. In the appropriate seasons, bear, coyotes, deer, and elk are hunted
here.

Campsites, facilities: There are 15 sites for
tents or RVs up to 40 feet long. Picnic tables
and fire rings are provided. Drinking water
and vault toilets are available. Garbage must
be packed out. Some facilities are wheelchair
accessible. Leashed pets are permitted.

Reservations, fees: Reservations are not
accepted. Sites are $8 per night, $4 per night
for an additional vehicle. Open late May-
November, weather permitting.

Directions: From John Day, take U.S. 395
south for 10 miles to Forest Road 15. Turn left
and on Forest Road 15 drive 16 miles to Forest
Road 16. Turn right on Forest Road 16 and
drive six miles to Forest Road 815. Turn right
and drive 0.5 mile to the campground on the
right.

Contact: Malheur National Forest, Prairie City
Ranger District, 541/820-3800, www.fs.usda.
gov/malheur.

96 TROUT FARM

Scenic rating: 6

near Prairie City in Malheur National Forest

Map 4.7, page 211

Trout Farm campground (4,900 feet elevation)
is situated on the Upper John Day River, which
provides good trout fishing with easy access

for people who don't wish to travel off paved
roads. A picnic shelter is available for family
picnics, and a small pond at the campground
has a wheelchair-accessible trail.

Campsites, facilities: There are six sites for
tents or RVs up to 21 feet long. Picnic tables
and fire rings are provided. Drinking water
and vault toilets are available. Garbage must
be packed out. Some facilities are wheelchair
accessible. Leashed pets are permitted.

Reservations, fees: Reservations are not accepted. Sites are $8 per night, $4 per night per
additional vehicle. Open June-mid-October,
weather permitting.

Directions: From John Day, drive east on U.S.
26 for 13 miles to Prairie City and Front Street.
Turn right on Front Street and drive 0.5 mile
to County Road 62. Turn left on County Road
62 and drive 15 miles to the campground entrance on the right.

Contact: Malheur National Forest, Prairie City
Ranger District, 541/820-3800, www.fs.usda.
gov/malheur.

97 ELK CREEK

Scenic rating: 8

on Elk Creek in Malheur National Forest

Map 4.7, page 211

This tiny, pretty camp at the confluence of the
north and south forks of Elk Creek (elevation
5,000 feet) has lots of hunting and fishing opportunities. The camp gets light use, except
during the hunting season. If full, North Fork
Malheur is an alternate camp in the area.

Campsites, facilities: There are five tent sites.
Picnic tables and fire rings are provided. Vault
toilets are available. There is no drinking water,
and garbage must be packed out. Leashed pets
are permitted.

Reservations, fees: Reservations are not accepted. There is no fee for camping. Open late
May-November, weather permitting.

Directions: From John Day, drive east on U.S.
26 for 13 miles to Prairie City and County Road

62. Turn right (southeast) on County Road 62 and drive 8.5 miles to Forest Road 13. Turn left and drive 16 miles to Forest Road 16. Turn right and drive 1.5 miles south to the campground on the right.

Contact: Malheur National Forest, Prairie City Ranger District, 541/820-3800, www.fs.usda.gov/malheur.

98 CROSSING

Scenic rating: 5

on Little Crane Creek in Malheur National Forest

Map 4.7, page 211

Quiet, primitive, private, and small: all these words describe this camp along the banks of Little Crane Creek at an elevation of 5,500 feet. The creek provides good trout fishing (only artificial bait and artificial lures are allowed). There are also some nice hiking trails in the area, the closest one at the north fork of the Malheur River, about 10 miles away. This is considered a dispersed camping site, so check current fire restrictions before lighting a campfire.

Campsites, facilities: There are four sites for tents or RVs up to 20 feet long. Picnic tables are provided. Vault toilets are available. There is no drinking water, and garbage must be packed out. Leashed pets are permitted.

Reservations, fees: Reservations are not accepted. There is no fee for camping. Open late May-November, weather permitting.

Directions: From John Day, drive east on U.S. 26 for 13 miles to Prairie City and County Road 62. Turn right and drive 8.5 miles to Forest Road 13. Turn left and drive 16 miles to Forest Road 16. Turn right and drive 5.5 miles south to the campground on the left.

Contact: Malheur National Forest, Prairie City Ranger District, 541/820-3800, www.fs.usda.gov/malheur.

99 NORTH FORK MALHEUR

Scenic rating: 7

on the north fork of the Malheur River in Malheur National Forest

Map 4.7, page 211

The secluded North Fork Malheur campground sits at an elevation of 4,700 feet along the banks of the north fork of the Malheur River, a designated Wild and Scenic River. Hiking trails and rough dirt roads provide additional access to the river and backcountry streams. (It's essential to obtain a U.S. Forest Service map.) Good fishing, hunting, and mountain biking opportunities abound in the area. Fishing is restricted to the use of artificial lures with a single, barbless hook.

Campsites, facilities: There are five sites for tents or RVs up to 21 feet long. Picnic tables and fire rings are provided. Vault toilets are available. There is no drinking water, and garbage must be packed out. Leashed pets are permitted.

Reservations, fees: Reservations are not accepted. There is no fee for camping. Open late May-November, weather permitting.

Directions: From John Day, drive east on U.S. 26 for 13 miles to Prairie City and County Road 62. Turn right and drive 8.5 miles to Forest Road 13. Turn left and drive 16 miles to Forest Road 16. Turn right and drive two miles south to a fork with Forest Road 1675. Take the left fork to Forest Road 1675 and drive two miles to the camp on the right.

Contact: Malheur National Forest, Prairie City Ranger District, 541/820-3800, www.fs.usda.gov/malheur.

100 ROCK SPRINGS FOREST CAMP
🥾 🐕 🚐 ⛺

Scenic rating: 5

at Rock Springs in Malheur National Forest

Map 4.7, page 211

If you want to camp in a big forest filled with the scent of ponderosa pines, Rock Springs Forest Camp is for you. This primitive camp has a sprinkling of pretty aspen and several little springs—in fact, it's located right on Rock Springs, with Cave Spring, House Creek Spring, and Sunshine Spring within a few miles. Do not count on the springs for drinking water, however, without a water filter. The elevation is 4,800 feet.

Campsites, facilities: There are 14 sites for tents or RVs up to 40 feet long. Picnic tables and fire grills are provided. Vault toilets are available. Drinking water is available from a spring (you must filter it first). Garbage must be packed out. Leashed pets are permitted.

Reservations, fees: Reservations are not accepted. Sites are $6 per night for first two vehicles, $3 per night for each additional vehicle. Open late May-mid-October, weather permitting.

Directions: From Burns, drive north on U.S. 395 for 30 miles to Van-Silvies Highway (County Road 73). Turn right on Van-Silvies Highway (which turns into Forest Road 17) and drive four miles to Forest Road 054. Turn right (south) and drive 0.75 mile to the camp on the left.

Contact: Malheur National Forest, Emigrant Creek Ranger District, 541/573-4300, www.fs.usda.gov/malheur.

101 WEST EAGLE MEADOW
🥾 🏊 🐕 ♿ 🚐 ⛺

Scenic rating: 7

near West Eagle Creek in Wallowa-Whitman National Forest

Map 4.8, page 212

West Eagle campground sits in a big, open meadow (5,200 feet elevation) about a five-minute walk from West Eagle Creek. The West Eagle Trail starts at the camp, providing access to the Eagle Cap Wilderness and offering a good opportunity to observe wildlife. The adjacent meadow fills with wildflowers in the summer. For campers with horses, there are new stock facilities with water available in a separate, adjacent campground.

Campsites, facilities: There are five sites for tents or RVs up to 30 feet long and seven walk-in sites for tents only. The adjacent campground at West Eagle Meadows has six sites for campers with horses. Picnic tables and fire rings are provided. Vault toilets are available. There is no drinking water, and garbage must be packed out. Stock facilities include corrals and hitching rails. Some facilities are wheelchair accessible. Leashed pets are permitted.

Reservations, fees: Reservations are not accepted. Sites are $5 per night per vehicle. Visitors to Eagle Cap Wilderness must obtain a free Wilderness Visitor Permit at the on-site self-service station (one permit per group). Open mid-June-late October, weather permitting.

Directions: From Baker City, drive north on I-84 for six miles to Highway 203. Turn east and drive 17 miles to the town of Medical Springs and County Road 71. Turn right (south) and drive two miles to Forest Road 67. Turn left and drive 12 miles to Forest Road 77. Turn left (north) and drive five miles to the camp on the right. Note: Segments of the road are narrow and steep.

Contact: Wallowa-Whitman National Forest, LaGrande Ranger District, 541/963-7186, www.fs.usda.gov/wallowa-whitman.

102 EAGLE FORKS

Scenic rating: 6

on Eagle Creek in Wallowa-Whitman National Forest

Map 4.8, page 212

This campground (3,000 feet elevation) is located at the confluence of Little Eagle Creek and Eagle Creek. A trail follows the creek northwest for several miles, making for a prime day hike, yet the spot attracts few people (except on holiday weekends). It's quite pretty and perfect for a weekend getaway or an extended layover.

Campsites, facilities: There are six single sites and two double sites for tents or RVs up to 21 feet long. Picnic tables and fire rings are provided. Drinking water and vault toilets are available. Garbage must be packed out. Some facilities are wheelchair accessible. Leashed pets are permitted.

Reservations, fees: Reservations are not accepted. Sites are $5 per night. Open May-late October, weather permitting.

Directions: From Baker City, drive east on Highway 86 for 42 miles to Richland and Newbridge. Turn north on Newbridge (after two miles on paved roads, it becomes Eagle Creek Road); then continue on Forest Road 7735 for seven miles to the campground entrance on the left.

Contact: Wallowa-Whitman National Forest, Whitman Ranger District, 541/742-7511, www.fs.usda.gov/wallowa-whitman.

103 TWO COLOR

Scenic rating: 6

on Eagle Creek in Wallowa-Whitman National Forest

Map 4.8, page 212

Two Color campground (4,800 feet elevation) sits on the banks of Eagle Creek, about a mile north of Tamarack. Evergreens shade the spacious campsites, and the creek is stocked with rainbow trout. If full, another option for campers is nearby Boulder Park campground, three miles northeast on Forest Road 7755.

Campsites, facilities: There are 11 sites for tents or RVs up to 16 feet long. Picnic tables and fire grills are provided. Vault toilets are available. There is no drinking water, and garbage must be packed out. Leashed pets are permitted.

Reservations, fees: Reservations are not accepted. There is no fee for camping. Open mid-June-late October, weather permitting.

Directions: From Baker City, drive north on I-84 for six miles to Highway 203. Turn east on Highway 203 and drive 17 miles to Medical Springs and County Road 71. Turn right (south) and drive two miles to Forest Road 67. Turn left and drive 12 miles to Forest Road 77. Turn left and drive one mile to Forest Road 7755. Turn right and drive one mile north to the camp.

Contact: Wallowa-Whitman National Forest, LaGrande Ranger District, 541/963-7186, www.fs.usda.gov/wallowa-whitman.

104 TAMARACK

Scenic rating: 5

on Eagle Creek in Wallowa-Whitman National Forest

Map 4.8, page 212

On the banks of Eagle Creek in a beautiful area with lush vegetation and abundant wildlife sits Tamarack campground at 4,600 feet elevation. This is a good spot for fishing and hiking in a remote setting; a short, accessible trail leads down to two creekside fishing platforms.

Campsites, facilities: There are 12 sites for tents or RVs up to 25 feet long. Picnic tables and fire rings are provided. Drinking water and vault toilets are available. Garbage must be packed out. Some facilities are wheelchair accessible. Leashed pets are permitted.

Reservations, fees: Reservations are not

accepted. Sites are $6 per night. Open June-late October, weather permitting.

Directions: From Baker City, drive east on Highway 86 for 42 miles to Richland and Newbridge. Turn north on Newbridge (after two miles on paved roads, it becomes Eagle Creek Road); then continue on Forest Road 7735 for 20 miles to the campground entrance.

Contact: Wallowa-Whitman National Forest, Pine Ranger District, 541/742-7511, www. fs.usda.gov/wallowa-whitman.

105 FISH LAKE

Scenic rating: 6

on Fish Lake in Wallowa-Whitman National Forest

Map 4.8, page 212

This is a pretty, well-forested camp with comfortable sites along the shore of 20-acre Fish Lake at an elevation of 6,600 feet. Fish Lake makes a good base for a fishing trip; side-trip options include hiking on nearby trails that lead to mountain streams. Bring mosquito repellent.

Campsites, facilities: There are 15 sites for tents or RVs up to 20 feet long. Six sites on the upper loop can accommodate longer RVs. Picnic tables and fire rings are provided. Drinking water and vault toilets are available. Garbage must be packed out. Boat-launching facilities (for small boats only) are nearby. Some facilities are wheelchair accessible. Leashed pets are permitted.

Reservations, fees: Reservations are not accepted. Sites are $6 per night. Open July-late October, weather permitting.

Directions: From Baker City, take I-84 north for four miles to Highway 86. Turn east on Highway 86 and drive 52 miles to Halfway and Main Street. Turn left (north) on Main Street and drive to Fish Lake Road. Turn right on Fish

Lake Road, then drive five miles to Forest Road 66. Continue north on Forest Road 66 for 18.5 miles to the campground on the left.

Contact: Wallowa-Whitman National Forest, Pine Ranger District, 541/742-7511, www. fs.usda.gov/wallowa-whitman.

106 SPRING RECREATION SITE

Scenic rating: 5

on the Snake River

Map 4.8, page 212

One of two camps in or near Huntington, this campground hugs the banks of the Brownlee Reservoir. Fishing is popular at this reservoir; it's known for large channel catfish. A more developed alternative, Farewell Bend State Recreation Area offers showers and all the other luxuries a camper could want.

Campsites, facilities: There are 35 sites for tents or RVs of any length. Group camping is available. Picnic tables, garbage service, and fire grills are provided. Drinking water (summer only) and vault toilets are available. Boat-launching facilities, a dock, and a fish-cleaning station are on-site. A seasonal camp host is on-site. Some facilities are wheelchair accessible. Leashed pets are permitted.

Reservations, fees: Reservations are not accepted. Sites are $5 per night per vehicle, with a 14-day stay limit. Open year-round, weather permitting; there is no fee October 31-April 1.

Directions: From Ontario (near the Oregon/Idaho border), drive northwest on I-84 for 28 miles to Huntington and Snake River Road. Turn right (northeast) on Snake River Road and drive three miles (paved road) to the campground.

Contact: Bureau of Land Management, Baker City Office, 541/523-1256, www.blm.gov.

107 FAREWELL BEND STATE RECREATION AREA

Scenic rating: 7

on the Snake River

Map 4.8, page 212

Farewell Bend campground offers a green desert experience on the banks of the Snake River's Brownlee Reservoir. Situated along the Oregon Trail, the camp has historic interpretive displays and an evening interpretive program at the amphitheater during the summer. The lake provides good numbers of catfish.

Campsites, facilities: There are 91 sites with partial hookups for RVs up to 60 feet long, 30 tent sites, a hiker-biker camp, two cabins, and one group site for up to 50 people. Picnic tables and fire rings are provided. Drinking water, garbage bins, restrooms with flush toilets and showers, a dump station, firewood, ice, a fish-cleaning station, basketball hoops, horseshoe pits, sand volleyball court, and boat-launching facilities are available. Some facilities are wheelchair accessible. Leashed pets are permitted.

Reservations, fees: Reservations are accepted at 800/452-5687 or www.reserveamerica.com ($8 reservation fee). RV sites are $24, tent sites are $18 per night, $5 per person per night for the hiker/biker camp, the group site is $76 per night, cabins are $44-54 per night, $5 per night per extra vehicle. Some credit cards are accepted. Open year-round, with limited winter facilities.

Directions: From Ontario (near the Oregon/ Idaho border), drive northwest on I-84 for 21 miles to Exit 353. Take that exit and drive one mile to the park.

Contact: Farewell Bend State Recreation Area, 541/869-2365 or 800/551-6949, www.oregon-stateparks.org.

108 BULLY CREEK PARK

Scenic rating: 7

on Bully Creek Reservoir

Map 4.8, page 212

Bully Creek Reservoir is located in a kind of high desert area with sagebrush and poplar trees for shade. It's beautiful if you like the desert, and the sunsets are worth the trip. People come here to boat, fish (mostly for warm-water fish, such as crappie and large- and smallmouth bass), swim, and water ski, and there is biking on the gravel roads. At 2,300 feet elevation, the primitive setting is home to deer, jackrabbits, squirrels, and many birds. No monthly rentals are permitted here—a big plus for overnighters.

Campsites, facilities: There are 40 sites with partial hookups for tents or RVs up to 40 feet in length; one site is pull-through. Picnic tables and fire pits are provided. Drinking water, restrooms with flush toilets and showers, ice, firewood, garbage bins, a dump station, picnic area, and boat ramp and dock are available. A camp host is on-site. A restaurant, café, convenience store, gasoline, propane gas, charcoal, and coin laundry are within nine miles. Some facilities are wheelchair accessible. Leashed pets are permitted.

Reservations, fees: Reservations are accepted at 541/473-2969. Sites are $15 per night. Open mid-April-mid-November, weather permitting.

Directions: From Ontario (near the Oregon/ Idaho border), drive west on U.S. 20/26 for 12 miles to Vale and Graham Boulevard. Turn right (northwest) on Graham Boulevard and drive five miles to Bully Creek Road. Turn right (west) and drive three miles to the park on the left.

Contact: Bully Creek Park, 541/473-2969; Malheur County Parks Department, 541/473-5191, www.malheurco.org.

THE
SOUTHERN
CASCADES

© PHONGPHOTOGRAPHY/DREAMSTIME.COM

The Southern Cascades is famous for Crater Lake, but it holds many recreation secrets. Crater Lake's cobalt-blue waters lie within clifflike walls; the lake's Rim Drive is on everybody's to-do list. Beyond the lake, you'll find stellar camping, fishing, and hiking. Neighboring Mount Washington Wilderness and Three Sisters Wilderness in Willamette National Forest are accessible via a beautiful drive on the McKenzie River Highway (Highway 126) east from Eugene. Crane Prairie, Waldo Lake, and Wickiup Reservoir provide boating, camping, and good fishing. The Umpqua and Rogue National Forests offer great water-sport destinations, including Diamond Lake, and the headwaters of the Rogue and North Umpqua Rivers. Upper Klamath Lake and the Klamath Basin are the number one wintering areas in America for bald eagles. Klamath Lake and the Williamson River provide a chance to catch huge but elusive trout.

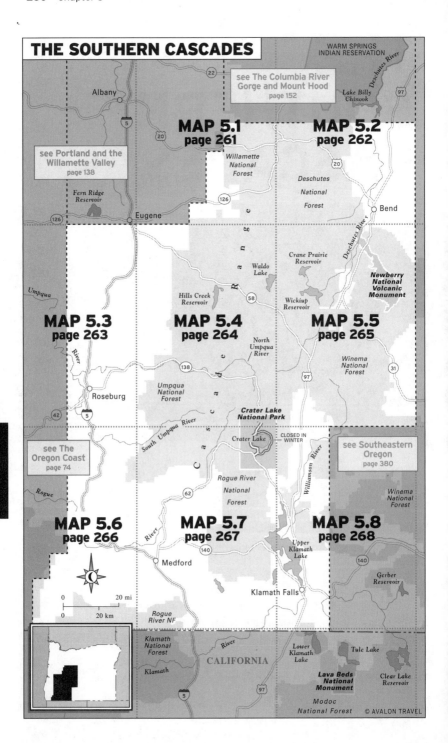

Map 5.1

Sites 1-16
Pages 269-275

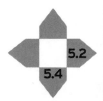

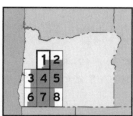

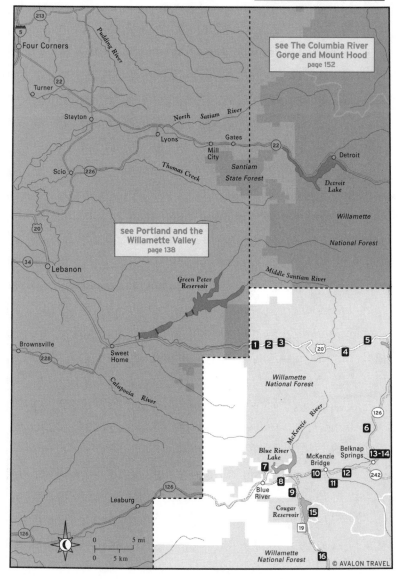

see The Columbia River Gorge and Mount Hood
page 152

see Portland and the Willamette Valley
page 138

© AVALON TRAVEL

Map 5.2
Sites 17-50
Pages 275-289

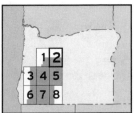

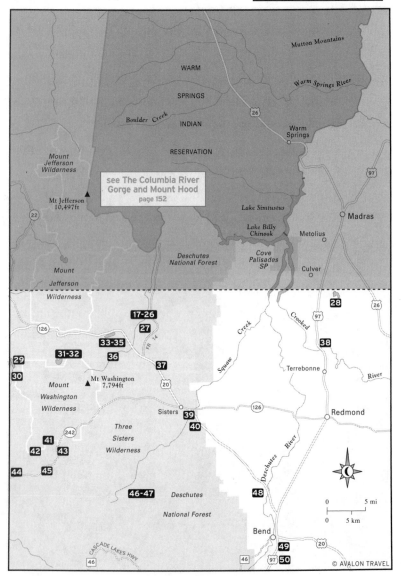

WARM

SPRINGS

INDIAN

RESERVATION

Mutton Mountains

Warm Springs River

Boulder Creek

Mount
Jefferson
Wilderness

Mt Jefferson
10,497ft

see The Columbia River
Gorge and Mount Hood
page 152

Warm
Springs

Lake Simtustus

Lake Billy
Chinook

Madras

Metolius

Mount
Jefferson

Deschutes
National Forest

Cove
Palisades
SP

Culver

Wilderness

126

17-26

27

33-35

36

29

31-32

30

FR 14

37

20

Mount
Washington
Wilderness

Mt Washington
7,794ft

Squaw Creek

Crooked

28

97

38

Terrebonne

River

242

41

42   43

44   45

Three
Sisters
Wilderness

Sisters

39

40

126

Redmond

Deschutes River

46-47

Deschutes

National Forest

48

N

0   5 mi

0   5 km

CASCADE LAKES HWY

46

Bend

49

97   50

20

© AVALON TRAVEL

Map 5.3

Sites 51-59
Pages 289-293

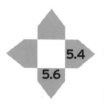

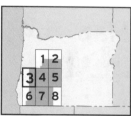

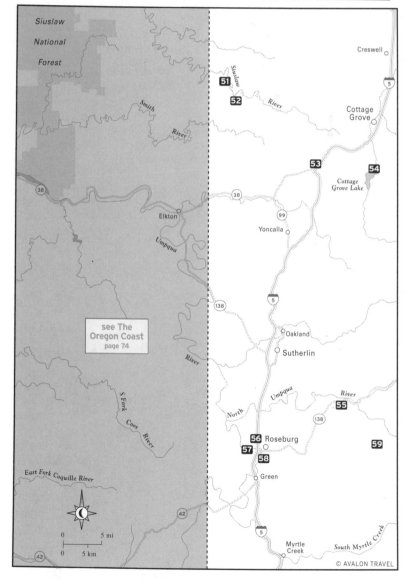

Map 5.4

Sites 60-117
Pages 293-318

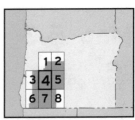

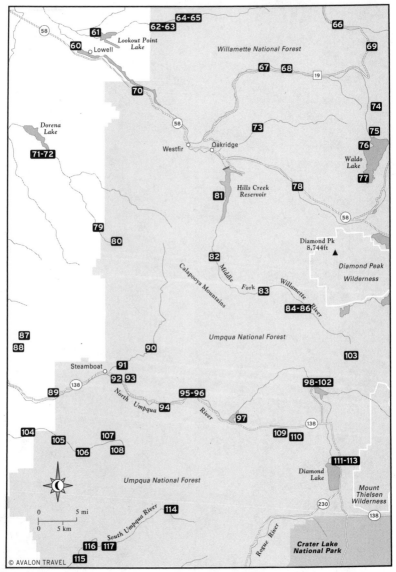

Map 5.5

Sites 118-179
Pages 318-343

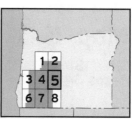

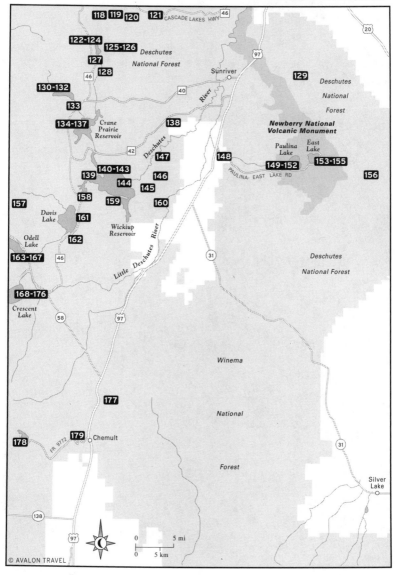

Map 5.6

Sites 180-201
Pages 344-353

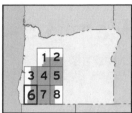

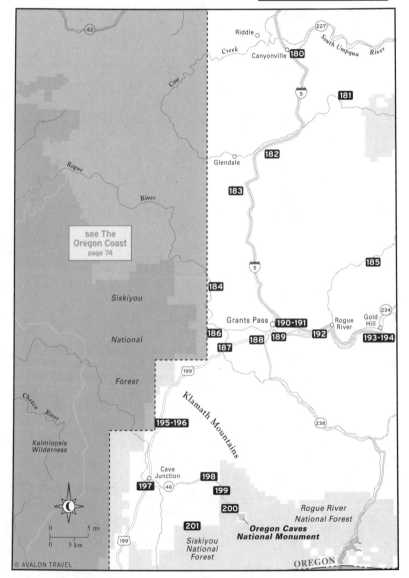

Map 5.7

Sites 202-250
Pages 353-374

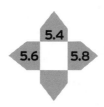

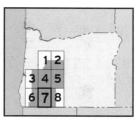

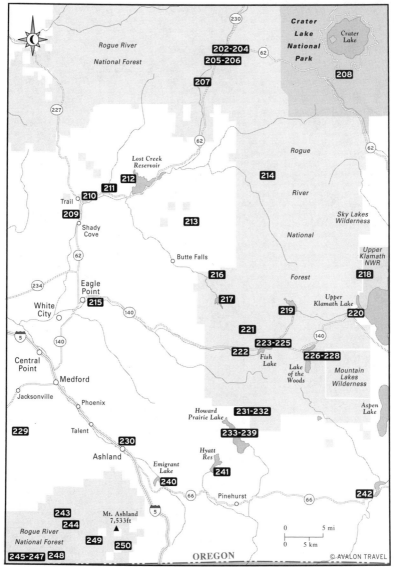

Map 5.8

Sites 251-257
Pages 375-377

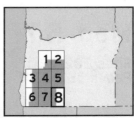

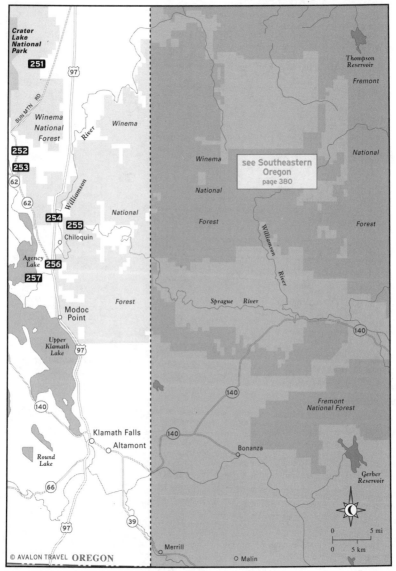

1 TROUT CREEK

🚶 🏊 🛶 🏕 🚻 ♿ 🚐 ⛰

Scenic rating: 8

on the South Santiam River in Willamette National Forest

Map 5.1, page 261

This campground is set along the banks of the South Santiam River at 1,200 feet in elevation, about seven miles east of Cascadia. Fishing and swimming are some of the recreation possibilities here. There is a historic shelter and the remains of stonework from the era of the Civilian Conservation Corps. The Trout Creek Trail, just across the highway, leads into the Menagerie Wilderness. The Long Ranch Elk Viewing Area is immediately west of the campground and, at the Trout Creek Trailhead, you'll also find a short trail leading to an elk-viewing platform. Nearby is the Old Santiam Wagon Road.

Campsites, facilities: There are 24 sites for tents or RVs up to 25 feet long, including eight sites that can accommodate RVs up to 32 feet long. Picnic tables, garbage bins, and fire grills are provided. Drinking water and vault toilets are available. Some facilities are wheelchair accessible. Leashed pets are permitted.

Reservations, fees: Reservations are accepted at 877/444-6777 ($10 reservation fee) or www.recreation.gov ($9 reservation fee). Sites are $15 per night, $5 per night per additional vehicle. Open May-October, weather permitting.

Directions: From Albany, drive east on U.S. 20 for 45 miles (19 miles past Sweet Home) to the campground entrance on the right.

Contact: Willamette National Forest, Sweet Home Ranger District, 541/367-5168, www.fs.usda.gov/willamette or www.linnparks.com.

2 YUKWAH

🚶 🏊 🛶 🏕 🚻 ♿ 🚐 ⛰

Scenic rating: 7

on the Santiam River in Willamette National Forest

Map 5.1, page 261

Yukwah campground is nestled in a second-growth Douglas fir forest on the banks of the Santiam River. The camp is 0.25 mile east of Trout Creek Campground and offers the same recreation possibilities. The camp features a 0.5-mile, compacted-surface interpretive trail that's barrier-free.

Campsites, facilities: There are 20 sites for tents or RVs up to 32 feet long, including a deluxe group site for up to 20 people. Picnic tables, garbage bins, and fire grills are provided. Drinking water, vault toilets, a picnic area, and a fishing platform are available. Some facilities, including the fishing platform, are wheelchair accessible. Leashed pets are permitted.

Reservations, fees: Reservations are not accepted. Sites are $18 per night, the deluxe site is $36 per night, $5 per night per additional vehicle. Open early May-late September, weather permitting.

Directions: From Albany, drive east on U.S. 20 for 45 miles (19 miles past Sweet Home) to the campground.

Contact: Willamette National Forest, Sweet Home Ranger District, 541/367-5168, www.fs.usda.gov/willamette or www.linnparks.com.

3 FERNVIEW

🚶 🏊 🛶 🏕 🚻 ♿ 🚐 ⛰

Scenic rating: 7

on the Santiam River in Willamette National Forest

Map 5.1, page 261

This campground is perched high above the confluence of Boulder Creek and the Santiam River, just south of the Menagerie Wilderness. A stepped walkway leads down to the river. Just across U.S. 20 lies the Rooster Rock Trail, which leads to—where else?—Rooster Rock, the site of an old lookout tower. The Old Santiam Wagon Road runs through the back of the campground. The camp is best suited for tent and small RV camping; the sites are small. The elevation is 1,400 feet.

Campsites, facilities: There are 11 sites for tents or RVs up to 22 feet long. The entire campground can be reserved as a group site. Picnic tables, garbage bins, and fire grills are provided. Drinking water and vault toilets are available. Some facilities are wheelchair accessible. Leashed pets are permitted.

Reservations, fees: Reservations are required for group camping at 877/444-6777 ($10 reservation fee) or www.recreation.gov ($9 reservation fee). Single sites are $18 per night, plus $5 per night per additional vehicle; the group campsite is $150 per night. Open May-October, weather permitting.

Directions: From Albany, drive east on U.S. 20 for 49 miles (23 miles past Sweet Home) to the campground entrance on the right.

Contact: Willamette National Forest, Sweet Home Ranger District, 541/367-5168, www.fs.usda.gov/willamette or www.linnparks.com.

4 HOUSE ROCK

Scenic rating: 8

on the Santiam River in Willamette National Forest

Map 5.1, page 261

House Rock campground is situated at the confluence of Sheep Creek and the South Santiam River. The camp is set in the midst of an old-growth forest and is surrounded by huge, majestic Douglas fir. Trout fishing can be good, particularly during summer evenings. Botany students come here from long distances to see firsthand many uncommon and spectacular specimens of plants. History buffs should explore the short loop trail out of camp, which passes by House Rock, a historic rock shelter for

Native Americans, and continues to the historic Old Santiam Wagon Road.

Campsites, facilities: There are 11 sites for tents or RVs up to 22 feet long and five tent-only sites. Picnic tables, garbage bins, and fire grills are provided. Vault toilets and drinking water are available. Some facilities are wheelchair accessible. Leashed pets are permitted.

Reservations, fees: Reservations are accepted at 877/444-6777 ($10 reservation fee) or www.recreation.gov ($9 reservation fee). Sites are $18 per night, $5 per night per additional vehicle. Open May-October, weather permitting.

Directions: From Albany, drive east on U.S. 20 for 52.5 miles (26 miles past Sweet Home) to Latiwi Road (Forest Road 2044). Turn right and drive a short distance to the campground.

Contact: Willamette National Forest, Sweet Home Ranger District, 541/367-5168, www.fs.usda.gov/willamette or www.linnparks.com.

5 LOST PRAIRIE

Scenic rating: 7

on Hackleman Creek in Willamette National Forest

Map 5.1, page 261

Lost Prairie campground hugs the banks of Hackleman Creek at 3,200 feet elevation in an area of Douglas fir and spruce. Three excellent hiking trails can be found within five miles of the camp: Hackleman Old-Growth Grove, Cone Peak, and Iron Mountain. The last two offer spectacular wildflower-viewing in the late spring and early summer. This camp provides an alternative to nearby Fish Lake.

Campsites, facilities: There are 10 sites for tents, two of which are suitable for RVs up to 24 feet long, and six walk-in sites for tents only. The entire campground may be reserved as a group site (single sites not available). Picnic tables, garbage bins, and fire grills are provided. Drinking water and vault toilets are available. Some facilities are wheelchair accessible. Leashed pets are permitted.

Reservations, fees: Reservations are accepted for the group site at 877/444-6777 ($10 reservation fee) or www.recreation.gov ($9 reservation fee). The group site is $150 per night. Single sites are $18 per night, $5 per night per additional vehicle. Open May-October, weather permitting.

Directions: From Albany, drive east on U.S. 20 for 63 miles (approximately 38 miles past Sweet Home) to the camp on the right.

Contact: Willamette National Forest, Sweet Home Ranger District, 541/367-5168, www.fs.usda.gov/willamette or www.linnparks.com.

6 OLALLIE

Scenic rating: 7
on the McKenzie River in Willamette National Forest

Map 5.1, page 261

Olallie campground sits at an elevation of 2,000 feet along the banks of the McKenzie River. Boating, fishing, and hiking are among its recreational opportunities, and fishing for rainbow trout usually is good. Other bonuses include easy access from Highway 126. The campground is two miles southwest of Trail Bridge Reservoir off Highway 126.

Campsites, facilities: There are 16 sites for tents or RVs up to 35 feet long. Picnic tables and fire grills are provided. Vault toilets, drinking water, and garbage service are available. A boat launch is nearby (non-motorized boats only). Leashed pets are permitted.

Reservations, fees: Reservations are accepted at 877/444-6777 ($10 reservation fee) or www.recreation.gov ($9 reservation fee). Sites are $18 per night, $7 per night per additional vehicle. Open late April-October, weather permitting.

Directions: From Eugene, drive east on Highway 126 for 47 miles to the town of McKenzie Bridge. Continue on Highway 126 for 11 miles to the campground on the left.

Contact: Willamette National Forest, McKenzie River Ranger District, 541/822-3381, www.fs.usda.gov/willamette.

7 MONA

Scenic rating: 8
near Blue River Reservoir in Willamette National Forest

Map 5.1, page 261

This forested campground (1,360 feet elevation) is set along the shore of Blue River Reservoir, close to where the Blue River joins it. A boat ramp is located across the river from the campground (at Lookout Campground); another boat ramp is situated at the south end of the reservoir. After launching a boat, campers can ground it near their campsite. Note that this camp is extremely popular when the reservoir is full.

Campsites, facilities: There are 23 sites for tents or RVs up to 36 feet long. Picnic tables, garbage bins, waste-water disposal, and fire grills are provided. Drinking water and flush toilets are available. Some facilities are wheelchair accessible. Leashed pets are permitted.

Reservations, fees: Reservations are accepted at 877/444-6777 ($10 reservation fee) or www.recreation.gov ($9 reservation fee). Single sites are $18 per night, double sites are $34 per night, $7 per night per additional vehicle. Open May-mid-September, weather permitting.

Directions: From Eugene, drive east on Highway 126 for 41 miles to Blue River. Continue east on Highway 126 for three miles to Forest Road 15. Turn left (north) and drive three miles to the campground on the left.

Contact: Willamette National Forest, McKenzie River Ranger District, 541/822-3381, www.fs.usda.gov/willamette.

8 PATIO RV PARK

Scenic rating: 7
near the South Fork of the McKenzie River

Map 5.1, page 261

This RV park is situated near the banks of the South Fork of the McKenzie River, not far from Cougar Lake, which offers opportunities for fishing, swimming, and waterskiing. Nearby recreation options include a golf course, hiking trails, and bike paths. The Hoodoo Ski Area is approximately 30 miles away.

Campsites, facilities: There are 60 sites with full hookups for RVs of any length and a grassy area for tents. Picnic tables are provided. Restrooms with flush toilets and showers, a recreation hall, group kitchen facilities, cable TV, Wi-Fi, a community fire pit, horseshoe pits, and a coin laundry are available. A store, gasoline, propane, and a café are within two miles. Some facilities are wheelchair accessible. Leashed pets are permitted.

Reservations, fees: Reservations are accepted at 541/822-3596 or via email at reservations@patiorv.com. RV sites are $30-37 per night, tent sites are $20 per night, $2 per person per night for more than two people. Group, weekly, and monthly rates are available. Some credit cards are accepted. Open year-round.

Directions: From Eugene, drive east on Highway 126 for 37 miles to the town of Blue River. Continue east on Highway 126 for six miles to McKenzie River Drive. Turn right and drive two miles to the park on the right.

Contact: Patio RV Park, 541/822-3596, www.patiorv.com.

9 DELTA

Scenic rating: 8
on the McKenzie River in Willamette National Forest

Map 5.1, page 261

This popular campground sits along the banks of the McKenzie River in a spot heavily forested primarily with old-growth Douglas fir. The Delta Old Growth Nature Trail, a 0.5-mile wheelchair-accessible interpretive trail, is adjacent to the campground. The camp also features an amphitheater. Nearby are Blue River and Cougar Reservoirs (seven and five miles away, respectively), both of which offer swimming, trout fishing, and waterskiing.

Campsites, facilities: There are 38 sites for tents or RVs up to 36 feet long. Picnic tables, garbage bins, and fire grills are provided. Drinking water, vault toilets, and waste-water disposal are available. Some facilities are wheelchair accessible. Leashed pets are permitted.

Reservations, fees: Reservations are accepted at 877/444-6777 ($10 reservation fee) or www.recreation.gov ($9 reservation fee). Single sites are $18 per night, double sites are $34 per night, and $7 per night per additional vehicle. Open late April-October, weather permitting.

Directions: From Eugene, drive east on Highway 126 for 37 miles to the town of Blue River. Continue east on Highway 126 for five miles to Forest Road 19 (Aufderheide Scenic Byway). Turn right (south) and drive 0.25 mile to Forest Road 400. Turn right and drive one mile to the campground.

Contact: Willamette National Forest, McKenzie River Ranger District, 541/822-3381, www.fs.usda.gov/willamette.

10 MCKENZIE BRIDGE

Scenic rating: 8
on the McKenzie River in Willamette National Forest

Map 5.1, page 261

McKenzie campground is set at 1,400 feet elevation along the banks of the McKenzie River, one mile from the town of McKenzie Bridge. During the summer, this stretch of river provides good evening fly-fishing for trout; only non-motorized boats are permitted on the river.

Campsites, facilities: There are 20 sites for tents or RVs up to 40 feet long. Picnic tables, garbage service, and fire rings are provided. Flush toilets and drinking water are available. A grocery store and restaurants are available within one mile. Some facilities are wheelchair accessible. Leashed pets are permitted.

Reservations, fees: Reservations are accepted at 877/444-6777 ($10 reservation fee) or www.recreation.gov ($9 reservation fee). Sites are $18 per night, $7 per night per additional vehicle. Open mid-April-late September, weather permitting.

Directions: From Eugene, drive east on Highway 126 for 46 miles to the campground entrance on the right (one mile west of the town of McKenzie Bridge).

Contact: Willamette National Forest, McKenzie River Ranger District, 541/822-3381, www.fs.usda.gov/willamette.

11 HORSE CREEK GROUP CAMP

Scenic rating: 9

on Horse Creek in Willamette National Forest

Map 5.1, page 261

This campground reserved for groups borders Horse Creek near the town of McKenzie Bridge. In spite of the name, no horse camping is permitted. Fishing is catch-and-release only; check current regulations. The camp sits at 1,400 feet elevation.

Campsites, facilities: This is a group camp with 60 sites for tents or RVs up to 27 feet long and space for up to 23 vehicles. Picnic tables and fire grills are provided. Vault toilets, drinking water, and garbage service are available. Leashed pets are permitted.

Reservations, fees: Reservations are accepted at 877/444-6777 ($10 reservation fee) or www.recreation.gov ($9 reservation fee). Sites are $40 per night for up to 49 people and $60 per night for 50-100 people. Open May-September, weather permitting.

Directions: From Eugene, drive east on Highway 126 for 47 miles to the town of McKenzie Bridge and Horse Creek Road. Turn right (south) on Horse Creek Road and drive one mile to the campground on the left.

Contact: Willamette National Forest, McKenzie River Ranger District, 541/822-3381, www.fs.usda.gov/willamette.

12 PARADISE

Scenic rating: 9

on the McKenzie River in Willamette National Forest

Map 5.1, page 261

Paradise campground (1,600 feet elevation), along the banks of the McKenzie River, may be right off the highway, but it offers a rustic, streamside setting with access to the McKenzie River National Recreation Trail. Trout fishing can be good here.

Campsites, facilities: There are 33 sites for tents or RVs of any length. Picnic tables, garbage service, and fire rings are provided. Flush and vault toilets, drinking water, a boat ramp, and firewood are available. Some facilities are wheelchair accessible. Leashed pets are permitted.

Reservations, fees: Reservations are accepted at 877/444-6777 ($10 reservation fee) or www.recreation.gov ($9 reservation fee). Single sites are $22 per night, double sites are $40 per night, $7 per night per additional vehicle. Open May-September, weather permitting.

Directions: From Eugene, drive east on Highway 126 for 47 miles to the town of McKenzie Bridge. Continue east on Highway 126 for 3.5 miles to the campground on the left.

Contact: Willamette National Forest, McKenzie River Ranger District, 541/822-3381, www.fs.usda.gov/willamette.

13 BELKNAP HOT SPRINGS RESORT

Scenic rating: 9

on the McKenzie River

Map 5.1, page 261   **BEST (**

This beautiful park, with 60 acres of developed and landscaped gardens, has been featured on at least one magazine cover. It's in a wooded, mountainous area on the McKenzie River. Trout fishing can be excellent here. If you're looking for hiking opportunities, the McKenzie River Trail can be accessed from camp. Other hiking opportunities include the Three Sisters and Mount Washington Wilderness Areas, both accessible by driving west of Sisters on Highway 242. Exceptionally scenic and pristine expanses of forest, they are well worth exploring. The Pacific Crest Trail runs north and south through both wilderness areas.

Campsites, facilities: There are 47 sites with full or partial hookups for RVs of any length, 25 sites for tents, a lodge with 18 rooms, and seven cabins. Picnic tables and fire pits are provided. Drinking water and restrooms with flush toilets and showers are available. A dump station is one mile away at Camp Yale. Recreational facilities include two hot-spring-fed swimming pools, and a recreation field. Some facilities are wheelchair accessible. Leashed pets are permitted at the campground and in some of the cabins and lodge rooms; pets are not permitted in the other cabins and lodge rooms.

Reservations, fees: Reservations are accepted at 541/822-3512 or www.belknaphotsprings. com. Tent sites are $30 per night, RV sites are $35-40 per night, cabins are $135-425 per night, lodge rooms are $110-185 per night, $8 per person per night for more than two people, $10 one-time pet fee. All fees include access to the hot springs. Some credit cards are accepted. Open year-round.

Directions: From Eugene, drive east on Highway 126 for 56 miles to Belknap Springs Road. Turn left and drive 0.5 mile until the road dead-ends at the lodge.

Contact: Belknap Hot Springs Resort, 541/822-3512, www.belknaphotsprings.com.

14 CAMP YALE

Scenic rating: 5

on the McKenzie River

Map 5.1, page 261

This is the "sister camp" to Belknap Hot Springs, just one mile away, and offers full access to Belknap's pools and gardens. It is surrounded by forest and meadows and offers spectacular views of the Cascade foothills and Frissel Ridge.

Campsites, facilities: There are 16 sites with full (110 and 30 amp) hookups for RVs to 65 feet and seven cabins. Picnic tables and fire pits are provided. Drinking water, restrooms with showers, a coin laundry, and a dump station are available. Some facilities are wheelchair accessible. Leashed pets are permitted.

Reservations, fees: Reservations are accepted at 541/822-3512 or www.belknaphotsprings. com. Sites are $30 per night, cabins are $225-325, $8 per person per night for more than two people, and a $10 one-time pet fee. All fees include access to the hot springs. Some credit cards are accepted. Open year-round.

Directions: From Eugene, drive east on Highway 126 for 56 miles to Highway 242. Turn right on Highway 242 and drive 0.5 mile to the campground.

Contact: Camp Yale, 541/822-3512, www. belknaphotsprings.com.

15 SLIDE CREEK

Scenic rating: 6

on Cougar Reservoir in Willamette National Forest

Map 5.1, page 261

Slide Creek campground sits on a hillside overlooking Cougar Reservoir, which covers about

1,300 acres, has a paved boat landing, and offers opportunities for fishing, swimming, and waterskiing. This pretty lakeside camp at 1,700 feet in elevation is quite popular, so plan to arrive early on weekends. If the camp is full, Cougar Crossing (off Road 19) and Sunnyside (off Road 500) are nearby alternatives.

Campsites, facilities: There are eight sites for tents or RVs up to 50 feet long. Picnic tables and fire grills are provided. Drinking water, garbage bins, and vault toilets are available. A boat ramp is also available. Leashed pets are permitted.

Reservations, fees: Reservations are accepted at 877/444-6777 ($10 reservation fee) or www.recreation.gov ($9 reservation fee). Single sites are $16 per night, double sites are $30 per night, $8 per night per additional vehicle. Open May-September, weather permitting.

Directions: From Eugene, drive east on Highway 126 for 41 miles to the town of Blue River. Continue east on Highway 126 for five miles to Aufderheide Scenic Byway. Turn right (south) and drive 11 miles (along the west shore of Cougar Reservoir, crossing the reservoir bridge) to Eastside Road (Forest Road 500). Turn left and drive 1.5 miles northeast to the campground set on the southeast shore of the lake.

Contact: Willamette National Forest, McKenzie River Ranger District, 541/822-3381, www.fs.usda.gov/willamette.

16 FRENCH PETE

Scenic rating: 8
on the South Fork of the McKenzie River in Willamette National Forest

Map 5.1, page 261

This quiet, wooded campground is set on the banks of the south fork of the McKenzie River and French Pete Creek at 1,800 feet in elevation. Fishing is catch-and-release only. A trail across the road from the campground provides access to the Three Sisters Wilderness (permit

required; contact district office). French Pete is only two miles from Cougar Reservoir, and the camp attracts campers wanting to use Cougar Reservoir facilities. Two more primitive camps (Homestead and Frissell Crossing) are located a few miles southeast on the same road.

Campsites, facilities: There are 17 sites for tents or RVs up to 40 feet long. Picnic tables, garbage containers, and fire grills are provided. Drinking water, vault toilets, and wastewater disposal are available. Leashed pets are permitted.

Reservations, fees: Reservations are not accepted. Sites are $16-32 per night, $7 per night per additional vehicle. Open May-September, weather permitting.

Directions: From Eugene, drive east on Highway 126 for 41 miles to the town of Blue River. Continue east on Highway 126 for five miles to Forest Road 19 (Aufderheide Scenic Byway). Turn right (south) and drive 12 miles to the campground on the right.

Contact: Willamette National Forest, McKenzie River Ranger District, 541/822-3381, www.fs.usda.gov/willamette.

17 CAMP SHERMAN

Scenic rating: 6
on the Metolius River in Deschutes National Forest

Map 5.2, page 262

Camp Sherman is set at an elevation of 2,950 feet along the banks of the Metolius River, where you can fish for wild trout. This place is for expert fly anglers seeking a quality fishing experience. Camp Sherman is one of five camps in the immediate area. It's advisable to obtain a map of the Deschutes National Forest that details back roads, streams, and trails.

A personal note: My late pal, John Korb, named his dog Sherman after this camp.

Campsites, facilities: There are eight sites for tents or RVs up to 40 feet long and one site for tents only. Picnic tables and fire grills are provided. Drinking water and garbage service are available mid-April-mid-October. Vault toilets and a picnic shelter are available. Leashed pets are permitted.

Reservations, fees: Reservations are accepted May-early September at 877/444-6777 ($10 reservation fee) or www.recreation.gov ($9 reservation fee); sites are first-come, first-served mid-October-December. In summer, sites are $14-18 per night, $8 per night per additional vehicle; October-April, sites are $12 per night, $6 per night per additional vehicle. Open year-round, weather permitting.

Directions: From Albany, drive east on U.S. 20 for 87 miles (near Black Butte) to the sign for Camp Sherman and Forest Road 14. Turn left on Forest Road 14 and drive five miles to Camp Sherman, the store, and Forest Road 900. Turn left on Forest Road 900 and drive 0.5 mile to the campground on the left.

Contact: Deschutes National Forest, Sisters Ranger District, 541/549-7700, www.fs.usda. gov/centraloregon.

18 ALLINGHAM

Scenic rating: 5

on the Metolius River in Deschutes National Forest

Map 5.2, page 262

One of five camps in the immediate area, Allingham sits along the banks of the Metolius River. The river is perfect for trout fishing, and fly anglers will find a quality fishing experience.

Campsites, facilities: There are 10 sites for tents or RVs up to 40 feet long. Picnic tables and fire grills are provided. Vault toilets, drinking water, and garbage service are available. A dump station is nearby. Leashed pets are permitted.

Reservations, fees: Reservations are not accepted. Sites are $16 per night, $8 per night per additional vehicle. Open May-September, weather permitting.

Directions: From Albany, drive east on U.S. 20 for 87 miles (near Black Butte) to the sign for Camp Sherman and Forest Road 14. Turn left on Forest Road 14 and drive five miles to Camp Sherman, the store, and Forest Road 900. Turn left on Forest Road 900 and drive one mile to the campground on the left.

Contact: Deschutes National Forest, Sisters Ranger District, 541/549-7700, www.fs.usda. gov/centraloregon; www.hoodoorecreation. com.

19 HOODOO'S CAMP SHERMAN MOTEL AND RV RESORT

Scenic rating: 6

near the Metolius River

Map 5.2, page 262

Camp Sherman offers a choice of graveled or grassy sites in a clean, scenic environment. This is a nice spot for bird-watching, fishing, and hiking.

Campsites, facilities: There are 15 sites with full or partial hookups for RVs to 45 feet and six motel rooms. Picnic tables and barbecues are provided. Restrooms with flush toilets and showers, a dump station, recreation room, and firewood are available. Propane gas, an additional dump station, a store, café, and ice are within three blocks. Some facilities are wheelchair accessible. Leashed pets are permitted.

Reservations, fees: Reservations are accepted. Sites are $32-34 per night, $3 per person per night for more than four people, $7 per additional vehicle (unless towed). Weekly and monthly rates are available. Some credit cards are accepted. Open year-round.

Directions: From Albany, drive east on U.S. 20 for 87 miles (near Black Butte) to the sign for Camp Sherman. Turn left (north) on Forest Road 1419 and drive four miles to a stop sign and the resort access road. Turn right and drive 0.25 mile to the park on the right.

Contact: Camp Sherman Resort, 541/595-6514, www.campshermanrv.com.

20 PINE REST

Scenic rating: 5

on the Metolius River in Deschutes National Forest

Map 5.2, page 262

Pine Rest campground is set at an elevation of 2,900 feet along the banks of the Metolius River. Fly-fishing and hiking are recreation options.

Campsites, facilities: There are eight tent sites. Picnic tables and fire grills are provided. Vault toilets and a picnic shelter are available. There is no drinking water. Garbage service is available in season. Leashed pets are permitted.

Reservations, fees: Reservations are not accepted. Sites are $12-16 per night, $6-8 per night per additional vehicle. Open year-round, weather permitting.

Directions: From Albany, drive east on U.S. 20 for 87 miles (near Black Butte) to the sign for Camp Sherman and Forest Road 14. Turn left on Forest Road 14 and drive five miles to Camp Sherman, the store, and Forest Road 900. Turn left on Forest Road 900 and drive two miles to the campground on the left.

Contact: Deschutes National Forest, Sisters Ranger District, 541/549-7700, www.fs.usda.gov/centraloregon; www.hoodoorecreation.com.

21 GORGE

Scenic rating: 5

on the Metolius River in Deschutes National Forest

Map 5.2, page 262

Here is another of the camps set along the banks of the Metolius River near Camp Sherman. Gorge campground is located at an elevation of 2,900 feet and is more open, with less vegetation than many of the others. Fly-fishing and hiking trails provide recreation opportunities.

Campsites, facilities: There are 18 sites for tents or RVs up to 40 feet long. Picnic tables and fire grills are provided. Vault toilets and garbage service are available. There is no drinking water. Leashed pets are permitted.

Reservations, fees: Reservations are accepted at 877/444-6777 ($10 reservation fee) or www.recreation.gov ($9 reservation fee). Sites are $12-16 per night, $6-8 per night per additional vehicle. Open May-September, weather permitting.

Directions: From Albany, drive east on U.S. 20 for 87 miles (near Black Butte) to the sign for Camp Sherman and Forest Road 14. Turn left on Forest Road 14 and drive five miles to Camp Sherman, the store, and Forest Road 900. Turn left on Forest Road 900 and drive 2.5 miles to the campground on the left.

Contact: Deschutes National Forest, Sisters Ranger District, 541/549-7700, www.fs.usda.gov/centraloregon; www.hoodoorecreation.com.

22 SMILING RIVER

Scenic rating: 5

on the Metolius River in Deschutes National Forest

Map 5.2, page 262

Smiling River sits along the banks of the Metolius River at an elevation of 2,900 feet. Another campground in the popular Camp Sherman area, Smiling River has access to fly-fishing and nearby hiking trails.

Campsites, facilities: There are 35 sites for tents or RVs up to 50 feet long. Picnic tables and fire grills are provided. Flush toilets, drinking water, and garbage service are available. Leashed pets are permitted.

Reservations, fees: Reservations are accepted at 877/444-6777 ($10 reservation fee) or www.recreation.gov ($9 reservation fee). Sites are $14-18 per night, $7-9 per night per additional vehicle. Open May-October, weather permitting.

Directions: From Albany, drive east on U.S. 20 for 87 miles (near Black Butte) to the sign for Camp Sherman and Forest Road 14. Turn left on Forest Road 14 and drive five miles to Camp Sherman, the store, and Forest Road 900. Turn left on Forest Road 900 and drive one mile to the campground on the left.

Contact: Deschutes National Forest, Sisters Ranger District, 541/549-7700, www.fs.usda.gov/centraloregon; www.hoodoorecreation.com.

23 ALLEN SPRINGS
🏃‍♀️🏊‍♀️🏠🐾🚐⛰️

Scenic rating: 7
on the Metolius River in Deschutes National Forest

Map 5.2, page 262

Shady Allen Springs campground is nestled in a conifer forest along the banks of the Metolius River, where fishing and hiking can be good. For an interesting side trip, head to the Wizard Falls Fish Hatchery about a mile away.

Campsites, facilities: There are 16 sites for tents or RVs up to 36 feet long. Picnic tables and fire grills are provided. Vault toilets and garbage service are available. Water is available from the river, but must be filtered. A store, café, and ice are within five miles. Leashed pets are permitted.

Reservations, fees: Reservations are accepted at 877/444-6777 ($10 reservation fee) or www.recreation.gov ($9 reservation fee). Single sites are $12-16 per night, $6-8 per night per additional vehicle. Open April-October, weather permitting.

Directions: From Albany, drive east on U.S. 20

for 87 miles (near Black Butte) to the sign for Camp Sherman and Forest Road 14. Turn left on Forest Road 14 and drive about nine miles to the campground on the left.

Contact: Deschutes National Forest, Sisters Ranger District, 541/549-7700, www.fs.usda.gov/centraloregon; www.hoodoorecreation.com.

24 LOWER BRIDGE
🏃‍♀️🏊‍♀️🏠🐾🚐⛰️

Scenic rating: 6
on the Metolius River in Deschutes National Forest

Map 5.2, page 262

Lower Bridge campground is set along the banks of the Metolius River at an elevation of 2,700 feet. The setting is similar to Pioneer Ford, but with less vegetation. A picnic area is located across the bridge.

Campsites, facilities: There are 12 sites for tents or RVs up to 30 feet long. Picnic tables and fire grills are provided. Vault toilets, drinking water, and garbage service are available. Leashed pets are permitted.

Reservations, fees: Reservations are accepted at 877/444-6777 ($10 reservation fee) or www.recreation.gov ($9 reservation fee). Sites are $12-16 per night, $6-8 per night per additional vehicle. Open May-October, weather permitting.

Directions: From Albany, drive east on U.S. 20 for 87 miles (near Black Butte) to the sign for Camp Sherman and Forest Road 14. Turn left on Forest Road 14 and drive 12 miles to the campground on the right.

Contact: Deschutes National Forest, Sisters Ranger District, 541/549-7700, www.fs.usda.gov/centraloregon; www.hoodoorecreation.com.

25 PIONEER FORD

Scenic rating: 7

on the Metolius River in Deschutes National Forest

Map 5.2, page 262

Quiet and serene Pioneer Ford campground is set along the banks of the Metolius River at an elevation of 2,750 feet. The wooded campground features grassy sites north of the Camp Sherman area. Hiking and fly-fishing are activities here.

Campsites, facilities: There are 20 sites for tents or RVs up to 50 feet long. Picnic tables and fire grills are provided. Drinking water and garbage service are provided. Vault toilets are available. Some facilities are wheelchair accessible. Leashed pets are permitted.

Reservations, fees: Reservations are accepted at 877/444-6777 ($10 reservation fee) or www.recreation.gov ($9 reservation fee). Sites are $18 per night, $8 per night per additional vehicle. Open May-September, weather permitting.

Directions: From Albany, drive east on U.S. 20 for 87 miles (near Black Butte) to the sign for Camp Sherman and Forest Road 14. Turn left on Forest Road 14 and drive 11 miles to the campground on the left.

Contact: Deschutes National Forest, Sisters Ranger District, 541/549-7700, www.fs.usda.gov/centraloregon; www.hoodoorecreation.com.

26 COLD SPRINGS RESORT

Scenic rating: 7

in Camp Sherman on the Metolius River

Map 5.2, page 262

This pretty, wooded RV park on the Metolius River is world-famous for its fly-fishing and features an acre of riverfront lawn. Birdwatching is also popular. Recreation options in the area include boating, swimming, waterskiing, and windsurfing. In addition, nearby facilities include a golf course, hiking and biking trails, a riding stable, and tennis courts. Winter activities vary from alpine and Nordic skiing to sledding, snowmobiling, and winter camping. A private footbridge leads from the resort to Camp Sherman; the towns of Sisters and Bend are nearby (15 miles and 35 miles, respectively).

Campsites, facilities: There are 24 sites, some with full hookups, for RVs of any length, eight cottages, and seven cabins on the river. Fire pits, picnic tables, and some patios are provided. Restrooms with flush toilets and showers, coin laundry, Wi-Fi, firewood, and a riverfront picnic facility are available. Propane gas, a convenience store, fishing and sport supplies, a café, a post office, and ice are within 0.25 mile. Leashed pets are permitted.

Reservations, fees: Reservations are accepted. Sites are $35-40 per night, $5 per person per night for more than two people, and $5 per pet per night. Weekly and monthly rates available. Some credit cards are accepted. Open year-round.

Directions: From Albany, drive east on U.S. 20 for 87 miles (near Black Butte) to the sign for Camp Sherman/Metolius River. Turn left (north) on Forest Road 14 and drive 4.5 miles to a stop sign. Turn right (still Forest Road 14) and drive about 300 feet to Cold Springs Resort Lane. Turn right and drive through the forest and the meadow, crossing Cold Springs Creek, to the resort.

Contact: Cold Springs Resort, 25615 Cold Springs Resort Lane, Camp Sherman, 541/595-6271 or 541/595-1400, www.coldspringsresort.com.

27 RIVERSIDE WALK-IN

Scenic rating: 7

on the Metolius River in Deschutes National Forest

Map 5.2, page 262

Riverside Walk-In is set 100 yards back from

the banks of the Metolius River, less than a mile from Metolius Springs at the base of Black Butte. Because this is a tent-only campground, and just far enough off the highway to be missed by most other people, it stays very quiet. You'll find plenty of solitude here. After parking along the road, you must walk to the campsites, carrying any gear in the process.

Campsites, facilities: There are 16 tent sites. Picnic tables and fire grills are provided. Vault toilets, garbage service, and drinking water are available. Leashed pets are permitted.

Reservations, fees: Reservations are accepted at 877/444-6777 ($10 reservation fee) or www.recreation.gov ($9 reservation fee). Sites are $12 per night, $6 per night per additional vehicle. Open May-September, weather permitting.

Directions: From Albany, drive east on U.S. 20 for 87 miles to the sign for Camp Sherman and Forest Road 14. Turn left and drive five miles to Forest Road 800. Turn left and drive a short distance to the campground.

Contact: Deschutes National Forest, Sisters Ranger District, 541/549-7700, www.fs.usda.gov/centraloregon.

28 HAYSTACK RESERVOIR
🎣 💦 🚐 🐕 🚙 ⛺

Scenic rating: 5
on Haystack Reservoir in Crooked River National Grassland

Map 5.2, page 262

This campground can be found in the high desert along the shore of Haystack Reservoir, a bright spot in an expansive desert landscape. The camps feature a moderate amount of privacy, as well as views of nearby Mount Jefferson. Haystack Reservoir receives moderate numbers of people who boat, camp, fish, swim, and water ski.

Campsites, facilities: There are 24 sites for tents or RVs up to 32 feet long; some sites are pull-through. Picnic tables and fire grills are provided. Vault toilets, drinking water, and covered picnic shelters are available. A store,

café, and ice are within five miles. Boat docks and launching facilities are nearby. Leashed pets are permitted.

Reservations, fees: Reservations are not accepted. Sites are $15 per night, $6 per night per additional vehicle. Open mid-May-mid-September.

Directions: From Madras, drive south on U.S. 97 for nine miles to Jericho Lane. Turn left and drive one mile to County Road 100. Turn right and drive two miles to Forest Road 96. Turn left (north) and drive 0.5 mile to the campground.

Contact: Crooked River National Grassland, 541/475-9272 or 541/416-6640, www.fs.usda.gov/centraloregon.

29 COLD WATER COVE
🚶 💦 🚐 🐕 ♿ 🚙 ⛺

Scenic rating: 10
on Clear Lake in Willamette National Forest

Map 5.2, page 262

Cold Water campground sits at 3,000 feet elevation on the south shore of Clear Lake, a spring-fed lake formed by a natural lava dam and the source of the McKenzie River. No motors are permitted on the lake, making it ideal for anglers in rowboats or canoes. The northern section of the McKenzie River National Recreation Trail passes by the camp.

Campsites, facilities: There are 35 sites for tents or RVs up to 40 feet long. Picnic tables and fire grills are provided. Vault toilets, drinking water, and garbage service are available. Boat docks, launching facilities, rowboats, a store, a café, and cabin rentals are available nearby at Clear Lake Resort. Some facilities are wheelchair accessible. Leashed pets are permitted.

Reservations, fees: Reservations are accepted at 877/444-6777 ($10 reservation fee) or www.recreation.gov ($9 reservation fee). Sites are $20 per night, $38 per night for double sites, $7 per night per additional vehicle. Open mid-May-mid-October, weather permitting.

Directions: From Eugene, drive east on Highway 126 for 47 miles to the town of

McKenzie Bridge. Continue on Highway 126 for 14 miles to Forest Road 770. Turn right (east) and drive to the campground.

Contact: Willamette National Forest, McKenzie River Ranger District, 541/822-3381, www.fs.usda.gov/willamette.

30 ICE CAP CREEK

Scenic rating: 9
on Carmen Reservoir in Willamette National Forest

Map 5.2, page 262

Ice Cap Creek campground is perched at 3,000 feet elevation on a hill above Carmen Reservoir, created by a dam on the McKenzie River. The McKenzie River National Recreation Trail passes by the camp, and Koosah Falls and Sahalie Falls are nearby. Clear Lake, a popular local vacation destination, is two miles away.

Campsites, facilities: There are 22 sites for tents or RVs up to 50 feet long; eight sites are walk-in. Picnic tables and fire grills are provided. Vault toilets and garbage service are available. There is no drinking water. Boat-launching facilities and boat rentals are two miles away at Clear Lake Resort. Only non-motorized boats are allowed on Carmen Reservoir. Leashed pets are permitted.

Reservations, fees: Reservations are not accepted. Sites are $16 per night, $7 per night per additional vehicle. Open mid-May-September, weather permitting.

Directions: From Eugene, drive east on Highway 126 for 47 miles to the town of McKenzie Bridge. Continue east on Highway 126 for 17.3 miles to the campground entrance road on the left. Turn left and drive 200 yards to the campground.

Contact: Willamette National Forest, McKenzie River Ranger District, 541/822-3381,

www.fs.usda.gov/willamette; Clear Lake Resort, 541/967-5030.

31 BIG LAKE

Scenic rating: 9
on Big Lake in Willamette National Forest

Map 5.2, page 262

This jewel of a spot on the north shore of Big Lake at 4,650 feet elevation offers a host of activities, including fishing, hiking, swimming, and waterskiing. Big Lake has heavy motorized boat use. One of the better hikes is the five-mile wilderness loop trail (Patjens Lakes Trail) that heads out from the south shore of the lake and cuts past a few small lakes before returning. There's a great view of Mount Washington from the lake. The Pacific Crest Trail is only 0.5 mile away.

Campsites, facilities: There are 49 sites for tents or RVs up to 35 feet long. Picnic tables and fire grills are provided. Drinking water, vault and flush toilets, and garbage service are available. Boat ramps are nearby. Some facilities are wheelchair accessible. Leashed pets are permitted.

Reservations, fees: Reservations are accepted at 877/444-6777 ($10 reservation fee) or www.recreation.gov ($9 reservation fee). Sites are $22 per night, $7 per night per additional vehicle. Open late May-mid-October, weather permitting.

Directions: From Eugene, drive east on Highway 126 for 47 miles to the town of McKenzie Bridge. Continue northeast on Highway 126 for 29.5 miles to Big Lake Road (Forest Road 2690). Turn right and drive 4.3 miles to the campground on the left.

Contact: Willamette National Forest, McKenzie River Ranger District, 541/822-3381, www.fs.usda.gov/willamette.

32 BIG LAKE WEST WALK-IN

Scenic rating: 9
on Big Lake in Willamette National Forest

Map 5.2, page 262

This spot, located west of the Big Lake Campground at an elevation of 4,650 feet, has many of the same attractions, but the walk-in sites offer some seclusion and quiet. The Mount Washington Wilderness and Patjens Lake access trails can be reached from here.

Campsites, facilities: There are 11 walk-in sites 200 feet from the road. Picnic tables and fire pits are provided. Vault toilets and garbage service are available. Drinking water is available in adjacent Big Lake Campground.

Reservations, fees: Reservations are accepted at 877/444-6777 ($10 reservation fee) or www.recreation.gov ($9 reservation fee). Single sites are $22 per night, double sites are $40 per night, $7 per night per additional vehicle. Open late May-early October, weather permitting.

Directions: From Eugene, drive east on Highway 126 for 47 miles to the town of McKenzie Bridge. Continue northeast on Highway 126 for 40 miles to Big Lake Road (Forest Road 2690). Turn right and drive four miles to the campground entrance on the left.

Contact: Willamette National Forest, McKenzie River Ranger District, 541/822-3381, www.fs.usda.gov/willamette.

33 SOUTH SHORE

Scenic rating: 6
on Suttle Lake in Deschutes National Forest

Map 5.2, page 262

This campground is at 3,500 feet elevation on the south shore of Suttle Lake, where waterskiing is permitted. A hiking trail winds around the lake and other popular activities include fishing and windsurfing. The camp often fills up on weekends and holidays, so reserve early.

Campsites, facilities: There are 38 sites for tents or RVs up to 50 feet long. Picnic tables and fire grills are provided. Vault toilets, drinking water, and garbage service are available. A fish-cleaning station, boat docks, launching facilities, and rentals are nearby. Leashed pets are permitted.

Reservations, fees: Reservations are accepted at 877/444-6777 ($10 reservation fee) or www.recreation.gov ($9 reservation fee). Single sites are $18 per night, double sites are $30 per night, $9 per night per additional vehicle. Open May-September, weather permitting.

Directions: From Albany, drive east on U.S. 20 to the junction with Highway 126. Continue east on Highway 126 for 12 miles to Forest Road 2070 (Suttle Lake). Turn right and proceed a short distance to the campground.

Contact: Deschutes National Forest, Sisters Ranger District, 541/549-7700, www.fs.usda.gov/centraloregon.

34 LINK CREEK

Scenic rating: 6
on Suttle Lake in Deschutes National Forest

Map 5.2, page 262

Link Creek campground is set at the west end of Suttle Lake at an elevation of 3,450 feet. The high-speed boating area is located on this end of the lake, making it a popular spot with water-skiers. Other activities include fishing, swimming, and windsurfing.

Campsites, facilities: There are 30 sites for tents or RVs up to 50 feet long, two double sites, and three yurts with bunk beds, a double-size futon, and a wood stove. Picnic tables and fire grills are provided. Vault toilets, drinking water, and garbage service are available. Boat docks, launching facilities, and rentals are nearby. Leashed pets are permitted.

Reservations, fees: Reservations are accepted for the yurts and some sites at 877/444-6777 ($10 reservation fee) or www.recreation.gov ($9 reservation fee). Single sites are $18 per night, double sites are $34 per night, yurts are $40 per night, $9 per night per additional vehicle. Open April-mid-October, weather permitting.

Directions: From Albany, drive east on U.S. 20 for 74 miles to the junction of U.S. 20 and Highway 126. Continue east on Highway 126 for 12 miles to Forest Road 2070 (Suttle Lake). Turn right and drive a short distance to the campground.

Contact: Deschutes National Forest, Sisters Ranger District, 541/549-7700, www.fs.usda. gov/centraloregon.

35 BLUE BAY

Scenic rating: 7
on Suttle Lake in Deschutes National Forest

Map 5.2, page 262

Blue Bay campground is situated along the south shore of Suttle Lake at an elevation of 3,450 feet. It's a quieter campground at the low-speed end of the lake, and with more tree cover than South Shore or Link Creek. Recreation activities include fishing, boating, and hiking.

Campsites, facilities: There are 21 single sites and three double sites for tents or RVs up to 50 feet long. Picnic tables and fire grills are provided. Vault toilets, drinking water, and garbage service are available. A fish-cleaning station, boat docks, launching facilities, and rentals are nearby. Leashed pets are permitted.

Reservations, fees: Reservations are accepted at 877/444-6777 ($10 reservation fee) or www. recreation.gov ($9 reservation fee). Single sites are $18 per night, double sites are $34 per night, $9 per night per additional vehicle. Open May-mid-September, weather permitting.

Directions: From Albany, drive east on U.S. 20 for 74 miles to the junction of U.S. 20 and Highway 126. Continue east on Highway 126 for 12 miles to Forest Road 2070 (Suttle Lake). Turn right and drive a short distance to the campground.

Contact: Deschutes National Forest, Sisters Ranger District, 541/549-7700, www.fs.usda. gov/centraloregon.

36 SCOUT LAKE GROUP

Scenic rating: 5
on Scout Lake in Deschutes National Forest

Map 5.2, page 262

Scout Lake is a group campground, with a mix of sunny and shady sites, at an elevation of 3,600 feet. The camp lies about 0.5 mile from Suttle Lake and is a good spot for swimming and hiking.

Campsites, facilities: There are 10 sites (single, double, and triple) for tents or RVs up to 40 feet long. The entire campground can accommodate up to 100 people. Picnic tables and fire grills are provided. Vault toilets, drinking water, garbage service, a picnic shelter, a volleyball court, and horseshoe pits are available. Leashed pets are permitted in the campground only (not in the day-use area) or in the lake.

Reservations, fees: Reservations are accepted at 877/444-6777 ($10 reservation fee) or www. recreation.gov ($9 reservation fee). Single sites are $18 per night, double sites are $34 per night, the triple site is $44 per night, $9 per night per additional vehicle. Open May-September, weather permitting.

Directions: From Eugene, drive east on Highway 126 for 74 miles to the junction of U.S. 20 and Highway 126. Continue east on Highway 126 for 12 miles to Forest Road 2070 (Suttle Lake). Turn right and drive to Forest Road 2066. Turn left and drive less than one mile to the campground.

Contact: Deschutes National Forest, Sisters Ranger District, 541/549-7700, www.fs.usda. gov/centraloregon.

37 BEND/SISTERS GARDEN RV RESORT

Scenic rating: 7
on Branchwater Lake

Map 5.2, page 262

This park is located amid wooded mountains

outside of Sisters at an elevation of 3,200 feet. Branchwater Lake, a three-acre lake at the campground, offers good trout fishing. (For hiking opportunities, explore the McKenzie River Trail or the Three Sisters and Mount Washington Wilderness Areas (west of Sisters on Highway 242). The Pacific Crest Trail runs north and south through both wilderness areas.

Campsites, facilities: There are 96 sites for RVs of any length (full hookups); many sites are pull-through. There are also two cabins and one luxury cottage. Picnic tables and fire rings are provided. Drinking water, restrooms with showers, a dump station, coin laundry, barbecue patio, Wi-Fi, video library, dog run, volleyball, badminton, miniature golf, convenience store, ice, RV supplies, and propane gas are available. Recreational facilities include a playground, horseshoes, a spa, and a seasonal heated swimming pool. Some facilities are wheelchair accessible. Leashed pets are permitted.

Reservations, fees: Reservations are accepted at 888/503-3588. Sites are $39-63 per night, $2-6 per person per night for more than two people, and $5 per night per additional vehicle. Weekly and monthly rates available. Some credit cards are accepted. Open year-round, weather permitting.

Directions: From Eugene, drive east on Highway 126 to its junction with U.S. 20. Turn east on U.S. 20 and drive 26 miles to Sisters. Continue southeast on U.S. 20 for three miles to the park on the right side of the highway.

Contact: Bend/Sisters Garden RV Resort, 541/516-3036 or 888/503-3588, www.bendsistersgardenrv.com.

38 CROOKED RIVER RANCH RV PARK

Scenic rating: 6

near Smith Rock State Park

Map 5.2, page 262   **BEST (**

Crooked River Ranch is a short distance from Smith Rock State Park, which contains unusual, colorful volcanic formations overlooking the Crooked River Canyon. Spectacular wildlife abounds in this area. Lake Billy Chinook to the north is a good spot for waterskiing and fishing for bass and panfish. The park has a basketball court and a softball field, and seasonal horseback riding is available. Nearby recreation options include fishing, golf, and tennis; one of Oregon's nicest golf courses is nearby.

Campsites, facilities: There are 90 sites with full or partial hookups for RVs of any length (some pull-through) and 20 tent sites. Picnic tables are provided. No open fires are allowed; propane is permitted. Restrooms with flush toilets and coin showers, a dump station, cable TV, Wi-Fi, a convenience store, coin laundry, ice, a covered picnic shelter, playground, horseshoe pits, basketball, pickleball, a tennis court, and a seasonal swimming pool are available. A café is nearby. Some facilities are wheelchair accessible. Leashed pets are permitted, with certain restrictions.

Reservations, fees: Reservations are accepted at 800/841-0563. RV sites are $38-40 per night; tent sites are $28 per night, additional tents are $10 per night. Some credit cards are accepted. Open mid-March-October, weather permitting.

Directions: From Redmond, drive north on U.S. 97 for six miles to Terrebonne and Lower Bridge Road. Turn left (west) on Lower Bridge Road and drive approximately two miles to 43rd Street. Turn right and drive two miles to a T-intersection with Chinook. Turn left on Chinook and drive approximately 4.5 miles (becomes Clubhouse Road, then Hays Road) to the ranch on the right.

Contact: Crooked River Ranch RV Park, 541/923-1441 or 800/841-0563, www.crookedriverranch.com.

39 INDIAN FORD
🏠 🚐 ⛰️

Scenic rating: 4
on Indian Ford Creek in Deschutes National Forest

Map 5.2, page 262

This campground sits on the banks of Indian Ford Creek at an elevation of 3,250 feet. Used primarily by overnighters on their way to the town of Sisters, the camp is subject to a lot of traffic noise from U.S. 20. The grounds are sprinkled with aspen trees, and great bird-watching opportunities are available.

Campsites, facilities: There are 25 sites for tents or RVs up to 50 feet long. Picnic tables, garbage service, and fire grills are provided. Vault toilets are available. There is no drinking water. Leashed pets are permitted.

Reservations, fees: Reservations are accepted at 877/444-6777 ($10 reservation fee) or www.recreation.gov ($9 reservation fee). Sites are $12 per night, $6 per night per additional vehicle. Open May-mid-October, weather permitting.

Directions: From Albany, drive east on U.S. 20 to the junction with Highway 126. Continue east on Highway 126 and drive 21 miles to the campground on the left.

Contact: Deschutes National Forest, Sisters Ranger District, 541/549-7700, www.fs.usda.gov/centraloregon; www.hoodoorecreation.com.

40 COLD SPRINGS
🏠 🚐 ⛰️

Scenic rating: 7
in Deschutes National Forest

Map 5.2, page 262

Wooded Cold Springs campground is set at 3,400 feet elevation at the source of a small seasonal creek. It's just far enough off the main drag to be missed by many campers. Spring and early summer are the times to come for great bird-watching in the area's abundant aspen trees.

Campsites, facilities: There are 22 sites for tents or RVs up to 50 feet long. Picnic tables, fire grills, and garbage service are provided. Vault toilets and drinking water are available. Leashed pets are permitted.

Reservations, fees: Reservations are accepted at 877/444-6777 ($10 reservation fee) or www.recreation.gov ($9 reservation fee). Sites are $14 per night, $7 per night per additional vehicle. Open May-October, weather permitting.

Directions: From Albany, drive east on U.S. 20 to the junction with Highway 126. Continue east on Highway 126 and drive 26 miles to Sisters and Highway 242. Turn right and drive 4.2 miles to the campground on the right.

Contact: Deschutes National Forest, Sisters Ranger District, 541/549-7700, www.fs.usda.gov/centraloregon; www.hoodoorecreation.com.

41 SCOTT LAKE WALK-IN
🏃 ≈ 🛶 🚐 🦌 ⛰️

Scenic rating: 10
on Scott Lake in Willamette National Forest

Map 5.2, page 262　　　　**BEST (**

Scott Lake Walk-In offers hike-in sites just over 0.1 mile from the road. The campground borders Scott Lake at an elevation of 4,680 feet; only non-motorized boats are allowed on the lake. Trails leading out of the camp provide access to several small lakes in the Mount Washington Wilderness, and there are great views of the Three Sisters Mountains. Be forewarned: Mosquitoes are heavy during the spring and early summer.

Campsites, facilities: There are 18 walk-in tent sites. Picnic tables and fire rings are provided. Vault toilets are available. There is no drinking water, and garbage must be packed out. Leashed pets are permitted.

Reservations, fees: Reservations are not accepted. Sites are $5 per night per vehicle. Open July-October, weather permitting.

Directions: From Eugene, drive east on Highway 126 for 54 miles to the junction with Highway 242 (part of the Santiam Scenic Byway). Turn right (east) on Highway 242 and drive 14.5 miles to Forest Road 260. Turn left and drive to the campground.

Note: Highway 242 is spectacularly scenic, but it's also very narrow, winding, and steep; it is not recommended for RVs or trailers. The maximum vehicle length is 35 feet.

Contact: Willamette National Forest, McKenzie River Ranger District, 541/822-3381, www.fs.usda.gov/willamette.

42 LAVA CAMP LAKE

Scenic rating: 4

near the Pacific Crest Trail in Deschutes National Forest

Map 5.2, page 262

Lava campground sits at an elevation of 5,300 feet among subalpine fir in the McKenzie Pass. It's not far from the Pacific Crest Trail, and a number of other trails provide additional hiking possibilities. Fishing is allowed, but don't expect to catch anything—perhaps that is why this campground gets such light use!

Campsites, facilities: There are 10 sites for tents or RVs up to 20 feet long. Picnic tables and fire grills are provided. Vault toilets are available. There is no drinking water, and garbage must be packed out. Leashed pets are permitted.

Reservations, fees: Reservations are not accepted. There is no fee for camping. Open June-October, weather permitting.

Directions: From Eugene, drive east on Highway 126 for 47 miles to the town of McKenzie Bridge. Continue east on Highway 126 for five miles to Highway 242. Turn right (east) and drive 14.6 miles on Highway 242 to the campground entrance on the right. Note: Highway 242 is spectacularly scenic, but also very narrow, winding, and steep. RVs and trailers are strictly held to a 35-foot length limit.

Contact: Deschutes National Forest, Sisters Ranger District, 541/549-9700, www.fs.usda.gov/centraloregon.

43 WHISPERING PINE HORSE CAMP

Scenic rating: 5

near the Trout Creek Swamp in Deschutes National Forest

Map 5.2, page 262

This wooded campground (elevation 4,400 feet) near Trout Creek Swamp is pretty, isolated, and private. Although generally not crowded, it's set up as a horse camp with corrals and is gaining in popularity; groups of horse users occasionally fill it up. Hikers, beware: You'll be sharing the trails with horses.

Campsites, facilities: There are nine primitive sites for tents or RVs up to 30 feet long and 36 individual box stalls. Picnic tables and fire grills are provided. Vault toilets and garbage service are available. There is stock water but no drinking water. Leashed pets are permitted.

Reservations, fees: Reservations are accepted at 877/444-6777 ($10 reservation fee) or www.recreation.gov ($9 reservation fee). Sites are $16 per night, $8 per night per additional vehicle. Open May-October, weather permitting.

Directions: From Albany, drive east on U.S. 20 to the junction with U.S. 126. Turn east on U.S. 126 and drive for 26 miles to Sisters and Highway 142. Turn right (east) and drive six miles on Highway 242 to Forest Road 1018. Turn left and drive four miles to the campground entrance. Note: Highway 242 is spectacularly scenic, but also very narrow, winding, and steep. RVs and trailers are discouraged (a 35-foot length limit is in effect).

Contact: Deschutes National Forest, Sisters Ranger District, 541/549-7700, www.fs.usda.gov/centraloregon; www.hoodoorecreation.com.

44 LIMBERLOST

Scenic rating: 9

on Lost Creek in Willamette National Forest

Map 5.2, page 262

Limberlost is a secluded campground set at 1,800 feet elevation along Lost Creek, about two miles from where it empties into the McKenzie River. Relatively unknown, the camp gets light use; it makes a good base camp for a trout-fishing trip.

Campsites, facilities: There are 12 sites for tents or RVs up to 16 feet long. Picnic tables, garbage service, and fire grills are provided. Vault toilets are available, but there is no drinking water. Some facilities are wheelchair accessible. Leashed pets are permitted.

Reservations, fees: Reservations are accepted at 877/444-6777 ($10 reservation fee) or www.recreation.gov ($9 reservation fee). Sites are $13 per night, $7 per night per additional vehicle. Open May-September, weather permitting.

Directions: From Eugene, drive east on Highway 126 for 47 miles to the town of McKenzie Bridge. Continue east on Highway 126 for five miles to Highway 242. Turn right (east) and drive 1.5 miles on Highway 242 to the camp. Note: Highway 242 is spectacularly scenic, but also very narrow, winding, and steep. RVs and trailers are discouraged (a 35-foot length limit is in effect). Highway 242 is closed in winter due to snow; check to make sure it's open if you are planning a trip in early or mid-spring.

Contact: Willamette National Forest, McKenzie River Ranger District, 541/822-3381, www.fs.usda.gov/willamette.

45 ALDER SPRINGS

Scenic rating: 7

in Willamette National Forest

Map 5.2, page 262

Remote Alder Springs campground sits at 3,600 feet elevation in the Willamette Forest. The camp features good hiking possibilities, including access to the Linton Lake Trail, a three-mile hike that leads to Linton Lake...and fishing. The Three Sisters Wilderness is just south of the highway.

Campsites, facilities: There are six tent sites. Picnic tables and fire grills are provided. Vault toilets are available. No drinking water is available, and garbage must be packed out. Some facilities are wheelchair accessible. Leashed pets are permitted.

Reservations, fees: Reservations are not accepted. There is no fee for camping. Open June-September, weather permitting.

Directions: From Eugene, drive east on Highway 126 for 47 miles to the town of McKenzie Bridge. Continue east on Highway 126 for five miles to Highway 242. Turn right (east) and drive 10 miles on Highway 242 to the campground on the left. Note: Highway 242 is spectacularly scenic, but also very narrow, winding, and steep; the road is closed during snow season and is often impassable until late spring. RVs and trailers are discouraged (a 35-foot length limit is in effect).

Contact: Willamette National Forest, McKenzie River Ranger District, 541/822-3381, www.fs.usda.gov/willamette.

46 DRIFTWOOD

Scenic rating: 9

on Three Creek Lake in Deschutes National Forest

Map 5.2, page 262   **BEST (**

This wooded campground, at 6,600 feet elevation, is often blocked by snowdrifts until early July. At this high elevation, the views of Tam McArthur Rim are spectacular. Although located on the lakeshore and hidden from outsiders, the area can get very crowded, and the campground is full most weekends from the Fourth of July through Labor Day. Some recreation options include boating (non-motorized only), fishing, hiking, and swimming.

Campsites, facilities: There are six sites for tents and RVs up to 40 feet long and 12 sites for tents only. Picnic tables and fire grills are provided. Vault toilets and garbage service are available. There is no drinking water. There is a small store open during the summer months. Leashed pets are permitted.

Reservations, fees: Reservations are not accepted. Sites are $14 per night, $7 per night per additional vehicle. Open June-October, weather permitting.

Directions: From Eugene, drive east on Highway 126 to its junction with U.S. 20. Turn east and drive 26 miles to Sisters and Forest Road 16. Turn right and drive 16.4 miles to the campground.

Contact: Deschutes National Forest, Sisters Ranger District, 541/549-7700, www.fs.usda.gov/centraloregon.

47 THREE CREEK LAKE AND THREE CREEK MEADOW HORSE CAMP

🚶 🏊 🚣 🛶 🚙 🐴 🚐 ⛺

Scenic rating: 8
on Three Creek Lake in Deschutes National Forest

Map 5.2, page 262

Three Creek Lake is in a pretty spot at 6,600 feet elevation; this forested campground lies along the south shore of its namesake lake. Boating (non-motorized only), fishing, hiking, swimming and horseback riding are the highlights. The camping area consists of two separate campgrounds; one campground is designed to accommodate campers who need to corral their stock animals. The Three Creek area has a beautiful view of the stretch from Sisters to Bend, as well as the Three Sisters Wilderness above it. Camping in the meadow is prohibited.

Campsites, facilities: There are 11 sites for tents or RVs up to 20 feet long, as well as nine equestrian sites with four corrals each, which can accommodate RVs and trailers of any size. Picnic tables and fire grills are provided. Vault toilets and garbage service are available. There is no drinking water. Leashed pets are permitted.

Reservations, fees: Reservations are accepted at 877/444-6777 ($10 reservation fee) or www.recreation.gov ($9 reservation fee). Sites are $14 per night, $7 per night per additional vehicle. Open June-October, weather permitting.

Directions: From Eugene, drive east on Highway 126 to Highway 20. Turn east and drive 26 miles to Sisters and Forest Road 16. Turn right and drive 17 miles to the campground.

Contact: Deschutes National Forest, Sisters Ranger District, 541/549-7700, www.fs.usda.gov/centraloregon or www.hoodoorecreation.com.

48 TUMALO STATE PARK

🚶 🚵 🏊 🛶 ❄ 🏕 🐴 ♿ 🚐 ⛺

Scenic rating: 7
on the Deschutes River

Map 5.2, page 262

Tumalo State Park sits along the banks of the Deschutes River, just four miles from Bend. Trout fishing can be good, and bird-watching is popular. The swimming area is generally safe and a good spot for children. Rafting is also an option here. Mount Bachelor is just up the road and provides plenty of winter recreation opportunities.

Campsites, facilities: There are 54 sites for tents or self-contained RVs, 23 sites with full hookups for RVs up to 44 feet long, a hiker/bicyclist area, seven yurts (two are pet friendly), and two group tent areas for up to 25 people each. Drinking water, fire grills, and picnic tables are provided. Restrooms with flush toilets and showers, firewood, and a playground are available. A store, café, and ice are within one mile. Some facilities are wheelchair accessible. Leashed pets are permitted.

Reservations, fees: Reservations are accepted

at 800/452-5687 or www.reserveamerica.com ($8 reservation fee). RV sites are $31 per night, tent sites are $21, $5 per person per night for hikers/bikers, $44-54 per night for yurts, $77 per night for the group areas, and $5 per night per additional vehicle. Some credit cards are accepted. Open year-round.

Directions: From Bend, drive north on U.S. 97 for two miles to U.S. 20 West. Turn west and drive five miles to Tumalo Junction. Turn left at Tumalo Junction onto Cook Avenue (the road becomes O. B. Riley), and drive one mile to the campground.

Contact: High Desert Management Unit, Oregon State Parks, 541/388-6055 or 800/551-6949, www.oregonstateparks.org.

49 SCANDIA RV PARK

Scenic rating: 5

near the Deschutes River

Map 5.2, page 262

This in-town park near the Deschutes River is close to bike paths, a golf course, a stable, and tennis courts. It is also within walking distance to Old Mill, Old Town, and the amphitheater.

Campsites, facilities: There are more than 60 sites for RVs of any length with full-hookups; 14 sites are pull-throughs. Picnic tables are provided. Restrooms with flush toilets and showers, Wi-Fi, cable TV, a picnic area, and a coin laundry are available. Propane gas, a dump station, store, café, and ice are within one mile. Some facilities are wheelchair accessible. Leashed pets are permitted.

Reservations, fees: Reservations are recommended. Sites are $35-58 per night. Some credit cards are accepted. Open year-round.

Directions: In Bend, drive south on Business U.S. 97 (3rd Street) for 0.5 mile to the park entrance on the right.

Contact: Scandia RV Park, 541/382-6206, www.scandiarv.com.

50 CROWN VILLA RV RESORT

Scenic rating: 6

near Bend

Map 5.2, page 262

This RV park offers large and landscaped grassy sites. Nearby recreation options include horseback riding and golf.

Campsites, facilities: There are 106 paved sites with full hookups for RVs of any length and 10 sites with partial hookups; some sites are pull-through. Picnic tables are provided. Restrooms with flush toilets and showers, cable TV, Wi-Fi, clubhouse, spa, a coin laundry, tennis court, pickleball, shuffleboard, disc golf, pool table, horseshoes, an off-leash dog park, a bistro, propane gas, and ice are available. A store and a café are within one mile. Some facilities are wheelchair accessible. Leashed pets are permitted with some restrictions.

Reservations, fees: Reservations are accepted at 541/388-1131. Sites are $55-99 per night, $3 per person per night for more than four people. Weekly and monthly rates available. Some credit cards are accepted. Open year-round.

Directions: From Bend, drive south on Business U.S. 97 (3rd Street) for two miles to Brosterhous Road. Turn left (east) and drive approximately one mile to a T intersection. Bear right to stay on Brosterhous Road. Continue about one mile to the park on the right.

Contact: Crown Villa RV Resort, 541/388-1131, www.crownvillarvresort.com.

51 WHITTAKER CREEK

Scenic rating: 7

near the Siuslaw River

Map 5.3, page 263

Whittaker Creek campground is home to one of the area's premier salmon spawning grounds, where annual runs of chinook, coho salmon, and steelhead can be viewed. Fishing is not allowed in Whittaker Creek. The (Whittaker Creek) Old Growth Ridge Trail, a national recreation trail, is accessible from the campground. This moderately difficult trail ascends 1,000 feet above the Siuslaw River through a stand of old-growth Douglas fir.

Campsites, facilities: There are 31 sites for tents or RVs up to 32 feet long. Picnic tables and fire rings are provided. Drinking water, vault toilets, garbage bins, a boat ramp, swimming beach, playground, horseshoe pits, and picnic shelter are available. A camp host is onsite. Some facilities are wheelchair accessible. Leashed pets are permitted.

Reservations, fees: Reservations are not accepted. Sites are $10 per night, $5 per night for each additional vehicle. Open mid-May-September, weather permitting.

Directions: From Eugene, drive west on Highway 126 for 33 miles to Siuslaw River Road. Turn left (south) and drive two miles to the first junction. Turn right and drive a short distance across Siuslaw River to the campground on the right.

Contact: Springfield Interagency Office, 541/683-6606, www.recreation.gov.

52 CLAY CREEK

Scenic rating: 7
near the Siuslaw River

Map 5.3, page 263

This campground gets a medium amount of use. Sites are situated in a forest of cedar, Douglas fir, and maple trees. Clay Creek Trail, a two-mile loop, takes you to a ridge overlooking the river valley and is well worth the walk. Fishing for trout and crayfish is popular.

Campsites, facilities: There are 21 sites for tents or RVs up to 32 feet long. Picnic tables and fire pits are provided. Drinking water, vault toilets, garbage bins, a swimming beach with changing rooms, a softball field, volleyball area, horseshoe pits, and two group picnic shelters with fireplaces are available. There is a camp

host. Some facilities are wheelchair accessible. Leashed pets are permitted.

Reservations, fees: Reservations are not accepted. Sites are $10 per night, $5 per night for each additional vehicle. Open May-November, weather permitting.

Directions: From Eugene, drive west on Highway 126 for 33 miles to Siuslaw River Road. Turn left (south) and drive 16 miles to BLM Road 19-7-2001 (signed for Clay Creek). Turn right and drive a short distance to the campground on the right.

Contact: Springfield Interagency Office, 541/683-6606, www.recreation.gov.

53 PASS CREEK COUNTY PARK

Scenic rating: 7
near Cottage Grove

Map 5.3, page 263

Pass Creek provides a decent layover spot for travelers on I-5. Situated in a wooded, hilly area, the camp features many shaded sites, and mountain views give the park scenic value. There is a covered pavilion and gazebo with barbecue grills for get-togethers. A bonus is the fishing pond with bluegill, crappie, and largemouth bass. There are no other campgrounds in the immediate area, so if it's late and you need a place to stay, grab this one.

Campsites, facilities: There is a grassy area for tents and 30 sites with full hookups (50 amp) for RVs up to 45 feet long. Picnic tables and fire rings or barbecues are provided. Drinking water, restrooms with flush toilets and showers, a coin laundry, and a playground are available. A store and ice are within one mile. Some facilities are wheelchair accessible. Leashed pets are permitted.

Reservations, fees: Reservations are accepted ($10 reservation fee) at 541/957-7001 or www. co.douglas.or.us. Sites are $17-25 per night, $3 per night for an additional vehicle unless towed. Discount available for Douglas County residents. Credit/debit cards are not accepted at the campground but may be used to make reservations. Open year-round.

Directions: On I-5, drive to Exit 163 (between Roseburg and Eugene). Take Exit 163 and turn west on Curtin Park Road. Drive west (under the freeway) for a very short distance to the park entrance.

Contact: Pass Creek County Park, 541/942-3281, www.co.douglas.or.us.

54 PINE MEADOWS

🏊 🛶 � 🏕 🐕 🎣 ♿ 🚐 ⛺

Scenic rating: 6

on Cottage Grove Reservoir

Map 5.3, page 263

Pine Meadows campground is surrounded by a varied landscape of forest, grassland, and marsh near the banks of Cottage Grove Reservoir. Campsites are within 200 feet of the water. Boating, fishing, swimming, and water-skiing are among the recreation options. It's an easy hop from I-5.

Campsites, facilities: There are 92 sites for tents or RVs of any length, with some pull-through sites. There are also 15 primitive sites for tents or small, self-contained RVs. Picnic tables and fire rings are provided. Drinking water, restrooms with flush toilets and showers, a dump station, garbage bins, a children's play area, an amphitheater, and a swimming area are available. A boat dock and launching facilities are nearby. Some facilities are wheelchair accessible. Leashed pets are permitted.

Reservations, fees: Reservations are accepted at 877/444-6777 ($10 reservation fee) or www.recreation.gov ($9 reservation fee). Sites are $14-20 per night, $6 per night for an additional vehicle. Primitive campers must have a permit, obtained at the entrance booth. Open mid-May-mid-September.

Directions: From Eugene, drive south on I-5 past Cottage Grove to Exit 172. Take that exit to London Road and drive south for 4.5 miles to Reservoir Road. Turn left and drive three miles to the camp entrance on the right.

Contact: U.S. Army Corps of Engineers, Recreation Information, Cottage Grove, 541/684-4300 or 541/942-5631, www.nwp.usace.army.mil.

55 WHISTLER'S BEND PARK

🏕 🛶 🚐 🏕 🐕 ♿ 🚐 ⛺

Scenic rating: 7

on the North Umpqua River

Map 5.3, page 263

This 175-acre county park along the banks of the North Umpqua River is an idyllic spot because it gets little pressure from outsiders, yet it is just a 20-minute drive from I-5. Two boat ramps accommodate boaters, and fishing is a plus. A wildlife reserve provides habitat for deer.

Campsites, facilities: There are 23 sites for tents or RVs up to 35 feet long (some with hookups) and two yurts. Three group camps are available. Picnic tables and fire rings are provided. Drinking water, restrooms with flush toilets and showers, a playground, disc golf, and launching facilities are available. Some facilities are wheelchair accessible. Leashed pets are permitted.

Reservations, fees: Reservations are accepted at 541/957-7001 ($10 reservation fee) or www.co.douglas.or.us. Sites with full hookups are $25 per night, sites without hookups are $17 per night, $3 per night per additional vehicle, $37 per night for yurts, $50 per night for the group camp for up to 50 people, $100 per night for the group camp for up to 100 people. Discount available for Douglas County residents. Credit/debit cards are not accepted at the campground but may be used to make reservations. Individual sites are open April-November; group sites and the yurts are open year-round.

Directions: From Roseburg, drive east on Highway 138 for 12 miles to Whistler's Bend Park Road (well signed). Turn left and drive two miles to the end of the road and the park entrance.

Contact: Whistler's Bend Park, 541/673-4863, www.co.douglas.or.us.

56 AMACHER PARK

Scenic rating: 5

on the Umpqua River

Map 5.3, page 263

A wooded Douglas County park set along the banks of the North Umpqua River, Amacher is a prime layover spot for I-5 RV cruisers. This park has one of the few myrtlewood groves in the country. Tent sites are located underneath the freeway next to the railroad tracks; trains come by intermittently. An 18-hole golf course and tennis courts are close by, riding stables are within a 20-minute drive, and Winchester Dam is within 0.25 mile.

Campsites, facilities: There are 10 sites for self-contained RVs and 20 sites with full or partial hookups for RVs up to 30 feet long (12-foot height limit). Picnic tables and fire rings are provided. Drinking water, restrooms with flush toilets and showers, a gazebo, and a picnic area are available. Propane gas, a store, café, coin laundry, and ice are within one mile. Boat-launching facilities are available. Some facilities are wheelchair accessible. Leashed pets are permitted.

Reservations, fees: Reservations are accepted ($10 reservation fee) at 541/957-7001 or www.co.douglas.or.us. Sites are $25 per night, $3 per night per additional vehicle. Credit/debit cards are not accepted at the campground but may be used to make reservations. Open year-round.

Directions: From Roseburg, drive five miles north on I-5 to Exit 129. Take that exit and drive south on Old Highway 99 for 0.25 mile to the park on the right (just across Winchester Bridge).

Contact: Amacher Park, 541/672-4901; Douglas County, 541/672-4901, www.co.douglas.or.us.

57 TWIN RIVERS VACATION PARK

Scenic rating: 6

near the Umpqua River

Map 5.3, page 263

This wooded campground is near the Umpqua River. It features large, shaded pull-through sites and more than 100 kinds of trees on the property. Groups are welcome and clubhouses are available for group use. Nearby recreation options include bike paths, a county park, and a golf course.

Campsites, facilities: There are 82 sites with full or partial hookups for RVs of any length; many are pull-through sites. Picnic tables and fire pits are provided. Restrooms with flush toilets and showers, cable TV, propane gas, firewood, a convenience store, a coin laundry, ice, Wi-Fi, clubrooms, and a playground are available. Boat-launching facilities are nearby. Leashed pets are permitted.

Reservations, fees: Reservations are accepted. Sites are $25-40 per night, $3 per person per night for more than two people. Some credit cards are accepted. Open year-round.

Directions: In Roseburg on I-5, take Exit 125 to Garden Valley Road. Drive west for five miles (over the river) to Old Garden Valley Road. Turn left and drive 1.5 miles to River Forks Road. Turn left and drive a short distance to the park entrance on the left.

Contact: Twin Rivers Vacation Park, 541/673-3811, www.twinriversrvpark.com.

58 DOUGLAS COUNTY FAIRGROUNDS RV PARK

Scenic rating: 8

on the South Umpqua River

Map 5.3, page 263

This 74-acre county park is very easily accessible off the highway. Nearby Umpqua River, one of Oregon's prettiest rivers, often has good fishing in season. Bike paths, a golf course, and tennis courts are nearby. Horse stalls and a boat ramp are available at the nearby fairgrounds.

Campsites, facilities: There are 50 sites with full or partial hookups for RVs of any length. Picnic tables are provided seasonally. Drinking water, restrooms with flush toilets and showers, and a dump station are available. A store, café, coin laundry, and ice are within one mile. Some facilities are wheelchair accessible. Leashed pets are permitted.

Reservations, fees: Reservations are not accepted. Sites are $26 per night, with a 14-day stay limit. Open year-round, except one week in August during the county fair. Phone ahead to confirm current status.

Directions: Heading south on I-5 in Roseburg, take Exit 123 and drive south under the freeway to Frear Street. Turn right and enter the park.

Contact: Douglas County Fairgrounds & Speedway, 541/957-7010, www.co.douglas. or.us/dcfair.

59 CAVITT CREEK FALLS
🏃 🚲 ⛵ 🏕 ♿ 🚐 ⛺

Scenic rating: 8
west of Roseburg

Map 5.3, page 263

The locals might try to hunt me down for revealing this spot, but here it is. This campground is located near a sensational swimming hole at the base of a 10-foot waterfall on Cavitt Creek. The elevation is 1,040 feet, and an abundant forest of fir, maple, and oak trees surrounds the campground. It is overlooked because it is set on land run by the Bureau of Land Management, not the Park Service or Forest Service. Fishing is closed on Cavitt Creek by the Oregon Department of Fish and Wildlife.

Campsites, facilities: There are 10 sites for tents or RVs up to 20 feet long (no hookups). Picnic tables, garbage bins, and fire rings are provided. Drinking water and vault toilets are available. A camp host is on-site. Some facilities

are wheelchair accessible. Leashed pets are permitted.

Reservations, fees: Reservations are not accepted. Sites are $10 per night, $4 per night for an additional vehicle. Open mid-May–mid-October, weather permitting.

Directions: From Roseburg, drive east on Highway 138 for 16.5 miles to Little River Road. Turn right (south) on Little River Road and drive 6.7 miles to the covered bridge. Turn right onto Cavitt Creek Road and drive 3.2 miles to Cavitt Creek Falls Recreation Site.

Contact: Bureau of Land Management, Roseburg District, 541/440-4930, www.or.blm. gov/or/resources/recreation.

60 HOODOO'S DEXTER SHORES RV PARK
🏃 ⛵ 🚐 🏕 ♿ 🚐 ⛺

Scenic rating: 7
near Dexter Reservoir

Map 5.4, page 264

If you're traveling on I-5, this RV park is well worth the 15-minute drive out of Springfield. It's across the street from Dexter Reservoir, where fishing and boating are permitted year-round. Speedboat races are held at Dexter in the summer. There is seasonal fishing for salmon and steelhead below Dexter dam. The local area is good for bird-watching. Nearby Lookout and Fall Creek Lakes offer sailing, swimming, waterskiing, and windsurfing. Many of the campsites have a lake view.

Campsites, facilities: There are 53 sites with full or partial hookups for RVs up to 40 feet long; 12 sites are pull-through. There are also eight tent sites. Picnic tables and fire pits are provided at tent sites; RV sites have tables only. Drinking water, restrooms with flush toilets and showers, a vault toilet, a dump station, cable TV, telephone hookups, Wi-Fi, putting green, a clubhouse, lending library, firewood, horseshoe pits, and a coin laundry are available. Propane gas, a café, restaurant, and ice are within three miles. Boat docks and launching facilities are nearby. Some facilities are wheelchair accessible. Leashed pets are permitted with size restrictions.

Reservations, fees: Reservations are accepted at 866/558-9777. RV sites are $34 per night, tent sites are $22 per night, $3 per person per night for more than four people, and $1 per pet per night. Weekly and monthly rates are available. Some credit cards are accepted. Open year-round.

Directions: From south Eugene on I-5, drive to Exit 188A and Highway 58. Take Highway 58 east and drive 11.5 miles to Lost Creek Road. Turn right (south) and drive several hundred feet to Dexter Road. Turn left (in front of the café) and drive east for half a block to the park on the right.

Contact: Dexter Shores RV Park, 541/937-3711 or 866/558-9777, www.dextershoresrv.com.

61 FALL CREEK STATE RECREATION AREA

Scenic rating: 7

in Fall Creek State Recreation Area

Map 5.4, page 264

There are two campgrounds here: Cascara and the group camp area, Fisherman's Park. Most of these spacious sites have Douglas fir and white fir tree cover. Water recreation is the primary activity here; boating and water skis are allowed. The lake level drops in August, and water temperatures are ideal for summer swimming.

Campsites, facilities: There are 39 primitive sites at Cascara Campground for tents or RVs up to 50 feet. Fisherman's Point Campground is a group area that accommodates up to 64 people and 16 RVs of any length. Picnic tables and fire rings are provided. Drinking water, vault toilets, garbage service, and firewood are available. A camp host is on-site. A boat launch, dock, and swimming area are also available. Some facilities are wheelchair accessible. Leashed pets are permitted.

Reservations, fees: Reservations are accepted for the RV group area at 800/452-5687 or www.reserveamerica.com. Sites are $17 per night, $7 per night per additional vehicle. The group RV area is $110 per night for up to 10 RVs, $11 per each additional RV, $7 per night per each additional car. Some credit cards are accepted. Open May 1-September 30.

Directions: From south Eugene on I-5, take Exit 188 to Highway 58. Drive 11 miles south to Lowell and Pioneer Street (at the covered bridge). Turn left on Pioneer Street and drive less than 0.25 mile to West Boundary Road. Turn left and drive one block to Lowell Jasper Road. Turn right and drive 1.5 miles to Unity and Place Road. Turn right and drive about one mile to a fork with North Shore Road (Big Fall Creek Road). Bear left onto Big Fall Creek Road and drive about eight miles to the head of Fall Creek Reservoir and Peninsula Road (Forest Road 6250). Turn right and drive 0.5 mile to the campground. The park is approximately 27 miles southeast of Eugene.

Contact: Fall Creek State Recreation Area, 541/937-1173 or 800/551-6949, www.oregonstateparks.org.

62 DOLLY VARDEN

Scenic rating: 6

on Fall Creek in Willamette National Forest

Map 5.4, page 264

This pretty campground is adjacent to Fall Creek and is at the lower trailhead for the scenic, 13.7-mile Fall Creek National Recreation Trail, which follows the creek and varies between 960 and 1,385 feet in elevation. This small campground gets moderate-heavy use. It is set on the inlet stream for Fall Creek Reservoir.

Campsites, facilities: There are five sites for tents or RVs up to 30 feet. Picnic tables and fire grills are provided. Vault toilets and garbage service are available. There is no drinking water. Leashed pets are permitted.

Reservations, fees: Reservations are not accepted. Sites are $14 per night, $7 per night per additional vehicle. Open May-September, weather permitting.

Directions: From south Eugene on I-5, take Exit 188 to Highway 58. Drive 11 miles south to Lowell and Pioneer Street (at the covered bridge). Turn left and drive 0.2 mile to West Boundary Road. Turn left and drive one block to Lowell Jasper Road. Turn right and drive 1.5 miles to Unity and Place Road. Turn right and drive about one mile to a fork with North Shore Road. Bear left onto North Shore Road (Big Fall Creek Road) and drive about 10 miles (the road becomes Forest Road 18) to the campground on the left.

Contact: Willamette National Forest, Middle Fork Ranger District, 541/782-2283, www. fs.usda.gov/willamette.

63 BIG POOL

Scenic rating: 6

on Fall Creek in Willamette National Forest

Map 5.4, page 264

Big Pool campground is quiet, secluded, and primitive. The camp sits along Fall Creek at about 1,000 feet elevation, and the scenic Fall Creek National Recreation Trail passes the camp on the other side of the creek, providing hiking opportunities. Sites are rather open, with only sparse vegetation between them.

Campsites, facilities: There are three tent sites and two sites for tents or RVs up to 24 feet long. Picnic tables, garbage containers, and fire grills are provided. Vault toilets and drinking water are available. Leashed pets are permitted.

Reservations, fees: Reservations are not accepted. Sites are $13 per night, $7 per night per additional vehicle. Open late May-September, weather permitting.

Directions: From south Eugene on I-5, take Exit 188 to Highway 58. Drive 11 miles south to Lowell and Pioneer Street (at the covered bridge). Turn left and drive 0.2 mile to West

Boundary Road. Turn left and drive one block to Lowell Jasper Road. Turn right and drive 1.5 miles to Unity and Place Road. Turn right and drive about one mile to a fork with North Shore Road. Bear left onto North Shore Road (Big Fall Creek Road) and drive about 12 miles (the road becomes Forest Road 18) to the campground on the right.

Contact: Willamette National Forest, Middle Fork Ranger District, 541/782-2283, www. fs.usda.gov/willamette.

64 BEDROCK

Scenic rating: 6

on Fall Creek in Willamette National Forest

Map 5.4, page 264

Bedrock lies along the banks of Fall Creek amid Douglas firs and cedars. This is one of the access points for the scenic Fall Creek National Recreation Trail, which in turn offers access to Jones Trail, a six-mile uphill climb. Swimming holes offer relief in summer.

Campsites, facilities: There are 18 single sites and one multiple site for tents or RVs up to 36 feet long. Picnic tables and fire grills are provided. Vault toilets and garbage service are available. There is no drinking water. Some facilities are wheelchair accessible. Leashed pets are permitted.

Reservations, fees: Reservations are not accepted. Single sites are $15 per night, $28 per night for double sites, and $7 per night per additional vehicle. Open May-mid-September, weather permitting.

Directions: From south Eugene on I-5, take Exit 188 to Highway 58. Drive 11 miles south to Lowell and Pioneer Street (at the covered bridge). Turn left and drive 0.2 mile to West Boundary Road. Turn left and drive one block to Lowell Jasper Road. Turn right and drive 1.5 miles to Unity and Place Road. Turn right and drive about one mile to a fork with North Shore Road. Bear left onto North Shore Road (Big Fall Creek Road) and drive about 14 miles (the road becomes Forest Road 18) to the campground on the left.

Contact: Willamette National Forest, Middle Fork Ranger District, 541/782-2283, www.fs.usda.gov/willamette.

65 PUMA

Scenic rating: 6

on Fall Creek in Willamette National Forest

Map 5.4, page 264

Puma campground hugs the banks of Fall Creek at an elevation of 1,100 feet. This is one of four camps in the immediate area, located across from the popular Fall Creek National Recreation Trail. The trail offers hiking opportunities, while Fall Creek provides a nice spot to cool off in summer.

Campsites, facilities: There are 11 sites for tents or RVs up to 36 feet long. Picnic tables and fire grills are provided. Vault toilets, drinking water, and garbage bins are available. Some facilities are wheelchair accessible. Leashed pets are permitted.

Reservations, fees: Reservations are not accepted. Sites are $15 per night, $7 per night per additional vehicle. Open late May-September, weather permitting.

Directions: From I-5 south of Eugene, take Exit 188 to Highway 58. Drive about 11 miles to Lowell. Turn left at Pioneer Street (at the covered bridge), drive 0.2 mile, and turn left on West Boundary Road. Drive one block and turn right at Lowell Jasper Road. Drive 1.5 miles to Place Road and turn right. Drive about one mile to a fork and bear left onto North Shore Road (Big Fall Creek Road). Drive about 16 miles (the road becomes Forest Road 18) to the campground on the left.

Contact: Willamette National Forest, Middle Fork Ranger District, 541/782-2283, www.fs.usda.gov/willamette.

66 FRISSELL CROSSING

Scenic rating: 8

near the Three Sisters Wilderness in Willamette National Forest

Map 5.4, page 264

If you're looking for solitude, this place should be heaven to you. Frissell campground (elevation 2,600 feet) sits on the banks of the South Fork of the McKenzie River, adjacent to a trailhead that provides access to the backcountry of the Three Sisters Wilderness. Note that Frissell Crossing is the only camp in the immediate area that has drinking water.

Campsites, facilities: There are 12 sites for tents or RVs up to 36 feet long. Picnic tables, garbage bins, and fire grills are provided. Hand-pumped drinking water and vault toilets are available. Leashed pets are permitted.

Reservations, fees: Reservations are not accepted. Single sites are $14 per night, double sites are $26 per night, $7 per night per additional vehicle. Open mid-May-mid-September, weather permitting.

Directions: From Eugene, drive east on Highway 126 for 37 miles to Blue River. Continue east on Highway 126 for five miles to Forest Road 19 (Aufderheide Scenic Byway). Turn right (south) and drive 21.5 miles to the camp on the left.

Contact: Willamette National Forest, McKenzie River Ranger District, 541/822-3381, www.fs.usda.gov/willamette.

67 BLAIR LAKE WALK-IN

Scenic rating: 6

on Blair Lake in Willamette National Forest

Map 5.4, page 264

If you're looking for a pristine, alpine lakeside setting, you'll find it here. The lake, set at 4,800 feet elevation, is small (only 35 acres) and shallow (20 feet). It supports a population of brook and rainbow trout and is stocked in the summer. The surrounding meadows and woods are well known for their wide range of wildflowers and huckleberries.

Campsites, facilities: There are seven walk-in tent sites. Picnic tables and fire rings are provided. Drinking water, a vault toilet, and garbage bins are available. Some facilities are wheelchair accessible. Leashed pets are permitted.

Reservations, fees: Reservations are not accepted. Sites are $8 per night for two vehicles, $4 per night per additional vehicle. Open mid-June-October, weather permitting.

Directions: From south Eugene on I-5, take Exit 188 to Highway 58. Drive 35 miles southeast on Highway 58 to Oakridge. Turn left at the signal to downtown and Salmon Creek Road. Turn east and drive nine miles (it becomes Forest Road 24) to Forest Road 1934. Turn left and drive eight miles to Forest Road 733. Turn right and continue for 1.25 miles to the campground.

Contact: Willamette National Forest, Middle Fork Ranger Station, 541/782-2283, www. fs.usda.gov/willamette.

68 KIAHANIE
🏕️🚴🏊🛻🐕♿🚗⛺️

Scenic rating: 5

on the North Fork of the Willamette River in Willamette National Forest

Map 5.4, page 264

This is one heck of a spot for fly-fishing (and the only kind of fishing allowed). Kiahanie is a remote campground that sits at 2,200 feet elevation along the North Fork of the Willamette River, a designated Wild and Scenic River. If you want beauty and quiet among enormous Douglas fir trees, you came to the right place. An even more remote campground, Box Canyon Horse Camp, is farther north on Forest Road 19.

Campsites, facilities: There are 19 sites for tents or RVs up to 24 feet long. Picnic tables and fire rings are provided. Drinking water, vault

toilets, garbage bins, and a recycling center are available. Some facilities are wheelchair accessible. Leashed pets are permitted.

Reservations, fees: Reservations are not accepted. Sites are $10 per night for two vehicles, $5 per night per additional vehicle. Open late May-late October, weather permitting.

Directions: From south Eugene on I-5, take Exit 188 to Highway 58. Drive 31 miles southeast on Highway 58 to Westfir. Take the Westfir exit and drive two miles to Westfir and the junction with Aufderheide Scenic Byway (Forest Road 19). Bear left (northeast) and drive 19 miles to the campground.

Contact: Willamette National Forest, Middle Fork Ranger Station, 541/782-2283, www. fs.usda.gov/willamette.

69 BOX CANYON HORSE CAMP
🏕️🏠🚗⛺️

Scenic rating: 4

near Chucksney Mountain in Willamette National Forest

Map 5.4, page 264

Only 80 miles from Eugene, this secluded campground with sparse tree cover offers wilderness trails, including the Chucksney Mountain Trail, Crossing-Way Trail, and Grasshopper Trail. It's a good base camp for a backpacking trip and is at 3,600 feet in elevation.

Campsites, facilities: There are 13 sites for tents or RVs up to 30 feet long that allow horse and rider to camp close together. Picnic tables, fire grills, stock water, and corrals are provided. Vault toilets are available. There is no drinking water, and garbage must be packed out. Leashed pets are permitted.

Reservations, fees: Reservations are not accepted. There is no fee for camping. Open June-late October, weather permitting.

Directions: From Eugene, drive east on Highway 126 for 41 miles to Blue River. Continue east on Highway 126 for five miles to Forest Road 19 (Aufderheide Scenic Byway). Turn right (south) and drive 33 miles to the camp on the right.

Contact: Willamette National Forest, McKenzie River Ranger District, 541/822-3381, www.fs.usda.gov/willamette.

70 BLACK CANYON

🏃 🚴 🛶 🚤 🏇 ♿ 🚙 ⛺

Scenic rating: 7

on the Middle Fork of the Willamette River in Willamette National Forest

Map 5.4, page 264

Black Canyon campground is set along the banks of the Middle Fork of the Willamette River, not far above Lookout Point Reservoir, where fishing and boating are available. The elevation is 1,000 feet. The camp is pretty and wooded and has comfortable sites. Within the camp is a one-mile-long nature trail with interpretive signs. You will hear train noise from the other side of the river.

Campsites, facilities: There are 70 sites for tents or RVs up to 40 feet long, and one group site is available. Picnic tables, garbage service, and fire grills are provided. Drinking water, vault toilets, and firewood are available. A dump station, café, and coin laundry are within six miles. Launching facilities are nearby at the south end of Lookout Point Reservoir. Some facilities are wheelchair accessible. Leashed pets are permitted.

Reservations, fees: Reservations are accepted for 17 sites at 877/444-6777 ($10 reservation fee) or www.recreation.gov ($9 reservation fee). Single sites are $20 per night, double sites are $38 per night, $7 per night per additional vehicle, and $85 for the group site. Open late April-early October, weather permitting.

Directions: From south Eugene on I-5, take Exit 188 to Highway 58. Drive southeast on Highway 58 for 27 miles to the camp on the left (six miles west of Oakridge).

Contact: Willamette National Forest, Middle Fork Ranger Station, 541/782-2283, www.fs.usda.gov/willamette.

71 BAKER BAY COUNTY PARK

🏃 🚴 🛶 🚤 🚣 ♿ 🏇 🚙 ⛺

Scenic rating: 6

on Dorena Lake

Map 5.4, page 264

Baker Bay is set along the shore of Dorena Lake, where boating, canoeing, fishing, sailing, swimming, and waterskiing are among the recreation options. Row River Trail follows part of the lake for a hike or bike ride, and there are covered bridges in the area. For golf, head to Cottage Grove.

Campsites, facilities: There are 48 sites for tents or self-contained RVs up to 40 feet, plus two group sites for up to 35 people each. Picnic tables and fire grills are provided. Drinking water, restrooms with flush toilets and coin showers, firewood, garbage bins, playground, reservable picnic areas, and a dump station are available. A concession stand with ice is in the park, and a store is within five miles. Boat docks, launching, and kayak rentals are nearby, with seasonal onshore facilities for catamarans. Some facilities are wheelchair accessible. Leashed pets are permitted.

Reservations, fees: Reservations are accepted at 541/682-2000 or http://reservations.lanecounty.org ($10 reservation fee). Sites are $30-32 per night, $7 for an additional vehicle. Group sites are $75 per night. Open April-October.

Directions: From Eugene, drive south on I-5 for 22 miles to Cottage Grove and Exit 174 (Dorena Lake exit). Take that exit to Row River Road and drive east for 4.4 miles (the road becomes Shore View Drive). Bear right on Shore View Drive and continue 2.8 miles to the campground entrance on the left.

Contact: Baker Bay County Park, 541/942-7669, www.lanecounty.org.

72 SCHWARZ PARK

Scenic rating: 7

on Dorena Lake

Map 5.4, page 264

This large campground sits below Dorena Lake on the Row River, where boating, fishing, swimming, and waterskiing are among the recreation options at the lake. Note that chances of rain are high May to mid-June and that there is a posted warning against consumption of fish from Dorena Lake. The Row River Trail, a paved trail for biking, walking, and shoreline access, parallels Dorena Lake's north shoreline and then extends 12 miles.

Campsites, facilities: There are 65 sites for tents or RVs of any length and six group sites for 15-50 people. Picnic tables and fire rings are provided. Restrooms with flush toilets and showers, drinking water, garbage bins, a playground, and a dump station are available. Boat-launching facilities are on the lake about two miles upstream. Some facilities are wheelchair accessible. Leashed pets are permitted.

Reservations, fees: Reservations are accepted at 877/444-6777 ($10 reservation fee) or www.recreation.gov ($9 reservation fee). Sites are $20-40 per night, group sites are $150 per night, and an additional vehicle is $6 per night. Open late April-late September.

Directions: From Eugene, drive south on I-5 for 22 miles to Cottage Grove and Exit 174. Take that exit to Shoreview Drive and drive one mile to Row River Road. Turn left and drive four miles east to the campground entrance.

Contact: U.S. Army Corps of Engineers, Recreation Information, Cottage Grove, 541/942-1418 or 541/942-5631, www.nwp.usace.army.mil.

73 SALMON CREEK FALLS

Scenic rating: 8

on Salmon Creek in Willamette National Forest

Map 5.4, page 264   **BEST (**

This pretty campground sits in a lush, old-growth forest, right along Salmon Creek at 1,500 feet in elevation. The rocky gorge area creates two small but beautiful waterfalls and several deep pools in the clear, blue-green waters. Springtime brings a full range of wildflowers and wild thimbleberries; hazelnuts abound in the summer. This area is a popular recreation spot.

Campsites, facilities: There are 14 sites for tents or RVs up to 40 feet long. Picnic tables, garbage bins, and fire grills are provided. Drinking water and vault toilets are available. A store, café, coin laundry, and ice are available within five miles. Leashed pets are permitted.

Reservations, fees: Reservations are not accepted. Sites are $15 per night, $7 per night per additional vehicle. Open late April-mid-September, weather permitting.

Directions: From south Eugene on I-5, take Exit 188 to Highway 58. Drive southeast on Highway 58 for 35 miles to Oakridge and the signal light for downtown. Turn left on Crestview Street and drive 0.25 mile to 1st Street. Turn right and drive five miles (the road becomes Forest Road 24, then Salmon Creek Road) to the campground entrance on the right.

Contact: Willamette National Forest, Middle Fork Ranger District, 541/782-2283, www.fs.usda.gov/willamette.

74 SKOOKUM CREEK

Scenic rating: 7

near the Three Sisters Wilderness in Willamette National Forest

Map 5.4, page 264

Skookum Creek, at 4,500 feet elevation, is a

popular starting point for backcountry fishing, hiking, and horseback riding. The Erma Bell Lakes Trail, a portal into the Three Sisters Wilderness, begins here. This trail is maintained for wheelchair accessibility, though it is challenging.

Campsites, facilities: There are nine walk-in tent sites. Picnic tables and fire rings are provided. Drinking water, hitching rails, garbage service, and vault toilets are available. Some facilities are wheelchair accessible. Leashed pets are permitted.

Reservations, fees: Reservations are not accepted. Sites are $5 per night. Open late May-mid-October, weather permitting.

Directions: From Eugene, drive east on Highway 126 for 37 miles to Blue River. Continue east for five miles to Forest Road 19 (Aufderheide Scenic Byway). Turn right and drive 35 miles south to Forest Road 1957. Turn right (south) and drive four miles to the campground.

Contact: Willamette National Forest, Middle Fork Ranger Station, 541/782-2283, www.fs.usda.gov/willamette.

75 NORTH WALDO

Scenic rating: 10
on Waldo Lake in Willamette National Forest

Map 5.4, page 264 **BEST (**

North Waldo is the most popular of the Waldo Lake campgrounds. Set at an elevation of 5,400 feet, Waldo Lake has the special distinction of being one of the three purest lakes in the world. The boat launch here is deeper than the others on the lake, which makes it more accommodating for large sailboats (gas motors are not allowed on the lake). Amphitheater programs are presented here on weekends late July-Labor Day. North Waldo is also a popular starting point to many wilderness trails and lakes, most notably Rigdon, Torrey, and Wahanna Lakes. The drier environment supports fewer mosquitoes, but they can still be plentiful in season.

Campsites, facilities: There are 58 sites for tents or RVs up to 40 feet long. Picnic tables and fire rings are provided. Drinking water, composting toilets, garbage bins, gray-water station, recycling center, swimming area, and amphitheater are available. Boat-launching facilities are available. Restrooms are wheelchair accessible. Leashed pets are permitted.

Reservations, fees: Reservations are accepted at 877/444-6777 ($10 reservation fee) or www.recreation.gov ($9 reservation fee). Single sites are $22 per night, double sites $40 per night, $7 per night per additional vehicle. A Northwest Forest Pass ($5 daily fee or $30 annual fee per vehicle) is required at the nearby boat launch and trailheads. Open early June-early October, weather permitting.

Directions: From Eugene, drive south on I-5 for four miles to Exit 188 and Highway 58. Turn southeast and drive about 60 miles to Waldo Lake Road (Forest Road 5897). Turn left and drive north on Waldo Lake Road for 14 miles to Forest Road 5898. Turn left and drive about two miles to the campground at the northeast end of Waldo Lake.

Contact: Willamette National Forest, Middle Fork Ranger District, 541/782-2283, www.fs.usda.gov/willamette.

76 ISLET

Scenic rating: 10
on Waldo Lake in Willamette National Forest

Map 5.4, page 264

You'll find sandy beaches and an interpretive sign at this campground at the north end of Waldo Lake. The winds blow consistently every afternoon, great for sailing. A picnic table placed strategically on the rock jetty provides a great spot to enjoy a sunset. A one-mile shoreline trail stretches between Islet and North Waldo Campground. Bring your mosquito repellent; June-August you'll need it.

Campsites, facilities: There are 55 sites, including four multiple sites, for tents or RVs up to 30 feet long. Picnic tables, garbage bins, a recycling center, and fire rings are provided. Drinking water and composting toilets are available. Boat-launching facilities are available nearby. Leashed pets are permitted.

Reservations, fees: Reservations are not accepted. Single sites are $22 per night, double sites are $40 per night, $7 per night per additional vehicle. A Northwest Forest Pass ($5 daily fee or $30 annual fee per parked vehicle) is required at the nearby boat launch and trailheads. Open July-October, weather permitting.

Directions: From Eugene, drive south on I-5 for four miles to Exit 188 and Highway 58. Turn southeast and drive about 60 miles to Waldo Lake Road (Forest Road 5897). Turn left and drive north on Waldo Lake Road for 14 miles to Forest Road 5898. Turn left and continue 1.5 miles to the campground at the northeast end of Waldo Lake.

Contact: Willamette National Forest, Middle Fork Ranger District, 541/782-2233, www.fs.usda.gov/willamette.

77 SHADOW BAY

Scenic rating: 10
on Waldo Lake in Willamette National Forest

Map 5.4, page 264

Shadow Bay campground, at 5,400 feet in elevation, is situated on a large bay at the south end of Waldo Lake. It has a considerably wetter environment than either North Waldo or Islet, supporting a more diverse and prolific ground cover—as well as more mosquitoes. The camp receives considerably lighter use than North Waldo. You have access to the Shore Line Trail and then the Waldo Lake Trail from here. Note that gas motors are not permitted on Waldo Lake.

Campsites, facilities: There are 92 sites for tents or RVs up to 44 feet long and three group sites for 30-120 people. Picnic tables, garbage bins, a recycling center, and fire grills are provided. Drinking water and vault and

composting toilets are available. A camp host is on-site in season. Boat-launching facilities and a swimming area are nearby. Leashed pets are permitted.

Reservations, fees: Reservations are accepted for 57 sites at 877/444-6777 ($10 reservation fee) or www.recreation.gov ($9 reservation fee). Single sites are $22 per night, double sites are $40 per night, and group sites are $100-350; $7 per night per additional vehicle. A Northwest Forest Pass ($5 daily fee or $30 annual fee per vehicle) is required at the nearby boat launch and trailheads. Open July-October, weather permitting.

Directions: From Eugene, drive south on I-5 for four miles to Exit 188 and Highway 58. Turn southeast and drive about 60 miles to Waldo Lake Road (Forest Road 5897). Turn left on Waldo Lake Road and drive north for 6.5 miles to the Shadow Bay turnoff. Turn left and drive on Forest Road 5896 to the campground at the south end of Waldo Lake.

Contact: Willamette National Forest, Middle Fork Ranger District, 541/782-2233, www.fs.usda.gov/willamette.

78 BLUE POOL

Scenic rating: 4
on Salt Creek in Willamette National Forest

Map 5.4, page 264

This campground is situated in an old-growth forest alongside Salt Creek at 1,900 feet elevation. The camp features a large picnic area along the creek with picnic tables, a large grassy area, and fire stoves built in the 1930s by the Civilian Conservation Corps. One-half mile east of the campground on Highway 58 is McCredie Hot Springs. This spot is undeveloped, without any facilities. Exercise caution when using the hot springs; they can be very hot.

Campsites, facilities: There are 24 sites for tents or RVs up to 25 feet. Picnic tables, garbage bins, a recycling center, and fire rings are provided. Drinking water, vault and flush toilets, and a gray-water station are available. Leashed pets are permitted.

Reservations, fees: Reservations are not accepted. Sites are $17 per night, $7 per night per additional vehicle. Open mid-May-late September, weather permitting.

Directions: From Eugene, drive south on I-5 for four miles to Exit 188 and Highway 58. Turn southeast and drive 35 miles to Oakridge. Continue east on Highway 58 for eight miles to the campground on the right.

Contact: Willamette National Forest, Middle Fork Ranger District, 541/782-2283, www. fs.usda.gov/willamette.

79 SHARPS CREEK

Scenic rating: 5

on Sharps Creek

Map 5.4, page 264

Like nearby Rujada, this camp on the banks of Sharps Creek is just far enough off the beaten path to be missed by most campers. It's quiet, primitive, and remote, and fishing, gold-panning, and swimming are popular activities in the day-use area.

Campsites, facilities: There are 10 sites for tents or RVs up to 25 feet long. Picnic tables and fire pits are provided. Drinking water and vault toilets are available. A camp host is here in summer. Some facilities are wheelchair accessible. Leashed pets are permitted.

Reservations, fees: Reservations are not accepted. Sites are $12 per night, $5 per night per additional vehicle. Open mid-May-September with a 14-day stay limit, weather permitting.

Directions: From Eugene, drive south on I-5 to Cottage Grove and Exit 174. Take that exit and drive east on Row River Road for 18 miles to Sharps Creek Road. Turn right (south) and drive four miles to the campground.

Contact: Bureau of Land Management, Eugene District, 541/683-6600 or 888/442-3062, www. blm.gov.

80 RUJADA

Scenic rating: 7

on Layng Creek in Umpqua National Forest

Map 5.4, page 264

Rujada campground is nestled on a river terrace on the banks of Layng Creek, right at the national forest border. The Swordfern Trail follows Layng Creek through a beautiful forest within a lush fern grotto. There is a fair swimming hole near the campground. Those with patience and persistence can fish in the creek. By continuing east on Forest Road 17, you reach a trailhead that leads 0.5 mile to beautiful Spirit Falls, a spectacular 60-foot waterfall. A bit farther east is another easy trail, which leads to Moon Falls, even more awe-inspiring at 125 feet. Another campground option is Cedar Creek, about six miles southeast on Brice Creek Road (County Road 2470).

Campsites, facilities: There are 15 sites for tents or RVs up to 22 feet long. Picnic tables, garbage bins, and fire pits are provided. Flush and vault toilets, drinking water, gray-water stations, and a softball field are available. Some facilities are wheelchair accessible. Leashed pets are permitted.

Reservations, fees: Reservations are not accepted. Sites are $12-24 per night, $5 per night per additional vehicle. Open late May-late September, weather permitting.

Directions: From Eugene, drive south on I-5 to Cottage Grove and Exit 174. Take that exit and drive east on Row River Road for 19 miles to Layng Creek Road (Forest Road 17). Turn left and drive two miles to the campground on the right.

Contact: Umpqua National Forest, Cottage Grove Ranger Station, 541/767-5000, www. fs.usda.gov/umpqua.

81 PACKARD CREEK

🏃 ⛵ 🏊 🛶 🏕 🐕 ♿ 🚐 ⛺

Scenic rating: 6

on Hills Creek Reservoir in Willamette National Forest

Map 5.4, page 264

Packard Creek campground is located on a large flat beside Hills Creek Reservoir. This camp is extremely popular with families and fills up on weekends and holidays. The mix of vegetation in the campground unfortunately includes an abundance of poison oak. The speed limit around the swimming area and boat ramp is 5 mph. The elevation is 1,600 feet.

One time at Hills Creek Reservoir my canoe flipped on a cold winter day and I almost drowned after 20 minutes in the icy water. After I'd gone down for the count twice, my brother Bob jumped in, swam out, grabbed the front of the flipped canoe, and towed me to shore. Then, once ashore, he kept me awake, preventing me from lapsing into a coma from hypothermia.

Thanks, Bob.

Campsites, facilities: There are 37 sites, including two multiple sites, for tents or RVs up to 40 feet long, and a group area for up to 75 people. Picnic tables and fire rings are provided. Drinking water, vault toilets, garbage bins, a recycling center, and firewood are available. Fishing and boat docks, boat-launching facilities, a roped swimming area, picnic shelter, and an amphitheater are available. Some sites have their own docks. Some facilities are wheelchair accessible. Leashed pets are permitted.

Reservations, fees: Reservations are accepted for 13 of the sites at 877/444-6777 ($10 reservation fee) or www.recreation.gov ($9 reservation fee). Single sites are $18 per night, double sites are $34 per night, $7 per night per additional vehicle, $145 for the group site. Open mid-April-mid-September, weather permitting.

Directions: From Eugene, drive south on I-5 for four miles to Exit 188 and Highway 58. Turn southeast and drive 35 miles to Oakridge.

Continue east on Highway 58 for two miles to Kitson Springs Road. Turn right and drive 0.5 mile to Forest Road 21. Turn right and continue six miles to the campground on the left.

Contact: Willamette National Forest, Middle Fork Ranger Station, 541/782-2283, www. fs.usda.gov/willamette.

82 SAND PRAIRIE

🏃 🚴 ⛵ 🛶 🏕 🐕 ♿ 🚐 ⛺

Scenic rating: 6

on the Willamette River in Willamette National Forest

Map 5.4, page 264

Situated at 1,600 feet elevation in a mixed stand of cedar, dogwood, Douglas fir, hazelnut, and western hemlock, this campground provides easy access to the Middle Fork of the Willamette River. An access road leads to the south (upstream) end of the Hills Creek Reservoir. The 27-mile Middle Fork Trail begins at the south end of the campground. Fishing is good here; you can expect to catch large cutthroat trout, rainbow trout, and suckers in the Middle Fork.

Campsites, facilities: There are 21 sites for tents or RVs up to 28 feet long. Picnic tables, garbage bins, and fire rings are provided. Vault and flush toilets and a group picnic area are available. There is no drinking water available. A camp host is on-site. A boat launch is nearby on Hills Creek Reservoir. Some facilities are wheelchair accessible. Leashed pets are permitted.

Reservations, fees: Reservations are not accepted. Sites are $13 per night, $7 per night per additional vehicle. Open late May-early September, weather permitting.

Directions: From Eugene, drive south on I-5 for four miles to Exit 188 and Highway 58. Turn southeast and drive 35 miles to Oakridge. Continue east on Highway 58 for two miles to Kitson Springs Road. Turn right and drive 0.5 mile to Forest Road 21. Turn right and continue 11 miles to the campground on the right.

Contact: Willamette National Forest, Middle Fork Ranger Station, 541/782-2283, www.fs.usda.gov/willamette.

83 SACANDAGA

Scenic rating: 5
on the Willamette River in Willamette National Forest

Map 5.4, page 264

Sacandaga campground sits along the middle fork of the Willamette River, where a segment of the historic Oregon Central Military Wagon Road is visible. Two trails from the campground access the Willamette River, and the Middle Fork Trail is in close proximity. Also, a short trail leads to a viewpoint with a bench, great for a short break. This campground gets low use, and the sites are well separated by vegetation. Count on solitude here. The elevation is 2,400 feet.

Campsites, facilities: There are 17 sites for tents or RVs up to 24 feet long. Picnic tables and fire rings are provided. Drinking water, vault toilets, and firewood are available. Leashed pets are permitted.

Reservations, fees: Reservations are not accepted. Sites are $8 per night, $4 per night per additional vehicle. Open mid-May-mid-November, weather permitting.

Directions: From Eugene, drive south on I-5 for four miles to Exit 188 and Highway 58. Turn southeast and drive 35 miles to Oakridge. Continue east on Highway 58 for two miles to Kitson Springs Road. Turn right and drive 0.5 mile to Forest Road 21. Turn right and drive 24 miles to the campground on the right.

Contact: Willamette National Forest, Middle Fork Ranger Station, 541/782-2283, www.fs.usda.gov/willamette.

84 CAMPERS FLAT

Scenic rating: 5
on the Willamette River in Willamette National Forest

Map 5.4, page 264

Small, pretty Campers Flat campground sits adjacent to the Middle Fork Willamette River, near Deadhorse Creek. Though the camp is right next to Forest Road 21, you're likely to hear more river than road. Fishing is a popular activity here, with good river access. For mountain bikers, the Young's Rock Trailhead awaits on the other side of the road. While at camp, be sure to check out the interpretive sign detailing the history of the Oregon Central Military Wagon Road.

Campsites, facilities: There are five sites for tents or RVs up to 40 feet long. Picnic tables, garbage bins, and fire grills are provided. Vault toilets and firewood are available. Well water may be available for drinking, but bring your own just in case. Leashed pets are permitted.

Reservations, fees: Reservations are not accepted. Sites are $13 per night, $7 per night per additional vehicle. Open late May-September.

Directions: From Eugene, drive south on I-5 for five miles to Exit 188 and Highway 58. Turn east and drive 35 miles to the town of Oakridge. From Oakridge, continue east on Highway 58 about two miles to Kitson Springs Road. Turn right and drive 0.5 mile to Forest Road 21. Turn right and drive 19 miles to the campground on the right.

Contact: Willamette National Forest, Middle Fork Ranger Station, 541/782-2283, www.fs.usda.gov/willamette.

85 SECRET

Scenic rating: 5

on the Willamette River in Willamette National Forest

Map 5.4, page 264

This small campground, set on the middle fork of the Willamette River, gets regular use from locals in the know. The tree cover is scant, but there is adequate vegetation to buffer the campsites from the nearby road noise. Fishing the Middle Fork Willamette is generally fair.

Campsites, facilities: There are six sites for tents or RVs up to 36 feet long. Picnic tables, garbage bins, and fire rings are provided. Pit toilets are available, but there is no drinking water. Leashed pets are permitted.

Reservations, fees: Reservations are not accepted. Sites are $13 per night, $7 per night per additional vehicle. Open May-late September, weather permitting.

Directions: From Eugene, drive south on I-5 for five miles to Exit 188 and Highway 58. Turn east and drive 35 miles to the town of Oakridge. From Oakridge, continue east on Highway 58 about two miles to Kitson Springs Road. Turn right and drive 0.5 mile to Forest Road 21. Turn right and drive 18 miles to the campground.

Contact: Willamette National Forest, Middle Fork Ranger Station, 541/782-2283, www. fs.usda.gov/willamette.

86 INDIGO SPRINGS

Scenic rating: 5

near the Willamette River in Willamette National Forest

Map 5.4, page 264

This small, semi-open tent campground sits at 2,800 feet elevation in a stand of old-growth Douglas fir. A nearby 250-foot walk leads to the origin of this cold-water spring. A remnant of the historic Oregon Central Military Wagon Road passes near the campground, with an interpretive sign explaining it.

Campsites, facilities: There are three sites for tents. Picnic tables and fire grills are provided. Vault toilets and firewood are available. There is no drinking water. Leashed pets are permitted.

Reservations, fees: Reservations are not accepted. There is no fee for camping. Open May-October, weather permitting.

Directions: From Eugene, drive south on I-5 for five miles to Exit 188 and Highway 58. Turn east and drive 35 miles to the town of Oakridge. From Oakridge, continue east on Highway 58 about two miles to Kitson Springs Road. Turn right and drive 0.5 mile to Forest Road 21. Turn right and drive 27 miles to the campground on the left.

Contact: Willamette National Forest, Middle Fork Ranger Station, 541/782-2283, www. fs.usda.gov/willamette.

87 ROCK CREEK

Scenic rating: 8

on Rock Creek

Map 5.4, page 264

Since I started roaming around the state 20 years ago, this campground on the banks of Rock Creek in a relatively obscure spot has been considerably improved by the Bureau of Land Management (BLM). It's not well known, either, so you're likely to have privacy as a bonus. No fishing is allowed in Rock Creek.

Campsites, facilities: There are 17 sites for tents or RVs up to 40 feet long. Picnic tables and fire grills are provided. A camp host is on-site, and vault toilets, drinking water, a reservable pavilion, horseshoe pits, volleyball area, and firewood are available. Some facilities are wheelchair accessible. Leashed pets are permitted but not in the swimming hole.

Reservations, fees: Reservations are not accepted. Sites are $10 per night, with a 14-day stay limit, and $4 per night per additional vehicle. Open late May-late September.

Directions: From Roseburg, drive east on Highway 138 for 22 miles to Rock Creek Road. Turn right (north) and drive seven miles to the campground on the right.

Contact: Bureau of Land Management, Roseburg District, 541/440-4930, www.blm.gov.

88 MILLPOND

Scenic rating: 8

on Rock Creek

Map 5.4, page 264

Rock Creek flows past Millpond and empties into the North Umpqua River five miles downstream. Just above this confluence is the Rock Creek Fish Hatchery, which is open year-round to visitors, with free access. This campground along the banks of Rock Creek is the first camp you'll see along Rock Creek Road, which accounts for its relative popularity in the area. Like Rock Creek Campground, it's primitive and remote. No fishing is allowed in Rock Creek.

Campsites, facilities: There are 12 sites for tents or RVs up to 42 feet long. Picnic tables, garbage service, and fire grills are provided. A camp host is on-site, and flush and vault toilets, drinking water, firewood, a ballfield, horseshoe pits, playground, and reservable pavilion are available. Some facilities are wheelchair accessible. Leashed pets are permitted, but not in the swimming hole.

Reservations, fees: Reservations are not accepted. Sites are $10 per night, $4 per night per additional vehicle. Open mid-May-late September with a 14-day stay limit.

Directions: From Roseburg, drive east on Highway 138 for 22 miles to Rock Creek Road. Turn right (north) and drive five miles to the campground on the right.

Contact: Bureau of Land Management, Roseburg District, 541/440-4930, www.blm.gov.

89 SUSAN CREEK

Scenic rating: 9

on the North Umpqua River

Map 5.4, page 264   **BEST (**

This popular and pretty campground borders the North Umpqua Wild and Scenic River. This lush setting features plenty of trees and river access. Highlights include two barrier-free trails, one traveling 0.5 mile to the day-use area. From there, a hike of about 0.75 mile leads to the 50-foot Susan Creek Falls. Another 0.4 mile up the trail are the Susan Creek Indian Mounds. These moss-covered rocks are believed to be a spiritual site and are visited by Native Americans in search of guardian spirit visions.

Campsites, facilities: There are 29 sites for RVs up to 48 feet long. Picnic tables, garbage service, and fire grills are provided. Restrooms with flush toilets and showers, drinking water, small amphitheater with seasonal interpretive programs, horseshoe pits, and firewood are available, and there is a camp host. Some facilities and trails are wheelchair accessible. Leashed pets are permitted.

Reservations, fees: Reservations are accepted by phone for 13 sites; the remaining sites are first-come, first-served. Sites are $14 per night, with a 14-day stay limit, and $4 per night per additional vehicle. Open mid-May-late September.

Directions: From Roseburg, drive east on Highway 138 for 29.5 miles to the campground (turnoff well signed).

Contact: Bureau of Land Management, Roseburg District, 541/440-4930, www.blm.gov.

90 STEAMBOAT FALLS

Scenic rating: 8

on Steamboat Creek in Umpqua National Forest

Map 5.4, page 264   **BEST (**

This Steamboat Creek campground boasts some excellent scenery. Beautiful Steamboat Falls features a fish ladder that provides passage for steelhead and salmon on their upstream migration. No fishing is permitted in Steamboat Creek. Other nearby camping options are Island and Canton Creek.

Campsites, facilities: There are seven sites for tents or RVs up to 24 feet long and three sites for tents only. Picnic tables, garbage bins, vault toilets, and fire grills are provided. There is no drinking water. Leashed pets are permitted.

Reservations, fees: Reservations are not accepted. Sites are $10 per night, $5 per night per additional vehicle. Open year-round, weather permitting.

Directions: From Roseburg on I-5, take Exit 120 to Highway 138. Drive east on Highway 138 to Steamboat and Forest Road 38. Turn left on Forest Road 38 (Steamboat Creek Road) and drive six miles to a fork with Forest Road 3810. Turn right and drive one mile on a paved road to the campground.

Contact: Umpqua National Forest, North Umpqua Ranger District, 541/496-3532, www.fs.usda.gov/umpqua.

91 SCAREDMAN

Scenic rating: 6

on Canton Creek

Map 5.4, page 264

Scaredman is a small campground along the banks of Canton Creek, virtually unknown to out-of-towners. Set in an old-growth forest, this private and secluded camp offers a chance to swim in the creek. Scaredman gets its name from an old legend that says some early settlers camped here, heard a pack of hungry wolves, and then ran off, scared to death. Although fishing is closed on Canton Creek and all Steamboat drainages, the North Umpqua River 3.5 miles downstream offers fly-fishing for steelhead or salmon.

Campsites, facilities: There are 10 sites for tents only. Picnic tables, garbage service, and fire grills are provided. Vault toilets and drinking water are available. Some facilities are wheelchair accessible. Leashed pets are permitted.

Reservations, fees: Reservations are not accepted. Sites are $10 per night, $5 per night for each additional vehicle. Open year-round, with limited services November-March.

Directions: From Roseburg, drive east on Highway 138 for 40 miles to Steamboat Creek Road. Turn left (north) and drive 0.5 mile to Canton Creek Road. Turn left (north) and drive three miles to the campground.

Contact: Bureau of Land Management, Roseburg District, 541/440-4930, www.blm.gov.

92 ISLAND

Scenic rating: 8

on the Umpqua River in Umpqua National Forest

Map 5.4, page 264

The North Umpqua is one of Oregon's most beautiful rivers, and this scenic campground borders its banks at a spot popular for both rafting and steelhead fishing. Note: Only fly-fishing is allowed here. A hiking trail that leads east and west along the river is accessible a short drive to the west.

Campsites, facilities: There are seven sites for tents or RVs up to 24 feet long. Picnic tables, garbage bins, gray-water waste sump, and fire grills are provided. There is no drinking water. Some facilities are wheelchair accessible. Leashed pets are permitted.

Reservations, fees: Reservations are not

accepted. Sites are $10 per night, $5 per night per additional vehicle. Open year-round, weather permitting.

Directions: From Roseburg, drive east on Highway 138 for 40 miles (just past Steamboat) to the camp on the right. The campground is along the highway.

Contact: Umpqua National Forest, North Umpqua Ranger District, 541/496-3532, www.fs.usda.gov/umpqua.

93 CANTON CREEK

Scenic rating: 8

near the North Umpqua River in Umpqua National Forest

Map 5.4, page 264

Set at an elevation of 1,195 feet at the confluence of Canton and Steamboat Creeks, this camp is less than a mile from the North Umpqua River and gets little overnight use—but lots of day swimmers come here in July and August. No fishing is permitted on Steamboat or Canton Creeks because they are spawning areas for steelhead and salmon. Steamboat Falls is six miles north on Forest Road 38.

Campsites, facilities: There are five sites for tents or RVs up to 22 feet long. Picnic tables and fire grills are provided. Drinking water, a covered picnic gazebo, and flush toilets are available. Garbage must be packed out. Leashed pets are permitted.

Reservations, fees: Reservations are not accepted. Sites are $10 per night, $5 per night per additional vehicle. Open mid-May-mid-October, weather permitting.

Directions: From Roseburg, drive east on Highway 138 for 39 miles to Steamboat and Forest Road 38 (Steamboat Creek Road). Turn left and drive 0.25 mile to the campground on the right.

Contact: Umpqua National Forest, North Umpqua Ranger District, 541/496-3532, www.fs.usda.gov/umpqua.

94 HORSESHOE BEND/ DEER FLAT GROUP

Scenic rating: 8

on the Umpqua River in Umpqua National Forest

Map 5.4, page 264

This campground, set at an elevation of 1,300 feet, is in the middle of a big bend in the North Umpqua River. This spot is a major launching point for white-water rafting. Fly-fishing is popular here and is the only type of fishing allowed.

Campsites, facilities: There are 23 sites and two double sites for tents or RVs up to 35 feet long. Deer Flat is a group site for up to 70 people. Picnic tables, fire grills, garbage bins, drinking water, gray-water sump, and flush toilets are provided. A store, gas, and propane are available one mile east. Raft-launching facilities are nearby. Some facilities are wheelchair accessible. Leashed pets are permitted.

Reservations, fees: Reservations are accepted for the Deer Flat group site at 877/444-6777 ($10 reservation fee) or www.recreation.gov ($9 reservation fee); reservations are not accepted for single sites. Sites are $15 per night, $5 per night per additional vehicle; the Deer Flat group site is $100 per night. Open mid-May-late September, weather permitting.

Directions: From Roseburg on I-5, take Exit 120. Drive east on Highway 138 for 47 miles to Forest Road 4750. Turn right and drive south a short distance to the campground entrance road on the right.

Contact: Umpqua National Forest, North Umpqua Ranger District, 541/496-3532, www.fs.usda.gov/umpqua.

95 EAGLE ROCK

Scenic rating: 9

on the North Umpqua River in Umpqua National Forest

Map 5.4, page 264

Eagle Rock camp sits next to the North Umpqua River and adjacent to the Boulder Creek Wilderness. It is named after Eagle Rock, which, along with Rattlesnake Rock, towers above the campground. The camp offers outstanding views of these unusual rock formations. It gets moderate use, heavy on weekends. The camp sits at 1,676 feet elevation near Boulder Flat, a major launch point for rafting. Fishing here is restricted to the use of artificial lures with a single barbless hook.

Campsites, facilities: There are 25 sites for tents or RVs up to 30 feet long, including two double sites. Picnic tables and fire grills are provided. Vault toilets, garbage bins, and gray-water disposal are available. There is no drinking water. A store, propane, and ice are within five miles. Some facilities are wheelchair accessible. Leashed pets are permitted.

Reservations, fees: Reservations are not accepted. Sites are $10 per night, $5 per night per additional vehicle. Open mid-May-October, weather permitting.

Directions: From Roseburg, drive east on Highway 138 for 53 miles to the campground on the left.

Contact: Umpqua National Forest, North Umpqua Ranger District, 541/496-3532, www. fs.usda.gov/umpqua.

96 BOULDER FLAT

Scenic rating: 8

on the North Umpqua River in Umpqua National Forest

Map 5.4, page 264   **BEST (**

Boulder Flat campground is nestled along the banks of the North Umpqua River at the confluence with Boulder Creek. There's good trout fishing here (fly-fishing only) and outstanding scenery. The camp sits at a major launching point for white-water rafting. Across the river from the campground, a trail follows Boulder Creek north for 10.5 miles through the Boulder Creek Wilderness, a climb in elevation from 2,000 to 5,400 feet. It's a good thumper for backpackers. Access to the trail is at Soda Springs Dam, two miles east of the camp. A little over a mile to the east you can see some huge, dramatic pillars of volcanic rock, colored with lichen.

Campsites, facilities: There are nine sites for tents or RVs up to 24 feet long. Picnic tables, garbage bins, and fire grills are provided. Vault toilets and gray-water sump are available. There is no drinking water. A store, propane, and ice are within five miles. A raft launch is on-site. Some facilities are wheelchair accessible. Leashed pets are permitted.

Reservations, fees: Reservations are not accepted. Sites are $10 per night, $5 per night per additional vehicle. Open year-round.

Directions: From Roseburg, drive east on Highway 138 for 54 miles to the campground on the left.

Contact: Umpqua National Forest, North Umpqua Ranger District, 541/496-3532, www. fs.usda.gov/umpqua.

97 TOKETEE LAKE

Scenic rating: 7

on Toketee Lake in Umpqua National Forest

Map 5.4, page 264

Located just north of Toketee Lake, this campground sits at an elevation of 2,200 feet. The North Umpqua River Trail passes near camp and continues east along the river for many miles. Die-hard hikers can also take the trail west toward the Boulder Creek Wilderness. Toketee Lake, a 97-acre reservoir, offers a good population of brown and rainbow trout and many recreation options. A worthwhile point of interest is Toketee Falls, just west of the lake turnoff. Another is Umpqua Hot Springs, a few miles northeast of the camp. The area sustains a wide variety of wildlife; you might see bald eagles, beavers, a variety of ducks and geese, great blue herons, kingfishers, and otters in fall and winter.

Campsites, facilities: There are 33 sites for tents or RVs up to 22 feet long and one group site for up to 50 people. Picnic tables and fire grills are provided. Vault toilets are available, but there is no drinking water or garbage disposal. Boat docks and launching facilities are nearby. Leashed pets are permitted.

Reservations, fees: Reservations are not accepted. Sites are $10-15 per night, $5 per night per additional vehicle, and $50 per night for the group site. Open year-round.

Directions: From Roseburg, drive east on Highway 138 for 59 miles to Forest Road 34. Turn left (north) and drive 1.5 miles to the campground on the right.

Contact: Umpqua National Forest, Diamond Lake Ranger District, 541/498-2531, www.fs.usda.gov/umpqua.

98 EAST LEMOLO

Scenic rating: 8
on Lemolo Lake in Umpqua National Forest

Map 5.4, page 264

This campground is on the southeastern shore of Lemolo Lake, where boating and fishing are some of the recreation possibilities. Boats with motors and personal watercraft are allowed. The North Umpqua River and its adjacent trail lie just beyond the north shore of the lake. If you hike for two miles northwest of the lake, you can reach spectacular Lemolo Falls. Large German brown trout, a wild, native fish, can be taken on troll and fly. Lemolo Lake also provides fishing for brook trout, kokanee, and a sprinkling of rainbow trout.

Campsites, facilities: There are 15 sites for tents or small RVs up to 22 feet long. Picnic

tables and fire rings are provided. Vault toilets are available. There is no drinking water and garbage must be packed out. Boat docks, launching facilities, boat rentals, dump station, restaurants, a store, coin laundry, and showers are nearby. Leashed pets are permitted.

Reservations, fees: Reservations are not accepted. Sites are $10 per night, $5 per night per additional vehicle. Open mid-May-late October, weather permitting.

Directions: From Roseburg, drive east on Highway 138 for 73 miles to Forest Road 2610 (three miles east of Clearwater Falls). Turn left (north) and drive three miles to Forest Road 2614. Turn right and drive two miles to Forest Road 2614-430. Turn left and drive a short distance to the campground at the end of the road.

Contact: Umpqua National Forest, Diamond Lake Ranger District, 541/498-2531, www.fs.usda.gov/umpqua.

99 POOLE CREEK

Scenic rating: 8
on Lemolo Lake in Umpqua National Forest

Map 5.4, page 264

Poole Creek campground on the western shore of Lemolo Lake isn't far from Lemolo Lake Resort, which is open for recreation year-round. The camp is just south of the mouth of Poole Creek in a lodgepole pine, mountain hemlock, and Shasta red fir forest. This is by far the most popular U.S. Forest Service camp at the lake, especially with water-skiers, who are allowed to ski in designated areas of the lake.

Campsites, facilities: There are 60 sites for tents or RVs up to 35 feet long and one group site for up to 60 people. Picnic tables and fire grills are provided. Drinking water and vault toilets are available. A grocery store, a restaurant, boat docks, launching facilities, and rentals are nearby. Leashed pets are permitted.

Reservations, fees: Reservations are accepted at 877/444-6777 or www.recreation.gov ($10 reservation fee). Single sites are $15 per night, double sites are $20 per night, $5 per night per additional vehicle, and $72-85 per night for the group camp. Open late April-late October, weather permitting.

Directions: From Roseburg, drive east on Highway 138 for 73 miles to Forest Road 2610 (Bird's Point Road). Turn left (north) and drive four miles to the signed turnoff for the campground entrance on the right.

Contact: Umpqua National Forest, Diamond Lake Ranger District, 541/498-2531, www.fs.usda.gov/umpqua.

100 INLET

Scenic rating: 5
on Lemolo Lake in Umpqua National Forest

Map 5.4, page 264

Inlet campground sits on the eastern inlet of Lemolo Lake, hidden in the deep, green, and quiet forest where the North Umpqua River rushes into Lemolo Reservoir. The camp is just across the road from the North Umpqua River Trail, which is routed east into the Oregon Cascades Recreation Area and the Mount Thielsen Wilderness. Lemolo Lake exceeds 100 feet in depth in some spots; boating and fishing for brook trout, kokanee, and rainbow trout are some recreation possibilities. (Boats with motors and personal watercraft are allowed.) Two miles northwest of the lake lies spectacular Lemolo Falls, a good hike.

Campsites, facilities: There are 14 sites for tents or RVs up to 22 feet long. Picnic tables and fire grills are provided. Vault toilets are available. There is no drinking water and garbage must be packed out. Boat docks, launching facilities, rentals, a restaurant, groceries, and a gas station are available nearby. Leashed pets are permitted.

Reservations, fees: Reservations are accepted at 877/444-6777 or www.recreation.gov ($10 reservation fee). Sites are $10 per night, $5 per night per additional vehicle. Open mid-May-late October, weather permitting.

Directions: From Roseburg, drive east on Highway 138 for 73 miles to Forest Road 2610. Turn left (north) and drive three miles to Forest Road 2614. Turn right (east) and drive three miles to the campground.

Contact: Umpqua National Forest, Diamond Lake Ranger District, 541/498-2531, www.fs.usda.gov/umpqua.

101 BUNKER HILL

Scenic rating: 7
on Lemolo Lake in Umpqua National Forest

Map 5.4, page 264

Bunker Hill campground, on the northwest shore of Lemolo Reservoir, is in a heavily wooded area of lodgepole pine. Fishing is excellent for kokanee as well as brook, rainbow, and large native brown trout. Nearby hiking trails lead to Lemolo Falls, the North Umpqua River, and the Pacific Crest Trail.

Campsites, facilities: There are eight sites for tents or RVs up to 22 feet long. Picnic tables and fire rings are provided. Vault toilets are available. There is no drinking water and garbage must be packed out. A boat ramp, boat rentals, a dump station, a restaurant, coin laundry, and coin showers are available 1.5 miles away at Lemolo Lake Resort. Leashed pets are permitted.

Reservations, fees: Reservations are not accepted. Sites are $10 per night, $5 per night per additional vehicle. Open May-October, weather permitting.

Directions: From Roseburg, drive east on Highway 138 for 73 miles to Bird's Point Road/Forest Road 2610. Turn left and drive 5.5 miles (crossing the dam) to Forest Road 2612. Turn right and drive to the camp at the north end of the lake.

Contact: Umpqua National Forest, Diamond Lake Ranger District, 541/498-2531, www.fs.usda.gov/umpqua; Lemolo Lake Resort 541/643-0750.

102 LEMOLO LAKE RV PARK

🚶🚴🛶🛥️🚂❄️🐕♿🚐⛺

Scenic rating: 7
in Umpqua National Forest

Map 5.4, page 264

Lemolo Lake is situated high in the Cascade Mountains at just over 4,000 feet elevation. This RV park is set up for folks to bring their own boats and enjoy the lake. Boating, waterskiing, wakeboarding, and Jet Skis are all popular, along, of course, with fishing and swimming, on the lake (40-mph speed limit). Each campground reservation includes free boat launch. There are also miles of hiking trails in the vicinity, plus Crater Lake National Park and Diamond Lake are a quick drive away. In winter, cross-country skiing is popular, and an extensive snowmobile loop runs through the property.

Campsites, facilities: There are 28 sites, some with full or partial hookups, for tents or RVs of any length; some sights are pull-through. There are also five cabins and a hotel available. Picnic tables and fire rings are provided. Drinking water, flush toilets, coin showers, and coin laundry are available. A restaurant and store are on the premises. A boat launch and boat rentals are available. Generators are not permitted. Some facilities are wheelchair accessible. Leashed pets are permitted.

Reservations, fees: Reservations are accepted at 541/643-0750. RV sites with full hookups are $35 per night, RV sites with partial hookups and/or tent sites are $30 per night, cabins are $180 per night, $2.50 per person for more than four adults, $15 per pet per night. Open year-round.

Directions: From Roseburg, drive east on Highway 138 (Diamond Lake Highway) for about 73 miles to Birds Point Road. Turn left on Birds Point Road and drive five miles to the resort.

Contact: Lemolo Lake RV Park, 541/643-0750, www.lemololakeresort.com.

103 TIMPANOGAS

🚶🛶🚂🐕♿🚐⛺

Scenic rating: 8
on Timpanogas Lake in Willamette National Forest

Map 5.4, page 264

Timpanogas Lake is the headwaters of the Middle Fork Willamette River. This campground, at 5,200 feet elevation, is situated in a stand of grand, noble, and silver fir. Fishing for brook trout and cutthroat is good; only non-motorized boating is permitted. Nearby activities include 23 miles of hiking trails in the Timpanogas Basin trails, with views of the Cowhorn Mountains, Diamond Peak, and Sawtooth. Warning: Time it wrong (July-August) and the mosquitoes will eat you alive if you forget insect repellent.

Campsites, facilities: There are 10 sites for tents or RVs up to 24 feet long. Picnic tables, garbage bins, and fire rings are provided. Drinking water, vault toilets, and firewood are available. A primitive boat ramp is nearby, but no boats with motors are allowed. Some facilities are wheelchair accessible. Leashed pets are permitted.

Reservations, fees: Reservations are not accepted. Sites are $8 per night, $4 per night per additional vehicle. Open June-October, weather permitting.

Directions: From Eugene, drive south on I-5 for five miles to Exit 188 and Highway 58. Turn east and drive 35 miles to the town of Oakridge. Continue east on Highway 58 for two miles to Kitson Springs Road. Turn right and drive 0.5 mile to Forest Road 21. Turn right and drive 32 miles to Forest Road 2154. Turn left and drive about 10 miles to the campground on the left.

Contact: Willamette National Forest, Middle Fork Ranger District, 541/782-2283, www.fs.usda.gov/willamette.

104 WOLF CREEK

Scenic rating: 6
on the Little River in Umpqua National Forest

Map 5.4, page 264

This pretty Little River camp is located at the entrance to the national forest, near the Wolf Creek Civilian Conservation Center. It is set at an elevation of 1,100 feet, with easy access to civilization. The campground has abundant wildflowers in the spring. If you want to get deeper into the Cascades, Hemlock Lake and Lake of the Woods are about 21 and 15 miles east, respectively.

Campsites, facilities: There are five sites for tents or RVs up to 30 feet long and three sites for tents only. There is also a group site for up to 150 people. Picnic tables and fire grills are provided. Flush toilets, drinking water, a covered pavilion for groups, garbage bins, horseshoe pits, a softball field, and a volleyball court are available. Note that if the group site is taken, some recreation facilities may not be available to single-site campers. Some facilities are wheelchair accessible. Leashed pets are permitted.

Reservations, fees: Reservations are accepted for the group site only at 877/444-6777 ($10 reservation fee) or www.recreation.gov ($9 reservation fee). Sites are $15 per night, $5 per night per additional vehicle, and $110 per night for the group site. Open mid-May-September, weather permitting.

Directions: From Roseburg on I-5, take Exit 120. Drive east on Highway 138 for 18 miles to Glide and County Road 17. Turn right (southeast) and drive 12 miles (the road becomes Little River Road) to the campground on the right.

Contact: Umpqua National Forest, North Umpqua Ranger District, 541/496-3532, www.fs.usda.gov/umpqua.

105 COOLWATER

Scenic rating: 6
on the Little River in Umpqua National Forest

Map 5.4, page 264

Coolwater campground (1,300 feet elevation) along the banks of the Little River gets moderate use. It features a pretty forest setting with some scenic hiking trails nearby. Overhang Trail is within 0.5 mile of the campground. Fishing and swimming are also options here. Scenic Grotto Falls can be reached by traveling north on Forest Road 2703 (across the road from the camp). Near the falls, you'll find Emile Grove, home of a thicket of old-growth Douglas fir and the huge "Bill Taft Tree," named after the former president.

Campsites, facilities: There are seven sites for tents or RVs up to 24 feet long. Picnic tables and fire grills are provided. Drinking water, vault toilets, and garbage disposal are available. Leashed pets are permitted.

Reservations, fees: Reservations are not accepted. Sites are $10 per night, $5 per night per additional vehicle. Open year-round, weather permitting.

Directions: From Roseburg on I-5, take Exit 120. Drive east on Highway 138 for 18 miles to Glide and County Road 17. Turn right (southeast) and drive 15.5 miles (County Road 17 becomes Little River Road) to the campground on the right.

Contact: Umpqua National Forest, North Umpqua Ranger District, 541/496-3532, www.fs.usda.gov/umpqua.

106 WHITE CREEK

Scenic rating: 6
on the Little River in Umpqua National Forest

Map 5.4, page 264

Hiking and fishing are two of the recreation options at this campground set at the confluence of White Creek and the Little River. There is a sandy beach on shallow Little River, and waterfalls are in the area.

Campsites, facilities: There is an open parking area for tents or RVs up to 16 feet long, as well as three walk-in sites and one site near the parking lot. Picnic tables, fire grills, and garbage bins are provided. Drinking water and vault toilets are available. Leashed pets are permitted.

Reservations, fees: Reservations are not accepted. Sites are $10 per night, $5 per night per additional vehicle. Open year-round, weather permitting.

Directions: From Roseburg on I-5, take Exit 120. Drive east on Highway 138 for 18 miles to Glide and County Road 17. Turn right (southeast) and drive 18 miles (the road becomes Little River Road) to Forest Road 2792 (Red Butte Road). Bear right and drive 0.25 mile to the campground on the left.

Contact: Umpqua National Forest, North Umpqua Ranger District, 541/496-3532, www. fs.usda.gov/umpqua.

107 LAKE IN THE WOODS

Scenic rating: 7

on Lake in the Woods in Umpqua National Forest

Map 5.4, page 264

The shore of little Lake in the Woods is the setting of this camp, which makes a nice home base for several good hikes. One of them leaves the camp and heads south for about three miles to the Hemlock Lake Campground. Two other nearby trails provide short, scenic hikes to either Hemlock Falls or Yakso Falls. The campground sits at 3,200 feet elevation. This is a man-made, four-acre lake, eight feet at its deepest point. Boats without motors are allowed.

Campsites, facilities: There are eight sites for tents or RVs up to 35 feet long, one site for tents only, and two double sites. Picnic tables, fire grills, and garbage bins are provided. Drinking

water and vault toilets are available. Leashed pets are permitted.

Reservations, fees: Reservations are not accepted. Sites are $10 per night, $5 per night per additional vehicle. Open late May-late October, weather permitting.

Directions: From Roseburg on I-5, take Exit 120. Drive east on Highway 138 for 18 miles to Glide and County Road 17. Turn right (southeast) and drive 18 miles (the road becomes Little River Road) to Forest Road 27. Continue 11 miles to the campground. The last seven miles are gravel.

Contact: Umpqua National Forest, North Umpqua Ranger District, 541/496-3532, www. fs.usda.gov/umpqua.

108 HEMLOCK LAKE

Scenic rating: 8

on Hemlock Lake in Umpqua National Forest

Map 5.4, page 264　　　　　　**BEST (**

This is a little-known jewel of a spot. For starters, it's set along the shore of Hemlock Lake at 4,400 feet elevation. This is a 28-acre, manufactured reservoir that is 33 feet at its deepest point. An eight-mile loop trail called the Yellow Jacket Loop is just south of the campground. Another trail leaves camp and heads north for about three miles to the Lake in the Woods campground. From there, it's just a short hike to either Hemlock Falls or Yakso Falls, both spectacularly scenic.

Campsites, facilities: There are nine sites for tents or RVs up to 35 feet long, three sites for tents only, and one double site. Picnic tables, fire grills, and garbage bins are provided. Vault toilets are available, but there is no drinking water. Boat docks and launching facilities are nearby. No motors are allowed on the lake. Leashed pets are permitted.

Reservations, fees: Reservations are not accepted. Sites are $10 per night, $5 per night per additional vehicle. Open year-round, weather permitting.

Directions: From Roseburg on I-5, take Exit 120. Drive east on Highway 138 for 18 miles to Glide and County Road 17. Turn right (southeast) and drive 32 miles to the campground on the right.

Contact: Umpqua National Forest, North Umpqua Ranger District, 541/496-3532, www.fs.usda.gov/umpqua.

109 WHITEHORSE FALLS

Scenic rating: 8

on the Clearwater River in Umpqua National Forest

Map 5.4, page 264

Whitehorse Falls campground sits along the Clearwater River, one of the coldest streams in Umpqua National Forest. Even though the camp is adjacent to the highway, the setting is primitive. It is shaded by old-growth Douglas fir and is located at an elevation of 3,790 feet. Pretty Clearwater Falls, a few miles east, makes for a good side trip. Other recreation options include fishing and hiking.

Campsites, facilities: There are five sites for tents or RVs up to 25 feet long. Picnic tables and fire grills are provided. Vault toilets are available, but there is no drinking water or garbage service. Leashed pets are permitted.

Reservations, fees: Reservations are not accepted. Sites are $10 per night, $5 per night per additional vehicle. Open June-late October, weather permitting.

Directions: From Roseburg, drive east on Highway 138 for 66 miles to the campground on the left.

Contact: Umpqua National Forest, Diamond Lake Ranger District, 541/498-2531, www.fs.usda.gov/umpqua.

110 CLEARWATER FALLS

Scenic rating: 8

on the Clearwater River in Umpqua National Forest

Map 5.4, page 264

The main attraction at this campground along the banks of the Clearwater River is the nearby cascading section of stream called Clearwater Falls. Hiking and fishing opportunities abound. The camp sits at an elevation of 4,100 feet.

Campsites, facilities: There are 12 sites for tents or RVs up to 30 feet long. Picnic tables and fire grills are provided. Vault toilets are available. There is no drinking water and garbage must be packed out. Leashed pets are permitted.

Reservations, fees: Reservations are not accepted. Sites are $10 per night, $5 per night per additional vehicle. Open mid-May-October, weather permitting.

Directions: From Roseburg, drive east on Highway 138 for 70 miles to a signed turn for Clearwater Falls. Turn right and drive to the campground.

Contact: Umpqua National Forest, Diamond Lake Ranger District, 541/498-2531, www.fs.usda.gov/umpqua.

111 BROKEN ARROW

Scenic rating: 6

on Diamond Lake in Umpqua National Forest

Map 5.4, page 264

Broken Arrow campground sits at 5,190 feet elevation near the south shore of Diamond Lake, the largest natural lake in Umpqua National Forest. Set back from the lake, it is surrounded by lodgepole pine and features views of Mount Bailey and Mount Thielsen. Bicycling, boating, fishing, hiking, and swimming keep visitors busy here. Diamond Lake is adjacent to Crater Lake National Park, Mount Bailey, and the

Mount Thielsen Wilderness, all of which offer a variety of recreation opportunities year-round. Diamond Lake is quite popular with anglers because of its good trout trolling, particularly in early summer.

Campsites, facilities: There are 130 sites for tents or RVs up to 40 feet long and four group sites that accommodate 40-104 people. Picnic tables, fire grills, and garbage bins are provided. Restrooms with flush toilets and showers, a dump station, and drinking water are available. Boat docks, launching facilities, and rentals are nearby. Some facilities are wheelchair accessible. Leashed pets are permitted.

Reservations, fees: Reservations are accepted at 877/444-6777 ($10 reservation fee) or www.recreation.gov ($9 reservation fee). Sites are $15-20 per night, $5 per night per additional vehicle, and the group sites are $70-165 per night. Open June-mid-September.

Directions: From Roseburg, drive east on Highway 138 for 78.5 miles to Diamond Lake Loop (Forest Road 4795). Turn right (south) and drive four miles (along the east shore) to the campground turnoff road. Turn right and continue one mile to the camp on the left at the southern end of the lake.

Contact: Umpqua National Forest, Diamond Lake Ranger District, 541/498-2531, www.fs.usda.gov/umpqua.

112 THIELSEN VIEW

Scenic rating: 7
on Diamond Lake in Umpqua National Forest

Map 5.4, page 264

This campground sits along the west shore of Diamond Lake in the shadow of majestic Mount Bailey. There is a beautiful view of Mount Thielsen from here.

Diamond Lake is popular with anglers and for boating, fishing, hiking, and swimming and the 11 miles of bike trails that keep everyone else busy. Nearby Crater Lake National Park, Mount Bailey, and the Mount Thielsen Wilderness offer recreation opportunities year-round.

Campsites, facilities: There are 60 sites for tents or RVs up to 30 feet long. Picnic tables, fire grills, and garbage bins are provided. Drinking water, vault toilets, and gray-water waste sumps are available. Boat docks and launching facilities are located adjacent to the campground, and boats can be rented at a resort five miles away. Some facilities are wheelchair accessible. Leashed pets are permitted.

Reservations, fees: Reservations are not accepted. Sites are $15-20 per night, $5 per night per additional vehicle. Open mid-May-mid-September, weather permitting.

Directions: From Roseburg, drive east on Highway 138 for 78.5 miles to Diamond Lake Loop (Forest Road 4795). Turn right and drive a short distance to the junction with the loop road. Continue on the loop road and drive four miles to the campground on the left.

Contact: Umpqua National Forest, Diamond Lake Ranger District, 541/498-2531, www.fs.usda.gov/umpqua.

113 DIAMOND LAKE

Scenic rating: 9
on Diamond Lake in Umpqua National Forest

Map 5.4, page 264

Diamond Lake is a true gem of the Cascades, and there's finally hope the trout fishing will return to its once famous status. This extremely popular camp along the east shore of Diamond Lake has all the luxuries: flush toilets, showers, and drinking water. There are campfire programs every Friday and Saturday night in the summer. Jet Skis and other motorized watercraft are not allowed. Bring your mosquito repellent.

Campsites, facilities: There are 238 sites for tents or RVs up to 45 feet long. Picnic tables, garbage bins, and fire grills are provided. Restrooms with flush toilets and showers, drinking water, a dump station, and an amphitheater are available. Boat docks, launching facilities, and a fish-cleaning station are available. Boat rentals are nearby. Leashed pets are permitted.

Reservations, fees: Reservations are recommended and are accepted at 877/444-6777 ($10 reservation fee) or www.recreation.gov ($9 reservation fee). Sites are $16-27 per night, $5 per night per additional vehicle. Open late April-late October, weather permitting.

Directions: From Roseburg, drive east on Highway 138 for 78.5 miles to Diamond Lake Loop (Forest Road 4795). Turn right and drive a short distance to the junction with a loop road. Turn right (south) and drive two miles (along the east shore) to the campground on the right.

Contact: Umpqua National Forest, Diamond Lake Ranger District, 541/498-2531, www.fs.usda.gov/umpqua.

114 CAMP COMFORT
🏃 🛖 🐕 ♿ 🚐 ⛺

Scenic rating: 6
on the South Umpqua River in Umpqua National Forest

Map 5.4, page 264

Camp Comfort is located near the upper South Umpqua River, deep in the Umpqua National Forest, at an elevation of 2,000 feet. Large old-growth cedars shade the campsites. No fishing is permitted. South Umpqua Falls (you will pass the access point while driving to this camp) makes a good side trip. Nearby trailheads provide access to Rogue-Umpqua Divide Wilderness (a map of Umpqua National Forest will be helpful in locating them).

Campsites, facilities: There are five sites for tents or RVs up to 22 feet long. Picnic tables and fire grills are provided. A vault toilet and garbage bins are available. There is no drinking water. Some facilities are wheelchair accessible. Leashed pets are permitted.

Reservations, fees: Reservations are not accepted. Sites are $10 per night, $5 per night per additional vehicle. Open May-October.

Directions: At Canyonville on I-5, take Exit 99 to County Road 1. Drive east on County Road 1 for 25 miles to Tiller and County Road 46. Turn left and drive six miles northeast (County Road 46 turns into South Umpqua Road/Forest Road 28). Continue northeast and drive 22 miles to the camp on the right.

Contact: Umpqua National Forest, Tiller Ranger District, 541/825-3100, www.fs.usda.gov/umpqua.

115 BOULDER CREEK
🏃 🛖 🐕 ♿ 🚐 ⛺

Scenic rating: 4
on the South Umpqua River in Umpqua National Forest

Map 5.4, page 264

Set at 1,400 feet elevation, this campground hugs the banks of the South Umpqua River near Boulder Creek. Unfortunately, no fishing is allowed here, but pleasant side trips include the fishing ladder and waterfall at nearby South Umpqua Falls.

Campsites, facilities: There are seven sites for tents or RVs up to 22 feet long. Picnic tables, fire grills, and garbage bins are provided. Vault toilets are available. There is no drinking water. Some facilities are wheelchair accessible. Leashed pets are permitted.

Reservations, fees: Reservations are not accepted. Sites are $10 per night, $5 per night per additional vehicle. Open May-October, weather permitting.

Directions: At Canyonville on I-5, take Exit 99 to County Road 1. Drive east on County Road 1 for 25 miles to Tiller and County Road 46. Turn left, then drive six miles northeast (County Road 46 turns into South Umpqua Road/Forest Road 28). Continue northeast and drive seven miles to the camp.

Contact: Umpqua National Forest, Tiller Ranger District, 541/825-3100, www.fs.usda.gov/umpqua.

116 DUMONT CREEK

Scenic rating: 4

on the South Umpqua River in Umpqua National Forest

Map 5.4, page 264

Dumont Creek is set at 1,300 feet elevation along the banks of the South Umpqua River, just above the mouth of Dumont Creek. Quiet, primitive, and remote, it gets moderate to heavy use. A short trail leads to a small beach on the river. No fishing is allowed at this camp, and there is no trailer turnaround here. Boulder Creek, just a few miles east, provides a camping alternative. A good side trip is nearby South Umpqua Falls, a beautiful, wide waterfall featuring a fish ladder and a platform so you can watch the fish struggle upstream.

Campsites, facilities: There are three sites for tents. Picnic tables, fire grills, and garbage bins are provided. Vault toilets are available, but there is no drinking water. Some facilities are wheelchair accessible. Leashed pets are permitted.

Reservations, fees: Reservations are not accepted. Sites are $10 per night, $5 per night per additional vehicle. Open May-October, weather permitting.

Directions: At Canyonville on I-5, take Exit 99 to County Road 1. Drive east on County Road 1 for 25 miles to Tiller and County Road 46. Turn left and drive six miles northeast (County Road 46 turns into South Umpqua Road/Forest Road 28). Continue northeast and drive 5.5 miles to the camp.

Contact: Umpqua National Forest, Tiller Ranger District, 541/825-3100, www.fs.usda.gov/umpqua.

117 COVER

Scenic rating: 4

on Jackson Creek in Umpqua National Forest

Map 5.4, page 264

If you want quiet, this camp set at 1,700 feet elevation along the banks of Jackson Creek is the right place, since hardly anyone knows about it. Cover gets light use during the summer. During the fall hunting season, however, it is known to fill. If you head east to Forest Road 68 and follow the road south, you'll have access to a major trail into the Rogue-Umpqua Divide Wilderness. Be sure not to miss the world's largest sugar pine tree, a few miles west of camp. No fishing is allowed here.

Campsites, facilities: There are seven sites for tents or RVs up to 22 feet long. Picnic tables, fire grills, and garbage bins are provided. Drinking water and vault toilets are available. Some facilities are wheelchair accessible. Leashed pets are permitted.

Reservations, fees: Reservations are not accepted. Sites are $10 per night, $5 per night per additional vehicle. Open May-October, weather permitting.

Directions: At Canyonville on I-5, take Exit 99 to County Road 1. Drive east on County Road 1 for 25 miles to Tiller and County Road 46. Turn left and drive five miles to Forest Road 29 (Jackson Creek Road). Turn right and drive east for 12 miles to the campground on the right.

Contact: Umpqua National Forest, Tiller Ranger District, 541/825-3100, www.fs.usda.gov/umpqua.

118 QUINN MEADOW HORSE CAMP

Scenic rating: 8

near Quinn Creek in Deschutes National Forest

Map 5.5, page 265

This scenic campground (elevation 5,100 feet) is open only to horse camping and gets high use. The Elk-Devil's Trail and Wickiup Plains Trail offer access to the Three Sisters Wilderness. There's also a horse route to Devil's Lake via Katsuk Trail.

Campsites, facilities: There are 26 sites for tents or RVs up to 40 feet long. Picnic tables and fire rings are provided. Horse corrals, stalls, and a manure-disposal site are available. Drinking water, vault toilets, and garbage bins are also available. Some facilities are wheelchair accessible. Leashed pets are permitted.

Reservations, fees: Reservations are accepted in summer at 877/444-6777 ($10 reservation fee) or www.recreation.gov ($9 reservation fee). Two-horse corral sites are $14, four-horse corral sites are $18, $7-9 per night per additional vehicle. Open late June-September, weather permitting.

Directions: From Bend, drive southwest on Cascades Lakes Highway (also called Century Drive Highway and County Road 46) for 31.2 miles to the campground entrance on the left.

Contact: Deschutes National Forest, Bend-Fort Rock Ranger District, 541/383-4000, www.fs.usda.gov/centraloregon.

119 DEVIL'S LAKE WALK-IN

Scenic rating: 8

on Devil's Lake in Deschutes National Forest

Map 5.5, page 265

This walk-in campground borders the shore of a scenic alpine lake with aqua-jade water and fishing access. Devil's Lake, set at 5,500 feet, is a popular rafting and canoeing spot, and several trailheads lead from the lake into the wilderness. No motorized boats are allowed. The Elk-Devil's Trail and Wickiup Plains Trail offer access to the Three Sisters Wilderness. There's also a horse route to Quinn Meadow Horse Camp via Katsuk Trail.

Campsites, facilities: There are 11 walk-in sites for tents only. Picnic tables and fire grills are provided. Vault toilets are available. There

is no drinking water, and garbage must be packed out. Leashed pets are permitted.

Reservations, fees: Reservations are not accepted. There is no fee, but a Northwest Forest Pass ($5 daily fee or $30 annual fee per parked vehicle) is required. Open June-October, weather permitting.

Directions: From Bend, drive southwest on Cascades Lakes Highway (Century Drive Highway, which becomes County Road 46) for 28.7 miles to the parking area. Walk 200 yards to the campground.

Contact: Deschutes National Forest, Bend-Fort Rock Ranger District, 541/383-4000, www.fs.usda.gov/centraloregon.

120 SODA CREEK

Scenic rating: 5

near Sparks Lake in Deschutes National Forest

Map 5.5, page 265

This campground, nestled between two meadows in a pastoral setting, is on the road to Sparks Lake. Boating—particularly canoeing—is ideal at Sparks Lake, about a two-mile drive away. Also at the lake, a loop trail hugs the shore; about 0.5 mile of it is paved and barrier-free. Only fly-fishing is permitted. The camp sits at 5,450 feet elevation.

Note: The Forest Service may close the campground for stream restoration work. Call to confirm access.

Campsites, facilities: There are six sites for tents or RVs up to 30 feet long and one multiple site. Picnic tables and fire grills are provided. Vault toilets are available. There is no drinking water, and garbage must be packed out. Leashed pets are permitted.

Reservations, fees: Reservations are not accepted. Single sites are $10 per night, multiple sites are $20 per night, $5 per night per extra vehicle. Open June-October, weather permitting.

Directions: From Bend, drive southwest on Cascades Lakes Highway (also called Century Drive Highway and County Road 46) for 26.2

miles to Forest Road 400 (at sign for Sparks Lake). Turn left (east) and drive 25 yards to the campground.

Contact: Deschutes National Forest, Bend-Fort Rock Ranger District, 541/383-4000, www.fs.usda.gov/centraloregon.

121 TODD LAKE HIKE-IN

Scenic rating: 8
near Todd Lake in Deschutes National Forest

Map 5.5, page 265

Todd Lake is a trailhead camp, with a trail access point here for hikers and horses to the Three Sisters Wilderness. One of numerous camps in the area that offer a pristine mountain experience yet can be reached by car, small Todd Lake campground sits 0.5 mile from the shore of an alpine lake at 6,200 feet elevation. It's popular for canoeing and offers great views. No bikes or horses are allowed on the trail around the lake.

Campsites, facilities: There are three hike-in tent sites. Picnic tables and fire grills are provided. A vault toilet is available. There is no drinking water, and garbage must be packed out. Leashed pets are permitted.

Reservations, fees: Reservations are not accepted. There is no fee for camping, but a Northwest Forest Pass ($5 daily fee or $30 annual fee per parked vehicle) is required. Open July-October, weather permitting.

Directions: From Bend, drive southwest on Cascades Lakes Highway (also called Century Drive Highway and County Road 46) for 24 miles to Forest Road 370. Turn right (north) and drive 0.5 mile to the parking area. Hike 0.5 mile to the campground.

Contact: Deschutes National Forest, Bend-Fort Rock Ranger District, 541/383-4000, www.fs.usda.gov/centraloregon.

122 POINT

Scenic rating: 8
on Elk Lake in Deschutes National Forest

Map 5.5, page 265

Point campground is situated along the shore of Elk Lake at an elevation of 4,900 feet. Fishing for kokanee salmon and brook trout can be good; hiking is another option. Swimming and water sports are popular during warm weather.

Campsites, facilities: There are eight sites for tents or RVs up to 26 feet long, and one group site. Picnic tables and fire grills are provided. Vault toilets and garbage service are available. Drinking water is usually available. Boat docks and launching facilities are on-site. A store, restaurant, and propane are at Elk Lake Resort, one mile away. Leashed pets are permitted.

Reservations, fees: Reservations are accepted at 877/444-6777 ($10 reservation fee) or www.recreation.gov ($9 reservation fee). Sites are $14 per night, $7 per night per additional vehicle; the group site is $26 for up to 15 people and four vehicles. Open late May-late September, weather permitting.

Directions: From Bend, drive southwest on Cascades Lakes Highway (Century Drive Highway, which becomes County Road 46) for 34 miles to the campground on the left.

Contact: Deschutes National Forest, Bend-Fort Rock Ranger District, 541/383-4000, www.fs.usda.gov/centraloregon.

123 ELK LAKE

Scenic rating: 8
on Elk Lake in Deschutes National Forest

Map 5.5, page 265

This campground hugs the shore of Elk Lake at 4,900 feet elevation. It is adjacent to Elk Lake Resort, which has a store, a restaurant, and propane. Elk Lake is popular for windsurfing and sailing.

Campsites, facilities: There are 22 sites for

tents or RVs up to 30 feet long, but sites are best suited for tents. Picnic tables and fire grills are provided. Vault toilets, drinking water, and garbage service are available. Boat-launching facilities are on-site. Boat rentals can be obtained nearby. Leashed pets are permitted.

Reservations, fees: Reservations are not accepted. Sites are $14 per night, $7 per night per additional vehicle. Open mid-May-mid-September, weather permitting.

Directions: From Bend, drive southwest on Cascades Lakes Highway (Century Drive Highway, which becomes County Road 46) and drive 33.1 miles to the campground at the north end of Elk Lake.

Contact: Deschutes National Forest, Bend-Fort Rock Ranger District, 541/383-4000, www.fs.usda.gov/centraloregon.

124 LITTLE FAWN

Scenic rating: 5
on Elk Lake in Deschutes National Forest

Map 5.5, page 265

Choose between sites on the water's edge or nestled in the forest at this campground along the eastern shore of Elk Lake. Afternoon winds are common here, making this a popular spot for sailing and windsurfing. Fishing for kokanee salmon and brook trout can be good; hiking is another option. Swimming and water sports are popular during warm weather. A play area for children can be found at one of the lake's inlets. The camp sits at 4,900 feet elevation, with Little Fawn Group Camp located just beyond Little Fawn campground.

Campsites, facilities: There are 20 sites for tents or RVs up to 36 feet long and eight group sites for up to 75 people. Picnic tables and fire grills are provided. Vault toilets, drinking water, and garbage service are available. Boat-launching facilities and rentals are on-site. Leashed pets are permitted.

Reservations, fees: Reservations are accepted at 877/444-6777 or www.recreation.gov ($10 reservation fee). Sites are $16 per night, $8 per night per additional vehicle, and $100 per night for the group sites. Open late May-September, weather permitting.

Directions: From Bend, drive southwest on Cascades Lakes Highway (Century Drive Highway, which becomes County Road 46) and drive 35.5 miles to Forest Road 4625. Turn left (east) and drive 1.7 miles to the campground.

Contact: Deschutes National Forest, Bend-Fort Rock Ranger District, 541/383-4000, www.fs.usda.gov/centraloregon.

125 MALLARD MARSH

Scenic rating: 8
on Hosmer Lake in Deschutes National Forest

Map 5.5, page 265   **BEST (**

Quiet Mallard Marsh campground is located on the shore of Hosmer Lake, at an elevation of 5,000 feet. The lake is stocked with brook trout and Atlantic salmon and reserved for catch-and-release fly-fishing only. You'll get a pristine, quality fishing experience here. The lake is ideal for canoeing. Only non-motorized boats are allowed.

Campsites, facilities: There are 15 sites for tents or RVs up to 26 feet long. Picnic tables, garbage service, and vault toilets are provided. No drinking water is available. Boat-launching facilities are nearby. Leashed pets are permitted.

Reservations, fees: Reservations are accepted at 877/444-6777 or www.recreation.gov ($10 reservation fee). Sites are $10 per night, $5 per night per additional vehicle. Open May-October, weather permitting.

Directions: From Bend, drive 35.5 miles southwest on Cascade Lakes Highway (Highway 46). Turn east onto Forest Road 4625 and drive 1.3 miles toward Hosmer Lake. South Campground will come up on the right side first and then Mallard Marsh.

Contact: Deschutes National Forest, Bend-Fort Rock Ranger District, 541/383-4000, www.fs.usda.gov/centraloregon; www.hoodoorecreation.com.

126 SOUTH

Scenic rating: 8

on Hosmer Lake in Deschutes National Forest

Map 5.5, page 265

South campground is located along the shore of Hosmer Lake, adjacent to Mallard Marsh, and enjoys the same fishing experience. It's a good option if Mallard Marsh is full.

Campsites, facilities: There are 23 sites for tents or RVs up to 20 feet long. Picnic tables, garbage service, and fire grills are provided. Vault toilets and boat-launching facilities are available. There is no drinking water. Leashed pets are permitted.

Reservations, fees: Reservations are accepted at 877/444-6777 or www.recreation.gov ($10 reservation fee). Sites are $12 per night, $6 per night per additional vehicle. Open mid-May-late September, weather permitting.

Directions: From Bend, drive southwest on Cascades Lakes Highway (Century Drive Highway, which becomes County Road 46) and drive 35.5 miles to Forest Road 4625. Turn left (east) and drive 1.2 miles to the campground on the right.

Contact: Deschutes National Forest, Bend-Fort Rock Ranger District, 541/383-4000, www.fs.usda.gov/centraloregon; www.hoodoorecreation.com.

127 LAVA LAKE

Scenic rating: 10

on Lava Lake in Deschutes National Forest

Map 5.5, page 265   BEST (

This well-designed campground sits on the shore of pretty Lava Lake at 4,750 feet elevation. Mount Bachelor and the Three Sisters are in the background, making a classic picture.

Boating and fishing are popular here. A bonus is nearby Lava Lake Resort, which has showers, laundry facilities, an RV dump station, store, gasoline, and propane.

Campsites, facilities: There are 44 sites for tents or RVs up to 40 feet long. Picnic tables, garbage service, and fire grills are provided. Vault toilets, drinking water, and a fish-cleaning station are available. Boat docks and launching facilities are on-site. Boat rentals are nearby. Some facilities are wheelchair accessible. Leashed pets are permitted.

Reservations, fees: Reservations are accepted at 877/444-6777 or www.recreation.gov ($10 reservation fee). Single sites are $16 per night, double sites are $30 per night, $8 per night per additional vehicle. Open mid-April-October, weather permitting.

Directions: From Bend, drive southwest on Cascades Lakes Highway (Century Drive Highway, which becomes County Road 46) and drive 38.4 miles to Forest Road 4600-500. Turn left (east) and drive one mile to the campground.

Contact: Deschutes National Forest, Bend-Fort Rock Ranger District, 541/383-4000, www.fs.usda.gov/centraloregon; www.hoodoorecreation.com.

128 LITTLE LAVA LAKE

Scenic rating: 8

on Little Lava Lake in Deschutes National Forest

Map 5.5, page 265

Little Lava Lake feeds into the Deschutes River; boating, fishing, hiking, and swimming are some of the recreation options here. Choose from lakeside or riverside sites set at an elevation of 4,750 feet.

Campsites, facilities: There are 15 sites for tents or RVs up to 40 feet long and a group site for up to 30 people. Picnic tables and fire grills are provided. Vault toilets, drinking water, and garbage service are available. A boat launch, docks, and rentals are nearby. There are also launching facilities on-site. Leashed pets are permitted.

Reservations, fees: Reservations are accepted at 877/444-6777 ($10 reservation fee) or www.recreation.gov ($9 reservation fee). Single sites are $14 per night, double sites are $26 per night, the group site is $50 per night, $7 per night per additional vehicle. Open early May-late October, weather permitting.

Directions: From Bend, drive southwest on Cascades Lakes Highway (Century Drive Highway, which becomes County Road 46) and drive 38.4 miles to Forest Road 4600-500. Turn left (east) and drive 0.7 mile to Forest Road 4600-520. Continue east for 0.4 mile to the campground.

Contact: Deschutes National Forest, Bend-Fort Rock Ranger District, 541/383-4000, www.fs.usda.gov/centraloregon; www.hoodoorecreation.com.

129 SWAMP WELLS HORSE CAMP
🏕 🐴 � 🏕

Scenic rating: 3
near the Arnold Ice Caves in Deschutes National Forest

Map 5.5, page 265

If you look at the map, this campground may appear to be quite remote, but it's actually in an area less than 30 minutes from Bend. Set at an elevation of 5,450 feet, this camp is a good place for horseback riding, but you don't need a horse to enjoy this spot. Trails heading south re-enter the forested areas. The system of lava tubes at the nearby Arnold Ice Caves is fun to explore; bring a bicycle helmet, a flashlight, and knee pads.

Campsites, facilities: There are five primitive sites for tents or RVs up to 16 feet long. Picnic tables and fire grills are provided. There are vault toilets, but no drinking water, and garbage must be packed out. Manure bins are available for horses. Leashed pets are permitted.

Reservations, fees: Reservations are not accepted. There is no fee for camping. Open April-late November, weather permitting.

Directions: From Bend, drive south on U.S. 97 for four miles to Forest Road 18/China Hat Road. Turn left (southeast) and drive 5.4 miles to Forest Road 1810. Turn right (south) and drive 5.8 miles to Forest Road 1816. Turn left (east) and drive three miles to the campground. The last mile is rough and primitive.

Contact: Deschutes National Forest, Bend-Fort Rock Ranger District, 541/383-4000, www.fs.usda.gov/centraloregon.

130 WEST CULTUS LAKE
🏕 🛶 🏊 � 🐴 🏕

Scenic rating: 5
on Cultus Lake in Deschutes National Forest

Map 5.5, page 265

This campground, set at 4,700 feet elevation along the west shore of Cultus Lake, is accessible by boat or trail only. It's about three miles by trail from the parking area to the campground. The lake is a good spot for fishing, swimming, and waterskiing. Trails branch out from the campground and provide access to numerous small backcountry lakes. Drinking water and boat-launching facilities are available at Cultus Lake.

Campsites, facilities: There are 12 boat-in or hike-in tent sites. Picnic tables and fire pits are provided. Vault toilets are available. There is no drinking water, and garbage must be packed out. Boat docks are available on-site; boat rentals are at Cultus Lake Resort. Leashed pets are permitted.

Reservations, fees: Reservations are not accepted. Sites are $15 per night. A Northwest Forest Pass ($5 daily fee or $30 annual fee per parked vehicle) is required. (The parking fee is waived if you park in the Cultus Lake Boat Launch lot.) Open May-late September, weather permitting.

Directions: From Bend, drive southwest on Cascades Lakes Highway (Century Drive

Highway, which becomes County Road 46) and drive 46 miles to Forest Road 4635. Turn right (west) and drive two miles to the parking area. Boat or hike in about three miles to the west end of the lake.

Contact: Deschutes National Forest, Bend-Fort Rock Ranger District, 541/383-4000, www.fs.usda.gov/centraloregon;· www.hoodoorecreation.com.

131 CULTUS LAKE

Scenic rating: 7
on Cultus Lake in Deschutes National Forest

Map 5.5, page 265

Located along the east shore of Cultus Lake at 4,700 feet elevation, this camp is a popular spot for fishing, hiking, swimming, waterskiing, and windsurfing. The sites fill up early on weekends and holidays.

Campsites, facilities: There are 55 sites for tents or RVs up to 36 feet long. Picnic tables and fire grills are provided. Vault toilets, drinking water, and garbage service are available. Boat docks and launching facilities are on-site. Boat rentals are nearby. A restaurant, gasoline, and cabins are available nearby at Cultus Lake Resort. Leashed pets are permitted.

Reservations, fees: Reservations are accepted at 877/444-6777 or www.recreation.gov ($10 reservation fee). Sites are $18 per night, $9 per night per additional vehicle. Open mid-April-late September, weather permitting.

Directions: From Bend, drive southwest on Cascades Lakes Highway (Century Drive Highway, which becomes County Road 46) and drive 46 miles to Forest Road 4635. Turn right (west) and drive two miles to the campground.

Contact: Deschutes National Forest, Bend-Fort Rock Ranger District, 541/383-4000, www.fs.usda.gov/centraloregon; www.hoodoorecreation.com.

132 CULTUS CORRAL HORSE CAMP

Scenic rating: 3
near Cultus Lake in Deschutes National Forest

Map 5.5, page 265

Located at 4,450 feet elevation, about one mile from Cultus Lake, this camp sits in a stand of lodgepole pine. Several nearby trails provide access to backcountry lakes. This is a good overflow campground for Quinn Meadow Horse Camp.

Campsites, facilities: There are 11 sites for tents or RVs up to 40 feet long. Picnic tables, garbage service, fire grills, and four-horse corrals are provided. Drinking water and vault toilets are available. Leashed pets are permitted.

Reservations, fees: Reservations are not accepted. Sites are $14 per night, $7 per night per additional vehicle. Open May-late September, weather permitting.

Directions: From Bend, drive southwest on Cascades Lakes Highway (Century Drive Highway, which becomes County Road 46) and drive 46 miles to Forest Road 4635. Turn right (west) and drive one mile to Forest Road 4630. Turn right and drive 0.75 mile to the campground on the right.

Contact: Deschutes National Forest, Bend-Fort Rock Ranger District, 541/383-4000, www.fs.usda.gov/centraloregon; www.hoodoorecreation.com.

133 LITTLE CULTUS LAKE

Scenic rating: 7
on Little Cultus Lake in Deschutes National Forest

Map 5.5, page 265

This campground is set near the shore of Little Cultus Lake at an elevation of 4,800 feet. It's a popular spot for boating (10-mph speed limit), fishing, hiking, and swimming. Nearby trails offer access to numerous backcountry lakes, and the Pacific Crest Trail passes about six miles west of the camp.

Campsites, facilities: There are 31 sites for tents or RVs up to 30 feet long. Picnic tables, garbage service, and fire grills are provided. Vault toilets and a boat launch are available. Check to confirm whether drinking water is available. Leashed pets are permitted.

Reservations, fees: Reservations are accepted at 877/444-6777 or www.recreation.gov ($10 reservation fee). Sites are $16 per night, $8 per night per additional vehicle. Open May-September, weather permitting.

Directions: From Bend, drive southwest on Cascades Lakes Highway (Century Drive Highway, which becomes County Road 46) and drive 46 miles to Forest Road 4635. Turn right (west) and drive two miles to Forest Road 4630. Turn left (south) and drive 1.7 miles to Forest Road 4636. Turn left (west) and drive one mile to the campground.

Contact: Deschutes National Forest, Bend-Fort Rock Ranger District, 541/383-4000, www.fs.usda.gov/centraloregon; www.hoodoorecreation.com.

134 COW MEADOW

Scenic rating: 6

on Crane Prairie Reservoir in Deschutes National Forest

Map 5.5, page 265

Cow Meadow campground is located near the north end of Crane Prairie Reservoir and near the Deschutes River. It's a pretty spot (elevation is 4,450 feet), great for fly-fishing and bird-watching.

Campsites, facilities: There are 18 sites for tents or RVs up to 30 feet long. Picnic tables, garbage service, and fire grills are provided. Vault toilets are available. There is no drinking water. A boat launch for small boats is nearby. Leashed pets are permitted.

Reservations, fees: Reservations are accepted at 877/444-6777 or www.recreation.gov ($10 reservation fee). Sites are $10 per night, $5 per night per additional vehicle. Open May-mid-October, weather permitting.

Directions: From Bend, drive southwest on Cascades Lakes Highway (Century Drive Highway, which becomes County Road 46) for 44.7 miles to Forest Road 40. Turn left (east) on Forest Road 40 and drive 0.4 mile to Forest Road 4000-970. Turn right (south) and drive two miles to the campground on the right.

Contact: Deschutes National Forest, Bend-Fort Rock Ranger District, 541/383-4000, www.fs.usda.gov/centraloregon; www.hoodoorecreation.com.

135 CRANE PRAIRIE

Scenic rating: 6

on Crane Prairie Reservoir in Deschutes National Forest

Map 5.5, page 265

This campground along the north shore of Crane Prairie Reservoir is a good spot for anglers and boaters. World-renowned for rainbow trout fishing, the reservoir is also popular for bass fishing. The Forest Service has erected osprey nesting platforms, which allow visitors a good look at these beautiful birds.

Campsites, facilities: There are 128 sites for tents or RVs of any length and one group site for up to 90 people. Picnic tables and fire grills are provided. Vault toilets, drinking water, and garbage service are available. Boat docks, launching facilities, and a fish-cleaning station are available on-site. Boat rentals, showers, gas, and a coin laundry are nearby. Some facilities are wheelchair accessible. Leashed pets are permitted.

Reservations, fees: Reservations are accepted at 877/444-6777 ($10 reservation fee) or www.recreation.gov ($10 reservation fee). Single sites are $16 per night, multi-sites are $30 per night, the group site is $90-200 per night, $8 per night per additional vehicle. Open April-October, weather permitting.

Directions: From Bend, drive south on U.S. 97 for 26.8 miles to Wickiup Junction and County Road 43. Turn right (west) on County Road 43 and drive 11 miles to Forest Road 42. Continue west on Forest Road 42 for 5.4 miles to Forest Road 4270. Turn right (north) and drive 4.2 miles to the campground on the left.

Contact: Deschutes National Forest, Bend-Fort Rock Ranger District, 541/383-4000, www.fs.usda.gov/centraloregon; www.hoo-doorecreation.com.

136 QUINN RIVER

Scenic rating: 5
on Crane Prairie Reservoir in Deschutes National Forest

Map 5.5, page 265

Set along the western shore of Crane Prairie Reservoir, this campground is a popular spot for anglers and a great spot for bird-watching. The area is also popular with a wide variety of mammals large and small, so don't leave any food out. A separate, large parking lot is available for boats and trailers. Boat speed is limited to 10 mph. The elevation is 4,450 feet.

Campsites, facilities: There are 41 sites for tents or RVs up to 45 feet long. Picnic tables and fire grills are provided. Vault toilets, drinking water, and garbage service are available. Boat-launching facilities are available. Some facilities are wheelchair accessible. Leashed pets are permitted.

Reservations, fees: Reservations are accepted at 877/444-6777 ($10 reservation fee) or www.recreation.gov ($10 reservation fee). Sites are $14 per night, $7 per night per additional vehicle. Open late April-September, weather permitting.

Directions: From Bend, drive southwest on Cascade Lakes Highway (Century Drive Highway, which becomes County Road 46) for 48 miles to the campground.

Contact: Deschutes National Forest, Bend-Fort Rock Ranger District, 541/383-4000, www.fs.usda.gov/centraloregon; www.hoo-doorecreation.com.

137 ROCK CREEK

Scenic rating: 5
on Crane Prairie Reservoir in Deschutes National Forest

Map 5.5, page 265

Rock Creek campground is set along the west shore of Crane Prairie Reservoir at an elevation of 4,450 feet. The setting is similar to Quinn River campground, and provides another good spot for anglers when that camp is full.

Campsites, facilities: There are 32 sites for tents or RVs up to 40 feet long, including two multi-sites. Picnic tables, garbage service, and fire grills are provided. Drinking water, a fish-cleaning station, and vault toilets are available. Boat docks and launching facilities are on-site. Leashed pets are permitted.

Reservations, fees: Reservations are accepted at 877/444-6777 ($10 reservation fee) or www.recreation.gov ($10 reservation fee). Single sites are $16 per night, multi-sites are $26 per night, $8 per night per additional vehicle. Open April-September, weather permitting.

Directions: From Bend, drive southwest on Cascade Lakes Highway (Century Drive Highway, which becomes County Road 46) for 48.8 miles to the campground.

Contact: Deschutes National Forest, Bend-Fort Rock Ranger District, 541/383-4000, www.fs.usda.gov/centraloregon; www.hoo-doorecreation.com.

138 FALL RIVER

Scenic rating: 5
on the Fall River in Deschutes National Forest

Map 5.5, page 265

Fall River is beautiful, crystal clear, and cold, and this campground is right on it at an elevation of 4,300 feet. Fishing is restricted to fly-fishing only, and it's wise to check the regulations for other restrictions. The Fall River Trail meanders along the river for 3.5 miles and is open for bicycling.

Campsites, facilities: There are 12 sites for tents or RVs up to 40 feet long. Picnic tables, garbage service, and fire grills are provided. Vault toilets are available. There is no drinking water. Leashed pets are permitted.

Reservations, fees: Reservations are accepted at 877/444-6777 ($10 reservation fee) or www.recreation.gov ($10 reservation fee). Sites are $10 per night, $5 per night per additional vehicle. Open early May-late October, weather permitting.

Directions: From Bend, drive south on U.S. 97 for 17.3 miles to the Vandevert Road exit. Take that exit and turn right on Vandevert Road. Drive 1.5 miles to Forest Road 42. Turn left and drive 12.2 miles to the campground.

Contact: Deschutes National Forest, Bend-Fort Rock Ranger District, 541/383-4000, www.fs.usda.gov/centraloregon; www.hoodoorecreation.com.

139 SHEEP BRIDGE

Scenic rating: 3

near Wickiup Reservoir in Deschutes National Forest

Map 5.5, page 265

This campground is set along the north Deschutes River Channel of Wickiup Reservoir in an open, treeless area that has minimal privacy and is dusty in summer. Dispersed sites here are popular with group campers. The elevation is 4,350 feet.

Campsites, facilities: There are 20 sites and three group sites for tents or RVs up to 40 feet long. Picnic tables, garbage service, and fire grills are provided. Drinking water, vault toilets, boat-launching facilities, and a picnic area are available. Leashed pets are permitted.

Reservations, fees: Reservations are at

877/444-6777 ($10 reservation fee) or www.recreation.gov ($9 reservation fee). Sites are $12 per night, the group sites are $30, $6 per night per additional vehicle. Open early May-October, weather permitting.

Directions: From Bend, drive south on U.S. 97 for 26.8 miles to Wickiup Junction. Turn right (west) on County Road 43 and drive 11 miles to Forest Road 42. Continue 4.6 miles west on Forest Road 42 to Forest Road 4260. Turn left (south) and drive 0.75 mile to the campground on the right.

Contact: Deschutes National Forest, Bend-Fort Rock Ranger District, 541/383-4000, www.fs.usda.gov/centraloregon; www.hoodoorecreation.com.

140 NORTH TWIN LAKE

Scenic rating: 6

on North Twin Lake in Deschutes National Forest

Map 5.5, page 265

Although small and fairly primitive, North Twin Lake has lake access and a pretty setting. The campground is located on the shore of North Twin Lake and is a popular weekend spot for families. Only non-motorized boats are permitted. The elevation is 4,350 feet.

Campsites, facilities: There are 20 sites for tents or RVs up to 40 feet long. Picnic tables and fire grills are provided. Vault toilets are available. There is no drinking water. Boat-launching facilities are on-site. There is also an RV dump station ($10 fee). Leashed pets are permitted.

Reservations, fees: Reservations are accepted at 877/444-6777 ($10 reservation fee) or www.recreation.gov ($9 reservation fee). Sites are $14 per night, $7 per night per additional vehicle. Open April-October, weather permitting.

Directions: From Bend, drive southwest on Cascade Lakes Highway (Century Drive Highway, which becomes County Road 46) for 52 miles and drive past Crane Prairie Reservoir to Forest Road 42. Turn east and drive four miles to Forest Road 4260. Turn right (south) and drive 0.25 mile to the campground.

Contact: Deschutes National Forest, Bend-Fort Rock Ranger District, 541/383-4000, www.fs.usda.gov/centraloregon; www.hoodoorecreation.com.

141 TWIN LAKES RESORT

Scenic rating: 8

on Twin Lakes

Map 5.5, page 265 **BEST (**

Twin Lakes Resort is a popular family vacation destination with a full-service marina and all the amenities, including beach areas. Recreational activities vary from hiking to boating, fishing, and swimming on Wickiup Reservoir. Nearby South Twin Lake is popular with paddleboaters and kayakers; it's stocked with rainbow trout.

Campsites, facilities: There are 23 sites with full hookups for RVs of any length. There are also 14 cabins. Picnic tables and fire rings are provided. Restrooms with flush toilets and coin showers, a dump station, coin laundry, convenience store, restaurant, ice, snacks, some RV supplies, propane gas, and gasoline are available. A boat ramp, rentals, and a dock are available; no motors are permitted on South Twin Lake. Some facilities are wheelchair accessible. Leashed pets are permitted.

Reservations, fees: Reservations are recommended. Sites are $32-35 per night, $5 per night per additional vehicle. Cabins are $80-220 per night. Some credit cards are accepted. Open late April-mid-October, weather permitting.

Directions: From Bend, drive south on U.S. 97 for 26.8 miles to Wickiup Junction. Turn right (west) on County Road 43 and drive 11 miles to Forest Road 42. Turn left and continue 4.6 miles west on Forest Road 42 to Forest Road

4260. Turn left (south) and drive two miles to the resort.

Contact: Twin Lakes Resort, 541/382-6432, www.twinlakesresort.net.

142 SOUTH TWIN LAKE

Scenic rating: 6

on South Twin Lake in Deschutes National Forest

Map 5.5, page 265

This campground is on the shore of South Twin Lake, a popular spot for boating (non-motorized only), fishing, and swimming. The elevation is 4,350 feet.

Campsites, facilities: There are 21 sites for tents or RVs up to 40 feet long. Picnic tables, garbage service, and fire grills are provided. Drinking water, vault and flush toilets, and dump station are available. Boat-launching facilities (small boats only), boat rentals, showers, and laundry facilities are nearby. Some facilities are wheelchair accessible. Leashed pets are permitted.

Reservations, fees: Reservations are accepted at 877/444-6777 ($10 reservation fee) or www.recreation.gov ($9 reservation fee). Single sites are $18 per night, multi-sites are $30 per night, $9 per night per additional vehicle. Open April-October, weather permitting.

Directions: From Bend, drive south on U.S. 97 for 26.8 miles to Wickiup Junction. Turn right (west) on County Road 43 and drive 11 miles to Forest Road 42. Continue west on Forest Road 42 for 4.6 miles to Forest Road 4260. Turn left (south) and drive two miles to the campground on the left.

Contact: Deschutes National Forest, Bend-Fort Rock Ranger District, 541/383-4000, www.fs.usda.gov/centraloregon; www.hoodoorecreation.com.

143 WEST SOUTH TWIN

Scenic rating: 4

on South Twin Lake in Deschutes National Forest

Map 5.5, page 265

A major access point to the Wickiup Reservoir, this camp is situated on South Twin Lake adjacent to the reservoir. It's a popular angling spot with very good kokanee salmon fishing. Twin Lakes Resort is adjacent to West South Twin. The elevation is 4,350 feet.

Campsites, facilities: There are 24 sites for RVs up to 40 feet long. Picnic tables and fire grills are provided. Drinking water, flush toilets, garbage service, and a dump station ($10 fee) are available. Boat-launching facilities are on-site, and boat rentals, a restaurant, showers, coin laundry, gas, propane, cabins, and a store are nearby. A dump station ($10) is located at Gull Point Campground. Leashed pets are permitted.

Reservations, fees: Reservations are accepted at 877/444-6777 ($10 reservation fee) or www.recreation.gov ($9 reservation fee). Sites are $16 per night, $8 per night per additional vehicle. Open April-mid-October, weather permitting.

Directions: From Bend, drive southwest on Cascade Lakes Highway (Century Drive Highway, which becomes County Road 46) for 40 miles (past Crane Prairie Reservoir) to Forest Road 42. Turn left (east) and drive four miles to Forest Road 4260. Turn right (south) and drive 0.25 mile to the campground.

Contact: Deschutes National Forest, Bend-Fort Rock Ranger District, 541/383-4000, www.fs.usda.gov/centraloregon; www.hoodoorecreation.com.

144 GULL POINT

Scenic rating: 5

on Wickiup Reservoir in Deschutes National Forest

Map 5.5, page 265

Located about two miles from West South Twin Campground, Gull Point is the most popular campground on Wickiup Reservoir. The campground sits in an open ponderosa stand on the north shore of the reservoir. You'll find good fishing for kokanee salmon here—though they are elusive and hard to catch. There are also brown trout in the 15-20-pound range.

Campsites, facilities: There are 78 sites for tents or RVs up to 40 feet long and two group sites for up to 30 people each. Picnic tables, garbage service, and fire grills are provided. Drinking water, a dump station, and flush and vault toilets are available. Boat-launching facilities and fish-cleaning stations are on-site. Coin showers and a small store are nearby. Some facilities are wheelchair accessible. Leashed pets are permitted.

Reservations, fees: Reservations are accepted at 877/444-6777 ($10 reservation fee) or www.recreation.gov ($9 reservation fee). Sites are $16 per night, double sites are $30 per night, $8 per night per additional vehicle, and $75 per night for group sites. Open mid-April-October, weather permitting.

Directions: From Bend, drive south on U.S. 97 for about 26.8 miles to County Road 43 (three miles north of LaPine). Turn right (west) on County Road 43 and drive 11 miles to Forest Road 42. Turn west on Forest Road 42 and drive 4.6 miles to Forest Road 4260. Turn left (south) and drive three miles to the campground on the right.

Contact: Deschutes National Forest, Bend-Fort Rock Ranger District, 541/383-4000, www.fs.usda.gov/centraloregon; www.hoodoorecreation.com.

145 BULL BEND

Scenic rating: 5

on the Deschutes River in Deschutes National Forest

Map 5.5, page 265

Bull Bend campground is located on the inside of a major bend in the Deschutes River at 4,300 feet elevation. For a mini float trip, start at the upstream end of camp, float around the bend, and then take out at the downstream end of camp. This is a low-use getaway spot.

Campsites, facilities: There are 12 sites for tents or RVs up to 40 feet long. Picnic tables, garbage service, fire grills, vault toilets, and boat-launching facilities are available. There is no drinking water. Leashed pets are permitted.

Reservations, fees: Reservations are accepted at 877/444-6777 ($10 reservation fee) or www. recreation.gov ($9 reservation fee). Sites are $10 per night, $5 per night per additional vehicle. Open early May-late September, weather permitting.

Directions: From Bend, drive south on U.S. 97 for 26.8 miles to Wickiup Junction. Turn right (west) on County Road 43 and drive eight miles to Forest Road 4370. Turn left (south) and drive 1.5 miles to the campground.

Contact: Deschutes National Forest, Bend-Fort Rock Ranger District, 541/383-4000, www.fs.usda.gov/centraloregon; www.hoodoorecreation.com.

146 PRINGLE FALLS

Scenic rating: 4

on the Deschutes River in Deschutes National Forest

Map 5.5, page 265

This campground fringing the Deschutes River is less than a mile from Pringle Falls. The camp gets light use and is pretty and serene.

Campsites, facilities: There are seven sites for tents or RVs up to 30 feet long. Picnic tables, garbage service, and fire grills are provided. Vault toilets are available. There is no drinking water. Leashed pets are permitted.

Reservations, fees: Reservations are accepted at 877/444-6777 ($10 reservation fee) or www. recreation.gov ($9 reservation fee). Sites are $10 per night, $5 per night per additional vehicle. Open May-October, weather permitting.

Directions: From Bend, drive south on U.S. 97 for 26.8 miles to Wickiup Junction. Turn right (west) on County Road 43 and drive 7.4 miles to Forest Road 4330-500. Turn north (right) and drive one mile to the campground.

Contact: Deschutes National Forest, Bend-Fort Rock Ranger District, 541/383-4000, www.fs.usda.gov/centraloregon; www.hoodoorecreation.com.

147 BIG RIVER

Scenic rating: 4

on the Deschutes River in Deschutes National Forest

Map 5.5, page 265

Big River is a good spot. Located between the banks of the Deschutes River and the road, it has easy access and is popular as an overnight camp. Fishing, motorized boating, and rafting are permitted.

Campsites, facilities: There are 10 sites for tents or RVs up to 40 feet long and three group sites for up to 40 people. Picnic tables, garbage service, and fire grills are provided. Vault toilets are available. There is no drinking water. Boat-launching facilities are on-site. Some facilities are wheelchair accessible. Leashed pets are permitted.

Reservations, fees: Reservations are accepted at 877/444-6777 ($10 reservation fee) or www. recreation.gov ($9 reservation fee). Sites are $10 per night, $5 per night per additional vehicle, and the group sites are $30 per night. Open early May-late October, weather permitting.

Directions: From Bend, drive south on U.S. 97 for 17.3 miles to the Vandevert Road exit. Take that exit and turn right on Vandevert Road. Drive 1.5 miles to Forest Road 42. Turn left and drive 7.9 miles to the campground.

Contact: Deschutes National Forest, Bend-Fort Rock Ranger District, 541/383-4000, www.fs.usda.gov/centraloregon; www.hoodoorecreation.com.

148 PRAIRIE

Scenic rating: 4

on Paulina Creek in Deschutes National Forest

Map 5.5, page 265

Here's another good overnight campground that is quiet and private. Set along the banks of Paulina Creek, Prairie is located about 0.5 mile from the trailhead for the Peter Skene Ogden National Recreation Trail. The elevation is 4,300 feet.

Campsites, facilities: There are 17 sites for tents or RVs up to 30 feet long. Picnic tables, garbage service, and fire grills are provided. Drinking water, firewood, vault toilets, and a dump station ($10) are available. Leashed pets are permitted.

Reservations, fees: Reservations are not accepted. Sites are $14 per night, $7 per night per additional vehicle. Open mid-May-late September, weather permitting.

Directions: From Bend, drive south on U.S. 97 for 23.5 miles to County Road 21 (Paulina/East Lake Road). Turn left (east) and drive 3.1 miles to the campground.

Contact: Deschutes National Forest, Bend-Fort Rock Ranger District, 541/383-4000, www.fs.usda.gov/centraloregon; www.hoodoorecreation.com.

149 PAULINA LAKE

Scenic rating: 8

on Paulina Lake in Deschutes National Forest

Map 5.5, page 265

This campground (6,350 feet elevation) is located along the south shore of Paulina Lake and within the Newberry National Volcanic Monument. The camp is adjacent to Paulina Lake Resort. The lake itself sits in a volcanic crater. Nearby trails provide access to the remains of volcanic activity, including craters and obsidian flows. My longtime friend, Guy Carl, caught the state's record brown trout here, right after I'd written a story about his unique method of using giant Rapala and Rebel bass lures for giant browns. The recreation options here include boating, fishing, hiking, mountain biking, and sailing. The boat speed limit is 10 mph. Note that food-raiding bears are common at all the campgrounds in the Newberry Caldera area and that all food must be kept out of reach. Do not store food in vehicles.

Campsites, facilities: There are 69 sites for RVs up to 30 feet long. Picnic tables, garbage service, and fire grills are provided. Drinking water and flush and vault toilets are available. Boat docks, launching facilities, boat rentals, coin showers, coin laundry, a small store, restaurant, cabins, gas, and propane are within five miles. The Newberry RV dump station ($10 fee) is nearby. Some facilities are wheelchair accessible. Leashed pets are permitted.

Reservations, fees: Reservations are accepted at 877/444-6777 ($10 reservation fee) or www.recreation.gov ($9 reservation fee). Sites are $18 per night, $9 per night per additional vehicle. Open May-late October, weather permitting.

Directions: From Bend, drive south on U.S. 97 for 23.5 miles to County Road 21 (Paulina/East Lake Road). Turn left (east) and drive 12.9 miles to the campground on the left.

Contact: Deschutes National Forest, Bend-Fort Rock Ranger District, 541/383-4000, www.fs.usda.gov/centraloregon; www.hoodoorecreation.com.

150 CHIEF PAULINA HORSE CAMP

Scenic rating: 4

on Paulina Lake in Deschutes National Forest

Map 5.5, page 265

Chief Paulina campground sits at an elevation of 6,400 feet, about 0.25 mile from the south shore of Paulina Lake, where fishing is good. Horse trails and a vista point are close by. Horse campers must use only certified weed-seed-free hay.

Campsites, facilities: There are 14 sites for tents or RVs up to 40 feet long. Picnic tables and fire grills are provided. A vault toilet, garbage service, and corrals are available. There is no drinking water. Boat docks and rentals and an RV dump station ($10 fee) are nearby. Leashed pets are permitted.

Reservations, fees: Reservations are accepted at 877/444-6777 ($10 reservation fee) or www. recreation.gov ($9 reservation fee). Two-horse stall sites are $14 per night, four-horse stall sites are $18, $7 per night per additional vehicle. Open May-late October, weather permitting.

Directions: From Bend, drive south on U.S. 97 for 23.5 miles to County Road 21 (Paulina/East Lake Road). Turn left (east) and drive 14 miles to the campground.

Contact: Deschutes National Forest, Bend-Fort Rock Ranger District, 541/383-4000, www.fs.usda.gov/centraloregon; www.hoodoorecreation.com.

151 LITTLE CRATER

Scenic rating: 8

near Paulina Lake in Deschutes National Forest

Map 5.5, page 265

Little Crater is a very popular campground (6,350 feet elevation) near the east shore of Paulina Lake in Newberry National Volcanic Monument, a caldera. Sites are situated on the scenic lake edge, perfect for fishing, and there are great hiking opportunities in the area. The place fills up most summer weekends.

Campsites, facilities: There are 50 sites for tents or RVs up to 40 feet long. Picnic tables and fire grills are provided. Vault toilets, drinking water, and garbage service are available. Boat docks and launching facilities are on-site, and boat rentals are nearby. Some facilities are wheelchair accessible. Leashed pets are permitted.

Reservations, fees: Reservations are accepted at 877/444-6777 ($10 reservation fee) or www. recreation.gov ($9 reservation fee). Sites are $18 per night, $9 per night for each additional vehicle. Open early May-late October, weather permitting.

Directions: From Bend, drive south on U.S. 97 for 23.5 miles to County Road 21 (Paulina/East Lake Road). Turn left (east) and drive 14.5 miles to Forest Road 2100. Turn left (north) and drive 0.5 mile to the campground on the left.

Contact: Deschutes National Forest, 541/383-4000, www.fs.usda.gov/centraloregon; www.hoodoorecreation.com.

152 NEWBERRY GROUP CAMP

Scenic rating: 7

west of Roseburg

Map 5.5, page 265

Newberry Group has a great location on Paulina Lake and is the only area on Newberry Monument designed exclusively for group camping. The parking area and roads are paved, and the group sites are separated from one another, although group sites B and C can be joined to accommodate large groups. One site accommodates groups of up to 35 people, while the other two accommodate up to 50. The entire campground can be reserved as well.

Campsites, facilities: There are three group sites for tents or RVs to 40 feet. Picnic tables and fire rings are provided. Drinking water and vault toilets are available. Leashed pets are permitted.

Reservations, fees: Reservations are accepted at 877/444-6777 ($10 reservation fee) or www.recreation.gov ($9 reservation fee). Sites are $60 per night for the smaller camp, $100 per night for the two larger camps, and $225 for all three camps. Open June-September, weather permitting.

Directions: From Bend, drive south on U.S. 97 for 23.5 miles to County Road 21 (Paulina/East Lake Road). Turn left (east) and drive 1.5 miles to the campground.

Contact: Deschutes National Forest, 541/383-4000, www.fs.usda.gov/centraloregon; www.hoodoorecreation.com.

153 CINDER HILL

Scenic rating: 7
on East Lake in Deschutes National Forest

Map 5.5, page 265

This campground hugs the northeast shore of East Lake at an elevation of 6,400 feet. Located within the Newberry National Volcanic Monument, Cinder Hill makes a good base camp for area activities. Boating, fishing, and hiking are among the recreation options here. Boat speed is limited to 10 mph.

Campsites, facilities: There are 55 sites, including pull-through sites, for tents or RVs of any length. Picnic tables and fire grills are provided. Drinking water, flush and vault toilets, and garbage service are available. A camp host is on-site. Boat docks and launching facilities are on-site, and boat rentals, a store, restaurant, coin showers, coin laundry, and cabins are nearby at East Lake Resort. Some facilities are wheelchair accessible. Leashed pets are permitted.

Reservations, fees: Reservations are accepted at 877/444-6777 ($10 reservation fee) or www.recreation.gov ($9 reservation fee). Sites are $18 per night, $9 per night per additional

vehicle. Open mid-May-September, weather permitting.

Directions: From Bend, drive south on U.S. 97 for 23.5 miles to County Road 21 (Paulina/East Lake Road). Turn left (east) and drive 17.6 miles to Forest Road 2100-700. Turn left (north) and drive 0.5 mile to the campground.

Contact: Deschutes National Forest, Bend-Fort Rock Ranger District, 541/383-4000, www.fs.usda.gov/centraloregon; www.hoodoorecreation.com.

154 EAST LAKE

Scenic rating: 8
on East Lake in Deschutes National Forest

Map 5.5, page 265

This campground is set along the south shore of East Lake at an elevation of 6,400 feet. Boating and fishing are popular here, and hiking trails provide access to signs of former volcanic activity in the area. East Lake Campground is similar to Cinder Hill, but smaller. Boat speed is limited to 10 mph.

Campsites, facilities: There are 29 sites for tents or RVs up to 40 feet long. Picnic tables and fire grills are provided. Drinking water, flush and vault toilets, and garbage service are available. A camp host is on-site. Boat docks, launching facilities, and rentals are nearby. Some facilities are wheelchair accessible. Leashed pets are permitted.

Reservations, fees: Reservations are accepted at 877/444-6777 ($10 reservation fee) or www.recreation.gov ($9 reservation fee). Sites are $18 per night, $9 per night per additional vehicle. Open early May-late October, weather permitting.

Directions: From Bend, drive south on U.S. 97 for 23.5 miles to County Road 21 (Paulina/East Lake Road). Turn left (east) and drive 16.6 miles to the campground on the left.

Contact: Deschutes National Forest, Bend-Fort Rock Ranger District, 541/383-4000, www.fs.usda.gov/centraloregon; www.hoo-doorecreation.com.

155 EAST LAKE RESORT AND RV PARK

Scenic rating: 7

on East Lake

Map 5.5, page 265

This resort offers shaded sites in a wooded, mountainous setting on the east shore of East Lake. Opportunities for boating, fishing, and swimming abound.

Campsites, facilities: There are 40 sites with partial hookups for tents or RVs up to 40 feet long, five sites for tents, and 16 cabins. Some sites are pull-through. Picnic tables and fire pits are provided. Drinking water, restrooms with flush toilets and coin showers, propane gas, firewood, a dump station, convenience store with fishing licenses, café, coin laundry, Wi-Fi, ice, boat-launching facilities, boat rentals, moorage, and a playground are available. Leashed pets are permitted.

Reservations, fees: Reservations are accepted. RV sites are $32 per night, tent sites are $25 per night, cabins are $85-250 per night. Monthly rates are available. Some credit cards are accepted. Open mid-May-September, weather permitting.

Directions: From Bend, drive south on U.S. 97 for 23.5 miles to County Road 21 (Paulina/East Lake Road). Turn left (east) and drive 18 miles to the park at the end of the road.

Contact: East Lake Resort and RV Park, 541/536-2230, www.eastlakeresort.com.

156 CHINA HAT

Scenic rating: 3

in Deschutes National Forest

Map 5.5, page 265

Remote China Hat campground is located at 5,100 feet elevation in a rugged, primitive area. There is direct trail access here to the East Fort Rock OHV Trail System. Hunters use China Hat as a base camp in the fall, but in summer it is a base camp for off-road motorcyclists.

Campsites, facilities: There are 14 sites for tents or RVs up to 30 feet long. Picnic tables and fire grills are provided. Vault toilets are available. Check to confirm whether drinking water is available. Garbage must be packed out. Leashed pets are permitted.

Reservations, fees: Reservations are not accepted. There is no fee for camping. Open April-early November, weather permitting.

Directions: From Bend, drive south on U.S. 97 for 29.6 miles to Forest Road 22. Turn left (east) and drive 26.4 miles to Forest Road 18. Turn left (north) and drive 5.9 miles to the campground on the left.

Contact: Deschutes National Forest, Bend-Fort Rock Ranger District, 541/383-4000, www.fs.usda.gov/centraloregon.

157 GOLD LAKE

Scenic rating: 8

on Gold Lake in Willamette National Forest

Map 5.5, page 265   BEST (

Gold Lake campground wins the popularity contest for high use. Although motors are not allowed on this small lake (100 acres and 25 feet deep), rafts and rowboats provide excellent fly-fishing access. A primitive log shelter built in the early 1940s provides a dry picnic area. In the spring and summer, this area abounds with wildflowers and huckleberries. The Gold Lake Bog is another special attraction where one can often see deer, elk, and smaller wildlife.

Campsites, facilities: There are 21 sites for tents or RVs up to 24 feet long. Picnic tables, garbage bins, and fire grills are provided. Drinking water, vault toilets, and a gray-water station are available. Boat docks and launching facilities are nearby. Some facilities are wheelchair accessible. Leashed pets are permitted.

Reservations, fees: Reservations are not accepted. Sites are $18 per night, $6 per night per additional vehicle. Open mid-May-October, weather permitting.

Directions: From Eugene, drive south on I-5 for five miles to Exit 188 and Highway 58. Turn east and drive 35 miles to the town of Oakridge. From Oakridge, continue east on Highway 58 for 28 miles to Gold Lake Road (Forest Road 500). Turn left (north) and drive two miles to the campground on the right.

Contact: Willamette National Forest, Middle Fork Ranger District, 541/782-2283, www. fs.usda.gov/willamette.

158 NORTH DAVIS CREEK

Scenic rating: 4

on North Davis Creek in Deschutes National Forest

Map 5.5, page 265

Set at an elevation of 4,350 feet, this remote, secluded campground is located along a western channel that feeds into Wickiup Reservoir. Fishing for brown and rainbow trout as well as kokanee salmon is good here. In late summer, the reservoir level tends to drop. The camp receives little use and makes a good overflow camp if campsites are filled at Wickiup.

Campsites, facilities: There are 14 sites for tents or RVs up to 26 feet long. Picnic tables and fire grills are provided. Vault toilets and garbage service are available. There is no drinking water. Boat-launching facilities are on-site. Leashed pets are permitted.

Reservations, fees: Reservations are accepted at 877/444-6777 ($10 reservation fee) or www. recreation.gov ($9 reservation fee). Sites are $10 per night, $5 per night per additional vehicle. Open April-early September.

Directions: From Bend, drive southwest on Cascade Lake Highway (Highway 46/Forest Road 46) for 56.2 miles to the campground on the left.

Contact: Deschutes National Forest, Bend-Fort Rock Ranger District, 541/383-4000, www. fs.usda.gov/centraloregon; www.hoodoorecreation.com.

159 RESERVOIR

Scenic rating: 4

on Wickiup Reservoir in Deschutes National Forest

Map 5.5, page 265

You'll find this campground along the south shore of Wickiup Reservoir, where the kokanee salmon fishing is good. The camp is best in early summer, before the lake level drops. This camp gets little use, so you won't find crowds here. The elevation is 4,350 feet.

Campsites, facilities: There are 21 sites for tents or RVs up to 24 feet long. Picnic tables, garbage service, and fire grills are provided. Boat-launching facilities and vault toilets are available, but there is no drinking water. Leashed pets are permitted.

Reservations, fees: Reservations are accepted at 877/444-6777 ($10 reservation fee) or www. recreation.gov ($9 reservation fee). Sites are $10 per night, $5 per each additional vehicle. Open April-September, weather permitting.

Directions: From Bend, drive southwest on Cascade Lakes Highway (Century Drive Highway, which becomes County Road 46) for 57.8 miles to Forest Road 44. Turn left (east) and drive 1.7 miles to the campground.

Contact: Deschutes National Forest, Bend-Fort Rock Ranger District, 541/383-4000, www.fs.usda.gov/centraloregon; www.hoodoorecreation.com.

160 LAPINE STATE PARK

Scenic rating: 7

on the Deschutes River

Map 5.5, page 265

This peaceful and clean campground sits next

to the trout-filled Deschutes River (a legendary fly-fishing spot) with many more high-mountain lakes in proximity. The camp is set in a subalpine pine forest populated by eagles or red-tailed hawks. Trails surround the campground; be sure to check out Oregon's "Big Tree." Skiing is a popular wintertime option in the area.

Campsites, facilities: There are 129 sites with full or partial hookups for tents or RVs of any length; only 20-amp service is available. There are also 10 cabins; five are rustic, five are deluxe, and two are pet friendly. Picnic tables and fire grills are provided. Drinking water, restrooms with flush toilets and showers, garbage bins, a dump station, a seasonal store, a day-use area with a sandy beach, a meeting hall that can be reserved, ice, and firewood are available. A boat launch is nearby. Some facilities are wheelchair accessible. Leashed pets are permitted.

Reservations, fees: Reservations are accepted at 800/452-5687 or online at www.oregonstateparks.org or www.reserveamerica.com ($8 reservation fee). Sites are $24-26 per night, $7 per night per additional vehicle. Rustic cabins are $44-54 per night, deluxe cabins are $87-97 per night. Some credit cards are accepted. Open year-round, weather permitting.

Directions: From Bend, turn south on U.S. 97 and drive 23 miles to State Recreation Road. Turn right and drive four miles to the park.

Contact: LaPine State Park, 541/536-2071 or 800/551-6949, www.oregonstateparks.org.

161 LAVA FLOW

Scenic rating: 8

on Davis Lake in Deschutes National Forest

Map 5.5, page 265

North Lava Flow campground is surrounded by old-growth forest along the northeast shore of Davis Lake, a very shallow lake formed by lava flow. The water level fluctuates here, and this campground can sometimes be closed in summer. There's good duck hunting during the fall.

Fishing can be decent, but only fly-fishing is allowed. Boat speed is limited to 10 mph. The south section of the campground may close in summer to protect nesting eagles.

Campsites, facilities: There are six sites for tents or RVs up to 30 feet long. Picnic tables and fire grills are provided. Vault toilets and firewood (which can be gathered from the surrounding area) are available. There is no drinking water, and garbage must be packed out. A primitive boat ramp is nearby. Leashed pets are permitted.

Reservations, fees: Reservations are not accepted. There is no fee for camping. Open April-December, weather permitting.

Directions: From Eugene, drive south on I-5 for five miles to Exit 188 and Highway 58. Turn east on Highway 58 and drive 86 miles to County Road 61. Turn left and drive three miles to Forest Road 46. Turn left and drive 7.7 miles to Forest Road 850. Turn left and drive 1.8 miles to the campground.

Contact: Deschutes National Forest, Crescent Ranger District, 541/433-3200, www.fs.usda.gov/centraloregon.

162 EAST DAVIS LAKE

Scenic rating: 7

on Davis Lake in Deschutes National Forest

Map 5.5, page 265

This campground sits nestled in the lodgepole pines along the south shore of Davis Lake. There was a large fire here a few years ago, and though it heavily impacted the surrounding vegetation—including the scenic view across the lake—a nice greenbelt along the creek where the sites are located, remains. Recreation options include boating (speed limit 10 mph), fly-fishing, and hiking. Leeches prevent swimming here. Bald eagles and sandhill cranes are frequently seen.

Campsites, facilities: There are 17 sites for tents or RVs up to 40 feet long and three double sites. Picnic tables, garbage service, fire grills, drinking water, and vault toilets are provided. Firewood may be gathered from the surrounding area. Primitive boat-launching facilities are available on-site. Some facilities are wheelchair accessible. Leashed pets are permitted.

Reservations, fees: Reservations are accepted at 877/444-6777 ($10 reservation fee) or www. recreation.gov ($9 reservation fee). Sites are $12 per night, $6 per night per additional vehicle. Open mid-April-late September, weather permitting.

Directions: From Eugene, drive south on I-5 for five miles to Exit 188 and Highway 58. Turn east and drive 73 miles to County Road 61. Turn left (east) and drive three miles to Forest Road 46. Turn left and drive 7.7 miles to Forest Road 850. Turn left and drive 0.25 mile to the campground entrance road on the right.

Contact: Deschutes National Forest, Crescent Ranger District, 541/433-3200, www.fs.usda. gov/centraloregon; www.hoodoorecreation. com.

163 TRAPPER CREEK
🏃🏊🛶🛥🐴🚐⛺

Scenic rating: 8
on Odell Lake in Deschutes National Forest

Map 5.5, page 265   **BEST (**

The west end of Odell Lake is the setting for this camp. Boat docks and rentals are available nearby at the Shelter Cove Resort. One of Oregon's prime fisheries for kokanee salmon and mackinaw (lake trout), this lake also has some huge brown trout.

Campsites, facilities: There are 18 sites for tents or RVs up to 40 feet long and three group sites. Picnic tables and fire grills are provided. Drinking water, vault toilets, garbage service, and a boat launch are available. Firewood may be gathered from the surrounding area. A store, coin laundry, and ice are within one mile. Leashed pets are permitted.

Reservations, fees: Reservations are accepted at 877/444-6777 ($10 reservation fee) or www. recreation.gov ($9 reservation fee). Sites are

$16-18 per night, $8 per night per additional vehicle, group sites are $30-34, $8 per night per additional vehicle. Open mid-May-October, weather permitting.

Directions: From Eugene, drive south on I-5 for five miles to Exit 188 and Highway 58. Turn east and drive 61 miles to the turnoff for Odell Lake and Forest Road 5810. Turn right on Forest Road 5810 and drive 1.9 miles to the campground on the left.

Contact: Deschutes National Forest, Crescent Ranger District, 541/433-3200, www.fs.usda. gov/centraloregon; www.hoodoorecreation. com.

164 SHELTER COVE RESORT & MARINA
🏃🚲🏊🛶🛥🐴🚐♿🚐⛺

Scenic rating: 9
on Odell Lake in Crescent

Map 5.5, page 265

Shelter Cove is a private resort along the north shore of Odell Lake, set at the base of the Diamond Peak Wilderness. The area offers opportunities for fishing, hiking, and swimming. The cabins sit right on the lakefront, and a general store and tackle shop are available.

Campsites, facilities: There are 72 sites with partial hookups for RVs up to 40 feet long; some sites are pull-through. There are also 13 cabins. Picnic tables and fire rings are provided. Drinking water, restrooms with flush toilets and showers, a dump station, Wi-Fi, an ATM, convenience store, propane, coin laundry, and ice are available. Boat docks, launching facilities, and boat rentals are on-site. Some facilities are wheelchair accessible. Leashed pets are permitted.

Reservations, fees: Reservations are recommended at 541/433-2548 or 800/647-2313. Sites start at $36 per night. Weekly and monthly rates are available. Some credit cards are accepted. Open year-round.

Directions: From Eugene, drive south on I-5 for five miles to Exit 188 and Highway 58. Turn east and drive 61 miles to the turnoff for Odell Lake and West Odell Lake Road. Turn right and drive south for 1.8 miles to the resort at the end of the road.

Contact: Shelter Cove Resort & Marina, 541/433-2548, www.highwaywestvacations. com.

165 ODELL CREEK

Scenic rating: 9

on Odell Lake in Deschutes National Forest

Map 5.5, page 265

You can fish, hike, and swim at this campground (4,800 feet elevation) along the east shore of Odell Lake. A trail from the nearby Crater Buttes trailhead leads southwest into the Diamond Peak Wilderness and provides access to several small lakes in the backcountry. Another trail follows the north shore of the lake. Boat docks, launching facilities, and rentals are available at the Odell Lake Lodge and Resort, adjacent to the campground. Windy afternoons are common here.

Campsites, facilities: There are 26 sites for tents or RVs up to 50 feet long. Picnic tables and fire grills are provided. Vault toilets, drinking water, and garbage service are available. Firewood may be gathered from the surrounding area. Some facilities are wheelchair accessible. Leashed pets are permitted.

Reservations, fees: Reservations are accepted at 541/433-2540 or at www.odelllakeresort. com. Sites are $14-18 per night, $5 per night per additional vehicle. Open May-late September, weather permitting.

Directions: From Eugene, drive south on I-5 for five miles to Exit 188 and Highway 58. Turn east and drive 68 miles to Odell Lake and Forest Road 680 (at the east end of the lake). Turn right on Forest Road 680 and drive 400 yards to the campground on the right.

Contact: Odell Lake Lodge, 541/433-2540, www.odelllakeresort.com.

166 SUNSET COVE

Scenic rating: 8

on Odell Lake in Deschutes National Forest

Map 5.5, page 265

Sunset Cove campground borders the northeast shore of Odell Lake. Boat docks and rentals are available nearby at Odell Lake Lodge and Resort. Campsites are surrounded by large Douglas fir and some white pine trees. The camp backs up to the highway; expect to hear the noise.

Campsites, facilities: There are 20 sites for tents or RVs up to 40 feet long. Picnic tables and fire grills are provided. Drinking water, vault toilets, garbage service, a boat launch and day-use area, and fish-cleaning facilities are available. Firewood may be gathered from the surrounding area. Some facilities are wheelchair accessible. Leashed pets are permitted.

Reservations, fees: Reservations are accepted at 877/444-6777 ($10 reservation fee) or www. recreation.gov ($9 reservation fee). Sites are $16 per night, multi-sites are $30 per night, $8 per night per additional vehicle. Open mid-May-mid-October, weather permitting.

Directions: From Eugene, drive south on I-5 for five miles to Exit 188 and Highway 58. Turn east and drive 67 miles to the campground on the right.

Contact: Deschutes National Forest, Crescent Ranger District, 541/433-3200, www.fs.usda. gov/centraloregon; www.hoodoorecreation. com.

167 PRINCESS CREEK

Scenic rating: 9

on Odell Lake in Deschutes National Forest

Map 5.5, page 265

This wooded campground is on the northeast shore of Odell Lake, but it backs up to the highway so expect traffic noise. Boat docks and rentals are available nearby at the Shelter

Cove Resort. Fishing, hiking, and swimming are popular activities at the lake. A trail from the nearby Crater Buttes trailhead leads southwest into the Diamond Peak Wilderness and provides access to several small lakes in the backcountry.

Campsites, facilities: There are 45 sites for tents or RVs up to 30 feet long. Picnic tables and fire grills are provided. Vault toilets, garbage service, and boat-launching facilities are available. There is no drinking water. Firewood may be gathered from the surrounding area. Showers, a store, coin laundry, and ice are within five miles. Leashed pets are permitted.

Reservations, fees: Reservations are accepted at 877/444-6777 ($10 reservation fee) or www.recreation.gov ($9 reservation fee). Sites are $14 per night, multi-sites are $26 per night, $7 per night per additional vehicle. Open April-September, weather permitting.

Directions: From Eugene, drive south on I-5 for five miles to Exit 188 and Highway 58. Turn east and drive 64 miles to the campground on the right.

Contact: Deschutes National Forest, Crescent Ranger District, 541/433-3200, www.fs.usda.gov/centraloregon; www.hoodoorecreation.com.

168 CONTORTA FLAT

Scenic rating: 8

on Crescent Lake in Deschutes National Forest

Map 5.5, page 265

This campground on Crescent Lake, near the top of Willamette Pass, was named for the particular species of lodgepole pine that grows here. It's worth the drive—the last few miles of which are on a gravel road—to discover that you may have this isolated lakeside campground all to yourself. The elevation is 4,850 feet.

Campsites, facilities: There are 18 sites for tents or RVs up to 40 feet long. Picnic tables and fire grills are provided. Vault toilets and

garbage bins are available. There is no drinking water. Leashed pets are permitted.

Reservations, fees: Reservations are accepted at 877/444-6777 ($10 reservation fee) or www.recreation.gov ($9 reservation fee). Sites are $12-22 per night, $6 per night per additional vehicle. Open June-October, weather permitting.

Directions: From Eugene, drive south on I-5 for five miles to Exit 188 and Highway 58. Turn east and drive 69 miles to County Road 60. Turn right (west) and drive 10 miles to the camp on the left.

Contact: Deschutes National Forest, Crescent Ranger District, 541/433-3200, www.fs.usda.gov/centraloregon; www.hoodoorecreation.com.

169 CRESCENT JUNCTION RV PARK

Scenic rating: 5

on Crescent Lake

Map 5.5, page 265

This campground is conveniently located off Highway 58, just two miles from Crescent Lake. Four-wheeling trails are nearby.

Campsites, facilities: There are 25 sites with full hookups for tents or RVs of any length. Picnic tables and fire grills are provided. Flush toilets, coin showers, coin laundry, and a recreation room are available. A store is nearby. Some facilities are wheelchair accessible. Leashed pets are permitted.

Reservations, fees: Reservations are accepted. Sites are $25-30 per night. Weekly and monthly rates are available. Open year-round.

Directions: From Eugene, drive south on I-5 for five miles to Exit 188 and Highway 58. Turn east and drive 69 miles to County Road 60. Turn right (west) and drive a short distance to the camp on the left.

Contact: Hoodoo Recreation, Crescent Junction RV Park, 20030 Crescent Lake Highway, Crescent Lake, 541/433-5300, www.crescentjunctionrv.com.

170 WINDY GROUP

Scenic rating: 8
on Crescent Lake in Deschutes National Forest

Map 5.5, page 265

Windy Group is located near the beaches on Crescent Lake. The lake warms up more easily than many high-mountain lakes, making swimming and waterskiing two popular options. Mountain biking and hiking are also available.

Campsites, facilities: There is one group site for tents or RVs up to 60 feet long and up to 40 people. Picnic tables and fire rings are provided. Vault toilets and garbage bins are available. There is no drinking water. Some facilities are wheelchair accessible. Leashed pets are permitted.

Reservations, fees: Reservations are accepted at 877/444-6777 ($10 reservation fee) or www.recreation.gov ($9 reservation fee). The site is $75 per night. Open May-September, weather permitting.

Directions: From Eugene, drive south on I-5 for five miles to Exit 188 and Highway 58. Turn east and drive 69 miles to County Road 60. Turn right (west) and drive 7.5 miles to the camp.

Contact: Deschutes National Forest, Crescent Ranger District, 541/433-3200, www.fs.usda.gov/centraloregon; www.hoodoorecreation.com.

171 SIMAX GROUP CAMP

Scenic rating: 8
on Crescent Lake in Deschutes National Forest

Map 5.5, page 265

This camp is set at an elevation of 4,850 feet on Crescent Lake and provides trails to day-use beaches. Fishing is variable year to year and is usually better earlier in the season. A boat launch is available at neighboring Crescent Lake, about two miles away. Nearby Diamond Peak Wilderness (free permit required) provides hiking options.

Campsites, facilities: There are three group sites for 30-50 people each and one group site (Site D) with electricity for up to 20 people. Picnic tables, fireplaces, and tent pads (tents must be placed on tent pads) are provided. Drinking water, restrooms with flush toilets and showers, garbage service, and a group shelter are available. Some facilities are wheelchair accessible. Leashed pets are permitted.

Reservations, fees: Reservations are accepted at 877/444-6777 ($10 reservation fee) or www.recreation.gov ($9 reservation fee). Site A is $80-100 per night, Sites B and C are $100-120 per night. (Note that Site C is best for RVs.) Site D is $75-140 per night. The group picnic area is $50 per day. Rates may be higher on weekends. Open mid-May-October, weather permitting.

Directions: From Eugene, drive south on I-5 for five miles to Exit 188 and Highway 58. Turn east and drive 70 miles to Crescent Lake Highway (Forest Road 60). Turn right and drive two miles to Forest Road 6005. Turn left and drive one mile to the campground on the right.

Contact: Deschutes National Forest, Crescent Ranger District, 541/433-3200, www.fs.usda.gov/centraloregon; www.hoodoorecreation.com.

172 CRESCENT LAKE

Scenic rating: 8
on Crescent Lake in Deschutes National Forest

Map 5.5, page 265

This campground is set along the north shore of Crescent Lake, and it is often windy here in the afternoon. Boat docks, launching facilities, and rentals are available at Crescent Lake Resort, adjacent to the campground. A trail from camp heads into the Diamond Peak Wilderness (free permit required; available on-site) and also branches north to Odell Lake.

Campsites, facilities: There are 47 sites for tents or RVs up to 36 feet long and three yurts. Picnic tables and fire grills are provided. Drinking water, vault toilets, garbage service, and boat-launching facilities are available. Firewood may be gathered from the surrounding area. Leashed pets are permitted.

Reservations, fees: Reservations are accepted at 877/444-6777 ($10 reservation fee) or www.recreation.gov ($9 reservation fee). Sites are $14-18 per night, $7-9 per night per additional vehicle, yurts are $40 per night. Open April-late October, weather permitting.

Directions: From Eugene, drive south on I-5 for five miles to Exit 188 and Highway 58. Turn east and drive 70 miles to Crescent Lake Highway (Forest Road 60). Turn right (west) and drive 2.2 miles southwest. Bear right to remain on Forest Road 60, and drive another 0.25 mile to the campground on the left.

Contact: Deschutes National Forest, Crescent Ranger District, 541/433-3200, www.fs.usda.gov/centraloregon; www.hoodoorecreation.com.

173 SPRING
🥾 🚲 🏊 🎣 ⛴ 🐕 🚐 ⛺

Scenic rating: 8
on Crescent Lake in Deschutes National Forest

Map 5.5, page 265

Spring campground is nestled in a lodgepole pine forest on the southern shore of Crescent Lake. Sites are open, with some on the lake offering Diamond Peak views. Boating, swimming, and waterskiing are popular activities, and the Windy-Oldenburg Trailhead provides access to the Oregon Cascades Recreation Area. The camp is at an elevation of 4,850 feet.

Campsites, facilities: There are 56 sites for tents or RVs up to 40 feet long, five sites for tents only, four multi-sites, and 12 sites that can be reserved as a group site for up to 70 people and 25 vehicles. Picnic tables and fire grills are provided. Drinking water, vault toilets, garbage service, boat-launching facilities, and firewood (may be gathered from the surrounding area) are available. Leashed pets are permitted.

Reservations, fees: Reservations are accepted at 877/444-6777 ($10 reservation fee) or www.recreation.gov ($9 reservation fee). Single sites are $18 per night, multiple sites are $34 per night, the group site is $125 per night, $9 per night per additional vehicle. Open May-September, weather permitting.

Directions: From Eugene, drive south on I-5 for five miles to Exit 188 and Highway 58. Turn east and drive 70 miles to Crescent Lake Highway (Forest Road 60). Turn right and drive eight miles west to the campground entrance road on the left. Turn left and drive one mile to the campground.

Contact: Deschutes National Forest, Crescent Ranger District, 541/433-3200 or 541/338-7869, www.fs.usda.gov/centraloregon.

174 CONTORTA POINT GROUP CAMP
🥾 🚲 🏊 🎣 ⛴ 🤸 🐕 🚐 ⛺

Scenic rating: 8
on Crescent Lake in Deschutes National Forest

Map 5.5, page 265

This campground (4,850 feet elevation) sits on the southern shore of Crescent Lake, where boating, swimming, and waterskiing are among the summer pastimes. A number of trails from the nearby Windy-Oldenburg Trailhead provide access to lakes in the Oregon Cascades Recreation Area. Motorized vehicles are restricted to open roads only.

Campsites, facilities: There are two group sites for tents or RVs up to 30 feet long that can accommodate up to 40 people each. There is no drinking water. Picnic tables and fire rings are provided. Vault toilets and garbage bins are available. Firewood can be gathered in surrounding forest. Boat docks and launching facilities are three miles away at Spring Campground. Leashed pets are permitted.

Reservations, fees: Reservations are accepted at 877/444-6777 ($10 reservation fee) or www.recreation.gov ($9 reservation fee). Sites are

$65 per night. Open May-September, weather permitting.

Directions: From Eugene, drive south on I-5 for five miles to Exit 188 and Highway 58. Turn east and drive 70 miles to Crescent Lake Highway (Forest Road 60). Turn right and drive 9.9 miles to Forest Road 280. Turn left and drive one mile to the campground.

Contact: Deschutes National Forest, Crescent Ranger District, 541/433-3200, www.fs.usda. gov/centraloregon; www.hoodoorecreation. com.

175 WHITEFISH HORSE CAMP

Scenic rating: 5

on Whitefish Creek in Deschutes National Forest

Map 5.5, page 265

This just might be the best horse camp in the state. Only horse camping is allowed here, and manure removal is required. High lines are not allowed; horses must be kept in stalls. On Whitefish Creek at the west end of Crescent Lake, this campground is set in lodgepole pine and has shaded sites. Although located in a flat area across the road from the lake, the campground has no lake view. Moderately to heavily used, it has access to about 100 miles of trail, leading to Diamond Peak Wilderness, the Metolius-Windigo National Recreation Trail, the Oregon Cascades Recreation Area, and many high mountain lakes. The camp sits at 4,850 feet elevation.

Campsites, facilities: There are 19 sites for tents or RVs up to 40 feet long. Picnic tables and fire rings are provided. Drinking water, garbage bins, vault toilets, horse corrals, and manure disposal site are available. Firewood may be gathered from the surrounding area. Leashed pets are permitted.

Reservations, fees: Reservations are accepted at 877/444-6777 ($10 reservation fee) or www. recreation.gov ($9 reservation fee). Sites are $14

per night for two stalls, $18 per night for four stalls, and $7-9 per night per additional vehicle. Open May-September, weather permitting.

Directions: From Eugene, drive south on I-5 for five miles to Exit 188 and Highway 58. Turn east and drive 70 miles to Crescent Lake Highway (Forest Road 60). Turn right (west) and drive 2.2 miles southwest. Stay to the right to remain on Forest Road 60, and drive six miles to the campground on the right.

Contact: Deschutes National Forest, Crescent Ranger District, 541/433-3200, www.fs.usda. gov/centraloregon; www.hoodoorecreation. com.

176 CRESCENT CREEK

Scenic rating: 7

on Crescent Creek in Deschutes National Forest

Map 5.5, page 265

One of the Cascades' classic hidden campgrounds, Crescent Creek camp sits along the banks of its namesake at 4,500 feet elevation. The buzzwords here are pretty, developed, and private. A registered bird-watching area is nearby. Hunters are the primary users of this campground, mainly in the fall. Otherwise, it gets light use. There's some highway noise here, and even if you can't hear it, traffic is visible from some sites.

Campsites, facilities: There are nine sites for tents or RVs up to 40 feet long. Picnic tables and fire grills are provided. Vault toilets, drinking water, and garbage service are available. Firewood may be gathered from the surrounding area. Leashed pets are permitted.

Reservations, fees: Reservations are accepted at 877/444-6777 ($10 reservation fee) or www. recreation.gov ($9 reservation fee). Single sites are $14 per night, multi-sites are $26 per night, $7 per night per additional vehicle. Open May-late September, weather permitting.

Directions: From Eugene, drive south on I-5 for five miles to Exit 188 and Highway 58.

Turn east and drive 73 miles to County Road 61. Turn left (east) and drive three miles to the campground on the right.

Contact: Deschutes National Forest, Crescent Ranger District, 541/433-3200, www.fs.usda. gov/centraloregon; www.hoodoorecreation. com.

177 CORRAL SPRINGS

Scenic rating: 4

in Fremont-Winema National Forest

Map 5.5, page 265

This flat campground with no water source is located next to Corral Springs at 4,900 feet elevation. The main attraction is solitude; it's primitive, remote, and quiet. The landscape features stands of lodgepole pine, interspersed by several small meadows.

Campsites, facilities: There are six sites for tents or RVs up to 50 feet long. Picnic tables and fire grills are provided. Vault toilets are available. There is no drinking water, and garbage must be packed out. A store, café, coin laundry, and ice are within five miles. Leashed pets are permitted.

Reservations, fees: Reservations are not accepted. There is no fee for camping. Open mid-May-late October, weather permitting.

Directions: From Eugene, drive southeast on Highway 58 for 86 miles to U.S. 97. Turn south and drive five miles to Forest Road 9774 (2.5 miles north of Chemult). Turn right and drive two miles west to the campground.

Contact: Fremont-Winema National Forest, Chemult Ranger District, 541/365-7001, www. fs.usda.gov/fremont-winema.

178 DIGIT POINT

Scenic rating: 7

on Miller Lake in Fremont-Winema National Forest

Map 5.5, page 265

This campground is nestled in a lodgepole pine and mountain hemlock forest at 5,600 feet elevation on the shore of Miller Lake, a popular spot for boating, fishing, and swimming. Nearby trails provide access to the Mount Thielsen Wilderness and the Pacific Crest Trail.

Campsites, facilities: There are 64 sites for tents or RVs up to 30 feet long. Picnic tables and fire grills are provided. Drinking water, flush toilets, garbage service, and a dump station are available. Boat docks and launching facilities are nearby. Some facilities are wheelchair accessible. Leashed pets are permitted.

Reservations, fees: Reservations are not accepted. Sites are $12 per night, $5 per night per additional vehicle. Open Memorial Day-mid-October, weather permitting.

Directions: From Eugene, drive southeast on Highway 58 for 86 miles to U.S. 97. Turn south and drive seven miles to Forest Road 9772 (one mile north of Chemult). Turn right and drive 12 miles west to the campground.

Contact: Fremont-Winema National Forest, Chemult Ranger District, 541/365-7001, www. fs.usda.gov/fremont-winema.

179 WALT HARING SNO-PARK

Scenic rating: 6

in Fremont-Winema National Forest near Chemult

Map 5.5, page 265

For eons, this has been a tiny, unknown, and free campground used as a staging area for snowmobiling and cross-country skiing in winter. In summer, it has primarily been a picnic site and layover spot. The elevation is 4,700 feet.

Campsites, facilities: There are five sites for tents or RVs. Picnic tables and fire rings are provided. Drinking water, vault toilets, and an RV dump station ($5 fee) are available. There is also a nice shelter with a woodstove. Some facilities are wheelchair accessible. Leashed pets are permitted.

Reservations, fees: Reservations are not accepted. There is no fee for camping; in winter, a parking permit is required and is available from the Oregon Department of Motor Vehicles. Open year-round.

Directions: From Eugene, drive southeast on Highway 58 for 86 miles to U.S. 97. Turn south and drive seven miles to Forest Road 9772 (one mile north of Chemult). Turn right on Forest Road 9772 (Miller Lake Road) and drive 0.5 mile to the campground.

Contact: Fremont-Winema National Forest, 541/365-7001, www.fs.usda.gov/fremont-winema; Oregon Department of Motor Vehicles, www.oregon.gov.

180 CHARLES V. STANTON PARK

Scenic rating: 7

on the South Umpqua River

Map 5.6, page 266

Charles V. Stanton Park, along the banks of the South Umpqua River, is an all-season spot with a nice beach for swimming in the summer and good steelhead fishing in the winter.

Campsites, facilities: There are 20 sites for tents or self-contained RVs (no hookups), 20 sites with full hookups for RVs up to 60 feet long, and one group area for up to 13 camping units. Picnic tables and fire rings or barbecues are provided. Drinking water, restrooms with flush toilets and showers, a dump station, pavilion, picnic area, Wi-Fi, and playground are available. Propane gas, a store, café, coin laundry, and ice are within one mile. Some facilities are wheelchair accessible. Leashed pets are permitted.

Reservations, fees: Reservations are accepted ($10 reservation fee) at 541/957-7001 or www.co.douglas.or.us. Sites are $17-25 per night. Call for group rates. Credit/debit cards are not accepted at the campground but may be used to make reservations. Open year-round.

Directions: Depending on which direction you're heading on I-5, there are two routes to reach this campground. In Canyonville northbound on I-5, take Exit 99 and drive one mile north on the frontage road to the campground on the right. Otherwise: In Canyonville southbound on I-5, take Exit 101. Turn right at the first stop sign, and almost immediately turn right again onto the frontage road. Drive one mile south on the frontage road to the campground on the left.

Contact: Charles V. Stanton Park, Douglas County Parks, 541/839-4483, www.co.douglas.or.us/parks.

181 CHIEF MIWALETA CAMPGROUND

Scenic rating: 7

on Galesville Reservoir, east of Azalea

Map 5.6, page 266

If location is everything, then this camp has got it. Wooded sites are set along the shore of beautiful Gales Reservoir, providing a base camp for a trip filled with fishing, boating, hiking, camping, and picnicking. A pavilion can be reserved in the day-use area.

Campsites, facilities: There are 20 sites with full hookups for RVs up to 60 feet long (some pull-through), 13 sites for tents only, and three cabins. Picnic tables and fire rings are provided. Drinking water, vault toilets, a reservable pavilion, a play structure, and a boat ramp are available. Some facilities are wheelchair accessible. Leashed pets are permitted.

Reservations, fees: Reservations are accepted at 541/957-7001 or www.co.douglas.or.us ($10 reservation fee). RV sites with full hookups are $25 per night, $3 per night per additional vehicle, tent sites are $17 per night, and the cabins are $37-52 per night. Discounts available for Douglas County residents. Some credit cards are accepted for reservations only. Open year-round.

Directions: From Azalea, take I-5 north about 0.5 mile to Exit 88 east to Upper Cow Creek Road. Merge onto Upper Cow Creek and drive eight miles to the campground on the left. GPS Coordinates: 42.85172, -123.164518

Contact: Chief Miwaleta County Campground, 541/837-3302, www.co.douglas.or.us/parks/campgrounds.asp.

182 MEADOW WOOD RV PARK

Scenic rating: 6

in Glendale

Map 5.6, page 266

Meadow Wood is a good option for RVers looking for a camping spot along I-5. It features 80 wooded acres and all the amenities. Nearby attractions include a ghost town, gold panning, and Wolf Creek Tavern.

Campsites, facilities: There are 25 tent sites and 75 pull-through sites with full or partial hookups for RVs up to 40 feet long. Picnic tables are provided. Drinking water, restrooms with flush toilets and showers, propane gas, a dump station, Wi-Fi, a coin laundry, a playground, and a seasonal heated swimming pool are available. Some facilities are wheelchair accessible. Leashed pets are permitted.

Reservations, fees: Reservations are accepted. Sites are $18-30 per night. Monthly rates are available. Open year-round.

Directions: From Grants Pass, drive north on I-5 to Exit 83 (near Glendale) and drive east for 0.25 mile to Autumn Lane. Turn right (south) on Autumn Lane and drive one mile to the park. Alternatively, if you are instead driving south from Roseburg, drive south on I-5 to Exit 86 (near Glendale). Take that exit and drive over the freeway and turn right onto the frontage road. Continue for three miles to Barton Road. Turn left (east) and drive one mile to Autumn Lane. Turn right (south) on Autumn Lane and drive 0.75 mile to the park.

Contact: Meadow Wood RV Park, 869 Autumn Ln., 541/832-3114.

183 WOLF CREEK PARK

Scenic rating: 6

near the town of Wolf Creek

Map 5.6, page 266

This rustic campground is located on Wolf Creek near the historic Wolf Creek Inn. A hiking trail leads to the top of London Peak through old-growth forest. Although close to I-5 and the town of Wolf Creek, this spot gets low to average use.

Campsites, facilities: There are 20 sites for tents only, 14 sites for tents or RVs up to 40 feet long (partial hookups), and two group sites for tents that accommodate up to 30 people each. Picnic tables and fire pits are provided. Drinking water, vault toilets, a dump station, softball field, playground, and a picnic shelter are available. A camp host is on-site. Supplies are available nearby. Some facilities are wheelchair accessible. Leashed pets are permitted.

Reservations, fees: Reservations are accepted at 800/452-5687 or www.reserveamerica.com ($9 reservation fee). Sites are $15-25 per night, $5 per night per additional vehicle, the group camps are $40 per night. Open May-early September.

Directions: From Grants Pass, drive north on I-5 for approximately 18 miles to Exit 76/Wolf Creek. Take that exit to Wolf Creek Road. Turn left and drive 0.5 mile to the town of Wolf Creek and Main Street. Turn left and drive 0.25 mile to the park.

Contact: Josephine County Parks, 541/474-5285, www.co.josephine.or.us.

184 INDIAN MARY PARK

Scenic rating: 9

on the Rogue River

Map 5.6, page 266   **BEST (**

This park is the crown jewel of the Josephine County parks. Set right on the Rogue River at an elevation of 900-1,000 feet, the park offers disc golf (Frisbee golf), fishing, hiking trails, a picnic shelter, a swimming beach (unsupervised), and volleyball. Rogue River is famous for its rafting, which can be done with a commercial outfit or on your own.

Campsites, facilities: There are 34 sites for tents or self-contained RVs (no hookups), 44 sites with full hookups, and 14 sites with partial hookups for tents or RVs of up to 40 feet, a group tent site for up to 20 people, and two yurts. Picnic tables and fire pits are provided. Drinking water, restrooms with flush toilets and coin showers, garbage bins, a dump station, boat ramp, day-use area, a reservable picnic shelter, playground, volleyball court, horseshoe pits, ice, and firewood are available. A camp host is on-site. A store and café are seven miles away, and a coin laundry is 16 miles away. Some facilities are wheelchair accessible. Leashed pets are permitted.

Reservations, fees: Reservations are accepted ($9 reservation fee) at 800/452-5687 or www.reserveamerica.com. Sites are $20-35 per night, $5 per night per additional vehicle, the group camp is $40-45 per night, and yurts are $40-45 per night. Open year-round.

Directions: From Grants Pass, drive north on I-5 for 3.5 miles to Exit 61 (Merlin-Galice Road). Take that exit and drive west on Merlin-Galice Road for 19 miles to Indian Mary Park on the right.

Contact: Josephine County Parks, 541/474-5285, www.co.josephine.or.us.

185 ELDERBERRY FLAT

Scenic rating: 7

on West Fork Evans Creek

Map 5.6, page 266

This camp is virtually unknown except to the off-highway vehicle (OHV) crowd. On weekends, this is usually not the place to find quiet and serenity. OHV and motorcycle activity is common here. It is located on the banks of Evans Creek, about a 30-minute drive from I-5. Small and primitive, it has access to swimming holes along the creek. No fishing is allowed in the creek.

Campsites, facilities: There are 11 sites for tents only. Picnic tables and fire grills are provided. Vault toilets and garbage service are available, but there is no drinking water. Some facilities are wheelchair accessible. Leashed pets are permitted.

Reservations, fees: Reservations are not accepted. There is no fee for camping, but there is a 14-day stay limit. Open April 1-October 31.

Directions: From Grants Pass, drive south on I-5 for 10 miles to the Rogue River exit. Take that exit, turn right on Depot Street, and drive to Pine Street. Turn left and drive 18 miles (it becomes East Evans Creek Road) to West Fork Evans Creek Road. Turn left and drive nine miles to the campground.

Contact: Bureau of Land Management, Medford District, 541/618-2200, www.or.blm.gov/medford.

186 GRIFFIN PARK

Scenic rating: 7

on the Rogue River

Map 5.6, page 266

This high-use campground and 16-acre park has grassy sites situated 100-150 yards from the Rogue River. The river current is slow in this area, so it is good for swimming and water play. Fishing and rafting are also popular. Hiking and bicycling are available nearby on Bureau of Land Management property.

Campsites, facilities: There are four sites for tents or RVs (no hookups), 15 sites for tents or RVs up to 40 feet long (full hookups), and one yurt. Picnic tables and fire pits are provided. Drinking water, restrooms with flush toilets and showers, a dump station, recreation field, playground, and horseshoe pits are available. A camp host is on-site. A boat ramp, convenience store, swimming area, and playground are within one mile. Some facilities are wheelchair accessible. Leashed pets are permitted.

Reservations, fees: Reservations are accepted ($8 reservation fee) at 800/452-5687 or www.reserveamerica.com. Sites are $20-30 per night, $5 per night per additional vehicle; yurts are $40 per night. Open year-round, but with no water November-early April; tent sites are closed mid-October-March 31.

Directions: From Grants Pass on I-5, take the U.S. 199 exit. Turn south on U.S. 199 and drive 6.7 miles to Riverbanks Road. Turn right and drive 6.2 miles to Griffin Park Road. Turn right and drive 0.5 mile to the park.

Contact: Josephine County Parks, 541/474-5285, www.co.josephine.or.us.

187 GRANTS PASS/ REDWOOD HIGHWAY CAMPGROUND

Scenic rating: 8

near Grants Pass

Map 5.6, page 266

This campground along a stream in the hills outside of Grants Pass attracts bird-watchers. It also makes a perfect layover spot for travelers who want to get away from the highway for a while. For an interesting side trip, drive south down scenic U.S. 199 to Cave Junction or Illinois River State Park.

Campsites, facilities: There are 40 sites for tents or RVs of any length (some with full hookups); some sites are pull-through. There are

also three cabins. Picnic tables are provided, and tent sites have fire pits. Restrooms with showers, drinking water, a dump station, coin laundry, convenience store, ice, RV supplies, propane gas, and limited Wi-Fi are available. There is also a playground and a recreation field. Leashed pets are permitted with certain restrictions.

Reservations, fees: Reservations are accepted and receive a 10 percent discount. RV sites are $29.50-45.50 per night, tent sites are $29 per night, cabins are $55 per night, $4 per person per night for more than two people, $3 per night for additional vehicle. Some credit cards are accepted. Open year-round.

Directions: In Grants Pass on I-5, take the U.S. 199 exit. Turn southwest on U.S. 199 and drive 14.5 miles to the campground on the right (at Milepost 14.5).

Contact: Grants Pass/Redwood Highway Campground, 541/476-6508 or 888/476-6508, www.redwoodhwycampground.com.

188 SCHROEDER

Scenic rating: 9

on the Rogue River

Map 5.6, page 266

Steelhead and salmon fishing, swimming, and boating are among the possibilities at this popular camp along the Rogue River. Just a short jog off the highway, it makes an excellent layover for I-5 travelers. A bonus for RVers is 50-amp service. The park is set close to Hellgate Excursions, which provides jet-boat trips on the Rogue River.

Campsites, facilities: There are 22 sites with partial hookups for tents or RVs, 29 sites with full hookups for tents or RVs of any length, and two yurts. Picnic tables and fire pits are provided. Restrooms with flush toilets and coin showers and a picnic shelter that can be reserved are available. Recreational facilities include ballfields, tennis and basketball courts, horseshoe pits, volleyball court, a dog park, picnic area, playground, and boat ramp. A camp host is on-site. Some facilities, including a fishing pier, are wheelchair accessible. Leashed pets are permitted.

Reservations, fees: Reservations are accepted ($8 reservation fee) at 800/452-5687 or www.reserveamerica.com. Sites are $20-30 per night, $5 per night per additional vehicle; yurts are $40 per night. Open year-round; tent sites are closed mid-October-March 31.

Directions: In Grants Pass on I-5, take Exit 55 to U.S. 199. Drive west on U.S. 199 for 0.7 mile to Redwood Avenue. Turn right and drive 1.5 miles to Willow Lane. Turn right and drive 0.9 mile to Schroeder Lane and the park.

Contact: Josephine County Parks, 541/474-5285, www.co.josephine.or.us.

189 ROGUE VALLEY OVERNITERS

Scenic rating: 5

near the Rogue River

Map 5.6, page 266

This park is just off the freeway in Grants Pass, the jumping-off point for trips down the Rogue River. The summer heat in this part of Oregon can surprise visitors in late June and early July. This is a nice, comfortable park with shade trees. About half of the sites are taken by monthly renters.

Campsites, facilities: There are 43 sites for RVs of any length (full hookups); some are pull-through sites. Picnic tables are provided. Restrooms with flush toilets and showers, Wi-Fi, cable TV, a dump station, meeting room, and coin laundry are available. Propane gas, a store, café, and ice are available within one mile. Leashed pets are permitted (limited to two).

Reservations, fees: Reservations are recommended. Sites are $33-37 per night, plus $2 per person per night for more than two people. Weekly and monthly rates are available. Open year-round.

Directions: In Grants Pass on I-5, take Exit 58 to 6th Street. Drive south on 6th Street for 0.25 mile to the park on the right.

Contact: Rogue Valley Overniters, 541/479-2208, www.roguevalleyoverniters.com.

190 WHITEHORSE

Scenic rating: 9

near the Rogue River

Map 5.6, page 266

This pleasant county park is set about 0.25 mile from the banks of the Rogue River. It is one of several parks in the Grants Pass area that provide opportunities for salmon and steelhead fishing, hiking, and boating. This is a popular bird-watching area. Wildlife Images, a wildlife rehabilitation center, is nearby. Possible side trips include Crater Lake National Park (two hours away), Kerby Museum, and Oregon Caves.

Campsites, facilities: There are 34 sites for tents or RVs of any length (no hookups), eight sites for RVs of any length (full hookups), and one yurt. Picnic tables and fire pits are provided. Restrooms with flush toilets and coin showers, a boat ramp, horseshoe pits, volleyball, a picnic shelter, and a playground are available. A camp host is on-site. Some facilities are wheelchair accessible. Leashed pets are permitted.

Reservations, fees: Reservations are accepted ($8 reservation fee) at 800/452-5687 or www.reserveamerica.com (search for "White horse"). Sites are $20-30 per night, $5 per night per additional vehicle. The yurt is $40 per night. Open year-round.

Directions: In Grants Pass on I-5, take Exit 58 to 6th Street. Drive south on 6th Street to G Street. Turn right (west) and drive approximately seven miles (the road becomes Upper River Road, then Lower River Road). The park is on the left at 7600 Lower River Road.

Contact: Josephine County Parks, 541/474-5285, www.co.josephine.or.us.

191 RIVER PARK RV RESORT

Scenic rating: 6

on the Rogue River

Map 5.6, page 266

This park has a quiet, serene riverfront setting, yet it is close to all the conveniences of a small city. Highlights here include 700 feet of Rogue River frontage for trout fishing and swimming. It's one of several parks in the immediate area.

Campsites, facilities: There are 47 sites with full hookups for RVs up to 40 feet long. Picnic tables are provided. Cable TV, Wi-Fi, restrooms with flush toilets and showers, a dump station, coin laundry, horseshoe pits, and ice are available. Leashed pets are permitted.

Reservations, fees: Reservations are accepted. Sites are $35-51 per night, $2 per person per night for more than two people, and $2 per night for an additional vehicle. Some credit cards are accepted. Open year-round.

Directions: In Grants Pass on I-5, take Exit 55 west to Highway 199. Drive west on Highway 199 for two miles to Parkdale. Turn left on Parkdale and drive one block to Highway 99. Turn left on Highway 99 and drive two miles to the park on the left.

Contact: River Park RV Resort, 541/479-0046 www.riverparkrvresort.com.

192 CHINOOK WINDS RV PARK

Scenic rating: 6

on the Rogue River

Map 5.6, page 266

This campground along the Rogue River is close to chartered boat trips down the Rogue and a golf course. Fishing and swimming access are available from the campground.

Campsites, facilities: There are 25 sites with full or partial hookups for RVs up to 40 feet; some are pull-through sites. Picnic tables are provided. Restrooms with flush toilets and showers, a dump station, Wi-Fi, coin laundry, boat dock, and ice are available. Some facilities are wheelchair accessible. Leashed pets are permitted.

Reservations, fees: Reservations are recommended. Sites are $35-45 per night, plus $3 per person per night for more than two people. Weekly and monthly rates are available. Cash or check only. Open year-round.

Directions: From Grants Pass, drive south on I-5 for 10 miles to Exit 48 at Rogue River. Take that exit west (over the bridge) to Highway 99. Turn right and drive west one mile to the park on the right.

Contact: Chinook Winds RV Park, 541/582-1686.

193 VALLEY OF THE ROGUE STATE PARK

Scenic rating: 7

on the Rogue River

Map 5.6, page 266

With easy highway access, this popular campground along the banks of the Rogue River often fills to near capacity during the summer. Recreation options include fishing and boating. This spot makes a good base camp for taking in the Rogue Valley and surrounding attractions: Ashland's Shakespeare Festival, the Britt Music Festival, Crater Lake National Park, historic Jacksonville, and Oregon Caves National Monument.

Campsites, facilities: There are 140 sites with full or partial hookups for tents or RVs up to 75 feet long, some with pull-through sites, and 14 sites for tents. There are also three group tent areas for up to 25 people each and eight yurts. Picnic tables and fire grills are provided. Restrooms with flush toilets and showers, drinking water, garbage bins, a dump station, firewood, Wi-Fi, coin laundry, a meeting hall, amphitheater, and playgrounds are available. A restaurant is nearby. Boat-launching facilities are nearby. Some facilities are wheelchair accessible. Leashed pets are permitted.

Reservations, fees: Reservations are accepted at 800/452-5687 or www.oregonstateparks.org ($8 reservation fee). Tent sites are $19 per night, RV sites are $26-29 per night, $7 per night per extra vehicle. Group areas are $71 per night; yurts are $41-51 per night. Some credit cards are accepted. Open year-round.

Directions: From Grants Pass, drive south on I-5 for 12 miles to Exit 45B/Valley of the Rogue State Park. Take that exit, turn right, and drive a short distance to the park on the right.

Contact: Valley of the Rogue State Park, 541/582-1118 or 800/551-6949, www.oregon-stateparks.org.

194 MEDFORD/GOLD HILL KOA

🏃 🚴 🏊 🛶 🚤 🐕 🎿 ♿ 🚐 ⛺

Scenic rating: 6

on the Rogue River

Map 5.6, page 266

This campground is set 0.5 mile from the Rogue River, with bike paths, a golf course, and the Oregon Vortex (the house of mystery) in the vicinity. It's one of the many campgrounds between Gold Hill and Grants Pass.

Campsites, facilities: There are 55 sites with full hookups, 21 sites with partial hookups for RVs of any length, 12 sites for tents, and four cabins. Some sites are pull-through. Picnic tables are provided, and tent sites have fire rings. Restrooms with flush toilets and showers, Wi-Fi, cable TV, propane gas, a dump station, firewood, a convenience store, coin laundry, ice, horseshoe pits, basketball hoop, a playground, and a seasonal swimming pool are available. A café is within one mile, and boat-launching facilities are within five miles. Some facilities are wheelchair accessible. Leashed pets are permitted.

Reservations, fees: Reservations are accepted at 800/562-7608. RV Sites are $40-42 per night, tent sites are $30 per night, cabins are $65 per night, plus $2 per person per night for more than two people. Some credit cards are accepted. Open year-round.

Directions: From Medford, drive north on I-5 for 10 miles to South Gold Hill and Exit 40. Take that exit, turn right, and drive 0.25 mile to Blackwell Road. Turn right (on a paved road) and drive 0.25 mile to the park.

Contact: Medford/Gold Hill KOA, 541/855-7710, www.koa.com.

195 LAKE SELMAC

🏃 🚴 🏊 🛶 🚤 🐕 🎿 ♿ 🚐 ⛺

Scenic rating: 9

on Lake Selmac

Map 5.6, page 266

Nestled in a wooded, mountainous area, this 300-acre park offers boating, hiking, sailing, swimming, and good trophy bass fishing on beautiful, 160-acre Lake Selmac. Horse trails are also available. There are seasonal hosts and a park ranger on-site.

Campsites, facilities: There are 113 sites for tents or RVs up to 40 feet long, some with full or partial hookups, a group area for up to 50 people, and five yurts. There are also six horse camps with corrals. Picnic tables and fire pits are provided. Drinking water, restrooms with flush toilets and coin showers, a dump station, convenience store, picnic area, horseshoe pits, playground, ballfields, two boat ramps, and a dock are available. Some facilities are wheelchair accessible. Leashed pets are permitted.

Reservations, fees: Reservations are accepted at 800/452-5687 or www.reserveamerica.com ($8 reservation fee). Sites are $20-30 per night, $5 per night per additional vehicle, horse sites are $19 per night, yurts are $40 per night. The group site is $40 per night for the first 12 people, $3 per person per night for more than 12 people. Open year-round, with some facility limitations in winter.

Directions: In Grants Pass on I-5, take the U.S. 199 exit. Turn south on U.S. 199 and drive for 23 miles to Selma. Continue 0.5 mile to the

Lake Selmac exit (Lakeshore Drive). Turn left (east) and drive 2.3 miles to the lake and the campground entrance.

Contact: Josephine County Parks, 541/474-5285, www.co.josephine.or.us.

196 LAKE SELMAC RESORT

🚶 🚴 🏊 🛶 🚐 🏕 🐕 ♿ 🚌 ⛺

Scenic rating: 7

on Lake Selmac

Map 5.6, page 266

This resort borders the shore of Lake Selmac, a 160-acre lake. Fishing is great for largemouth bass (the state record has been set here three times). Bluegill, catfish, crappie, and trout are also catchable here. Fishing derbies are held during the summer. There is a 5-mph speed limit on the lake. Watch for waterfowl, including eagles, geese, ospreys, and swans. A trail circles the lake, and bikers, hikers, and horses are welcome. A disc golf course is 1.5 miles away at the county park, and a golf course is about six miles away. Oregon Caves National Monument, about 30 miles away, makes a good side trip.

Campsites, facilities: There are 29 sites with full or partial hookups for tents or RVs of any length; most sites are pull-through. Two cabins and a rental trailer are also available. Picnic tables and fire rings are provided. Drinking water, restrooms with flush toilets and showers, coin laundry, a general store with fishing and hunting licenses, bait and tackle, firewood, ice, Wi-Fi, and a play area with miniature golf, volleyball, tetherball, and horseshoe pits are available. Boat docks and launching facilities are nearby, and rentals are on-site. Some facilities are wheelchair accessible. Leashed pets are permitted, with breed restrictions.

Reservations, fees: Reservations are accepted. Sites start at $35 per night, $3 per night per additional vehicle, $5 per person per night for more than four. Monthly rates are available. Some credit cards are accepted. Open year-round, with limited winter facilities.

Directions: In Grants Pass on I-5, take the U.S. 199 exit. Turn southwest on U.S. 199 and drive 23 miles to Selma and the Lake Selmac exit (Lakeshore Drive). Turn left (east) and drive 2.5 miles to the lake and the resort on the left.

Contact: Lake Selmac Resort, 541/597-2277, www.lakeselmacresort.com.

197 MOUNTAIN MAN RV PARK

🏊 🚐 🏕 🚌 ⛺

Scenic rating: 7

on the Illinois River

Map 5.6, page 266

This park on the Illinois River provides good opportunities for swimming and boating (no motors are permitted). And yes, there is a mountain man here who often shows up in costume in the evening when camp groups build a fire. Great Cats World Park, a wildlife park, is 1.5 miles away. Other nearby side trips include Oregon Caves National Monument (21 miles) and Grants Pass (31 miles). Crescent City is 50 miles away. Note that a majority of the campground is taken by monthly rentals, with the remainder available for overnighters. This park was previously known as Town and Country RV Park.

Campsites, facilities: There are 51 sites for tents or RVs of any length (full hookups); some sites are pull-through. Picnic tables are provided, and some sites have fire rings. Drinking water, cable TV, restrooms with flush toilets and showers, coin laundry, a community fire ring, ice, horseshoe pits, Wi-Fi, and a clubhouse are available. Leashed pets are permitted.

Reservations, fees: Reservations are accepted. RV sites are $30 per night, tent sites are $20 per night, $4 per person per night for more than two people. Weekly and monthly rates are available. Open year-round.

Directions: In Grants Pass on I-5, take the U.S. 199 exit. Go 30 miles west on U.S. 199 (past Cave Junction) to the park on the right.

Contact: Mountain Man RV Park, 541/592-2656, www.mountainmanrvpark.com.

198 COUNTRY HILLS RESORT

🚶 🚲 🏊 🐕 🚙 ⛺

Scenic rating: 7

near Oregon Caves National Monument

Map 5.6, page 266

Lots of sites at this wooded camp border Sucker Creek, a popular spot for swimming. Several wineries are located within two miles. Lake Selmac and Oregon Caves National Monument provide nearby side-trip options.

Campsites, facilities: There are 12 sites for tents only and 20 sites with partial or full hookups for RVs of any length; some are pull-through sites. There are also six cabins and a five-unit motel. Picnic tables and fire rings are provided. Restrooms with flush toilets and coin showers, a dump station, Wi-Fi, drinking water, firewood, a convenience store, coin laundry, basketball hoops, volleyball, horseshoe pits, seasonal ice cream parlor, seasonal café, and ice are available. Leashed pets are permitted.

Reservations, fees: Reservations are accepted. RV sites are $30-32 per night, tent sites are $18 per night, $3 per night per additional vehicle, $5 per night per pet. Some credit cards are accepted. The campground is open February-November, weather permitting; the resort is open year-round.

Directions: In Grants Pass on I-5, take the U.S. 199 exit. Go 28 miles on U.S. 199 to the junction of Cave Junction and Highway 46/Oregon Caves. Turn left on Highway 46 and drive eight miles to the resort on the right.

Contact: Country Hills Resort, 541/592-3406, www.countryhillsresort.com.

199 GRAYBACK

🚶 🚣 🏕 🐕 ♿ 🚙 ⛺

Scenic rating: 7

near Oregon Caves National Monument in Rogue River-Siskiyou National Forest

Map 5.6, page 266

This wooded campground (2,000 feet elevation) along the banks of Sucker Creek has sites with ample shade. It's a good choice if you're planning to visit Oregon Caves National Monument, about 10 miles away. The camp, set in a grove of old-growth firs, is also a prime place for bird-watching. A 0.5-mile trail cuts through the camp.

Campsites, facilities: There are 39 sites for tents and one site with full hookups for RVs up to 42 feet long. Picnic tables, garbage bins, and fire grills are provided. Vault toilets and drinking water are available. Some facilities are wheelchair accessible, including a 0.5-mile trail. Leashed pets are permitted.

Reservations, fees: Reservations are not accepted. Sites are $15 per night, $7 per night per vehicle. Open May-September, weather permitting.

Directions: In Grants Pass on I-5, take Exit 55 for U.S. 199. Bear southwest on U.S. 199 for 30 miles to Cave Junction and Highway 46. Turn east on Highway 46 and drive 12 miles to the campground on the right.

Contact: Rogue River-Siskiyou National Forest, Wild Rivers Ranger District, 541/592-4000, www.fs.usda.gov/rogue-siskiyou.

200 CAVE CREEK

🚶 🚣 🐕 🚙 ⛺

Scenic rating: 7

near Oregon Caves National Monument in Rogue River-Siskiyou National Forest

Map 5.6, page 266

No campground is closer to Oregon Caves National Monument than this U.S. Forest Service camp, a mere four miles away. There is even a two-mile trail out of camp that leads directly to the caves. The camp, at an elevation of 2,500 feet, lies in a grove of old-growth timber along the banks of Cave Creek, a small stream with some trout fishing opportunities (catch-and-release only). The sites are shaded, and an abundance of wildlife can be spotted in the area. Hiking opportunities abound.

Campsites, facilities: There are 18 sites for tents or RVs up to 16 feet long. Picnic tables and fire rings are provided. Drinking water, garbage bins, and vault toilets are available. Showers are within eight miles. Leashed pets are permitted.

Reservations, fees: Reservations are not accepted. Sites are $10 per night, $5 per night per additional vehicle. Open mid-May-mid-September, weather permitting.

Directions: In Grants Pass on I-5, take Exit 55 for U.S. 199. Bear southwest on U.S. 199 for 30 miles to Cave Junction and Highway 46. Turn east on Highway 46 and drive 16 miles to the campground on the right.

Contact: Rogue River-Siskiyou National Forest, Wild Rivers Ranger District, 541/592-4000, www.fs.usda.gov/rogue-siskiyou.

201 BOLAN LAKE

🏕️ 🛶 🚐 🐎 🐕 🚌 ⛺

Scenic rating: 9

on Bolan Lake in Rogue River-Siskiyou National Forest

Map 5.6, page 266   **BEST (**

Very few out-of-towners know about this camp, with pretty, shaded sites along the shore of 15-acre Bolan Lake. The lake is stocked with trout, and the fishing can be good. Only non-motorized boats are allowed. A trail from the lake leads up to a fire lookout and ties into miles of other trails, including the Bolan Lake Trail. This spot is truly a bird-watcher's paradise, with a variety of species to view. The camp is set at 5,500 feet elevation.

Campsites, facilities: There are 12 sites for tents or RVs up to 16 feet long. An unfurnished lookout is also available for rent. Picnic tables and fire grills are provided. Vault toilets and

firewood are available. There is no drinking water. Garbage must be packed out. Leashed pets are permitted.

Reservations, fees: Reservations are accepted for the lookout only at 877/444-6777 ($10 reservation fee) or www.recreation.gov ($9 reservation fee). Sites are $10 per night, $5 per each additional vehicle, the lookout is $65 per night. Open June-early October, weather permitting.

Directions: From Grants Pass, drive south on U.S. 199 for 30 miles to Cave Junction and Rockydale Road (County Road 5560). Turn left (southeast) on Rockydale Road and drive eight miles to County Road 5828 (also called Waldo Road and Happy Camp Road). Turn southeast and drive 14 miles to Forest Road 4812. Turn left (east) and drive four miles to Forest Road 4812-040. Turn left (south) and drive two miles to the campground. This access road is very narrow and rough. Large RVs are strongly discouraged.

Contact: Rogue River-Siskiyou National Forest, Wild Rivers Ranger District, 541/592-4000, www.fs.usda.gov/rogue-siskiyou.

202 FAREWELL BEND

🏕️ 🛶 🐎 ♿ 🚌 ⛺

Scenic rating: 7

on the Upper Rogue River in Rogue River-Siskiyou National Forest

Map 5.7, page 267

Extremely popular Farewell Bend campground is set at an elevation of 3,400 feet along the banks of the Upper Rogue River near the Rogue River Gorge. A 0.25-mile barrier-free trail leads from camp to the Rogue Gorge Viewpoint and is definitely worth the trip. The Upper Rogue River Trail passes near camp. This spot attracts a lot of the campers visiting Crater Lake.

Campsites, facilities: There are 61 sites for tents or RVs up to 40 feet long. Picnic tables, fire grills, and fire rings are provided. Drinking water, firewood, and flush toilets are available. Some facilities are wheelchair accessible. Leashed pets are permitted.

Reservations, fees: Reservations are accepted at 877/444-6777 ($10 reservation fee) or www.recreation.gov ($9 reservation fee). Sites are $23 per night, $10 per night per additional vehicle. Open mid-May-late October, weather permitting.

Directions: From Medford, drive northeast on Highway 62 for 57 miles (near Union Creek) to the campground on the left.

Contact: Rogue River-Siskiyou National Forest, Prospect Ranger District, 541/560-3400, www.fs.usda.gov/rogue-siskiyou; Rogue Recreation, 541/560-3900, www.roguerec.com.

203 UNION CREEK

Scenic rating: 8

near the Upper Rogue River in Rogue River-Siskiyou National Forest

Map 5.7, page 267

One of the most popular camps in the district, this spot is more developed than the nearby camps of Mill Creek, Natural Bridge, and River Bridge. It sits at 3,200 feet elevation along the banks of Union Creek, where the creek joins the Upper Rogue River. The Upper Rogue River Trail passes near camp. Interpretive programs are offered in the summer, and a convenience store and restaurant are within walking distance.

Campsites, facilities: There are 78 sites for tents or RVs up to 30 feet long and three RV sites with full hookups. Picnic tables and fire grills are provided. A restroom with flush toilets, vault toilets, drinking water, and garbage service are available. Firewood is available for purchase. An amphitheater is available for programs. A store and restaurant are within walking distance. Some facilities are wheelchair accessible. Leashed pets are permitted.

Reservations, fees: Reservations are accepted at 877/444-6777 ($10 reservation fee) or www.recreation.gov ($9 reservation fee). Sites are $21 per night, $8 per night per additional vehicle; RV sites with full hookups are $32 per night. Open mid-May-mid-October, weather permitting.

Directions: From Medford, drive northeast on Highway 62 for 56 miles (near Union Creek) to the campground on the left.

Contact: Rogue River-Siskiyou National Forest, Prospect Ranger District, 541/560-3400, www.fs.usda.gov/rogue-siskiyou; Rogue Recreation, 541/560-3900, www.roguerec.com.

204 NATURAL BRIDGE

Scenic rating: 8

on the Upper Rogue River Trail in Rogue River-Siskiyou National Forest

Map 5.7, page 267   **BEST (**

Expect lots of company in midsummer at this popular camp, which sits at an elevation of 3,200 feet, where the Upper Rogue River runs underground. The Upper Rogue River Trail passes by the camp and follows the river for many miles to the Pacific Crest Trail in Crater Lake National Park. There is an interpretive area and a spectacular geological viewpoint adjacent to the camp. A 0.25-mile, barrier-free trail is also available.

Campsites, facilities: There are 17 sites for tents or RVs up to 30 feet long. Picnic tables and fire grills are provided. Vault toilets are available. There is no drinking water and garbage must be packed out. Some facilities are wheelchair accessible. Leashed pets are permitted.

Reservations, fees: Reservations are not accepted. Sites are $15 per night, $7 per night per additional vehicle. Open May-early November, weather permitting.

Directions: From Medford, drive northeast on Highway 62 for 55 miles (near Union Creek) to Forest Road 300. Turn left and drive one mile west to the campground on the right.

Contact: Rogue River-Siskiyou National Forest, Prospect Ranger District, 541/560-3400, www.fs.usda.gov/rogue-siskiyou.

205 ABBOTT CREEK

Scenic rating: 8

on Abbott and Woodruff Creeks in Rogue
River-Siskiyou National Forest

Map 5.7, page 267   **BEST (**

Situated at the confluence of Abbott and
Woodruff Creeks about two miles from the
Upper Rogue River, this camp is a better choice
for visitors with children than some of the others along the Rogue River. Abbott Creek is
small and tame compared to the roaring Rogue.
The elevation here is 3,100 feet.

Campsites, facilities: There are 25 sites for
tents or RVs up to 35 feet long, including five
OHV sites. Picnic tables, garbage service, and
fire grills are provided. Vault toilets and firewood are available. There is no drinking water.
Leashed pets are permitted.

Reservations, fees: Reservations are not accepted. Sites are $14 per night, $10 per night
per additional vehicle. Open mid-May-late
October, weather permitting.

Directions: From Medford, drive northeast on
Highway 62 for 50 miles (near Union Creek) to
Forest Road 68. Turn left and drive 3.5 miles
west to the campground on the left.

Contact: Rogue River-Siskiyou National
Forest, Prospect Ranger District, 541/560-
3400, www.fs.usda.gov/rogue-siskiyou; Rogue
Recreation, 541/560-3900, www.roguerec.com.

206 MILL CREEK

Scenic rating: 7

near the Upper Rogue River in Rogue
River-Siskiyou National Forest

Map 5.7, page 267

This campground (elevation of 2,800 feet)
along the banks of Mill Creek, about two miles
from the Upper Rogue River, features beautiful, private sites and heavy vegetation. One in a
series of remote, primitive camps near Highway

62 missed by out-of-towners, this camp is an
excellent choice for tenters.

Campsites, facilities: There are 10 sites for
tents. Picnic tables and fire grills are provided.
Vault toilets are available. There is no drinking
water and garbage must be packed out. Leashed
pets are permitted.

Reservations, fees: Reservations are not accepted. Sites are $15 per night, $7 per night per
additional vehicle. Open early May-November,
weather permitting.

Directions: From Medford, drive north on
Highway 62 for 46 miles (near Union Creek)
to Forest Road 6200-030. Turn right (southeast) and drive one mile to the campground
on the left.

Contact: Rogue River-Siskiyou National
Forest, Prospect Ranger District, 541/560-3400,
www.fs.usda.gov/rogue-siskiyou.

207 RIVER BRIDGE

Scenic rating: 7

on the Upper Rogue River in Rogue
River-Siskiyou National Forest

Map 5.7, page 267

River Bridge campground, situated at 2,900 feet
elevation along the banks of the Upper Rogue
River, is particularly scenic, with secluded
sites and river views. This is a calmer part of
the Wild and Scenic Upper Rogue River, but
swimming and rafting are not recommended.
The Upper Rogue River Trail passes by the
camp and follows the river for many miles to
the Pacific Crest Trail in Crater Lake National
Park.

Campsites, facilities: There are 11 sites for
tents or RVs up to 25 feet long. Picnic tables and
fireplaces are provided. Vault toilets are available, but there is no drinking water. Leashed
pets are permitted.

Reservations, fees: Reservations are not accepted. Sites are $15 per night, $7 per night per
additional vehicle. Open early May-November,
weather permitting.

Directions: From Medford, drive northeast on Highway 62 (Crater Lake Highway) for 42 miles (before reaching Union Creek) to Forest Road 6210. Turn left and drive one mile to the campground on the right.

Contact: Rogue River-Siskiyou National Forest, Prospect Ranger District, 541/560-3400, www.fs.usda.gov/rogue-siskiyou.

208 MAZAMA

Scenic rating: 6

near the Pacific Crest Trail in Crater Lake National Park

Map 5.7, page 267

One of two campgrounds at Crater Lake, this camp sits at 6,000 feet elevation and is known for cold nights, even in late June and early September. (I once got caught in a snowstorm here at the opening in mid-June.) The Pacific Crest Trail passes through the park, but the only trail access down to Crater Lake is at Cleetwood Cove. Seasonal boat tours and junior ranger programs are available. Note that winter access to the park is from the west only on Highway 62 to Rim Village.

Campsites, facilities: There are 213 sites for tents or RVs up to 50 feet long; some have partial hookups. Picnic tables and fire rings are provided. Drinking water, restrooms with flush toilets and coin showers, bear-proof food lockers, garbage bins, a dump station, coin laundry, gasoline, mini-mart, restaurant, gift shop, firewood, and ice are available. Some facilities are wheelchair accessible. Leashed pets are permitted in the campground and on paved roads only.

Reservations, fees: Reservations are recommended at 888/774-2728 or www.craterlakelodges.com. RV sites are $32-36 per night, tent sites are $23 per night, $3.50 per person per night for more than two people. There is a $15 park entrance fee per vehicle. Some credit cards are accepted. Open early June-September, weather permitting.

Directions: From I-5 at Medford, turn east on Highway 62 and drive 72 miles into Crater Lake National Park and to Annie Springs junction. Turn left and drive a short distance to the national park entrance kiosk. Just beyond the kiosk, turn right to the campground and Mazama store entrance.

Contact: Crater Lake National Park, 541/594-3000, www.nps.gov/crla.

209 FLY CASTERS RV PARK

Scenic rating: 6

on the Rogue River

Map 5.7, page 267

This spot along the banks of the Rogue River is a good base camp for RVers who want to fish or hike. The county park, located across the river in Shady Cove, offers picnic facilities and a boat ramp. Lost Creek Lake is about a 15-minute drive northeast. Note that about half of the sites are taken by long-term rentals.

Campsites, facilities: There are 47 sites with full hookups for RVs of any length; two are pull-through sites. Five mobile homes are also available. Picnic tables are provided and a loaner fire pit is available. Restrooms with flush toilets and showers, satellite TV, Wi-Fi, a clubhouse, barbecue area, horseshoe pits, and coin laundry are available. A store, café, and ice are within one mile. Boat-launching facilities are nearby. Some facilities are wheelchair accessible. Leashed pets are permitted.

Reservations, fees: Reservations are recommended. Sites are $36-46 per night, $2.50 per person for more than two people. Some credit cards are accepted. Weekly and monthly rates are available. Open year-round.

Directions: From Medford, drive northeast on Highway 62 for 21 miles to the park on the left.

Contact: Fly Casters RV Park, 541/878-2749, www.flycastersrv.com.

210 BEAR MOUNTAIN RV PARK

Scenic rating: 7

on the Rogue River

Map 5.7, page 267

This campground is set in an open, grassy area on the Rogue River about six miles from Lost Creek Lake, where boat ramps and picnic areas are available for day use. The campsites are spacious and shaded.

Campsites, facilities: There is a grassy area for tent sites and 37 sites with full or partial hookups for RVs of any length. Picnic tables are provided. Drinking water, restrooms with flush toilets and showers, coin laundry, ice, and a playground are available. A store and café are within one mile. Boat docks and launching facilities are nearby. Leashed pets are permitted.

Reservations, fees: Reservations are accepted at 541/878-2400. RV sites are $30 per night, tent sites are $25 per night, $2 per person per night for more than two adults. Cash or check only; credit cards are not accepted. Open year-round.

Directions: From Medford, drive northeast on Highway 62 to the junction with Highway 227. Continue east on Highway 62 for 2.5 more miles to the park on the left.

Contact: Bear Mountain RV Park, 541/878-2400.

211 ROGUE ELK CAMPGROUND

Scenic rating: 8

on the Rogue River east of the city of Trail

Map 5.7, page 267

Right on the Rogue River at an elevation of 1,476 feet, the park has creek swimming (unsupervised), a Douglas fir forest, fishing, hiking trails, rafting, and wildlife on 33 acres of space with 0.75 mile of river frontage. The forest is very beautiful here. Lost Creek Lake on Highway 62 makes a good side trip.

Campsites, facilities: There are 38 sites for tents or RVs of up to 25 feet long; some have partial hookups. Picnic tables and fire pits are provided. Drinking water, restrooms with flush toilets and coin showers, garbage bins, a dump station, boat ramp, and playground are available. A café, mini-mart, ice, coin laundry, and firewood are available within three miles. Some facilities are wheelchair accessible. Leashed pets are permitted.

Reservations, fees: Reservations are accepted ($8-10 reservation fee). Sites are $20-24 per night, $6 per night per additional vehicle. Open mid-March-mid-October.

Directions: From Medford, take Exit 30 for the Crater Lake Highway (Highway 62) and drive northeast on Highway 62 for 29 miles to the park entrance on the right.

Contact: Jackson County Parks, 27766 Highway 62, Trail 97541, 541/774-8183, www.jacksoncountyor.org.

212 JOSEPH H. STEWART STATE RECREATION AREA

Scenic rating: 7

on Lost Creek Reservoir

Map 5.7, page 267

This state park is on the shore of Lost Creek Reservoir, about 40 miles from Crater Lake National Park, and is home to 11 miles of hiking and biking trails, a lake with a beach, boat rentals, and a marina. Grassy sites are spacious and sprinkled with conifers. The Cole River Hatchery is available for tours.

A blue-green algae health advisory may be in effect. Call for updates.

Campsites, facilities: There are 151 sites with partial hookups for tents or self-contained RVs, including some sites for RVs of any length, and 50 sites with water for tents or self-contained RVs. There are also two group areas for tents and RVs for up to 50 people each. Picnic tables and fire grills are provided. Restrooms with flush toilets and showers, garbage bins, drinking water, a dump station, firewood, and a playground with volleyball and horseshoes are available. Boat rentals, launching facilities, a swimming area, and a picnic area that can be reserved are nearby. Some facilities are wheelchair accessible. Leashed pets are permitted.

Reservations, fees: Reservations are at 800/452-5687 or www.oregonstateparks.org ($8 reservation fee). Sites are $17-22 per night, $7 per night per additional vehicle. Group sites are $71 per night for up to 25 people and one RV, $3 per person per night for more than 25 people; up to four additional RVs are permitted for $10 each. Some credit cards are accepted. Open March 1-October 31, weather permitting.

Directions: From Medford, drive northeast on Highway 62 for 34 miles to the Lost Creek Reservoir and the campground on the left.

Contact: Joseph H. Stewart State Recreation Area, 541/560-3334 or 800/551-6949, www.oregonstateparks.org.

213 WHISKEY SPRINGS

Scenic rating: 9

near Butte Falls in Rogue River-Siskiyou National Forest

Map 5.7, page 267

This campground at Whiskey Springs, near Fourbit Ford Campground, is one of the larger, more developed backwoods U.S. Forest Service camps in the area. A one-mile, wheelchair-accessible nature trail passes nearby. You can see beaver dams and woodpeckers here. The camp is set at 3,200 feet elevation.

Campsites, facilities: There are 34 sites for tents or RVs up to 30 feet long. Picnic tables, garbage service, and fire grills are provided. Drinking water and vault toilets are available. Some facilities are wheelchair accessible. Leashed pets are permitted.

Reservations, fees: Reservations are accepted at 877/444-6777 ($10 reservation fee) or www.recreation.gov ($9 reservation fee). Sites are $16 per night, $8 per night per additional

vehicle. Open mid-May-September, weather permitting.

Directions: From Medford, drive northeast on Highway 62 for 14 miles to the Butte Falls Highway. Turn right and drive east for 16 miles to the town of Butte Falls. Continue southeast on Butte Falls Highway for nine miles to Forest Road 3065. Turn left on Forest Road 3065 and drive 300 yards to the campground on the left.

Contact: Rogue River-Siskiyou National Forest, Butte Falls Ranger District, 541/865-2700, www.fs.usda.gov/rogue-siskiyou; Rogue Recreation, 541/560-3900, www.roguerec.com.

214 IMNAHA

Scenic rating: 7

near the Sky Lakes Wilderness in Rogue River-Siskiyou National Forest

Map 5.7, page 267

Located along Imnaha Creek at an elevation of 3,800 feet, this campground makes a good base camp for a wilderness trip. Trailheads at the ends of the nearby forest roads lead east into the Sky Lakes Wilderness; there are also two shorter interpretive trails.

Campsites, facilities: There is one group site for tents or RVs up to 30 feet long. A cabin is also available. Picnic tables and fire grills are provided. Vault toilets, drinking water, and garbage service are available. Leashed pets are permitted.

Reservations, fees: Reservations are accepted at 877/444-6777 ($10 reservation fee) or www.recreation.gov ($9 reservation fee). The site is $50 per night and the cabin is $125 per night. Open mid-May-October, weather permitting.

Directions: From Medford, drive northeast on Highway 62 for about 35 miles to Prospect and Mill Creek Drive. Turn right and drive one mile to County Road 992/Butte Falls Prospect Highway. Turn right and drive 2.5 miles to Forest Road 37. Turn left and drive 10 miles east to the campground.

Contact: Rogue River-Siskiyou National

Forest, Butte Falls Ranger Station, 541/865-2700, www.fs.usda.gov/rogue-siskiyou.

215 MEDFORD OAKS RV PARK

Scenic rating: 6

near Eagle Point

Map 5.7, page 267

This park is in a quiet, rural setting among the trees. Just a short hop off I-5, it's an excellent choice for travelers heading to or from California. The campground is located along the shore of a pond that provides good catch-and-release fishing (barbless hooks only). Most sites are filled with monthly renters.

Campsites, facilities: There are 55 sites with full or partial hookups for RVs of any length and six sites for tents; most sites are pull-through. There are also three cabins. Restrooms with flush toilets and coin showers, a dump station, Wi-Fi, coin laundry, limited groceries, ice, and RV supplies are available. Recreational facilities include a seasonal, heated swimming pool, movies, horseshoe pits, table tennis, a recreation field for baseball, basketball, football, and volleyball, and a playground. Leashed pets are allowed with certain restrictions.

Reservations, fees: Reservations are recommended. RV sites are $30-35 per night, tent sites are $20 per night, $3 per person per night for more than four people. Group rates are available. Some credit cards are accepted. Open year-round.

Directions: From Medford, drive northeast on Highway 62 for five miles to Exit 30 and Highway 140. Turn east on Highway 140 and drive 6.8 miles to the park on the left.

Contact: Medford Oaks RV Park, 541/826-5103, www.medfordoaks.com.

216 FOURBIT FORD

Scenic rating: 6

on Fourbit Creek in Rogue River-Siskiyou National Forest

Map 5.7, page 267

Fourbit Ford campground, situated at an elevation of 3,200 feet along Fourbit Creek, is one in a series of hidden spots tucked away near County Road 821.

Campsites, facilities: There are seven sites for tents or trailers up to 16 feet long. Picnic tables and fire grills are provided. Vault toilets, drinking water, and garbage service are available. There is no drinking water. Leashed pets are permitted.

Reservations, fees: Reservations are accepted at 877/444-6777 ($10 reservation fee) or www.recreation.gov ($9 reservation fee). Sites are $14 per night, $7 per extra vehicle per night. Open mid-May-late September, weather permitting.

Directions: From Medford, drive northeast on Highway 62 for 14 miles to Butte Falls Highway. Turn right and drive 16 miles east to the town of Butte Falls and County Road 821. Turn left and drive nine miles southeast to Forest Road 3065. Turn left and drive one mile to the campground on the left.

Contact: Rogue River-Siskiyou National Forest, Butte Falls Ranger District, 541/865-2700, www.fs.usda.gov/rogue-siskiyou; Rogue Recreation, 541/560-3900, www.roguerec.com.

217 WILLOW LAKE RESORT

Scenic rating: 9

on Willow Lake

Map 5.7, page 267

This campground sits on the shore of Willow Lake. Located at the base of Mount McLoughlin at an elevation of 3,200 feet, it encompasses 927 wooded acres. The lake has fishing opportunities for bass, crappie, and trout. A hiking trail starts near camp. Waterskiing is allowed at the lake.

Campsites, facilities: There are 32 sites for tents or RVs (no hookups), 31 sites for tents or RVs (full or partial hookups), and a group area with 11 sites that can accommodate up to 150 people. There are also four cabins and two yurts. Picnic tables and fire rings are provided. Restrooms with flush toilets and coin showers, a dump station, and firewood are available. A store, boat ramp, and boat rentals are on-site. Some facilities are wheelchair accessible. Leashed pets are permitted.

Reservations, fees: Reservations are accepted ($8-10 reservation fee) for groups, yurts, and cabins only at 541/774-8183. Sites are $20-30 per night, yurts are $35 per night, cabins are $100-125 per night, $6 per night per additional vehicle. The group area is $175 per night. Open mid-April-October.

Directions: From Medford, drive northeast on Highway 62 for 15 miles to Butte Falls Highway. Turn east and drive 25 miles to Willow Lake Road. Turn right (south) and drive two miles to the campground.

Contact: Jackson County Parks, 541/774-8183, www.jacksoncountyor.org.

218 ODESSA

Scenic rating: 4

near Klamath Lake in Fremont-Winema National Forest

Map 5.7, page 267

This campground (4,100 feet elevation) borders Odessa Creek, near the shore of Upper Klamath Lake. The lake is the main attraction, with fishing the main activity. The lake can provide excellent fishing for rainbow trout on both flies and Rapalas. Boating is also popular. Campsites sit among scattered mixed conifers and native brush.

Campsites, facilities: There are five tent sites. Picnic tables, garbage bins, and fire grills are provided. Vault toilets are available, but there is no drinking water. Leashed pets are permitted.

Reservations, fees: Reservations are not accepted. There is no fee for camping. Open year-round, weather permitting.

Directions: From Klamath Falls, drive west on Highway 140 about 18 miles to Forest Road 3639. Turn right (northeast) and drive one mile to the campground.

Contact: Fremont-Winema National Forest, Klamath Ranger District, 541/885-3400, www.fs.usda.gov/fremont-winema.

219 FOURMILE LAKE

Scenic rating: 8

at Fourmile Lake in Fremont-Winema National Forest

Map 5.7, page 267

This beautiful spot is the only camp on the shore of Fourmile Lake. Several nearby trails provide access to the Sky Lakes Wilderness. The Pacific Crest Trail passes about two miles from camp. Primitive and with lots of solitude, it attracts a calm and quiet crowd. Afternoon winds can be a problem, and in the evening, if the wind isn't blowing, the mosquitoes often arrive. Although this campground is near the foot of Mount McLoughlin (9,495 feet), there is no view of the mountain from here. Go to the east side of the lake for a good view.

Campsites, facilities: There are 28 sites for tents or RVs up to 22 feet long and one double site. Picnic tables, garbage bins, and fire grills are provided. Drinking water and vault toilets are available. Some facilities are wheelchair accessible. Leashed pets are permitted.

Reservations, fees: Reservations are accepted at 877/444-6777 ($10 reservation fee) or www.recreation.gov ($9 reservation fee). Single sites are $15 per night, the double site is $30 per night, $6 per night per additional vehicle. Open June-late September, weather permitting.

Directions: From Medford, drive northeast on Highway 62 for five miles to Exit 30 and

Highway 140. Turn east on Highway 140 and drive approximately 40 miles to Forest Road 3661. Turn left (north) and drive six miles to the campground.

Contact: Fremont-Winema National Forest, Klamath Ranger District, 541/885-3400, www.fs.usda.gov/fremont-winema.

220 ROCKY POINT RESORT

Scenic rating: 7

on Upper Klamath Lake

Map 5.7, page 267

Rocky Point Resort, at the Upper Klamath Wildlife Refuge, boasts 10 miles of canoe trails, along with opportunities for motorized boating and fishing. Ponderosa pines and Douglas firs create a quite picturesque setting for stellar sunsets and a peaceful retreat.

Campsites, facilities: There are 25 sites with partial or full hookups for RVs to 40 feet, five sites for tents, four cabins, and five motel rooms. Some sites are pull-through. Picnic tables and fire rings are provided. Restrooms with flush toilets and showers, drinking water, a convenience store, firewood, coin laundry, ice, fishing licenses, and a marina with boat gas, boat launch, and boat and canoe rentals are available. A restaurant and lounge overlook the lake. Some facilities are wheelchair accessible, including a fishing dock. Leashed pets are permitted.

Reservations, fees: Reservations are accepted. RV sites are $25-30 per night, tent sites are $25 per night, $3-4 per person per night for more than two people, $3 per pet per night, and $5 per night per additional vehicle. Weekly and monthly rates are available. Some credit cards are accepted. Open April 1-November 1.

Directions: From Klamath Falls, drive northeast on Highway 140 for 25 miles to Rocky Point Road. Turn right and drive three miles to the resort on the right.

Contact: Rocky Point Resort, 541/356-2287, www.rockypointoregon.com.

221 WILLOW PRAIRIE HORSE CAMP

Scenic rating: 7

near Fish Lake in Rogue River-Siskiyou National Forest

Map 5.7, page 267

There are two campgrounds here, including one for equestrian campers. This spot is located near the origin of the west branch of Willow Creek and next to a beaver swamp and several large ponds that attract deer, ducks, elk, geese, and sandhill cranes. A number of riding trails pass nearby. A map of Rogue River-Siskiyou National Forest details the back roads and can help you get here. Fish Lake is four miles south.

Campsites, facilities: There are 10 sites for tents or RVs up to 16 feet long, one primitive cabin with cots, and 10 equestrian sites. Picnic tables and fire grills are provided. Drinking water, vault toilets, and garbage service are available. The equestrian camp has 10 sites for tents or small RVs, two stock water troughs, and horse corrals. A store, café, ice, boat docks, launching facilities, and rentals are nearby. A camp host is on-site. Leashed pets are permitted.

Reservations, fees: Reservations are accepted only for the horse camp and cabin at 877/444-6777 ($10 reservation fee) or www.recreation.gov ($9 reservation fee). Sites are $15 per night, $7 per night per additional vehicle. The cabin is $65 per night. Open late May-late October, weather permitting.

Directions: From Medford, drive northeast on Highway 62 for five miles to Exit 30 and Highway 140. Turn east on Highway 140 and drive 31.5 miles to Forest Road 37. Turn left and drive north 1.5 miles to Forest Road 3738. Turn left and drive one mile west to Forest Road 3735. Turn left and drive 100 yards to the campground. For the equestrian camp, continue for 0.25 mile to the campground entrance.

Contact: Rogue River-Siskiyou National Forest, High Cascades Ranger District, 541/560-3400, www.fs.usda.gov/rogue-siskiyou.

222 NORTH FORK

🏃🚴🛶🛥🐎🏕🛢🚐🔺

Scenic rating: 7

near Fish Lake in Rogue River-Siskiyou
National Forest

Map 5.7, page 267

Here is a small, pretty campground with easy access from the highway and proximity to Fish Lake. Situated on the north fork of Little Butte Creek at an elevation of 4,500 feet, it's fairly popular, so grab your spot early. Excellent fly-fishing can be found along the Fish Lake Trail, which leads directly out of camp.

Campsites, facilities: There are nine sites for tents or RVs up to 24 feet long. Picnic tables and fire grills are provided. Vault toilets and drinking water are available. Garbage must be packed out. A camp host is on-site. Boat docks, launching facilities, and rentals are nearby. Some facilities are wheelchair accessible. Leashed pets are permitted.

Reservations, fees: Reservations are accepted at 877/444-6777 ($10 reservation fee) or www.recreation.gov ($9 reservation fee). Sites are $14 per night, $7 per night per additional vehicle. Open May-mid-November, weather permitting.

Directions: From Medford, drive northeast on Highway 62 for five miles to Exit 30 and Highway 140. Turn east on Highway 140 and drive 31.5 miles to Forest Road 37. Turn right (south) and drive 0.5 mile to the campground.

Contact: Rogue River-Siskiyou National Forest, High Cascades Ranger District, 541/560-3400, www.fs.usda.gov/rogue-siskiyou; Rogue Recreation, 541/560-3900, www.roguerec.com.

223 FISH LAKE

🏃🚴🏊🛶🛥🐎🏕🛢🚐🔺

Scenic rating: 8

on Fish Lake in Rogue River-Siskiyou National Forest

Map 5.7, page 267

Bicycling, boating, fishing, and hiking are among the recreation options at this campground on the north shore of Fish Lake. Easy, one-mile access to the Pacific Crest Trail is also available. If this campground is full, Doe Point and Fish Lake Resort are nearby.

Campsites, facilities: There are 17 sites for tents or RVs up to 40 feet long and three walk-in tent sites. Picnic tables, fire grills, and garbage bins are provided. Drinking water, flush toilets, a picnic shelter that can be reserved, a store, café, firewood, and ice are available. A camp host is on-site. Boat docks, launching facilities, boat rentals, coin laundry, dump station, and coin showers are nearby. Some facilities are wheelchair accessible. Leashed pets are permitted.

Reservations, fees: Reservations are accepted at 877/444-6777 ($10 reservation fee) or www.recreation.gov ($9 reservation fee). Sites are $23 per night, $20 per night per additional vehicle. Open mid-May-mid-October, weather permitting.

Directions: From Medford, drive northeast on Highway 62 for five miles to Exit 30 and Highway 140. Turn east on Highway 140 and drive 30 miles to the campground on the right.

Contact: Rogue River-Siskiyou National Forest, Siskiyou Mountains District, 541/899-3800, www.fs.usda.gov/rogue-siskiyou; Rogue Recreation, 541/560-3900, www.roguerec.com.

224 DOE POINT

Scenic rating: 8

on Fish Lake in Rogue River-Siskiyou National Forest

Map 5.7, page 267

This campground (at 4,600 feet elevation) sits along the north shore of Fish Lake, nearly adjacent to Fish Lake Campground. Doe Point is slightly preferable because of its dense vegetation, offering shaded, quiet, well-screened sites. Privacy, rare at many campgrounds, can be found here. Recreation options include biking, boating, fishing, and hiking, plus an easy, one-mile access trail to the Pacific Crest Trail.

Campsites, facilities: There are 25 sites for tents or RVs up to 30 feet long and five walk-in sites for tents. Picnic tables and fire grills are provided. Drinking water, garbage service, flush toilets, a store, café, firewood, and ice are available. Boat docks, launching facilities, boat rentals, showers, and a dump station are nearby. Some facilities are wheelchair accessible. Leashed pets are permitted.

Reservations, fees: Reservations are accepted at 877/444-6777 ($10 reservation fee) or www.recreation.gov ($9 reservation fee). Sites are $23 per night, $10 per night per additional vehicle. Open mid-May-late September, weather permitting.

Directions: From Medford, drive northeast on Highway 62 for five miles to Exit 30 and Highway 140. Turn east on Highway 140 and drive 30 miles to the campground on the right.

Contact: Rogue River-Siskiyou National Forest, High Cascades District, 541/560-3400, www.fs.usda.gov/rogue-siskiyou; Rogue Recreation, 541/560-3900, www.roguerec.com.

225 FISH LAKE RESORT

Scenic rating: 7

on Fish Lake

Map 5.7, page 267

This resort along Fish Lake is privately operated under permit by the U.S. Forest Service and offers a resort-type feel, catering primarily to families. This is the largest and most developed of the three camps at Fish Lake. Bicycling, boating, fishing, and hiking are some of the activities here. Cozy cabins are available for rent. Boat speed on the lake is limited to 10 mph.

Campsites, facilities: There are 12 sites for tents, 45 sites with full hookups for RVs up to 40 feet long, and 11 cabins. Some sites are pull-through. Picnic tables and fire rings are provided. Drinking water, restrooms with flush toilets and coin showers, propane gas, dump station, recreation hall, convenience store, café, coin laundry, ice, garbage bins, boat docks, boat rentals, and launching facilities are available. Some facilities are wheelchair accessible. Leashed pets are permitted, with breed restrictions.

Reservations, fees: Reservations are accepted at 541/949-8500 or www.fishlakeresort.net. RV sites are $44 per night, tent sites are $22-32 per night, $3 per person per night for more than four people, $5 per extra vehicle per night. Weekly, monthly, and group rates are available. Some credit cards are accepted. Open year-round, weather permitting, with limited winter facilities.

Directions: From Medford, take I-5 to Exit 30 and go to Highway 140. Turn east on Highway 140 and drive 30 miles to Fish Lake Road. Turn right (south) and drive 0.5 mile to the resort on the left.

Contact: Fish Lake Resort, 541/949-8500, www.fishlakeresort.net.

226 LAKE OF THE WOODS RESORT

🚶 🚴 🚣 🛶 ⛴ ⛷ 🐕 ♿ 🚐 ⛺

Scenic rating: 9
on Lake of the Woods

Map 5.7, page 267　　　　**BEST (**

On beautiful Lake of the Woods, this resort offers fishing (four kinds of trout, catfish, and bass) and boating in a secluded forest setting. It's on one of the most beautiful lakes in the Cascade Mountains, surrounded by tall pine trees. A family-oriented campground, it has all the amenities. In the winter, snowmobiling and cross-country skiing are popular. Attractions in the area include the Mountain Lakes Wilderness and the Pacific Crest Trail.

Campsites, facilities: There are 22 sites with full or partial hookups for tents or RVs up to 35 feet long and 32 cabins. Picnic tables and fire rings are provided. Restrooms with showers, a dump station, coin laundry, general store, ice, snacks, a restaurant, lounge, barbecue area, gasoline, and propane gas are available. There is also a boat ramp, dock, marina, and boat rentals. Some facilities are wheelchair accessible. Leashed pets are permitted.

Reservations, fees: Reservations are accepted at 866/201-4194 or www.lakeofthewoodsresort. com. Sites are $40-50 per night, $5 per night per additional vehicle, and $1 per pet per night. Monthly and winter rates are available. Some credit cards are accepted. Open spring-fall, weather permitting; call for winter availability.

Directions: In Medford on I-5, take Exit 14 to Highway 62. Go six miles on Highway 62 to Highway 140/Lake of the Woods. Drive 59.6 miles on Lake of the Woods Road to the resort on the left.

Contact: Lake of the Woods Resort, 541/949-8300, www.lakeofthewoodsresort.com.

227 ASPEN POINT

🚶 🚣 🛶 ⛴ 🐎 🐕 ♿ 🚐 ⛺

Scenic rating: 8
on Lake of the Woods in Fremont-Winema National Forest

Map 5.7, page 267　　　　**BEST (**

This campground (at 5,000 feet elevation) is near the north shore of Lake of the Woods, adjacent to Lake of the Woods Resort. It's heavily timbered with old-growth fir and has a great view of Mount McLoughlin (9,495 feet). A hiking trail just north of camp leads north for several miles, meandering around Fourmile Lake and extending into the Sky Lakes Wilderness. Other trails nearby head into the Mountain Lakes Wilderness. Boating, fishing, swimming, and waterskiing are among the activities here. Note that of the 39 campsites, 20 are available by reservation; the rest are first-come, first-served.

Campsites, facilities: There are 18 single sites and two double sites for tents or RVs up to 55 feet long. Picnic tables, garbage bins, and fire grills are provided. Drinking water, a dump station, and flush toilets are available. Boat docks, launching facilities, and rentals are nearby. Some facilities are wheelchair accessible. Leashed pets are permitted.

Reservations, fees: Reservations are accepted at 877/444-6777 ($10 reservation fee) or www.recreation.gov ($9 reservation fee). Single sites are $20 per night, double sites are $40 per night, $6 per night per each additional vehicle. A group site is available for $90-95 per night. Open late May-early September, weather permitting.

Directions: In Ashland on I-5, take Exit 14 to Highway 66. Drive east for less than a mile to Dead Indian Memorial Road. Turn left (east) and drive 40 miles to Lake of the Woods. Continue along the east shore to the campground turnoff on the left.

Contact: Fremont-Winema National Forest, Klamath Ranger District, 541/885-3400, www.fs.usda.gov/fremont-winema; Lake of the Woods Resort, 541/949-8300, www.lake-ofthewoodsresort.com.

228 SUNSET

Scenic rating: 8

near Lake of the Woods in Fremont-Winema National Forest

Map 5.7, page 267

Sunset campground, near the eastern shore of Lake of the Woods, is fully developed and offers a myriad of recreation options. It's particularly popular for both fishing and boating. The elevation is 5,000 feet.

Campsites, facilities: There are 64 sites for tents or RVs up to 50 feet long. Picnic tables, garbage bins, and fire grills are provided. Drinking water and flush toilets are available. Boat docks, launching facilities, and rentals are nearby. Some facilities are wheelchair accessible. Leashed pets are permitted.

Reservations, fees: Reservations are accepted for some sites at 877/444-6777 ($10 reservation fee) or www.recreation.gov ($9 reservation fee). Sites are $20 per night, $6 per night per additional vehicle. Open late May-early September.

Directions: In Ashland on I-5, take Exit 14 to Highway 66. Drive east for less than a mile to Dead Indian Memorial Road. Turn left (east) and drive 40 miles to Lake of the Woods. Continue along the east shore to Forest Road 3738. Turn left (west) and drive 0.5 mile to the camp.

Contact: Fremont-Winema National Forest, Klamath Ranger District, 541/885-3400, www.fs.usda.gov/fremont-winema; Lake of the Woods Resort, 541/949-8300, www.lake-ofthewoodsresort.com.

229 CANTRALL-BUCKLEY PARK & GROUP CAMP

Scenic rating: 8

on the Applegate River

Map 5.7, page 267

This county park outside of Medford offers pleasant, shady sites in a wooded setting. Encompassing 88 acres of land, the camp has 1.75 miles of frontage along the Applegate River, which has good trout fishing.

Campsites, facilities: There are 30 sites for tents or self-contained RVs up to 25 feet long and one group area for up to 100 people. Picnic tables and fire pits are provided. Drinking water, restrooms with flush toilets and coin showers, and a reservable picnic area are available. Recreational facilities include horseshoes, a playground, and a recreation field. Some facilities are wheelchair accessible. Leashed pets are permitted.

Reservations, fees: Reservations are accepted only for the group site at 541/774-8183. Sites are $16 per night; the group site is $65 for the first night and $50 each night thereafter. Some credit cards are accepted with reservations only. Open mid-April-mid-October.

Directions: In Medford on I-5, take the Jacksonville exit to the Jacksonville Highway. Drive west on the Jacksonville Highway (Highway 238) for seven miles to Jacksonsville. Bear left on Highway 238 and drive to Hamilton Road. Turn left (south) on Hamilton Road and drive approximately 0.4 mile to Cantrall Road. Turn right on Cantrall and drive approximately 0.5 mile to the campground.

Contact: Jackson County Parks, 154 Cantrall Road, Ruch, 541/774-8183, www.jacksoncountyor.org.

230 GLENYAN CAMPGROUND OF ASHLAND

Scenic rating: 7

near Emigrant Lake

Map 5.7, page 267

This campground, located within seven miles of Ashland and less than one mile from Emigrant Lake, offers shady sites. Recreation options in the area include a golf course and tennis courts. It's an easy jump from I-5 at Ashland.

Campsites, facilities: There are 22 tent sites and 46 sites with full or partial hookups for tents or RVs of any length. Picnic tables and fire rings are provided. Drinking water, restrooms with flush toilets and showers, propane gas, a dump station, Wi-Fi, firewood, a recreation hall, seasonal convenience store, coin laundry, ice, a playground, horseshoe pits, and a seasonal heated swimming pool are available. Some facilities are wheelchair accessible. Leashed pets are permitted.

Reservations, fees: Reservations are accepted at 877/453-6926 or www.glenyancampground. com. RV sites are $37-40 per night, tent sites are $25-28, $3 per person per night for more than five people. Weekly and monthly rates are available. Some credit cards are accepted. Open year-round.

Directions: From Ashland, drive east on Highway 66 for 3.5 miles to the campground on the right.

Contact: Glenyan Campground of Ashland, 541/488-1785, www.glenyancampground.com.

231 DALEY CREEK GROUP

Scenic rating: 6

on Daley Creek in Rogue River-Siskiyou National Forest

Map 5.7, page 267

Daley Creek campground is a primitive alternative to some of the more developed spots in the area. Situated at 4,500 feet elevation, the camp borders the banks of Daley Creek near the confluence of Beaver Dam and Daley Creek. The Beaver Dam Trail heads right out of camp, running along the creek. Fishing can be decent downstream.

Campsites, facilities: There is one group site for RVs up to 18 feet long. Picnic tables and fire grills are provided. There is no drinking water, and garbage must be packed out. Some facilities are wheelchair accessible. Leashed pets are permitted.

Reservations, fees: Reservations are not accepted. The site is $50 per night. Open early May-mid-November, weather permitting.

Directions: In Ashland on I-5, take Exit 14 to Highway 66. Drive east for less than a mile to Dead Indian Memorial Road. Turn left (east) and drive 22 miles to Forest Road 37. Turn left (north) and drive 1.5 miles to the campground.

Contact: Rogue River-Siskiyou National Forest, High Cascades Ranger District, 541/560-3400, www.fs.usda.gov/rogue-siskiyou.

232 BEAVER DAM GROUP

Scenic rating: 5

on Beaver Dam Creek in Rogue River-Siskiyou National Forest

Map 5.7, page 267

This group campground sits at an elevation of 4,500 feet along Beaver Dam Creek. There's not much screening around the site, but it's a pretty, rustic, and quiet spot, with unusual vegetation along the creek. The trailhead for the Beaver Dam Trail is also here and the camp is adjacent to Daley Creek.

Campsites, facilities: There is one group site for tents or RVs up to 16 feet long. Picnic tables and fire grills are provided. Vault toilets are available. There is no drinking water and garbage must be packed out. Leashed pets are permitted.

Reservations, fees: Reservations are not

accepted. The site is $50 per night. Open early May-early November, weather permitting.

Directions: In Medford on I-5, take Exit 14 to Highway 66. Drive east for less than a mile to Dead Indian Memorial Road. Turn left (east) and drive 22 miles to Forest Road 37. Turn left (north) and drive 1.5 miles to the campground.

Contact: Rogue River Siskiyou National Forest, Ashland Ranger District, 541/552-2900, www.fs.usda.gov/rogue-siskiyou.

233 HOWARD PRAIRIE RESORT

Scenic rating: 7

on Howard Prairie Lake

Map 5.7, page 267

This wooded campground is located along the shore of Howard Prairie Lake, where boating, fishing, hiking, and swimming are among the recreation options. This is one of the largest campgrounds in over 100 miles and is Jackson County's most popular park.

Campsites, facilities: There are 243 sites with full or partial hookups for tents or RVs of any length and one furnished cabin. Some sites are pull-through. Picnic tables and fire rings are provided. Restrooms with flush toilets and showers, propane gas, a dump station, firewood, 24-hour security, a convenience store, café, coin laundry, boat docks, boat rentals, moorage, and launching facilities are available. Leashed pets are permitted.

Reservations, fees: Reservations are accepted ($8-10 reservation fee). Sites are $18-30 per night, $6 per night for more than two vehicles. The cabin is $150 per night. Some credit cards are accepted. Open mid-April-October.

Directions: In Ashland on I-5, take Exit 14 to Highway 66 and drive for less than a mile to Dead Indian Memorial Road. Turn left and drive 17 miles to Hyatt Prairie Road. Turn right and drive 3.5 miles to the resort.

Contact: Howard Prairie Lake Recreational Area, Jackson County Parks, 3249 Hyatt Prairie Road, 541/774-8183, www.jacksoncountyor.org.

234 APSERKAHA

Scenic rating: 5

on Howard Prairie Lake

Map 5.7, page 267

This park's 66 acres offer almost half a mile of lake frontage. Secluded lake access is a big feature at Apserkaha, along with breathtaking scenery.

Campsites, facilities: There are nine sites with partial hookups for RVs up to 65 feet long and 12 rustic sleeping cabins. The entire park may be reserved for group camping. Picnic tables and fire pits are provided. Drinking water, vault toilets, covered dining shelter, group campfire rings, and a swimming beach are available. Showers and an enclosed commercial kitchen are available to group reservations only. Some facilities are wheelchair accessible. Leashed pets are permitted.

Reservations, fees: Reservations are accepted ($8-10 reservation fee). RV sites are $24 per night, cabins are $30 per night, group camping is $350-450 for 50-120 people. Some credit cards are accepted. Open mid-April-October, weather permitting.

Directions: In Ashland on I-5, take Exit 14 to Highway 66. Drive east for 0.25 mile to Dead Indian Memorial Road. Turn left and drive 17 miles to Hyatt Prairie Road. Turn right on Howard Prairie Road and drive five miles to Dam Road. Turn left and drive 2.5 miles to Apserkaha.

Contact: Howard Prairie Lake Recreational Area, Jackson County Parks, 541/774-8183, www.jacksoncountyor.org.

235 LILY GLEN

Scenic rating: 6

near Howard Prairie Lake

Map 5.7, page 267

Set along the shore of Howard Prairie Lake, this horse camp is a secluded, primitive getaway. Trout fishing is available. Tubb Springs Wayside State Park and the nearby Rogue River-Siskiyou National Forest are possible side trips. There is also nearby access to the Pacific Crest Trail. The elevation is 4,500 feet.

Campsites, facilities: There are 12 sites for tents or self-contained RVs and two group sites for up to 75 people. Picnic tables and fire rings are provided. Drinking water, vault toilets, and corrals are available. Some facilities are wheelchair accessible. Leashed pets are permitted.

Reservations, fees: Reservations are accepted for group sites only at 541/774-8183. Sites are $18 per night, $6 per night per additional vehicle, $1 per pet per night, and $2 per horse per night for more than two horses; group sites are $75-125 per night. Some credit cards are accepted for reservations. Open mid-April-October, weather permitting.

Directions: In Ashland on I-5, take Exit 14 to Highway 66. Drive east for less than a mile to Dead Indian Memorial Road. Turn left (east) and drive 21 miles to the campground on the right.

Contact: Howard Prairie Lake Recreational Area, Jackson County Parks, 541/774-8183, www.jacksoncountyor.org.

236 GRIZZLY

Scenic rating: 7

near Howard Prairie Lake

Map 5.7, page 267

One of a series of seven county campgrounds at Howard Prairie Lake, Grizzly features well-spaced campsites amid a forest and lake setting. The lake level is known to fluctuate; in

low-water years, this camp is sometimes shut down. It gets moderate use. The elevation is 4,550 feet.

Campsites, facilities: There are 21 sites for tents or RVs (no hookups). Picnic tables and fire rings are provided. Drinking water, vault toilets, garbage bins, and a boat ramp are available. A store, café, laundry facilities, and boat rentals are available within two miles. Some facilities are wheelchair accessible. Leashed pets are permitted.

Reservations, fees: Reservations are not accepted. Sites are $18 per night, $6 per night per additional vehicle, and $1 per pet per night. Open mid-April-mid-September, weather permitting.

Directions: In Ashland on I-5, take Exit 14 to Highway 66. Drive east for less than a mile to Dead Indian Memorial Road. Turn left (east) and drive 17 miles to Howard Prairie Road. Turn right (south) and drive eight miles to Howard Prairie Dam Road. Turn left (east) and drive 0.25 mile to the campground.

Contact: Howard Prairie Lake Recreational Area, Jackson County Parks, 541/774-8183, www.jacksoncountyor.org.

237 WILLOW POINT

Scenic rating: 7

near Howard Prairie Lake

Map 5.7, page 267

Willow Point is similar to Grizzly (see listing in this chapter), offering flat tent sites in an area well covered by trees. The lake is stocked with about 100,000 trout annually.

Campsites, facilities: There are 41 sites for tents or self-contained RVs. Picnic tables and fire rings are provided. Drinking water, vault toilets, garbage bins, fish-cleaning station, and a boat ramp are available. A store, café, laundry facilities, and boat rentals are available within four miles. Some facilities are wheelchair accessible. Leashed pets are permitted.

Reservations, fees: Reservations are accepted

($8-10 reservation fee). Sites are $18 per night, $6 per night per additional vehicle, $1 per pet per night. Open mid-April-October.

Directions: In Ashland on I-5, take Exit 14 to Highway 66. Drive east for less than a mile to Dead Indian Memorial Road. Turn left (east) and drive 17 miles to Howard Prairie Road. Turn right (south) and drive three miles to the reservoir.

Contact: Howard Prairie Lake Recreational Area, Jackson County Parks, 541/774-8183, www.jacksoncountyor.org.

238 KLUM LANDING

Scenic rating: 7

near Howard Prairie Lake

Map 5.7, page 267

Klum Landing is one of seven county campgrounds on Howard Prairie Lake. A bonus at this one is that coin-operated showers are available.

Campsites, facilities: There are 30 sites for tents or self-contained RVs at Klum Landing, Picnic tables and fire rings are provided. Drinking water, garbage bins, and restrooms with flush toilets and coin showers, firewood, and boat-launching facilities are available. Some facilities are wheelchair accessible.

A boat ramp is nearby. A store, café, laundry facilities, and boat rentals are available at Howard Prairie Lake Resort. Leashed pets are permitted.

Reservations, fees: Reservations are not accepted for Klum Landing. Sites are $20 per night, $6 per night per additional vehicle, and $1 per pet per night. Reservations are accepted for Sugar Pine Group; the group camp is $150-200 per night. Open mid-April-mid-September.

Directions: In Ashland on I-5, take Exit 14 to Highway 66. Drive east for less than a mile to Dead Indian Memorial Road. Turn left (east) and drive 17 miles to Howard Prairie Road. Turn right (south) and drive eight miles to

Howard Prairie Dam Road. Turn left (east) and drive one mile to reach Klum Landing.

Contact: Jackson County Parks, 541/774-8183, www.jacksoncountyor.org.

239 SUGAR PINE GROUP

Scenic rating: 7

near Howard Prairie Lake

Map 5.7, page 267

Sugar Pine Group camp offers a more primitive group camping experience than the other Jackson County campgrounds in this area.

Campsites, facilities: There is one group site for tents or self-contained RVs that can accommodate up to 100 people. Vault toilets, a group fire ring, and horseshoe pits are available. A boat ramp is nearby. A store, café, laundry facilities, and boat rentals are available at Howard Prairie Lake Resort. Some facilities are wheelchair accessible. Leashed pets are permitted.

Reservations, fees: Reservations are accepted. The site is $150-200 per night. Open mid-April-mid-September.

Directions: In Ashland on I-5, take Exit 14 to Highway 66. Drive east for less than a mile to Dead Indian Memorial Road. Turn left (east) and drive 17 miles to Howard Prairie Road. Turn right (south) and drive eight miles to Howard Prairie Dam Road. Turn left (east) and drive 0.25 mile to Sugar Pine Group camp on the right.

Contact: Jackson County Parks, 541/774-8183, www.jacksoncountyor.org.

240 EMIGRANT LAKE CAMPGROUND

Scenic rating: 8

on Emigrant Lake

Map 5.7, page 267

This camp is nestled among the trees above Emigrant Lake, a well-known recreational area.

Activities at this park include boating, fishing, hiking, swimming, and waterskiing. There are also two 280-foot water slides. The park has its own swimming cove (unsupervised). Side-trip possibilities include exploring nearby Mount Ashland, where a ski area operates in the winter, as well as visiting Ashland's world-renowned Shakespeare Festival, the Britt Music Festival, and historic Jacksonville.

Campsites, facilities: There are two camp-grounds: Point RV Park and Oak Slope Campground. Point RV Park has 32 sites with full hookups for RVs to 45 feet. Oak Slope has 42 sites for tents. There is also a group camp area for up to 100 people. Restrooms with flush toilets, coin showers, a dump station, snacks in summer, firewood, and a barbecue are available. A group picnic and day-use area that can be reserved are also available. Recreational facilities include horseshoe pits, volleyball, a swim cove, a waterslide, and a playground. Two boat ramps are available. Laundry and food are within six miles. Some facilities are wheelchair accessible. Leashed pets are permitted in designated areas only.

Reservations, fees: Reservations are accepted ($8-10 reservation fee). RV sites with full hookups are $30 per night, tent sites are $20 per night, $6 per night per additional vehicle. The group site is $125-175 per night. Some credit cards are accepted for reservations. Point RV Park is open year-round; Oak Slope is open April 1-mid-October, weather permitting.

Directions: From Ashland, drive east on Highway 66 for five miles to the campground on the left.

Contact: Jackson County Parks, 5505 Highway 66, 541/774-8183, www.jacksoncountyor.org.

south end of Hyatt Reservoir, which has six miles of shoreline. Fishing is good for brook and rainbow trout and smallmouth bass. The boat speed limit here is 10 mph. The Pacific Crest Trail runs next to the campground. Another campground option is Wildcat, about two miles north, with 12 sites.

Campsites, facilities: There are 47 sites for tents or RVs up to 40 feet long (no hookups), five equestrian sites, seven walk-in tent sites, and one group site for up to 50 people. Picnic tables and fire grills are provided. Drinking water, restrooms with flush toilets and showers, garbage service, dump station, fish-cleaning station, group kitchen, day-use area, softball fields, volleyball, a playground, horseshoe pits, firewood, docks, and two boat ramps are available. Some facilities are wheelchair accessible. Leashed pets are permitted.

Reservations, fees: Reservations are accepted only for the group camp or horse camp at 541/482-2031 or www.recreation.gov. Sites are $7-15 per night, $3 per night per additional vehicle, with a 14-day stay limit. Equestrian sites are $10 per night; the group site is $95-150 per night. Sites at nearby primitive Wildcat Campground are $7 per night. Pacific Crest Trail hikers pay $2 per person per night for camping. Open late April-October, weather permitting.

Directions: From Ashland, drive east on Highway 66 for 17 miles to East Hyatt Lake Road. Turn north and drive three miles to the campground entrance on the left.

GPS Coordinates: 42.170430, -122.463300

Contact: Bureau of Land Management, Ashland Resource Area, 541/618-2200, www. blm.gov.

241 HYATT LAKE

Scenic rating: 8

on Hyatt Lake

Map 5.7, page 267

Hyatt Lake campground is situated on the

242 TOPSY

Scenic rating: 7

on the Upper Klamath River

Map 5.7, page 267

This campground is on Boyle Reservoir near

the Upper Klamath River, a good spot for trout fishing. Swimming is not recommended because of the murky water. This is a top river for rafters (experts only, or non-experts with professional, licensed guides). There are Class IV and V rapids about four miles southwest at Caldera, Hells Corner, and Satan's Gate. I flipped at Caldera and ended up swimming for it, finally getting out at an eddy. Luckily, I was wearing a dry suit and the best life jacket available, perfect fitting, which saved my butt.

Campsites, facilities: There are 13 sites for RVs up to 32 feet long. Picnic tables and fire grills are provided. Drinking water, vault toilets, garbage service, and a dump station are available. Boat-launching facilities are on-site. A camp host is on-site in season. Some facilities are wheelchair accessible. Leashed pets are permitted.

Reservations, fees: Reservations are not accepted. Sites are $7 per night, $4 per night per additional vehicle, with a 14-day stay limit. Open mid-May-mid-September, weather permitting.

Directions: From Klamath Falls, drive west on Highway 66 for 20 miles to Topsy Road. Turn south on Topsy Road and drive 1.5 miles to the campground on the right.

Contact: Bureau of Land Management, Klamath Falls Resource Area, 541/883-6916, www.blm.gov.

243 JACKSON

Scenic rating: 7

on the Applegate River in Rogue River-Siskiyou National Forest

Map 5.7, page 267

Jackson campground is nestled in an old mining area at 1,700 feet elevation. Situated between the Applegate River and the road, under a canopy of ponderosa pine, it features a swimming hole and good trout fishing. An interpretive trail is across the road from the campground. Mine tailings can be seen

from the camp. Trailers and large RVs are not allowed.

Campsites, facilities: There are eight sites for tents only, two sites for RVs up to 25 feet, and one group site. Picnic tables and fire rings are provided. Drinking water, garbage service, and flush toilets are available. Some facilities are wheelchair accessible. Leashed pets are permitted.

Reservations, fees: Reservations are accepted at 877/444-6777 ($10 reservation fee) or www.recreation.gov ($9 reservation fee). Sites are $20 per night, the group site is $40 per night, $5 per night per additional vehicle. Open year-round, weather permitting, with limited services in winter.

Directions: In Medford on I-5, take the Jacksonville exit to the Jacksonville Highway. Drive west on the Jacksonville Highway (Highway 238) for seven miles to Jacksonville. Bear left on Highway 238 and drive eight miles to the town of Ruch and Upper Applegate Road (County Road 10). Turn left and drive 10 miles to the campground on the right.

Contact: Rogue River-Siskiyou National Forest, Siskiyou Mountains District, 541/899-3800, www.fs.usda.gov/rogue-siskiyou; concessionaire, 541/899-9220, www.applegatelake.com.

244 BEAVER SULPHUR GROUP

Scenic rating: 7

on Beaver Creek in Rogue River-Siskiyou National Forest

Map 5.7, page 267

This group camp is well hidden along the banks of Beaver Creek. It is set at an elevation of 2,100 feet and situated in an area with mixed tree cover, including tall Douglas fir, live oak, and maple. The camp is about nine miles from Applegate Reservoir, features attractive shaded sites, and offers easy access to the creek.

Campsites, facilities: There is one group

site for up to 50 people. Picnic tables and fire grills are provided. Vault toilets and garbage bins (summer only) are available. There is no drinking water. Some facilities are wheelchair accessible. Leashed pets are permitted.

Reservations, fees: Reservations are accepted at 877/444-6777 ($10 reservation fee) or www.recreation.gov ($9 reservation fee). The site is $75 per night. Open May-mid-September, weather permitting.

Directions: In Medford on I-5, take the Jacksonville exit to the Jacksonville Highway. Drive west on the Jacksonville Highway (Highway 238) for seven miles to Jacksonville. Bear left on Highway 238 and drive eight miles to the town of Ruch and Upper Applegate Road (County Road 10). Turn left (south) and drive 9.5 miles to Forest Road 20. Continue three miles to the campground on the right.

Contact: Rogue River–Siskiyou National Forest, Siskiyou Mountains District, 541/899-3800, www.fs.usda.gov/rogue-siskiyou.

245 HART-TISH PARK WALK-IN

Scenic rating: 7

on Applegate Lake, Rogue River-Siskiyou National Forest

Map 5.7, page 267

This concessionaire-managed campground on Applegate Lake has shaded sites and a great view of the lake. Bald eagles and ospreys nest in the area, and it's a treat to watch them fish. A boat launch with boat and kayak rentals is available nearby. The walk-in campsites are only 200 yards from the parking area; wheelbarrows are provided to carry your gear.

Campsites, facilities: There are seven walk-in tent sites and eight lakeside sites in the parking lot for RVs up to 45 feet long. There is also one group site for 30 people. Picnic tables and fire pits are provided. Drinking water, flush toilets, and garbage bins are provided. Firewood is available at a small on-site store. A day-use area

is nearby. Some facilities are wheelchair accessible. Leashed pets are permitted.

Reservations, fees: Reservations are accepted at 877/444-6777 ($10 reservation fee) or www.reserveamerica.com ($9 reservation fee). Sites are $20 per night, $5 per night per additional vehicle; the group site is $40 per night. Open mid-April-September, weather permitting.

Directions: In Medford on I-5, take the Jacksonville exit to the Jacksonville Highway. Drive west on the Jacksonville Highway (Highway 238) for seven miles to Jacksonville. Bear left on Highway 238 and drive eight miles to the town of Ruch and Upper Applegate Road (County Road 10). Turn left (south) and drive 15.5 miles to the campground on the left.

Contact: Rogue River-Siskiyou National Forest, Siskiyou Mountains District, 541/899-3800, www.fs.usda.gov/rogue-siskiyou; concessionaire, 541/899-9220, www.applegatelake.com.

246 WATKINS

Scenic rating: 6

on Applegate Lake in Rogue River-Siskiyou National Forest

Map 5.7, page 267

Set on the southwest shore of Applegate Reservoir, this pretty campground is small and quite primitive—like Carberry Walk-In and French Gulch—and offers the same recreation options. Few campers know about this spot, so it usually doesn't fill up quickly. There are good views of the lake and the surrounding Siskiyou Mountains. The Seattle Bar day-use area at the lake is approximately two miles away. The elevation is 2,000 feet.

Campsites, facilities: There are 14 walk-in sites for tents only. Picnic tables, fire grills, and garbage facilities are provided. Vault toilets are available. There is no drinking water and garbage must be packed out. A general store, boat docks, and launching facilities are within two miles. Leashed pets are permitted.

Reservations, fees: Reservations are not accepted. Sites are $15 per night, $5 per night per additional vehicle. Open year-round, weather permitting.

Directions: In Medford on I-5, take the Jacksonville exit to the Jacksonville Highway. Drive west on the Jacksonville Highway (Highway 238) for seven miles to Jacksonville. Bear left on Highway 238 and drive eight miles to the town of Ruch and Upper Applegate Road (County Road 10). Turn left (south) and drive 17 miles to the campground.

Contact: Rogue River-Siskiyou National Forest, Siskiyou Mountains District, 541/899-3800, www.fs.usda.gov/rogue-siskiyou; concessionaire, 541/899-9220, www.applegatelake.com.

247 CARBERRY WALK-IN

Scenic rating: 5

near Applegate Reservoir in Rogue River-Siskiyou National Forest

Map 5.7, page 267

You'll find recreational opportunities aplenty, including boating, fishing, hiking, mountain biking, and swimming, at this campground on Cougar Creek near the southwest shore of Applegate Reservoir. Dense forest covers the campsites, providing much-needed shade. This camp is similar to Watkins Walk-in.

Campsites, facilities: There are 10 walk-in sites for tents and three spaces in the parking lot for RVs up to 25 feet long. Picnic tables and fire grills are provided. Vault toilets are available. There is no drinking water. A general store, firewood, boat docks, and launching facilities are within two miles. Some facilities are wheelchair accessible. Leashed pets are permitted.

Reservations, fees: Reservations are not accepted. Sites are $15 per night, $5 per night per additional vehicle. Open late May-early September, weather permitting.

Directions: In Medford on I-5, take the Jacksonville exit to the Jacksonville Highway. Drive west on the Jacksonville Highway (Highway 238) for seven miles to Jacksonville. Bear left on Highway 238 and drive eight miles to the town of Ruch and Upper Applegate Road (County Road 10). Turn left (south) and drive 18 miles to the campground parking area. A short walk is required.

Contact: Rogue River-Siskiyou National Forest, Siskiyou Mountains District, 541/899-3800, www.fs.usda.gov/rogue-siskiyou; concessionaire, 541/899-9220, www.applegatelake.com

248 SQUAW LAKE HIKE-IN

Scenic rating: 10

on Squaw Lake in Rogue River-Siskiyou National Forest

Map 5.7, page 267   **BEST (**

"Paradise Found" should be the name of this campground. The setting on the shore of spectacular Squaw Lake is more intimate than that of larger Applegate Reservoir to the west. Numerous trails crisscross the camp and the area attracts the canoe and kayak crowd. This spot has a mix of developed and primitive sites and it's also more popular. In fact, it's the only campground in the district that requires reservations, so be sure to reserve ahead for a space. Campers with disabilities are welcome, but should make arrangements in advance with the local U.S. Forest Service office. The elevation is 3,000 feet.

Campsites, facilities: There are 17 walk-in sites for tents and two family group sites that can accommodate up to 10 people each. Picnic tables and fire grills are provided. Vault toilets are available. Drinking water is available at one end of the camp during the summer only. Garbage must be packed out. Leashed pets are permitted.

Reservations, fees: Reservations are accepted and are recommended at 877/444-6777 ($10 reservation fee) or www.reserveamerica.

com ($9 reservation fee). Sites are $15 per night, group sites are $40 per night. Open mid-May-mid-September, weather permitting.

Directions: In Medford on I-5, take the Jacksonville exit to the Jacksonville Highway. Drive west on the Jacksonville Highway (Highway 238) for seven miles to Jacksonville. Bear left on Highway 238 and drive eight miles to the town of Ruch and Upper Applegate Road (County Road 10). Turn left (south) and drive 15 miles to Forest Road 1075. Continue eight miles to Squaw Lake and the trailhead. Hike is from 150 feet to one mile to the campsites.

Contact: Rogue River-Siskiyou National Forest, Siskiyou Mountains District, 541/899-3800, www.fs.usda.gov/rogue-siskiyou; concessionaire, 541/899-9220, www.applegatelake.com.

249 WRANGLE
🧍 🐴 ⛺

Scenic rating: 10
near the Pacific Crest Trail in Rogue River-Siskiyou National Forest

Map 5.7, page 267

This campground is located at the headwaters of Glade Creek in the Siskiyou Mountains at an elevation of 6,400 feet. The Pacific Crest Trail passes near camp. Dutchman Peak Lookout, built in the late 1920s and featured in the National Historic Register, is within five miles. This lovely campground, in a beautiful, high-country setting, boasts huge Shasta red firs and views of the Siskiyou Mountains. Wrangle is along the Scenic Siskiyou Loop driving tour.

Campsites, facilities: There are five sites for tents. Picnic tables and fire grills are provided. Vault toilets, a pole shelter, and a community kitchen are available. There is no drinking water, and garbage must be packed out. Leashed pets are permitted.

Reservations, fees: Reservations are not accepted. There is no fee for camping. Open early July-late October, weather permitting.

Directions: In Ashland on I-5, take the

Jacksonville exit. Drive east on the Jacksonville Highway to Jacksonville and Highway 238. Bear left on Highway 238 and drive eight miles to the town of Ruch and County Road 10 (Upper Applegate Road). Turn left and drive 9.5 miles to Forest Road 20. Turn left and drive 21 miles to Forest Road 2030. Continue one mile on Forest Road 2030 to the campground.

Contact: Rogue River-Siskiyou National Forest, Siskiyou Mountains District, 541/899-3800, www.fs.usda.gov/rogue-siskiyou.

250 MOUNT ASHLAND
🧍 🐴 🚙 ⛺

Scenic rating: 8
on the Pacific Crest Trail in Klamath National Forest

Map 5.7, page 267   **BEST (**

Set at 6,600 feet elevation along the Pacific Crest Trail, this beautiful camp is heavily wooded and has abundant wildlife. On a clear day, enjoy great lookouts from nearby Siskiyou Peak, particularly to the south, where California's 14,162-foot Mount Shasta is an awesome sight. Mount Ashland Ski Resort is one mile east of the campground and has mountain bike trails. Remember, this is bear country, so keep your food secured.

Campsites, facilities: There are nine sites for tents or RVs up to 28 feet long, with extremely limited space for RVs. Picnic tables and fire grills are provided. Vault toilets are available. There is no water. Garbage must be packed out. Leashed pets are permitted.

Reservations, fees: Reservations are not accepted. There is no fee for camping, but donations are accepted. Open May-late October, weather permitting.

Directions: From Ashland, drive south on I-5 for 12 miles to Mount Ashland Ski Park Road (County Road 993). Turn west and drive 10 miles (the road becomes Forest Road 20) to the campground.

Contact: Klamath National Forest, Happy

Camp/Oak Knoll Ranger District, 530/493-2243, www.fs.usda.gov/klamath.

251 SCOTT CREEK

Scenic rating: 6

in Fremont-Winema National Forest near Chemult

Map 5.8, page 268

This small, remote campground in a mixed conifer forest is popular with the fall hunting crowd. The campsites are nicely shaded and you may spot the occasional trout swimming in Scott Creek, which meanders through the north side of the campground.

Campsites, facilities: There are six sites for tents or RVs up to 30 feet long. Picnic tables and fire grills are provided. A vault toilet is available. There is no drinking water and garbage must be packed out. Leashed pets are permitted.

Reservations, fees: Reservations are not accepted. There is no fee for camping. Open mid-May-late October, weather permitting.

Directions: Scott Creek Campground is located 45 minutes southwest of Chemult. From Chemult, take U.S. Highway 97 south toward Klamath Falls for approximately 16 miles, then turn right onto Millitary Crossing. Turn left onto Sun Mountain Road and then turn right onto Forest Service (FS) Road 2310. Make a left off Forest Service Road 2310 and look for Scott Creek Campground on the left.

Contact: Fremont-Winema National Forest, Chemult Ranger District, 541/365-7001, www.fs.usda.gov/fremont-winema.

252 JACKSON F. KIMBALL STATE PARK

Scenic rating: 7

on the Wood River

Map 5.8, page 268

This primitive state campground at the headwaters of the Wood River is another nice spot just far enough off the main drag to remain a secret. A trail from camp leads to a nearby spring. Fishing from canoe is good on the Wood River.

Campsites, facilities: There are 10 primitive sites for tents or self-contained RVs up to 45 feet long. Picnic tables, fire grills, and garbage bins are provided. Vault toilets are available. There is no drinking water. Leashed pets are permitted.

Reservations, fees: Reservations are not accepted. Sites are $5-11 per night, $7 per night per additional vehicle. Open year-round, weather permitting.

Directions: From Klamath Falls, drive north on U.S. 97 for 21 miles to Highway 62. Turn left (northwest) on Highway 62 and drive 10 miles to Highway 232/Sun Pass Road (near Fort Klamath). Turn right (north) and drive three miles to the campground.

Contact: Jackson F. Kimball is managed by Collier Memorial State Park, 541/783-2471 or 800/551-6949, www.oregonstateparks.org.

253 CRATER LAKE RESORT

Scenic rating: 6

on the Wood River

Map 5.8, page 268

The campground at Crater Lake Resort is dotted with huge pine trees on the banks of the beautiful, crystal-clear Fort Creek. It's located just outside Fort Klamath, the site of numerous military campaigns against the Modoc people in the late 1800s.

Campsites, facilities: There are 14 sites with

full or partial hookups for RVs of any length, five sites for tents, and 11 cabins. Picnic tables and fire rings are provided. Drinking water, restrooms with flush toilets and showers, Wi-Fi, a recreation hall, playground, store, ice, and a coin laundry are available. Propane gas and a café are within 12 miles. Leashed pets are permitted.

Reservations, fees: Reservations are accepted. RV sites are $30-35 per night, $5 per person per night for more than two people, and $5 per pet per night. Tent sites are $20 per night. Some credit cards are accepted. Open mid-April-mid-October.

Directions: From Klamath Falls, drive north on U.S. 97 for 21 miles to Highway 62. Bear left on Highway 62 and drive 12.5 miles north to the resort (just before reaching Fort Klamath).

Contact: Crater Lake Resort, 541/381-2349, www.craterlakeresort.com.

254 COLLIER MEMORIAL STATE PARK

Scenic rating: 7

on the Williamson River

Map 5.8, page 268

This campground sits at the confluence of Spring Creek and the Williamson River, both of which are superior trout streams. An area for equestrian campers is situated at a trailhead for horses. A nature trail is also available. The park features a pioneer village and a logging museum. Movies about old-time logging and other activities are shown on weekend nights during the summer.

Campsites, facilities: There are 50 sites for tents or RVs of any length (full hookups), 18 sites for tents or self-contained RVs up to 50 feet (no hookups), and an area for up to four groups of equestrian campers. Some sites are pull-through. Picnic tables, fire grills, and garbage bins are provided. Drinking water, restrooms with flush toilets and showers, a dump station, firewood, coin laundry, playground,

and day-use hitching area are available. Some facilities are wheelchair accessible. Leashed pets are permitted.

Reservations, fees: Reservations are accepted at 800/452-5687 or www.reserveamerica.com ($8 reservation fee). RV sites are $26 per night, tent sites are $19 per night, $7 per night per additional vehicle. The equestrian area is $19 per night. Some credit cards are accepted. Open year-round, weather permitting.

Directions: From Klamath Falls, drive north on U.S. 97 for 28 miles to the park (well signed).

Contact: Collier Memorial State Park, 800/551-6949 or 541/783-2471, www.oregonstateparks.org.

255 WILLIAMSON

Scenic rating: 6

near Collier Memorial State Park in Fremont-Winema National Forest

Map 5.8, page 268

Another great little spot is discovered, this one at 4,200 feet elevation, with excellent trout fishing along the banks of the Williamson River, a world-famous fly-fishing river. Mosquitoes are numerous in spring and early summer, which can drive people away. A map of Fremont-Winema National Forest details the back roads and trails. Collier Memorial State Park provides a nearby side-trip option.

Campsites, facilities: There are 20 sites for tents or RVs up to 30 feet long. Picnic tables, garbage bins, and fire grills are provided. Drinking water and vault toilets are available. A restaurant is within five miles. Some facilities are wheelchair accessible. Leashed pets are permitted.

Reservations, fees: Reservations are not accepted. Sites are $10 per night, $4 per night per additional vehicle. There is no fee in winter. Open late April-late November, weather permitting.

Directions: From Klamath Falls, drive north on U.S. 97 for 30 miles to Chiloquin. Continue north on U.S. 97 for 5.5 miles to Forest Road 9730. Turn right (northeast) and drive one mile to the campground.

Contact: Fremont-Winema National Forest, Chiloquin Ranger District, 541/883-6714, www.fs.usda.gov/fremont-winema.

256 WALT'S RV PARK

Scenic rating: 7
on the Williamson River

Map 5.8, page 268

This heavily treed campground, across the highway from the Williamson River near Collier Memorial State Park, is one of three camps in the immediate area. The Williamson River has excellent trout fishing. For those looking for a more remote setting, head east to Potter's Park.

Campsites, facilities: There are 20 sites for tents and 14 sites with full or partial hookups for RVs of any length; some are pull-through sites. Picnic tables and fire pits are provided. Drinking water, restrooms with flush toilets and showers, firewood, and ice are available. A café is within 0.25 mile and there is a grocery and a hardware store in Chiloquin. Some facilities are wheelchair accessible. Leashed pets are permitted with breed restrictions.

Reservations, fees: Reservations are accepted. RV sites are $22-28 per night, tent sites are $18 per night, $4 per person per night for more than three people, and $1 per night for air-conditioning. Open year-round, weather permitting.

Directions: From Klamath Falls, drive north on U.S. 97 for 24 miles to Chiloquin Junction. Continue north for 0.25 mile to the campground (adjacent to the Chiloquin Ranger Station) on the left.

Contact: Walt's RV Park, 541/783-2537, www.waltsrvpark.com.

257 AGENCY LAKE RESORT

Scenic rating: 5
on Agency Lake

Map 5.8, page 268

This campground sits along Agency Lake in an open, grassy area with some shaded sites. The resort has more than 700 feet of lakefront property, offering world-class trout fishing. Look across the lake and watch the sun set on the Cascades. Note that some sites are filled with monthly renters.

Campsites, facilities: There are 15 sites for tents, 25 sites with full or partial hookups for tents or RVs of any length, and three cabins. Picnic tables are provided. Drinking water, restrooms with flush toilets and showers, Wi-Fi, a general store (with hunting and fishing licenses), ice, boat docks, and launching facilities are available. Leashed pets are permitted.

Reservations, fees: Reservations are accepted. RV sites are $20-30 per night, tent sites are $18-20 per night, cabins are $55-75 per night, $10 per night for more than two people or pets. Some credit cards are accepted. Open year-round, weather permitting.

Directions: From Klamath Falls, drive north on U.S. 97 for 17 miles to Modoc Point Road. Turn left and drive about 10 miles to the resort on the left.

Contact: Agency Lake Resort, 541/783-2489, www.agencylakeresort.net.

SOUTHEASTERN OREGON

Some people think that southeastern Oregon is one big chunk of nothing. This high-desert region is dry and foreboding, with many miles between campgrounds. However, it is so under-visited that you'll often have vast areas to yourself. Highlights include the Newberry National Volcanic Monument, with East and Paulina Lakes set within its craters, trailhead camps with access to Gearhart Mountain Wilderness in Fremont-Winema National Forest, and camps at Steens Mountain Recreation Lands. Some of the most remote drive-to campgrounds in Oregon are in underused Ochoco and Malheur National Forests. The Owyhee River watershed is like a miniature Grand Canyon, with steep, orange walls and the river cutting a circuitous route through the desert. I have paddled a canoe through most of it—from remote stretches below the Jarbidge Mountains in Nevada through Idaho and into Oregon.

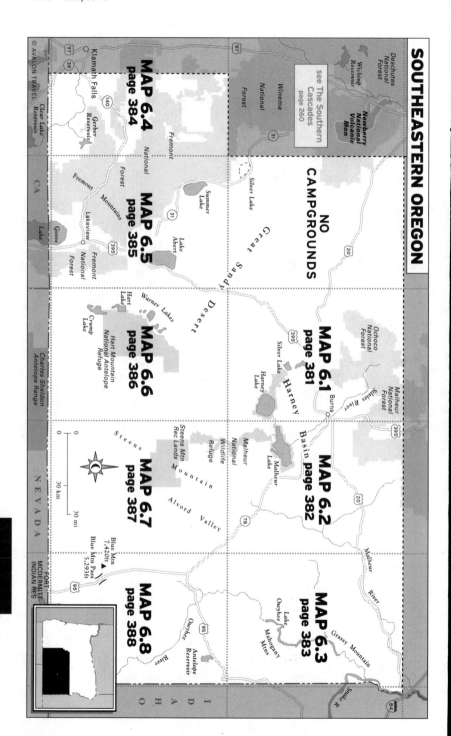

SOUTHEASTERN OREGON

© AVALON TRAVEL

see The Southern
Cascades
page 260

MAP 6.4
page 384

Klamath Falls

Deschutes
National
Forest

Wickiup
Reservoir

Winema
National
Forest

**Newberry
National
Volcanic
Mon**

NO
CAMPGROUNDS

Gerber
Reservoir

Fremont
National
Forest

MAP 6.5
page 385

Silver Lake

Summer
Lake

Great
Sandy
Desert

Ochoco
National
Forest

Malheur
National
Forest

MAP 6.1
page 381

Silver Lake

Lakeview

Lake
Abert

Fremont
Mountains

Fremont
National
Forest

Goose
Lake

Clear Lake
Reservoir

CA

MAP 6.6
page 386

Warner Lakes

Hart
Lake

Crump
Lake

Hart Mountain
National Antelope
Refuge

Harney
Lake

Silver Lake

Harney
Basin
page 382

MAP 6.2

Burns

Silvies River

Malheur
National
Refuge

Malheur
Lake

MAP 6.7
page 387

Steens Mtn
Rec Lands

Steens
Mountain

Alvord
Valley

MAP 6.3
page 383

Malheur
River

Lake
Owyhee

Mahogany
Mtns

Grassy Mountain

Charles Sheldon
Antelope Range

NEVADA

Blue Mtn
7,420ft

Blue Mtn Pass
5,293ft

FORT
McDERMITT
INDIAN RES

MAP 6.8
page 388

Owyhee
Reservoir

Antelope
Reservoir

Owyhee
River

Snake R.

I
D
A
H
O

0   0
       30 km
       30 mi

Map 6.1

Sites 1-5
Pages 389-390

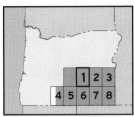

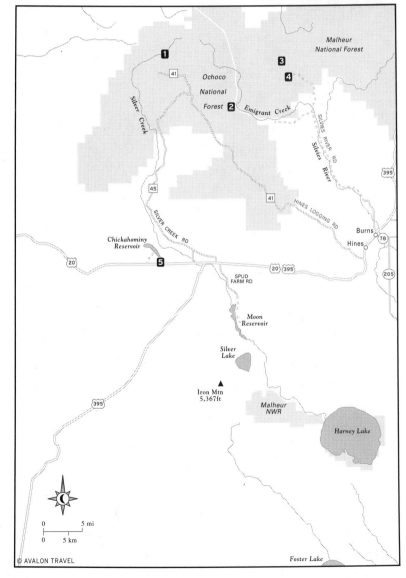

Map 6.2

Sites 6-9
Pages 391-392

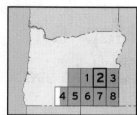

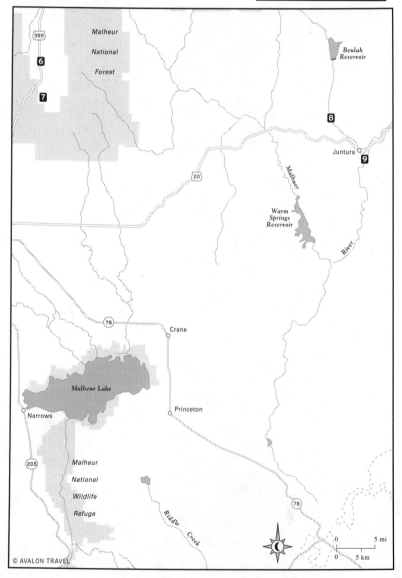

Map **6.3**

Sites 10-13
Pages 392-393

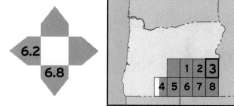

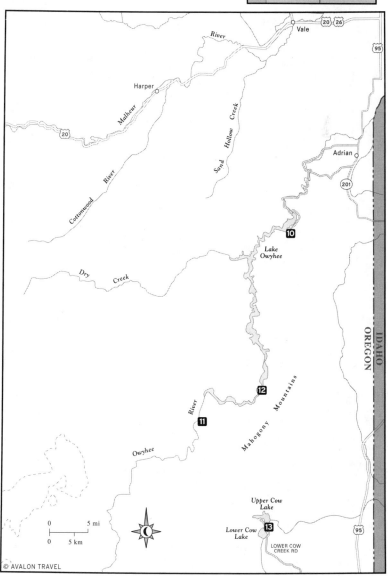

Map 6.4

Sites 14-19
Pages 394-396

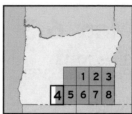

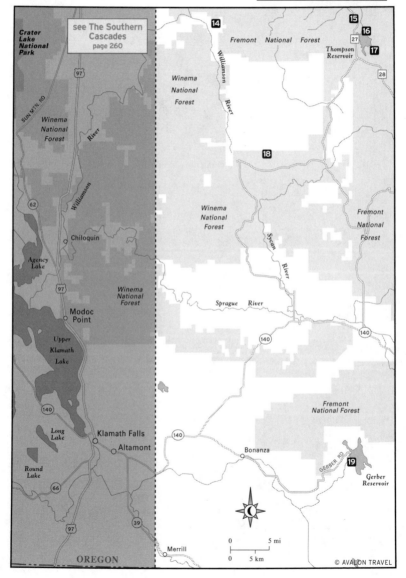

Crater Lake National Park

see The Southern Cascades page 260

Fremont National Forest

Thompson Reservoir

Winema National Forest

Williamson River

Winema National Forest

Winema National Forest

Fremont National Forest

Sycan River

Sprague River

Chiloquin

Agency Lake

Winema National Forest

Modoc Point

Upper Klamath Lake

Fremont National Forest

Long Lake

Klamath Falls

Altamont

Bonanza

Gerber Reservoir

Round Lake

Merrill

OREGON

0   5 mi
0   5 km

© AVALON TRAVEL

Map 6.5

**Sites 20-36
Pages 397-403**

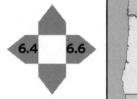

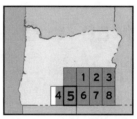

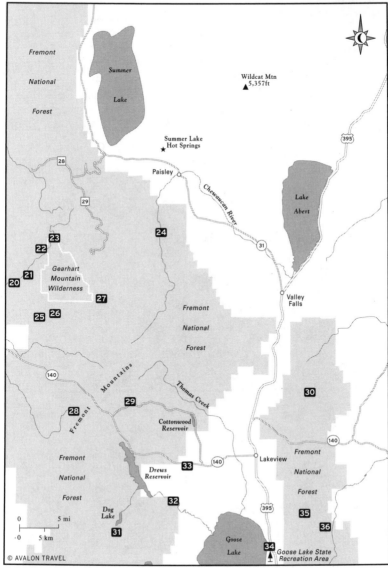

Fremont

National

Forest

Summer
Lake

Wildcat Mtn
▲ 5,357ft

Summer Lake
★ Hot Springs

28

Paisley

Chewaucan River

29

31

Lake
Abert

24

23

22

21

20

Gearhart
Mountain
Wilderness

27

Valley
Falls

25   26

Fremont

National

Forest

140

Mountains

Thomas Creek

30

28

29

Cottonwood
Reservoir

Fremont

140

140

Lakeview

Fremont

National

National

33

Drews
Reservoir

Forest

Forest

Dog
Lake

32

35

395

36

31

Goose
Lake

34

Goose Lake State
Recreation Area

0   5 mi

0   5 km

© AVALON TRAVEL

Map 6.6

Site 37
Page 404

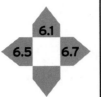

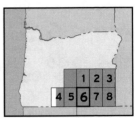

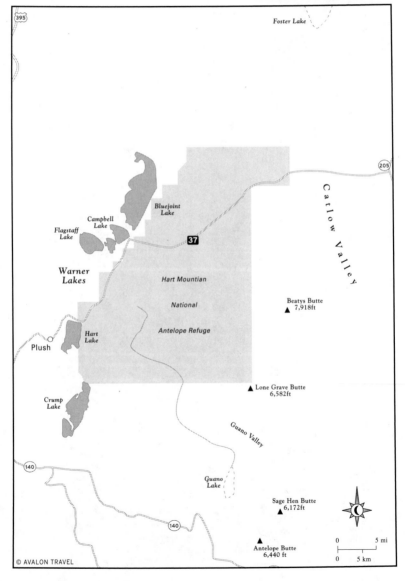

Map 6.7

Sites 38-44
Pages 404-407

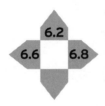

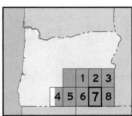

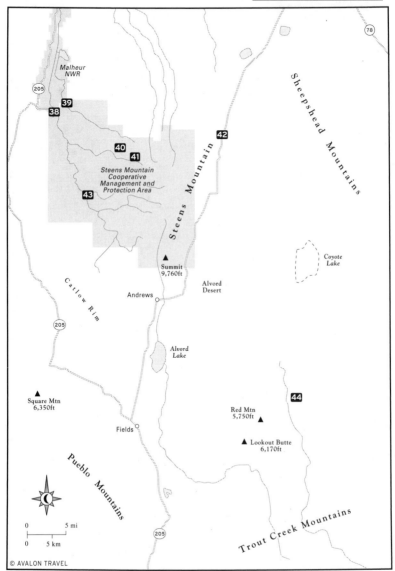

Map **6.8**
Sites 45-47
Pages 407-408

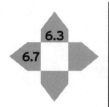

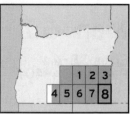

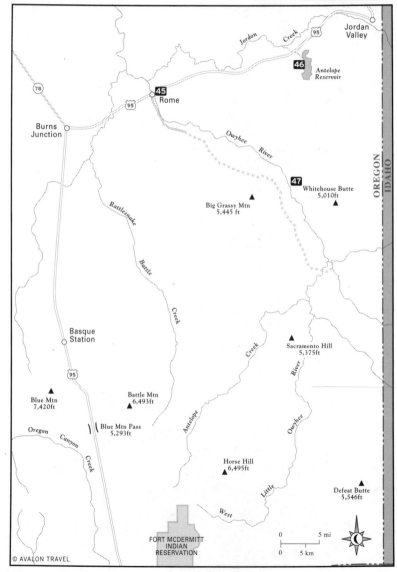

© AVALON TRAVEL

1 DELINTMENT LAKE

🏕 🏊 🛶 ⛴ 🐴 ♿ 🚐 ⛺

Scenic rating: 7

on Delintment Lake in Malheur National Forest

Map 6.1, page 381

This very pretty, forested camp skirts the shore of Delintment Lake. Originally a beaver pond, the lake was gradually developed to its current size of 62 acres. It is now pretty and blue and is stocked with trout, providing good bank and boat fishing. Note that electric motors only are allowed on the lake. Insider's note: Rainbow trout here average 12-18 inches.

Campsites, facilities: There are 29 sites for tents or RVs up to 30 feet long and six walk-in tent-only sites. Picnic tables and fire grills are provided. Drinking water, vault toilets, garbage service, a group picnic area, and boat-launching facilities are available. Some facilities are wheelchair accessible. Leashed pets are permitted.

Reservations, fees: Reservations are not accepted. Sites are $10 per night, $5 per night for an additional vehicle. Open May-October, weather permitting.

Directions: From Burns, drive southwest on U.S. 20 for three miles to County Road 127. Turn right (northwest) and drive 11 miles to Forest Road 41. Turn left on Forest Road 41 and drive about 26.5 miles (staying on Forest Road 41 at all junctions, paved all the way) to the campground at the lake.

Contact: Malheur National Forest, Emigrant Creek Ranger District, 541/573-4300, www.fs.usda.gov/malheur.

2 EMIGRANT

🏕 🚴 🛶 🐴 ♿ 🚐 ⛺

Scenic rating: 4

near Emigrant Creek in Malheur National Forest

Map 6.1, page 381

One of two camps in the immediate area, Emigrant is set at an elevation of 5,200 feet in Malheur National Forest, in a meadow near Emigrant Creek. You'll get peace and quiet here, because this spot is usually not crowded. There's good fly-fishing in the spring and early summer, and several nearby backcountry dirt roads are fun for mountain biking. Falls camp, two miles away, is busier but has drinking water.

Campsites, facilities: There are seven sites for tents or RVs up to 28 feet long. Picnic tables and fire grills are provided. Vault toilets and garbage service are available. There is no drinking water (but drinking water is available nearby at Falls campground). Some facilities are wheelchair accessible. Leashed pets are permitted.

Reservations, fees: Reservations are not accepted. Sites are $8 per night, $4 per night for an additional vehicle. Open May-October, weather permitting.

Directions: From Burns, drive southwest on U.S. 20 for three miles to County Road 127. Turn right (northwest) and drive 25 miles (passing Forest Road 41 on the left) to Forest Road 43 and the junction for Allison Guard Station, Delintment Lake, and Paulina. Turn left on Forest Road 43 and drive 9.75 miles to Forest Road 4340-050. Turn left and drive on Forest Road 4340-050 to the campground.

Contact: Malheur National Forest, Emigrant Creek Ranger District, 541/573-4300, www.fs.usda.gov/malheur.

3 YELLOWJACKET

🏕 🚴 🛶 🐟 ⛴ 🐴 🚐 ⛺

Scenic rating: 8

on Yellowjacket Lake in Malheur National Forest

Map 6.1, page 381

This quiet and crowd-free campground is set at an elevation of 4,800 feet in the ponderosa pines along the shore of Yellowjacket Lake. Fishing for rainbow trout can be very good in the summer; boats without motors are allowed.

Campsites, facilities: There are 20 sites for tents or RVs up to 22 feet long and a group camping area. Picnic tables are provided. Drinking water, vault toilets, and garbage service are available. A boat launch is nearby. Leashed pets are permitted.

Reservations, fees: Reservations are not accepted. Sites are $10 per night, $5 per night for an additional vehicle. Open late May-October, weather permitting.

Directions: From Burns, drive southwest on U.S. 20 for three miles to County Road 127. Turn right (northwest) and drive 32 miles to Forest Road 47. Turn right and drive three miles to Forest Road 3745. Turn right and drive one mile to the campground on the right.

Contact: Malheur National Forest, Emigrant Creek Ranger District, 541/573-4300, www. fs.usda.gov/malheur.

4 FALLS

Scenic rating: 5

near Emigrant Creek in Malheur National Forest

Map 6.1, page 381

Falls camp is set in a beautiful meadow next to Emigrant Creek and is surrounded by ponderosa pine forests. This is a great place to see wildflowers in the early summer. A short trail leads to a small waterfall on the creek, which gives the camp its name. Fly-fishing and mountain biking are good here, as well as at nearby Emigrant, located two miles down the road. The elevation is 5,200 feet.

Campsites, facilities: There are six sites for tents or RVs up to 28 feet long. Picnic tables and fire grills are provided. Drinking water, vault toilets, and garbage service are available. Some facilities are wheelchair accessible. Leashed pets are permitted.

Reservations, fees: Reservations are not accepted. Sites are $8 per night, $4 per night for an additional vehicle, except for towed vehicles. Open May-October, weather permitting.

Directions: From Burns, drive southwest on

U.S. 20 for three miles to County Road 127. Turn right (northwest) and drive 25 miles (passing Forest Road 41 on the left) to Forest Road 43 and the junction for Allison Guard Station, Delintment Lake, and Paulina. Turn left on Forest Road 43 and drive eight miles to the campground on the left.

Contact: Malheur National Forest, Emigrant Creek Ranger District, 541/573-4300, www. fs.usda.gov/malheur.

5 CHICKAHOMINY RESERVOIR

Scenic rating: 4

on Chickahominy Reservoir

Map 6.1, page 381

While a good spot for group camping, this camp is located in the high desert with no shade. Weather conditions can be extreme, so come prepared to tie everything down when the wind blows (a common occurrence). The camp is used primarily as an overnight stop for travelers driving through the area. Boats with motors are allowed on the reservoir. There is an access road on the northwest side of the reservoir for day use. The nearest services are five miles east (via U.S. 20) in Riley.

Campsites, facilities: There are 28 sites for tents or RVs up to 35 feet long. Picnic tables, garbage bins, and fire grills are provided. Drinking water (summer only, subject to fluctuations), vault toilets, a fish-cleaning station, and a boat launch are available. Some facilities are wheelchair accessible. Leashed pets are permitted.

Reservations, fees: Reservations are not accepted. Sites are $8 per night per vehicle, with a stay limit of 14 days. Open year-round, with limited winter facilities.

Directions: From Burns, drive west on U.S. 20 for 30 miles to the campground on the right.

Contact: Bureau of Land Management, Burns District, 541/573-4400, www.blm.gov.

6 JOAQUIN MILLER HORSE CAMP

Scenic rating: 5

in Malheur National Forest

Map 6.2, page 382

Set among mature ponderosa pines and adjacent to a meadow, campsites here are spread out, and there's a fair amount of privacy at this camp. It does receive some highway noise, though. Lots of old logging roads are available for biking, horseback riding, and walking. The camp gets low use, and while it caters to horse campers, all are welcome. Campers with horses are strongly advised to arrive early, before the weekend, to claim the campsites nearest to the corrals.

Campsites, facilities: There are eight sites for tents or RVs up to 28 feet long. Picnic tables and fire rings are provided. Drinking water (supplied by a solar-powered water system), vault toilets, and garbage service are available. Stock facilities include four corrals and two hitching rails. Some facilities are wheelchair accessible. Leashed pets are permitted.

Reservations, fees: Reservations are not accepted. Sites are $8 per night, $4 per night per additional vehicle. Open mid-May-November, weather permitting.

Directions: From Burns, drive north on U.S. 395 for 19 miles to the campground on the left (this turnoff is easy to miss; watch for a very small green sign on the right that says Joaquin Miller Horse Camp).

Contact: Malheur National Forest, Emigrant Creek Ranger District, 541/573-4300, www. fs.usda.gov/malheur.

7 IDLEWILD

Scenic rating: 8

in Devine Canyon in Malheur National Forest

Map 6.2, page 382

This campground sits at an elevation of 5,300 feet in Devine Canyon, a designated winter Sno-Park that's popular with locals for snowmobiling and cross-country skiing. Several hiking and biking trailheads start here, including the Divine Summit Interpretive Loop Trail and the Idlewild Loop Trail. Since it provides easy access and a pretty setting, it's also a popular spot for visitors traveling up U.S. 395 and in need of a stopover. Bird-watching for white-headed woodpeckers and goshawks is popular. Expect to hear some highway noise. But the ponderosa pine forest and area trails are so beautiful that this area can feel divine, even if Devine Canyon and neighboring Devine Ridge were named back in the good old days when nobody worried about spelling.

Campsites, facilities: There are 19 single sites for tents and RVs up to 28 feet long, three double sites, and one group site for 20-50 people. Picnic tables and fire grills are provided. Drinking water, vault toilets, picnic areas, and garbage service are available. A group shelter can be reserved. Some facilities are wheelchair accessible. Leashed pets are permitted.

Reservations, fees: Reservations are accepted for the group shelter only at 877/444-6777 ($10 reservation fee) or www.recreation.gov ($9 reservation fee). Sites are $10 per night, $5 per night for an additional vehicle, except for towed vehicles. Open late May-mid-October, weather permitting.

Directions: From Burns, drive north on U.S. 395 for 17 miles to the campground on the right.

Contact: Malheur National Forest, Emigrant Creek Ranger District, 541/573-4300, www. fs.usda.gov/malheur.

8 CHUKAR PARK

Scenic rating: 7

on the north fork of the Malheur River

Map 6.2, page 382

Chukar Park campground hugs the banks of the north fork of the Malheur River. The general area provides habitat for chukar, an upland game bird species. Hunting can be good in season during the fall but requires much hiking in rugged terrain. Trout fishing is also popular here. Bureau of Land Management (BLM) asks that visitors please respect the surrounding private property.

Campsites, facilities: There are 18 sites for tents or RVs up to 28 feet long. Picnic tables, fire rings, and garbage service are provided. Drinking water (May-October only) and vault toilets are available. Firewood is not available. Some facilities are wheelchair accessible. Leashed pets are permitted.

Reservations, fees: Reservations are not accepted. Sites are $5 per night per vehicle, with a 14-day stay limit. Open year-round, with limited winter facilities.

Directions: From Burns, drive north on U.S. 395 for three miles to U.S. 20. Take U.S. 20 east and drive 55 miles to Juntura and Beulah Reservoir Road. Turn northwest and drive six miles to the campground.

Contact: Bureau of Land Management, Vale District, 541/473-3144, www.blm.gov.

9 OASIS CAFÉ, MOTEL & RV PARK

Scenic rating: 6

in Juntura

Map 6.2, page 382

One of the only camps in the area, this well-maintained RV park is close to Chukar Park. The general area provides habitat for chukar, an upland game bird species. Hunting during the fall and trout fishing are recreation opportunities here.

Campsites, facilities: There are 22 sites with full hookups for RVs of any length, two cabins, and seven motel rooms. Some sites are pull-through. Picnic tables are provided. Restrooms with flush toilets and showers, a café, and ice are available. Leashed pets are permitted.

Reservations, fees: Reservations are not accepted. Sites are $31 per night. Some credit cards are accepted. Open year-round.

Directions: From Burns, drive north on U.S. 395 for three miles to U.S. 20. Turn east and drive 55 miles to Juntura (a very small town). The park is on the left along U.S. 20.

Contact: Oasis Café, Motel & RV Park, 5838 U.S. 20, 541/277-3605.

10 LAKE OWYHEE STATE PARK

Scenic rating: 7

on Owyhee Lake

Map 6.3, page 383

There are two campgrounds here: McCormack and Indian Creek, which are located 1.5 miles apart. This state park is situated along the shore of 53-mile-long Owyhee Lake, a good lake for waterskiing in the day and fishing for warm-water species in the morning and evening. Owyhee is famous for its superb bass fishing; the place even has floating restrooms. Other highlights include views of unusual geological formations and huge rock pinnacles. Bighorn sheep, coyotes, golden eagles, mountain lions, mule deer, pronghorn antelope, and wild horses live in the area.

Campsites, facilities: McCormack has 31 sites with partial hookups for tents and RVs of any length, eight tent sites, and two tepees. Indian Creek has 26 sites with partial hookups for tents or RVs up to 50 feet and nine tent sites. Drinking water, picnic tables, and fire grills are provided. Vault toilets, garbage bins, firewood, a dump station, and a picnic area are available. Restrooms with flush toilets and showers are available at McCormack. Boat launches are at Indian Creek, Gordon Gulch day-use, and near the dam. Fuel and ice are available at the park. Marine fuel is available at Indian Creek. Some facilities are wheelchair accessible. Leashed pets are permitted.

Reservations, fees: Reservations are accepted at 800/452-5687 or www.reserveamerica.com

($8 reservation fee). RV sites are $22 per night, tent sites are $17 per night, tepees are $41 per night, $5 for the hiker/biker site at Indian Creek, and $7 per night for an additional vehicle. Some credit cards are accepted. Open year-round.

Directions: From Ontario (near the Oregon/Idaho border), drive south on U.S. 20/26 for six miles to the Nyssa exit. Turn south and drive eight miles to Nyssa and Highway 201. Turn left (southeast) on Highway 201 and drive eight miles to Owyhee. Turn east and drive about 20 miles to road's end and the entrance to the park, approximately 33 miles from Nyssa.

Contact: Lake Owyhee State Park, 541/339-2331 or 800/551-6949, www.oregonstateparks.org.

11 COW LAKES

Scenic rating: 6

near Cow Lakes

Map 6.3, page 383

Cow Lakes is a little-used campground adjacent to an old lava flow. The lake is shallow and murky, which makes fishing popular here. The campsites are open and treeless, and the road is rutted and rough in places.

Campsites, facilities: There are 10 sites for tents or very small RVs. Picnic tables and fire rings are provided. A vault toilet and a primitive boat ramp are available. No drinking water or firewood is available, and garbage must be packed out. Leashed pets are permitted.

Reservations, fees: Reservations are not accepted. There is no fee for camping. Open year-round, weather permitting.

Directions: From Burns Junction, drive east on U.S. 95 for 30 miles to Danner Loop Road. Turn left (north) and drive 14 miles (past Danner) to Cow Lakes and the campground.

Contact: Bureau of Land Management, Vale District, 541/473-3144, www.blm.gov.

12 SLOCUM CREEK

Scenic rating: 6

on Owyhee Lake

Map 6.3, page 383

This campground sits on the eastern shore of Owyhee Lake, about 20 miles from the Oregon/Idaho border. Hiking, warm-water fishing, and waterskiing are among the recreation options in this high-desert area. Lake Owyhee State Park provides the other developed recreation destination on the lake.

Campsites, facilities: There are 12 sites for tents or RVs up to 20 feet long. Picnic tables are provided. Vault toilets and garbage service are available. There is no drinking water on-site, but some can be found 05.-mile away. Firewood is not available. Boat-launching facilities (for boats less than 17 feet long) are available on-site. Some facilities are wheelchair accessible. Leashed pets are permitted.

Reservations, fees: Reservations are not accepted. There is no fee for camping. Open early March–mid-November.

Directions: From U.S. 95 where it crosses the Idaho/Oregon border, drive north for five miles to McBride Creek Road. Turn west and drive 10 miles to Leslie Gulch Road. Turn left (west) and drive 15 miles to the campground.

Contact: Bureau of Land Management, Vale District, 541/473-3144, www.blm.gov.

13 BIRCH CREEK HISTORIC RANCH

Scenic rating: 9

near the Owyhee River

Map 6.3, page 383

This is one of the most remote campgrounds in Oregon. When I stayed here, it was known as "Hole in the Ground." The official name, Birch Creek Ranch, is the collective name for two ranches founded about 100 years ago. The remote setting is an oasis in the arid, scenic Owyhee River Canyon, its green fields contrasting strongly with the sun-drenched cream- and chocolate-colored formations and the red and black volcanic rocks that soar up from the edges of its narrow meadows. This section of the Owyhee River holds Class III, IV, and V+ rapids. Hiking options include the Jordan Crater, a 4,000-year-old caldera offering domes, kipukas, lava tubes, trenches, and more. The Owyhee Canyon rim looks like a miniature Grand Canyon. This camp/ranch's stone walls, water wheel, and barn contribute to its inclusion on the National Register of Historic Places. I canoed nearly the entire length of the Owyhee, from the headwaters below the Jarbidge Mountains in Nevada, through Idaho and into Oregon.

Campsites, facilities: There are five sites for tents or small RVs. Picnic tables and fire rings are provided. A vault toilet is available. There is no drinking water, but water can be found within 0.25 mile. Garbage must be packed out. There is access to the Owyhee River by self-registration for non-motorized boats only. Some facilities are wheelchair accessible. Leashed pets are permitted.

Reservations, fees: Reservations are not accepted. There is no fee for camping. Open mid-March–mid-October, weather permitting.

Directions: From Jordan Valley, take U.S. 95 north for 10 miles to Cow Creek Road at the Jordan Craters sign. Turn left (west) on Cow Creek Road and follow BLM Owyhee River access signs 28 miles to campground. High-clearance 4WD vehicles recommended. Road may be impassable when wet.

Contact: Bureau of Land Management, Vale District, 541/473-3144, www.blm.gov.

14 JACKSON CREEK

Scenic rating: 8

on Jackson Creek in Fremont-Winema National Forest

Map 6.4, page 384   **BEST (**

Jackson Creek is a remote campground in a beautiful stand of old-growth ponderosa pine at an elevation of 4,600 feet. Horseback riding and mountain biking are popular. Wildlife-viewing can be outstanding some years. Note that there are many mosquitoes in spring and early summer, so bring repellent. The campground borders private land, so watch for forest boundary signs to avoid trespassing.

Campsites, facilities: There are 12 sites for tents or RVs up to 25 feet long. Picnic tables and fire grills are provided. Vault toilets are available. There is no drinking water. Garbage must be packed out. Leashed pets are permitted.

Reservations, fees: Reservations are not accepted. There is no fee for camping. Open year-round, weather permitting.

Directions: From Chemult and Highway 97, drive south for 25 miles to Silver Lake Road (County Road 676). Turn left (northeast) and drive 22 miles to Forest Road 49. Turn right (southeast) and drive five miles to the camp.

Contact: Fremont-Fremont-Winema National Forest, Chemult Ranger District, 541/365-7001, www.fs.usda.gov/fremont-winema.

15 SILVER CREEK MARSH

Scenic rating: 4

near Silver Creek in Fremont National Forest

Map 6.4, page 384

A trailhead and terminus for segments of the National Recreational Trail are located at this small, quiet, and primitive camp that gets little attention. It's a short walk to the creek, a popular fishing spot, and the camp is also close to a wildlife area boundary.

Campsites, facilities: There are 14 sites for

tents or RVs up to 50 feet long. Picnic tables and fire grills are provided. Drinking water, vault toilets, garbage bins, and hitching rails and corrals for horses are available. Note that drinking water and garbage service availability is uncertain. Firewood is available nearby. Leashed pets are permitted.

Reservations, fees: Reservations are not accepted. Sites are $6 per night, $2 per night per additional vehicle. There is a 14-day stay limit. Open May-mid-November, weather permitting.

Directions: From Bend, drive south on U.S. 97 for 32 miles to Highway 31. Turn southeast on Highway 31 and drive 48 miles to County Road 4-11 (one mile west of the town of Silver Lake). Turn right and drive six miles (the road becomes Forest Road 27). Continue south for five miles to the campground entrance road on the left.

Contact: Fremont-Fremont-Winema National Forest, Silver Lake Ranger District, 541/576-2107, www.fs.usda.gov/fremont-winema.

16 THOMPSON RESERVOIR
🚶 🏊 ⛵ 🛶 🏕 🐎 🚐 ⛰

Scenic rating: 3
on Thompson Reservoir in Fremont National Forest

Map 6.4, page 384

Located on the north shore of Thompson Reservoir among black-bark ponderosa pines the height of telephone poles, this simple and pretty camp features shaded sites close to the water. The area is popular for fishing and boating. Water in the reservoir fluctuates and sometimes nearly dries up altogether in late summer.

Campsites, facilities: There are 19 sites for tents or RVs up to 22 feet long, plus a separate group camping area. Picnic tables and fire grills are provided. Drinking water, garbage bins, and vault toilets are available. Boat-launching facilities are nearby. Leashed pets are permitted.

Reservations, fees: Reservations are not accepted. Sites are $6 per night, $2 per night per

additional vehicle. Open May-mid-November, weather permitting.

Directions: From Bend, drive south on U.S. 97 for 32 miles to Highway 31. Turn southeast on Highway 31 and drive 48 miles to County Road 4-11 (one mile west of the town of Silver Lake). Turn right and drive six miles (the road becomes Forest Road 27) and continue south for nine miles to the campground entrance road. Turn left and drive one mile to the camp.

Contact: Fremont-Fremont-Winema National Forest, Silver Lake Ranger District, 541/576-2107, www.fs.usda.gov/fremont-winema.

17 EAST BAY
🚶 🏊 ⛵ 🛶 🏕 🐎 ♿ 🚐 ⛰

Scenic rating: 3
on Thompson Reservoir in Fremont National Forest

Map 6.4, page 384

This campground on the east shore of Thompson Reservoir has paved roads, but it's still a long way from home, so be sure to bring all of your supplies with you. A day-use area is adjacent to the camp. Nearby Silver Creek Marsh Campground provides an even more primitive setting along a stream.

Campsites, facilities: There are 17 sites for tents or RVs up to 50 feet long and one double site. Picnic tables and fire grills are provided. Drinking water, garbage bins, vault toilets, and a fishing pier are available. Boat-launching facilities are nearby. Some facilities are wheelchair accessible. Leashed pets are permitted.

Reservations, fees: Reservations are not accepted. Sites are $10 per night, $5 per night per extra vehicle. Open May-mid-November, weather permitting.

Directions: From Bend, drive south on U.S. 97 for 32 miles to Highway 31. Turn southeast on Highway 31 and drive 49 miles to Silver Lake. Continue east a short distance on Highway 31 to Forest Road 28. Turn right on Forest Road 28 and drive 13 miles to Forest Road 014. Turn right on Forest Road 014 and drive two miles to the campground.

Contact: Fremont-Fremont-Winema National Forest, Silver Lake Ranger District, 541/576-2107, www.fs.usda.gov/fremont-winema.

18 HEAD OF THE RIVER

Scenic rating: 8

on the Williamson River in Fremont-Winema National Forest

Map 6.4, page 384

Almost nobody knows about this small, extremely remote spot on the edge of a meadow in the lodgepole and ponderosa pines, though hunters use it in the fall. The only camp for miles around, it's set at 4,500 feet elevation along the Williamson River headwaters, where you can actually see the beginning of the river bubbling up from underground springs. Be prepared for mosquitoes in early summer.

Campsites, facilities: There are five sites for tents or RVs up to 30 feet long. Picnic tables, garbage bins, and fire pits are provided. A vault toilet is available. There is no drinking water. Leashed pets are permitted.

Reservations, fees: Reservations are not accepted. There is no fee for camping. Open Memorial Day weekend-late November, weather permitting.

Directions: From Klamath Falls, drive north on U.S. 97 for 30 miles to Chiloquin and Sprague River Highway. Turn right (east) on Sprague River Highway and drive five miles to Williamson River Road. Turn left (northeast) and drive 20 miles to Forest Road 4648. Turn left (north) on Forest Road 4648 and drive 0.5 mile to the campground.

Contact: Fremont-Fremont-Winema National Forest, Klamath Ranger District, 541/885-3400, www.fs.usda.gov/fremont-winema.

19 GERBER NORTH, SOUTH, AND HORSE CAMP

Scenic rating: 6

on Gerber Reservoir

Map 6.4, page 384

This camp can be found at an elevation of 4,800 feet alongside the west shore of Gerber Reservoir. Off the beaten path, Gerber attracts mainly locals. Recreation options include boating (10-mph speed limit), fishing, and hiking. Swimming is not popular here because the water is murky with algae.

Campsites, facilities: There are 50 sites for tents or RVs up to 30 feet at Gerber North and Gerber South. Gerber Horse Camp has seven equestrian sites about 0.25 mile above Gerber North. Some dispersed primitive sites are also available; these have no garbage service. Picnic tables and fire grills are provided at the three developed campgrounds. Drinking water, a dump station, vault toilets, two boat ramps with docks, and two fish-cleaning stations are available at Gerber North and Gerber South. Drinking water, a dump station, vault toilets, and corrals are available at Gerber Horse Camp. Garbage service, restroom maintenance, and a camp host are available in summer only. Some facilities are wheelchair accessible. Leashed pets are permitted.

Reservations, fees: Reservations are not accepted. Sites are $7 per night, $4 per night for an additional vehicle. Open year-round, weather permitting; equestrian sites are open May-October. Drinking water and garbage service are only available May-mid-September.

Directions: From Klamath Falls, drive east on Highway 140 for 16 miles to Dairy and Highway 70. Turn right (south) on Highway 70 and drive seven miles to Bonanza and East Langell Valley Road. Turn left (east) on East Langell Valley Road and drive 11 miles to Gerber Road. Turn left on Gerber Road and drive eight miles to the campground on the right.

Contact: Bureau of Land Management,

Klamath Falls Resource Area, 541/883-6916, www.blm.gov.

20 LEE THOMAS

Scenic rating: 6

near the north fork of the Sprague River in Fremont National Forest

Map 6.5, page 385

Lee Thomas is located near the trailhead that provides access to the Dead Horse Rim Trail. Nestled along the north fork of the Sprague River in the interior of Fremont National Forest, this small, cozy camp is a genuine hideaway, with all the necessities provided. It is set in a meadow at an elevation of 6,306 feet and, like Sandhill Crossing Campground (two miles downstream), it's popular with anglers and hunters in the fall.

Campsites, facilities: There are eight sites for tents or RVs up to 16 feet long. Picnic tables and fire grills are provided. Drinking water and vault toilets are available. Garbage must be packed out. Some facilities are wheelchair accessible. Leashed pets are permitted.

Reservations, fees: Reservations are not accepted. There is no fee for camping. Open June-late October, weather permitting.

Directions: From Lakeview, drive north on U.S. 395 for 23 miles to Highway 31. Turn northwest and drive 22 miles to Paisley. Continue on Highway 31 for 0.5 mile to Mill Street. Turn west on Mill Street and drive 20 miles (the road becomes Forest Road 33) and continue to the T intersection with Forest Road 28. Turn right on Forest Road 28 and drive 0.5 mile to Forest Road 3411. Turn right and drive one mile to the campground on the right.

Contact: Fremont-Fremont-Winema National Forest, Paisley Ranger District, 541/943-3114, www.fs.usda.gov.

21 SANDHILL CROSSING

Scenic rating: 6

on the north fork of the Sprague River in Fremont National Forest

Map 6.5, page 385

If you're looking for a combination of beauty and solitude, you've found it. This camp (6,306 feet elevation) sits on the banks of the designated Wild and Scenic North Fork Sprague River, where fishing is superior. Although a low-use camp, it is popular with anglers and hunters in the fall. A nearby trailhead leads into the Gearheart Wilderness.

Campsites, facilities: There are five sites for tents or RVs up to 25 feet long. Picnic tables and fire grills are provided. Vault toilets and drinking water are available. Garbage must be packed out. Some facilities are wheelchair accessible. Leashed pets are permitted.

Reservations, fees: Reservations are not accepted. There is no fee for camping. Open June-October, weather permitting.

Directions: From Lakeview, drive north on U.S. 395 for 23 miles to Highway 31. Turn northwest and drive 22 miles to Paisley. Continue on Highway 31 for 0.5 mile to Mill Street. Turn west on Mill Street and drive 20 miles (the road becomes Forest Road 33); continue to the T intersection with Forest Road 28. Turn right and drive 11 miles to Forest Road 3411. Turn left and drive eight miles to the campground on the left.

Contact: Fremont-Fremont-Winema National Forest, Paisley Ranger District, 541/943-3114, www.fs.usda.gov/fremont-winema.

22 DEAD HORSE LAKE

Scenic rating: 9

on Dead Horse Lake in Fremont National Forest

Map 6.5, page 385

The shore of Dead Horse Lake is home to this

camp sitting at 7,372 feet elevation; it generally fills up on most weekends and holidays. A hiking trail winds around the perimeter of the lake, hooking up with other trails along the way. One original Civilian Conservation Corps canoe, a relic of the 1930s, remains in the lake. No gas motors are permitted on the lake, and a 5-mph speed limit is in effect. Nearby Fremont National Forest provides good side trips.

Campsites, facilities: There are 14 sites for tents or RVs up to 25 feet long and a separate group area for up to 40 people. Picnic tables and fire grills are provided. Drinking water and vault toilets are available, but garbage must be packed out. A boat launch and day-use area are nearby. Leashed pets are permitted.

Reservations, fees: Reservations are not accepted. Sites are $6 per night, $2 per night per additional vehicle. Open July-October, weather permitting.

Directions: From Lakeview, drive north on U.S. 395 for 23 miles to Highway 31. Turn northwest and drive 22 miles to Paisley. Continue on Highway 31 for 0.5 mile to Mill Street. Turn west on Mill Street and drive 20 miles (the road becomes Forest Road 033); continue to the T intersection with Forest Road 28. Turn right and drive 11 miles (watch for the turn to Campbell-Dead Horse Lakes) to Forest Road 033. Turn left and drive three miles (gravel road) to the campground.

Contact: Fremont-Fremont-Winema National Forest, Paisley Ranger District, 541/943-3114, www.fs.usda.gov/fremont-winema.

23 CAMPBELL LAKE

Scenic rating: 9

on Campbell Lake in Fremont National Forest

Map 6.5, page 385   BEST (

This campground on the pebbled shore of Campbell Lake is located near Dead Horse Lake Campground. These high-elevation, crystal-clear lakes were formed during the glacier period, evidence of which can be found on the nearby Lakes Trail system. Both camps are very busy, filling up most weekends in July and August. No gas motors are permitted on Campbell Lake, and a 5-mph speed limit is in effect. A U.S. Forest Service map details the back roads.

Campsites, facilities: There are 18 sites for tents or RVs up to 25 feet long. Picnic tables and fire grills are provided. Drinking water and vault toilets are available. Garbage must be packed out. A boat launch and day-use area are adjacent to the camp. Boats with electric motors are permitted, but gas motors are prohibited. Leashed pets are permitted.

Reservations, fees: Reservations are not accepted. Sites are $6 per night, $2 per night per additional vehicle. Open July-late October, weather permitting.

Directions: From Lakeview, drive north on U.S. 395 for 23 miles to Highway 31. Turn northwest and drive 22 miles to Paisley. Continue on Highway 31 for 0.5 mile to Mill Street. Turn west on Mill Street and drive 20 miles (the road becomes Forest Road 33) and continue to the T intersection with Forest Road 28. Turn right and drive eight miles to Forest Road 033. Turn left and drive two miles to the campground.

Contact: Fremont-Fremont-Winema National Forest, Paisley Ranger District, 541/943-3114, www.fs.usda.gov/fremont-winema.

24 MARSTER SPRING

Scenic rating: 6

on the Chewaucan River in Fremont National Forest

Map 6.5, page 385

The largest of several popular camps in this river corridor, Marster Spring sits right on the banks of the Chewaucan River at an elevation of 4,845 feet. This pretty campground is set among ponderosa pine trees in a good fishing area, yet is close to the town of Paisley. The Fremont National Recreation Trail is accessible at the Chewaucan Crossing Trailhead, 0.25 mile to the south.

Campsites, facilities: There are 10 sites for tents or RVs up to 22 feet long. Picnic tables and fire grills are provided. Drinking water and vault toilets are available. Leashed pets are permitted.

Reservations, fees: Reservations are not accepted. Sites are $6 per night, $2 per night per additional vehicle. Open May-October, weather permitting.

Directions: From Lakeview, drive north on U.S. 395 for 23 miles to Highway 31. Turn northwest and drive 22 miles to Paisley. Continue on Highway 31 for 0.5 mile to Mill Street. Turn west on Mill Street and drive 7.5 miles (the road becomes Forest Road 33) to the campground on the left.

Contact: Fremont-Fremont-Winema National Forest, Paisley Ranger District, 541/943-3114, www.fs.usda.gov/fremont-winema.

25 CORRAL CREEK

Scenic rating: 4
near the Gearhart Mountain Wilderness in Fremont National Forest

Map 6.5, page 385

Set along Corral Creek, this camp is adjacent to a trailhead that provides access into the Gearhart Mountain Wilderness, making it a prime base camp for a backpacking trip. Access is also available from camp to the Palisade Rocks, a worthwhile side trip. Another option is Quartz Mountain Sno-Park, which is 14 miles east of the campground. The elevation is 6,000 feet.

Campsites, facilities: There are six sites for tents or RVs up to 22 feet long. Picnic tables and fire grills are provided. Vault toilets are available. There is no drinking water, and garbage must be packed out. Stock facilities include hitching posts, stalls, and corrals. Some facilities are wheelchair accessible. Leashed pets are permitted.

Reservations, fees: Reservations are not accepted. There is no fee for camping. Open mid-May-late October, weather permitting.

Directions: From Klamath Falls, drive east on Highway 140 for 53 miles to the town of Bly. Continue east on Highway 140 for one mile to Campbell Road. Turn left and drive 0.5 mile to Forest Road 34. Turn right and drive 15 miles to Forest Road 012. Turn right and drive to the campground.

Contact: Fremont-Fremont-Winema National Forest, Bly Ranger District, 541/353-2700, www.fs.usda.gov/fremont-winema.

26 DAIRY POINT

Scenic rating: 6
on Dairy Creek in Fremont National Forest

Map 6.5, page 385

This campground, elevation 5,200 feet, is situated next to the Dairy Creek Bridge in a stand of ponderosa pine and white fir at the edge of a large and open meadow. The setting is beautiful and peaceful, with a towering backdrop of mountains. In the spring, wildflowers are a sight to behold; bird-watching can also be excellent this time of year. Fishing and inner tubing are popular activities at Dairy Creek. Warning: This campground is suitable for large groups and is often full on holidays and most weekends.

Campsites, facilities: There are four sites for tents or self-contained RVs up to 25 feet long. Picnic tables and fire grills are provided. A vault toilet and drinking water are available. Garbage must be packed out. Leashed pets are permitted.

Reservations, fees: Reservations are not accepted. There is no fee for camping. Open mid-May-October, weather permitting.

Directions: From Lakeview, drive north on U.S. 395 for 23 miles to Highway 31. Turn northwest and drive 22 miles to Paisley. Continue on Highway 31 for 0.5 mile to Mill Street. Turn west on Mill Street and drive 20 miles (the road becomes Forest Road 33); continue to the T intersection with Forest Road 28. Turn left and drive two miles (crossing the Dairy Creek Bridge) to Forest Road 3428. Turn left and drive to the campground (just past the intersection on the left).

Contact: Fremont-Fremont-Winema National Forest, Paisley Ranger District, 541/943-3114, www.fs.usda.gov/fremont-winema.

27 HAPPY CAMP

Scenic rating: 6
on Dairy Creek in Fremont National Forest

Map 6.5, page 385

Here's a pleasant spot with open sites along Dairy Creek, though only one site is close to the water. The camp features some old 1930s Civilian Conservation Corps shelters, preserved in their original state. Fishing is available for rainbow trout, though the creek is no longer stocked. The camp sits at 5,289 feet elevation.

Campsites, facilities: There are nine sites for tents or RVs up to 16 feet long. Picnic tables and fire grills are provided. Vault toilets, picnic shelters, and horseshoe pits are available. There is no drinking water (drinking water is available 1.5 miles west on Forest Road 047 at Clear Spring). Garbage must be packed out. Leashed pets are permitted.

Reservations, fees: Reservations are not accepted. There is no fee for camping. Open mid-May-late October, weather permitting.

Directions: From Lakeview, drive north on U.S. 395 for 23 miles to Highway 31. Turn northwest and drive 22 miles to Paisley. Continue on Highway 31 for 0.5 mile to Mill Street. Turn west on Mill Street and drive 20 miles (the road becomes Forest Road 33); continue to the T intersection with Forest Road 28. Turn left and drive two miles (just before Dairy

Creek) to Forest Road 047. Turn right and drive two miles to the campground on the left.

Contact: Fremont-Fremont-Winema National Forest, Paisley Ranger District, 541/943-3114, www.fs.usda.gov/fremont-winema.

28 LOFTON RESERVOIR

Scenic rating: 6
on Lofton Reservoir in Fremont National Forest

Map 6.5, page 385

This remote campground sits on the shore of Lofton Reservoir, a small lake that can provide the best trout fishing in this region. Other nearby lakes are accessible by forest roads. This area marks the beginning of the Great Basin, a high-desert area that extends to Idaho. A large fire burned much of the surrounding forest about 20 years ago, making this campground an oasis of sorts.

Campsites, facilities: There are 22 sites for tents or RVs up to 25 feet long and four double sites. Picnic tables and fire grills are provided. Vault toilets are available. There is no drinking water and garbage must be packed out. Boat docks and launching facilities are nearby. A camp host is on-site. Some facilities are wheelchair accessible. Leashed pets are permitted.

Reservations, fees: Reservations are not accepted. Sites are $6 per night, $2 per night per additional vehicle. Open mid-May-late October, weather permitting.

Directions: From Klamath Falls, drive east on Highway 140 for 54 miles to Bly. Continue east on Highway 140 for 13 miles to Forest Road 3715. Turn right and drive seven miles to Forest Road 013. Turn left on Forest Road 013 and drive one mile to the campground.

Contact: Fremont-Fremont-Winema National Forest, Bly Ranger District, 541/353-2700, www.fs.usda.gov/fremont-winema.

29 COTTONWOOD COMPLEX CAMPGROUND

Scenic rating: 6

on Cottonwood Meadow Lake in Fremont National Forest

Map 6.5, page 385

Cottonwood Recreation Area, along the upper shore of Cottonwood Meadow Lake, is one of the better spots in the vicinity for fishing and hiking. The camp is set at an elevation of 6,130 feet in a forested setting with aspen and many huge ponderosa pines. Boats with electric motors are allowed on the lake, but gas motors are prohibited. Three hiking trails wind around the lake, and facilities for horses include hitching posts, feeders, water, and corrals.

Campsites, facilities: There are 25 sites for tents or RVs up to 35 feet long and nine tent sites. Picnic tables and fire grills are provided. Drinking water and vault toilets are available, but garbage must be packed out. A camp host is on-site. Boat docks are nearby. No gasoline motors are allowed on the lake. The boating speed limit is 5 mph. Leashed pets are permitted.

Reservations, fees: Reservations are not accepted. Sites are $6 per night, $2 per night per additional vehicle. Open early June-mid-October, weather permitting.

Directions: From Lakeview, drive west on Highway 140 for 21 miles to Forest Road 3870. Turn right and drive about eight miles to the campground.

Contact: Fremont-Fremont-Winema National Forest, Lakeview Ranger District, 541/947-6300, www.fs.usda.gov/fremont-winema.

30 MUD CREEK

Scenic rating: 4

on Mud Creek in Fremont National Forest

Map 6.5, page 385

Remote and quiet, this camp sits at 6,600 feet elevation in an isolated stand of lodgepole pines along the banks of Mud Creek. Fishing in Mud Creek is fairly good, and Drake Peak (8,405 feet elevation) is nearby. There are no other camps in the immediate vicinity.

Campsites, facilities: There are seven sites for tents or RVs up to 16 feet long. Picnic tables and fire grills are provided. Drinking water and vault toilets are available. Garbage must be packed out. Leashed pets are permitted.

Reservations, fees: Reservations are not accepted. There is no fee for camping. Open June-mid-October, weather permitting.

Directions: From Lakeview, drive five miles north on U.S. 395 to Highway 140. Turn right on Highway 140 and drive eight miles to Forest Road 3615. Turn left and drive seven miles to the campground.

Contact: Fremont-Fremont-Winema National Forest, Lakeview Ranger District, 541/947-6300, www.fs.usda.gov/fremont-winema.

31 DOG LAKE

Scenic rating: 5

on Dog Lake in Fremont National Forest

Map 6.5, page 385   **BEST**

This campground is located on the west shore of Dog Lake at an elevation of 5,100 feet. Native Americans named the lake for its resemblance in shape to the hind leg of a dog. The lake provides a popular fishery for bass, crappie, and perch. Boats with motors are permitted, though speeds are limited to 5 mph. Prospects for seeing waterfowl and eagles are good.

Campsites, facilities: There are 12 sites for tents or RVs up to 40 feet long and four double sites. Picnic tables and fire grills are provided. Vault toilets are available. There is no drinking water. Garbage must be packed out. A boat launch is nearby. Leashed pets are permitted.

Reservations, fees: Reservations are not accepted. Sites are $6 per night, $2 per night per additional vehicle. Open mid-April-mid-October, weather permitting.

Directions: From Lakeview, drive west on

Highway 140 for seven miles to County Road 1-13. Turn left on County Road 1-13 and drive four miles to County Road 1-11D (Dog Lake Road). Turn right and drive four miles (the road becomes Forest Road 4017) into national forest. Continue on Forest Road 4017 for 12 miles (two miles past Drew Reservoir) to Dog Lake and the campground entrance on the left.

Contact: Fremont-Fremont-Winema National Forest, Lakeview Ranger District, 541/947-3334, www.fs.usda.gov/fremont-winema.

32 DREWS CREEK

Scenic rating: 9

near Lakeview in Fremont National Forest

Map 6.5, page 385   **BEST (**

This exceptionally beautiful campground is set along Drews Creek at 4,900 feet elevation. Gorgeous wild roses grow near the creek, and several unmarked trails lead to nearby hills where campers can enjoy scenic views. A great spot for a family trip, Drews Creek features horseshoe pits, an area for baseball, and a large group barbecue, making it equally popular with group campers. Fishing is available in nearby Dog Lake, which also provides facilities for boating. Waterskiing is another option at Drews Reservoir, two miles to the west.

Campsites, facilities: There are three sites for tents or RVs up to 25 feet long and two group sites for 20-50 people. Picnic tables, fire grills, and vault toilets are provided. There is no drinking water and garbage must be packed out. Leashed pets are permitted.

Reservations, fees: Reservations are not accepted. There is no fee for camping. Open early mid-May-mid-October, weather permitting.

Directions: From Lakeview, drive west on Highway 140 for 10 miles to County Road 1-13. Turn left and drive four miles to County Road 1-11D. Turn right and drive six miles (the road will become Forest Road 4017) to the bridge that provides access to the campground.

Contact: Fremont-Fremont-Winema National Forest, Lakeview Ranger District, 541/947-3334, www.fs.usda.gov/fremont-winema.

33 JUNIPERS RESERVOIR RV RESORT

Scenic rating: 6

on Junipers Reservoir

Map 6.5, page 385

This resort on an 8,000-acre cattle ranch is situated in a designated Oregon Wildlife Viewing Area, and campers may catch glimpses of seldom-seen species. Many nature-walking trails meander through the park, and guests can also take driving tours. Fishing for catfish and trout can be good and, because it is a private lake, no fishing license is required. The summer climate is mild and pleasant. Antelope and elk can be spotted in this area.

Campsites, facilities: There is a grassy area for tents and 40 pull-through sites with full or partial hookups (some 50 amp) for RVs up to 80 feet; a 20-foot camping trailer is also available. Group camping, with group rates, is available. Picnic tables are provided. Weather permitting, small campfires are allowed in the meadow. Drinking water, restrooms with showers, a dump station, Wi-Fi, coin laundry, community fire pit, and ice are available. Recreational facilities include a recreation hall, a volleyball court, and horseshoe pits. Some of the facilities are wheelchair accessible. Leashed pets are permitted.

Reservations, fees: Reservations are recommended. Tent sites are $20 per night, and RV sites are $32-39 per night; weekly and monthly rates are available. Open May 1-mid-October.

Directions: From Lakeview, drive west on Highway 140 for 10 miles to the resort (at Milepost 86.5) on the right.

Contact: Junipers Reservoir RV Resort, 541/947-2050, www.junipersrv.com.

34 GOOSE LAKE STATE PARK

Scenic rating: 7

on Goose Lake

Map 6.5, page 385

This park is situated on the east shore of unusual Goose Lake, which lies half in Oregon and half in California. The fishing at the lake is poor, but better fishing is available in nearby streams. Waterfowl from the Pacific flyway frequent this out-of-the-way spot, as do many other species of birds and wildlife, like the mule deer that frequent the shaded campground. Note that only 15- and 20-amp service is available for RVs.

Campsites, facilities: There are 48 sites with partial hookups (water and electricity) for tents or RVs up to 50 feet long. Tent-only hiker/biker sites are available. Picnic tables, fire grills, garbage bins, and drinking water are provided. A camp host is on-site. Restrooms with flush toilets and showers, a dump station, ice, and firewood are available. Leashed pets are permitted.

Reservations, fees: Reservations are not accepted. Sites are $22 per night, $7 per night for an additional vehicle. Open mid-April–mid-October.

Directions: From Lakeview, drive south on U.S. 395 for 14 miles to the California border and Stateline Road. Turn right (west) and drive one mile to the campground.

Contact: Goose Lake State Park, 541/947-3111 or 800/551-6949, www.oregonstateparks.org.

35 WILLOW CREEK

Scenic rating: 4

near Willow Creek in Fremont National Forest

Map 6.5, page 385

This campground (at 5,800 feet elevation) is situated in a canyon among tall pines and quaking aspen not far from the banks of Willow Creek. Campsites are private, and some are located along the creek. Watch for wildflowers

blooming in the spring. A hiking trail offers access to the Crane Mountain Trail, and a nearby dirt road heads north to Burnt Creek.

Campsites, facilities: There are eight sites for tents or RVs up to 22 feet long. Picnic tables and fire grills are provided. There is no drinking water, and garbage must be packed out. Vault toilets are available. Leashed pets are permitted.

Reservations, fees: Reservations are not accepted. There is no fee for camping. Open June–mid-October, weather permitting.

Directions: From Lakeview, drive five miles north on U.S. 395 to Highway 140. Turn right (east) on Highway 140 and drive seven miles to Forest Road 3915. Turn right and drive nine miles to Forest Road 4011. Turn right and drive one mile to the campground on the right.

Contact: Fremont-Fremont-Winema National Forest, Lakeview Ranger District, 541/947-3334, www.fs.usda.gov.

36 DEEP CREEK

Scenic rating: 8

on Deep Creek in Fremont National Forest

Map 6.5, page 385

Shaded by huge ponderosa pines and cottonwoods and nestled on the banks of Deep Creek, this pretty, little-used campground is the place if you're after privacy. Deep Creek is a good fishing stream. Magnificent spring wildflowers are a highlight here. The camp sits at an elevation of 5,600 feet.

Campsites, facilities: There are five sites for tents or RVs up to 22 feet long. Picnic tables and fire grills are provided. Vault toilets are available. There is no drinking water, and garbage must be packed out. Leashed pets are permitted.

Reservations, fees: Reservations are not accepted. There is no fee for camping. Open June–mid-October, weather permitting.

Directions: From Lakeview, drive five miles north on U.S. 395 to Highway 140. Turn right (east) on Highway 140 and drive six miles to Forest Road 3915. Turn right on Forest Road 3915 and drive 14 miles to Deep Creek and the campground entrance road on the right (Forest Road 4015). Turn right and drive one mile to the campground on the right.

Contact: Fremont-Fremont-Winema National Forest, Lakeview Ranger District, 541/947-3334, www.fs.usda.gov/fremont-winema.

37 HART MOUNTAIN NATIONAL ANTELOPE REFUGE
🚶 🚴 💦 🐕 ♿ 🚐 ⛺

Scenic rating: 6

near Adel

Map 6.6, page 386

The U.S. Fish and Wildlife Service operates very few areas with campgrounds—Hart Mountain is one of them. This unusual refuge features canyons and hot springs in a high-desert area. There are three primitive campgrounds: Hot Springs Campground, Post Meadows Horse Camp, and Camp Hart Mountain (CCC Camp). Hot Springs gets the highest use in the summer. Some of Oregon's largest antelope herds roam this large area, and the campground is popular with hunters in the fall.

Campsites, facilities: Hot Springs Campground has 25 primitive sites for tents or RVs up to 20 feet long. Post Meadows Horse Camp has six primitive sites with corrals, hitching posts, and stock water (100 yards away) available; pellet (or certified weed-free) feed is required for horses. Camp Hart Mountain has eight primitive tent sites. Some sites have fire rings. Pit toilets are provided, and there is a seasonal camp host. There is no drinking water except at Camp Hart Mountain or at headquarters, which you pass on the way in. Firewood is not available. Garbage must be packed out. Supplies are available in the town of Plush. Some facilities are wheelchair accessible. Leashed pets are permitted.

Reservations, fees: Reservations are not

accepted. There is no fee for camping, but there is a 14-day stay limit. Open year-round, weather permitting.

Directions: From Lakeview, drive north on U.S. 395 for five miles to Highway 140. Turn east on Highway 140 and drive 16 miles to the Plush-Hart Mountain Cutoff. Turn left (signed for Hart Antelope Refuge) and drive north for 43 miles (first paved, then gravel) to the refuge headquarters. Continue 0.5 mile to CCC Campground, four miles to Hot Springs Campground (the road is often impassable in the winter). For the Post Meadows Horse Camp, follow the above directions to the refuge headquarters. At headquarters, turn onto Blue Sky Road and drive 10 miles to the camp.

Contact: Hart Mountain National Antelope Refuge, 541/947-3315 or 541/947-2731, www.fws.gov/refuges.

38 STEENS MOUNTAIN WILDERNESS RESORT
🚶 🚴 💦 🐕 ♿ 🚐 ⛺

Scenic rating: 9

on the Blitzen River

Map 6.7, page 387

The self-proclaimed "gateway to Steens Mountain," this resort is bordered by the Malheur National Wildlife Refuge on three sides, and it has great views. The mile-high mountain and surrounding gorges make an excellent photo opportunity. Hiking and hunting are other possibilities in the area. Fishing is available on the Blitzen River, with easy access from the camp.

Campsites, facilities: There are 14 tent sites, 37 pull-through sites with full hookups (30 or 50 amps), and 39 sites with partial hookups for tents or RVs of any length, plus eight cabins and one rental home. Picnic tables and fire pits are provided. Drinking water, restrooms with showers, a dump station, coin laundry, limited groceries and fishing supplies, and ice are available. Some facilities are wheelchair accessible. Leashed pets are permitted.

Reservations, fees: Reservations are accepted at 800/542-3765 or www.steensmountainresort.com. Tent sites are $15 per night, RV sites are $27-32 per night, $5 per person per night for more than two people. Some credit cards are accepted. Open year-round.

Directions: From Burns, drive east on Highway 78 for two miles to Highway 205. Turn right (south) on Highway 205 and drive 59 miles to Frenchglen and Steens Mountain Road. Turn left (east) and drive three miles to the resort on the right.

Contact: Steens Mountain Wilderness Resort, 541/493-2415, www.steensmountainresort.com.

39 PAGE SPRINGS

Scenic rating: 7

near Malheur National Wildlife Refuge

Map 6.7, page 387

Page Springs campground lies adjacent to the Malheur National Wildlife Refuge at an elevation of 4,200 feet. Sites are shaded by juniper and cottonwood, with some near the Donner und Blitzen River. Activities include hiking on the area trails, bird-watching, fishing, hunting, and sightseeing. The Frenchglen Hotel (three miles away) is administered by the state parks department and offers overnight accommodations and meals.

Campsites, facilities: There are 36 sites for tents or RVs up to 35 feet. Picnic tables and fire rings are provided. Drinking water, vault toilets, a day-use area with a shelter, garbage bins, and a seasonal camp host are available. Some facilities are wheelchair accessible. Leashed pets are permitted.

Reservations, fees: Reservations are not accepted. Sites are $8 per vehicle per night, with a 14-day stay limit. Open year-round.

Directions: From Burns, drive east on Highway 78 for two miles to Highway 205. Turn south on Highway 205 and drive 60 miles to Frenchglen and Steens Mountain Loop Road.

Turn left (east) and drive three miles to the campground.

Contact: Bureau of Land Management, Burns District, 541/573-4400, www.blm.gov.

40 FISH LAKE

Scenic rating: 8

on Fish Lake

Map 6.7, page 387

The shore of Fish Lake is the setting for this primitive but pretty camp. Set among the aspen at 7,400 feet elevation, it can make an excellent weekend-getaway spot for sightseeing. Trout fishing is an option, made easier by the boat ramp near camp.

Campsites, facilities: There are 23 sites for tents or RVs up to 20 feet long. Picnic tables and fire grills are provided. Drinking water and vault toilets are available. Garbage must be packed out. Boat-launching facilities are on-site (non-motorized boats only). Leashed pets are permitted.

Reservations, fees: Reservations are not accepted. Sites are $8 per vehicle per night, with a 14-day stay limit. Open mid-June-October, weather permitting.

Directions: From Burns, drive east on Highway 78 for two miles to Highway 205. Turn south on Highway 205 and drive 60 miles to Frenchglen and Steens Mountain Loop Road. Turn left (east) and drive 17 miles to the campground.

Contact: Bureau of Land Management, Burns District, 541/573-4400, www.blm.gov.

41 JACKMAN PARK

Scenic rating: 8

near Fish Lake

Map 6.7, page 387

One of four camps in the area, Jackman Park sits at 7,800 feet elevation in the eastern Oregon desert. This scenic campground, with its aspen and willow trees, is known as one of the best places to view the golden aspen leaves on Steens Mountain in the fall. Fish Lake is 2.5 miles away. Note that trailers and RVs are not recommended in the campground.

Campsites, facilities: There are six sites for tents only. Picnic tables and fire rings are provided. Drinking water and vault toilets are available. Garbage must be packed out. Leashed pets are permitted.

Reservations, fees: Reservations are not accepted. Sites are $6 per vehicle per night, with a 14-day stay limit. Open mid-June-October, weather permitting.

Directions: From Burns, drive east on Highway 78 for two miles to Highway 205. Turn south on Highway 205 and drive 60 miles to Frenchglen and Steens Mountain Loop Road. Turn left (east) and drive 22 miles to the campground.

Contact: Bureau of Land Management, Burns District, 541/573-4400, www.blm.gov.

42 MANN LAKE

Scenic rating: 8

on Mann Lake

Map 6.7, page 387

Mann Lake sits at the base of Steens Mountain. This scenic, high-desert camp is mainly used as a fishing camp—fishing can be very good for cutthroat trout. Wintertime ice fishing, rockhounding, and wildlife-viewing are also popular. Sites are open, with sagebrush and no trees. There is a small boat ramp and a 10-horsepower limit on motors. Weather can be extreme. Nearby Alvord Desert is also an attraction.

Note: Please respect private property on parcels of land next to the lake.

Campsites, facilities: There are dispersed sites for tents or RVs of up to 35 feet long on each side of the lake. Vault toilets and a boat ramp are available. There is no drinking water

and garbage must be packed out. Leashed pets are permitted.

Reservations, fees: Reservations are not accepted. There is no fee for camping. A 14-day stay limit is enforced. Open year-round.

Directions: From Burns, drive southeast on Highway 78 for 65 miles to East Steens Road. Turn right (south) and drive 22 miles to the campground at Mann Lake.

Contact: Bureau of Land Management, Burns District, 541/573-4400, www.blm.gov.

43 SOUTH STEENS FAMILY AND EQUESTRIAN

Scenic rating: 6

near Steens Mountain Wilderness

Map 6.7, page 387

This campground hugs the edge of the Steens Mountain Wilderness. The area features deep, glacier-carved gorges, volcanic uplifts, stunning scenery, and a rare chance to see elk and bighorn sheep. Redband trout fishing is nearby at Donner und Blitzen Wild and Scenic River and its tributaries, a designated reserve. Trails are accessible from the campground.

Campsites, facilities: There are 36 sites for tents or RVs up to 25 feet at the family camp; there are 15 sites designated for horse campers at the equestrian camp. Picnic tables and fire grills are provided. Drinking water and vault toilets are available. Corrals and hitching posts are available at the equestrian campground. Leashed pets are permitted.

Reservations, fees: Reservations are not accepted. Sites are $6 per vehicle per night. There is a 14-day stay limit. Open May-November, weather permitting.

Directions: From Burns, drive east on Highway 78 for two miles to Highway 205. Turn south on Highway 205 and drive 60 miles to Frenchglen. Continue south on Highway 205 for 10 miles to Steens South Loop Road. Turn left (east) and drive 18 miles to the campground on the right.

Contact: Bureau of Land Management, Burns District, 541/573-4400, www.blm.gov.

44 WILLOW CREEK HOT SPRINGS

Scenic rating: 7

near Whitehorse Butte

Map 6.7, page 387

A very small campground with no privacy, Willow Creek features campsites about 100 feet from the hot springs, which consist of two connected, smaller pools. This campground can be difficult to find, and only the adventurous should attempt this trip. Despite being out of the way, it still attracts travelers from far and wide. The surrounding scenery features rocky hills, not a flat expanse.

Campsites, facilities: There are four sites for tents or small RVs. Picnic tables and fire rings are provided. A vault toilet is available. Drinking water and firewood are not available, and garbage must be packed out. Leashed pets are permitted.

Reservations, fees: Reservations are not accepted. There is no fee for camping. Open year-round, weather permitting.

Directions: From Burns, drive southeast on Highway 78 for 105 miles to Burns Junction and U.S. 95. Turn right (south) on U.S. 95 and drive 20 miles to Whitehorse Road. Turn right (southwest) and drive 21 miles (passing Whitehorse Ranch); continue for 2.5 miles to a fork (look for the telephone pole). Bear left and drive two miles to the campground.

Contact: Bureau of Land Management, Vale District, 541/473-3144, www.blm.gov.

45 ROME LAUNCH

Scenic rating: 6

on the Owyhee River

Map 6.8, page 388

Rome Launch campground is used mainly by folks rafting the Owyhee River and overnighters passing through. A few cottonwood trees and sagebrush dot the camp, with some sites adjacent to the Owyhee River. Rome Launch is also good for wildlife-viewing; mountain lions and bobcats have been spotted, and there are some farms and ranches in the area. This is a popular spot to fish for trout and catfish.

The Owyhee Canyon is quite dramatic, like a miniature Grand Canyon. I have canoed most of the Owyhee from the headwaters in Nevada below the Jarbidge Mountains all the way through Idaho and into Oregon, and I would rate this river as one of the top canoeing destinations in North America. Note: No motorized boats are allowed on the river.

Campsites, facilities: There are five sites for tents or small RVs. Picnic tables and fire rings are provided. Drinking water, vault toilets, and a boat launch are available. No firewood is available. Garbage must be packed out. Some facilities are wheelchair accessible. Leashed pets are permitted.

Reservations, fees: Reservations are not accepted. There is no fee for camping. Open March-November, weather permitting.

Directions: From Burns Junction, drive east on U.S. 95 for 15 miles to Jordan Valley and the signed turnoff for the Owyhee River and BLM-Rome boat launch. Turn south and drive 0.25 mile to the campground.

Contact: Bureau of Land Management, Vale District, 541/473-3144, www.blm.gov.

46 ANTELOPE RESERVOIR

Scenic rating: 3

on the Antelope Reservoir

Map 6.8, page 388

This campground gets little use, except during hunting season. An open area on a slope above the reservoir, the camp has no tree cover—be prepared for extreme weather. Water levels fluctuate at shallow Antelope Reservoir and it can dry up.

Campsites, facilities: There are four sites for tents or small RVs. Picnic tables and fire rings are provided. Vault toilets and primitive boat access are available. No drinking water is available, and garbage must be packed out. Some facilities are wheelchair accessible. Leashed pets are permitted.

Reservations, fees: Reservations are not accepted. There is no fee for camping. Open year-round, weather permitting.

Directions: From Burns Junction, drive east on U.S. 95 for 36 miles to the signed turnoff for Antelope Reservoir. Turn south and drive one mile to the campground on the left.

Contact: Bureau of Land Management, Vale District, 541/473-3144, www.blm.gov.

47 THREE FORKS

Scenic rating: 9

near the Owyhee River

Map 6.8, page 388

This remote camp is set along the east bank of the Owyhee River, where several warm streams snake through tall grass to the river. The area offers fishing for brown trout in the river and day hiking to secluded springs and a waterfall pool in the upper Owyhee Canyon (swimwear optional). Clusters of 95°F springs are located on both sides of the river, and the rugged Owyhee Canyon forms a magnificent backdrop. To the west are a number of wild horse herds. (The BLM recreation map has the general locations of the herds.)

Campsites, facilities: There are four sites for tents or small RVs. Picnic tables and fire rings are provided. Vault toilets are available. There is no drinking water, and garbage must be packed out. There is access to the Owyhee River by permit for non-motorized boats only. Leashed pets are permitted.

Reservations, fees: Reservations are not accepted. There is no fee for camping. Open year-round, weather permitting.

Directions: On U.S. 95 (15 miles southwest of Jordan Valley), turn south on Three Forks Road and drive 35 miles to the campground. High-clearance vehicles recommended. Road may be impassable when wet.

Contact: Bureau of Land Management, Vale District, 541/473-3144, www.blm.gov.

RESOURCES

NATIONAL FORESTS

The U.S. Forest Service provides many secluded camps and allows camping anywhere except where it is specifically prohibited. If you ever want to clear the cobwebs from your head and get away from it all, this is the way to go.

Many Forest Service campgrounds are remote and have no drinking water. You usually don't need to check in or make reservations, and sometimes there is no fee. At many Forest Service campgrounds that provide drinking water, the camping fee is often only a few dollars, with payment made on the honor system. Because most of these camps are in mountain areas, they are subject to winter closure due to snow or mud.

Dogs are permitted in national forests with no extra charge. Always carry documentation of current vaccinations.

Northwest Forest Pass

A Northwest Forest Pass is required for certain activities in some Oregon national forests. The pass is required for parking at participating trailheads, non-developed camping areas, boat launches, picnic areas, and visitors centers.

Daily passes cost $5 per vehicle; annual passes are $30 per vehicle. Combined recreation passes for Washington and Oregon are also available. You can buy Northwest Forest Passes at national forest offices and dozens of retail outlets and online vendors. Major credit cards are accepted at most retail and online outlets and at some Forest Service offices.

More information about the Northwest Forest Pass program, including a listing of retail and online vendors, can be obtained at www.fs.usda.gov.

An Interagency Pass is available for $80 annually in lieu of a Northwest Forest Pass. The Interagency Pass is honored nationwide at all Forest Service, National Park Service, Bureau of Land Management, Bureau of Reclamation, and U.S. Fish and Wildlife Service sites charging entrance or standard amenity fees. Valid for 12 months from the month of purchase, the America the Beautiful Pass is available at most national forest or grassland offices or online at www.discovernw.org.

National Forest Reservations

Some of the more popular camps and most of the group camps are on a reservation system. Reservations can be made up to 240 days in advance and up to 360 days in advance for groups. To reserve a site, call 877/444-6777 or visit www.recreation.gov. The reservation fee is usually $10 for a campsite in a national forest, but group site reservation fees are higher. Major credit cards are accepted.

National Forest Maps

National Forest maps are among the best you can get for the price. They detail all backcountry streams, lakes, hiking trails, and logging roads for access and can be obtained in person at Forest Service offices or online at www.nationalforestmapstore.com.

Forest Service Information

Forest Service personnel are most helpful for obtaining camping or hiking trail information. Unless you are buying a map or Adventure Pass, it is advisable to phone in advance to get the best service.

For further information on individual national forests, contact the following offices:

U.S. Forest Service
Pacific Northwest Region
1220 SW 3rd Avenue
Portland, OR 97204
503/808-2468
www.fs.usda.gov

Deschutes National Forest
63095 Deschutes Market Road
Bend, OR 97701
541/383-5300
www.fs.usda.gov/deschutes

Fremont-Winema National Forests
1301 South G Street

Lakeview, OR 97630
541/947-2151
www.fs.usda.gov/fremont-winema

Malheur National Forest
431 Patterson Bridge Road
John Day, OR 97845
541/575-3000
www.fs.usda.gov/malheur

Mt. Hood National Forest
16400 Champion Way
Sandy, OR 97055
503/668-1700
www.fs.usda.gov/mthood

Ochoco National Forest
3160 NE 3rd Street
Prineville, OR 97754
541/416-6500
www.fs.usda.gov/ochoco

Rogue River-Siskiyou National Forest
3040 Biddle Road
Medford, OR 97504
541/618-2200
www.fs.usda.gov/rogue-siskiyou

Siuslaw National Forest
4077 SW Jefferson Way
Corvallis, OR 97331
541/750-7000
www.fs.usda.gov/siuslaw

Umatilla National Forest
72510 Coyote Road
Pendleton, OR 97801
541/278-3716
www.fs.usda.gov/umatilla

Umpqua National Forest
2900 NW Stewart Parkway
Roseburg, OR 97471
541/957-3200
www.fs.usda.gov/umpqua

Wallowa-Whitman National Forest

1550 Dewey Avenue
Suite A
Baker City, OR 97814
541/523-6391
www.fs.usda.gov/wallowa-whitman

Willamette National Forest
3106 Pierce Parkway, Ste. D
Springfield, OR 97477
541/225-6300
www.fs.usda.gov/willamette

NATIONAL PARKS AND RECREATION AREAS

The national parks and recreational areas in Oregon are natural wonders, varying from the spectacular Columbia River Gorge to the breathtaking Crater Lake National Park. Reservations are available at some of the campgrounds at these parks and recreation areas.

For information about each of the national parks in Oregon, contact the parks directly:

Columbia River Gorge National Scenic Area
902 Wasco Avenue, Suite 200
Hood River, OR 97031
541/308-1700
www.fs.usda.gov/crgnsa

Crater Lake National Park
P.O. Box 7
Crater Lake, OR 97604
541/594-3000
www.nps.gov/crla

Crooked River National Grassland
274 SW 4th Street
Madras, OR 97741
541/416-6640
www.fs.usda.gov/ochoco

Hells Canyon National Recreation Area
Wallowa-Whitman National Forest
1550 Dewey Avenue, Suite A
Baker City, OR 97814
541/523-6391

www.fs.usda.gov/wallowa-whitman

Oregon Dunes National Recreation Area
Visitor Center
855 Highway 101
Reedsport, OR 97467
541/271-6000
www.fs.usda.gov/siuslaw

STATE PARKS

The Oregon State Parks system provides many popular camping spots. Reservations are often a necessity during the summer. The camps include drive-in numbered sites, tent spaces, and picnic tables, with showers and bathrooms provided nearby. Although some parks are well known, there are still some little-known gems in the state parks system where campers can find seclusion, even in the summer.

State Park Reservations

Many of the state park campgrounds are on a reservation system, and campsites can be booked up to nine months in advance at these parks. Reservations can be made for 44 Oregon state parks through Reserve America at 800/452-5687 or online at www.reserveamerica.com. A nonrefundable reservation fee of $8-10 and the first night's fee will be required as a deposit, charged to a MasterCard or Visa credit card (debit cards linked to MasterCard or Visa also accepted).

Oregon Parks and Recreation Department State Parks
725 Summer St. NE, Ste. C
Salem, OR 97301
800/551-6949
www.oregon.gov

STATE FORESTS

Oregon Department of Forestry
2600 State Street
Salem, OR 97310
503/945-7200

Tillamook State Forest
http://tillamookstateforest.blogspot.com

Forest Grove District
801 Gales Creek Road
Forest Grove, OR 97116-1199
503/357-2191

Tillamook State Forest
5005 3rd Street
Tillamook, OR 97141-2999
503/842-2545

U.S. ARMY CORPS OF ENGINEERS

Some of the family camps and most of the group camps operated by the U.S. Army Corps of Engineers are on a reservation system. Reservations can be made up to 240 days in advance for family camps and up to 360 days in advance for groups. To reserve a site, call 877/444-6777 or visit www.recreation.gov. The reservation fee is usually $10 for a campsite, but group site reservation fees are higher. Major credit cards are accepted.

Portland District
333 SW 1st Ave
Portland, OR 97204
503/808-4327
www.nwp.usace.army.mil

BUREAU OF LAND MANAGEMENT (BLM)

Most BLM campgrounds are primitive and in remote areas. Often, there is no fee charged for camping.

Oregon Office
1220 SW 3rd Avenue
Portland, OR 97204
503/808-6001
www.blm.gov

Burns District
28910 Highway 20 West
Hines, OR 97738
541/573-4400

Coos Bay District
1300 Airport Lane
North Bend, OR 97459
541/756-0100

Lakeview District
1301 South G Street
Lakeview, OR 97630
541/947-2177

Medford District
3040 Biddle Road
Medford, OR 97504
541/618-2200

Northwest Oregon District
1717 Fabry Road, SE
Salem, OR 97306
503/375-5622

Prineville District
3050 NE 3rd Street
Prineville, OR 97754
541/416-6700

Roseburg District
777 NW Garden Valley Boulevard
Roseburg, OR 97471
541/440-4930

Vale District
100 Oregon Street
Vale, OR 97918
541/473-3144

OTHER VALUABLE RESOURCES

Oregon Department of Fish and Wildlife
4034 Fairview Industrial Drive SE
Salem, OR 97302
503/947-6000
www.dfw.state.or.us

Oregon State Department of Transportation
355 Capitol Street NE, MS 11
Salem, OR 97301
888/275-6368
www.oregon.gov/odot

U.S. Geological Survey
888/275-8747
www.usgs.gov

Index

Acknowledgments

The following state and federal resource experts provided critical information and galley reviews regarding changes in reservations, fees, directions, and recreational opportunities. I am extremely grateful for their timely help and expert advice.

U.S. Forest Service

Jan Nelson-Dean, Deschutes National Forest

Amy Tinderholt, Deschutes National Forest, Bend-Fort Rock Ranger District

Bob Hennings, Deschutes National Forest, Sisters Ranger District

Alan Grubb, Clark Higgler, Erica Hupp, Heidi Ratliff, Jeremy Sugden, Vicky Zacharias, Fremont-Winema National Forests

Larry Hills, Fremont-Winema National Forests, Bly and Lakeview Ranger Districts

Tim Stack, Fremont-Winema National Forests, Silver Lake Ranger District

Phil McNeil, Klamath National Forest, Happy Camp/Oak Knoll Ranger District

Shawna Clark, Melissa Walker, Malheur National Forest

Chris Bentley, Rachel Drake, Delva Nelson, Jenny Wade, Mount Hood National Forest

Katherine Martin, Ochoco National Forest, Paulina Ranger District

Pam Carr, Virginia Gibbons, Rogue-Siskiyou National Forest

Melonie Smeltz, Rogue-Siskiyou National Forest, Butte Ranger District

Teresa Miller, Jackie Ringulet, Rogue-Siskiyou National Forest, Gold Beach Ranger District

Nancy Wallace, Rogue-Siskiyou National Forest, Powers Ranger District

Carl Tollestrup, Rogue-Siskiyou National Forest

Nancy Schwieger, Siskiyou National Forest, Gold Beach Ranger District

David Wickwire, Siskiyou National Forest, Galice Ranger Districts

Marcus Elder, Siuslaw National Forest

Briana Guenther, George Vogel, Siuslaw National Forest, Hebo Ranger District

Zack Hayes, Siuslaw National Forest, Waldport Ranger District

Kathy Rankin, Umatilla National Forest, Heppner Ranger District

Janelle Lacey, Umatilla National Forest, North Fork John Day Ranger District

Jeff Bloom, Umatilla National Forest, Walla Walla Ranger District

Dennis Scott, Umpqua National Forest, North Umpqua Ranger District

Mariance Spence, Wallowa-Whitman National Forest

Mike Montgomery, Wallowa-Whitman National Forest, LaGrande Ranger District

Yvonne Santiago, Wallowa-Whitman National Forest, Wallowa Valley Ranger District/Eagle Cap Ranger District/Hells Canyon National Recreation Area

Annie Moore, Wallowa-Whitman National Forest, Whitman Ranger District

Linda Watson, Willamette National Forest, Chilla Ranger District

Angela Stagg, Willamette National Forest, Clackamas Ranger District

Ellaine Burnett, Jeff Lunsford, Willamette National Forest, Detroit Ranger District

Shelly Parsons, Willamette National Forest, Hood River Ranger District

Jennifer McDonald, Willamette National Forest, McKenzie Ranger District

Holly Cotton, Willamette National Forest, Middle Fork Ranger District

Isabel Shackelford, Willamette National Forest, Sweet Home Ranger District

Dave Sanders, Willamette National Forest

Roe Namitz, Diana Campos, United States Forest Service

Bureau of Land Management

Dennis Byrd, Ashland Resource Area

Kevin McCoy, Brett Paige, Baker City Office

Trish Lindemann, Medford District

Greg Currie, Prineville District

Greg Morgan, Roseburg District

Traci Meredith, Salem District

Deb Drake, Tillamook District
David Draheim, Vale District

National Parks, Recreation Areas, and Refuges

Diana Camcho, Columbia River Gorge National Scenic Area
Annie Whittenberg, Grasslands National Recreation Area
Vicky Mugnai, Jacob Rhone, Oregon Dunes National Recreation Area

State Parks

Chris Havel, Sheri Miller, Renee Okerman, Oregon State Parks
Allison Mangini, Beverly Beach State Park
Paul Wayne, Cape Blanco State Park
Mary Nulty, Carl G. Washburne State Park
Linda Brege, Deschutes State Recreation Area
Debi Hill, Fort Stevens State Park
Larry Moniz, Goose Lake State Park
Cathi Dunn, Harris Beach Management Unit
Rick Duda, Milo McIver State Park

Ami Ericdon, Nehalam Bay State Park
Linda Taylor, South Beach State Park
Janet Sobezak, Sunset Bay State Park
Sandy Anderson, Umpqua Lighthouse State Park
Jorge Moreno, California State Parks

Other

Clara Johnson, Crook County Parks and Recreation
Kathy Hammons, Douglas County Parks
JoAnn Woelfle, Lane County Parks
Kristi Mosier, Lane County, Richardson Park
Julie Smith, Linn County Parks
Peggy Murphy, Lost Lake Resort
Jill Hammond, Jackson County Parks
Alisha Howard, Josephine County Parks
Bill Doran, Metro Regional Parks and Green Spaces
Kirsti Cason, Morrow County Parks
Lynn Studley, Portland General Electric
Joanne Mead, PG&E camp host
Ken Hill, Port of Siuslaw

MOON OREGON CAMPING

Avalon Travel
Hachette Book Group
1700 Fourth Street
Berkeley, CA 94710, USA
www.moon.com

Editor and Series Manager: Sabrina Young
Copy Editor: Kim Runciman
Production and Graphics Coordinator: Krista Anderson
Cover Design: Faceout Studios, Charles Brock
Moon Logo: Tim McGrath
Map Editor: Mike Morgenfeld
Proofreader: Alissa Cyphers

ISBN-13: 978-1-64049-807-5

Printing History
1st Edition – 2002
5th Edition – April 2018
5 4 3 2 1

Front cover photo: Cape Lookout State Park, Tillamook County, Oregon, USA © David L. Moore - Oregon | Alamy Stock Photo

Title page photo: Cannon Beach in Oregon © Dan Breckwoldt | Dreamstime.com

Back cover photo: © John Beath

Additional photos: page 3 © Natalia Bratslavsky | 123rf.com; page 4 © Craig Hanson | 123rf.com; page 5 © Kevin Wells | Dreamstime.com

Printed in Canada by Friesens

Avalon Travel is a division of Hachette Book Group, Inc. Moon and the Moon logo are trademarks of Hachette Book Group, Inc. All other marks and logos depicted are the property of the original owners.

31901063030177